Connection of R.F.&P.&R.&P. R.R.
City Rail Road.

REFERENCES

b 2nd Baptist Church
   2nd Presbyterian
c Cemetery   M.E.
d United Presbyter
e St Pauls Church (Episcopal)
f St Peters Church (Catholic)
g St James Church (Episcopal)
h Bethlehem's   Lutheran
i St Mary's   Catholic
k St Josephs Asylum
   Female Institute
   Presbyterian Church
   Street Methodist
   Episcopal Church
   Baptist
   African
   College
   Church (Disciples)
   Church M.E.
       (Epis)
   rial's   (Cath)
   Presbyterian Church
   Leigh St. Baptist
   Grace Church
   2nd Baptist
aa Masons Castle
bb Clay Street Methodist Church
cc Friends Meetinghouse
dd New Masonic Hall
ee St Marks Church (Episc)
ff Lutheran Church
gg Universalist
hh St Johns Lutheran (German)
ii Female Orphan Asylum
kk Builders Exchange
ll Tobacco
mm Pearl Flour
       2-24 Fire Alarm boxes

UNION

VENABLE

BYRD

CARRINGTON

CHURCH HILL

CHIMBORAZO HILL

LEIGH

GRACE

FRANKLIN

MAIN

Masonic Hall

Union Hotel

CARY

WATER

Union Church

Depot

RIVER

23

24

21

2

12

THE JEWISH
CONFEDERATES

★

The Jewish Confederates

★ ★ ★ ★ ★ ★ ★ ★ ★ ★

ROBERT N. ROSEN

University of South Carolina Press

© 2000 University of South Carolina

Published in Columbia, South Carolina, by the
University of South Carolina Press

Manufactured in the United States of America

04 03 02 01 00   5 4 3 2 1

Library of Congress Cataloging-in-Publication Data

Rosen, Robert N., 1947–
     The Jewish Confederates / Robert N. Rosen.
          p.   cm.
     Includes bibliographical references (p.) and index.
     ISBN 1-57003-363-3 (cloth)
     1. Jews—Southern States—History—19th century.   2. Jews—Confederate
States of America—History—19th century.   3. United States—History—Civil
War, 1861–1865—Jews.   4. Confederate States of America. Army—Officers—
Biography.   5. Jewish soldiers—United States—Biography.   I. Title.
F220.J5 R67   2000
975.004'924—dc21   00-009492

Endpapers: Street map of Richmond, Virginia, from the 1871 *Richmond
City Directory,* published by B. W. Gillis of Richmond. This map identifies
the locations of both the German synagogue, Beth Ahabah (near "House of
Jeff Davis"), and the Portuguese synagogue, K. K. Beth Shalome, near the
state capitol.

For Susan, again,
for her perseverance and love
To our three incomparable children
Annie, for her humor and insight
Ali, for her enthusiasm and inspiration
Will, for his exuberance and perspective
and to
Gustavus Poznanski Jr. and Isaac Valentine,
who died for their people at Secessionville
June 1862

There is only one baptism that can consecrate a man to a nationality: that is the baptism of blood shed in a common battle for freedom and fatherland.

> —Gabriel Riesser, a German Jewish lawyer who led the fight to emancipate Jewry in early nineteenth-century Germany

★　★　★

And as thou led'st thy chosen people forth
From Egypt's sullen wrath, oh King of Kings!
So smite the armies of the cruel North
And bear us to our hopes "on eagles' wings."

> —Capt. Samuel Yates Levy, poem written
> in Savannah, November 2, 1863

★　★　★

In time to come, when our grief shall have become, in a measure, silenced, and when the malicious tongue of slander, ever so ready to assail Israel, shall be raised against us, then, with feeling of mournful pride, will we point to this monument and say: *"There* is our reply."

> —Appeal of the Hebrew Ladies' Memorial Association of
> Richmond, "To the Israelites of the South," 1866, to raise
> funds for a monument to the Jewish Confederate dead

CONTENTS

★

PREFACE

★

THE WORLD OF THE JEWISH CONFEDERATES is a lost world. Although in the long history of the Jewish people 140 years is but the blink of an eye, both the South and American Jewry have undergone such monumental changes since 1861 that one traveling back in time must be prepared to visit a very different land populated by very different people.

My interest in this subject grew out of my curiosity about Charleston Jewry and the Civil War. In writing *Confederate Charleston*, I was determined to tell the story of African Americans, the Irish, and the Jews as well as the traditional story of the war. I knew that the old Jewish families had supported the Confederacy, but I was struck by the depth of their commitment to the cause. I wanted to understand why Southern Jews—most of whom were recent immigrants who at Passover each year celebrated the Exodus from their own enslavement in Egypt—were so committed to the Confederate States of America. Like most contemporary Jews, I was struck by the apparent irony of their story. I also believed I was in familiar territory, as the focal points, I thought, would be Charleston, Savannah, and Richmond.

What I discovered was much more complex. Jewish Confederates were, for the most part, not "old families" at all, but German, Polish, Hungarian, and Russian Jews. There were, to be sure, many prominent old Sephardic and Americanized Jewish Confederates from South Carolina and Virginia, but the typical "Hebrew" or "Israelite" soldiers, as they then called themselves, were German-speaking immigrants from Louisiana, a state that was home to approximately one-third of all Jews in the South in 1861. There were also large communities of these immigrants in Memphis, Nashville, Mobile, and Shreveport, as well as scattered communities in Arkansas and Mississippi. But Louisiana was a phenomenon. In 1861, Judah P. Benjamin was one of the state's U.S. senators; Henry M. Hyams, his cousin, served as lieutenant governor of Louisiana during the Civil War; and Edwin W. Moise had just retired as Speaker of the Louisiana House to become the Confederate district judge.[1] Here was an unusual—and unknown—moment in American Jewish history. When the war ended, Louisiana sent a former Jewish Confederate soldier, Benjamin Franklin Jonas of Fenner's Battery, to the U.S. Senate to lead its fight against Reconstruction. He was the first practicing Jew in the Senate, yet no historian had ever written about him.

The Jews of the South were committed to the cause of Southern independence because they were committed to their homeland, their new fatherland. The immigrants from Bavaria, Prussia, and Central Europe, struck by the freedom they now enjoyed, repaid that gift with patriotic fervor. While Gratz Cohen of Savannah bemoaned prejudice against the Jews in the South in 1864—"intolerance & prejudice cast their baneful seed throughout the land," he wrote his father—Cohen did not hesitate to give to the Confederacy, in Rabbi Bertram Korn's poignant words, "the greatest service in his power to offer—his life."[2] It will surprise many to know that, although there was anti-Semitism in the South, there was little anti-Semitism in the armies of Robert E. Lee and Joseph E. Johnston, or in Jefferson Davis's executive offices—while Ulysses S. Grant and William Tecumseh Sherman issued blatantly anti-Jewish orders and proclamations. Although there were anti-Jewish outbursts in the South during the war, the Confederate South was, contrary to popular belief, the exact opposite of the image of the Old South held by most contemporary Americans.

Until recent years, the Jewish Confederates' story has not been told for a variety of reasons. After the war, the South was devastated and the small Jewish population failed to adequately write its own history. More importantly, Jewish historians have focused on the "bigger" issues in American history—immigration, anti-Semitism, political and economic success, and the large centers of Jewish population, primarily in New York and the Northeast. Political correctness is also a culprit. Typical is this statement by Lawrence Fuchs: Jews have been "Tories, Confederates, and Know-Nothings as well as Socialists, Progressives and liberal Democrats," as if being a Confederate equated to disloyalty in the American Revolution and being a radical nativist in the 1850s.[3] Nathaniel Weyl summarized the point quite colorfully in *The Jew in American Politics:* "The prominent role of Jews in the Confederacy is generally either ignored or condensed into shamefaced footnotes by those historians of American Jewry whose opinions conform to the liberal-leftist stereotype. While these writers are happy to expatiate on the deeds of comparatively insignificant Jewish Socialists and needle trade organizers, the most pertinent thing they have to say about Judah P. Benjamin is that he did not believe in the tenets of Judaism. By this criterion, Benedict Spinoza, Karl Marx, Sigmund Freud and Albert Einstein would also have to be denied inclusion in the ranks of Jewry."[4]

I have tried to bring this lost Southern Jewish world back to life, to reintroduce old names and families to today's readers, and to do so without apologies. This is not without its difficulties. Modern-day Jews are very uncomfortable with the notion that antebellum Southern Jews owned slaves and that a few were in the business of slave trading. After all, Jews are unique among people in telling the story of their own enslavement.[5] Tony Horwitz writes of Charleston in *Confederates in the Attic* that the "image of Southern Jewish foot soldiers discomfitted me. I thought of my draft-dodging great-grandfather and of the Passover service, with its leitmotif of liberation from slavery in Egypt. Yet here were young Jews—a rabbi's son, even, who had perhaps recited the four questions at his family's Seder—going off to fight and die in defense of the South and its Pharaonic institution."[6] Of course, given the horror of slavery and the terrible damage and injustice it inflicted on millions of innocent people, Jewish Americans are understandably ill at ease at the mention of "Israelites with Egyptian principles," as Sen. Benjamin Wade once described Judah P. Benjamin.

Few Jewish Confederate soldiers owned slaves. Indeed, the great majority of Jewish soldiers were relatively poor clerks, peddlers, artisans, tailors, shopkeepers, and petty merchants who not only never owned a slave but had no realistic hope or ambition to do so. Being from the German states, some likely opposed slavery in private, although it cannot be said that Southern Jews were any different from their neighbors in matters of race and slavery. And while clearly the Civil War was brought about by the controversy over slavery, Confederate soldiers did not necessarily *fight* for slavery.

Jewish soldiers, as we shall see, fought for the South for many reasons, but the chief reason was to do their duty as they saw it.[7] It was a cardinal belief of anti-Semites and others in the nineteenth century that "the Wandering Jew" was a citizen of no country, that they were cowards and they were disloyal. This had been a staple of Judeophobia in Europe since the Middle Ages. Thus, like African American soldiers who fought for the Union army to prove they were men and equals, many a Jewish soldier enlisted to prove he was a man and a worthy citizen. Fighting for the Confederacy did not equate to fighting for slavery. Many who opposed secession and had misgivings about slavery fought for the South, Robert E. Lee being the foremost example. "You are all now going to the devil," one South Carolina unionist said, "and I will go with you. Honor and patriotism require me to stand by my state, right or wrong."[8]

The purpose of this book is to describe the Jewish Confederates in the context of their time and to give the reader a picture of them, warts and all. They neither need, nor would they want, a defense from a historian writing more than 130 years after an event and a cause to which they so willingly gave their energy, their property, and their lives.

Because, as Hasia Diner wrote, it is fashionable today to make a "public statement of the baggage one brings to a project," I confess to being a native third-generation Southerner whose grandparents were all immigrants or the children of immigrants. I have no Confederate ancestors. As a Southerner, however, I feel a kinship to the Southern Jews of the 1860s. It is hard to sit at Beth Elohim in Charleston and not feel a connection with the congregation's past members. And, because the South has been so deeply misunderstood, especially in relation to its Jewish citizens, I feel obliged to try to correct this misperception. Near the end of his life, Robert E. Lee told a visitor, "Doctor, I think some of you gentlemen that use the pen should see that justice is done us."[9]

In 1820 James Madison wrote Dr. Jacob De La Motta of Savannah to thank him for the doctor's speech at the dedication of Mikva Israel. "The history of the

Jews," Madison wrote, "must for ever be interesting. The modern part of it is at the same time so little generally known, that every ray of light on the subject has its value."[10] This one ray of light will hopefully illuminate and allow us to glimpse again the Jewish Confederates.

ACKNOWLEDGMENTS

★

THERE ARE SIX PEOPLE WITHOUT whose help this book could not have been written. First and foremost is my wife, Susan, who, like Robert E. Lee, persevered when others would have surrendered. She has cajoled, argued, typed, and helped me in every way possible. I have been extremely fortunate in having had the generous assistance of two experts on Jews in the Civil War: Mel Young of Chattanooga, Tennessee, and Robert Marcus of Springfield, Virginia. I called Mel out of the blue eight years ago, and he pledged his help, saying in Hebrew, "La dor, Va dor" ("from generation to generation"). Bob Marcus has been equally generous and kind, sharing his extensive collection of photographs, research, and knowledge with me and correcting my many errors. Not being a military historian, I could not have deciphered the military records without the expertise and intellectual curiosity of Lt. Col. James A. Gabel, U.S. Air Force (Ret.). Without his meticulous attention to detail, dedication to accuracy, and hard work, I would have fallen into even more errors. Dr. Belinda Gergel of Columbia College was my personal historical tutor. Claudia Kelley, my administrative assistant, has gone far, far above and beyond the call of duty. Without her time, patience, hard work, and generosity, this book would not have been finished.

Andrea Mëhrlander of Berlin was of inestimable help in giving me perspective and technical assistance on German immigrants, as well as encouragement from a brilliant historian. My editor, Alex Moore, of the University of South Carolina Press, pulled this overloaded literary cart out of the ditch, and Barbara A. Brannon gave it a final push. Dr. Moore's sympathetic and tactful suggestions have been critical. Solomon Breibart, my high school history teacher, has not only used his red pencil on my work, but has given me something more important—the encouragement of a respected mentor. Mark Greenberg of the Museum of the Southern Jewish Experience read the manuscript and offered expert advice. Tim Belshaw made the maps. A special thanks to my publisher, Catherine Fry, who always believed fervently in this project when I doubted it and held onto that belief for five long years.

Numerous people have helped me in my research. Cathy Kahn was a most hospitable host in New Orleans and shared her vast knowledge of Louisiana Jewry; her family photographs and documents; Cecile Levin, her cousin; and Fred Kahn, her knowledgeable husband. Eric Brock was extremely generous with his excellent work on the Jewish community of Shreveport as well as his personal photograph collection. Herbert Heltzer of Richmond opened many doors for me in Richmond, to important archives as well as good restaurants. Dale Rosengarten of the College of Charleston has been a helpful and patient colleague. Richard Gergel of Columbia has been a friend as well as a constant advisor and excellent listener.

I particularly want to thank the American Jewish Archives in Cincinnati. This book would not have been possible without the AJA. Kathy Spray and the entire staff has responded efficiently to my numerous and, at times, amateurish requests. The AJA is a precious resource for American Jewish history and deserves the support of all who care about American history.

I was fortunate over the years to have had the assistance of hardworking and intelligent research assistants, especially Karen Reilly, Jennifer Cohen, Suzanne Krebsbach, and Ben Steele. My lifelong friend, Michael Levkoff, patiently took numerous photographs of historical sites in Charleston and Savannah while listening to my many complaints.

I also wish to express my gratitude to the following for their assistance, advice, counsel and material: Elliott Ashkenazi of Washington, D.C., who shared his wisdom, his time, and his files; Tony Horwitz (who told me "a book is never finished; it is abandoned"); Moise Steeg, Esq., of New Orleans; Sandy and Chuck Marcus, Tom Houck, Beryl Weiner, Esq., and Jacob Haas of Atlanta; Kay Kole and Harriet Meyerhoff of Savannah; Nancy Greenberg and Rabbi Arnold Task of Alexandria, Louisiana; Michael D. Robbins, Esq., of San Antonio, Texas; Mary Ann F. Plaut of El Paso, Texas; Juliet George of Dallas, Texas, for sharing her outstanding thesis; Jack Steinberg of Augusta, Georgia, for his history of Children of Israel; Tom Brooks of Ontario, Canada (for the Max Neugas material); Stephen Paulovitch; Lynn M. Berkowitz; Rachel Hamovitz; Andrew Felber; Van Hart of Montgomery and Carol Hart, Esq., of New Orleans; Robert I. Zeitz of Mobile; the Felsenthal family of Tennessee; Ken Libo and Eli Evans of New York; and Barbara Stender, Bob Schindler, Carolyn Rivers, Leah Chase, and Elizabeth Moses of Charleston, South Carolina. Many, many others have kindly sent me family records and photographs, and I have acknowledged their kindness and generosity in endnotes and illustration credits. Without the help of the descendants of Jewish Confederates and local historians of the Southern Jewish experience, the story of Jewish Confederates could not be told.

I have had the pleasure of working at many archives, libraries, historical societies, and museums. The staff of the Charleston County Library has been both efficient and courteous. I wish to thank Shannon Glasheen, Claudia Kheel-Cost, and Katherine Page of the Louisiana State Museum in New Orleans; Wilbur Menerary and the staff of the Special Collections Department at Tulane University; the efficient staff of the Williams Research Center of the Historic New Orleans Collection; the staff at the Georgia Historical Society in Savannah; Sandra Berman and the Atlanta Jewish Federation Archives; Shirley Berkowitz and Lynn Kelsey of the Beth Ahabah Archive in Richmond; John Coski and Terri Hudgins of the Museum of the Confederacy; Miriam K. Syler of the Cob Memorial Archives, Valley, Alabama;

the staffs of the Library of Virginia, the Virginia Historical Society, the South Carolina Historical Society (especially Pat Hash), and the Library Society of
Charleston; and the American Jewish Historical Society.

I particularly want to thank Jennifer Gregory Priest, the splendid archivist at
Ohef Sholom in Norfolk.

I never met Rabbi Bertram Korn or Dr. Jacob Rader Marcus, but I wish to
acknowledge their pioneering works in this field. Rabbi Korn had planned to write
the history of Southern Jewry. "If God spares me," he wrote in *The Early Jews of
New Orleans,* "I still hope to move on to an evaluation of the nature of Jewish life
in the South prior to the outbreak of the Civil War." God did not spare him. He
died too young at age sixty-one. All students of American Jewish history owe both
of these "teachers in Israel" a great debt.

Edward McCrady, a Charleston lawyer, wrote in his introduction to his mag-
isterial *The History of South Carolina* (1897) that his study had been made "amidst
the engagements of a busy professional life, in hours snatched from that jealous
mistress—the law." My fellow shareholders, associates, paralegals, and staff at
Rosen, Goodstein & Hagood know firsthand what Mr. McCrady meant, and I
deeply appreciate their support.

No one can write a book without imposing upon his family, friends, and associates. My gratitude to my daughters, Annie and Ali, who have lived with Jewish
Confederates for eight years; and to my son, Will, who was born after the search for
Jewish Confederates began, thereby making this, for him, a lifelong project; to my
ever-supportive father, Morris Rosen; Betty Palmer; Richard, my brother, and Mar-
ianne Rosen; Debra Rosen, my sister; my mother-in-law, Joyce Ann Corner (for the
best writer's retreat in the world, Bald Peak Colony Club); and my in-laws, Alison
and Bob Adkins and Sue and Buzz Corner, for putting up with all this. I also wish
to thank Dutch and Mortie Cohen; Marvin and Julie Cohen; Carolyn Cohen and
Alan Dershowitz; Alan Rosen; Franklin and Dottie Ashley; Steve and Harriett
Steinert; Diane and Arnold Goodstein; Dr. Charles Peery; Senator Ernest L. Pas-
sailaigue; James Quackenbush, Esq.; Marty Perlmutter; Zoe and Alexander M.
Sanders; Peter Fuge; Barbara Rice; Donald B. Clark; Sabrina R. Grogan; Alexandra
D. Varner; Lisa D. Magnan; Marcia F. Jones; and Barbara M. Dear for being good
listeners; and Dottie Frank, a world-class author.

I am extremely grateful to the many descendants of Jewish Confederates and
their families for allowing me to utilize their records and family photographs. I am
indebted to Alice Dale Cohan of New York for the Solomon photographs; Anne
Jennings of Charleston for the Moses photograph; Max and Marcelle Furchgott;
Eric Brock of Shreveport; Julian Hennig Jr. of Columbia for the Kohn photographs;
Caroline L. Triest and Larry W. Freudenberg of Charleston; as well as Jane Meyer-
son, Gloria Felsenthal, and Betty Santandrea; Joan and Thomas Gandy of Natchez;
Mrs. P. A. Silverstein; and last, but hardly least, Robert A. Moses of Sumter.

ILLUSTRATIONS

★

Many of the illustrations are reproduced from Clarence C. Buel and Robert U.
Johnson, eds., *Battles and Leaders of the Civil War*, 4 vols. (New York: Century,
1888).

ABBREVIATIONS

★

AJA   American Jewish Archives, Hebrew Union College, Cincinnati, Ohio

AJA   *American Jewish Archives,* journal published by American Jewish Archives

AJH   *American Jewish History,* journal of the American Jewish Historical Society

AJHQ   *American Jewish Historical Quarterly,* New York, 1961–

AJHS   Library of the American Jewish Historical Society, Waltham, Massachusetts, and New York City

BA   Beth Ahabah Museum and Archive, Richmond, Va.

CC   College of Charleston, Jewish Heritage Collection, Charleston, S.C.

CSR   Compiled Service Records, National Archives, Washington, D.C.

DAB   *Dictionary of American Biography* (New York, 1946)

GHS   Georgia Historical Society, Savannah, Ga.

HNOC   Williams Research Center, Historic New Orleans Collection, New Orleans, La.

JE   *Jewish Encyclopedia* (New York, 1901–1905)

JPSA   Jewish Publication Society of America

NA   National Archives, Washington, D.C.

OR   U.S. War Department, *War of the Rebellion: Official Records of the Union and Confederate Armies*

ORN   U.S. Navy Department, *Official Records of the Union and Confederate Navies in the War of Rebellion*

PAJHS   *Publications of the American Jewish Historical Society,* Baltimore and New York, 1893–1960

SCHS   South Carolina Historical Society, Charleston, S.C.

TU   Tulane University, New Orleans, La.

UNC   Southern Historical Collection, University of North Carolina, Chapel Hill, N.C.

VHS   Virginia Historical Society, Richmond, Va.

VSL   Virginia State Library (now the Library of Virginia), Richmond, Va.

Our Sons Will Defend This Land

> To every thing there is a season and a time to every purpose
> under the heaven: . . . A time to love, and a time to hate; a
> time of war, and a time of peace.
>
> Eccelsiastes 3:1–8

ON MARCH 19, 1841, one of the oldest Jewish congregations in the United States, Kahal Kadosh Beth Elohim (Holy Congregation House of God) in Charleston, invited the entire community to the consecration of its new synagogue on Hasell Street. Constructed so that worshipers faced Jerusalem, the handsome neoclassical building, the first in the city to be constructed in the form of a Greek Doric temple, overflowed with Charlestonians of many faiths. "The public spirit of the Israelites of our city," the *Courier* wrote, "is worthy of the highest praise in rearing a temple of such classical mode." It was likely the most imposing synagogue building in America. The trustees, six of the oldest congregants, the *parnass* (president), and rabbi carried the sacred Torah (scrolls containing the Five Books of Moses) from the tabernacle next door to the new building. The ancient *shofar* (ram's horn) was sounded four times. The rabbi, Gustavus Poznanski, spoke for generations of Jewish Charlestonians when he exclaimed that "this synagogue is our *temple,* this city our *Jerusalem,* this happy land our *Palestine,* and as our fathers defended with

K. K. Beth Elohim as it appeared in the 1920s. It was, in a sense, the mother synagogue of Southern Judaism. Its rabbis and congregants assumed leadership roles throughout the South. (Raisin, "Centennial Booklet.")

The bombardment of Fort Sumter. The dramatic beginning of the Civil
War in Charleston harbor in April 1861 as depicted by Currier & Ives.
(Courtesy of the Library of Congress.)

their lives *that* temple, *that* city and *that* land, so will their sons defend *this* temple, *this* city, and *this* land."[1]

Twenty years later, on April 12, 1861, the Civil War began in Charleston harbor. Charleston Jewry, proud of their history and patriotism dating from the Revolution, rallied to the cause. Lt. Jacob Valentine commanded one of the chief artillery batteries in the bombardment of Fort Sumter. After the fort surrendered, Moses Cohen Mordecai's steamship, the *Isabel*, named for Mrs. Mordecai, transported Maj. Robert Anderson and his garrison to the waiting federal fleet. The Jews of Charleston enlisted in various units, and Rabbi Poznanski's son, Gustavus Jr., joined the Sumter Guard of the Charleston Battalion.[2]

Eight days after the bombardment of Fort Sumter and 275 miles away in Columbus, Georgia, a nineteen-year-old boy named Albert Luria sat with his family around the breakfast table when a message came that his company was to leave for Norfolk, Virginia, in two hours. Albert buttoned up his Confederate uniform, packed his trunk, and said his good-byes. He set out for town and stopped at his cousins' house, where he bid them an affectionate farewell.

Albert joined his company, the Columbus City Light Guards, Company A, 2d Georgia Infantry Battalion, and marched to the depot, where, amidst the crowd, were young Albert's family. His aunts, uncles, and cousins had walked to Columbus to send young Albert off to fight, although they were all prosperous planters accustomed to riding horseback or in carriages. It was Saturday, and, after all, the

Lt. Albert Luria. Luria served in the City Light Guards of Columbus, Georgia. He later was commissioned as a second lieutenant, Company I, 13th North Carolina Volunteers/23d North Carolina State Troops. In this photograph, he is seventeen years old and at military school in North Carolina. (Courtesy of Raphael J. Moses of Boulder, Colorado.)

family members were Orthodox Jews. "I did not anticipate seeing them," the young soldier wrote in his journal, "for as it was Saturday I knew they could not ride & hardly expected they would pay me the compliment of walking in."[3]

His parents, Eliza and Raphael J. Moses, were born and raised in observant Jewish homes in Charleston and descended from a long line of Jewish Southerners. Raphael Moses was so proud of his Sephardic ancestry that, not wanting his old family names to die out, he named one son, Albert, "Luria" and another son, Israel, "Nunez" to carry on those old Sephardic names. A successful lawyer and planter in Columbus, Moses also volunteered for the Confederate army and achieved the rank of major as Gen. James Longstreet's chief of commissary. In addition to Albert Luria, two other sons of Raphael J. Moses served in the Confederate armed forces.

Albert Luria saw action with his company on May 19, 1861, at Sewell's Point, near Norfolk, Virginia. There, he picked up a live bombshell that had been lobbed into the Confederate fort by a Union gunboat in Hampton Roads, and he threw it over the works before it could explode. He saved the lives of many men but refused a promotion. Had he been a British soldier, his regimental history stated, his heroic act "would have brought him the Victoria Cross and caused the world to ring his name."[4] He may have given thanks to God at synagogue B'nai Jaacov in Norfolk.

Albert's thirteen-year-old cousin Eliza, nicknamed "Lize," wrote in her journal in July 1861, "now he expects to go to Manassas junction, where he has longed to be ever since he left it. Why?—because it is the most dangerous place. He is now among all his friends that are left from that large battle. . . . If his precious life could be insured I would be sorry that he had not an opportunity to distinguish himself again; but everything happens for the best." On May 27, 1861, Albert had asked another cousin, Julia, to remember him to Lize and to thank her for her assistance in communicating his romantic feelings toward her, "even though I should never return to thank you in person."[5]

On May 31, 1862, Albert Luria, now a second lieutenant in the 23d North Carolina, was severely wounded as he led his men over the enemies' works at the Battle of Seven Pines in the Peninsular Campaign. Major Moses, his father, was stationed in Richmond and set out to find his son. Moses went to the hospital where the ambulance had carried Albert. He saw a group of ladies standing by a cot and heard one of them say: "What a handsome young man!" Major Moses recalled in his memoir: "I crossed over to the cot, and my shock was beyond my power of expression when I saw my son Albert lying unconscious with a wound to his head." His father took him to a relative's home, where he died. And thus, his father later wrote, "passed away a bright, promising youth of nineteen."[6]

Mary Chesnut, the wife of South Carolina Sen. James Chesnut, knew the Moses family well. She wrote in her famous diary:

> Miriam's Luria—and the coincidence of his life. Luria (born Moses) and the hero of the bombshell. His mother was at a hotel in Charleston. Kind hearted Anna DeLeon Moses went for her sister-in-law, gave up her own chamber to her, that her child might be born in the comfort and privacy of a home. Only our people [that is, Southerners] are given to such excessive hospitality. So little Luria was born in Anna DeLeon's chamber. After Chickahominy, when this man was mortally wounded—again Anna, who is now living in Richmond, found him, and again she brought him home—her house being crowded to the doorsteps. Again she gave up her chambers to him—and as he was born in her room, so he died.[7]

Albert Luria was buried at his family's plantation, The Esquiline, in Columbus. His cousin Eliza, the young girl Albert left behind, found comfort in her ancient faith: "God, who knows and does all things for the best, has seen fit to deprive me of my greatest treasure, so I must bow in submission to his will. . . . God knows he did his duty to his country, and he died as he said he wanted to die—on the field of battle."[8]

Gustavus Poznanski Jr.'s tomb at the Coming Street Cemetery, Charleston. (Author's collection. Photograph by Michael Levkoff.)

Albert Luria's story was repeated many times during the war. On June 21, 1862, three Jewish boys were killed at the Battle of Secessionville on James Island defending Charleston. They were Pvt. Robert Cohen, Cpl. Isaac D. Valentine, and the former rabbi's son Pvt. Gustavus Poznanski Jr. "Thus has fallen," the *Charleston Mercury* said of young Poznanski, "a gallant youth, of singular promise." The *Charleston Daily Courier* wrote, "No one more willingly gave a life to free the soil from the invader."[9] Like Albert Luria, Gustavus Poznanski was "a bright, promising youth of nineteen." And, like Albert Luria, Gustavus Poznanski Jr. died defending his temple, his city, and his land, just as his father said he would from the pulpit of Kahal Kadosh Beth Elohim on Hasell Street twenty-one years before.

PART 1

This Happy Land, Our Palestine

★ ★ ★ ★ ★ ★ ★ ★ ★ ★

FREEDOM AND EQUALITY IN THE OLD SOUTH

In a free and independent country like America, where civil and religious freedom go hand in hand, where no distinctions exist between the clergy of different denominations, where we are incorporated and known in law; freely tolerated; where in short we enjoy all the blessings of freedom in common with our fellow citizens, you may readily conceive we pride ourselves under the happy situation which makes us feel we are men, susceptible of that dignity which belongs to human nature, by participating in all the rights and blessings of this happy country.

Letter of Beth Elohim to London's Sephardic community
(1806), quoted in Faber, *The Jewish People in America*

K. K. Beth Elohim Synagogue, Charleston,
South Carolina, in 1794 (the print is mislabeled
1749). (Raisin, "Centennial Booklet.")

CHAPTER 1

★

The Free Air of Dixie

FROM ABRAHAM LINCOLN'S ELECTION as president of the United States in November 1860, through the secession winter of 1860, to the bombardment of Fort Sumter in April 1861, Jewish Southerners from Virginia to Texas weighed their devotion to the Union and to their states. "A storm, vast and terrible, is impending," Rabbi James K. Gutheim of New Orleans told his congregation.[1] Some were the sons and daughters—indeed, the grandsons and the granddaughters—of Southerners born and bred in Dixie. Some were slaveholders. A very few were planters. Some were descended from Sephardic Jews whose ancestors had been expelled from Spain and Portugal in the year Columbus set sail for the Orient.

Most Jewish Southerners, however, were Ashkenazi immigrants who in the 1840s and 1850s had fled Bavaria, Prussia, Alsace, Hesse, Baden, Swabia, Westphalia, Hungary, Poznań (Posen), and Silesia in Prussian Poland and Russian Poland to America, the fabled land of freedom.[2] "There is," one Hessian Jew wrote his brother in America, "only one land of liberty, which is ruled according to natural, reasonable laws, and that is the Union."[3] Rabbi Gutheim, himself an immigrant, reminded his congregation in a Thanksgiving sermon in 1860 that in the Old Country, the Jewish people endured "a life of tribulation and misery." But now, in America, the blessings of Providence "have been showered upon us."[4] They were peddlers and clerks, shopkeepers and saloon keepers, businessmen, liquor dealers, tobacco merchants, watchmakers, tanners, tailors, bakers, auctioneers, innkeepers, music teachers, grocers, and apothecaries. Thousands were young men who had fled their German fatherlands to avoid serving a tyrannical government in brutal, anti-Semitic armies. "Whatever you and many others may say about America," teacher Charles Mailert wrote, "you do not know European slavery, German oppression, and Hessian taxes."[5] Ludwig Börne exclaimed: "[B]ecause I was born a bondsman, I therefore love liberty more than you. Yes, because I have known slavery, I understand freedom more than you. Yes, because I was born without a fatherland my desire for a fatherland is more passionate than yours."[6]

Now they had to choose, the Sephardic grandee and the German peddler; the shipping tycoon Moses Cohen Mordecai, who lived in a great mansion south of Broad Street in Charleston and had served as *parnass* of Beth Elohim, and Henry Gintzberger, the immigrant peddler who had arrived penniless in Salem,

Bird's-eye view of Charleston in 1850. By 1861 there was an old and established Jewish community in Charleston. Jews had been living in South Carolina since 1695. There were three synagogues, the Hebrew Orphan Society building next to the courthouse on Broad Street, and prominent Jewish Charlestonians in all walks of life. (Courtesy of the South Carolina Historical Society.)

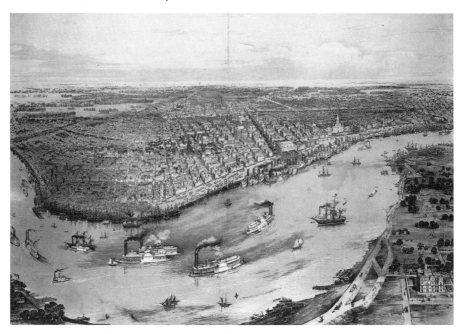

Bird's-eye view of New Orleans. In 1861 New Orleans was the Confederacy's largest city by far. It was also home to the largest Jewish community in the South. (Courtesy of Library of Congress.)

Virginia, in 1860. They had chosen freedom over tyranny and now they had to choose between two versions of freedom—one Union and one Confederate.[7]

★   ★   ★

Judah P. Benjamin in 1860. (*Battles and Leaders of the Civil War*.)

On December 31, 1860, the senior senator from Louisiana rose in the Senate Chamber to defend the right of the Southern states to secede from the Union. It was the Christmas season, and the Senate galleries were thronged with a crowd in high spirits. The senator wore a simple black suit. A pocket watch with a long chain hung across his vest. He was a short portly man with black curly hair and black eyes. He was an affable and cosmopolitan man, a popular senator, a dapper dresser, an inveterate gambler whose unusual voice was "silvery [and] sweet and beautifully modulated." He privately felt that secession would be a disaster, but in a few months he would become the Confederacy's lawyer. Over the course of the war, he would become its spymaster.

He spoke for more than an hour. His voice, Mrs. Jefferson Davis recalled in later years, "rose over the vast audience distinct and clear . . . he held his audience spellbound . . . so still were they that a whisper could have been heard." He reminded his colleagues that incessant attacks upon "the feelings and sensibilities of a high-spirited people by the most insulting language and the most offensive epithets" would lead to secession. He ridiculed Republican suggestions of coercion without war.

As he reached the end of his remarks, one hand was in his pocket, the other toying with his watch chain. "And now, senators," he said softly, "within a few weeks we part to meet as senators in one common council chamber of the nation no more forever. We desire, we beseech you, let this parting be in peace. . . . What may be the fate of this horrible contest, no man can tell, none pretend to foresee; but this much I will say: the fortunes of war may be adverse to our arms; you may carry desolation into our peaceful land, and with torch and fire you may set our cities in flames . . . you may, under the protection of your advancing armies, give shelter to the furious fanatics who desire, and profess to desire, nothing more than to add all the horrors of a servile insurrection to the calamities of civil war; you may do all this,—and more, too, if more there be—but you never can subjugate us."

Here, the senator released his grasp of his watch chain, as if the chains which held the South to the Union were now severed. He put his other hand in his pocket, and as he turned to take his seat, he added, "An enslaved and servile race you can never make of us—never! never!"[8] The whole gallery burst into uncontrollable applause so loud that the presiding officer, Sen. James M. Mason, attempted to clear the galleries. But the crowd was wild with enthusiasm.

It was one of the most dramatic moments in the history of the U.S. Senate. The senator was Judah P. Benjamin, the brilliant lawyer from New Orleans and the first senator of acknowledged Jewish descent in American history. Benjamin was a Southerner who lived by the Southern code of honor. In 1858, he clashed with Mississippi Sen. Jefferson Davis on the floor of the Senate. Davis declared in a stage whisper that he had "no idea that he was to be met with the arguments of a paid attorney in the Senate chamber." Benjamin challenged Davis to a duel without asking for a withdrawal or explanation. To his credit, Davis apologized publicly the next day.[9]

On December 31, 1860, Judah Benjamin was at the height of a remarkable career. He was married to a beautiful Louisiana Creole lady. He possessed great wealth, a successful legal practice, and the admiration of the people of Louisiana and the South. He had even declined a seat on the U.S. Supreme Court. He was now about to give up everything he held dear, including the company of his beloved sisters, nieces, and nephews, to support the South, to become the Confederacy's lawyer and counselor, the friend and ally of Jefferson Davis, and ultimately, to become the chief of espionage operations. Judah Benjamin made his choice.

On January 5, 1861, after South Carolina had seceded, eleven influential Southern senators, including Jefferson Davis, met in Washington. Two of them, Judah Benjamin and David Levy Yulee of Florida, were Southerners of Jewish origin. Most of them had long resisted secession, but now they had all made the fateful choice. They prepared resolutions calling for the secession of the Southern states and a convention in Montgomery, Alabama, in February to create a new government.

Judah Benjamin soon left Washington for New Orleans. He made arrangements to leave his family, his friends, his law practice, and all of his business interests. He made his last public address in New Orleans on February 22 and left for Montgomery. He would never return or see his brothers or sisters again. On February 25 he was unanimously confirmed as attorney general of the Confederacy. David Yulee stayed in Washington hoping to save the Union but also to gather information on the military situation in Florida in the event of secession. He arrived in Fernandina in early February and reported to Jefferson Davis, whom he had known for years. "Everywhere along the route I found among all classes a warm response to [your election which] has quieted concern and raised the popular heart in hopefulness. I doubt if Washington in his day had more entire hold upon public confidence."[10] A few weeks later he wrote Davis: "I hope you will not have occasion to take the field, but if there is a war . . . you have the example of Napoleon before you."[11]

The Solomon Cohen family of Savannah in 1851. Young Gratz Cohen is on
the left. (From the collection of Louis Schmier, Valdosta, Georgia.)

Abraham Charles Myers, the great-grandson of Moses Cohen, the first rabbi
of Charleston, a career soldier, and a graduate of West Point, surrendered the Federal supply depot in New Orleans to the Louisiana authorities and resigned his
hard-earned commission the same day. "South Carolina, the State where I was
born," his letter read, "and Louisiana, the State of my adoption, having in convention passed ordinances of secession from the United States, I am absolved from my
allegiance to the Federal government."[12]

"Now we of the South," Solomon Cohen of Savannah wrote his aunt in
Philadelphia, "seeing that public opinion, the law of the land in the North, is against
all that we hold valuable . . . and that the government is about to pass into the hands
of those who hate us and our institutions, feel that prudence and self-defense

demand that we should protect ourselves." Samuel Yates Levy, also from Savannah, joined the City Light Guard and was stationed on Tybee Island. His nephew, seventeen-year-old Octavus Cohen, volunteered for the Savannah Artillery. Isaac Hermann, a French immigrant, had arrived at Castle Garden in New York in 1859 and settled in Sandersville, Georgia. He joined the Washington Rifles, 1st (Ramsey's) Georgia Infantry in June.[13]

Young Jewish Southerners flocked to the Confederate banner. Haiman Kaminski, from Posen, and Solomon Emanuel, also an immigrant, both now living in Georgetown, South Carolina, joined Company A, 10th South Carolina.[14] In May, Adolph Proskauer, the son of a Prussian immigrant from Breslau, enlisted in Capt. Augustus Stikes's company, the Independent Rifles of Mobile, Alabama, which became Company C, 12th Alabama. He was appointed first corporal. A Polish immigrant to Texas, Herschell Kempner (now called Harris Kempner), joined the Ellis County Blues, a local militia unit that eventually became Company H of William H. Parsons's 12th Texas Cavalry. Lewis Leon, a recent immigrant from Germany, left his parents' home on Norfolk Street on the lower east side of New York City in 1858 at the age of seventeen. He settled in Charlotte, North Carolina, and when the war came he enlisted in the Charlotte Grays, 1st North Carolina Volunteers. Eugene Henry Levy of New Orleans enlisted as a private in Dreux's Battery. Two of his brothers, Joseph Calhoun and Julian, also volunteered.[14]

When the Richmond Light Infantry Blues left the capital of Virginia for battle in April 1861, fifteen of its ninety-nine members were Jews, including Ezekiel ("Zeke") J. Levy, its fourth sergeant. There was a Jewish contingent in the Richmond Grays. Myer Angle, the president of Beth Ahabah, the German synagogue, eventually had six sons in the Confederate army. Recent German Jewish immigrants from all over Virginia enlisted: Max Guggenheimer Jr. of Lynchburg, a native of Hurben, Bavaria, in the 11th Virginia; Aaron and Isadore Reinach of Petersburg in the 12th Virginia; and Leopold and Sampson Levy, natives of Altenstadt, Bavaria, in the 1st Virginia Cavalry. Fellow Bavarian Emanuel Gerst of Halifax County joined the 6th Virginia Cavalry.[15]

Thus, overwhelmingly, almost unanimously, some with fear and trepidation, others with courage and enthusiasm, some with reservations, others with a firm unflinching resolve, Southern Jewry cast its lot with the Confederate States of America. Many, like "Ike" Hermann, had found the land of Canaan. Others, like Gustavus Poznanski, had found their Jerusalem, their Palestine. Still others, like Marcus Baum, Jacob Samuels, Adolph Proskauer, and Herschell Kempner, had finally found their fatherland.

When in March 1865 Eugenia Levy Phillips's brother, Capt. Samuel Yates Levy, wrote his father from Johnson's Island, a Union prisoner of war camp, he spoke from his heart: "I long to breathe the free air of Dixie."[16]

★　　★　　★

Southern Jews had been breathing the free air of Dixie for two hundred years. No one knows who the first Southern Jews were. Elias Legardo has been said to be America's first known Jew, arriving in Virginia on the *Abigail* in 1621. The first confirmed documentation of a Jew living in Carolina was in 1695. John Locke's Fundamental Constitution of Carolina granted freedom of religion to "Ye Heathens, Jues [*sic*] and other Disenters." It was the first constitution in history to guarantee religious freedom to Jews. South Carolina was, according to Leonard Dinnerstein, the colony "most hospitable to Jews." It was little wonder, then, that the persecuted Jew, like the persecuted Huguenot and German Palatine, emigrated to South Carolina "to find a haven of rest."[17] When the planter Francis Salvador, an immigrant from England, was elected to the provincial Congresses of South Carolina between 1773 and 1776, he became the first Jew in modern history anywhere in the world to be elected to a popular assembly.[18]

The small Jewish community of Charles Town grew rapidly. Beth Elohim was founded in 1749. By 1820, there were 700 Jews in Charleston and 550 in New York City. In 1820 South Carolina boasted the largest Jewish population in the United States, and Charleston was the foremost Jewish community in the nation.[19] London Jewry sent a group of Jews to Georgia aboard the *William and Sarah,* which arrived in Savannah on July 11, 1733. In 1735 they founded K. K. Mikve Israel (Holy Congregation Hope of Israel), the third congregation in America, after New York and Newport, Rhode Island. Richmond's Jewish community established K. K. Beth Shalome (House of Peace) in 1789. By the 1820s, the immigrant Jews of Petersburg, Virginia, organized an informal congregation, and in 1858 Rodef Shalom was organized on Sycamore Street. There were Jewish families and merchants in Charlottesville, where David Isaacs sold goods to Thomas Jefferson, including, so the story goes, the ball of twine Mr. Jefferson used to lay out the first building of the University of Virginia.[20] Jacob De La Motta, a physician, spoke for Southern Jewry when he exclaimed at the dedication of Mikve Israel in Savannah in 1820: "On what spot in this habitable Globe does an Israelite enjoy more blessings, more privileges, or is more elevated in the sphere of preferment and more conspicuously dignified in respectable stations?"[21]

In the 1820s, New Orleans Jews organized Shangarai Chased (Gates of Mercy), the city's first synagogue, located in the French Quarter, where many Jews lived and worked. A New Yorker, Jacob de Silva Solis was in New Orleans on business during Passover in 1826 and was unable to buy matzo, the unleavened bread used during the Passover Seder. He determined to remedy the situation and, together with a number of German and French Jews, organized the first congregation.[22]

The Jews of the South lived in a slaveholding society, and they accepted the institution as part of everyday life. Living in cities and towns, those Jews who owned slaves utilized them as domestic servants, as workers in their trades, or they hired them out. "Acceptance of slavery was," Leonard Dinnerstein wrote, "an

16   aspect of southern life common to nearly all its white inhabitants." Indeed, it was
common to its free black inhabitants, who owned more slaves by far than Southern Jews. The free blacks of Charleston, for example, owned three times the number of slaves owned by Charleston Jewry.[23] Mark I. Greenberg points out that Jews
adopted the Southern way of life, including the code of honor, dueling, slavery, and
Southern notions about race and states' rights.[24]

In 1840 three-fourths of all heads of families in Charleston owned at least
one slave, and the incidence of slaveholding among Jews likely paralleled that of
their neighbors.[25] In Richmond, a few auctioneers sold slaves, and there was one
Jewish slave dealer, Abraham Smith. Richmond's rabbis supported slavery. George
Jacobs of Richmond hired a slave to work in his home, although he owned no
slaves.[26] Reverend Max Michelbacher prayed during the war that God would protect his congregation from slave revolt and that the Union's "wicked" efforts to
"beguile [the slaves] from the path of duty that they may waylay their masters, to
assassinate and slay the men, women, and children . . . be frustrated." Reverend
Michelbacher believed, together with the Christian clergy, that slavery was divinely
ordained. "The man servants and maid servants Thou has given unto us," he
prayed during the war, "that we may be merciful to them in righteousness and bear
rule over them, the enemy are attempting to seduce . . . [and] invite . . . to insurrection. . . . In this wicked thought, let them be frustrated, and cause them to fall
into the pit of destruction."[27]

The 1840s and 1850s brought a sea change to the Jewish population of the
United States. Between 1800 and 1860, 100,000 Jewish immigrants arrived from
Poland, Central Europe, and the German states such as Prussia and particularly
Bavaria, which "stood first in the row of intolerant states," infamous for "its
Pharaoh-like registration laws," its restriction of trade, marriage, and even the Jew's

Shearith Israel (Remnant of Israel)
Synagogue, Wentworth Street in
Charleston (between Anson and
Meeting Streets). The Orthodox
members of Beth Elohim seceded to
build this synagogue in the 1840s
when Beth Elohim installed an organ
and liberalized the service. The building was shelled in the Union bombardment. Charleston Jewry could
not support Beth Elohim, Shearith
Israel, and Berith Shalome after the
war. Shearith Israel was closed, and
this building was demolished in the
twentieth century. (Courtesy of K. K.
Beth Elohim Archive, Charleston,
South Carolina.)

right to reside in the place of his choice. Thus, while the Sephardim had been the earliest settlers, by 1860 Southern Jewry was overwhelmingly Ashkenazic, that is, German and Eastern and Central European. Some of these Ashkenazic Jews were "Anglicized," or "Americanized," Jews who had intermarried with and adopted the ways of the earlier Sephardim, who were masters of acculturation. These Ashkenazic Jews identified with Sephardic ideals, considered themselves Southerners, and looked upon the new German-Jewish immigrants as foreigners who needed to be taught local customs.[28]

The older established Southern Jewish families—whether Sephardic or Ashkenazic, German, Polish, English, assimilated, Reform, or Orthodox—were not prepared for this wave of German and Ashkenazic immigrants in the 1840s and 1850s. Their attitude toward the newcomers changed as the numbers increased. Some Sephardic families even said a Kaddish (prayer for the dead) when a Sephardi "intermarried" with a German Jewish immigrant. By 1860 there were few Sephardic Jews left in the South, most having intermarried with Gentiles and Ashkenazic Jews. Dr. Malcolm H. Stern concluded that "almost the entire early Sephardic community became completely absorbed by the Ashkenazic."[29]

When the Civil War began, Southern Jewry was an integral part of the Confederate States of America. Louisiana boasted at least five congregations. New Orleans had the seventh largest Jewish population in the United States (Boston was sixth and Chicago eighth).[30] "In Charleston," I. J. Benjamin wrote, "Israelites occupy the most distinguished places." With the addition in 1855 of a Polish and German congregation, Berith Shalome, located in a house on St. Philip Street near Calhoun Street, there were now three synagogues in Charleston, as well as the Hebrew Orphan Society building on Broad Street and dozens of Jewish-owned businesses on King Street. There were sizable Jewish communities in Columbia, Sumter, and Georgetown. In 1846 the Shearith Israel (Remnant of Israel) congregation was formed in Columbia. The DeLeon family, Sephardim from Leon, Spain, lived in Charleston, Camden, and Columbia, and by 1860 had become one of the leading Jewish families of the state. Dr. Mordecai H. DeLeon served as mayor of Columbia and was a close friend of the controversial Dr. Thomas Cooper, president of South Carolina College. DeLeon's sons, David Camden, Edwin, and Thomas Cooper (named for Dr. Cooper), were all to play a prominent role in the life of the Confederacy.[31]

There were Jewish communities throughout Georgia. In 1861, Mikve Israel was located near Chippewa Square, and Jewish businessmen prospered. There were 2,500 Jews in Savannah, Augusta, Macon, Atlanta, Columbus, and numerous small towns and villages throughout Georgia. Jews had lived in Augusta since 1802, and a large influx of German immigrants arrived in the 1840s. By 1846, B'nai Israel (Children of Israel) was founded when the "scattered Israelites of Augusta, Georgia and Hamburg, South Carolina, desirous of uniting as a band of brothers, with a view of publicly worshiping the God of Abraham, Isaac, and Jacob," formed a congregation.[32] In 1854 twenty Jewish families in Columbus founded Temple B'nai Israel. In 1859 they bought a house to use as a synagogue.[33]

Eleven German Jews organized Beth Israel (House of Israel) in Macon in 1859. By 1861 members of the congregation were active in the unfolding of events: R. Einstein was a delegate to the state Democratic Party convention, which supported the pro-Southern candidate for president. The Macon German Artillery, consisting of German immigrants, both Christian and Jewish, was ordered into state service in September 1861, and four Binswangers, two Sangers, and an Einstein, a Nordlinger, a Kahn, and other Macon Jews went with their company.[34]

Atlanta, that creation of cotton and the railroad, was a wilderness in 1836. But it grew dramatically after the railroad arrived in the 1840s and 1850s. From 20 families in 1845 it grew to 9,554 in 1860. Its population consisted of native Southern whites and a few immigrants. The first Atlanta Jews came for the same reason non-Jews came: economic opportunity. Jacob Haas and Henry Levi, peddlers from Hessendarmstadt, came in 1845 to open a dry goods store. They soon built one of the town's largest stores. Aaron Alexander, a Sephardi from Charleston, came in 1848 and operated a drugstore at the "Sign of the Negro and the Mortar," where he, like many Jewish merchants, sold medical and dental supplies, paint, window glass, perfume, and wine and liquor. Aaron Alexander's wife, Sarah Moses Alexander, established the first Jewish Sabbath school, which, as Henry Aaron Alexander wrote in 1954, "she conducted in the forest around her home with fallen logs for benches," stressing the Ten Commandments and how and when to say the *Shema*, then pronounced *Shemang* ("Hear, O Israel, the Lord our God, the Lord is One").[35]

Georgia Jewry reflected the variety of the Jewish experience in the South. Louis Merz from Durkheim, Bavaria, emigrated in 1853, arrived at Philadelphia, and went to live in LaGrange in westernmost Georgia for a time. A peddler, he eventually settled in the small town of West Point between LaGrange and Columbus when the railroad came to the town. He was a merchant, a quiet, intellectual man who became a part of small-town Georgia life. His sister Betty also came to America and settled in Cincinnati. She later married Herman Heyman, her brother's partner, and moved to West Point. Their brother Daniel also came to West Point, while Merz's parents and one sister remained in Bavaria. Merz was to enlist in the West Point Guards, Company D of the 4th Georgia.[36]

Not far from West Point in Columbus, Georgia, Raphael J. Moses, a fifth-generation Sephardic Jew, lived on his plantation, The Esquiline, named for one of the Roman hills. Moses had worked as a peddler, retail merchant, and a farmer, and eventually became a planter and a lawyer after speculating in land in Florida. One of the first Georgians to successfully grow and market peaches and plums, Moses is credited with shipping the first peaches from the South. His family was completely acculturated into Columbus society while remaining devout Jews.

Moses became involved in politics and, being a South Carolinian by heritage and upbringing, was a committed secessionist.[37]

Moses had always been a strong supporter of states' rights. He had favored nullification in the 1830s, was opposed to popular sovereignty in the 1840s, and supported secession in the 1850s. When the war broke out, he had forty-seven slaves. Thus, it was natural that Raphael Moses was in the forefront of secession and war. Like many other Georgians, he and his son, Albert Luria, were in Milledgeville, Georgia, in January 1861 to show the delegates to the secession convention that the people were for it.[38]

Many Richmond Jews likely agreed with Raphael Moses's states' rights position. Richmond's Jewish community had grown so that by 1860 the capital of Virginia was home to three congregations and dozens of thriving Jewish-owned mercantile establishments. There were still a few Sephardic and Anglicized families, but the great majority were Ashkenazic Jews from Bavaria, the Palatinate (western Germany), and the North. Richmond's Jewry could look with pride on its success. In 1861, Beth Shalome, the old Sephardic synagogue, was located on Mayo Street near Franklin. The German Jews had established K. K. Beth Ahabah (House of Love) in 1841 and built a synagogue on Eleventh Street between Marshall and Clay (near the Valentine Museum) in 1848. A Polish congregation, Kenesseth Israel (Congregation of Israel) was established in 1856. As in other Southern communities, Richmond had had a Jewish mayor and Jews were active in civic and military affairs.[39]

German immigrants also lived in Alexandria, Lynchburg, Harrisonburg, Staunton, Fredericksburg, and Norfolk, Virginia. A small congregation, Beth El, was organized in Alexandria in 1859. Norfolk's early Jewish community was revitalized by the German Jews in the 1840s. Jacob Umstadter, who had been trained

K. K. Beth Shalome (Holy Congregation of the House of Peace) Synagogue, Mayo Street, Richmond. Richmond's first synagogue, consecrated in 1822, was built in the center of the city near the capitol. The congregation was founded in 1789. In 1860 it was also called the Portuguese Synagogue. This photograph was taken in 1890. The building was demolished in 1935, and Mayo Street itself became a victim of urban growth. The site today is in the middle of a modern government complex. (Courtesy of the Jacob Rader Marcus Center, American Jewish Archives, Cincinnati, Ohio.)

House of Jacob Synagogue, Norfolk, Virginia. The first synagogue in Norfolk, built in 1859 just before the war began. It was named in honor of its founder, Jacob Umstadter. Later called the Cumberland Street Shul, it housed the congregation until 1878, when it became Beth-El synagogue. (Courtesy of Ohef Sholom Temple and the Norfolk Public Library, Sargeant Memorial Room.)

as a *shochet* and *hazzan* (cantor), helped organize Chevra B'nai Jaacov (Association of the Sons of Jacob, or House of Jacob) in 1848. By 1859 they had built a synagogue on Cumberland Street.[40]

After Richmond and Appomattox, Manassas is the most well-known place-name in Virginia's Civil War history. It was named for a Jew who kept an inn there in the eighteenth century. In the Bible, Manasseh (*Menasheh* in Hebrew) was the name of Joseph's firstborn son and also one of the twelve tribes of Israel. There was an innkeeper named Manasseh who, according to the *Richmond Enquirer* in August 1861, was "a caterer for the traveling public, we believe a Jew, who for a long time had his house of entertainment there." The innkeeper was widely known and much esteemed for his good cheer, and many a horseman would travel a little longer "that he might spend the night with 'Old Manasseh.' . . . In short, he was as well known as his gap, and from him the latter caught its name of Manasseh's Gap."[41]

On the eve of the Civil War, there were approximately two thousand Jews in the Old Dominion. Most agreed with Edmund Myers, who wrote to his uncle, Sam Mordecai, "I am with [Virginia]—bound to her for the issue be it weal or for woe."[42]

Native Jewish Southerners and German Jewish immigrants, like their fellow Southerners and Americans, went west during the antebellum period and helped settle Alabama, Mississippi, Tennessee, Louisiana, Arkansas, and Texas, the

Gates of Heaven, Mobile, Alabama. This synagogue, also known as the Jackson Street synagogue, stood at the northeast corner of St. Michael and Jackson. It was occupied by the congregation from 1853 to 1907. This photograph was taken in 1907. (Courtesy of Gates of Heaven [Sha'arai Shomayim] Temple Archives and Robert J. Zietz, Mobile, Alabama.)

The Interior of Gates of Heaven. This photograph, taken in 1907, shows the interior of the Jackson Street synagogue. Note the balconies for the women, who must sit in a separate section from the men according to Orthodox Judaism. (Courtesy of Gates of Heaven [Sha'arai Shomayim] Temple Archives and Robert J. Zietz, Mobile, Alabama.)

remaining states of the Confederacy. Many Jews from the German states and Central Europe settled in Mobile in the 1840s and 1850s. The first congregation in Alabama, Sha'arai Shomayim U-Maskil El Dol (Congregation of the Gates of Heaven and Society of the Friends of the Needy) was organized in the early 1840s. A synagogue on Jackson Street was dedicated in 1853. Protestant and Catholic clergy attended. "The synagogue is worthy in all respects the high character of our Jewish brethren for wealth, intelligence and character," the *Mobile Register* exclaimed. "How proud must the enfranchised descendants of the patriarchs have felt yesterday who were some time since the slaves and serfs of Russia, Austria and Prussia." A second synagogue on Jackson Street burned down in 1856, and a new synagogue was built on Jackson Street between St. Louis and St. Michael in 1858. There were congregations in Montgomery and other smaller Alabama towns.[43]

Mayer Lehman arrived in Montgomery, Alabama, at the age of eighteen from the village of Rimpar near Würzburg, Bavaria, in 1850. His older brother Chaim, who changed his name to Henry, had arrived four years earlier and became a peddler. Another brother, Emanuel, came in 1847. The brothers opened a shop on Commerce Street. Eventually, Henry Lehman & Brothers moved to 17 Court Square near the courthouse. As Montgomery and the cotton trade grew, so did the Lehmans' business. Montgomery became the state capital and a center of the booming cotton economy. Warehouses and cotton trading abounded. One traveler noted that the people "buy cotton, sell cotton, think cotton, eat cotton, drink cotton, and dream cotton. They marry cotton wives, and unto them are born cotton children." The Lehmans became cotton dealers as well as grocers, dry goods merchants, and suppliers to the cotton planters. Emanuel traveled to New York and Henry to New Orleans to buy goods and broker cotton. When Henry died of yellow fever in 1856, the two younger brothers, Mayer and Emanuel, carried on the family business.[44]

On the eve of the Civil War, Lehman Brothers was a large and successful cotton brokerage house with offices in New York City. Emanuel moved to New York. Mayer married Babette Newgass of New Orleans, also an immigrant from Würzburg, and they lived in Montgomery. The Lehmans were prominent citizens of Montgomery. Alan Nevins wrote that they lived in a house "roomy enough to permit the clerks in the general store to come in—after a general custom of the time—for meals. This was no great hardship to the young wife, for they had household slaves." They traveled back and forth to New Orleans on business and for family and social occasions. Mayer Lehman was a typical Alabama merchant. A staunch Democrat, he was well connected in political circles. He was also a practicing Jew in a town with a small but active Jewish community.[45]

In Mississippi and Arkansas, German and Central European Jews settled in small towns and hamlets, opening stores and putting down roots. There were small Jewish communities in Woodville, Natchez, Vicksburg, Fayette, and Jackson. B'nai

Mayer Lehman. The Lehmans, immigrants from Bavaria, settled in Montgomery and became successful cotton brokers and dry goods merchants prior to the war. Lehman made strenuous efforts to aid the Alabama Confederate prisoners held in Union prisoner of war camps. He was the father of Sen. Herbert H. Lehman of New York, whom he named for his lawyer, a Confederate colonel. (Courtesy of the Jacob Rader Marcus Center, American Jewish Archives, Cincinnati, Ohio.)

Israel in Natchez was organized in 1840, although no synagogue was built prior to the war. Typical of Mississippi Jewry, Aaron Beekman emigrated in the 1840s from Forets, Germany, opened a store on Franklin Street in Cotton Square, and helped oversee the Natchez Hebrew School with twenty-five children. Other congregations were also founded in Mississippi prior to the war. Gemiluth Chassed was organized in Port Gibson in 1859, and a congregation gathered upstairs at Bernard Yoste's Levee Street building in Vicksburg. Congregation Beth Israel built a synagogue in early 1861 in Jackson on South State and South Streets, which was burned by Union troops during the war.[46]

Louisiana in 1860 was a phenomenon in American Jewish history. That keen correspondent for the *London Times,* William Howard Russell, the author of *My Diary North and South,* wrote: "It is a strange country, indeed; one of the evils which afflicts the Louisianians, they say, is the preponderance and influence of South Carolinian Jews, and Jews generally, such as [Edwin Warren] Moise, Mordecai, Josephs, and Judah Benjamin, and others. The subtlety and keenness of the Caucasian intellect give men a high place among a people who admire ability and dexterity, and are at the same time reckless of means and averse to labor. The Governor is supposed to be somewhat under the influence of the Hebrews."[47]

Canal Street in the Civil War era. Many Jewish businesses were located on Canal Street, as was the Dispersed of Judah synagogue prior to 1860. (Courtesy of the Louisiana State Museum, New Orleans.)

The Jewish Orphans House in New Orleans. By 1856 the large and prosperous Jewish community of New Orleans was able to build the only such Jewish home in America. Unfortunately, the city's epidemics made such an institution necessary. The building no longer exists. (Courtesy of the Louisiana State Museum, New Orleans.)

Judah Benjamin was the most famous of these "South Carolinian Jews." Lt. Gov. Henry M. Hyams was Benjamin's cousin, having come to Louisiana with Benjamin from Charleston in 1828. Edwin Warren Moise had served as Speaker of the Louisiana House and was to serve as a Confederate judge. When young Salomon de Rothschild, of the great French Jewish banking family, arrived in New Orleans in 1861, he was amazed at the success of the Jews of Louisiana. "What is astonishing here . . . is the high position occupied by our coreligionists, or rather by those who were born into the faith and who, having married Christian women, and without converting, have forgotten the practices of their fathers. Benjamin, the attorney general of the Confederate States, is perhaps the greatest mind on this continent. Hyams, the [lieutenant] governor of Louisiana, Moyse . . . [that is, Edwin W. Moise, the Speaker of the House], etc. And, what is odd, all these men have a Jewish heart and take an interest in me, because I represent the greatest Jewish house in the world."[48]

Estimates of the Jewish population are wholly unreliable, but in 1860 Louisiana was home to at least 8,000 Jews, and likely many more. The total number of Jews in the eleven states of the Confederacy was in the range of 20,000 to 25,000, which means that Louisiana was home to 25 percent to 40 percent of Southern Jewry. New Orleans in 1860,was the South's largest city by far. Its population of 168,675 dwarfed Charleston's (40,522), Richmond's (37,910), Mobile's (29,258), and Savannah's (22,292). Like the growing cities of the North and West, New Orleans beckoned to immigrants and they came.[49]

By 1850 New Orleans Jewry supported a number of Jewish institutions. In 1845 the small Sephardic community had organized its own congregation, K. K. Nefutzoth Yehudah (The Dispersed of Judah), rejecting an appeal to join with the German synagogue. In 1847, the philanthropist Judah Touro purchased an Episcopal church at the corner of Canal and Bourbon Streets in the French Quarter, renovated it, and presented it to the Dispersed of Judah congregation. In 1856, Dispersed of Judah built a larger facility on Carondelet near Julia Street. In 1851 Gates of Mercy moved to a new building on Rampart Street between St. Louis and Conti.[50]

In the 1850s Central European and German Jewish immigrants in the working-class suburb of Lafayette City, just up the river from downtown New Orleans, founded Shaarai Tefillah (Gates of Prayer). This area was populated by the Irish and the Jews and was later known as the Irish Channel, the Garden District, and part of Central City. Most members of this congregation worked in the clothing or dry goods business, or were petty merchants or peddlers who arrived from Bavaria and Alsace. In 1855, the congregation bought a little schoolhouse at the corner of St. Mary and Fulton Streets, known as the "Old Lafayette Schule." The last New Orleans synagogue to be founded before the Civil War was the "Polish Congregation," Temime Derech (the Right Way), organized in 1857.[51]

26 The Solomon family of New Orleans was typical of older Southern Jewish families. Solomon and Emma Solomon were born and raised in South Carolina. Sephardim, they traced their ancestry to England and possibly the British West Indies. They were part of the Jewish "haute bourgeoisie," who, according to Elliott Ashkenazi, "were reasonably successful financially, mixed well with the general white southern population, intermarried regularly, and adopted many southern customs, including slave ownership, but still retained a Jewish identity." Their teenage daughter, Clara Solomon, was very Americanized in her speech and writing, but occasionally used a Yiddish expression (such as *ponum* for "face"). She had many Christian friends and acquaintances. The Solomons belonged to Dispersed of Judah and attended services on Carondelet Street, within walking distance of their home on Hercules Street (now Rampart) in the lower Garden District.[52]

In 1861 the New Orleans Jewish community was the largest in the South by far, numbering an estimated four thousand souls. A 1905 history of the Jewish Orphan's Home puts the number of Jews at two thousand in 1854, the year after the yellow fever epidemic, which was the immediate cause of the creation of the home. If these figures are accurate, then the size of the Jewish community in New Orleans doubled in the seven years preceding the Civil War, a fact which is consistent with the city's general history.[53]

New Orleans Jewry, like the city's population in general, was a different mix from Charleston or Savannah. Like Macon and Mobile, it consisted largely of recent immigrants. There were relatively few old New Orleans Jewish families. While there were four congregations, most Jews had little identification with the Jewish community. The Jewish leadership did not necessarily influence the Jewish population. Unlike Charleston, Savannah, or Richmond, where Jewish families considered themselves a long-established part of the city, New Orleans's most

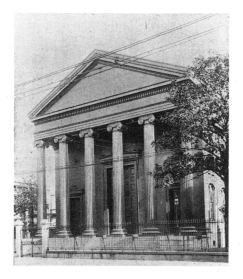

K. K. Nefutzoth Yehudah (Holy Congregation of the Dispersed of Judah). This Sephardic or "Portuguese" congregation was organized in 1845, rejecting an appeal to join with the German synagogue, Gates of Mercy. By the Civil War, the synagogue was located on Carondelet near Julia Street. Gates of Mercy and Dispersed of Judah merged after the Civil War in 1881 to form the Touro Synagogue. The building is no longer in existence, although the Touro Synagogue congregation still exists in a handsome building on St. Charles Avenue near Napoleon. (Courtesy of the Touro Infirmary Archives, New Orleans. Photograph from *The History of the Jews of Louisiana*, likely taken in the early 1900s.)

(*Above*) One of six Solomon girls, Clara was sixteen when the war broke out. She was studying at the Louisiana Normal School to become a teacher. (Courtesy of Alice Dale Cohan of Great Neck, New York.)

K. K. Shangarai Chased (Gates of Mercy), "the Old Deutsche Shule." The congregation, New Orleans's first, was founded in the 1820s. It was known as "the German congregation." By the 1860s, the congregation was worshiping at this synagogue on North Rampart Street. The building was demolished. (Courtesy of the Touro Infirmary Archives, New Orleans.)

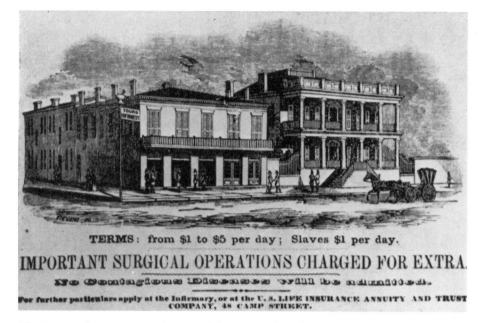

TERMS: from $1 to $5 per day; Slaves $1 per day.

IMPORTANT SURGICAL OPERATIONS CHARGED FOR EXTRA.

No Contagious Diseases will be admitted.

For further particulars apply at the Infirmary, or at the U. S. LIFE INSURANCE ANNUITY AND TRUST COMPANY, 48 CAMP STREET.

The Touro Infirmary, New Orleans. Judah Touro endowed this hospital, which served the entire New Orleans community. It was located at New Levee and Gaiennie streets, south of Canal Street. (Courtesy of the Touro Infirmary Archives, New Orleans.)

successful Jews had completely assimilated and lost their Jewish identity. Thus, this large mass of immigrants lacked a strong link to the past and to the traditions of the city. And New Orleans was a different city from the other great Southern cities in the East. In 1850 one-fourth of the free population of Louisiana was foreign born, and this figure was undoubtedly much higher for New Orleans.[54]

Rural Louisiana was also home to many Jews. Many recent immigrants set out to make their living in the small towns, villages, and crossroads of rural Louisiana. By 1860 the number of Jews living in rural Louisiana equaled the Jewish population of New Orleans.[55] The experience of the Hyams family, although hardly typical, is illustrative.

A merchant family, the Hyamses were originally from Charleston, where they were members of Beth Elohim. In 1828, at the age of twenty-two, Henry Michael Hyams came to New Orleans with his cousin Judah P. Benjamin. Young Hyams had been a founding member of the Reformed Society of Israelites in 1825. He explored Louisiana looking for opportunities and began his career as a cashier at the Canal Bank in Donaldsonville in the early 1830s. He became a planter, amassing a fortune and becoming one of the largest landholders in Louisiana. In 1835 Hyams was active in anti-abolitionist activities and served on a vigilance committee whose mission was to stop antislavery propaganda in the area.

In 1840 he owned forty-two slaves. Over the years, Hyams was involved in the railroad and insurance business, real estate, planting, politics, and law. In 1859 he became lieutenant governor of Louisiana, the first Jew elected to that office in American history. In 1861 the impressionable young Salomon de Rothschild found Hyams to be "a topnotch man . . . on whose shoulders rests all the work of the State of Louisiana." Although he married outside the faith, Hyams always regarded himself as a practicing Jew and attended services at Dispersed of Judah. He was proud of his Jewish lineage, which was both Sephardic and Ashkenazic.

In 1860 the second largest Jewish community in Louisiana was in Shreveport, a town in northwestern Louisiana at the opposite end of Louisiana from New Orleans. Jewish immigrants from all over Europe came to Shreveport. By 1850 there were thirty Jews in the town, and in 1859 the Har El (Mountain of God) congregation was chartered. When the war came, at least seventy-eight Jews from Shreveport served in the Confederate armed services. Almost all of them were German, Polish, or Central European. The congregation resolved in May 1861 to "scorn and repel" the advice of the *Jewish Messenger* of New York to stand by the union and affirmed their devotion to the Confederacy.[56]

Jews settled up the Mississippi in Memphis, Tennessee. According to tradition, a Charleston Jew, Joseph J. Andrews, the son-in-law of the Revolutionary patriot Haym Salomon, was the founder of Memphis Jewry.[57] B'nai Israel (Children of Israel) was founded in 1853. Judah Touro bequeathed the small congregation $2,000, and in 1858 the former Farmers and Mechanics Bank Building on the corner of Main and Exchange Streets in Memphis was rented by the congregation and dedicated as the first synagogue in Tennessee. There had been individual Jews in and around Nashville since the late 1790s, but it was not until the late 1840s that services were held at the home of Isaac Garritson. In August 1852 Garritson wrote Isaac Leeser that the Hebrew Benevolent Society "is at present very small yet numbering only 5 families and about 8 young men." This simple description illustrates the preponderance of young men in the new immigrant Jewish population of the South in the years leading up to the war. K. K. Mogen David (Shield, or Star, of David) was chartered by the legislature in 1854 and was located on North Market Street. Tradition has it that the name was chosen in honor of Davidson County, in which Nashville was located. A second Orthodox congregation, Ohava Emes, was founded in 1859 and was located over Fry's store on South Market.

The Felsenthals of Tennessee came from Alsace. The family took its name from *Fels und thal* ("rock and dale"), and family tradition has it that Herz Felsenthal attended the historic Sanhedrin assembled by Napoleon in 1806. Jacob ("Jake") Felsenthal left Munchweiler, in the Alseng, for America and settled in Brownsville, Tennessee. He was soon followed by his brother, Joseph. In 1856 they established a mercantile business that became Felsenthal Department Store. The brothers married two sisters in Germany. Joseph married Regina, and Jacob married

Pvt. Joseph Felsenthal of Company B, 9th
Tennessee. (Courtesy of Betty Santandrea
and the Felsenthal family.)

Karolina. Cecilia Felsenthal, a descendant, wrote that "their home became a haven
for other relatives. Two nieces lived with them and, in due time, there was to be a
double wedding." Since Brownsville had no newspaper, Uncle Jake had handbills
printed announcing "Double Jewish Wedding at the First Baptist Church."[58]

Texas was America's Southern frontier in the 1850s. "Thousands of acres of
land can be bought, within settled portions of the state, for the small sum of from
25 cents to $1 per acre," Lewis A. Levy wrote a New York Jewish newspaper from
Houston in 1850. He advised fellow Jews to come to Texas, "where a man can
make his living to his liking, and [be] more independent than the Autocrat of Russia, or the Emperor of Austria." Beginning in the early nineteenth century, Jews
began trickling into the Lone Star State. Spanish Jews came as well as Ashkenazic.
Jacob De Cordova, for example, was born in Jamaica to a planter family and emigrated to New Orleans and then Texas. He arrived in Galveston in 1837 and
became a merchant, served in public office, and eventually became an important
land developer who publicized Texas in three books and through his land agency.
In 1858 he wrote that, as Texas was an agricultural country, the "immigration of the
children of Israel has been very limited." However, he continued, Texas "is a country where the poor man can easily obtain land." And while the state was indeed "a
'land flowing with milk and honey,' it is necessary to FIRST MILK THE COWS
AND GATHER THE HONEY." He moved to Houston, then to Bosque County
near Waco, in the 1850s. During the war he was a tax collector.[59]

A typical Texas Jew in this era, Harris Kempner arrived in New York City in
1854, "another face in a boatload of Polish immigrants," according to a descendant.
He was seventeen, a German-speaking Pole escaping from the czar's tyrannical

rule of Russian Poland. "Harris" was the Americanized version of "Herschell," his Hebrew name. A tall, muscular youth, ambitious and aggressive, Kempner began his career at twenty cents an hour as a bricklayer's assistant, and, by dint of hard work, saved his money and moved to Texas. He settled in Cold Springs, San Jacinto County, a cotton-growing and timbering region in southeast Texas, which may have reminded him of his boyhood village. Beginning as a peddler, he built a general merchandise store and developed a good reputation.[60]

Texas had a small Jewish community in 1860. There were, for example, only 108 Jews in Houston in 1860, only one of whom had been born in Texas. Most had come from Germany, some from Poland and Eastern Europe. Many were single men from Bavaria and Poland.[61] Galveston was a bustling pioneer town in the 1850s. Michael Seeligson was elected mayor in 1853, but no synagogue was built until after the war. (The first synagogue in Texas, B'nai Israel, was built in Galveston in 1871.) Congregation Beth Israel in Houston was founded in 1854 and chartered in 1859.

As we have seen, the Old South was remarkably free of prejudice against Jews. Historians, travelers, residents, newspapers, business leaders, and all contemporary observers agree that the Old South was a hospitable climate for Jewish Southerners. Historians of the American Jewish experience reached a consensus long ago that Jews were more accepted in the antebellum South than in the North. "For Southern Jews," Howard M. Sacher wrote in *A History of the Jews in America,* "loyalty to the Confederacy often was a matter of intense personal gratitude. Nowhere else in America had they experienced such fullness of opportunity or achieved comparable political and social acceptance."[62]

Joseph Kershaw, the founder of Camden, South Carolina, left "To God's Anticent [*sic*] people the Jews [a lot] for a Burying ground and place of worship whenever they may incline to build upon the same." In Savannah, the Gentile community helped fund the renovation of Mikve Israel in the 1850s. In 1859, an improbable journalist, Israel Joseph Benjamin, set out to emulate a famous medieval traveler, Benjamin of Tudela, who had made a circuit of the known world about 1170 "to describe the scattered remnants of the tribes of Israel."[63] Benjamin, from the Turkish province of Moldavia, wrote his accounts from 1859 to 1862. He reached this conclusion about Southern Jewry: "The southern states, however, for natural reasons, outdid, in many respects, the northern states in hospitality. The white inhabitants felt themselves united with, and closer to, other whites—as opposed to the Negroes. Since the Israelite there did not do the humbler kinds of work which the Negro did, he was quickly received among the upper classes and easily rose to high political rank. For this reason, until now, it was only the South which sent Jews to the Senate. Benjamin came from Louisiana; Yulee from Florida; Louisiana has elected Hyams lieutenant governor."[64]

I. J. Benjamin's belief that Jews, being white, were a welcome ally against blacks is simplistic. The Jews were in mercantile trade, which was more respectable than manual labor, and they were frequently more accepted in Southern society than the Irish.[65] The South attracted few immigrants, and white minorities were therefore more readily accepted. Most importantly, the planter elite and Southern aristocracy were more tolerant in matters of religion than of social class. Unlike New England in the eighteenth and early nineteenth centuries, where Puritanism spawned anti-Semitism, the Southern leadership tended to be Episcopalians, Presbyterians, and Methodists, the most tolerant of the Protestant denominations, and were cosmopolitan and educated people who appreciated those qualities in their Jewish neighbors. While the "mob calls him, 'Mr. Davis's pet Jew,' a King Street Jew," Mary Chesnut wrote of Judah P. Benjamin, her husband, Senator Chesnut, thought Benjamin "the very cleverest man we had in the Senate."[66] The Southern aristocrats were not threatened by Jews as competitors, and their quality of life was enhanced by the presence of Jewish teachers, musicians, innkeepers, lawyers, doctors, druggists, merchants, and men of learning. The planters certainly did not need the Jews as allies against the blacks. First, the Jews were an insignificant fraction of the population, and, second, the planters could have persecuted the Jews *and* kept the blacks enslaved as was amply demonstrated by the Ku Klux Klan in the twentieth century. The acceptance of the Jews in the Old South was a simple matter of a small, law-abiding, educated, and productive minority who brought diversity to Southern life, together with much-needed mercantile skills and loyalty to the existing order.

Mary and James Chesnut of South Carolina were typical of aristocratic Southerners. The Jews they knew were cosmopolitan and educated, qualities Mary admired.[67] But Jews were different, and Mary was keenly aware of that difference.

Gen. Robert E. Lee's headquarters flag. Lee's flag was flown at his headquarters when he encamped. According to Joseph H. Crute Jr. in *Emblems of Southern Valor*, its star pattern represents the Ark of the Covenant and was "symbolic of the Bread of Life which is the symbol of spiritual nourishment." Nineteenth-century Southerners identified Jews with the ancient Hebrews and were much taken with Old Testament symbols. Whether Lee's flag actually depicted the Ark of the Covenant or not, the imagery was consistent with Southerners' fascination with ancient Israel. (Courtesy of the Museum of the Confederacy, Richmond, Virginia. Photograph by Katherine Wetzel.)

She referred to her friend Miriam ("Mem") DeLeon Cohen in her diary as "My Hebrew friend" or "Jewish angel." Mem was a practicing Jew, and Mary respected her friend's religion.[68] She wrote, "Mem is proud of her high lineage," and "Cohen is a high name among Jews."[69]

Southerners believed fervently in the God of the Old Testament and respected their Jewish neighbors' knowledge of the Bible. The learned Jew of a small Southern town often settled theological disputes among Christians. Isidor Straus's family came to Talbotton, Georgia, in the 1850s. "Our family was received with kindness and hospitality," Straus recalled. "My father, always a student and well versed in biblical literature and the Bible, which he read in the original, was much sought by the ministers of the various denominations, several of whom habitually dined at our house when in Talbotton on their circuit. At such times the discussion usually ran along theological lines. One of my earliest recollections is hearing my father take passages from the Old Testament and translate them literally for the information of these ministers."[70]

Southerners frequently used Jewish references from the Bible and saw the Jewish people of ancient times as noble and heroic. For example, David Clopton wrote to Sen. Clement C. Clay, "Delay is submission, 'to your tents O! Israel' and let the God of battles decide the issue."[71] Mary Chesnut likened the "stay-at-home men" working their plantations to "the old Jews while Noah was building the Ark," and compared Southerners to Jews for believing they were "the chosen people of God. And that he is fighting for us." Keenly aware of the differences in theology, Mary Chesnut wrote that Willie [William B.] Myers "was so angelically beautiful that at first they thought he must be their still expected messiah."[72] Stonewall Jackson was perceived by his men as Moses-like, leading the Southern people across the Red Sea. A well-known Civil War song, "Stonewall Jackson's Way," published in 1862, contained these lines:

> Lay bare thine arm,
> Stretch forth thy rod,
> Amen.
> *That's* Stonewall Jackson's way![73]

An 1861 Southern song, "The Southrons' Chaunt of Defiance" ("You Can Never Win Us Back"), contains these verses:

> But the Battle to the Strong
> Is not given,
> While the Judge of Right and
> Wrong sits in heaven.
> And the God of David still
> Guides the Devil with his will.
> There are giants yet to kill.[74]

Rev. J. William Jones remembered that General Lee's "orders and reports always gratefully recognized 'the Lord of hosts' as the 'Giver of victory.'"[75] Lee believed fervently in the God of the Old Testament, who was sometimes called the Lord of Hosts (Hebrew *Yahweh Sabaoth* actually means "God of Armies"). Because God was unconquerable, defeat in the eyes of the ancient Jews was caused by the faithlessness of the Israelites. In August 1863, after his defeat at Gettysburg, Lee issued an order recognizing August 21 as a day of prayer, and he reminded his soldiers that "we have sinned against Almighty God" and that, by confessing, "He will give us a name and place among the nations of the earth."[76]

Thus, it is not curious at all that Yulee and Benjamin, the first senators of Jewish descent, were from the South. Nor is it surprising that of the six Jewish members of Congress elected before the Civil War, three were from the South and three were from the North, despite the fact that there were fewer than 25,000 Jews in the South and 120,000 in the North.[77] Numerous Southern Jews served in the state legislatures, city councils, and in other positions of authority. In 1850 a Richmond rabbi, Rev. Julius Eckman, gave the opening prayer at a session of the Virginia House of Delegates, the first time a rabbi had so officiated before a state legislature.[78] In the 1840s the Jews of South Carolina, angered that Gov. Henry Hammond had issued a Thanksgiving Day Proclamation addressed to Christians only, wrote the governor, "we do not sue for toleration, we un-mask it." Their audacity, Abraham J. Peck wrote, was unprecedented.[79] Hammond's successor, Gov. William Aiken, issued a new proclamation on his first day in office excising Christian passages. Aiken's close political relationship with M. C. Mordecai was at work. Even Hammond, who privately called Mordecai's brother "a miserable Jew," described Senator Mordecai as "a man of force and influence in Charleston." As Frederic Jaher has written, "Often descended from old clans that had grown up with the city, Charleston's Jews were rarely labeled alien upstarts or intruders."[80]

This is not to say that there was no prejudice against Jews in the antebellum South. Anti-Semitism was a fact of life in the nineteenth century. Emma Holmes of Charleston wrote in her diary that she disliked "Sumter very much from the prevalence of sand & Jews, my great abhorrences." By 1862 she blamed all of her ills on the Jews. Jews came into conflict with the majority Christian society on issues such as conducting retail businesses on Sunday. In many states, North and South, Jewish businessmen tested or refused to obey these Sabbatarian laws. And, of course, Southerners often found Jewish customs strange. Maria Bryan Connell of Hancock County, Georgia, had a Jewish houseguest. "I did not at all comprehend the trouble occasioned by their notions of unclean and forbidden food until I had a daughter of Abraham under the roof. She will not eat one mouthful of the finest fresh pork or the most delicate ham," she wrote. It was not, Maria concluded, "an unimportant consideration with her. Pray let this be entre nous, for I feel as if I am in some respect violating the duties of hospitality in speaking of it."[81]

The Northern states were not as hospitable as the South to the Jews prior to the Civil War. Colonial Massachusetts, for example, was a hotbed of anti-Semitism. The first known Jew in Boston was "warned out" in the 1640s.[82] Unlike in colonial Charleston, where Jews flourished, Jews were not allowed to live in early colonial Boston.[83] John Quincy Adams referred to David Yulee as the "squeaking Jew delegate from Florida," and Rep. Albert G. Marchand of Pennsylvania as "a squat little Jew-faced rotundity." Indeed, when the South seceded, the *Boston Evening Transcript,* a Brahmin publication, blamed secession on the Southern Jews. Calling Benjamin "the disunion leader in the U.S. Senate," and Yulee ("whose name has been changed from the more appropriate one of Levy or Levi") an ultra fire-eater, the newspaper claimed that "this peculiar race . . . having no country of their own," desired "that other nations shall be in the same unhappy condition."[84] The *New York Times* contended in May 1860 that Jonas Phillips Levy, Comdr. Uriah P. Levy's brother, was "laying pipes for a ticket to consist of Senators Benjamin and Yulee (representing Louisiana and Florida) as the President and Vice-President of a Southern Jerusalem." By 1864, the *Times* castigated the Democratic Party because its chairman, August Belmont, was "the agent of foreign jew bankers."[85]

Southern Jewry, more secure in their place in Southern society than their coreligionists in the North, accepted their responsibilities when war came. They had experienced a freedom unknown to Jews anywhere else in the world. They had been accepted by their fellow citizens of the Old South, more accepted as Jews than at any other time since the Golden Age of Jewry in medieval Spain. And they repaid that freedom and respect, that right to breathe "the free air of Dixie," by loyalty to their homeland.

It is difficult to determine the opinion of Jewish Southerners about secession. Edwin DeLeon was pro-secession, while his brother Camden DeLeon, an officer in the army, was clearly uncomfortable with disloyalty to his government.[86] Many were concerned about Lincoln's election and the elevation of an avowed opponent of slavery to the presidency. Simon Baruch, a Prussian immigrant and a medical student, carried a lantern in a parade to celebrate secession bearing the words, "There is a point beyond which endurance ceases to be a virtue."[87] Baruch's fellow South Carolinian, the poet Penina Moise, celebrated the Palmetto State's secession in a war ditty, "Cockades of Blue." Solomon Cohen wrote from Savannah that with Lincoln's election, "our enemies have triumphed," and he was worried about control of the Federal government by "those who hate us and our institutions."[88] His son, Gratz, believed the Union was at an end and it was the duty of every Southern state to secede.[89] Like all Southerners, they defended their homeland. "It was quite natural," A. E. Frankland of Memphis wrote, "they sided with the section that was their home."[90] They reacted with anger at Jewish periodicals and rabbis who took up the abolitionist cause. Jacob A. Cohen of New Orleans, soon to be an officer in the Confederate army, returned a lithograph of Rabbi Max Lilienthal of

Rev. Dr. M. Lilienthal.

Lithograph of Rev. Doctor Max Lilienthal. By May 1861 Jacob A. Cohen of New Orleans
was disgusted with Rabbi Lilienthal's abolitionist activities. He scrawled a highly critical
message over Lilienthal's picture and sent it to him. Notice that Cohen gives his address as
"S.C.A." rather than "U.S.A." Cohen became a captain of the Shepherd Guards, Company
A, 10th Louisiana, and was killed at Second Manassas in 1862. (Courtesy of the Western
Jewish History Center, Judah L. Magnes Museum, Berkeley, California.)

Ohio to him with this message written over the rabbi's face: "Sir, Since you have discarded the Lord and taken up the sword in the defense of a Negro government—your picture which has occupied a place in our Southern homes we herewith return that you may present them to your beloved Black Friends as they will not be permitted in our dwellings. . . . I shall be engaged actively in the field and should be happy to rid Israel of the disgrace of your life."[91]

Rabbi Simon Tuska of Memphis denounced "rabid" abolitionists. "The Jews of Memphis," he said, "are ready, in common with their Christian brethren, to sacrifice their property and their lives in defense of southern rights."[92]

Northern Jews perceived Southern Jewry as proslavery and pro-secession. In 1862 Bernhard Felsenthal, the abolitionist rabbi, wrote an article entitled "Die Juden und die Sclaverei" (The Jews and Slavery), in which he asserted that the "Israelites residing in New Orleans are man by man—with very few exceptions—ardently in favor of secession, and many among them are 'sincere fire-eaters.' . . . The reason why these gentlemen take such interest in secession has always been a miracle to me." Felsenthal explained this seeming anomaly by recalling the condition under which the Jews had lived in Germany: suppression, isolation, and persecution. Felsenthal also believed that because many Germans were "to their immortal honor . . . outspoken enemies of slavery," some "Jewish Germans are in favor of it." He also pointed to the Southern press in Richmond, Charleston, and New Orleans, which published articles entitled "The Jews Are for Us," referring to Benjamin, Yulee, and some Northern proslavery rabbis. (Felsenthal, a Northerner, concluded that "despite stupidity, narrow-mindedness, and the efforts of a few demagogues the large majority of the American Jewry can be found on the side of freedom.")[93]

The plain fact of the matter is that, as Rabbi Bertram Wallace Korn has written, "No Jewish political figure of the Old South ever expressed reservations about the justice of slavery or the rightness of the Southern position."[94] Nor is there any evidence that Jews supported slavery as a result of intimidation or fear of reprisals. The Talmud taught the Jews that "the law of the land is the law," and slavery was the law of the land. Opponents of slavery, Jewish or Gentile, were a distinct minority even in the North. While there were many Jews in the North who actively opposed slavery, few Jews were conspicuous as abolitionists. Indeed, Rabbi Morris J. Raphall of B'nai Jeshurun in New York City fiercely criticized abolitionists. "How dare you . . . denounce slaveholding as a sin?" he asked them. "When you remember that Abraham, Isaac, Jacob, Job—the men with whom the Almighty conversed, with whose names he emphatically connects his own most holy name . . . all these men were slaveholders."[95] Solomon Cohen wrote his aunt that "God gave laws to his chosen people for the government of their slaves, and did not order them to abolish slavery."[96] Oscar Straus put it best when he wrote in his memoirs, "As a boy brought up in the South I never questioned the rights or wrongs of slavery. Its existence I regarded as matter of course, as most other customs or institutions."[97]

When in April 1861 the *Jewish Messenger* of New York City called upon American Jewry to "rally as one man for the *Union* and the *Constitution*," the Jews of Shreveport responded with a resolution denouncing the newspaper and its editor. "[W]e, the Hebrew congregation of Shreveport," the resolution began, "scorn and repel your advice, although we might be called Southern rebels; still, as law-abiding citizens, we solemnly pledge ourselves to stand by, protect, and honor the flag, with its stars and stripes, the Union and Constitution of the Southern Confederacy, with our lives, liberty, and all that is dear to us." The resolution, in true Southern fashion, condemned the newspaper "as a black republican paper" and deplored its editor's advice "to act as traitors and renegades to our adopted country," meaning the South. Max Baer, the president of the congregation, asked that newspapers friendly to the Southern cause publish their resolution.[98]

Jewish Southerners perceived New Englanders as abolitionists who were frequently anti-Semitic.[99] Theodore Parker, a leading abolitionist minister, believed Jews' intellects were "sadly pinched in those narrow foreheads," that Jews were "lecherous" and "did sometimes kill a Christian baby at the Passover."[100] William Lloyd Garrison, editor of the *Liberator*, once described Judge Mordecai Manuel Noah of New York as "the miscreant Jew," a "Shylock," "the enemy of Christ and liberty," and a descendent "of the monsters who nailed Jesus to the cross."[101] Similar sentiments came from Edmond Quincy, Lydia Maria Child, William Ellery Channing, and Sen. Henry Wilson of Massachusetts, all leading abolitionists. Child thought Judaism rife with superstition, claiming that Jews "have humbugged the world." John Quincy Adams opposed slavery and derided Jews.[102] It is little wonder then that there was no great love lost between Southern Jews, who were accustomed to being treated as equals, and New Englanders. Southern Jews had even more reason, if it is possible, to dislike the officious New Englanders than did other Southerners, and this undoubtedly influenced their view of secession.[103] Isaac Harby, the Charleston journalist and pioneer of the Reform movement, was typical in his denunciation of "the abolitionist society and its secret branches."[104] Isaac Scherck, a Prussian immigrant who settled in Summit, Mississippi, and enlisted as a private in Company E, 3d Mississippi Battalion, described the North as filled with "puritanic bigotry & humbug." It came as no surprise to South Carolina Jewry to see reprinted in their local newspaper in March 1861 the following from the *Boston Journal*: "The Jew, [Benjamin] Mordecai, at Charleston, who gave ten thousand dollars to the South Carolina Government, had just settled with his Northern creditors by paying fifty cents on the dollar. The ten thousand was thus a Northern donation to secession." The *Charleston Daily Courier* called the story "a willful, unmitigated and deliberate falsehood."[105]

Thus, when South Carolina seceded, its Jewish citizens went with their state. The DeLeons, typical of men with their background, stood by the Palmetto State. This was not an easy decision. Like Robert E. Lee, Maj. David Camden DeLeon

Maj. David Camden DeLeon of South Carolina reluctantly resigned his commission in the U.S. Army to join the Confederate army. He became the first acting surgeon general of the Confederacy from May 6 to July 12, 1861. He served later as the medical director of the Army of Northern Virginia and then left the army for reasons unknown. His military career was undistinguished. (Portrait by Solomon Carvalho. Courtesy of Jacob Rader Marcus Center, American Jewish Archives, Cincinnati, Ohio and the Jewish Museum of New York.)

was a career army officer. He had been a hero in the Mexican War. "Treason and patriotism are next door neighbors," he wrote his younger brother Edwin, "and only accident makes you strike the right knocker. Revolution is treason even if right, if unsuccessful." DeLeon agonized over the decision he knew was coming. "A Southern Confederacy seeming as near a fixed fact as human foresight can dive into the future. The wire pullers have fixed their line so that electricity has been infused into the masses." Having spent his career as a surgeon in the army, Major DeLeon found it difficult to cast aside his loyalty. "I have loved my country. I have fought under its flag and every star and stripe is dear to me. I can forgive and forget."[106]

But events forced Major DeLeon to choose. "If time comes when war is inevitable," he wrote his brother Edwin, "I know my sides, and they will find the difference between howling demagogues and the men of action. As long as I hold the commission I do, I make no promises. But when a Southern Confederacy is acknowledged or inaugurated, then I shall take my stand." He took that stand a month later in February 1861 when he resigned. His letter of resignation went to Gen. Winfield Scott, his old friend and commander in the Mexican War. Scott pleaded with DeLeon, as he did with many senior Southern officers, to remain in the army and accept a post in the Northwestern frontier, far from his Southern homeland. He was even threatened with arrest if he resigned. "Camden DeLeon, M.D., called fresh from Washington," Mary Chesnut recorded in February 1861, "says General Scott is using all of his power and influence to prevent officers from the South from resigning their commissions. Among other things, promising that they should never be sent against us in case of war."[107] DeLeon fled South. Camden's brother, the journalist Edwin DeLeon, also supported secession. "Of

Secession, I may say with the Irish statesman, on a somewhat similar occasion, 'I sat by its cradle, I followed its hearse,'" he recalled in his memoirs.[108]

State Sen. Moses Cohen Mordecai was not fervent for secession. He had been one of the owners of the *Southern Standard,* which was established in 1851 to oppose the immediate secession of South Carolina without the other Southern states. The majority of South Carolinians in the early 1850s opposed the secession of their state without the cooperation of other slave states. "The Resistance or Co-operation Party of the State was not divided as to her right to secede," William L. King wrote in a history of Charleston's newspapers, "but many were convinced that such a movement at that time, would be fatal." The *Standard* represented these cooperationist views and was successful in bringing about a test vote in 1851 by the people of South Carolina which rejected separate secession. The newspaper flourished for a time but ceased publication in the summer of 1858. By then, most South Carolinians wanted to secede. Mordecai likely held his counsel if he still had doubts about secession.[109] Solomon Cohen of Savannah was a delegate to the Democratic Party's national convention in Charleston in 1860. He was a member of the minority that stayed when the ultra-secessionists walked out. Avery wrote in his history of Georgia that Cohen was "a gentleman of high social standing and considerable speaking ability. He and his colleagues, while in sympathy with the seceders in principle, remained behind hoping that a better spirit might prevail and justice be done to the South by the Northern Democrats."[110] Clearly, Cohen, like Mordecai, was a reluctant secessionist.

Moses Cohen Mordecai and Isabel Lyons Mordecai. M. C. Mordecai (pronounced "Mor de key" in the South at the time) was the most prominent Jewish Charlestonian of the 1850s and 1860s. He served as state senator from Charleston and owned the Mordecai Steamship Line. The Mordecais lived on Meeting Street, a prestigious address below Broad Street and near St. Michael's Church. (Author's collection.)

Some of Savannah's German Jews were among the city's German community who met at Armory Hall on May 15, 1861, to "show by words and acts that the German inhabitants of the city were ready with heart and hand to defend the home of their choice." Joseph Lippman called the assembly to order. Magnus Loewenthal served on the program committee and read his committee's resolution, which likened the Southern cause to the 1848 Revolution and the Venetians' hatred for Austrian rule. While they deplored "the necessity forced upon us of perhaps imbruing our hands in the blood of brothers of our dear old Fatherland, yet the cause of the South being our cause, we accept the gage of hostility." E. W. Solomons of Effingham County near Savannah was a delegate to the Georgia Secession Convention and signed the ordinance.[111]

There were at least two Jewish delegates to the Louisiana Secession Convention held in January 1861 in Baton Rouge: Isaac N. Marks, representing Orleans Parish, and Leon D. Marks, representing Caddo Parish (Shreveport). Samuel Hyams was nominated as the secretary to the convention, and a Mr. Leovy of New Orleans was nominated to be the official printer, but neither was elected. Governor Moore orchestrated the secession of Louisiana, and Lt. Gov. Henry Hyams, a loyal Moore ally, was undoubtedly active on its behalf although he was presiding over the Senate and was not a delegate to the convention. (The *Daily Picayune* reported on March 26, 1861, that Hyams "made a most beautiful and touching response" in the Senate to a resolution thanking him for his services.)[112]

Unlike the Hyamses, the Lemann family of Donaldsonville opposed the war. According to Elliott Ashkenazi in *The Business of Jews in Louisiana, 1840–1875,* Jacob Lemann's career was "a success story in the best tradition of Jewish immigrants

Benjamin Mordecai was a patriotic Charleston merchant. He received a great deal of notoriety in both the Northern and Southern press for his "magnificent" donation of $10,000 to the State of South Carolina to be used by the governor "for such purposes as will best advance the interests and honor of our noble commonwealth." "This evidence of your devoted patriotism," the governor's aide-de-camp replied, "is most gratifying and is most highly appreciated by His Excellency Gov. Pickens." He was thanked by a resolution of the Secession Convention (Mordecai to Governor Pickens, January 1, 1861; Lucas to Mordecai, January 1, 1861, AJA). (Courtesy of South Carolina Historical Society).

to the American South." Lemann emigrated to Donaldsonville from the Duchy of Hesse in 1836, and he soon graduated from peddler to owner of a general store to commercial banker and real estate investor. He married Marie Berthelcor, a Gentile who converted and even formally adopted Judaism before a rabbinical court in New York in 1852. She changed her name to Miriam. He continued trading with the owners of sugar plantations, the wealthiest in Louisiana, right up to 1861. He also continued keeping his personal accounts in his native Yiddish, which also guaranteed secrecy. The Lemanns were living in New York, Newport, and Louisiana in the mid-1850s and apparently had no truck with the Southern cause. The family purchased a mansion in Newport in 1854 and lived in the North more than the South. The self-indulgent son of the Lemann family, Bernard, left Louisiana a month after Sumter for Europe. His diary, replete with references to historic sites, monuments, parties, and high society, never mentions the war being fought by the young men of his generation. Clearly, the family went to Europe to escape the conflict as Bernard returned to Donaldsonville in December of 1863 and declared his allegiance to the Union.[113]

In New Orleans, unlike Charleston, Richmond, and Savannah, some Jews questioned the wisdom of secession and were reluctant to fight in a war in which they perceived no stake.[114] "Secession was never as popular in Louisiana as in her sister States of the lower South," Ralph A. Wooster concluded, and its large immigrant population may have been one of the reasons.[115] Christian German immigrants were divided on the wisdom of the war. A leading German American, New Orleans attorney Michael Hahn, was an outspoken abolitionist, and many German immigrants were opposed to slavery. John Frederick Nau concludes in *The German People of New Orleans, 1850–1900,* that many German New Orleanians "looked upon the conflict as purely an American 'family' affair and did not take an enthusiastic or active part in it."[116] The same was true of other immigrant groups. And, of course, not every native Southerner favored secession.

Jake Weil, a German immigrant, veteran of the Mexican War, and a cotton factor in Montgomery, enlisted in the 4th Alabama Home Guard and enthusiastically endorsed secession as the only realistic alternative. He was at the capital in Montgomery when Jefferson Davis was inaugurated. He found Davis to be "a man both imposing and impressive," but, he wrote his brother Josiah, "I fear he has not the stomach nor the verstandt [understanding] to lead us through the struggle that ensues." Weil felt there was "no place left" for a man of reason; of "two evils I choose the one more familiar. This land has been good to all of us," he wrote his brother Josiah in Prussia. "We shall not be deprived of rights or property. . . . I shall fight to my last breath and to the full extent of my fortune to defend that in which I believe." Weil was not a proponent of slavery. He and his brother Henry had set their slaves free, except for their household servants, when there were enough settlers in Montgomery to lease their lands. "In truth one man never has right another man to own," he wrote Josiah. "But," he continued, "one man has no right to sell property to another and after he has invested the proceeds claim that the buyer is evil and should divest himself of his property."[117]

The Jews of Richmond favored secession but hoped for peace. Both Reverend Jacobs of Beth Shalome and Reverend Michelbacher of Beth Ahabah published prayers in the newspapers in January 1861 in response to President Buchanan's request for prayers of national unity. Likening Southerners to the Children of Israel crossing the Red Sea, Michelbacher asked that if "union and peace may not be preserved, because of perpetual and opposing interests," then "grant, Father of all, that a way may be opened whereby we, the people of the South, may pass with dry feet safely to the position of peace and plenty, attended with the Protection which Thou gavest to thy chosen people of old." Jacobs asked that God instill in "the hearts of all classes the knowledge that, as brethren how good and how beautiful it is for us to dwell together in unity." But that "if it be Thy will, O Lord! Who weighest the destinies of all nations," that secession was to come, then let it come without "the horrors of civil warfare . . . [and] that brother shall not lift up hand against his brother, but that an equitable and peaceful separation may take place."[118]

Both Jacobs and Michelbacher soon became ardent supporters of the Confederate cause. The Mordecai family of Virginia and North Carolina was sorely divided. Major E. T. D. Myers, whose mother was a Mordecai, wrote his uncle Samuel Mordecai from Georgetown near Washington, D.C., that "impending ruin frowns heavily here. . . . I . . . can truly sympathize with Mr. Hunter of the State Department who assured me the other day that he was ashamed to look the delegates of foreigners in the face!" But, he would go with his state. Capt. Alfred Mordecai, Samuel Mordecai's brother and the most respected Jewish officer in the U.S. Army in 1860, agonized over his future course. He declined an offer of a commission from Jefferson Davis, but his older sister Ellen, who lived in Richmond, begged him to fight for the South: "I avail myself of a private opportunity," she wrote him in May 1861, "to express to you the anxiety I feel with every member of our family and all our friends that you should come where you are not only desired but needed in directing the military affairs of your native state. All eyes of the south are turned towards you, and from various places, wishes expressed that you should come." Mordecai was married to a Northern woman and his son was raised in Pennsylvania. He resigned his commission and spent the war years in Philadelphia, unable to lift his sword against his native South or his Northern family. His son, Alfred Mordecai Jr., became an officer in the Union army. This infuriated the family that had sent four young Mordecais to serve in the Confederate army. Dr. Solomon Mordecai of Mobile, another brother, wrote Ellen: "I do not see how he could conscientiously have acted otherwise. . . . Yet how deeply this is to be regretted! His services in our cause would have been invaluable."[119] Mordecai was not

Congressman Philip Phillips of
Mobile, Alabama. (Courtesy of the
Library of Congress.)

(*Right*) Map of Charleston showing
key Jewish Confederate sites. Map
drawn by Tim Belshaw.

alone. Other Southern Jews had serious reservations about secession. Edwin Warren Moise, a Charlestonian living in Columbus, Georgia, opposed secession, while
his employer, Raphael J. Moses, supported it.

Eugenia and Philip Phillips of Mobile disagreed about slavery and secession.
As in many marriages, the partners differed markedly in their temperament.
Philip, one of the most respected Jewish lawyers in America, was calm and moderate, a conservative who supported the Union. Eugenia, the daughter and friend
of Southern aristocrats, was an ardent Southern partisan. Her entire family supported the war. Sister Phoebe recalled that the "women of the South had been
openly and violently rebellious from the moment they thought their states' rights
touched. They incited the men to struggle in support of their views, and whether
right or wrong, sustained them nobly to the end. They were the first to rebel—the
last to succumb." Philip thought secession foolhardy and slavery an impediment to
the South's progress. He even attempted a mission to the South on behalf of President Buchanan to stem the tide of secession. Phillips knew that the South would
never give up slavery or that "the spirit of abolitionism which now dominated the
North would be content with anything less." Yet, like many Southerners, he did not
believe that Lincoln's election justified secession. "I looked with profound amaze-
ment," he later recalled, "upon the efforts made by many of the Southern leaders
to induce the South to believe that secession would be peacefully acquiesced in by
the North. . . . What little influence I possessed was exerted to prevent the proposed action of the Southern states."[120]

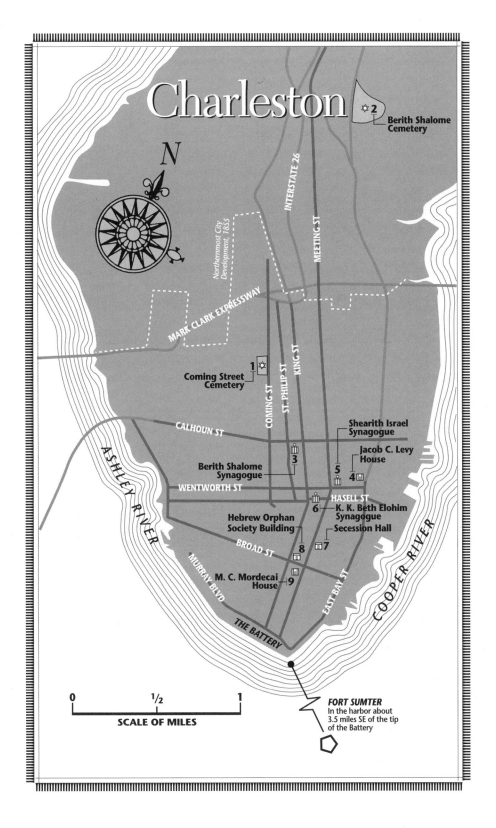

Charleston

✡2 **Berith Shalome Cemetery**

N

INTERSTATE 26

MEETING ST

Northernmost City Development, 1835

MARK CLARK EXPRESSWAY

ASHLEY RIVER

COMING ST

ST. PHILIP ST

KING ST

1 ✡ **Coming Street Cemetery**

CALHOUN ST

Shearith Israel Synagogue

3

Jacob C. Levy House

5

4

Berith Shalome Synagogue

WENTWORTH ST

HASELL ST

6 **K. K. Beth Elohim Synagogue**

Hebrew Orphan Society Building

Secession Hall

BROAD ST

8

7

MURRAY BLVD

M. C. Mordecai House

9

EAST BAY ST

THE BATTERY

COOPER RIVER

0   ½   1
SCALE OF MILES

FORT SUMTER
In the harbor about
3.5 miles SE of the tip
of the Battery

Maj. Robert Anderson, the Union commander at Fort Sumter in Charleston harbor, did all he could to avert war, but in April President Lincoln sent a relief expedition to the beleaguered fort. Jefferson Davis ordered an attack on Fort Sumter before it could be reinforced. In the early morning hours of April 12, 1861, a heavy mist covered Charleston harbor and the nearby islands. Through the gloom came "the brilliant flash of exploding shells from the batteries all around the bay, while the deep hoarse tones of talking cannons echoed over the waters."

In that mist and gloom, among the soldiers ringing Fort Sumter were Jewish Confederates from Charleston. Moses E. Lopez served as a private in the Palmetto Guards. He was assigned to the Ironclad Battery on Morris Island on this fateful day. A Jewish physician, Columbus DaVega, apparently designed and served in a ten-bed hospital attached to a floating battery used in the attack on Sumter. Also in that mist and in command of a few of those "talking cannons" was Lt. Jacob Valentine of Company K, 1st South Carolina, a veteran of the Mexican War who had been wounded at Churubusco. There were four Valentine boys—Emanuel, Jacob, Isaac, and Hertz. Their ancestors had, according to family legend, served "with credit" in the Prussian army during the Napoleonic Wars. Valentine commanded the enfilade battery at the end of Sullivan's Island nearest Charleston and overlooking Fort Sumter. It was the mission of this battery, consisting of four cannons, to rake the enemy line.[121]

The bombardment was furious and constant for the first two and a half hours. "There stands the bold defiant fort," one observer wrote, "as quiet as death." After daybreak, Sumter fired back. "The firing from Fort Sumter against our battery was heavy," Valentine reported to Lt. Col. Roswell S. Ripley, "but, I am happy to say ineffective, and resulted in neither injury to the battery or to the men." The bombardment had commenced at 4:30 a.m. and firing became general at 5:00 a.m. from the ring of forts and batteries on Sullivan's Island, Morris Island, and James Island. Fort Sumter returned fire at 7:00 a.m. with a vigorous assault on Cummings Point. "The enemy next directed his fire upon the enfilade battery on Sullivan's Island," the official report continued.[122]

The bombardment continued into Saturday, April 13. Thousands of people watched, including Eleanor Cohen, a young Jewish girl from Charleston, and Perry Moses of Sumter, who was a student at the Citadel. Sumter was firebombed, and the officers' quarters and barracks caught fire. Beauregard was concerned that Maj. Robert Anderson, his old instructor at West Point now facing him as his enemy, would be injured by an explosion of the fort's magazine before he could surrender. Beauregard therefore sent a boat with a fire engine over to Sumter under the direction of M. H. Nathan, chief of the fire department, to put out the fire. Prominent in the Jewish community, Nathan served as a commissioner of markets in the 1850s.[123]

Fort Sumter surrendered on Sunday, April 14, while the Federal fleet floated outside the bar of Charleston harbor. At 11:00 a.m., a Mordecai Lines steamer, the

The *Isabel*, named for Isabel Lyons Mordecai, was owned by the Mordecai Steamship Line. It transported Major Anderson and his men from Fort Sumter to the awaiting federal fleet. (Courtesy of the Maryland Historical Society.)

Isabel, arrived at Sumter's wharf. Major Anderson stood on the deck of the *Isabel* while his cannon fired a salute to the American flag. Two of Anderson's men were accidentally killed in the salute, the first casualties of the Civil War. They were laid in a grave in the middle of the parade ground, "after the earth had been heaped upon the sacred spot, a volley was fired, the drum beat its solemn roll, and the garrison was transferred to The Isabel." The steamer took the small Union garrison out to the Federal fleet waiting off the bar. The Palmetto flag was raised over the fort by Franklin J. Moses Jr. and J. L. Dearing of the governor's staff. Fire Chief Nathan was sent to put out the fires.[124]

The war no one believed would happen, the war Solomon Cohen and M. C. Mordecai dreaded and Eugenia Phillips and Raphael J. Moses welcomed, was under way, and the Jewish Confederates made their choice—to go to war.

Why did Southern Jewish boys and men flock to the Confederate banner? What was their motivation? Why did men who, in many cases, had only recently come to the South risk their life and limb for the Southern cause? It is a truism that the Civil War was brought about by the dispute over slavery. One need only consult the secession conventions' resolutions to ascertain their reasons for seceding or, in the South's view, declaring independence. The South Carolina Declaration of the Immediate Causes of Secession rests the case for secession on slavery: "The Northern states 'have denounced as sinful the institution of slavery,' they have encouraged abolitionist societies, and have incited 'servile insurrection.' Lincoln has declared himself an enemy of slavery and the Republican Party 'announced . . . that a war must be waged against slavery.'"[125] And this resolution, together with the convention's address to the slaveholding states, constituted South Carolina's official reasons for seceding from the Union. Texas adopted a "declaration of causes," which included the election of Lincoln and the lack of protection of slavery in the territories.[126] Gov. Thomas O. Moore of Louisiana called for a secession convention because he did not feel that "it comports with the honor and self-respect of Louisiana, as a slaveholding state to live under the government of a Black Republican."[127] Solomon Cohen of Savannah perceived early on that the war was about slavery. "I fear," he wrote his aunt, "that the epitaph long since written for us is about to be engraved upon the tomb of the Union: 'Here lies a people who in seeking the liberty of the Negro, lost their own.'"[128]

Some Jewish Confederates, like many of their Gentile comrades, fought for what they termed their "liberty" and freedom, which included the right to own slaves. Pvt. Eugene Henry Levy of New Orleans reflected the sentiments of many a Johnny Reb when he wrote in his diary in October 1864 that he objected to a proposal made by Judah P. Benjamin that slaves who fought for the Confederacy be freed. The principle "that slaves are in their proper sphere as they are at present situated within the boundaries of the Confederacy is one of the grand incentives to the waging of war against the United States."[129] Like their fellow Johnny Rebs, a small percentage of Jewish Confederates owned slaves themselves, although many came from slaveholding families, and all came from slaveholding communities where relatives, friends, business associates, and customers owned slaves. And even those who owned no slaves had a stake in the South's racial caste system.

Pvt. Simon Mayer of the Natchez Southrons detested the Yankee invaders and believed them to be a gang of abolitionists. "I sympathize," he wrote his family with "the poor victims of abolition despotism." He accused the "damnable followers & supporters of Abraham Lincoln" of "making war upon decrepit old age, defenseless women & helpless infancy," of "rapine, destruction & murder," of burning Southern homes and of "starving our people" into subjugation and even "their new doctrine of 'miscegenation.'" "I doubt not," he concluded, "that the amalgamation doctrine would be of benefit to the *Yankee* race."[130]

It is also true, however, that individual Confederate soldiers had their own reasons for fighting which did not include slavery or race. In fact, most Jewish Johnny Rebs, like their fellow countrymen, believed they were fighting for their own liberty and in defense of their homes. They believed they were patriots fighting for independence, life, liberty, and property as the soldiers of 1776 had done.[131] Gustavus Poznanski Jr., the son of the former rabbi at K. K. Beth Elohim in Charleston, came back to his native Charleston from Canada to join his comrades in the defense of his native city. At "the breaking out of the war," his obituary reads, Poznanski "was temporarily residing at the North where his parents were forced to spend much of their time on account of impaired health. . . . His parents are still in Canada having been unable to obtain the requisite passes to come South."

Obviously, neither he nor his parents, who were residing in Canada, owned slaves. And it strains credulity that Poznanski returned to South Carolina and gave his life at the age of nineteen to defend the institution of slavery. "No one more willingly gave a life," another Poznanski obituary read, "to free the soil from the invader. In giving it away, he had that glorious consolation that has cheered the dying moments of so many who have fallen for liberty."[132]

Jewish Johnny Rebs were also motivated by a sense of duty and honor, powerful emotions in Victorian America. "Victorians," McPherson wrote, "understood duty to be a binding moral obligation involving reciprocity: one had a duty to defend the flag under whose protection one had lived." A fallen Jewish Confederate, Cpl. Isaac Valentine, mortally wounded in the same battle as his comrade Poznanski, said on his deathbed that he had done his duty and died for his country.[133]

Letters, memoirs, and obituaries reflect the Jewish soldiers' chief reasons for fighting: To do their duty, to protect their homeland, to protect Southern rights and liberty and, once the war began, loyalty to their comrades in arms. Philip Rosenheim of Richmond had just returned home from marching to the Chickahominy and had "fallen into sweet slumber" when his sister Rebecca awoke him. The bells had tolled, informing his militia company to gather. "I was very weak and had a severe headache," he wrote his family, "but still I dressed myself buckled on my accouterments, thinking I would not shrink from my duty and would follow the company wherever it goes, as our Flag says, when duty calls tis ours to obey."[134] Julius Yaretzky, a Polish immigrant who lived in Shuqualak, Mississippi, and served as first sergeant in Company A, 33d Alabama, spoke for many of his fellow Jewish

Moses Ezekiel of Richmond at the age of twelve. Ezekiel was too young to enlist when the war began, but he saw action later as a VMI cadet and participated in the famous Battle of New Market. After the war, with the encouragement of Robert E. Lee, he pursued his dream of becoming a sculptor. This photograph was taken in 1856. (Courtesy of American Jewish Historical Society, Waltham, Massachusetts, and New York City.)

50   Confederates when he wrote his son after the war, "The war between the states was for principles of states' rights."[135] "We were thoroughly imbued with the idea," Moses Ezekiel of Richmond wrote in his memoirs, "that we were not fighting for the perpetuation of slavery, but for the principle of State's rights and free trade, and in the defense of our homes, which were being ruthlessly invaded."[136]

Slavery was an evil that Virginia had inherited, and "we wanted to get rid of . . . [Virginia] tried to arbitrate for peace . . . but it failed. No slavery question entered the matter at all, but when [Lincoln] called upon Virginia to furnish her quota of troops to help subjugate her sister Southern states . . . Virginia . . . seceded from the Union."[137] Isaac Hirsch of Fredericksburg, a soldier in the 30th Virginia, visited the battlefield at Second Manassas, where Stonewall Jackson defeated General Pope's army. "It is bad," he wrote in his diary, "that the dead Yankees could not be buried as I don't like to see any human being lay on the top of the earth and rot, but it is a fit emblem for the invader of our soil for his bones to bleach on the soil he invades, especially of a people that wish to be left alone and settle down to their own peaceful pursuits."[138] J. Gottlieb wrote from Corinth, Mississippi, in June 1861 on stationery decorated with the Stars and Bars that he wished "to face the Lincolnites as soon as possible. Our cause is a right one & we will be victorious."[139]

Jewish men, like other Southern men, were encouraged to fight by their mothers and sisters. At the start of the war, Catherine Ezekiel, Moses's mother, said "she would not own a son who would not fight for his home and country."[140] Mary Chesnut wrote of her friend "Mem" Cohen's dedication to the cause. "Our soldiers, thank God, are men after our own heart, cries Miriam of the house of Aaron," Mary wrote in her diary in May 1862.[141] Phoebe Pember recalled that the women of the South had urged their men to resist the enemy with force if necesary[142]; see page 44.

It speaks volumes about the South that many a Jewish youth left the German fatherland to *avoid* military service only to *voluntarily* enlist in the Confederate army soon after arriving in Dixie. Myer Schwabacher left Germany to avoid military service and arrived in Richmond just as the war began. He enlisted, although as a foreigner he had no obligation to do so. Charles Wessolowsky's parents sent him to America in 1858 because they dreaded his being forced into the Prussian army. His older brother, Asa, had settled in Georgia, a place, he said in letters home, which was a land of freedom and opportunity. When Charles arrived, his brother sent him off to peddle goods in the "wilds" of rural Georgia. Given his experience with anti-Semitic Prussians, Charles was afraid to go out into this strange land. But he found, to his surprise, that his customers, the rural farmers of Georgia, were definitely not prejudiced Prussians. Instead, he was warmly received. Asa and Charles had the respect of their countrymen and they enlisted on May 7, 1862, in Company G, 57th Georgia (later Company E, 32d Georgia).[143]

Pvt. Theodore Kohn was a young immigrant from Fürth, Bavaria, who settled in Orangeburg, South Carolina. When war was imminent, his father, who lived in New York, practically ordered him to leave the South and come live with him so that he would not have to "serve as a soldier-slave for an unjust cause." Kohn, however, enlisted in the Edisto Rifles, Company A, of Hagood's 1st South Carolina Volunteers. (Courtesy of Julian Hennig Jr. of Columbia.)

Theodore Kohn of Orangeburg, South Carolina, came from Fürth, Bavaria, to live with his uncle. His parents settled in New York. In February 1861 Theodore's mother wrote that she hoped "no civil war will break out," but if it did, the "ones guilty of high treason will be all hanged." When war was imminent, Philip Kohn wrote his son, Theodore, in German: "I want to tell you my very desire, that you leave this un-happy country [South Carolina] as soon as possible, because it will be ruined within a few years. . . . I got [you] away from the old world, from the old 'rust' fatherland, so that [you would not have] to serve as a soldier-slave for an unjust cause. For what? . . . the Lord make your mind clear and lead you as soon as possible!" Ignoring his father's earnest entreaties, Theodore enlisted enthusiastically in Company A, Hagood's 1st S.C. Volunteers, the Edisto Rifles, one of the first to volunteer. His sergeant, William V. Izlar, recalled Kohn in his company history as being "thoroughly Southern in sentiment and principle," and that he had been among the first to heed the call to arms. He served throughout the war, rising to the rank of corporal in Company G, 25th South Carolina, the Eutaw Regiment, and saw action in Charleston, North Carolina, and Virginia. Kohn fought at First Manassas, Battery Wagner, Petersburg, Cold Harbor, and Drewry's Bluff, where he was wounded. Holding up his hand he told his sergeant, "Look here, Willie, what the d—d Yankees have done to me."[144]

The social pressure to enlist was also a strong factor in many a young Confederate's decision to join the army. According to Gary W. Gallagher, 75 to 85 percent of the Confederacy's available draft-age white population served in the military.[145] And a young Southern male had a difficult time in 1862 and 1863 explaining why he was not in uniform. Simon Baruch, a Prussian from Schwersenz, immigrated to Camden, South Carolina, as did his younger brother Herman. When Simon enlisted he admonished Herman to stay out of the war. But Herman joined the cavalry because, as he told Simon, "I could no longer stand it. I could no longer look into the faces of the ladies."[146]

There was also the adventure of war and the bounty paid in advance. Young men who worked at jobs they disliked, such as peddlers, mechanics, and store clerks, saw a chance to escape. Lewis Leon was such a clerk. An unmarried immigrant who spoke German as well as English, he enlisted for six months at the age of nineteen in the Charlotte Grays, Company C, 1st North Carolina. (In six months, most Southerners believed, the war would be over.) He was issued a fine uniform. "We were all boys between the ages of eighteen and twenty-one. . . . Our trip was full of joy and pleasure, for at every station where our train stopped the ladies showered us with flowers and Godspeed. We marched to the Fair Grounds. The streets were lined with people, cheering us." But Leon also believed he was right. "I still say," he concludes in his diary, "our Cause was just, nor do I regret one thing that I have done to cripple the North."[147] Asa and Charles Wessolowsky enlisted in the 57th Georgia in May, 1862, hoping to avoid the battlefield, but glad of the fifty-dollar sign-up bounty. Asa's daughter recalled that the bonus "looked mighty inviting and was a lot of money for doing nothing."[148] The 57th was redesignated the 32d, and the Wessolowsky brothers found themselves doing hard fighting at Secessionville, at Morris Island, and in Florida. Charles participated in the defense of Atlanta in 1864 and was captured.

Another young Jewish volunteer, Isaac ("Ike") Hermann, sounded the same theme: "I found in this country [the South] an ideal and harmonious people; they treated me as one of their own; in fact for me, it was the land of Canaan where milk and honey flowed." Hermann believed his fellow countrymen were imposed upon by their Northern brethren, and that is why he joined in their defense. Hermann, like Leon, was an immigrant. He arrived from Alsace-Lorraine in 1859 in a four-masted schooner at Castle Garden, a massive structure at the tip of Manhattan, and settled in Sandersville, Washington County, Georgia. His cousin Abe Hermann was a merchant and ran a store at Fenns Bridge. From the beginning of the war to the end of his life, Hermann believed in the righteousness of the Southern cause. The "Slave States . . . had a perfect right" to secede, he argues in his 1911 *Memoirs of a Veteran, Who Served as a Private in the 60s in the War between the States.*[149]

Jewish Confederates, like other immigrants and African Americans, had a special burden during the war. They had to prove that Jews would fight. One of the staples of nineteenth century anti-Semitism was that the Jews were citizens of no country except the Jewish Nation. The "Wandering Jew" was a staple of folk anti-Semitism, found in prose, poetry, music, and even in names of plants and birds. Jews were said to be disloyal, unpatriotic, and cowardly. They had lived in ghettos in Europe, kept to themselves, refused to intermarry or assimilate with their neighbors, and had fled Europe to avoid military service.[150] Many a Southern Jewish boy set out to disprove these calumnies.

Simon Mayer was as fervent in his support of the Confederate cause in 1864 as he was when the war began. In a letter to his family in April 1864, he unsuccessfully urged his brother Henry, who had not enlisted, to join his unit, the "Natchez Southrons" or, failing that,

> to at least join the Army now battling for our rights and independence. I hope he has awakened to the realities of the situation, & no longer can remain passive to the scenes that are daily enacted in the grand drama now in full play upon this continent, but that he sees that he too has a part to play, and will with light heart & strong arm, backed by a determination to do or die, come forth and take his place on the broad arena. I am in full earnest in regard to the course I have marked out for him, and I do not want it said, when Peace shall once more gladden our hearts, that a brother of mine, who had nothing to keep him back, acted the coward, and was afraid to come out & meet his would be masters, and subjugators. I hope that my pleadings in the last few letters that I have written are not in vain.[151]

Marx Mitteldorfer of the 1st Virginia Cavalry, on hearing the remark that the Jewish soldiers were in the habit of firing and falling back, invited the accuser to follow him. "Mitteldorfer rode so far to the front (needless to say, alone) that his captain had to send him word to return to the ranks or he might be shot by his comrades," wrote Herbert T. Ezekiel and Gaston Lichtenstein in *The History of the Jews of Richmond,* published in 1917.[152]

Other Jews fought to make a place in Southern society for the Jews who would come after them. Philip Whitlock wrote in his memoir that "especially when I was of the Jewish Faith I thought that if I am negligent in my duty as a citizen of this country, it would unfavorably reflect on the whole Jewish race and religion."[153] Charles Wessolowsky said after the war that "sometimes he felt like a Jewish missionary among the Gentiles to show the way for other Jews to follow." Early-twentieth-century Jewish historians were anxious to defend the courage and bravery of the generation that preceded them. "There existed no occasion to threaten the young or, for that matter, the middle-aged, with the 'white feather,'" Ezekiel and Lichtenstein wrote. "None held back or hesitated. . . . The Jewish youth were no

54   different from the others. Virginia needed them—that was sufficient. . . . That they did their duty is a matter of such common note as to excite no comment."[154]

Finally, Jewish tradition also played a part. From the Book of Esther and from Jeremiah ("Seek the welfare of the city to which I have exiled you," Jer. 29:7) to rabbinical law, Judiaism taught respect and obedience to the established goverment. Jews had traditionally aligned themselves with monarchs and conservative regimes for self-protection from the masses. The traditional Jewish prayer for the government, dating to the sixteenth century, called upon God to "bless, guard, protect, help, exalt, magnify, and highly aggrandize" the king and the royal family and inspire them with benevolence "toward us and all Israel our brethren." In short, as the new Confedracy was now their lawful government, Jewish tradition demanded loyalty and obedience to it.[155]

Thus, Jewish Johnny Rebs went off to war for a variety of reasons: Patriotism and love of country; to defend their homeland, their yearning for a fatherland they could believe in; Jewish tradition as they understood it; to demonstrate to the North that their rights, liberty, and property, including slaves, could not be assailed; hatred for the Yankees; social and peer pressure; being caught up in the frenzy of secession and war; to escape from home and everyday work and see the world; for adventure, pay, and excitement; and to prove that Jews would fight. "The Jews of the Confederacy had good reason to be loyal to their section," Rabbi Korn concluded. "Nowhere else in America—certainly not in the ante-bellum North—had Jews been accorded such an opportunity to be complete equals as in the old South."[156]

Jewish Southerners would not seek shelter nor would they escape from this storm, no matter how "vast and terrible." They had grown accustomed to breathing the free air of Dixie and were determined, like the Jews of Shreveport, to stand by, protect, and honor the flag of the Confederacy.

Two Sephardic Senators

BOTH JUDAH PHILIP BENJAMIN and David Levy Yulee were Sephardic Jews born in the West Indies, were raised in the South, and were U.S. senators on the eve of the Civil War. Both played a prominent role in secession. Benjamin became a Confederate cabinet officer. Yulee returned to Florida to protect his business interests. But each supported the Confederacy in his own way. Benjamin was born a British citizen on August 11, 1811, in St. Croix in the Virgin Islands, and Yulee (born David Levy) on the island of St. Thomas, then a Danish colony. Benjamin's mother, Rebecca de Mendes, claimed descent from one of the most prominent Jewish families of Spain, although her mother was of Ashkenazic ancestry.[1] The family left the Iberian Peninsula for London and thence to the West Indies. Judah's father, Philip Benjamin, was less illustrious. The elder Benjamin was described by one historian as "a Talmudic scholar, naïve, lackluster, far more concerned with study than with making a living." Pierce Butler was less kind. He described the senior Benjamin as "that *rara avis*, an unsuccessful Jew."[2]

Rebecca, Philip, and their young children moved to North Carolina in 1813 and then in 1821 to Charleston, South Carolina. Philip Benjamin became an American citizen in Charleston in 1826. It was a large family by 1821 with eight children: Rebecca ("Sis" or "Penny"), Solomon, Judah, Joseph, Hannah (whom Philip called "Harriet" or "Hatty"), Julia, Penina, and Jacob.[3] Life was not easy in Charleston. Although free to practice their religion and participate in the life of the community, the Benjamin family were poor. Judah's parents owned a small and not particularly profitable fruit stand on King Street. Mrs. Benjamin kept it open on Saturday, the Jewish Sabbath, much to the dismay of the Jewish community. As a boy, Judah worked in the shop.

For a time, Judah's father was active in the affairs of Beth Elohim. He joined a group of co-religionists in 1824 in their attempt to "reform" and Americanize the orthodox Jewish service by shortening the service and increasing the use of English. While the early records of Beth Elohim have been lost, Benjamin's modern biographer, Eli N. Evans, believes that "it is probable that Judah was one of the first children confirmed in the new Reformed Society." According to Rabbi Malcolm H. Stern, Benjamin's father had the distinction of being the only member expelled, apparently on account of his failure to pay his dues. Judah was educated

David Yulee as a young man.
(Courtesy of the Jacob Rader
Marcus Center, American Jewish
Archives, Cincinnati, Ohio.)

at the Hebrew Orphan Society and was probably sent to Yale College by Moses
Lopez, a prominent Jewish merchant. He may have taken a Hebrew psalter
(prayer book) with him when he left for New Haven.[4]

David Yulee had a more affluent boyhood. He was known as David Levy
from the day of his birth until 1845, when he changed his name to David Levy
Yulee, apparently to suit his new bride, Nancy Wickliffe, the daughter of a former
governor of Kentucky.[5] (In the interest of clarity, he is referred to in this work as
"David Yulee.") His family claimed an even more exotic ancestry than the Benjamins. Yulee's father, Moses Elias Levy, was born in Mogador, Morocco, in 1782,
reputedly the son of the grand vizier (counselor) of the emperor of Morocco. Levy
told a friend, Maj. George R. Fairbanks, that his father had discovered a conspir-
acy on the part of the heir to the throne, and the grand vizier caused the young pre-
tender to be imprisoned. When the emperor died and the son came to the throne,
the vizier was, in Fairbank's version, forced to flee, taking his family to Gibraltar.
In fact, Yulee's grandfather was one of a number of courtiers to the sultan.[6]

Moses Levy left home at a young age and settled in St. Thomas by 1800. A variety of business interests made him wealthy. Judah Benjamin's father or uncle and Moses Levy may have been in business together on St. Thomas in the firm of Levy, Benjamin and Robles.[7] Florida was still a part of the Spanish empire and was governed from Cuba, but he realized that it was only a matter of time before Florida became a part of the United States. Moses Levy purchased a large tract of land in North Florida and in and around St. Augustine, which he intended to turn into a colony for European Jews. With his family, and possibly co-religionists, he became an American citizen. By all accounts Moses Elias Levy was a highly educated, observing Jew, actively involved in Jewish affairs.[8]

Thus, young Yulee grew up in an affluent, cosmopolitan, educated Jewish family. On one of his many trips to the United States, Moses Levy brought his son, David, age nine, not to Florida, which was then a rural backwater, but to Norfolk, Virginia, where he placed him with his good friend Moses Myers, the great merchant. Young David lived with the Myers family in Norfolk for eight years, from 1819 until 1827, when he turned seventeen. According to Yulee's son, C. Wickliffe Yulee, Yulee attended the prestigious Norfolk Academy. These early years were spent in one of the most venerable cities of the Old South, and Yulee's values, beliefs, and social outlook were influenced by antebellum Virginia.[9]

Unlike Yulee, Benjamin had few advantages. As he grew to young manhood, Judah Benjamin built his career on intellectual prowess and a legendary capacity for hard work. He studied at Yale from the age of fourteen to seventeen but left under mysterious circumstances. His enemies later charged him with theft. Benjamin denied it, and the record is inconclusive. After leaving Yale, young Judah and his older cousin Henry M. Hyams moved to New Orleans to seek their fortunes. New Orleans in 1828 was booming. Purchased by the United States in 1803, Louisiana was still very much a multinational and multicultural state. The population was exploding; shipping, trade, and sugar production were rapidly expanding. It was a place where a young Jewish man with talent and determination could succeed.[10]

Judah Benjamin's rise in New Orleans was meteoric. He made friends rapidly, learned French, and studied law in his spare time. He was admitted to the bar in 1832 and began a remarkable legal career. He coauthored a legal digest with a Yale classmate, Thomas Slidell, the brother of John Slidell, the leading politician of antebellum Louisiana. Benjamin perfected his skills in the courtroom, especially as an appellate lawyer. By the early 1840s, Benjamin was widely recognized as an outstanding attorney. A little volume published in 1846, *Sketches of Life and Character in Louisiana*, stated that he was "emphatically the *Commercial* Lawyer of our city, and one of the most successful advocates at our bar. . . . To his many scholarly acquirements he adds the French language, which he speaks with fluency and elegance." He was admitted to the bar of the Supreme Court of the United States at the same term as Abraham Lincoln.[11]

Judah P. Benjamin's townhouse at 327 Bourbon Street in New Orleans. This house has
been identified as Benjamin's townhouse in the
Julius Bisno manuscript collection. Benjamin
practiced law in New Orleans before the war
and could walk up Bourbon Street to his law
office across Canal Street at 37 Camp Street,
now demolished. Henry Hyams's law office
was nearby, at 165 Canal Street. (Author's collection. Photograph by Susan Rosen.)

Unfortunately, Benjamin could not depend upon his wife for support of
any kind. In 1833, when he was twenty-one, he had married Natalie St. Martin, a
beautiful, witty, vivacious sixteen-year-old Creole from a prominent Catholic family. One daughter, Ninette, was born ten years later. The match was not a good one.
Although in the early years the Benjamins lived with the St. Martins and Judah was
close to the St. Martin family all his life, his wife did not want to share his life.
When he purchased a sugar plantation, Belle Chasse, Natalie found it dull and left
for France in 1845, taking their only child with her. Yet he supported her and his
daughter for the rest of his life. He visited them in Paris, and on his death left them
the bulk of his estate. After his wife left him, Benjamin invited his mother, by then
separated from his father, to live with him.[12]

Benjamin climbed the political ladder the old-fashioned way as campaign
worker, manager, lawyer, and finally as a candidate for office. He was "a veritable
dynamo in the Whig organization in Louisiana," according to Louis Gruss. He was
elected to the Louisiana House of Representatives from New Orleans in 1842 and
was an active participant in the constitutional conventions of 1844–45 and 1852,
called to rewrite the state constitution. His brilliant performance at the 1852 constitutional convention won him many supporters, and he was elected to the
Louisiana Senate as a Whig that same year. At the right place at the right time—
and with the right connections—Benjamin was elected to the U.S. Senate, a
vacancy having coincidentally occurred around the same time.[13]

When he was elected, Benjamin was the first acknowledged Jew in the
Senate. Yulee was the first American of Jewish descent to be elected to the Senate,

but Yulee denied his connection to Judaism. Benjamin, according to Eli Evans, "acknowledged his Judaism." He was never a member of a synagogue but never renounced Judaism or converted to Christianity (although, on his deathbed, his wife had the last rites of the Catholic church performed). Benjamin was keenly aware of his Jewish appearance. "I first met him at dinner at President Pierce's house." Varina Howell Davis later wrote, "His type was decidedly Hebrew; he had not a marked line in his face which was boyish in the extreme . . . [He] had rather the air of a witty *bon vivant* than that of a great Senator." On one occasion Benjamin went before a justice of the peace to secure an affidavit. The judge inserted the name "Judas" where "Judah" should have been, whereupon Benjamin was said to have grabbed the paper, thrown it down on the desk, and exclaimed, "My God, man, is not Judah Jew enough?"[14]

On the other hand, Benjamin was a close friend to Jews in his political circle. He was close to David Yulee while they served together in the Senate, and Gustavus Myers, the leading Jewish lawyer in Richmond while Benjamin served there in the Confederate cabinet. He always welcomed Jewish visitors and made no pretense of being anything other than Jewish. Young Pvt. Eugene H. Levy of New Orleans visited Benjamin in wartime Richmond and brought regards from his father, "old Jack Levy," whom Benjamin knew.[15] The 1846 *Sketches of Life and Character in Louisiana* told its readers what they were undoubtedly curious about: "Mr. Benjamin is by birth, and as his name imports, an Israelite. Yet how far he still adheres to the religion of his fathers, I cannot tell, though I should doubt whether the matter troubled him much." The *New Orleans Courier* stated in 1844, "Of Mr. Benjamin's religious views we know nothing."[16]

In point of fact, Benjamin was completely unconcerned about religion. Pierce Butler, Benjamin's first biographer, accurately described Benjamin's feelings: "He did not forswear Judaism or conceal his Jewish origin; he remained always . . . a firm believer in immortality and in a personal Divinity; he was not ashamed, rather justly proud, of his lineage, and in temperament always retained much of the best of the traits of his people; but he had ceased to hold any active communion with Judaism." Substitute Christianity for Judaism and this would be an accurate description of Abraham Lincoln's and Thomas Jefferson's religious views. Benjamin *"had no positive or active interest in Jews or in Judaism,"* Rabbi Korn concluded.[17]

Benjamin's Jewishness, although always an impediment to his political career, was not a major stumbling block. He had no public connection to Judaism, and organized religion played no role in his life. And he had married into a Creole Catholic family. He had strong promoters in his law partners and friends at the bar. He was a close friend of the powerful Slidell clan and a protégé of John Slidell. Louisiana in the 1850s was an extraordinarily fluid society with a variety of religious, national, and ethnic groups, unlike any other American state at that time.

60   These factors combined with Benjamin's personality and his urban and plantation ties, to make his candidacy a logical one in the Louisiana of the 1850s.[18]

Like Judah Benjamin, David Yulee had a poor relationship with his father. In 1827 David and his older brother, Elias, were embroiled in some sort of controversy with their father. The disagreement led the elder Levy to terminate his sons' education. Elias was forced to leave Harvard and David left Norfolk. Both returned to one of their father's sugar plantations in Alachua County, Florida, which they managed for several years. Although he lived in relative isolation, David visited St. Augustine often and clearly had his mind set on bigger and better things than farming. Bright and energetic, Yulee decided on a career in law. He studied with Judge Robert R. Reid, later territorial governor of Florida, was admitted to the bar in 1832 at age twenty-one, and practiced in St. Augustine for a few years.[19] Yulee had a natural aptitude for politics. He became clerk to the Territorial Legislature before Florida became a state. In 1837 he was elected to the Florida legislature and in 1838 was a delegate to the convention which wrote Florida's constitution. In 1841 Yulee campaigned for the office of Territorial Delegate from Florida to the U.S. Congress. He and his fellow Jacksonian Democrats denounced the "Federal, Aristocratic, Bank Paper, Stock Jobbing Party"—that is, the Whigs. The Whigs denounced Yulee as a Jew. He was elected anyway and served in that capacity until 1845, when he was elected Florida's first U.S. senator.[20] Before Moses Levy died in 1854, father and son, who were completely estranged, attempted a reconciliation, but David's commitment to his Christian religious beliefs and Moses Levy's desire to control not only his son's but his daughter-in-law's religious beliefs made that impossible. In a loving but firm December 1842 letter to his father, Yulee wrote that he deplored but understood his father's refusal to address him as his son, reflecting the Orthodox Jewish custom of treating those who convert or marry outside of the faith as dead. "I cannot but pray that time and circumstances will gradually lessen the breach which has divided you from your child," he told his father.[21]

Yulee devoted his time as Territorial Delegate to what we would now call constituent service. Wheeling and dealing in Washington was his forte. He led the drive to bring Florida into the Union and was the Father of Florida statehood. He was an early advocate of Southern rights. The Southern bloc embraced him, and he was well hated by some New Englanders. John Quincy Adams, the former one-term president, was a member of Congress when Yulee (then called Levy) served as Territorial Delegate from Florida. He disliked Levy intensely on account of his being Jewish. Adam's diary mentions Levy often: "I found Levy, the Jew Delegate from Florida, making a red hot speech against the President's message declaring his intention to put an end to the Florida war." On another occasion Adams refers to Levy as "the alien Jew Delegate from Florida," and by 1843 he wrote: "Weller moved a reconsideration to let Levy make another hour speech, which he did. I was provoked to the boiling point, but made no reply."[22]

Once Florida was in the Union, Yulee embarked on a campaign to be elected to the U.S. Senate. It was a bitter campaign complete with the now familiar anti-Semitic slurs. But Yulee prevailed. He served two terms in the Senate, the first from 1845 to 1851 and the second from 1856 until he resigned in 1861. The year 1845 was momentous for Yulee. On March 10, the state of Florida named Levy County in his honor. On July 1, he was sworn in as a senator, and, on December 29, he had his name changed by act of the Florida legislature to David Levy Yulee. It was his grandfather's name (or one of them) and it was a well-known Jewish name. Soon after, he married Nancy Wickliffe, a great beauty whom he probably met at the White House during John Tyler's administration. Julia Tyler, the president's daughter, and Nancy Wickliffe were friends, and Nancy's father, Charles A. Wickliffe, was postmaster general. Nancy's brother Robert C. Wickliffe served as governor of Louisiana from 1856 to 1860. She was a devout Christian and was known to her contemporaries as the "Wickliffe Madonna."[23]

We do not know what went on in Yulee's mind with regard to his name change. We do know that he had left the practice of Judaism and had now embraced Christianity, although he apparently never formally converted. His marriage seemed to precipitate his name change, and he may very well have agreed to embrace Christianity in deference to his wife's wishes. Yulee also began to identify with his grandfather Yulee rather than his father.[24]

Yulee became a Presbyterian, as his letters to his wife of many years attest, but he did not regularly attend church. It was, his daughter recalled in the 1930s, "an event in the Yulee household when he did." But he was fervent in his religious beliefs. Yulee continued to associate and befriend Jews. He was close to Judah Benjamin when they served together in the Senate, and it was Yulee who convinced Benjamin not to resign from the Senate during Benjamin's travails with his promiscuous wife. Yulee certainly could never escape being called a Jew. It was an issue in all of his elections. Even though their parents were Presbyterians, the Yulee children—Wickliffe, Margaret, Nancy (or Nannie Christian), and Florida—were brought up as Episcopalians, and Yulee's son claimed that his grandfather, Moses Elias Levy, was a "Mahometan" and was not Jewish at all. The grandson, who may never have known his grandfather, simply ignored the pioneering efforts Moses Levy made to settle and develop the state of Florida.[25]

Yulee's service in the Senate was workmanlike. His son accurately described his father's contribution as giving his time "to that valuable work which is called routine, because there is nothing spectacular about it." Yulee was a practical man. During his senatorial career, he was a friend to Stephen A. Douglas and a protégé of John C. Calhoun. He represented the views of his constituents and defended the institution of slavery. He was a slaveholder and planter as well as a businessman, lawyer, real estate developer, and railroad promoter. He thus appealed to a wide spectrum of Florida's electorate, knowing firsthand the feelings of planters and farmers, businessmen and entrepreneurs.[26]

Although Yulee's father had long been an advocate of the abolition of slavery, Yulee was in the forefront of the defense of the peculiar institution. According to Yulee's son, the senator was "always solicitous as to the happiness of those dependent upon him," and would never sell a slave nor buy one if it meant separating families. He did break this rule once, when, according to young Yulee, the slave husband of a shrewish wife insisted on the sale, saying, "Massa, please don't put yoself out 'bout dat." Yulee "became an associate and an ardent admirer of Calhoun," Dorothy Dodd wrote, "who occasionally honored him by utilizing him as an instrument for the expression of his own views." Yulee deserves much of the credit for the development of the Southern position on the issue of slavery in the territories, arguing long before the Dred Scott decision that the territories belonged to all of the people and therefore slaveholders had a right to take their property wherever they wished. Yulee was an early supporter of Southern rights, was a member of the Congressional caucus which adopted Calhoun's famous 1849 address, and prepared a detailed memorandum on the proposal for a Southern convention, which ultimately materialized in the Nashville Convention of 1850.[27]

Yulee's views on secession were initially radical but, within the context of Southern political thought, became more moderate the closer the nation drew toward civil war. Like all Southern senators, he insisted on the constitutional right of slaveholders to take slaves into the territories. He felt that the North had violated the Missouri Compromise by even proposing the Wilmot Proviso. He signed Calhoun's Address to the Southern People. In the absence of a constitutional amendment protecting Southern rights, Yulee argued for immediate secession. He wrote to Calhoun in 1849 that, absent such an amendment, "the best policy [would be] to take steps at once for a separation." He was intensely involved in the debate on the admission of California as a free state, which he opposed; he voted against the abolition of slavery in the District of Columbia; and he opposed the Compromise of 1850 in any form. Newspapers called him the "Florida Fire Eater."[28]

Yulee's views, as it turned out, were too radical for the Florida of the early 1850s. In 1851, Yulee was defeated in an extremely close reelection bid to the senate. Yulee's father-in-law, Governor Wickliffe, wrote Mrs. Yulee, "Mr. Yulee can now devote himself to his own affairs for a few years." And Yulee did turn his attention from politics to his own affairs—namely, developing Florida's railroads.[29]

Judah Benjamin served in the Senate continuously from 1853 to the eve of war. He was on friendly terms with Franklin Pierce, who entertained Benjamin at the White House. Indeed, Benjamin had a national reputation even before his senatorial career. In the late winter of 1852–53, Benjamin was nominated by President Millard Fillmore to the U.S. Supreme Court, an honor he declined. He was, therefore, the first Jew nominated to the Court.[30]

In the Senate, the Whig Benjamin actively promoted Louisiana's commercial interests. He involved himself in trade, treaties, and the development of the railroad. The 1850s, however, were not ordinary times, and slavery, the territories, and sectional conflict dominated the Senate. As the political temperature rose, Benjamin, like his fellow Southern senators, warmed to the subject of the South's right to hold slaves and expand the institution to Kansas, Nebraska, and beyond. Benjamin ably defended slavery and Southern rights in debate. He once replied to Henry Wilson of Massachusetts by pointing out that the Pilgrims enslaved the Indians and sold them as slaves in the West Indies. He was one of the few senators who could stand his ground against Charles Sumner of Massachusetts, one of the Senate's most scholarly members. Yet he was widely respected by all factions and was his own man. Alone of the Southern senators, he publicly disapproved when South Carolina Rep. Preston S. Brooks assaulted Sen. Sumner and beat him with a cane.[31]

Benjamin was a slave owner who, by all accounts, treated his slaves decently. "Some few of his slaves were still living a year or two since," Butler wrote in 1907, "and would tell visitors all sorts of tales of the master of long ago;—none but kindly memories, and romantic legends of the days of glory on the old place."[32] Benjamin thought of slavery as a necessary evil much as Thomas Jefferson did. He was not, like Calhoun or Jefferson Davis, a proslavery ideologue. In 1860, for example, as chairman of the Senate Judiciary Committee, he reported a bill allowing the Federal government to contract with such organizations as the African Colonization Society to return Africans captured by slave traders engaged in illegal slave trading. Benjamin opposed all of the prominent leaders of his own party to vote for the bill. Benjamin was among the first to propose a Confederate emancipation plan toward the end of the Civil War. He believed slavery to be contrary to natural law.

Benjamin foresaw, as many could not, the ultimate end of the debate over the extension of slavery. In 1854, seven years before the firing on Fort Sumter, he wrote to a fellow Southern Whig: "I am sorry, my dear Sir, that I cannot take quite so hopeful a view of the future as you seem to anticipate." Arguing that the Whigs would divide on sectional lines, Benjamin wrote, "If I be right in this prediction, God knows what awaits us. . . . What becomes of the Union?"[33]

His responsibilities as a senator were not as time-consuming as those of his modern counterparts in Congress, and Benjamin continued to practice law. Living in Washington allowed him to practice before the Supreme Court, which was then conveniently located in the basement of the Capitol. He continued to negotiate contracts and to represent major commercial clients traveling to distant places. His ability to speak and write fluently in Spanish and French and his encyclopedic knowledge of international law and the law of foreign countries added to his reputation. He was, however, always thought of as a Jew. Once, after making an eloquent argument before the Supreme Court, a justice told his adversary, "You had better look to your laurels, for that little Jew from New Orleans has stated your case out of court."[34]

For a variety of reasons, including the rise of antislavery sentiment in the northern states, the Whig Party fell apart during the 1850s, just as Benjamin predicted it would. Former Whigs were forced to choose a new party. Benjamin joined the Democratic Party. In 1856, he announced his decision while speaking on the Kansas issue. He argued that the South, which the North perceived as "so excited, so passionate, so violent," was willing to submit the issue of the extension of slavery into Kansas to the Supreme Court; whereas the "calm, cold, quiet, calculating North" refused to be bound by the Constitution. Sen. John P. Hale of New Hampshire lamented Benjamin's eloquence. "I have listened," Hale told the Senate, "with great pleasure, as I always do, on account of [Senator Benjamin's] acknowledged ability, his great eloquence, his very persuasive powers, his mellifluous voice, his winning and graceful manner. All this only makes me regret that he is in a wrong position."[35]

Not all of Benjamin's colleagues were so kind. Sen. Benjamin Wade of Ohio, a violent opponent of slavery, said: "Why, sir, when old Moses, under the immediate inspiration of God Almighty, enticed a whole nation of slaves, and ran away, not to Canada, but to old Canaan, I suppose that Pharaoh and all the chivalry of old Egypt denounced him as a most furious abolitionist . . . there were not those who loved Egypt better than they loved liberty. . . . They were not exactly Northern men with Southern principles; but they were Israelites with Egyptian principles."[36]

Meanwhile, Yulee, out of office, continued to build his railroad empire. He bought a fleet of steamships to complement the railroad. A trunk line was built and the town of Fernandina, owned by the company and located just south of the Georgia line, began to grow into an important port. Floridian boosters saw Fernandina as an eventual rival of New Orleans. Yulee was able to convince northern shipping and railroad interests to invest in the company, and his support and that of his wife's family for Stephen A. Douglas won him important friends at the Illinois Central Railroad, with which all new railroads hoped to connect.

Yulee, however, could not get politics out of his blood. He had continued to be active in politics and was a leader in Democratic Party politics. Fortunately for his career, the Whig Party collapsed and Florida became solidly Democratic. Thus, in 1855, when a senate seat was once again open, Yulee perceived that the political landscape had changed. Floridians now saw danger in the growing Republican Party, and Yulee's positions, considered radical in 1850, now drew considerable support. Yulee had also moderated his positions, bringing him closer to the mainstream.

Like all Southern leaders, Yulee was deeply concerned about the growth of the abolitionist movement and the Republican Party. Because of his defeat in 1851, or because he now realized the catastrophe disunion would bring—especially to the railroad industry—Yulee took a more pro-Union stance. He was seen as a political power broker with too much power as well as a candidate and elected official. His enemies campaigned against what they called the "Jew Dynasty" and portrayed

Sen. David Yulee of Florida, the Father of Florida Statehood.
(Courtesy of the National Archives, Washington, D.C.)

Yulee as an "alien, traitor, and proselyte." But Yulee was an archetypal Jacksonian Democrat who wanted to open up economic opportunities, for the small businessman, the artisan, and the small farmer. He was the embodiment of what Edward Pessen has called the Jacksonian politician: an "astute realist . . . ambitious for material gain, worldly success and prestige." Yulee was immensely well liked at this stage of his career. "Although frequently denounced as an alien and a Jew," Adler concludes, "Yulee became the most popular man in Florida."[37]

During his second term as senator, Yulee was more interested in building the Florida Railroad Company than in the great issues of the day. As chairman of the Committee on Post Offices and Post Routes, he helped his brother-in-law Joseph Holt (Holt and Yulee had both married Wickliffe sisters) become postmaster general and influenced the awarding of postal contracts to steamship companies. One postal route, for example, was changed from Charleston/Key West to Charleston/Fernandina, where Yulee and Holt had substantial real estate holdings. It is likely that Yulee saw to it that Holt had an economic interest in Fernandina. He secured a mail contract between Charleston and New Orleans for the Florida Railroad, which was worth $160,000 annually. In the battle over the funding of the post office department late in the Buchanan administration, Holt and Yulee had a falling-out.[38]

Yulee opposed the withdrawal of the Southern delegates from the Democratic Party national convention in Charleston in 1860, but he was still adamant that the South never compromise on the issue of slavery in the territories. "I have never," he wrote the editor of the *Tallahassee Floridian,* "in any form, nor to any degree . . . [countenanced] . . . the idea that the inhabitants of a territory have any power to exclude slave holders." He urged the South never to abandon that right, or "as I once expressed it, the Liberty of Growth." He nevertheless urged his fellow Democrats not to send delegates to the ultra-Southern breakaway faction of the party meeting in Richmond, but instead endorsed the action of the regular party convention which was then meeting in Baltimore. This was an unpopular position for a Southern senator at the time. Yulee only broke with Douglas when all was lost and Douglas repudiated the right of secession. Yulee ended up supporting John C. Breckinridge for president in 1860, but his heart was not in it.[39]

Yulee opposed immediate secession in the months leading up to the presidential election. As late as October 1860 he was in favor of preserving the Union. While his fire-eating stance ten years earlier has caused him to be grouped with the radicals, in fact Yulee did not wholeheartedly support secession until after the election of Lincoln. He was actually a "cooperationist"; that is, he favored a solution short of secession until secession became inevitable. He was hopeful a crisis could be averted in November and December, although he notified the legislature in November that he intended to "promptly and joyously" return to Florida if the state seceded. Yulee encouraged Jefferson Davis to serve on the Committee of Thirteen, a group of senators dedicated to compromise. But by January 1861 Yulee had made up his mind to go with his state. He began planning for the secession of Florida. He wrote a blunt letter to the Florida state authorities advising them to seize and occupy Federal forts and arsenals in his state. "The Naval Station and forts at Pensacola are first in consequence. For this a force is necessary," he wrote, adding that Gov. Joseph E. Brown of Georgia would send a sufficient force to take these facilities if need be. "Lose no time," he urged, "for my opinion is, troops will be very soon despatched to reinforce and strengthen the forts in Florida." He urged the organization of a Southern government:

> What is advisable is the earliest possible organization of a Southern Confederacy and of a Southern Army. The North is rapidly consolidating against us upon the plan of force. A strong government, as eight States will make, promptly organized, and a strong army with Jeff. Davis for General in Chief, will bring them to a reasonable sense of the gravity of the crisis. . . .

I shall give the enemy a shot next week before retiring. I say enemy. Yes. I am theirs and they are mine. . . .

Yours in haste,

D. L. YULEE

This letter would come back to haunt him.[40]

On January 7, he wrote another letter which enclosed copies of resolutions drawn by a group of Southern senators and explained that "the States should go out at once" and organize "a Confederate Government" no later than February 15. Florida seceded on January 10, 1861, and Senator Yulee was one of the first of the Southern senators to announce the secession of a Southern state on the floor of the U.S. Senate.[41] It was a dignified—and sorrowful—farewell.

Yulee was always remembered as an ardent secessionist because of his original support for it. Just a month before, in December 1860, Sen. Andrew Johnson had attacked Yulee and the State of Florida as unappreciative of being a part of the United States. He chastised Yulee and his fellow Floridians, pointing out that $100,000 had been spent by the United States in negotiating for Florida; $6 million to purchase the state; and $25 million to fight and relocate the Seminole Indians. Was Florida going back to Spain, Johnson asked, or to the Seminoles? But Yulee's views had moderated. Even when secession was an accomplished fact, he urged caution. He counseled against the firing on Fort Sumter. Even as war began, Fernandina remained a stronghold for peace.[42]

By a stroke of bad luck, Joseph Holt, Yulee's estranged former brother-in-law (Holt's wife had died), became secretary of war just as the Union was breaking apart. It was said that within five minutes of his appointment, Holt made plans to provision Fort Sumter and set in motion the sailing of the *Star of the West* for Charleston harbor. Holt, a Kentuckian who had lived in Mississippi, remained fiercely loyal to the Union and convinced President Buchanan to reinforce the Pensacola forts and take a more aggressive stand for the Union. Holt's actions were an affront to the state of Florida and obviously affected Yulee. It was around this time in early January that Yulee wrote his pro-secession letters. It was also around this time that both Yulee and his fellow Florida senator, Stephen R. Mallory, attempted to procure from Holt information on munitions, equipment, and the Florida arsenals. Holt refused to provide the requested information and undoubtedly resented the request, made twice by Mallory and Yulee. All semblance of a relationship between Yulee and Holt ended. [43]

Before leaving Washington, Yulee participated in the Peace Conference called by the governor of Virginia. (His father-in-law, Charles Wickliffe, was chairman of the rules committee.) He also kept his friends informed about the movement of troops and ships. On January 28, 1861, he sent this telegram home: "The Brooklyn is bound to Pensacola. Two companies on board." [44]

Yulee's controversial personality has, with some justification, colored history's view of him. His role in the Civil War was hardly heroic, and his motives in supporting secession have been questioned. Robert L. Clarke argues that it was most likely Yulee's substantial financial interest in the Florida Railroad Company that caused him to "quickly and heartily" endorse secession. The Florida railroad *was* heavily in debt to northern banks. This was a contemporary charge in the northern press. The *New York Times* in an anti-Semitic outburst charged that Yulee was no longer getting the "fat mail contracts and subsidies" he had received and "it is well known that it was because his Jew heart did not get all it craved that he urged the secession of Florida—and like the base Judean, threw away a pearl richer than all his tribe." (The Northern Jewish press took great umbrage at this slur, as Yulee was no longer a Jew but "had been an Israelite, long, long ago.")[45]

But, it can just as well be argued that Yulee's investment in the railroad was a reason to *oppose* secession, which, in fact, his son suggests in his biography. Adler argues flatly that "economic factors [that is, the railroad] were primarily responsible" for Yulee's change of heart. In any event, Yulee was and always had been in favor of the *right* of secession, and many Southerners saw the creation of a Southern confederacy as an opportunity to establish economic independence from the North, to create new wealth, and even to repudiate debts.[46]

The Lincoln-Douglas debates, the Dred Scott decision, and John Brown's raid on Harpers Ferry polarized public sentiment on slavery and secession. Feelings reached a fever pitch by early 1860. Judah Benjamin disagreed with both Lincoln and Douglas: "I have no stomach for a fight in which I am to have the choice between the man who denies me all my rights, openly and fairly [Lincoln], and a man who admits my rights but intends to filch them [Douglas]." Unlike some other Southern politicians, he never underestimated Lincoln and in fact stated frankly that "it is impossible not to admire [his] perfect candor and frankness."[47]

Benjamin, though ultimately a secessionist, was not a leader in the movement.[48] Like many Southern politicians, Benjamin failed to grasp the popularity of secession. From August to November of 1860, Benjamin was involved in a trial in California. By October it was clear that Lincoln could be elected, but opinion in Louisiana was divided on secession. The emotion sweeping westward from South Carolina, however, was overwhelming. According to one historian, the Louisiana leadership, including Benjamin, now "thought it wise to fall in line and even when possible to lead the fast-growing parade . . . lest their office-holding futures and reputations as loyal Southerners be seriously impaired."[49]

On December 14, 1860, Benjamin signed the "Address of Certain Southern Members of Congress to Our Constituents" urging secession and on December 31 made his eloquent speech defending the right of secession. Louisiana seceded on January 26, 1861, and Benjamin bade farewell to the Senate on February 4. "We are told," he said, "that . . . the South is in rebellion without cause and that her citizens are traitors. Rebellion. The very word is a confession. . . . When, sir, did millions of people as a single man rise in organized, deliberate unimpassioned rebellion against justice, truth and honor?"[50] As if to illustrate what the future held, he wore a pistol.

On Washington's birthday, February 22, he gave the main address to 20,000 people in New Orleans, where he noted soberly that "our independence is not to

The first Confederate cabinet. Clockwise from top center: Robert A. Toombs of Georgia, secretary of state; Leroy Pope Walker of Alabama, secretary of war; Judah P. Benjamin of Louisiana, then attorney general; John H. Reagan of Texas, postmaster general; Stephen R. Mallory of Florida, secretary of the Navy; and Christopher G. Memminger of South Carolina, secretary of the Treasury. Stephen Mallory of Florida was a close friend of Eugenia Phillips. Robert Toombs was a close friend of Raphael J. Moses of Columbus, Georgia. (Author's collection.)

be maintained without the shedding of our blood." This was the last public speech he would ever make in his adopted home. He made provisions for his sisters, who were living in his New Orleans residence, urging them to stay there if war came. He then left for Montgomery, Alabama, where the new Confederate Congress was in session. He never saw his sisters, his nephews and nieces, or the Crescent City again.[51]

On February 25, 1861, Judah P. Benjamin was confirmed as attorney general of the Confederate States of America. "A Hebrew of Hebrews, for the map of the Holy City was traced all over his small, refined face, the attorney-general was of the highest type of his race," Thomas Cooper DeLeon recalled in *Belles, Beaux, and Brains of the '60s*. "Small and rotund, he was yet of easy grace in manner, and his soft voice was not only pleasant of sound, but always carried something worth hearing. That he was a great and successful lawyer all knew, and that he was an omnivorous devourer of books and of wonderful assimilative capacity." His high profile as a former Southern senator and a Southern Jew sparked blatantly anti-Semitic criticism. Henry Wilson, senator from Massachusetts, exclaimed that Benjamin was part of a "foul and wicked plot to . . . overthrow the government of his adopted country which gives equality of rights even to that race that stoned prophets and crucified the Redeemer of the world."[52] Andrew Johnson referred to him as a "Jew—that miserable Benjamin!" and attacked Benjamin for belonging "to that tribe that parted the garments of our Savior and for his vesture cast lots" and as "a sneaking, Jewish, unconscionable traitor."[53] A Boston newspaper in a reference to Benjamin hissed: "We ask whether the Jews, having no country of their own, desire to put other nations in the same unhappy condition."[54] A Jew in the spotlight of national politics was rare in the nineteenth century, Benjamin Disraeli notwithstanding. William H. Russell, correspondent of the *London Times*, in his famous Civil War memoir, *My Diary North and South,* wrote of the new attorney general that he was a "short, stout man, with a full face, olive-colored, and most decidedly Jewish features, with the brightest large black eyes, one of which is somewhat diverse from the other, and a brisk, lively, agreeable manner, combined with much vivacity of speech and quickness of utterance." He also described Benjamin as "the most brilliant perhaps of the whole of the famous Southern orators," and the most "open, frank, and cordial" as well.[55]

Judah Benjamin was not a close personal friend of Jefferson Davis before the war. He was chosen for his new post because he was one of the South's leading constitutional and commercial lawyers, and Davis wanted each state to have a place in his cabinet. All of Benjamin's biographers agree that it was a waste of talent. Meade writes that Benjamin was unsuited for the position because "it was too unimportant a place for a man of his ability."[56] The Confederacy, after all, had no courts and when war came, there was little litigation. *Inter arma silent leges* (In time of war, the laws are silent).

His good humor and his grasp of the situation at hand commended him to the president, the members of the cabinet, and the leadership of the new nation. While the capital of the Confederacy was still temporarily in Montgomery, Benjamin was addressing the practical problems of the new nation. Leroy P. Walker, the first Confederate secretary of war, noted Benjamin's foresight in an anecdote: At the time, Mr. Walker said, he believed there would be no war. In fact, he had gone about the state promoting secession and promising to "wipe up with my pocket-handkerchief all the blood that would be shed." Walker recalled that when the Confederate cabinet met, there was only one man who grasped the real situation, and that was Benjamin. Benjamin proposed that the government purchase as much cotton as it could, at least 100,000 bales, and ship it to England. With the proceeds of a part of it he advised the purchase of arms and munitions. The rest of the cotton was to be held for credit. "'For,' said Benjamin, 'we are entering on a contest that must be long and costly.' All the rest of us fairly ridiculed the idea of a serious war," Walker concluded. "Well, you know what happened."[57]

While Benjamin's talents were wasted in the attorney general's office, his energetic and affable personality were well suited to Confederate Richmond. He became a popular member of Richmond society. Thomas Cooper DeLeon recalled that Benjamin was highly sought after at social occasions. He was that "polished and smooth brevet bachelor . . . with the plus sign. There was no circle, official or otherwise, that missed his soft, purring presence, or had not regretted so doing. . . . He moved into and through the most elegant or the simplest assemblage on natural rubber tires and well-oiled bearings, a smile of recognition for the mere acquaintance, a reminiscent word for the intimate, and a general diffusion of placid *bonhomie*."[58]

Jefferson Davis began to rely on his attorney general for advice and support. When Secretary Walker resigned, Davis asked Benjamin to serve as acting secretary of war. Davis, early in the war, perceived in Benjamin a capacity for hard work and personal loyalty that was lacking in other subordinates. Benjamin proved efficient as well as devoted to Davis personally. He served as acting secretary of war from September 17, 1861, to November 21, 1861, when he was confirmed as secretary of war by the Confederate Senate.[59]

His appointment was greeted with favor by the press and the public. The *Richmond Examiner* mentioned the new secretary as a possible candidate for vice president. Benjamin inherited severe problems. His predecessor resigned for many reasons, but the most obvious were a lack of supplies and transportation and of organizational ability. The plan to purchase arms, for example, had foundered. Unfortunately, the new secretary was not a military strategist, and this was not a propitious time to learn how to communicate with military men. Benjamin had written a note to General Beauregard in which he acknowledged that he was only a civilian "who knows nothing of war." One Confederate soldier agreed: "Mr.

72   Benjamin was a brilliant lawyer, but he knew as much about war as an Arab knows of the Sermon on the Mount." In fact, Jefferson Davis acted as his own secretary of war. "In Judah Benjamin," Evans concludes, Davis "developed the perfect alter-ego and technician." To some degree, Benjamin was the lightning rod for Davis, but this was also true of other cabinet members.[60]

Benjamin brought to the War Department his well-known capacity for hard work and his organizational abilities. He made the department more efficient; he recognized the problems of inadequate railroads, communication, equipment, arms, ordnance, ammunition, and a lack of trained officers and troops, and he did his best to remedy them. He worked closely with Col. Josiah Gorgas, the chief of ordnance in the War Department, but he failed in his relationships with generals and eventually with the Congress. Early on he earned the enmity of Joseph E. Johnston and P. G. T. Beauregard, two of the Confederacy's highest-ranking generals and foes of Jefferson Davis. He also quarreled with the heroic but dour Stonewall Jackson and lost the encounter when Jackson threatened to resign. Benjamin did, however, have a consistently pleasant relationship with Robert E. Lee.[61]

Benjamin was bombarded with requests for reinforcements of the defenses of Roanoke Island. The North Carolina coast guarded a water route from Norfolk, Virginia, and the railroad, an important link with Richmond, was nearby. The defense of Roanoke Island was in the hands of an aristocratic but not particularly competent Charlestonian, Maj. Gen. Benjamin Huger. On January 7, 1862, a former governor of Virginia, Brig. Gen. Henry A. Wise, was in charge of the island and reported to Huger. Wise wanted more men. Benjamin looked to General Huger, who demurred. Wise went out of the chain of command and spoke directly to the secretary of war, a gross violation of military law. Benjamin ordered Wise back to his post. When Roanoke Island fell to the Union army and navy in February 1862, 2,500 Confederates, including many prominent Richmonders, were taken prisoner. Governor Wise's popular young son was killed, and the new secretary of war was held accountable for the debacle. There was bitter criticism of Benjamin, Huger, and President Davis as well. Benjamin had relied on Huger, a graduate of West Point, but his reliance was misplaced.[62]

The Roanoke Island defeat hurt Benjamin's reputation in Richmond. Not only could it have been avoided, but the soldiers involved were Virginians from the capital city itself. There was constant criticism of the secretary, who, after all, was in charge of the war department. "Laws," Benjamin remarked, "cannot suddenly convert farmers into gunsmiths."[63] There was a clamor for Benjamin's resignation when the news arrived that Brig. Gen. Ulysses S. Grant captured Fort Henry and Fort Donelson in Tennessee, and Gen. Albert Sidney Johnston's retreat from Nashville confirmed low opinions of his military judgment.

A no-confidence resolution was introduced in the Confederate Congress in March 1862, which unleashed a torrent of anti-Benjamin, anti-Semitic rhetoric.

Congressman Henry S. Foote of Tennessee, a rabid anti-Semite and virulent opponent of Davis, referred to Benjamin as "Judas Iscariot Benjamin" and the "Jewish puppeteer" behind the "Davis tyranny." There was a congressional investigation, and the secretary of war told the committee repeatedly that he took personal responsibility for the defeat at Roanoke.[64]

Davis did not seek Benjamin's confirmation as secretary of war under the new, permanent constitution, but instead on March 17, 1862, appointed Benjamin secretary of state of the Confederate States of America, a promotion, as one contemporary observed, in "the very teeth of criticism." He had served six long months as secretary of war and was now among the highest-ranking officers of the Confederacy. John M. Daniel of the *Richmond Examiner* reacted to Benjamin's appointment as secretary of state by remarking that "the representation of the Synagogue is not diminished; it remains full."[65]

While Judah Benjamin labored in wartime Richmond, David Yulee protected his railroads in Florida. He held no political or military office during the war. Given Yulee's interest in politics, it is puzzling that he sought no appointed or elected position in the Confederate government. He was asked to run, and he would likely have been elected to the Confederate Senate. Perhaps his reasons were just what he said they were: He had tired of politics and wished only "to enjoy the relief of a home life" and tend to his business concerns. Unlike Judah Benjamin and many other politicians, Yulee had a happy marriage and did in fact wish to tend to his businesses. Service in Richmond, away from his family, had no allure for him, and he may have doubted the success of the South's war for independence. He had no military training and never served in the armed forces, although, according to his son, he paid the expenses of "a couple of companies of infantry" to protect his home county.[66]

His son, Wickliffe, saw a little fighting as a volunteer in a cavalry company but never joined the army. According to family tradition, Yulee's brother, Elias, became an officer in the Washington (Georgia) Rifles. Mrs. Yulee was an adamant Confederate. "I pity those who have no country to love or to fight for!" she wrote from her home in Florida. "It is this very country of yours and mine that induces me to write this letter. . . . Tax! tax! tax our people to half we have, if necessary, but let the world know we are paying! Ten victories will not give the Yankees such a blow as this fact . . . we are not discouraged. I have never felt a doubt of my country, but dark and painful trials are yet before us, perhaps!"[67] Yulee acted as a kind of unofficial ombudsman helping his former constituents with their problems, injecting his opinions about everything from military strategy to taxes, legislation, and the conduct of the war, and as an ambassador-at-large and roving counselor to the governor, to generals, and to the Confederate cabinet.[68]

Yulee used the war to wrest control of the Florida Railroad Company from its northern stockholders. While the Florida line, like most Southern railroads, remained local in nature, Yulee envisioned a Florida line tied into a national network. He also realized early that, as the irascible war clerk John B. Jones phrased it, "The iron was wanted more than anything else but men." Yulee's involvement with the railroad constitutes his most significant activity during the war. The northern stockholders may have had control before secession, but they were now "enemy aliens," and Yulee, the largest Southern stockholder, was able to take over the company.[69]

War is beyond the control of businessmen, and the Union invasion of coastal Florida severely limited the use of the railroad. Yulee asked Gen. Robert E. Lee, who in the early days of the war was given the lackluster assignment of defending Florida, Georgia, and South Carolina, for assistance in protecting the line. Lee took a steamer to Fernandina in November 1861 to meet with Yulee and informed him that Brig. Gen. James H. Trapier, whose appointment Yulee had helped engineer, was under orders to establish himself at Fernandina and protect the harbor. But Lee politely declined to devote his limited resources to protecting Yulee's railroad. This did not deter Yulee, who continued to try and convince anyone who would listen that the defense of Fernandina and the railroad were "vital for the defense of the entire Gulf States region." He personally arranged for General Trapier to purchase a steamer, which he thought would make "a capital gun boat" to protect Fernandina, and then wrote his old Senate colleague Stephen Mallory, now secretary of the Confederate navy, to pay for it. "We have no boat, in Florida upon which a gun can be carried," he wrote Mallory, "Georgia & So Ca have monopolized them & this is the only boat available." Men were sent to defend Fernandina and Amelia Island as a result of his efforts.[70]

Yulee traveled to Richmond early in the war to take the measure of the Confederate government; influence the selection of military commanders in Florida; lobby for his railroad and for the defense of Fernandina; and to reinforce his contacts, particularly his relationship with his old friend Judah Benjamin, now acting secretary of war. He lobbied successfully for the appointment of General Trapier as commander of the Department of Eastern and Middle Florida. At times, it seemed to those in the state government that Yulee was running the Confederate military operation in Florida. He wrote Benjamin in October 1861 asking him to direct General Trapier to raise ten companies and bring "the post at Fernandina under better command." Benjamin immediately complied. Lee continued to communicate directly with Yulee about the defense of the Florida coast sometimes to the exclusion of the Florida government. Lee tried to convince the state to protect itself and Yulee tried to convince Lee to send Confederate troops and a naval defense. Typical were Lee's telegrams to Yulee of December 14 and 16, 1861: "I will reinforce all I can," and "Call the Florida troops to Fernandina—they are not wanted [that is, not needed] elsewhere."[71]

He tried his best to keep the railroad and port facilities in both Fernandina and Cedar Key operational, but the Union army and navy would not cooperate.

Yulee continually implored the Confederate government to send men. In January 1862, he complained to Benjamin that Trapier's department was partly in Lee's command and partly in another's and that this was inefficient. He requested two more cannons and added a postscript: "General Lee is a capital commander." In January 1862, the Federal navy landed a small detachment at Cedar Key. They spiked cannons and burned eight ships, seven freight cars, the railroad depot, and a warehouse. Yulee sent a train to evacuate the women and children. In February 1862 he wrote Lee, "The line across the peninsula between Ferna[ndina] and C Key constitutes the necessary base of all military operations in Florida. I think the constant presence & vigilance of a competent head upon this line is indispensable." Lee replied that he had referred the matter to General Trapier, but that in his opinion the Yankees were unlikely to try to capture the entire railroad.[72]

By 1862 Yulee had moved his family from Fernandina to his Gulf Coast home, Margarita, on Tiger Tail Island at the mouth of the Homosassa River. There they remained safely for two years. Fernandina was captured in March of 1862, and Yulee was on the last train to escape. He was forced to remove his business operations to Gainesville, which remained his headquarters from 1862 to 1864. Yulee turned his attention to safeguarding the Cedar Key terminus and procuring a military presence. He could not visit his family very often on the Gulf Coast because the Union army and navy were looking for him and the area swarmed with Union gunboats. A letter from a captured Confederate soldier, who was an involuntary passenger on such a gunboat, confirmed that the Yankees wanted to arrest Yulee and that "when in possession of him, he would be hung as a traitor. They also said that they knew where his plantation was, & that they did not mean to let him make any more sugar for the rebels, as they styled us."[73]

Federal troops occupy Fernandina, Florida. (Author's collection.)

Judah Philip Benjamin was the first attorney general, the second secretary of war, and the third secretary of state of the Confederate States of America. He was a lawyer who turned down a nomination to the U.S. Supreme Court and a slave owner who proposed freeing slaves to fight for the Confederacy. This photograph was taken early in the war by Charles Anthony. (Courtesy of Bob Marcus, Springfield, Virginia.)

Back in Richmond, Benjamin served as secretary of state from March 1863 until the last days of the Confederacy in April 1865. He was to the civilian government what Lee was to the military: a loyal, stalwart, indefatigable, and uncomplaining patriot. He was the most well-known Confederate official next to the president and vice president and third in order of succession.[74] Historians early on referred to him as the "brains of the Confederacy," and Varina Howell Davis called him her husband's "right arm."[75] Charles P. Roland described Benjamin as "the President's most intimate friend and counselor."[76] His office was located near Davis's in an executive office building, formerly the Federal customs house, in downtown Richmond, and the two men worked "like galley-slaves, early and late," according to Mrs. Davis. "Mr. Davis came home . . . perfectly exhausted," she added, "but Mr. Benjamin was always fresh and buoyant."[77] While the War Department had thousands of employees, the State Department had six clerks. His chief assistant was Lucius Quinton Washington, a distant relative of the first president.

Like his predecessors, the new secretary's main goals when he took office were to achieve foreign recognition of the Confederacy and to lift the Union blockade. Failing that, he hoped to preserve European neutrality, secure shipments of material, and borrow money from European bankers. He failed to obtain recognition but succeeded in borrowing money. The European powers were wary of recognizing a country that could not achieve military victory. The British and French governments, as opposed to the British and French people, hoped for the success of the Confederacy, and early in the war there may have been some chance of recognition. From the diplomatic point of view, the South's most optimistic moment probably came in the fall of 1862. In October, William Gladstone, then chancellor of the exchequer, said, "Jefferson Davis and other leaders of the South have made an army; they are making, it appears, a navy; and they have made what is more than either—they have made a nation." But Gladstone's oratorical flourish proved to be a political mirage.[78]

The opportunity quickly faded. After Gettysburg and Vicksburg in the summer of 1863, recognition was not a real option. From March 1862 until that fateful July 1863, however, Benjamin used all of his considerable energy in trying to convince, cajole, and even bribe the British and French governments.

Confederate two-dollar bill. Benjamin's portrait is at left. He may be the only Jewish American whose likeness has appeared on currency. (Author's collection.)

Jefferson F. Davis, president of the Confederate States of America. Davis had longstanding relationships with many Jewish Southerners both before and during the war. He was a close friend of the Phillips family in the 1850s. Judah P. Benjamin was his closest advisor, and according to Eli Evans, the beleaguered president's alter ego. This daguerreotype was taken prior to 1860. (Courtesy of the Chicago Historical Society, Chicago, Illinois.)

Benjamin's real value as secretary of state was a personal acquaintance with European political figures, lawyers, bankers, and businessmen. His wife and daughter lived in Paris, and John Slidell, his political mentor and former Senate colleague, was the Confederacy's emissary to France. Louisiana had considerable economic and social connections with France, and Benjamin was an experienced international lawyer. He was familiar with the court of Emperor Napoleon III and knew it to be corrupt. His strategy for obtaining French recognition was simple. Shortly after his appointment, he instructed Slidell to offer the emperor commercial concessions such as the duty-free importation of French products and 100,000 bales of cotton valued at $4.5 million or more if necessary. He would also support the emperor's military and political adventures in Mexico. Napoleon III's position was too insecure to allow him to take the offer. Indeed, the emperor tried in vain to convince the British and the Russians to propose an armistice and an end to the Union blockade. But the British could not be moved, and Napoleon felt that the risk of supporting the South—even for a $5 million bribe—was too great.[79]

Benjamin, however, continued to press the French connection because it appeared to have a greater potential for success than the British. The famous Erlanger loan, in which the Confederacy received $2.5 million in badly needed cash, was an outgrowth of foreign policy initiatives and previous efforts by the Confederacy to borrow money against Southern cotton crops. Benjamin personally negotiated the loan with Baron Emile Erlanger in Richmond. He hoped the involvement of the banking house of Erlanger & Cie and the Erlanger family, close friends and advisors of the emperor of France, would somehow bring the French government closer to the Southern cause.[80]

John Slidell's daughter was engaged to marry Baron Erlanger. The connection was obvious. (The Slidells were further connected to the Jewish community through the marriage of Slidell's niece to August Belmont, the well-known New York lawyer who represented the Rothschild family.) The Erlangers hoped to reap a substantial profit from the transaction, and the original plan called for a loan of $25 million to be repaid with bonds and the sale of cotton. The Erlangers wanted a 23 percent commission and various concessions for handling the bonds at 8 percent. Benjamin thought the terms usurious; but, because the Confederacy was so desperate for money, the government had agreed in principle to the terms requested by the Erlangers. After extensive face-to-face negotiations in Benjamin's office between the South's leading diplomat and France's leading banker, Benjamin was able to modify the arrangement in the Confederacy's favor. "The conflict of these two Jewish brains—Benjamin and Erlanger—caused modification very beneficial to the Confederate Government," Burton J. Hendrick concluded. The interest rate declined to 7 percent, and the Erlanger profits were reduced.[81]

Speculators and investors in Europe snapped up the bonds, and the Erlangers made a handsome profit. The Confederacy received a timely infusion of much-needed cash. The pro-Davis faction thought Benjamin brilliant. "Everything Mr. Benjamin said, we listened to," Mary Chesnut wrote, "bore it in mind, gave heed to it diligently." The anti-Davis faction thought Benjamin an enemy of the people: "On the occasion of the recent visit of Mr. Erlanger," Congressman Foote huffed and puffed, "Minister Plenipotentiary, Envoy Extraordinaire from his Highness, the Emperor of France, to his Highness the would-be Emperor of the Confederate States, Judas Iscariot Benjamin had spoke for two hours in French." In the end, European speculators lost a great deal of money on the transaction.[82]

None of it mattered. Napoleon III refused to risk recognition of the Confederacy without Great Britain, and Great Britain, under the cautious leadership of Lord John Russell, the foreign secretary, and Lord Palmerston, the prime minister, would not budge. Benjamin focused his diplomacy on Great Britain. In April of 1862, he drafted instructions to the Confederacy's ambassador arguing against the legality of the Union blockade and its ineffectiveness. Under international law, an ineffective blockade was not legally binding on neutral nations. He pointed out how Lord Russell had misunderstood, or deliberately misconstrued, applicable treaties which demonstrated his point—but to no avail. Cotton was not king after all. To Russell, the risk of war with the United States and the risk of alienating the great majority of the British public were too great. Judah Benjamin had to bow to these basic facts. By August 1863 Benjamin was thoroughly disenchanted with the British treatment of the Confederacy and its minister, James Murray Mason. He recalled Mason and asked for the recall of all British consuls in the Confederacy. Benjamin had exhausted his diplomatic arsenal.[83]

As the war dragged on, the Confederacy's options dwindled. On February 12, 1864, the Confederate Congress voted in secret session to create "bodies for the capture and destruction of the enemies' property." The Bureau of Special and Secret Service came into existence, and funding for these operations went to the State Department. Benjamin, as secretary of state, was the likely head of the bureau and chief of Confederate covert activities. Shortly thereafter, important agents of the Confederacy arrived in Montreal. "A few months later," Roy Z. Chamlee Jr. writes in *Lincoln's Assassins*, "John Wilkes Booth opened a bank account in the same Montreal bank used by the Rebels."[84]

Benjamin had now taken on the most dangerous assignment Davis had given him—and his last assignment for the Confederacy—that of spymaster. He established spy rings and sent political propagandists to the North and to Canada. He enlisted the seductive Belle Boyd, the "Cleopatra of Secession," to travel abroad, rallying public opinion for the southern states. He sent emissaries and agents to Ireland to stem the tide of Irish volunteers entering the Union army. He planned the burning of Federal medical stores in Louisville and the burning of bridges and boats in strategic locations across the occupied South. He also oversaw the suppression of treason against the Confederacy. Special commissioners who investigated and arrested those disloyal to the government reported to Benjamin. For example, Col. Henry J. Leovy, a close friend of Benjamin from New Orleans, served as a military commissioner in southwest Virginia. His job was ferreting out traitors.[85]

Benjamin, like many other Confederate leaders, believed the Northern public would not support Lincoln indefinitely. Serious efforts were made to exploit the difference between the eastern and western states, to increase public disaffection in the North for the war, and to raid prisoner of war camps. Provocateurs attempted to capture Federal property in the far north. Confederate agents tried to disrupt the monetary system by urging people to convert paper money to gold. There was even an attempt—probably unknown to Benjamin but involving his agents—to set New York City on fire. Benjamin oversaw the most ambitious mission, a $1 million Canadian covert operation headed by Jacob Thompson. Canada was a potential Confederate ally. Its governor was friendly, and it provided a base for blockade-running, spy operations, and offensive military operations. In April 1864, the State Department requested $1 million from the Confederate treasury, an astronomical sum by the standards of the time. The warrant for the funds was issued pursuant to the Secret Service Act and signed by Davis "in favor of Hon. J. P. Benjamin, Secretary of State."[86] Thompson reported to Benjamin.

Meanwhile, in Florida David Yulee continued to grow sugar, which was desperately needed by the Confederacy. In early July 1863, the Confederate army tried to purchase sixty-four hogsheads of Yulee's sugar weighing 49,898 pounds, but would not pay the market price. The Confederate commissary officer, using a fixed schedule to pay for goods which fluctuated dramatically in price, then impressed—that is, took—the sugar, and years of litigation followed until Yulee recovered his right to fair compensation. The case was decided in the Florida Supreme Court.[87] In partnership with other investors, Yulee also engaged in blockade-running, exporting cotton and tobacco to Cuba, and bringing in rum, paper, quinine, and clothing.[88]

A year earlier, in March 1862, the Confederate army had become a bigger threat to the Florida Railroad Company than the Federals had been. Yulee's friend Trapier agreed with the Confederate command that the rails were needed. "Railroads are," he had said in December of 1861, "at one and the same time the *legs* and the *stomach* of an army." The Confederacy, however, did not have the capacity to manufacture rails. According to Robert C. Black, not a single new rail was manufactured in the Confederacy after 1861, and the Confederate government proved incapable of coordinating the use of the Southern railroads. Existing lines became valuable as "iron mines," as the Confederate government realized that its railroads could only be maintained by cannibalizing existing rails. After Fernandina fell, General Trapier ordered the taking up of the rails to a defensible point inland so that another line, the Lawton-Live Oak route, could be built further west.[89]

Yulee's rail line ran east-west, but the Confederate government needed to ship Florida's foodstuffs, particularly beef, north. Yulee had the rails. The Confederacy wanted them. Florida Gov. John Milton, who, unlike other Southern governors, prided himself on his cooperation with the Richmond government, ordered the arrest of anyone who interfered. He urged Yulee to support the cause of Southern independence "rather than engage in a neighborhood fight for a little railroad iron." Yulee, however, not only refused to cooperate, he went into state court and obtained an injunction restraining the Confederate army from removing the rails. "I humbly trust," he had previously informed Gov. John Milton, "I may not be wanting at any time in necessary & dutiful sacrifices & contribution to the great cause in which all citizens are engaged, and will gladly unite with yourself & other Trustees [of the Internal Improvement Fund] in liberal & patriotic devotion of our own means. But, I have not the right to make myself free with the property of others, nor to seek merit for a generous patriotism at another's cost." This angered the Confederate military, the governor, and Jefferson Davis.[90]

Yulee delayed the Confederate army for two years while Northern stockholders prodded the Union army to take every step possible to regain control of the line. The Battle of Olustee in February 1864 was the final straw for the Confederate government. "Had the gap between Lawton and Live Oak been filled by a line of railroad," Gen. P. G. T. Beauregard complained, "the enemy would at once have been driven out of Florida." In May 1864 a young Confederate lieutenant, J. M. Fairbanks, decided to ignore the state court injunction and take up Yulee's rails. When he informed Yulee of his intention to do so, and also informed him that it was Confederate government policy to buy or replace the rails within six months after the end of the war, Yulee went back to court. Judge James B. Dawkins, incensed that the army did not obey his order, ordered Fairbanks to appear before him on contempt charges. Fairbanks escaped arrest only because his soldiers kept the local sheriff from carrying out Judge Dawkins's order. Although he disagreed with the order, Governor Milton was angry that the army would not obey an order of a Florida court. The Confederate government then filed suit on behalf of the Sequestration Fund, claiming the assets of the company because it was owned by alien Northerners.[91]

Yulee was protecting his investment. In this, he was not alone. Black observes in *The Railroads of the Confederacy,* "The owners of companies designated as iron mines were normal men." When war came, they committed their resources to the Confederate cause, but when asked to give up their rails, they offered pretexts, they got angry, and rallied to the banner of states' rights. They soon resorted to litigation, going into state courts and obtaining injunctions against the Confederate government. Yulee fought off the Confederate lawyers just as he fought off the armies of both sides. He delayed the sequestration proceedings by various strategies, including muddying the facts about his own personal financial relationship with the company. The war ended before any of these issues were resolved, although some of the rails were taken up by the Confederate army.[92]

Wickliffe Yulee's explanation for his father's seemingly unpatriotic behavior was that he was protecting the assets of the railroad in his fiduciary capacity as president of the company and that he was protecting the interests of his Northern partners. His partners, however, did not see it that way. Neither did the Confederate government. Although it was untrue, Yulee believed that a warrant had been issued by the Confederacy for his arrest. The arrest incident led to a lifelong estrangement between Davis and Yulee. The Northern press seized on this incident in the spring of 1864 and reported that Yulee was in favor of abandoning the war and for reconstruction of the Union. Yulee vehemently denied these allegations and further denied that he had declined the office of Confederate senator because of a lack of commitment to the Southern cause. He said he wholeheartedly supported the Confederacy and the prosecution of the war "until the Sovereignty of the Confederate States is allowed." But the combination of Yulee's fight against the Confederacy for his railroad line, his failure to seek office, and the Fernandina area's general desire for peace led many to believe he was a Union sympathizer.[93]

Preservation of the Florida Railroad Company and its rails was not just a matter of money to Yulee. He had dedicated his adult life to bringing Florida into the modern world, first by bringing it into the Union, and then by joining Florida to the Union by rail. Indeed, one historian concludes that "the completion of the Florida Railroad must rank as one of his most notable achievements," and it became "his main ambition in life."[94]

By 1864 Judah Benjamin was convinced that unless slaves could be drafted or persuaded to fight for the Confederacy, the South would soon exhaust its manpower. He privately argued for the use of black troops and granting freedom to slaves who would fight for the Confederacy. It was clear to Benjamin that slavery was at an end. That fact was less clear to most Confederate leaders and the great majority of white Southerners. Cooperating with Varina Davis and Robert E. Lee, both of whom agreed with his assessment, Benjamin finally convinced Jefferson Davis to act. The president authorized his secretary of state to send an emissary to the British government to offer gradual emancipation in exchange for recognition. Benjamin then began to work in earnest behind the scenes to convince the Confederate Congress and the public of the need to use black troops. It was an exhausting ordeal. Benjamin offered to give a public speech "to feel the pulse of the people," Mrs. Davis recalled.

On February 9, 1865, Jefferson Davis's lawyer argued his last public case for the Confederacy to more than ten thousand people assembled in and around the

African Church near Capitol Square.[95] After the invocation, Jefferson Davis made an impassioned speech against Lincoln, Yankee rule, Grant, and Sherman, and pledged that the South would never return to the Union as "a conquered people." Sen. Robert M. T. Hunter of Virginia spoke vigorously in the same vein.[96] When it was Benjamin's turn, he appealed to the patriotism of the assembled crowd. He argued that Southerners should reject Lincoln's demands "that you should bend the knee, bow the neck, and meekly submit to the conqueror's yoke." The "fire of freedom burns unquenchably in your souls." But more was needed, he said. Cotton and tobacco must be sacrificed for the Confederacy. The crowd applauded. Cheers interrupted him. Men were needed, both black and white, he said. "I am going to open my whole heart to you," Benjamin confided to his audience. "Look to the trenches below Richmond. Is it not a shame that men who have sacrificed all in our defense should not be reinforced by all the means in our power?" He then spoke in exaggerated figures of the difference in manpower: 3,000,000 men fighting for the North; 1,644,000 for the South. More were needed. "Our resources of white population have greatly diminished," he thundered, but the South still had 680,000 black men of fighting age. Could "Divine prophecy have told us of the fierceness of the enemy's death grapple at our throats—could we have known what we now know, that Lincoln has confessed, that without 200,000 negroes which he stole from us, he would be compelled to give up the contest, should we have entertained any doubts upon the subject?" Benjamin then publicly advanced the proposition that slaves who fought for the Confederacy be freed: "Let us say to every Negro who wishes to go into the ranks on condition of being made free—'Go and fight; you are free.' If we impress [draft] them, they will go against us."[97]

Reactions varied to this radical proposal. Varina Davis believed that Benjamin had never been more eloquent. But a resolution in the Confederate Congress which stated that Benjamin was "not a wise and prudent Secretary of State" failed on a tie vote. Benjamin offered to resign, but Davis would not consider it. In early March, a month before Appomattox, the Confederate Congress passed a watered-down act allowing slaves to fight for the Confederacy if their masters "volunteered" them. Emancipation was not included. Benjamin had lost his last case for the Confederate States of America.

The Southern nation began to dissolve. Casualties were high in Lee's army. Survivors deserted. Desperate, Davis and Benjamin considered their options. Surrender was not one of them. A plot to kidnap Lincoln and blow up the White House was. (For more on this episode, see chapter 8, pp. 314–15.)[98]

As the war came to an end in 1865, Judah Benjamin prepared to escape from Richmond with Jefferson Davis and the Confederate cabinet. David Yulee, his plantation, business, and railroads in shambles, prepared to face an uncertain

future. These two former powerful Southern senators, these two Sephardic senators, had made their respective choices. Each now had to face the disastrous consequences and whatever fate had in store.

PART 2

Be Strong and
of a Good Courage

★ ★ ★ ★ ★ ★ ★ ★ ★ ★

THE SOLDIERS

Have not I commanded thee? Be strong and of a good courage; be not afraid, neither be thou dismayed: for the Lord thy God *is* with thee whithersoever thou goest.

—Joshua 1:9

Capt. Ezekiel J. Levy of the
Richmond Blues. (Author's collection.)

★

CHAPTER 3

Hebrew Officers
and Israelite Gentlemen

Like Judah P. Benjamin and David Yulee, the Jewish officers of the Confederate armed forces and officials of the government were part and parcel of Southern society. They accepted their responsibility to defend their homeland. Lt. Simon Mayer, an officer in the Mississippi brigade, implored his brother Henry to join the army, telling him he could "no longer . . . remain passive to the scenes that are daily enacted in the grand drama." He urged his brother to join "with light heart & strong arms, backed by a determination to do or die . . . to come out & meet his would be masters, and subjugators."[1] Some, like Maj. Raphael J. Moses of Columbus, Capt. Edwin Warren Moise of Charleston, Lt. James Madison Seixas of New Orleans, the DeLeons of Columbia, and Col. Samuel M. Hyams of Natchitoches Parish, were descended from old Sephardic families. Others, like Col. Leon Dawson Marks of Shreveport, Samuel Yates Levy of Savannah, and Abraham Charles Myers of Georgetown, South Carolina, were from old Southern families whose ancestors, both Ashkenazic and Sephardic, had settled in the South generations before Fort Sumter. Most had grown to manhood in the South even if their parents were the first of their family to become Southerners. Capt. Ezekiel J. Levy's father, Jacob A. Levy, had moved to Richmond from Holland as a young man, but "Zeke" was raised as a Richmonder.[2] Simon Mayer's father had settled in Natchez. These young Confederate officers, men in their twenties and early thirties, had grown up in the fiercely partisan decades preceding the war. Unlike their parents, the younger generation spent their formative years in a South defensive about slavery and hostile to what their generation perceived as Northern aggression and condescension toward the South.[3]

Some Jewish officers were first generation immigrants. Maj. Adolph Proskauer of Mobile came to America when his father Julius left Prussia after the failed 1848 Revolution. The name Proskauer was, in typical German Jewish fashion, taken from the small town of Proskau near Breslau. Young Proskauer had lived in Philadelphia and Richmond before settling in Mobile and becoming a merchant. By 1861 he was a Southern partisan.[4] Maier Triest of Charleston was born in Bavaria, served as a militia captain in Charleston before and for the first year of the war, and enlisted in

Maj. Adolph Proskauer at Gettysburg. Major Proskauer, an immigrant from Prussia to Mobile, led the 12th Alabama Infantry at Culp's Hill during the Battle of Gettysburg. This 1999 painting re-creates the moment described in the history of the regiment by Capt. Robert Emory Park, "Our gallant Jew Major smoked his cigars calmly and cooly in the thickest of the fight." (Painting by Dan Nance of Charlotte, North Carolina. Author's collection.)

the South Carolina 24th as sergeant major. Simon Baruch from Posen in Prussia became a surgeon in the 3d South Carolina Battalion. Edwin Kursheedt, an immigrant from Jamaica, came to New Orleans in 1838 and rose to the rank of adjutant in the famed Washington Artillery. An Alsatian immigrant, Leon Fischel of Vicksburg enlisted in the cavalry even before the bombardment of Fort Sumter.[5]

Jewish officers were accepted into the Confederate ranks and were well respected by both their superior officers and their subordinates. Lt. Col. Samuel M. Hyams Sr. was beloved by his men. Proskauer successfully led his regiment at the Battle of Gettysburg. Ezekiel Levy became captain of the elite Richmond Blues, whose first wartime captain was the son of former Gov. Henry A. Wise. Jacob S. Valentine of Charleston was the commandant of Fort Moultrie. And there were

Lt. James Madison Seixas, 5th Company, Washington Artillery. Born in Charleston in 1829, Seixas (pronounced "Sayshus") moved to New Orleans in 1853. He was a cotton broker and law partner of Brig. Gen. Adley Hogan Gladden, also a native of South Carolina. Their firm was Gladden and Seixas at 55 Charles Street. Seixas enlisted as a private in the 5th Company (which served in the western theater), was promoted to lieutenant for gallantry on the field, later served as an agent for the War Department in Wilmington, and was promoted to captain. He married Julia Deslonde, sister of Mrs. John Slidell and Mrs. P. G. T. Beauregard. ("Information" sheet by a Gladden descendent, courtesy of Bruce S. Allardice, in the possession of the author. Courtesy of the Louisiana State Museum.)

dozens of young Jewish lieutenants like Octavus Cohen of Savannah, who fought at Secessionville; Ezekiel Levy, at the Battle of the Crater; and Joshua Lazarus Moses, at Fort Blakely near Mobile. When Lt. Albert Luria was killed at Seven Pines, the men of his company inscribed the bombshell he had thrown out of their earthworks at Sewell's Point with the words, "The pride of all his comrades, the bravest of the brave."[6] There are few cases of anti-Semitism directed at Jewish officers.[7]

There were no Jewish Confederate generals and few colonels. This is not surprising given the small number of Jews in the "old army"; the lack of a military tradition among most nineteenth-century Jews; the paucity of Jewish West Point, Virginia Military Institute, and South Carolina Military Academy (Citadel) graduates; and the intensely political nature of the appointment of general officers. Confederate officers were successful, educated, and affluent. Many had important family connections. In the Army of Northern Virginia, for example, the majority of majors, lieutenant colonels, and colonels were lawyers, judges, planters, politicians, doctors, or teachers. One-half of the officers in the Army of Northern Virginia graduated from colleges and universities, 44 percent from Virginia institutions. Many Confederate officers were, like Robert E. Lee and Joseph E. Johnston, veterans of the Mexican War.[8]

Jewish officers fit this profile. Abraham Charles Myers served as quartermaster general of the Confederacy and was a career soldier. Myers graduated from West Point in 1833 and served in the Seminole Wars in Florida. In the Mexican War, he served under both Zachary Taylor and Winfield Scott and was breveted for meritorious conduct at the Battle of Palo Alto and at Resaca de la Palma in May

Simon Levy Jr. of Shreveport. This photograph was taken in 1869. Local tradition holds that Levy served as a captain. (Courtesy of Eric Brock, Shreveport, Louisiana.)

(*Below*) William B. Myers. Gustavus Myers's son, Will Myers, served as a lieutenant, as an engineer officer, and as an adjutant for Major Generals Samuel Jones and William W. Loring. DeLeon described him as "witty and full of quaint satire . . . a good and reliable soldier" (Crute, *Confederate Staff Officers*). DeLeon has him as an adjutant to General John C. Breckinridge (*Belles, Beaux, and Brains of the '60s*).

1846.[9] After the Mexican War, Myers served as a quartermaster at a number of Southern posts. He was chief quartermaster of the Department of Florida, where he married the daughter of Maj. Gen. David Emanuel Twiggs. In the late 1840s, Twiggs was in charge of the defense of Florida, which was plagued by Indian attacks. In 1850, in response to one such attack, he ordered the rebuilding of a fort on the Caloosahatchee River and named it Fort Myers in honor of his prospective son-in-law. The post to be called "Fort Myers, by order of Major General Twiggs," came into existence in February 1850. Thus, the city of Fort Myers, Florida, is named for Abraham Myers.[10]

Jacob Valentine was also a veteran of the Mexican War, having fought at Churubusco.[11] William Mallory Levy, originally from Isle of Wight County, Virginia, graduated from William and Mary and was a lieutenant with the Virginia Volunteers in the Mexican War.[12] David Camden

Capt. Isaac L. Lyons. Rachel Lyons's brother and the nephew of Henry Lyons, mayor of Columbia, South Carolina, Lyons commanded Company A (Shepherd Guards), 10th Louisiana. His predecessor as captain of the company was Jacob A. Cohen, who was killed in battle. Lyons settled in New Orleans after the war. (DeLeon, *Belles, Beaux, and Brains of the '60s.*)

DeLeon of South Carolina graduated from South Carolina College in 1833 and obtained a medical degree from the University of Pennsylvania in 1836. He, too, fought the Seminole Indians in Florida and served with Gen. Zachary Taylor's army from Matamoros to Vera Cruz.[13]

As the infantry was the largest branch of the army, it had the largest number of officers. There were dozens of Jewish Confederate infantry lieutenants, and according to Mel Young, sixteen Jewish infantry lieutenants were killed in battle.[14]

Typical of young Jewish officers was Michael Levy of Arkansas. He and his brother, Julius, enlisted as privates. Michael enlisted for one year with Capt. Samuel G. Smith's Company E, the "Dixie Grays" of the 6th Arkansas. Julius likely enlisted at the same time in Company A, the "Capitol Guards" of the same regiment.[15] Julius was killed at the Battle of Shiloh (Pittsburgh Landing) near the border of Tennessee and Mississippi in early April 1862. At least nine other Jewish Confederates were killed at Shiloh.[16] Michael Levy survived and was promoted to fourth corporal, then sergeant. He was detailed to the ordnance department. By July 8, 1862, Levy was promoted to lieutenant and reported to the chief of ordnance at the depot at Okalona, Mississippi. He continued to serve in the Artillery Corps but was detailed as an ordnance officer.[17]

The career of Octavus Cohen demonstrates how a young man from a prominent Jewish family became a lieutenant. At the age of seventeen, this son of a successful and acculturated Savannah family volunteered as an artilleryman, even

94 though underage for military duty. His father used his family connection with Eugenia Phillips, his sister-in-law, in his attempts to secure a cadetship in the Confederate army for his son. (Eugenia, in turn, used her feminine wiles on her friend, Stephen R. Mallory, secretary of the navy.) Brigadier General Lawton wrote a letter of recommendation citing Cohen's service at Fort Pulaski and stating that he would "be gratified to have him appointed . . . and attached to my command." Octavus Cohen Sr. wrote directly to Judah Benjamin seeking his assistance. When the campaign to secure a cadetship failed, Cohen's family used its political clout to secure a lieutenant's commission for him. Meanwhile, Cohen served in the Signal Corps in Savannah. His family's efforts continued into 1863 with letters from all of his superior officers, including the endorsement of Brig. Gen. Hugh Mercer, commander of the District of Georgia, who wrote, "From his experience in the service both in the line & the staff & his unexceptionable private character, I consider him eminently worthy to wear a sword in the service of the Confederacy."[18]

In June 1862 Cohen fought at Secessionville while serving as a volunteer aide to Gen. William Duncan Smith, second in command to Brig. Gen. Nathan "Shanks" Evans. Cohen was on Smith's staff, in combat and on picket duty. He brought his body servant, George, along. The Union forces shelled James Island day and night. "We have a pretty hard time riding all day without eating anything & at night sleeping on the hard floor. I must say that soldiering is a hard life sleeping

Lt. Michael Levy enlisted, as did his brother Julius, as a private. Levy served with "the Dixie Grays" of the 6th Arkansas and later became first lieutenant of artillery. This photograph shows him with the two collar stripes of a first lieutenant. His brother, Julius, was killed at Shiloh. (Courtesy of Mrs. Jay [Pearl Anne] Silverstein, Chattanooga, Tennessee.)

[in] our clothes all night, etc." He added a postscript: "If you hear of anyone writing [his first cousin] Gratz [Cohen] please ask them to tell him that I will be happy to hear from him but have not time to write him. I tell you what that we are in a Yankee nest on this Island."[19]

He served with Smith on James Island from June to October 1862. In July he was able to go to Charleston on a furlough to see his father and his uncle Solomon Cohen, and he enjoyed a cocktail at his Uncle Jack's. Cohen was detailed to the Signal Corps in October 1862 and served in that assignment until June 1863.[20]

On June 5, 1863, Cohen was finally appointed to second lieutenant, Company G, 32d Georgia. This regiment, which was to distinguish itself throughout the war, was sent to Charleston at the urgent request of General Beauregard in the summer of 1863 to defend Charleston.[21]

The Union army under Gen. Quincy Gillmore was preparing a major assault, and men were badly needed on James Island across the Ashley River from Charleston to free up other units to man Battery Wagner at the tip of Morris Island. Cohen arrived on James Island in June 1863 with his body servant, George, and spent a hot few weeks on picket duty. He was superseded in command of his company by a more experienced and senior Lt. Morris Dawson. Despite all the trouble his father had gone to secure his position, Cohen did not object to being relieved of command of one of the advanced posts in the Confederate line of

Lt. Octavus Cohen of Savannah. (Courtesy of Bob Marcus, Springfield, Virginia.)

defense, "as I thought myself too young for the position."[22] He wrote his mother, "We expect to leave for Morris Island in a few hours & have but a little time to write. This is no play soldiering."[23] Morris Island was difficult duty and George could not accompany him.

In July 1863 Morris Island was to become, in Bruce Catton's words, "the deadliest sandpit on earth." The Union army, in a surprise attack on July 10, captured the southern half of Morris Island, but Batteries Wagner and Gregg on the northern end of the island, between Fort Sumter and the Union army, held. "With additional guns, a fresh garrison, and a new commander in Brig. Gen. William B. Taliaferro," Stephen R. Wise wrote, "the Confederates prepared to meet their enemy." That a major assault on Wagner would be made was obvious to its defenders. Eight days later, on July 18, 1863, it began: artillery bombardment, naval assault, and then a massive infantry attack on Wagner itself. On that same day, the 32d Georgia was rushed over to Morris Island. Led by Brig. Gen. Johnson Hagood, they arrived in time to seal off the escape route of Union troops caught in the killing fire of the fort's salient, the defensive ditch dug in front of the fort to trap invaders. The 32d Georgia was one of the units that was rotated in and out of Battery Wagner for the remainder of the siege. Colonel Harrison became the fort's acting commander again in mid-August.[24] Cohen was there with him. In August 1863 Cohen described a fierce bombardment and fight. "I never expected to live that night through in the midst of the enemies severest firing of shells, Grape cannister & shrapnel & musketing."[25]

By 1864 the Lincoln administration was trying to hurry the end of the war by granting amnesty to the rebels who would bring Southern states back into the Union. Florida was a serious possibility, and plans were made to occupy the Jacksonville area. There was intense fighting at Baldwin and a major battle at Olustee (Ocean Pond), where the Confederates turned back the Union advance. Octavus Cohen was in the thick of the fighting as aide-de-camp to Colonel Harrison, who had command of a brigade. Although it was "the finest country" Cohen had ever seen, water was scarce and the men drank ditch water. The fight, he wrote his mother, was "a pretty affair. . . . We lost . . . about 800, the enemy lost upwards of 3,000 [actually 1,861] . . . if our cavalry had been worth any thing, we would have captured the whole force, as they were very much demoralized. . . . Our Regt fought splendidly." Thus ended the only large campaign fought on Florida soil.[26]

When Colonel Harrison was again assigned the command of a brigade in December 1864, Cohen became acting brigade ordnance officer. He continued in this duty through the end of the war. December 1864 through early 1865 found him stationed at Pocotaligo near Beaufort, handling arms, wagons, and ammunition for the entire brigade. He surrendered with the 32d Georgia on April 26, 1865, and was paroled on May 1, 1865, at Greensboro, North Carolina, with the forces under Gen. Joseph E. Johnston.[27]

Capt. Ezekiel ("Zeke") J. Levy was a merchant in Richmond and the secretary of Beth Ahabah when the war began. He was elected fourth sergeant of the Richmond Light Infantry Blues in April 1861. He served most of the war as a lieutenant and attained the rank of captain. He was in command of the Blues, Company A of the 46th Virginia, at the Battle of the Crater at Petersburg. (Courtesy of the Jacob Rader Marcus Center, American Jewish Archives, Cincinnati, Ohio.)

At the beginning of the war, prominent men raised and outfitted companies and made themselves captains. Officers were mostly elected by the men during the first year of the war, although this practice was discontinued in the spring of 1862.[28] There were a number of Jewish infantry captains, including Ezekiel J. Levy of Richmond, who earned his captain's rank in combat.

Levy served most of the war as a lieutenant but had succeeded through attrition to captain of the Richmond Light Infantry Blues of the 46th Virginia late in the war. Levy had been a member of the Blues, a prestigious militia company, since 1855. When the company was called into service in April 1861, he was elected fourth sergeant. His younger brother Isaac J. Levy enlisted as a private in his company in March, as did a number of other Jewish soldiers. By June, Levy was first sergeant. The company went to western Virginia under Capt. O. Jennings Wise and soon became Company A of the 46th Virginia Regiment of Brigadier General and former Virginia Gov. Henry A. Wise's Legion. Capt. Wise was killed and more than half the company was captured when Roanoke Island fell in February 1862. The company next served on the Peninsula around Yorktown. Levy was elected second lieutenant in May 1862, and the company saw action during the Battle of Seven Pines and the Seven Days in the summer of 1862. (General Wise said that the Blues "were the damnest hardest set of men to manage he ever had anything to do with, but they were perfect devils in a fight.")[29]

The Levy brothers tried to keep kosher and observe their religious rites during the war. Ezekiel Levy went to great lengths to make a proper Passover Seder while in the Charleston area. This did not affect Levy's standing with the men of his company. By March 1864, he was in command of the company although just a lieutenant. The Blues returned to Virginia from Charleston and arrived in Petersburg in early May. On May 16, as the 46th Virginia went into action north of Petersburg, Lt. Levy was again in command of the Blues. (His captain was temporarily commanding a battalion of several companies of the 46th Virginia.) Afterward, the company was engaged in hard, brutal trench warfare around Petersburg, which did not end until they were surrendered at Appomattox eleven months later.[30]

Levy saw a great deal of combat and led his men courageously during a hard and trying ordeal. The enemy made several charges on the works, which the regiment occupied around Petersburg in the middle of June. During the first charge, Captain Carter was mortally wounded and the first lieutenant put out of action. During the charge the next day, Levy was wounded but remained on the field. He finally went into Petersburg three days later to have his wound dressed, but returned early the next morning. Levy was promoted to first lieutenant in July as a result of Captain Carter's death.[31]

Levy was still in command when the tremendous mine explosion beneath the Confederate works commenced the Battle of the Crater on July 30. Four tons of powder exploded in what has been described as the most awesome spectacle of the war. One soldier reported feeling "a jar like an earthquake." An officer wrote of "a vast cloud of earth borne upward." The Blues were in position about two hundred yards from the explosion. They defended the trenches to the right of the breach that tore a hole in the center of Brig. Gen. Stephen Elliott's brigade. Levy was soon promoted to captain in recognition of his command of the company.[32] His brother, Isaac, who had survived being hit by a spent musket ball two days after the Battle of the Crater, was killed by an exploding shell on August 21.

Samuel Yates Levy, a member of the distinguished Charleston and Savannah Levy family, had an easier time becoming a captain. His sisters were Phoebe Yates Levy Pember and Eugenia Levy Phillips. A tall, dark-complexioned man, Levy was thirty-four when the war began. He joined the City Light Guard of Savannah in August 1861. From that time on he commanded this unit, which became Company D, 1st (Olmstead's) Regiment Georgia Infantry. The company was stationed at various locations in the Savannah area and was at Causten's Bluff Battery from May to November 1862.[33]

Captain Levy described camp life at Causten's Bluff Battery in a letter to his father, written on September 29, 1862, as busy and dangerous: "almost every moment of my time from sunrise to sunset is fully occupied, and the exigencies of the times, forbidding us candles, render it impossible to write at night, or in fact to do anything else, except to sit round the fire, talk and smoke pipes." Levy told his father that he had never worked so hard in his life as he had since he took command of the batteries. The men were constantly plagued by mosquitoes and sand flies. They were sick on account of the unhealthy conditions and the inefficiency of the quartermaster in providing supplies. Some had died. Bread and coffee, which he had

Capt. Samuel Yates Levy. The
brother of Phoebe Pember and
Eugenia Phillips, Levy enlisted in
the City Light Guard of Savannah,
1st (Olmstead's) Georgia. He served
mostly in the Savannah area as a
captain but was captured in June
1864 at Marietta, Georgia.
(Courtesy of Bob Marcus, Springfield, Virginia.)

not had for months, were luxuries. They lived on rice and all the fresh shrimp they wanted whenever the men decided to go to the trouble of casting nets in the creeks.[34]

This letter also revealed Levy's pessimism about victory at this early date. He could see for himself the energetic preparation made by the Union navy in building improved gunboats. "As for ourselves," he wrote his father, "I cannot see that we have done anything to increase our means of resistance." His command had done nothing all summer, its leaders "looking to the achievement of the Army of Virginia." Levy told his father that he would not be surprised if his superiors abandoned their lines and fell back to Savannah. Levy felt that all he did was build and then dismantle batteries. He was, however, happy that General Beauregard was now in charge of the defense of Georgia and South Carolina: "we shall now probably have less of the 'Sleepy Hollow' course of proceedings," he wrote. "The Yanks will never relinquish the fat pickings of the South," he concluded. "Charleston and Savannah may therefore expect to pass through the fire."[35]

Despite their lack of food, whiskey, or decent clothing, Levy and the men in his unit were cheerful. They had their relaxing moments: "round the camp fire at night and in the free enjoyment of indisputable clay pipes, there is nothing but fun and laughter. Whiskey had become a myth," he wrote his father, "and ranks in the same category as some of the forgotten tipples of the Babylonians." He closed his letter: "Rain, rain, rain: nothing but rain for the past month: it is so disagreeable in camp that I begin to think it, Lincoln's reign. My paper has run out and so I am yours affectionately, Yates Levy."[36]

Levy was not an experienced soldier. He was, however, highly literate and well educated. He spent most of 1862 and 1863 serving as judge advocate in court-martial proceedings in Savannah. He was recommended for promotion to major, but he apparently was not promoted, although *The Roster of Georgia Troops in Confederate Service* states that he was "Elected Major November 1861."

Levy commanded his company in combat in June 1864 at Marietta, Georgia. At Pine Mountain near Atlanta, Levy's company became separated from his command and, concluding that "discretion was the better part of valor," Levy surrendered his men to the 15th Ohio. He became a prisoner of war and was transferred to the military prison at Louisville, Kentucky, then to Nashville, and finally to Johnson's Island, Ohio.[37]

Levy was clearly a man of peace, an intellectual who hated war. In 1862 he wrote his father reminiscing about the long talks they used to have about "old friendly authors," and wondered, "will those days ever come again, or is Mars to be in the ascendant for the rest of our time?" In November of 1863, after the fall of Vicksburg and defeat at Gettysburg, he had written a long poem entitled "Prayer for Peace." Like many Southerners, he felt that the Union victories were divine punishment for the sins of the South:

> We know our sins are manifold, oh Lord
> And that thy wrath against us is but right
> For we have wandered wildly from thy word
> and things committed wrongful in thy sight.[38]

Johnson's Island Prison was located in Sandusky Bay on Lake Erie. One mile from the mainland, the prison consisted of army barracks on forty acres. There were three thousand prisoners held there by April 1865, most of them officers. The prisoners ate rats to supplement their poor diet. Deadly brawls took place over bits of food. Clothing was inadequate to the cold, and some prisoners froze to death. Levy wrote home about the "long and bitterly cold winter." It was, in Maj. Henry Kyd Douglas's words, "just the place to convert visions to the theological belief that Hell has torments of cold instead of heat."[39] Yates Levy was released after taking the oath on June 15, 1865, and returned to Savannah.[40]

The few Jewish infantry colonels were native-born Southerners. Col. Leon Dawson Marks, for example, was one of the highest-ranking Jewish infantry officers of the line—that is, a commander who saw combat. Born at Bayou Sara, Louisiana, in 1829, he fought in the Mexican War, practiced law in Shreveport, and edited a weekly newspaper, the *Caddo News*. His father was a German Jew. His mother was Christian, a Dawson from the St. Francisville area. In 1859 Marks, who was a practicing Jew, married Amelia Jordan of Shreveport, a cousin of Julia Dent, the wife of Ulysses S. Grant, and a Christian.[41]

Col. Leon Dawson Marks. One of the highest-ranking Jewish Confederate officers of the line, Marks was a lawyer in Shreveport before the war. A colonel, he helped construct the defenses at Vicksburg, where he was mortally wounded. (Courtesy of Eric Brock of Shreveport, Louisiana.)

Marks was a delegate to the Louisiana secession convention and helped organize the "Shreveport Greys," which became Company D, 1st Louisiana Special Battalion (Dreux's Rifles). Once the battalion was formed in Virginia, he served as the battalion adjutant. In April 1862 he returned to Louisiana, where he was appointed colonel of the 27th Louisiana. He served for a period in March 1863 as "commandant of the Post of Vicksburg." On June 28, 1863, during the brutal siege of Vicksburg by the Union army and navy, Marks was mortally wounded by shrapnel from an exploding Union Parrott bomb. He had risked his life in battle on many occasions, but this time he was wounded as he ate his dinner. Vicksburg fell on July 4, and Marks was brought back to Shreveport to be with his family. He died on September 23, 1863, at the age of thirty-four, leaving a widow and a five-year-old son.[42]

Alexander "Alex" Hart, a native of New Orleans and a store clerk, was twenty-two years old when the war broke out.[43] He joined the 2d Company of the Orleans Cadets, Louisiana Militia, on May 4, 1861. Hart was recognized as a leader and was appointed first lieutenant of this company, which became Company E, 5th Louisiana Infantry, in June. He was promoted to captain upon the resignation of Capt. Charles Hobday and was with the 5th Louisiana in the Peninsular Campaign, Seven Days Campaign, Cedar Mountain, and Second Manassas.

The 5th Louisiana went to Richmond as part of Major General Magruder's army. Unlike most Confederate regiments, it was made up of common laborers, "denizens of the New Orleans waterfront," and clerks from the retail district of the Crescent City. Many were immigrants. The Orleans Cadets, Hart's company, for example, was 46 percent foreign-born. By the end of the war, 161 of the 5th

Maj. Alexander Hart of New Orleans. One of the highest-ranking Jewish Confederate infantry officers, Major Hart served with the 5th Louisiana. He served at Sharpsburg, Fredericksburg, Gettysburg, Wilderness, Spotsylvania, North Anna, and Third Winchester. (Reproduced from Ginsberg, *Chapters on the Jews of Virginia, 1658–1900*; courtesy of Shirley Ginsberg, Petersburg, Va.)

Louisiana's 1,074 men would be killed; 66 died of disease. Thirteen officers were killed. One soldier claimed that the regiment was mostly "uneducated Irishmen." Many of the immigrants were from Ireland, but they were also from the German states, England, and France. It was certainly a rough lot and became a part of the famous 1st Louisiana Brigade known as the Louisiana Tigers. One company, the Perret Guards, was said to consist mostly of gamblers. A soldier wrote that "to be admitted one must be able to cut, shuffle, and deal on the point of a bayonet."[44]

The Louisiana Tigers fought valiantly at Antietam. As Stephen W. Sears has written, that "strict Presbyterian Stonewall Jackson always regarded the habits and pleasures of the Louisiana 'foreigners' with some suspicion, but there was no question of their worth in battle." On September 17, 1862, they charged across the pasture at Antietam and toward the cornfield where they were shelled by Union batteries. Hart was seriously wounded in this battle, and his wound would plague him for the remainder of the war. He was hit in his left thigh by grape shot and remained on medical furlough in Richmond for five months. Ezekiel and Lichtenstein relate a story about Hart which probably relates to this time: A surgeon said Captain Hart's leg must be amputated. The lady of the house where he had been taken after the battle begged the surgeon to wait and give her a chance to nurse Hart back to health. "So young and handsome a man should not lose a leg," she said. She nursed him back to health. After the war, Major Hart visited his friend every year. On one occasion when the lady's daughter-in-law complained there was no ham on the table, the old lady said "No, there shall be no ham on my table when my 'Jewish son' is here."[45]

While on leave, Hart was appointed major of the regiment. He returned to his unit in time to participate in the Chancellorsville campaign, where the 5th Louisiana was heavily engaged a prelude and sideshow to Lee's greatest victory. The 5th provided the primary opposition to the Federal crossing of the Rappahannock River at Fredericksburg on April 29 and was with Maj. Gen. Jubal Early's division at Fredericksburg while the Battle of Chancellorsville raged. Afterward, at the Battle of Salem Church, the 1st Louisiana Brigade was at the center of the Confederate line which charged the Union army and incurred heavy losses. The 1st Louisiana Brigade also marched with Lee to Gettysburg and led the drive through the town of Gettysburg, pushing the Federals out onto Cemetery Hill. They assaulted the Federal position and carried the crest of Cemetery Hill, but were forced to retreat at great loss of life. Hart was wounded again at Gettysburg by a gunshot to his left hand. He spent the rest of the summer of 1863 recuperating. In November he was certified as permanently disabled and assigned to the Department of Henrico under Brig. Gen. John H. Winder.

Hart chafed to get back into active service. He demanded a medical examining board review his fitness two months before the next review was scheduled. He was declared fit for duty and, by April 30, 1864, had rejoined his command. During his absence, much of his brigade and all of his regiment except one captain had been captured at Rappahannock Station in November 1863. Most of the men were exchanged, and Hart was probably with his command during their heavy fighting at the Wilderness, Spotsylvania, and North Anna. Hart was briefly admitted to a hospital again but went back into action in July 1864, leading a temporary command of men on their way back to rejoin their units in the Shenandoah Valley. He rejoined his regiment in time to participate in the battle at Kernston, Virginia. Hart requested a promotion to colonel as the senior surviving officer of the regiment, but it was never acted upon.

In August he crossed the Potomac and marched through Sharpsburg. "Moved at sunrise," he wrote in his diary on August 6. "Passed the old battle field.

Saw the place I had been wounded at 17th Sept., 1862." He must have been out of sorts on August 12, as he wrote in his diary:

> I am a man,
> so weary with disast[er], with fortune
> That I could set my life on any chance,
> To mend it or be rid on't.

He continued: "When once sordid interest seizes on the heart, it freezes up the source of every warm and liberal feeling."[46] Hart's diary is full of references to hard fighting. "Formed line of battle at Leetown," he wrote on August 25. "Engaged the Yankee cavalry. Had a rousing fight." He acted as field officer of the day on the 26th and as a pallbearer for Colonel Monaghan, commander of the 6th Louisiana, killed in action the day before, with other high-ranking officers. "Wet and miserable," he wrote on September 5. "No shelter from rain." Then came the third Battle of Winchester against Maj. Gen. Philip Sheridan on September 19, 1864. The Louisiana brigade fought bravely, at one point holding the Federal attackers at bay virtually alone. All of the mounted officers of the brigade were wounded. Hart's horse was killed, and he was captured.[47]

Hart, now a prisoner of war, was sent to Fort McHenry, Maryland; and ultimately to Savannah, Georgia, where he and many others were exchanged in November 1864. The joyous Confederates were taken to the Pulaski House, Savannah's premier hotel, where they were treated to a sumptuous dinner. "Crowds waiting to receive us all cheer'd lustily," he noted. The ladies, he wrote, "did everything in their power to make us comfortable." He stayed with the Alexander Abrams family in Savannah for two days.[48]

On November 15, 1864, Major Hart was paroled, and he set off for Richmond. He stopped in Columbia, South Carolina, where he visited friends, including Joe Mark. He stayed in Charlottesville, Virginia, with the Heilbrun family. "Received splendidly," he wrote in his diary. He arrived in Richmond on November 20, where his fiancée, Leonora, "cried some." Part of the time in Richmond he was confined to the Louisiana hospital. Part of the time he was "having a good time generally." He likely was waiting to be officially discharged. On December 8 he applied for retirement. In January 1865, Major Hart was ordered to report to his command but was found unfit for field duty. He was allowed to retire to the Invalid Corps in March 1865.[49] He took his time leaving Richmond and made it out on one of the last trains as Richmond was being evacuated in April. He was finally paroled in Atlanta, Georgia, in early May.

Another native-born, high-ranking Jewish Confederate officer and leader of his community was William Mallory Levy. He commenced his military service as a captain of the LeCompte Guard from Natchitoches Parish, a company of the 2d Louisiana in May 1861. The regiment was dispatched to the front in Virginia. On

May 21, 1861, the regiment reported to Col. John Bankhead Magruder, who had just been appointed to command the forces on the Peninsula, near Richmond. A week after the Battle of Bethel Church in June, the 2d Louisiana was sent in to occupy the area. On June 18, Magruder sent Captain Levy under a flag of truce to Fort Monroe, and he returned with the intelligence that an expedition of some magnitude was under way, prompting Magruder to move back to Yorktown. In July Levy was back in his old college town, Williamsburg, where his regiment was active in securing the defenses. Undoubtedly, Levy took this opportunity to visit friends and family in and around Richmond. When Col. Lewis G. DeRussy resigned to take a position on the staff of Maj. Gen. Leonidas Polk, Levy was elected colonel of the regiment.[50]

By the spring of 1862, the 2d Louisiana was in the 2d Brigade, 2d Division, Army of the Peninsula, commanded by Brig. Gen. Howell Cobb. General McClellan's campaign to capture the Peninsula began in April. Colonel Levy led his men at the battle at Dam Number 1 (Lee's Mill) at the center of Magruder's defensive line across the Peninsula. He wrote his wife that he was "hearty, healthy and lively. My regiment participated in the skirmish which took place at this position on the 16th [of April] and I am unhurt . . . We defeated them in beautiful style . . . killing a large number of them." Major General Magruder, in his report, cited Colonel Levy's "judgment, courage, and high soldierly qualities of conduct and arrangements, which I desire specially to commend." Levy reported to his wife that "our troops behaved with great gallantry and have been highly complimented." On the morning of April 19, Colonel Levy carried a message under a flag of truce proposing a cessation of hostilities so that the Union troops could collect their dead lying in front of the Confederate works.

Despite his success, Levy failed to win reelection as colonel and was replaced by Isaiah T. Norwood, who was killed two months later at Malvern Hill. Levy tried to secure another command. "I beg you to be cheerful and hopeful," he wrote his wife from the Peninsula. "The cause is a righteous one and God is on our side and will watch over us."[51] He wrote to General Magruder in July 1862 that his "sense of duty as well as inclination will keep me in the army as long as the war or my life may last even in the capacity of a private in the ranks."[52]

Like many an officer who failed to secure a promotion, Levy went to Richmond in search of an appointment. Louisiana Gov. Thomas O. Moore wrote Secretary of War Randolph that Levy "failed, as did nearly every good officer, in a re-election, because he discharged his duties with great fidelity and judgment, and I am desirous that he shall renew his service & if possible in this state."[53] Magruder asked Randolph to appoint Levy a brigadier general, and Howell Cobb said in a bit of an overstatement that the loss of Levy's services would be *"a public calamity."*[54] In July Levy offered to take command of a brigade near Monroe, Louisiana, to be under command of General Magruder in his newly appointed capacity as commander of the Trans-Mississippi Department. His knowledge of the Trans-Mississippi country and its people and his status with the citizens of the area suited him for the position.[55]

Magruder's departure for the new assignment was held up until the conclusion of the Seven Days Battle, which had all of Richmond on high alert. But Levy was unlucky. Magruder was replaced by Maj. Gen. Theophilus Holmes in July, and Magruder was detained in Richmond until October, answering charges arising out of his conduct during the Seven Days Battle. When new orders came, Magruder was reassigned to Texas.

Levy now had no chance for a command of his own. In July he obtained an appointment as a major in the adjutant general's department. He was confirmed by the Confederate Congress in October. He joined Maj. Gen. Richard Taylor's staff as assistant adjutant general when Taylor became commander of the Western District of Louisiana. Levy briefly commanded the post at Fort DeRussy, Louisiana, on the Red River, but was soon at Taylor's side in the field, a position he retained until the war ended. Taylor was an important Confederate military commander. A son of President Zachary Taylor and a former brother-in-law of Jefferson Davis, an influential planter, and Louisiana state senator, Taylor became an outstanding field commander and was promoted to brigadier general, then major general, then lieutenant general. He won many a battle and achieved his greatest success in the Red River campaign in Louisiana.[56] Levy was Taylor's closest aide.

From December 1863 to June 1864, Levy served as General Taylor's commissioner of exchange, negotiating the exchange of prisoners of war with his counterparts under Major Generals William B. Franklin and Nathaniel P. Banks. He helped raise a cavalry unit among the Louisiana Creoles. He also apparently continued to raise or broker cotton throughout the war. Taylor relied heavily on Levy's judgment. In an April 1864 report covering the Red River Campaign, Taylor lamented that he "was deprived of the very valuable services of Major William M. Levy," who was, Taylor wrote, "[d]istinguished time and again for gallantry on the field as well as for patient labor in office work."[57]

Taylor asked to be relieved of his command of the Trans-Mississippi Department in June 1864. He was promoted to lieutenant general, and in September he assumed command of the Department of Alabama, Mississippi, and East Louisiana. He brought Levy with him. Because there was a senior staff already in place, Taylor had the unpleasant duty of choosing which senior officers he would retain and which he would relieve or reassign. "Majors Surget and Levy," he wrote Gen. Samuel Cooper, "have long been with me, and am particularly desirous to retain them. They are fine officers." Levy was retained and in October 1864 was promoted to lieutenant colonel and senior assistant inspector general of the department. With the exception of a few weeks, Levy remained at General Taylor's side. Levy officially surrendered May 4, 1865, and was paroled May 10 at Meridian, Mississippi.[58]

Maj. Adolph Proskauer of Mobile, a
Prussian immigrant, rose from the
rank of corporal to major of the 12th
Alabama. He served at Sharpsburg
(Antietam), where he was wounded.
He led the 12th "amid a perfect rain
of bullets, shot and shell" at Gettys-
burg. (Courtesy of the Jacob Rader
Marcus Center, American Jewish
Archives, Cincinnati, Ohio.)

Adolph Proskauer of Mobile was among the few Jewish immigrants who rose
to be a higher-ranked Confederate officer. Proskauer had been educated at the
gymnasium in Breslau until he came to America at age sixteen. In May 1861, he
enlisted in Capt. Augustus Stikes' company, the Independent Rifles, for twelve
months.[59] He was appointed first corporal. The company went to Richmond and in
July was combined with other companies to form the 12th Alabama Infantry. It
became Company C. Like the 5th Louisiana, the 12th Alabama was a cosmopolitan regiment that included a large portion of Germans, French, Irish, and Spanish, sailors and dockworkers from Mobile, and mountain boys from north
Alabama.[60] They were noted as foragers, recalled one of its officers, Capt. Robert
Emory Park, "and the vast majority of them suffered very little from hunger"
despite limited rations.

By December, Proskauer had been promoted to sergeant. In April 1862 he
was commissioned as a first lieutenant. He served in that rank for only twenty-six
days before being promoted to captain in May, replacing Stikes, who became a
major of the regiment. As captain, Proskauer was remembered as handsome and
the "best dressed man in the regiment."

Proskauer participated in many of the fiercest battles of the war. As lieutenant of Company C, he fought in the Siege of Yorktown (April–May 1862),
including the Battle of Williamsburg. As captain, he helped lead the 12th Alabama
at the Battle of Seven Pines, where the 12th made a "gallant charge . . . into the
very jaws of death." The regiment suffered heavy casualties: sixty officers and men

were killed outright, including their commander. This was the regiment's first experience in real battle. The men were worn out and were glad to "stretch themselves upon the wet ground and sleep soundly," one officer recalled, "though the air was filled with the agonizing cries and groans of the wounded and dying men and animals by whom they were surrounded." The 12th was at Gaines Mill in June and at Malvern Hill on July 1 during the Seven Days Battle before Richmond.[61]

Proskauer and his regiment marched north in Lee's Maryland campaign as part of Rodes's brigade. Proskauer was in combat at the Battle of South Mountain and Sharpsburg (Antietam), where he was wounded. On September 17, 1862, the single bloodiest day in the Civil War, Lee's Army of Northern Virginia faced George B. McClellan's Army of the Potomac. There were 4,710 men killed, 18,440 wounded.[62] Proskauer was among the wounded, having been shot in the abdomen during intense fighting along the Sunken Road, later called the "Bloody Lane." He recuperated from September until January 1863 and returned to his company at Orange Court House, Virginia.

While the 12th was encamped near Fredericksburg in 1863, Proskauer, now the senior captain in the regiment, formally applied to become major. Major Stikes had resigned his commission and returned to Mobile. Col. Samuel B. Pickens did not favor his appointment, preferring a junior captain who was apparently well qualified for the position. Colonel Pickens had an examining board appointed. Made up of distinguished senior officers, two generals and a colonel, the board, Pickens hoped, would find Proskauer unsuited for the rank and deny his application. "It was stated in camp," Captain Park recalled in his *Sketch*, "that Colonel Pickens hinted to this Committee of Examiners that he hoped they would be so rigid that Captain Proskauer could not pass the examination." Let Captain Park continue the story as he set it down in 1906, some forty-three years later:

> During the day of the examination there was an unusual interest felt by the officers of the camp, and especially by the Colonel. Late in the afternoon, after an all-day examination had been concluded, one of the officers rode rapidly up to Col. Pickens' headquarters and in reply to an anxious inquiry, was told that the Committee had done all they could to defeat Capt. Proskauer, but that after an examination [in] squad drill, in company drill, in regimental drill, in brigade drill, in drill by echelon, and in the army movements as suggested in Jomini's tactics, Captain Proskauer did not fail to answer promptly and accurately every question. The general added, "he knows more about tactics than any of the Examining Committee, and we were forced to recommend his position."[63]

Bertram Korn read into Park's account that Colonel Pickens "was so prejudiced against Jews" that he attempted to block Proskauer's promotion.[64] Yet Park does not say that, nor does his recollection prove this charge. Indeed, Park's personal admiration of Proskauer, his pointed criticism of Colonel Pickens, the interest of the other officers in Proskauer's success, Park's relish in telling the story, and the crucial fact that the board found Proskauer unusually qualified (and he was therefore promoted to major) all attest to the lack of anti-Semitism in the Confederate army.

Proskauer was a popular officer with his men. He was at the Battle of Chancellorsville in May of 1863, when the 12th fought as a part of Stonewall Jackson's famous flanking attack on Major General Hooker's Union army. On the morning of May 3 (still captain) Proskauer led the regiment as Colonel Pickens assumed command of a portion of the brigade after the commander was wounded. Proskauer was wounded in the battle and was transferred to General Hospital No. 4 in Richmond. He was promoted to major by Colonel Pickens while he was in the hospital. His promotion was ultimately confirmed by the Confederate Congress, but not until early 1864.

The 12th Alabama had broken camp on June 4, 1863, on their way to Maryland and Pennsylvania with the Army of Northern Virginia. Major Proskauer caught up with his command on the road and was fit for duty at the Battle of Gettysburg on July 1, 1863. A part of Rodes's division, the 12th suffered heavy casualties at Oak Ridge, northeast of Gettysburg. The poor leadership of both Maj. Gen. Robert Rodes and Col. Edward A. O'Neal, commanding the Alabama Brigade, cost many of Proskauer's men their lives. "Unwarned, unled as a brigade, we went to our death," one soldier recalled. There were 696 of O'Neal's 1,688 men killed or wounded along the Mummasburg Road early in the battle. Union artillery fire killed many others. Colonel Pickens sent Captain Park to the field hospital on Proskauer's horse. Years later, on learning of the major's death, Park wrote Mrs. Proskauer: "I can see him now, in mental view, as he nobly carried himself at Gettysburg, standing coolly and calmly, with cigar in his mouth, at the head of the Twelfth Alabama, amid a perfect rain of bullets, shot and shell. He was the personification of intrepid gallantry, of imperturbable courage." All of Company C's officers were wounded and half of its men.[65] As the Union troops withdrew to Cemetery Hill south of Gettysburg, the 12th Alabama moved into town the next day.

On July 3 the 12th proceeded into Gettysburg, where it participated in the unsuccessful assault on Culp's Hill, the tip of the Union "fishhook" line at Gettysburg. Culp's Hill looked down on Cemetery Hill and Cemetery Ridge, areas of immense tactical importance. If the Confederates could capture Culp's Hill, they could take Cemetery Hill and defeat the enemy. Lee hoped the attck on Culp's Hill would pull men away from General Meade's center, where he planned to send Col. George E. Pickett on that fateful day.[66]

But at 4:30 a.m., as the sun rose, the artillery of the Union XII Corps opened fire on the Confederates. They, too, appreciated the value of Culp's Hill. The fighting raged for seven hours, as the musket fire of thousands of soldiers literally destroyed a forest of oak trees. "The wonder is," the Union commander wrote, "that the rebels persisted so long in an attempt that in the first half hour must have seemed useless." Stopped at almost every advance, the Confederate army, including Major Proskauer and the 12th Alabama, tried again and again against impossible odds to take Culp's Hill. Finally they withdrew. "For decades thereafter," Champ Clark wrote in *Gettysburg: The Confederate High Tide,* "on Culp's Hill a ghostly forest would stand, its trees shorn of their limbs and stripped of their bark by flying metal—testimony to the savagery of a contest that would nevertheless be overshadowed by events still to come."[67]

Pickett's charge failed, and on July 4, 1863, Lee retreated from Pennsylvania. Major Proskauer and the 12th Alabama, "suffering, wet and anxious," on a dark, dreary, rainy night retreated south. They camped near Orange Courthouse during the remainder of the summer of 1863. Fighting continued in Virginia, and in October Major Proskauer led a force of half the regiment on a mission to destroy railroad tracks near Warrenton Junction.[68]

In November, the 12th saw action at Kelly's Ford on the Rappahannock and during the Mine Run Campaign. Proskauer was in command of the regiment at this time, as Colonel Pickens had been injured and the lieutenant colonel was absent from camp. In late December, Proskauer led the regiment to Paine's Mill to help saw planks for the Orange Road. The army was in winter quarters, and Proskauer was granted a furlough around April 21, 1864.[69]

The war, however, was far from over. The 12th Alabama, now a part of Battle's Alabama brigade, was heavily engaged on the Orange Turnpike early in the afternoon of May 5, when the Battle of the Wilderness began. Temporarily overwhelmed, the 12th rallied and drove back the Union invaders. The regiment saw action again on May 8 at Spotsylvania Court House, where Major Proskauer received his third wound of the war. The surgeon's report described the bullet "entering in front and near lobe of left ear, passing through parotid gland—ranging obliquely downwards . . . and making its exit on posterium of right side of neck." The war was over for Adolph Proskauer. He was retired to the Invalid Corps in January 1865 and was assigned to the Alabama State Reserve Forces. In February he requested a leave of absence to go to Europe to recuperate. The request was approved and forwarded to Richmond, but the capital was evacuated before the Confederate government could act on his request.[70]

★ ★ ★

Jewish officers also fought in Confederate artillery units. Officers commanded gunners and crews who transported, maintained, and fired increasingly complex and deadly cannons or fieldpieces. Artillery units needed ammunition, equipment, horses, and tools. A unit might be as large as a battalion, such as the

2d Alabama Artillery Battalion or the Washington Artillery Battalion consisting of five companies, or it could be an independent battery (a company-size unit).[71] A large number of Jews from Macon, Georgia, for example, served in the Macon German Artillery. Wolf estimated that one-third of the men were "of Hebrew faith" and wrote that Nathan Binswanger served as second lieutenant.

Edwin I. Kursheedt (pronounced "Kur-shet") of New Orleans was an outstanding officer of the famed Washington Artillery.[72] Born in Jamaica in 1838, Kursheedt came to New Orleans with his family as a child. Raised in an observant Jewish household, he attended its schools and became a merchant. When South Carolina seceded, Edwin was twenty-three years old; joined the Washington Artillery Company in December 1860. This company took possession of the U.S. Arsenal at Baton Rouge and then returned in triumph to New Orleans. Three more companies were added, and the Washington Artillery Battalion volunteered for the war in May 1861. Kursheedt was mustered into Confederate service as a private in Capt. Harry M. Isaacson's 1st Company, which undoubtedly contained a number of New Orleans Jews. Isaacson was Jewish, and Clara Solomon referred to the Washington Artillery as "Our Battalion."[73]

Born in Jamaica, Lt. Edwin I. Kursheedt came to New Orleans with his family. He joined the Washington Artillery as a private and served at First Manassas (Bull Run), the Peninsular Campaign, Sharpsburg, Gettysburg, and Petersburg. He was the adjutant of Lt. Col. Benjamin F. Eshleman. (Courtesy of the Jacob Rader Marcus Center, American Jewish Archives, Cincinnati, Ohio.)

The battalion left New Orleans by train for the Virginia front, arrived in Richmond a week later, and was sent to Manassas, where Kursheedt was assigned to the first section of the 1st Company manning a three-inch, eight-pound rifled cannon. This section had the honor of firing the Washington Artillery's first shot against the enemy. Private Kursheedt was in the midst of the Battle of First Manassas (Bull Run) in late July 1861. Early on, his section was placed on Henry House Hill, which soon became the center of the battle. "The Washington Artillery of New Orleans," Clara Solomon wrote with pride in her diary, "did great execution."[74] The unit remained with the Army of Northern Virginia and its predecessors throughout the remainder of the war.

Kursheedt was promoted to lance corporal by September 1861. He saw action in September at Great Falls, Maryland, and at Yorktown in the Peninsula Campaign and fought with his company through all of the various engagements, including the Seven Days Battle.[75]

New Orleans fell on April 25, 1862. On April 27 Kursheedt, at his camp near Williamsburg, wrote Sarah ("Sallie") Levy complaining about marching "in a drenching rain—'for the rain it raineth every day.'" He could not believe New Orleans had been captured. "We are in receipt of the telegraphic news 'Fall of New Orleans &c' but do not credit it,'" he wrote. He felt good about his army's position at Yorktown: "Our position is very strong—our left rests on Yorktown—the centre at Lee's Mills, & right on Mulberry Island." He felt his unit might be ordered to Fredericksburg, "as it is believed Massa Geo. B. McClellan [the Union commander] is trying to force a passage to Richmond via that point." Not only was Kursheedt's military position strong, but he had plenty to eat. "We are luxuriating in quantities of shad & fresh beef, vegetables, bakers bread & c. So we feast one day and starve the next." He also looked forward to a visit to Williamsburg. "I intend going into town to see 'one of the chosen' whose name was given to me by Eugene Levy, whom I was very pleased to meet here, so au revoir."[76]

Kursheedt's unit was under frequent bombardment during the Peninsula campaign. We "are not afar off from our Yankee friends," he wrote Sarah Levy. He and his men were "enjoying the constant music of their heavy guns." He and 250 men were crammed in a schooner that brought them from Richmond to the front: "[W]e felt like a lot of chickens cooped up, but were willing to 'die game.'" Miss Levy had sent him a package of food, which enabled him "to live very high up to yesterday, but had to come down to rations this morning viz, Bacon & crackers—I enjoyed the latter, but have not made up my mind to partake of the former." Kursheedt was still trying to keep kosher and avoid eating pork.[77]

By June Kursheedt began referring to Sarah Levy as "My Dear Miss Sarah" and wrote her frequently about his activities. On June 25 he told her it had been his intention to come to visit her, but his orders prevented it. "I will be busy this evening issuing orders &c to the various Batteries under the Colonel so will not be able to see you." He had been acting as an adjutant since at least June 9, 1862.[78]

The 1st Company concluded the Seven Days Campaign by successfully attacking General McClellan's transport ships on the James River on July 6 and 7, doing considerable damage. After a month's rest, the Army of Northern Virginia began to move north from Richmond. Kursheedt's company was in an artillery battle at Beverley's Ford and Rappahannock Station on August 23, 1862. On August 25 Kursheedt wrote Sarah a long letter detailing his participation in the various engagements: "Last Saturday the 3rd Company and our Battery together with others, engaged the enemy at Rappahannock Station & after a hard fight of 4 hours drove the enemy from his position occupying his camp in the evening. The loss of our two companies was very heavy." He also reported that "The little *Battle Flag* is pretty well cut up by the shells of the enemy and we are all very proud of it." It was the "hottest place we have ever been," but Kursheedt felt that the Confederacy was now winning the war. "The tables have been turned & we are now pressing the enemy to the wall." He knew the army was heading toward Manassas and believed he was about to be involved in a "quite heavy" engagement.[79]

Like many soldiers writing loved ones, Kursheedt was concerned that this might be his last letter. "By the Protection of a kind Providence," he told Sarah, "I am again spared after having had some very narrow escapes. I write today for the purpose of informing you of my safety." He also wrote to tell other Jewish families that "Eugene Levy & brother are both well—we fought side by side in both engagements." And never forgetting one of the strong bonds between him and Sarah, he wrote: "There is no telling when we shall see Richmond as we might march into the Enemy's Country, but I shall certainly try to come down for the Holy days" (Jewish High Holidays, Rosh Hashanah—New Year—and Yom Kippur—Day of Atonement—usually take place in September and early October of each year).[80]

Kursheedt marched north with the Washington Artillery with Lee into Maryland in September 1862. As the troops marched toward Boonsboro, the rear ammunition chest of a caisson exploded. Contrary to the orders of his officers, a private had sat atop a caisson loaded with gunpowder and proceeded to smoke his pipe. The powder exploded and the soldier was hurled twenty feet into the air, fell on the road, was burned from head to foot, and lost all of his clothing. Miraculously, he was not seriously injured. The soldier was barely removed from the scene when the live shells in the chest began to explode. Officers and men ran as far as they could. "Then," in the words of one eyewitness, "Corporals Kursheedt and Ruggles, of the First Company, stepped to the front, and, going deliberately up to the smoking chest, emptied their canteens of water upon the burning cotton used for packing; then taking the shells, some already ignited, threw them into the ditch of water alongside the road, where some exploded, making an awful scatteration of mud and water, but fortunately hurting no one. The danger over, the march was

114   resumed. For this gallant act these corporals quite modestly received the warm approbation of their comrades, and no more was thought of it. But the 'Victoria' and the 'Cross of the Legion of Honor' have been pinned to a soldier's breast for acts of lesser heroism."[81]

The Washington Artillery was now at Sharpsburg, Maryland, near Antietam Creek. Posted on a hill east of the town, the 1st Company was equipped with two three-inch rifles and two ten-pound Parrott cannons. They fired upon Federal troops as they attacked across Rohrbach's Bridge on the southern end of the battlefield while themselves under constant artillery fire. Attacked four times by Union infantry, the company fought back with the assistance of the Confederate infantry. Kursheedt may have been wounded at Sharpsburg.

The Army of Northern Virginia next redeployed to Fredericksburg. Three of the Washington Artillery's four companies, including Kursheedt's 1st Company, were positioned on Marye's Heights overlooking the town. The artillery was "spreading havoc among the enemy's ranks," and the Washington Artillery was encouraged by Major Sorrel, General Longstreet's assistant adjutant general, to hold its position despite the ferocity of the Union assault. The battalion's historian recalled the battle this way: "We are fighting under the very eyes of Lee and Longstreet. 'Now, boys, do your level best!' A solid rifle cannon-ball tears its way

The Washington Artillery on Marye's Hill firing on the Union columns forming for the assault. A number of New Orleans Jews served in the Washington Artillery, including Edwin Kursheedt, its adjutant (*Battles and Leaders of the Civil War*).

through the redoubt, scattering dirt and dust in our faces. Kursheedt picks it up, and says, laughingly, 'Boys, let's send this back to them again.' An instant later it is in the gun, and despatched on its mission back to the enemy." Not too long after this show of bravado Kursheedt was wounded. By April 1863 Kursheedt, now only twenty-five years old, was promoted to battalion sergeant major.[82]

The Washington Artillery marched to Pennsylvania with the Army of Northern Virginia and fought at Gettysburg under a new commander, Maj. Benjamin F. Eshleman,[83] who used Kursheedt as his adjutant. After Gettysburg, the Washington Artillery returned to Virginia and Kursheedt officially became the adjutant with the rank of first lieutenant. The battalion went into winter quarters at Petersburg rather than accompany Longstreet to Georgia. Kursheedt was granted a much-deserved leave of absence in the fall. The unit was called back into action in May 1864, when Maj. Gen. Benjamin Butler began his Bermuda Hundred Campaign. Men of the battalion were rushed north to meet the invaders. On May 14, Kursheedt was with Lieutenant Colonel Eshleman and Major Owen on an inspection of their lines south of Drewry's Bluff when they came under heavy fire from enemy sharpshooters. The party halted behind some log cabins. "To go forward or retreat was equally hazardous," Owen later wrote, "so we held a council of war, and determined to run the gauntlet across an open field." The men rode in a bunch so that there would be a small target, and gathering their horses "well in hand, gave them the spur and started. . . . Instantly the sharp-shooters began firing, and the bullets flew by us like the buzzing of a swarm of bees. Our good steeds seemed conscious of our peril, and went like the wind. Some close shots were made, but no hits. Finally we heard a 'thud' of a bullet, and Eshleman's horse rose up on his hind legs, and Kursheedt and I thought he was a goner, but he came down again, and away we went. We reached the ridge, and were hid from view, right thankful we had run the gauntlet so successfully and with whole skins."[84]

In June the battalion marched north to confront Grant's Army on the Chickahominy River, east of Richmond. By June 18 the men returned to Petersburg, where they were to remain until forced out in April 1865. The battalion was part of the determined Confederate force resisting the brutal siege of Petersburg for almost a year, from June 1864 until April 1865. The Army of the Potomac besieged the small but important railroad town twenty miles south of Richmond for ten months. It was trench warfare at its worst and became a death struggle for the Confederate army, which faced starvation, desertion, and sickness.

In December 1864 Kursheedt wrote to Miss Sallie: "I have not been able to see the Chanucka lights this year. Last year I was with my aunt and officiated in reading the service as I always did at home, for in addition to lighting the lamps in Synagogue we always did so at home. That was our Christmas, as children and we always rec'd presents & enjoyed ourselves—but those times have passed and I only expect to see them again when I shall have a family of my own to hand down these

116   ceremonies to. Don't you say so too my Pet? . . . After I shall have been with you in February not many weeks will elapse ere Pesach [Passover]."[85]

When the Army of Northern Virginia retreated toward Appomattox Courthouse, all of the artillery battalions but two were sent off to attempt to reach North Carolina. These units were attacked by Union Calvary on April 8, and some escaped and rejoined Lee's Infantry. The Washington Artillery destroyed their gun carriages, buried their guns in the woods, and escaped into the mountains to the west. Kursheedt was later paroled in Lynchburg, Virginia, in April 1865.

★   ★   ★

There were a few Jewish officers in the Confederate cavalry. Exceptional riding skill, which few Jewish Southerners possessed, was a prerequisite for a cavalry officer. An urban and mercantile people, Jewish Southerners were rarely qualified to command these units. But there were a few who served in the cavalry, Edwin Warren Moise and members of the Hyams family among them.

The most illustrious of the Moise family, Edwin Warren Moise grew up in Charleston, where his family belonged to Beth Elohim. His father was a lawyer and a leader in the Reform movement, and young Edwin was brought up as an observing Jew. At fourteen, he left school to help support his family, first as a clerk and then in his own business. He married Esther Lyon of Petersburg, Virginia, in 1854 and soon accepted a position with Raphael J. Moses of Columbus, Georgia, to operate his flour mill, keep his books, and study law.[86]

Moise was opposed to secession, but he volunteered and raised a company of "Partisan Rangers," or cavalry, in May 1862. According to Harold Moise, of the company's 120 men, Captain Moise mounted 50 at his own expense, "costing him $10,000—all of his little fortune. This company was officially named the Moise Rangers." It is the only company named for a Jewish officer, with the possible exceptions of Joseph Benjamin's company and Capt. Samuel Yates Levy's company, neither of which is listed in Marcus Wright's 1876 official list.[87]

The Moise Rangers enrolled in the Confederate service on July 1, 1862. Moise was appointed captain, not elected, because it was a Confederate army unit, not a state volunteer unit. The unit went to North Carolina and joined Col. William C. Claiborne's 7th Confederate Cavalry. Moise's Rangers now became Company A of the 7th Regiment.[88]

The regiment was sent to Ivor, Isle of Wight County, Virginia, near the Blackwater River. The 7th served its entire career either in the southeastern corner of Virginia between Petersburg and Suffolk or in North Carolina. Moise's company engaged in a foraging expedition in January 1863 at Kelly's Store, then was stationed near Petersburg.

In February 1864 Captain Moise and his company had the unusual experience of capturing and destroying a Federal gunboat on Chuckatuck Creek near

Smithfield, Virginia. The Union forces sent a joint army-navy expedition to capture some "rebel troops (said to be about 40) and tobacco." When one Union party ran into a much superior force of Confederates, they retreated to Smithfield to the gunboat *Smith Briggs*. As the Union soldiers attempted to board, Moise's men came charging down a hill, "opened a murderous fire," and captured the gunboat. They next turned the *Smith Briggs'* gun on the other Federal launches, driving them from the scene. Moise removed the boat's equipment before setting it ablaze.

Moise's company served in the defenses around Petersburg during the Bermuda Hundred Campaign of May 1864. The 7th Cavalry was part of Dearing's brigade. On May 31 Dearing's men attacked the Federal position at Spring Hill but were opposed by Union infantry, artillery, and gunboats on the Appomattox River. Moise's horse was killed. (The next day, he requested reimbursement of $2,500 for his horse, which had been conscripted into Confederate service but for which he had not yet been paid.) The 7th Cavalry continued to harry the Union army. In June it was sent to the Jerusalem Plank Road south of Petersburg to protect the Weldon Railroad. In July it was back on the James River. (On August 14, Moise received his $2,500. He now was able to buy 2 ¼ yards of officer's cloth for a new uniform and two weeks later a new pair of shoes.)

Shortly after Lee selected Maj. Gen. Wade Hampton to succeed the late J. E. B. Stuart as commander of his cavalry corps, Hampton organized what came to be known as the "Great Beefsteak Raid." Dearing's brigade and Moise's men had a key role in guarding the right flank of the main party raiding the Union army's corrals, which contained thousands of cattle. The Confederate raiders brought in 2,468 cattle, covered one hundred miles, fought the enemy twice, and captured 304 prisoners and a large quantity of supplies with a loss of only ten killed and forty-seven wounded. The Confederate soldiers were also delighted to take cigars, liquor, butter, cheese, sardines, pickles, boots, blankets, and firearms. "Who that was there can ever forget the wild grandeur of the scene?" one member of the raiding party recalled five years later. The sunset, the shot and shell, the waving of battle flags, "the galloping of staff officers and couriers over the field, the defiant shouts of our men calling to the Yankees to 'come and get some beef for supper,' all made up a scene strangely mingling the sublime and the ridiculous."[89] This raid cemented a close relationship between Hampton and Moise, which continued for thirty-seven years after the war.

In November 1864 Moise's company became part of the 10th Georgia Cavalry. In January 1865, Hampton led his troopers south to attempt to counter General Sherman's invasion of the Palmetto State. Moise saw action at the Battle of Monroe's Crossroads (humorously known as the "Battle of Kilpatrick's Pants" because Maj. Gen. Judson Kilpatrick was chased out of his camp in his bedclothes). Moise was also at the last major battle of the Civil War, Bentonville. He was with his command on the retreat to Smithville. He and his men were assigned the unenviable task of burning the bridge over the Neuse River to delay the Federal advance. This he accomplished under a hail of bullets from the Federals, who were in pursuit of the retreating Confederates. Captain Moise was paroled at Greensboro on April 26 as a soldier in Gen. Joseph E. Johnston's army.

★　　★　　★

The urban mercantile experience which denied most Southern Jews the background to serve in the cavalry made them highly qualified as quartermasters, adjutants, and commissaries. Quartermasters supply clothing and equipment. Adjutants are administrative officers who write orders and keep a commanding officer's paperwork organized. Commissaries supply food and other equipment. These jobs, while less glamorous than others, are vital to an army's success in battle. "An army," Napoleon is said to have remarked, "travels on its stomach." There were numerous Jewish officers in these departments throughout the Confederate army.

One of the highest-ranking Jewish Confederates was the quartermaster general of the Confederacy, Col. Abraham Charles Myers.[90] Myers and much of the general staff was formally appointed in March 1861. As quartermaster general, Myers was charged with supplying the army with clothing, supplies, and transportation. His was one of the chief supply bureaus of the Confederate army, along with the Commissary Department headed by Lucius B. Northrop, the commissary general; the Bureau of Ordnance headed by Josiah Gorgas, chief of ordnance; the adjutant and inspector general's department headed by Gen. Samuel Cooper; and the Medical Department first headed by David Camden DeLeon, surgeon general.[91]

Col. Abraham Myers' job, like that of his cohorts, would prove to be impossible. As Richard D. Goff wrote in *Confederate Supply,* "The financial base and the transportation network of the Slave States were feeble. Their industrial output was comparatively minuscule." And, while the Upper South had some semblance of heavy industry, the "Cotton States had little to offer a sustained military effort."[92]

But Abraham Myers had faced formidable odds in Mexico and undoubtedly believed that the war would be short and that the South could prevail. Myers began with uniforms, tents, and equipment. He advertised for bids. He negotiated with contractors. He was president of the military board, which designed the first Confederate uniform. (It was not gray, but consisted of a blue flannel shirt, gray flannel pants, a red flannel undershirt, cotton drawers, wool socks, boots, and a cap.) Myers ordered from suppliers he knew in New Orleans and later branched out to mills in Georgia and Virginia. He created supply depots all over the South, from San Antonio to Mobile to Charleston to Richmond. He contracted with steamboat and railroad companies to haul men and material. But the men in the supply corps lacked expertise, and problems arose at the local level, where quartermasters and commissaries, although theoretically responsible to their bureau chiefs, tended to side with field commanders.[93]

Col. Abraham Charles Myers was the great-grandson of the
first rabbi of Beth Elohim. After graduating from West Point, he
became a career army officer and served in the Mexican War. Fort
Myers, Florida, then literally a fort, was named in his honor by his
father-in-law, Gen. David Emanuel Twiggs. Colonel Myers served
as quartermaster general of the Confederate army. (Photograph
[carte de visite] by Rees, Richmond, Virginia. Courtesy of Bob
Marcus, Springfield, Virginia.)

The capital of the Confederacy moved from Montgomery to Richmond as
soon after the firing on Fort Sumter as it could. Jefferson Davis arrived in late May.
Abraham and Marion Twiggs Myers moved to Richmond. Mrs. Myers immediately
became immersed in the Richmond social scene and was a popular member of
wartime society.[94]

Myers set up his offices on the southwest corner of 9th and Main Streets,
near Capitol Square. His offices were on the second floor of the quartermaster's

building. He eventually administered the largest Confederate supply bureau, with eighty-eight clerks versus sixty-one in the inspector general's office, twenty-one in the surgeon general's, and thirty-six in the commissary department. The Quatermaster Department included quartermasters in each state, paymasters and quartermasters in the field, manufacturing plants, special units such as the Tax-in-Kind Office, purchasing agents abroad, and depot and post quartermasters. Colonel Myers reported to the secretary of war.[95]

Despite deficiencies in supply, the Battle of Manassas in July 1861 was a Confederate victory. Both armies were inexperienced and, as President Lincoln put it in response to his commander, "You are green, it is true, but they are green, also; you are all green alike."[96] Nevertheless, this first battle pointed up the critical importance of supply. Many Southerners believed that if the Southern army had been better supplied it could have marched to Washington and won the war.

Public concern, then anger, then outrage at the Commissary and Quartermaster Departments would be a constant theme in the Confederacy as the war went on.[97] It was understandable, if unjustified, that the officers in charge of food, clothing, and supplies would be blamed for the ills of the army. Northrop was the Confederate Congress's main scapegoat; his nomination to full colonel and confirmation as commissary general provoked heated debate. Myers's nomination to full colonel and confirmation as quartermaster general was immediately approved. (By then, Judah Benjamin was making his exit as secretary of war.) T. C. DeLeon believed that Myers's "bureau was managed with an efficiency and vigor that could scarcely have been looked for in so new an organization."[98] Early in the war, Myers enjoyed a good reputation as a competent and honest department head. An 1862 investigating committee found the quartermaster general's conduct "most favorable and satisfactory" with regard to "prudence, economy, integrity and efficiency," according to a letter to the *Charleston Courier*.[99]

It soon became clear that the war would not be a short one and even clearer that supplying an army of up to 400,000 men would prove to be a formidable task. "You are somewhat in error," Myers wrote to Brig. Gen. J. B. Magruder on August 21, 1861, "as to the resources of the C.S. . . . You do not know how difficult it is to get any, the most common, thing heretofore abundant." As early as 1861 Myers had to give up on supplying Texas, telling his quartermasters he could not send supplies from the East. Prices rose as the blockade tightened and Northern sources of supply dwindled. States' rights played a part in the Confederacy's problems. North Carolina, for example, supplied its own troops in return for an agreement that the quartermaster would not purchase clothing from its factories. Myers reorganized his supply system, consolidating his efforts in fewer regional depots. To some degree he had been lucky. Blockade-running met with success early in the war. People and states gave generously of clothing. But the Southern economy could not keep pace with the army's huge appetite for supplies, and it fell to Myers

and his men to gather every kind of supply from shoes and clothes to horses and
fodder in a shrinking economy.[100]

The Union victories of 1862 were a disaster for the Confederacy and especially for the quartermaster general. The loss of key border states, New Orleans
and other coastal areas, and the Mississippi Valley constricted the area from which
supplies, manufactured goods, and raw materials could be obtained. Blockade-
running was severely curtailed, interfering with the importation of European
goods. New Orleans had manufactured shoes and clothing. By August 1862 Lee
complained that his army lacked "much of the materials of war, . . . [was] feeble in
transportation, the animals being much reduced, and the men . . . poorly provided
with clothes, and in thousands of instances . . . destitute of shoes." This was an
indictment of the quartermaster operation, and, indeed, Lee's invasion of Maryland in 1862 was partly necessitated by supply considerations. Part of Lee's problems after Second Manassas was the simple lack of shoes.[101]

The government now realized that Myers had been correct in his recommendation to send purchasing agents abroad. He received permission to send Maj.
J. B. Ferguson, a former merchant, to Europe. He also used the war department's
powers to detail men to work in textile factories by allowing them an exemption
from military service. Shops were set up to sew uniforms, relying, in many
instances, on soldiers' wives and other women desperate to work.[102]

Myers's reorganized department divided the country into eleven purchasing
districts, each headed by a principal purchasing agent who controlled purchasing
and prices. "On the whole," Goff concludes, "Myers had, by mid-1863, built up a
going and growing concern." Congress enacted a new supply law to solve the subsistence problem. Called "the tithe," the law provided for a tax-in-kind rather than
money. Thus, a percentage of the South's crops and livestock raised for slaughter
would be paid to the Confederate government. Myers's department was charged
with enforcement. A chief quartermaster in each state and district quartermasters
in each congressional district, together with post quartermasters at regional depots,
were appointed to collect the supplies.[103]

Of all Myers's headaches, the railroad was perhaps his greatest.[104] Deeply
conservative by upbringing, temperament, and training, Myers did not seek and at
times actively resisted government control of the rails. When the president of one
railroad company suggested that the government build its own system, Myers
opposed the idea.[105] In the first years of the war, the railroads were hardly regulated
at all. As the war progressed, however, Myers realized that the failure of transportation was hampering the war effort and that his conservative approach had
failed. While he continued to oppose seizure of the railroads or control by field
commanders, by October 1862 Myers recommended the appointment of "an able,
methodical, and energetic person" to regulate the railroads. Congress demurred,
but the secretary of war, James A. Seddon, acted. Without consulting Myers, the

secretary appointed William M. Wadley superintendent of railroads with the rank of lieutenant colonel and assigned him to the office of the adjutant and inspector general. Myers complained that this decision would "occasion difficulty and embarrassment to this department," but he received no reply. His relationship with the secretary of war and the president was souring. The railroad industry and the Confederate Congress got involved. Secret sessions were held. Finally, Congress enacted a bill giving the government broad power to control the rails. It lodged that power in the quartermaster general's department. Congress had more faith in Myers than in the secretary of war. The new law gave Myers authority to supervise the Confederacy's railroads, promulgate regulations, dictate freight schedules, and take equipment, rolling stock, and rails as necessary. Myers initially opposed impressment, the practice of appropriating or condemning property and paying a price established by the government, but was forced to resort to it. Yet in a circular to his subordinates, he restricted impressment to instances where "absolutely demanded by the public necessities."[106]

Another Confederate dilemma was the sale of cotton. The early Confederate position, that cotton was king, had failed. Myers's approach was to rely on purchasing agents abroad and to pay for the goods at Southern ports with cotton. Judah Benjamin, then secretary of war, disagreed, preferring to rely on contracts with private parties. Eventually, the government decided to sell cotton in order to buy military supplies, Myers having been among the first to realize that cotton was not king. He supported a change in Confederate policy which forbade trading for supplies through enemy lines. The law had been violated, of necessity and because of greed, from the beginning. By late 1862, it was obvious to those charged with obtaining supplies that there was no choice.[107]

As the war dragged on, the Quartermaster Department came in for severe criticism. The *Savannah Daily News* noted the suspicion in the public mind "that peculation and plunder, and misuse of authority for private purpose, have often been put before public duty and public service." The *Richmond Enquirer* complained that "Quartermasters sometimes get rich—they ought never to get rich. . . . Unfaithful, incompetent, or dishonest quartermasters or commissaries could plunge the country into ruin." Despite the criticism, the leading historian of Confederate supply, Richard Goff, concluded that the Quartermaster Department under Myers "appears to have been as well organized and as efficient as circumstances would allow."[108]

James McPherson concludes in *Battle Cry of Freedom* that Q.M. Gen. Abraham Myers could never supply the army with enough tents, uniforms, blankets, shoes, or horses and wagons. "Consequently, Johnny Reb often had to sleep in the open under a captured blanket, to wear a tattered homespun butternut uniform, and to march and fight barefoot unless he could liberate shoes from a dead or captured Yankee." In an evaluation which gives new meaning to the phrase "damned by faint praise," Richard Goff concludes: "By Confederate standards his bureau was well run, and his contemporaries praised him. On all major policy innovations Myers had been at or near the forefront, except for railroad regulation, where he shared the conservative outlook of the President."[109]

Myers's friends in Congress sought to promote him to brigadier general, and in March 1863 the Congress passed a law providing that the rank and pay of the quartermaster general "shall be those of Brigadier General in the provisional army." Seventy-six members of Congress sent the president a letter recommending that Colonel Myers be promoted to general. "We think he has shown himself able, honest, and diligent in the discharge of his responsible and laborious duties," the letter read, "and take pleasure in bearing our testimony to his services and his merits."[110] Ironically, the law would be used by Jefferson Davis to dismiss Myers from office altogether. On August 7, 1863, Jefferson Davis fired Abraham Myers and replaced him with his old friend Alexander R. Lawton. The only reason Davis gave was that it was in the interest of efficiency.[111] And there does seem to be some basis for the charge. Both the secretary of war and General Lee, among others, had expressed dissatisfaction with Myers's operation of the department. After Chancellorsville in May 1863, Lee's army was never again adequately supplied with horses.[112] Capt. Robert G. H. Kean complained in his diary that "Our troops in Lee's army are barefooted—failure to provide shoes and blankets during all this year conclusive of mismanagement of Q.M.D."[113] Lee had experienced severe problems at Gettysburg due to a lack of supplies of shoes, clothing, overcoats, and blankets.[114]

Some said that Myers and Davis had feuded in the old army years before.[115] But the true reason, according to Richmond gossip, was that Marian Myers, who considered herself the social superior of Mrs. Davis, had called the president's wife "an old squaw," Mrs. Davis being of a somewhat dark complexion.[116] Assistant Secretary of War A. T. Bledsoe passed along the insult in early 1862. The remark was repeated and became well known.[117] Mrs. Myers had apparently made offensive remarks about Mrs. Davis, but the precise role of the quartermaster general's wife in the controversy is uncertain.[118] "The Congress of 1863," Mary Chesnut wrote, "gave up its time to fighting the battle of Colonel Myers—Mrs. Myers." Congress was indeed angry. Myers's old friend William Porcher Miles stood by him.[119] Not only had the tactless (some said arrogant) president failed to promote Myers, he now utilized a law enacted to help him to fire Myers. Davis's argument was that the congressional act, which Davis knew was designed to promote Myers, was an unconstitutional encroachment on the president's authority to award promotions and, therefore, Congress must have meant that a brigadier general should replace the current occupant of the office. Davis sought a replacement from June to August and found a brigadier general, Lawton, who had been appointed to that rank in April 1861. Congress was incensed. It devoted the winter of 1863 to debating the issue and, in a colorful description by Mrs. Chesnut, "to a hand-to-hand fight with Mr. Davis on account of Mr. Quartermaster General Myers. Here again, who pulled the wires? Not Colonel Myers, surely? Who cared a fig for him? The friends of Mrs. Myers, led by Mr. [William Porcher] Miles, and the enemies of Mr. Davis formed a brigade of great strength."[120]

Richmond society, government officials, and the newspapers joined the Senate in feeling that Myers had been treated unfairly. Mary Chesnut likened the feud to Andrew Jackson's famous defense of Peggy Eaton, the wife of his secretary of war, who was accused of impropriety. "And now, she wrote, "Richmond plays old Hickory with its beautiful Mrs. M."[121] Captain Kean wrote in his diary: "The event which has put the gossips agog in the last two days is the taking off of the Quartermaster General's head." Josiah Gorgas confided to his diary: "[Myers] has fulfilled his duties very well. . . . [The President] has, I fear, little appreciation of services rendered, unless the party enjoys his good opinion."[122] Society belle Sallie B. Putnam, author of *Richmond during the War,* recalled Myers as "one of the most prudent, sagacious and efficient officers under the government." The controversy was "bitterly acrimonious, and gave rise to some unpleasant *on dits* of a personal character," which, being a lady, Mrs. Putnam deigned not to repeat.[123]

There is no evidence that anti-Semitism played any role in Myers's firing, despite the glee expressed by John Beauchamp Jones, a clerk in the War Department whose memoir, *A Rebel War Clerk's Diary,* was published in 1866. Jones called Myers the "Jew Quarter-Master General" and claimed he replied, "let them suffer," when told of soldiers' pleas for blankets.[124] But Sallie Putnam, who had no love for the Jews, thought Myers was mistreated and, most importantly, Jefferson Davis not only had no prejudice against Jews, but, to the contrary, maintained warm relationships with many Southern Jews.

Myers was crushed by his termination. In January 1864 he was ill in bed.[125] The Senate in a 15–6 vote resolved "1st. That in the opinion of the Senate, A. C. Myers is now Quartermaster General of the Confederate States army, and is by law authorized and required to discharge the duties thereof. 2nd. That A. R. Lawton is not authorized by law to discharge the duties of said office."[126] But the Confederate Congress was not about to create a constitutional crisis over the issue, and when Davis sent Lawton's name to the Senate for confirmation in early February, the Senate complied.[127] Myers could have served under Lawton but refused. It is unclear what Myers's position was. By June 1864 the attorney general gave an opinion that Myers was no longer in the army, a position Myers himself took at first.[128] Later, he said he was a colonel and a commissioned officer and remained on the army list.

Myers remained bitter for the rest of his life. He had no income, and he and his family went to live in Georgia, where they survived with the help of friends.[129] He tried to secure a field command and wrote to Gen. Braxton Bragg on a number of occasions to ascertain his place in the army. Bragg apparently did nothing and would not see Myers. In August, Myers wrote Bragg that his situation "was painful in the extreme . . . it is very humiliating to be obliged to live as I do, very much upon the charity of friends and almost in want."[130]

Abraham Myers was an actor in a drama on the national stage. But there were quartermasters in every regiment in the army. A typical quartermaster in the trenches was Maier Triest of Charleston. Triest immigrated from Bavaria in 1850. He was thirty years old when the war started, and he served as captain of Triest's Company (Beat 2), 16th South Carolina Militia, from November 9 to December 20, 1861. Like Triest, most young, able-bodied Charlestonians had served in militia units prior to the war. In January 1862 Triest and hundreds of other South Carolinians enlisted in a regiment being raised by Col. Clement H. Steven, who had formerly commanded Triest's militia regiment and likely knew Triest. The regiment was originally organized by Stevens and Lt. Col. Ellison Capers for twelve months of Confederate service. Six companies were raised for one year when state law changed in March 1862 to require service for the duration of the war. All the men agreed to so serve, and four additional companies were added. The 24th South Carolina then went into Confederate service in April.[131]

Colonel Stevens, during the formative period, chose Triest to be sergeant major of the regiment, whereupon Triest reenlisted at that rank on January 20,

Maier Triest, another Bavarian immigrant, was active in Charleston Jewish affairs and served in the militia prior to the war. He served as regimental quartermaster sergeant in the 24th South Carolina. He returned to Charleston when the war ended, and his descendants are members of Beth Elohim today. (Courtesy of Caroline L. Triest and Larry W. Freudenberg, Charleston.)

126   1862. In January 1863 he was promoted to regimental quartermaster sergeant, a position he held throughout the war. Rabbi Elzas, who knew Triest's family, wrote that Triest was promoted twice to acting assistant adjutant general, once by General Stevens, who died before the commission was returned, and again by General Capers just before the close of the war.[132]

The 24th saw action throughout the war at Secessionville, South Carolina; Jackson, Mississippi (Vicksburg campaign); Atlanta; Franklin; Nashville; and the Carolinas. Triest was with the 24th in the weeks before the final capitulation of Vicksburg, when Grant was getting between Vicksburg, the Confederate stronghold on the Mississippi River, and the Confederate forces at Jackson, a city and rail hub to the east of Vicksburg.[133] The South Carolinians were determined to prevent Jackson from falling to Grant's army and engaged in fierce, hand-to-hand combat with the 10th Missouri. At Wright's Farm, a ball hit Col. Ellison Capers's horse, and a number of men of the 24th were killed. Capers wrote afterward that Triest had given him "a most welcomed drink of whiskey." Capers said it was the only time he ever took a drink during the war.[134]

As regimental quartermaster sergeant, it was Triest's job to see to it that the entire regiment was supplied. During the Jackson campaign, for example, he traveled to Canton and Meridian, Mississippi, to obtain shoes and clothing which had been left behind in storage at the beginning of the campaign. He traveled throughout July and August 1863, retrieving and transporting boxes of clothing, cooking utensils, and supplies. In early October 1863, while at Chickamauga, Braxton Bragg sent Triest to Columbia and Charleston to act as agent for the collection of winter clothes, blankets, and other supplies from the South Carolina Relief Association. He returned on October 28, having used his own funds for drayage (movement by wagon) and cooperage (crating) at stops along the way. (The funds were refunded to him.) Triest surrendered with the consolidated and redesignated 16th/24th South Carolina Regiment with Gen. Joseph E. Johnston's army on April 26, 1865. He was paroled on May 1. According to Elzas, Triest was wounded at Atlanta.[135]

★   ★   ★

The job of the commissary is to provide food and related supplies to the army. In Raphael J. Moses, the Confederate army found its most colorful and dedicated commissary. Moses was a native of Charleston and a resident of Columbus, Georgia, where he lived on a plantation, The Esquiline, named, in true Southern fashion, for one of the Seven Hills of Rome. He was, according to Douglas Southall Freeman, Robert E. Lee's biographer, "the best commissary of like rank in the Confederate service. Moses's stories were endless; his narrative flawless. The darkest, dullest night at headquarters he could enliven." He was a "most intelligent, efficient officer," according to G. Moxley Sorrel, the chief of Longstreet's staff. At the end of his life, Moses prided himself on his service to the cause; prized his memories of Lee, Longstreet, and other luminaries at Gettysburg; and in 1893 his calling card still read, "Major Raphael J. Moses, C.S.A."[136]

Moses and three of his sons—Raphael J. Moses Jr., Albert Moses Luria, and Israel Moses Nunez—fought in the Confederate armed forces.[137] Moses himself was fifty years old, but, while in Virginia on business in April 1861, he volunteered. Moses's old friend Robert Y. Toombs had become a powerful senator. He was seriously considered for the presidency of the Confederacy and was named its first secretary of state.[138] Toombs opposed the firing on Fort Sumter, predicting that it was like striking a hornet's nest and "legions now quiet will swarm out and sting us to death."[139] Toombs found his office unimportant and resigned, becoming a brigadier general, and Moses sought a field position in his brigade. Toombs offered Moses the position of commissary, but Moses declined, preferring a combat role. Howell Cobb, another prominent Georgian, who had resigned from Buchanan's cabinet and was now serving as president of the Provisional Confederate Congress, convinced Moses that he ought to accept, as it was a difficult job to fill with a competent man and, Moses recalled, "he was sure that I could do more good in that position than any other." Toombs and Cobb knew their man. Moses committed four years of his life and his formidable talent to supplying Toombs's brigade, then as commissary officer of Gen. David R. Jones's Division, Army of Northern Virginia, and then in November 1862 as chief commissary officer of Gen. James Longstreet's corps.[140]

Raphael J. Moses was in Virginia in 1862 serving as Toombs's commissary during the Peninsular Campaign, when Gen. Joseph E. Johnston's and then Robert E. Lee's Army of Northern Virginia faced Gen. George B. McClellan's Army of the Potomac on the Peninsula between the James and the York Rivers. Commissaries were charged with the responsibility of feeding the soldiers, but they often were caught in a battle. During this campaign, a Texas commissary's head was blown off. Moses related the story that there were those in the army who said that it served him right. After all, "what the devil right had a Commissary to be in the battle; he should have been with his wagons looking after the commissary stores. On this hint I did not speak, but said to myself if this is the way they talk about Commissaries with their heads shot off, I'll so conduct myself hereafter as to avoid similar comments."[141]

At one point during the campaign, Moses ran Toombs's headquarters. For two or three days, Lee found this headquarters to be the most convenient place for him to locate, and so he sent his cot and personal things down by a wagon. His staff followed. Moses found Lee to be as calm "as a summer cloud." He gave his orders "with precision and courtesy." Moses recalled a dinner at which an officer arrived, saluted, and said, "I am ordered by General Longstreet to inform you that General McClellan has retired." Lee bowed to the officer and then said to Moses, "Well,

Major, you can see what trouble that young man has given me!" That was all Lee said. After dinner, Lee moved back to his own headquarters.[142]

Moses's position brought him into contact with many of the major officers of the Confederate army. John Bell Hood, who commanded one of Longstreet's divisions at Gettysburg and was later promoted to temporary full general, was, according to Moses, "one of the best Brigadiers and poorest commanders in the army." Moses remembered "Jeb" Stuart as "a splendid Cavalry Officer, but, oh, how frivolous. He carried a banjo player with him wherever he went, and his favorite pastime when not dancing with the girls was to have his banjo player thrum and sing, 'Come, jine the Cavalry.' . . . He was as vain and frivolous as he was brave and dashing." Moses saw Robert E. Lee almost daily during his service in Virginia because Lee's headquarters was frequently near Longstreet's. Moses described Lee as "a plain, splendid looking, courteous gentleman, with such wonderful self control . . . in victory and defeat the same, unruffled exterior, kind to his men and kind to animals." He was present on one occasion when Lee contrived to convince the enemy that reinforcements had arrived when they had not. Lee ordered the men to cut brush and have the horses drag it along the road to cause an immense dust to arise and make it appear that fresh troops had arrived. The ruse worked.[143]

The Army of Northern Virginia was reorganized in 1862 into two corps: the 1st Corps commanded by Longstreet, and the 2d Corps by Jackson. When the staff assignments were completed, Moses was promoted to chief commissary of subsistence in Longstreet's corps, which now consisted of five divisions totaling 41,000 soldiers.[144] Moses became a member of Longstreet's inner circle of his top officers. "He soon became a favorite with the younger members of Longstreet's staff because of his wit and seemingly endless string of stories and anecdotes," concludes Longstreet's biographer, Jeffrey Wert.[145] Moses was with Longstreet at Second Manassas when Lee routed a much bigger Union army under Gen. John Pope and forced it to retreat back to Washington.[146] Moses had been on foraging excursions during these campaigns procuring food and supplies for Lee's army. On one excursion, Moses spied some cattle and sent a detail to drive them along with his unit's herd. After a half mile or so, an old woman came up to him in great distress and said that one of the cattle was her "pet heifer" and wanted to know whether Moses intended to kill it. She seemed almost brokenhearted at the apparent fate of her pet, and Moses's sympathies got the better of him. He said, "Certainly not, take her back." Years later, he reminisced: "I shall never forget the joy that illuminated the old woman's face . . . as she went back with her pet heifer. . . . This is a small matter . . . but . . . it is one of my good deeds that comes back to memory and cheers me in my waning years."[147]

Some of Moses's excursions lasted weeks and were both dangerous and fatiguing. He arrived in camp the morning before the Battle of Sharpsburg (Antietam) after a two-week foray, and the next night he and his men were forced to retreat and leave the supplies they had so laboriously procured. Moses let the soldiers take what they could in their knapsacks and even on their bayonets. The "adornment of a flitch of bacon being in no case objected to," he recalled, "and except for what was thus saved and the cattle which we could drive, my two weeks labor was lost. So much for the uncertainties of a boarding house keeper in the midst of War, and as I had, including teamsters and other noncombatants, a family of nearly 54,000 to provide for, this depletion of the larder was a very serious matter."[148]

In November 1862 Moses was chief commissary of the right wing, Longstreet's corps of the Army of Northern Virginia, and the next month participated in the first battle of Fredericksburg. One of his small contributions was to locate a friendly home where Mrs. Longstreet could stay.[149] Longstreet's official report after that battle thanked his staff, including Moses, for "the valuable services in their respective departments."[150] Moses next served as acting commissary officer of Gen. Lafayette McLaw's division. He was relieved of that assignment on February 25, 1863, and was ordered to report to General Longstreet at Petersburg, Virginia.

Longstreet's area of operation was now the coastal areas of the Carolinas and Southeast Virginia, areas occupied by Union forces. Moses was chosen to forage and raid in enemy-occupied territory because his skill as a commissary officer was well known. "Longstreet," Freeman writes in *Lee's Lieutenants*, "had a justly high opinion of Moses and he promptly forwarded to the commanding General the report prepared by the commissary."[151] Lee agreed with Longstreet that it was "of the first importance to draw from the invaded districts every pound of provision and forage we can. It will lighten the draught from other sections and give relief to our citizens." Lee and Longstreet, based on Moses's report of available supplies, determined to capture Suffolk, Virginia, in an effort to pin down the Union forces so that Moses could forage for badly needed supplies behind enemy lines. The troops at Fredericksburg were in need of supplies, and there was no place to obtain them except on the coast of North Carolina, where there were quantities of fish and bacon. Moses and Longstreet agreed that the capture of Suffolk would prevent the Federal troops from interfering with Moses's mission and "gobbling up" all the supplies. Suffolk was taken. Moses and his men and trains went to the coast of North Carolina and procured a large quantity of supplies, which were then sent to Fredericksburg.[152]

While Longstreet's corps was away, the rest of the army fought the second battle of Fredericksburg and the Battle at Chancellorsville. The next great Confederate offensive of the war was the Gettysburg campaign, and for it Longstreet's corps had rejoined the rest of the Army of Northern Virginia. This meant that Raphael Moses was charged with keeping the 1st Corps supplied with food from Virginia to Pennsylvania. The 1st Corps was ordered to proceed along the east side of the Blue Ridge mountains and to cross into Maryland. Moving on to

Pennsylvania, Longstreet's corps was in Chambersburg on June 27. Moses had orders to seize property from stores but not private homes and to pay for goods in Confederate money.[153] The storekeepers hid their most valuable goods or closed shop. Moses's job was made more difficult by the fact that General Ewell's corps had just come through a week before. Moses was excited, however, when he discovered a large supply of felt hats hidden away in a cellar, which he "annexed," as he put it, at once.[154] Moses had been ordered to secure three days' rations for the whole army, either voluntarily or by seizing or "impressing" supplies. The town officials had disappeared as had keys to the stores. When Moses's men began using axes to open the stores, however, the keys and townspeople reappeared. Moses and his men worked long hours attempting to find provisions. He returned to the camp very late one evening, having endured much abuse and insults from the local women, who called him "a thievish little rebel scoundrel" and other names. This did not annoy him so much as the hiding of goods in private homes, which he was not allowed to search by General Lee's orders. Next, he had to endure the chaffing of his fellow officers, who, with good humor, made him continually repeat the different names he had been called. He said that at first the women refused his Confederate "trash" [money] with great scorn, but they ended being very anxious to receive the exact amount due.[155]

The Battle of Gettysburg was fought over three days, from July 1 to July 3, 1863. Moses was privy to all of the top-level discussions, even those involving civilian spies. In his memoirs, for example, Moses remembered two spies, Harrison and Schrieber, who gave Lee the exact position of the Union army, but Lee distrusted the men and refused to rely on their reports, which turned out to be correct.[156]

"Moses, like his ancestor in the wilderness," Jacob Marcus wrote, "had to feed an army." By all accounts he succeeded admirably. Moses was well liked and respected by Lee's staff at Gettysburg. "He was much older than most of us," General Sorrel recalled in his memoirs, "but 'bon comrade,' and had an exhaustless fund of incident and anecdote, which he told inimitably."[157] Moses got along famously with Maj. John W. Fairfax, the aristocratic Virginian who owned James Monroe's plantation and volunteered to serve on Longstreet's staff.[158] Courageous and brave, pious and a bon vivant, Fairfax was something of a character. He always had a sack with two pockets, one for his bottle of whiskey and the other for his Bible. One Sunday when Fairfax was drunk, Moses entered his tent and wrote on one sheet of paper, "This in a moment brings me to an end," and on another sheet, "While this informs me I shall never die." He fixed the first to the bottle of whiskey and put the second between the pages of the Bible. When Fairfax awoke, he read the notes and exclaimed, "Moses, by the Lord!"[159]

One event which Moses understandably omits from his memoir (which was written for his family and not for publication) was the theft of his trunk containing more than $10,000 in government funds from his tent during the early morning hours of July 4. His military records contain his affidavit explaining the theft, which Moses felt was not his fault, as iron safes had not been provided by the government. He was not disciplined on account of the incident, and his superiors obviously accepted his explanation without question.[160]

Another of the colorful characters at Gettysburg was Col. Arthur J. L. Fremantle of the British army's Coldstream Guards, who was present as a military observer. Fremantle was a guest in Moses's tent.[161] The colonel later published a memoir of his experience and wrote of Major Moses: "He is the most jovial, amusing, and clever son of Israel I ever had the good fortune to meet."[162]

Moses was not far from Lee during much of the Battle of Gettysburg. "I had a splendid view of the grand and disastrous battle. The thunder of the artillery was terrifically grand, the charge of Pickett's division right up a long hill in the face of Federal cannon was not exceeded in valor by the charge of the six hundred [the Charge of the Light Brigade]." But the Confederate army suffered its worst defeat of the war. Colonel Freemantle related his return to Moses's tent, where he found "that worthy commissary in very low spirits."[163] And then came the retreat amidst a terrible rain storm. "I laid down in a fence corner and near by on the bare earth in an India rubber [sheet] lay General Lee biding the pelting storm."[164]

After the retreat from Gettysburg, Longstreet's corps was sent to Tennessee to reinforce the Army of Tennessee, commanded by Gen. Braxton Bragg. Major Moses, as Longstreet's chief commissary, continued his responsibilities for the subsistence of this corps. A portion of Longstreet's corps arrived in time to participate

The retreat from Gettysburg. (*Battles and Leaders of the Civil War.*)

132   in the Confederate victory at Chickamauga. Afterward, the Corps participated in major campaigns around Chattanooga and Knoxville, Tennessee. Moses's job in this war-ravaged state was difficult. His reports relay the near impossibility of securing tens of thousands of pounds of flour and meat, the competition between commissary officers of different divisions, and the refusal of civilians to cooperate. In Sweet Water, Tennessee, for example, a railroad engineer refused to move the train, and Moses took forcible possession of the railroad and ran the engine with an officer detailed from one of the Tennessee regiments. Despite his best efforts, the troops, on occasion, went two to three days and sometimes longer without flour rations.[165]

The Tennessee campaigns went badly for the Confederates. General Bragg suffered defeats at Lookout Mountain and Missionary Ridge, and Longstreet failed to push the enemy out of Knoxville. Longstreet took up winter quarters in the mountainous region of northeast Tennessee, where the terrain was rugged and much of the population pro-Union. Nevertheless, Moses kept the army supplied for six months after Longstreet thought he would be forced to retreat for lack of supplies. Moses's experience in business enabled him to obtain much-needed wheat from reluctant farmers. He obtained the wheat thrashers' records identifying those who brought in wheat to be thrashed. When the farmers hid the wheat, Moses and his men went after the sheep that wandered about the hill country. The sheep were not fit to eat, but the farmers wanted to shear the wool for winter clothing. Thus, when Moses seized the flocks (and gave receipts as commissary), he could bargain two pounds of sheep for one pound of bacon. This, he recalled, "unlocked the secret places in which the bacon was hid, and sheep proving good currency, I got nearly all the bacon necessary for rationing the Corps." He was forced at times to feed the troops sheep meat, which proved to be very unpopular.[166] Longstreet's biographer credits Moses's "wizardry of swapping confiscated sheep for bacon, of running mills day and night, and of commandeering trains" with having "fed the men in those difficult weeks in East Tennessee."[167]

A number of Jewish Confederate doctors, surgeons, and assistant surgeons served in the Confederate army. Indeed, the first surgeon general of the Confederate army was David Camden DeLeon of Columbia. Like many Confederate officers, DeLeon left the regular army to serve the Confederacy. A major in the medical corps of the "old" army, he was appointed surgeon in the Confederate army and chief of the medical staff of Gen. Braxton Bragg's army in Pensacola. In May, he was appointed surgeon general of the Confederacy, but, according to H. H. Cunningham, "his occupancy of the Surgeon General's office, consisting of only one room at that time, was of brief duration."[168] He was relieved on July 12, 1861. It is not clear whether DeLeon was replaced by Samuel Preston Moore because Moore outranked DeLeon in the "old Army," or whether DeLeon was not competent to head the Confederacy's medical department, or whether he had a drinking problem. After all, DeLeon's former military career was a distinguished one.

David Camden DeLeon's Confederate career appears to have been a disaster. The records of the Medical Corps were destroyed in the burning of Richmond, and so the details are lost. In his brief tenure as surgeon general, he sat on a board which designed the Confederate uniform with fellow South Carolinian Abraham Myers.[169] He certainly enjoyed the social life of early wartime Richmond, visiting with the Chesnuts, for example. He gave Mrs. Chesnut a miniature silver gondola he had bought in Venice. He told her he gave it to her as opposed to a Miss Sanders on account of Mrs. Chesnut's "Superior pulchritude."[170]

His career was steadily downhill after being replaced as surgeon general. He was assigned to Gen. Benjamin Huger's forces at Norfolk, where he served briefly as medical director. On June 3, 1862, he became medical director of Lee's Army of Northern Virginia and served in the Seven Days Battle. He was again relieved of duty within a month of his appointment. He resigned his commission in July 1862.[171]

DeLeon may have rejoined the Confederate army in Texas or he may have gone to Europe as an aide to his brother Edwin DeLeon. Charles Cullop writes in *Confederate Propaganda in Europe* that Dr. David Camden DeLeon was in Europe on Medical Department business in January 1863 and carried dispatches for his brother Edwin.[172] When the war ended, DeLeon left Texas for Mexico with other Confederate officers. He lived in Mexico for a year, returned to New Mexico, took up the practice of medicine, and lived quietly gardening and engaging in "his favorite amusement . . . to break the wild mustangs." He never returned to South Carolina. He never visited his family.[173]

DeLeon was afflicted with some kind of disgrace, drinking problem, or mental illness. Mary Chesnut noted in March of 1862 that Dr. DeLeon had been drinking and that he repeated "every thing, over & over" and "bored us to death."[174] In June she evidently felt DeLeon had acted improperly: "Edward Boykin told me he heard that old beast of a Camden DeLeon brag of his having given me that silver Gondola. I wish he had it back."[175] In July 1861 she wrote: "Camden DeLeon is sure to lose his place as surgeon general. Dr. Gibbs wants it. Dr. Nott is looked upon by many as a fit person for it. DeLeon is always drunk."[176] In an 1860 letter to his brother Edwin, Camden described an "unaccountable mental depression foreign to my naturally sanguine temperament. I attribute it to the effect of the Climate [he was touring the Middle East and Europe] and think that my namesake Old King David who was a bad man as well as myself and occasionally was guilty of much indiscretion must have suffered in a similar way."[177]

More successful and distinguished medical service was rendered by Simon Baruch, a Prussian immigrant from Camden, South Carolina. Baruch was born in Schwersenz, Posen, Prussia, in 1840. Like many a Prussian Jew, he came to America

Dr. Joseph Bensadon (pronounced Ben *say'* dun), a Sephardic Jew from Charleston, was educated at the College of Charleston, served in the Mexican War, and moved to New Orleans in 1847. He was a successful physician, counting Judah Touro among his patients. When Touro established the Touro Infirmary, Dr. Bensadon was its first director. He served as a surgeon in the Confederate army. (Courtesy of the Touro Infirmary Archives, New Orleans.)

to avoid conscription in the Prussian army. He lived in South Carolina with Mannes Baum, a native of his hometown who operated a small general store in Camden with his brother Marcus. Baruch was a bookkeeper for Baum, but soon went to Charleston to study medicine. He acculturated quickly into South Carolina society. By December 1860, at the age of twenty, this Prussian immigrant was marching in a parade in Charleston to celebrate signing the secession ordinance. When the war began, Baruch continued in his studies at the Medical College of Virginia in Richmond. He could not resist joining the Confederate army and enlisted in April 1862. His mentor, Mannes Baum, gave Baruch a uniform and sword.[178]

Baruch did not need a sword. What he needed were medical instruments, as he was appointed an assistant surgeon "without even having lanced a boil," as he used to tell his children.[179] As an assistant surgeon, Baruch had a rank equivalent to a captain. He was promoted to surgeon in November 1864. (A surgeon was equivalent to a major.)

Baruch joined the 3d South Carolina Battalion in April 1862.[180] His first combat experience was during the preliminary fighting before Second Manassas, when he marched through bursting shells at Thoroughfare Gap to set up his medical tent. His brigade reached the battlefield in time to receive "a volley of minie balls, the first I had ever heard zipping," even though Pope's Union army was in full retreat. It was here that Baruch saw his first wounded man. "While engaged in removing the first dressing a solid shot fell on the other side [of a protecting fence], scattering earth over us."[181] After the battle at Groveton (Second Manassas), Baruch's medical unit camped on the field and "awoke amid the ghastliest scenes of real war. Long lines of ambulances that had come from Washington under flag of truce [*sic*] were passing with the union wounded to Washington while we stood with bared heads in token of respect for our brave enemy." Details of men from both armies buried their dead. Baruch went to the nearest battlefield hospital, which was in a small house. An operating table was set up by laying a door upon a barrel and a box. Men were waiting to be operated upon. When the surgeon saw Baruch, his face pale, and recognized his uniform as that of an assistant surgeon, he "banteringly offered me the knife, saying, 'Doctor, perhaps you would like to operate.' I accepted the challenge. This was my first surgical operation of any kind. The surgeon was kind enough to commend my work."[182]

The next day, Baruch marched north with his corps, forded the Potomac, and entered upon the first Maryland invasion. Just before the Battle of Antietam, Baruch was involved in the Battle of South Mountain. When he reached the battlefield, the Confederates were in full retreat. Baruch was ordered to stay with the wounded men at Boonsboro, Maryland, while the Union army pursued the retreating Confederates. Baruch was captured and spent six weeks in Boonsboro before being sent to Fort McHenry at Baltimore. Captured officers were treated well in 1862, and Baruch had the run of the town until he was exchanged. (Doctors were exchanged quickly so that the sick and wounded soldiers would have medical treatment.) Indeed, Baruch was entertained at a dance which lasted until two in the morning.[183] According to his son Bernard Baruch's memoir, Simon Baruch and his fellow Confederate officers rode in a carriage to a photographer's studio the next morning and posed for their pictures. ("A copy of this photograph," Bernard Baruch recalled, "which Father's female admirers paid for, hung in our Camden home when I was a boy.")[184] The next day, Simon Baruch was on his way back to Virginia.

Baruch was with the 3d South Carolina Battalion, Kershaw's brigade at Gettysburg. He arose before dawn and marched until noon. He was at the famous Peach Orchard, where he saw "for the first time the charge of the entire division while infantry and artillery were mowing them down with shot and shell that flew around and above my first aid station." Sent to the Black Horse Tavern, where the division hospital was established, Baruch spent two days and two nights in constant operations and vigils, treating ambulance after ambulance of seriously wounded men.[185] The Union advance on July 5 after Lee's army began withdrawing placed the hospital in grave danger. Soon shells shrieked overhead and burst all around. The surgeons ran up a yellow flag to signal that they were in a hospital. The doctors treated the wounded while a hail of artillery fire exploded nearby.[186]

When Lee retreated, Baruch was again ordered to remain with his patients. Once again, he was not at the front. The front lines had moved behind him. Dr. Pearce, the surgeon in charge, ordered Baruch to carry a message of surrender to the approaching Yankees because, he said, "You understand these Yankees."[187] Baruch hastily donned his gray coat and green sash. "As I approached the line," he recalled, "with the nearest cavalryman's pistol dangerously pointed at me, I held up my hand and said, 'I surrender. Where is your captain?' The man yelled in a distinct Irish brogue, 'Say, Cap, here is a Reb wants to see you.'"[188] The captain asked if there were many Rebels around to which Baruch replied "only the wounded."

Baruch spent six weeks treating his men at Gettysburg. The Union medical officers shared their supplies, but many men died, six from lockjaw. Baruch was given a wagon for his supplies, and an officer gave him the *New York Herald* and told him he could now "learn what has become of General Lee. Read it until one of our wagons arrives." Some among the local people also came with supplies to help the wounded Confederate soldiers. A physician from Baltimore presented Baruch with "a fine case of instruments" with his name engraved on it.[189]

Once again, Baruch was taken to Fort McHenry in Baltimore as a prisoner of war. Being marched through the hot streets of Baltimore was a trying experience. "What a contrast," Baruch recalled, "between this tramp through dirty streets and my previous year's drive through the fashionable streets of Baltimore in a victoria!"[190] His stay this time was not so happy, but was not oppressive. The officers were put in a barracks, and they ate hardtack and coffee for supper; pork and corned beef for dinner. They were allowed to roam the grounds, play ball, exercise, swim, and even receive visitors. It was here that Dr. Baruch wrote a medical paper later published as "Two Penetrating Bayonet Wounds of the Chest." Eventually Baruch and the other doctors were exchanged for Union medical personnel in October 1863. ("The case of instruments which I had sent to my home in Camden, S.C., was captured eighteen months later by General Sherman.")[191]

In December 1863 Baruch reported for duty at Newnan, Georgia. The 3d South Carolina Battalion was then with Longstreet in Tennessee. In August 1864, he was ordered to report to the medical director of Longstreet's corps. He was assigned to the 13th Mississippi stationed in Richmond and was promoted to surgeon. He was with Maj. Gen. Joseph B. Kershaw's division as it went to reinforce Lt. Gen. Jubal A. Early's army in the Shenandoah Valley. Baruch recounted a humorous episode at the close of the Battle of Cedar Creek in October 1864. When inspired by the sight of General Early waving a flag and imploring his men to stop the rout, he "foolishly undertook with a colleague to check the flight of a group of soldiers." Galloping toward the front, Baruch yelled, "Rally, men, for God's sake rally." When a shell exploded over his head and his horse bolted and ran away, the men yelled after him, "Why in hell don't you rally?"[192]

Baruch later suffered from some kind of medical disability and spent a part of the remainder of the war in hospitals as a patient. He was relieved from duty with the 13th Mississippi on a certificate of disability and ordered to Raleigh, North Carolina, where he was again in service in Confederate hospitals. He was in charge

Simon Baruch, Bernard Baruch's father, was a Prussian immigrant to Camden, South Carolina. He served as a surgeon in the Confederate army (with the equivalent rank of major) and was left behind to care for the wounded at Boonsboro, Maryland, and at Gettysburg. He was active in the Confederate Veterans after the war. (Courtesy of South Carolina Historical Society.)

of a smallpox hospital in Goldsboro. He treated the wounded after the Battle of Kinston, North Carolina, and treated Union prisoners as well. "They were raw Germans," Baruch recalled, "unable to speak English, and were delighted when I addressed them in their own language." He organized a hospital at Thomasville and there treated men who had been wounded at Averasboro. He commandeered wagons, gathered pine straw for bedding, persuaded college girls to help as nurses, went house to house seeking food, and cleaned up abandoned factories to use as hospitals. He came down with typhoid fever and was unconscious for two weeks. When he awoke, the war was over for him and he had been paroled.[193]

★　　★　　★

The Confederate government was concerned about disloyalty and treason, and special commissioners were appointed with military and judicial authority to investigate and prosecute treason, espionage, harboring deserters, or trading with the enemy. These commissioners were part prosecutor, part judge, part police. Many were distinguished lawyers, including a former attorney general of the Confederacy.[194] There was at least one Jewish military commissioner in the Confederate army, and he had quite an interesting career. Henry J. Leovy was a talented Jewish lawyer from New Orleans.[195] He codified the laws of the City of New Orleans, which were published from 1856 to 1872. After the war he served as city attorney of New Orleans. In addition, Leovy was the principal owner of the *Delta* newspaper, which he operated until it was seized by Gen. B. F. Butler in 1862, when New Orleans was occupied by the Union army.

Leovy left New Orleans before its capture and joined the Confederate forces. Brig. Gen. Hamilton Prioleau Bee, Gen. Bernard E. Bee's brother, was in contact with Leovy in the fall of 1863. Bee was in Brownsville, Texas, trading cotton for ammunition and war material, and Leovy was somehow involved in the operation. "If you hear that I am killed by a Mexican," Bee wrote, "I want you to kill a dozen or so before you leave the frontier—not the poor devils, but the officials."[196] Leovy was apparently a kind of "troubleshooter," or special assignment agent, for the Confederate government. He went to Richmond undoubtedly at the behest of his old friend Judah P. Benjamin, who likely assigned Leovy the arduous and dangerous task of investigating and routing out spies, deserters, and disloyal citizens.

The area to which Leovy was assigned, Southwestern Virginia, was sorely divided on the issues of secession, slavery, and loyalty to the Confederacy. Many remained loyal to the Union. Many who had supported the Confederacy early in the war had been alienated by the government's inefficiency and now called for a return to the Union. Judah Benjamin, as secretary of state, concerned himself with espionage issues and trusted Leovy to handle this potentially explosive situation. Indeed, the government at Richmond had convinced itself, according to Kenneth W. Noe, that "southwest Virginia, so important strategically as a source of war material and as a transportation corridor, was overrun with 'Red Strings,' members of the unionist Heroes of America." These Appalachian counties, peopled with Scotch Irish and Germans, often clashed with their fellow Virginians to the east over a variety of issues, including slavery, internal improvements, and taxes.[197]

As the war progressed, economic conditions worsened. The currency became worthless, the black market drove prices up, and military impressment depleted stores. The Confederate "tax in kind" and the draft added fuel to the fire. By late 1863 the majority of people in this area were "tired of the war and thoroughly dissatisfied with Richmond's conduct of it," according to Noe.[198] It was into this hornet's nest that the Confederate War Department sent Major Leovy.

Leovy went to Southwestern Virginia in the summer of 1864. He interrogated suspects and those in custody. He brought in detectives, who spent time pretending to be prisoners in jail with some of those arrested, gained their confidence, and learned all about the secret organizations.[199]

The secretary of war gave a detailed report to President Davis on November 8, 1864, describing the secret association dedicated to protecting and hiding deserters and escaped prisoners, and attempting to organize a new state of Southwest Virginia. Seddon's report credited Leovy's "zeal and vigilance" in successfully concluding the investigation and passed on Leovy's recommendation to the president.[200] In December 1864 Leovy was appointed president of the military court for the Department of Southwestern Virginia.[201] He was officially appointed colonel of cavalry and judge.[202]

There were also Jewish Confederate officers in the Confederate navy, which defended coastal cities and raided the Union merchant fleet. Perry DeLeon was twenty years old when his native South Carolina seceded. One week later, he was among the first officers to resign from the U.S. Army. From May 1861 until October 1862, he served as a volunteer in the Wise and Hampton Legions and fought at Gaines' Mill and Malvern Hill. In October 1862 he was assigned to duty by the Confederate secretary of the navy as an assistant paymaster. He served in the navy from October until the war ended, serving on the CSS *Harriet Lane*, the *Savannah (Oconee)*, the *Stono*, and the *Albemarle*.[203] DeLeon volunteered for a commando expedition to free Confederate prisoners on Johnson's Island on Lake Erie in the fall of 1863. A group of fifteen Confederate naval officers and sailors left North Carolina, ran the blockade, and traveled to Montreal, where they made plans to capture a Union ship on the Canadian side of the lake and use it to free two thousand prisoners of war. The plan was foiled when the Canadian authorities were alerted to the plot, and the men were forced to return home empty handed.[204]

DeLeon served at the battles of Plymouth, North Carolina, and Albemarle Sound on the ironclad *Albemarle*. The CSS *Albemarle* was built in 1864 on the Roanoke River to defend the North Carolina coast. It was 152 feet long and carried two 6.4-inch Brooke guns. Commissioned on April 17, 1864, the *Albemarle* attacked Union gunboats at Plymouth, North Carolina, two days later. "In Albemarle Sound," DeLeon recalled, "we fought nine boats of the enemy carrying 69 guns, with our little boat carrying two guns. This in April, 1864." He recalled years later, "Our boat did splendid work." In October 1864, however, the *Albemarle's* luck ran out. Lt. William B. Cushing with seven Union volunteers, "blew us up with a torpedo at the wharf of Plymouth. We captured his boat and crew but not him. We retreated to Halifax and were building another boat when the war ended. I was paroled at Norfolk in May, 1865." The *Albemarle* sank.[205] Although his rank was denominated "assistant paymaster," DeLeon was a combat naval officer with the relative rank of a captain in the army.

DeLeon was proud of his family's service to the Confederacy. His brief memoir begins: "In our war with the North, every male descendant of Jacob DeLeon between the ages of 15 and 60 served the Confederacy, save one," an uncle with nine children and other family members to support. Of the eleven grandsons and great-grandsons of Jacob DeLeon, two served the Confederacy in civilian capacities: Edwin DeLeon as a diplomat and Thomas Cooper DeLeon as a clerk; eight served in the army and navy. Of the eight, Perry DeLeon wrote simply, "four gave their lives for the Confederacy." [206]

A career naval officer, Capt. Levi Charles Harby of Galveston, Texas, joined the Confederate cause when his native South Carolina seceded. Born in 1793,

140   Harby was sixty-eight years old when he resigned his commission in the Revenue Service (the early Coast Guard) of the United States and gave up command of the revenue cutter *Henry Dodge* in Galveston. Having served as a midshipman in the War of 1812 and in the War for Texas Independence, Harby was an experienced officer and a committed patriot. Indeed, the entire Harby family entered the fray, as Captain Harby's two sons, Henry J. Harby and J. D. Harby, also enlisted— Henry in the 26th Texas Cavalry and J. D. in the Texas Light Artillery. Given his age, Harby was asked to train artillerymen and served his adopted state in the Texas Maritime Service. He was likely commissioned as a lieutenant but, because of his former rank in the Revenue Service, was frequently addressed as "captain." Later he apparently was actually promoted to captain.[207]

Harby was among the Texans who recaptured Galveston from the occupying Union army and navy on New Year's Day 1863. A combined Confederate land and sea force under Gen. John Bankhead ("Prince John") Magruder launched a surprise attack that day. It was so dangerous that men were asked to volunteer. Col. Thomas Green addressed the men at Harrisburg and asked them to step forward: "Soldiers, you are called upon to volunteer in a dangerous expedition," he said. "I have never deceived you; I will not deceive you now. I regard this as the most dangerous

The Battle of Galveston, New Year's Day, 1863. Seventy-year-old Capt. Levi Charles Harby of Galveston commanded two guns on the small Confederate packet *Neptune*, which successfully attacked the 619-ton Union warship *Harriet Lane*. (*Battles and Leaders of the Civil War.*)

enterprise that men ever engaged in." The whole line stepped forward. These Texas soldiers and cavalrymen, none of them sailors, became "horse marines" and agreed to serve as artillerymen, sharpshooters, and boarding parties on "high-pressure cotton steamers," protected from Union shot and shell only by cotton bales. The Confederates referred to the two small ships, the *Neptune* and the *Bayou City,* as "cottonclads."[208]

Captain Harby, now seventy years old, was asked to command the two twenty-four-pound howitzer guns on the *Neptune,* one of the two ships designated to ram and capture the *Harriet Lane,* a large side-wheel steamer used as a blockading cruiser carrying five guns, while Magruder's troops attacked Kuhn's Wharf on Galveston Bay. Harby was in command of a small company of infantry acting as artillerymen.[209]

Between 4:00 a.m. and 5:00 a.m. on January 1, 1863, Magruder's forces commenced their attack. The *Harriet Lane* and other blockading Union warships opened an intense bombardment of the Confederate attackers near Kuhn's Wharf. The Confederate ships "puffing and snorting from their high pressure steam," aimed for the Federal fleet.[210] Harby was in one of the most dangerous positions, commanding the guns on a small mail packet which was ordered to attack a 619-ton Union warship. When one of the nervous sharpshooters asked his colonel whether the cotton bales would protect them, his reply was: "None whatever, not even against grape shot; our only chance is to get along side before they hit us."[211] This is about what actually happened. The plan was for the two "cottonclads" to attack the *Harriet Lane* from opposite sides. The *Neptune* was badly damaged in its collision with the *Harriet Lane;* many men were killed on board; Federal gunners blew a hole in the *Neptune*'s hull, and it began to sink.[212] Fortunately, it sank in eight feet of water, so Harby and his artillerymen and the sharpshooters continued firing. "We had two 24-pounders on board," Joseph Faust recalled, "that roared with extraordinary loud report."[213] This diverted the *Harriet Lane* so that the *Bayou City* could successfully ram the Union ship; and its crew boarded the *Lane,* killed its officers, and captured the vessel with its crew of 109. Magruder recaptured Galveston in one of the most daring battles of the war. Jefferson Davis congratulated Magruder on his "brilliant exploit."[214]

Harby had done his part in the great victory. Magruder thanked all of the successful officers in his official report: "Captain Harby, and the officers and crew of the ship, likewise deserve, as they have received, my thanks for their participation in this brilliant battle."[215] He also reported to the governor of Texas, where he again thanked "The gallant Texans, under their devoted leaders," including Captain Harby."[216] Harby had lost eight out of fifteen men; his lieutenant was killed at his side. He was the last to leave the *Neptune.*[217]

When the war ended, Captain Harby was in command of the harbor of Galveston. He died in 1870 in Galveston, having never sought a pardon from the United States for his role in the war.

The youngest son of Maj. Raphael J. Moses, Raphael J. Moses Jr. also served in the Confederate navy. Born in Florida in 1844, young Moses was called "Lea" or "Lee."[218] He matriculated at Annapolis in September 1860, when he was not yet sixteen. A popular and lively student, young Raphael resigned when Georgia seceded from the Union. In July he joined the Confederate States navy as a midshipman and was soon in combat. Assigned to the CSS *Savannah,* young Moses fired several "excellent shots . . . [while] commanding the after-gun," according to Capt. Josiah Tattnall's report. He was promoted to the rank of master, in line of promotion, in the Confederate navy. He also served on the CSS *Arctic* out of Wilmington, North Carolina. When yellow fever struck the ship, Moses was left as the senior officer. He had the good fortune to spot a ship on Frying Pan Shoals just below the mouth of the Cape Fear River. The vessel was deserted by her crew except one survivor. Moses's crew saved the survivor and brought the ship to port. "To my surprise," Moses wrote in a letter years later, "I shortly afterwards received form [*sic*] the prize court $3000.00 in gold and my share of the prize money."[219]

In the fall of 1862 Moses was sent to the CSS *Georgia* and was involved in several engagements off the coast of Europe. The *Georgia* was an iron-hulled merchant crew ship, originally named *Japan,* which was purchased by Confederate agents in Scotland in 1863. One officer called it "a poor miserable little tin kettle." Nevertheless, it captured nine merchantmen prizes while cruising the Atlantic Ocean and, like the *Alabama,* created panic in Northern shipowners.[220]

In March 1863 the Confederate government sent Moses to England to help take charge of two turreted ironclads known as the Laird Rams, being built for the Confederacy. The British government, however, seized the ships. Young Moses then went to Paris for a year and was ordered to the CSS *Alabama,* but that legendary vessel was sunk by the USS *Kearsage* off Cherbourg before he arrived. In September 1864 he returned to the South by running the blockade. Sent to a naval artillery battery known as the Semmes Batteries fifteen miles below Richmond on the James River, he commanded a battery of six eight-inch cannons and had almost daily artillery duels with the Union army. Moses was also assigned the dangerous duty of laying mines (called "torpedoes" during the Civil War) at night in the river. "We had to go with muffled oars in a row boat," he recalled, "pick out a night particularly dark, then tow these torpedoes to the points we wished and anchor them with just sufficient rope to keep the torpedo concealed and as it was concealed from the enemy, it was equally concealed from us on our return trip."[221]

Young Moses was an exacting commander and drove the men in his command hard. For Christmas in 1864, he decided to treat his men to a good Christmas dinner, and, seeing some corn across the river in enemy territory, he decided to raid the cornfield and sell the corn in Richmond to raise the funds. After three boatloads, however, he was captured. He was sent first to the Old Capitol Prison in Washington and then to Fort Delaware, where he passed time usefully, studying

law. This he did partly for future use and partly to divert himself and fellow prisoners from the horrors of their surroundings, doing such things as holding mock
court with trials by jury.[222]

Two other Jewish Confederates played important roles in the Confederate
navy. David Lopez, a builder and contractor in Charleston, was put in charge of
much of South Carolina's arms production and repair. The builder of Institute Hall
in Charleston, where South Carolina's Ordinance of Secession was signed, Lopez
was responsible for building one or more of the innovative torpedo boats that
attacked the Union ships blockading Charleston. One, the CSS *David,* was
involved in a number of attempts to break the Union blockade of Charleston harbor by ramming Union warships. Harry Simonhoff claims that the *David* was
named for Lopez, but it was likely named David because its foes were Union
Goliaths.[223]

Col. Henry J. Leovy, the military judge and special commissioner, was also
involved in naval affairs. Leovy, a lawyer, was Horace L. Hunley's friend. Hunley
was a fellow New Orleans lawyer and inventor of the CSS *H. L. Hunley,* the first
submarine in history to successfully attack a ship during wartime. Leovy helped
Hunley build his submarine. He acted as a surety on the bond necessary to procure the letter of marque authorizing the vessel to attack enemy ships.[224] When
Hunley died in one of the submarine's test dives, it was Leovy who acted as executor of his estate. (Hunley's will, incidentally, requested Leovy to dispose of his
sugar and tobacco stores and "use the money for speculation or running the blockade till the end of the war."[225])

Many Southern Jewish families gave more than one officer to the Southern
cause. The Hyams and Jonas clans of Louisiana contributed numerous high-ranking officers to the Confederacy. Henry M. Hyams, an observant Jew, served as lieutenant governor of the state throughout the war.[226] Hyams's sons, his brother
Samuel Myers Hyams, and his nephews all saw service in the Confederate army,
most as officers. At least three of Henry Hyams's sons served in the armed forces:
Isaac Smith Hyams, Kosciusko Ravenkamp Hyams, and Henry M. Hyams Jr.

Henry Hyams had always wanted Isaac to be a soldier. Born in 1837, Isaac
entered West Point in 1854, but left the academy in 1856. When the war began,
Isaac was twenty-four years old. He joined Company A, 1st Regiment in the
Louisiana State Army in January 1861 and was commissioned second lieutenant.
When he mustered into Confederate service in March, he was first lieutenant of
Company B. Father and son enlisted the aid of their cousin, Judah Benjamin, then
attorney general, to write the Confederate secretary of war to obtain a commission
for young Hyams in the Confederate States regular army, preferably in the artillery
corps. While in Montgomery, Benjamin wrote a request to Leroy Pope Walker, the

Judah Benjamin's letter to Leroy Pope Walker. The Hyamses eagerly sought commissions as officers. In this letter, written less than two weeks before the bombardment at Fort Sumter, Judah P. Benjamin, then just appointed attorney general, asked the newly appointed secretary of war, Leroy Pope Walker, to give Isaac Hyams a lieutenant's commission "in the Regular C.S. Army in the artillery if possible." Isaac's father, Henry, was Benjamin's first cousin. "I make *special* application & feel deep personal interest in his behalf," Benjamin concluded. (Courtesy of National Archives, Isaac Hyams compiled service record.)

secretary of war, on April 1, 1861: "Mr. Hyams has been two years at West Point & is now 1st Lieutenant in the State army, in the Infantry. . . . This young gentleman is the son of the Lieut. Governor of La. & is of a family which has been foremost in defense of our case—I make *special* application & feel deep personal interest in his behalf." Benjamin's recommendation had its effect. Young Hyams was appointed a second lieutenant of infantry in the regular Confederate army in April 1861. He was "temporarily" assigned to Company B of the Confederate States Marine Corps from New Orleans, which was pitted against the Union forces holding Fort Pickens. The men were being drilled in the use of heavy guns, and Hyams was likely an instructor. He saw combat and was commended by Capt. Alfred C. Van Benthuysen for his "cool and gallant conduct" in an artillery duel in November. It was Isaac Hyams's first experience under fire.[227] Hyams served with this company of the CSMC for ten months.

In 1862 Hyams reported to Maj. Gen. Edmund Kirby Smith for duty as a drillmaster. He was next assigned to the 39th North Carolina and was acting adjutant of the regiment at the Battle of Murfreesboro, Tennessee (Stones River), in December 1862 and January 1863.

Hyams's bravery at the battle led to his selection by the men of his regiment as one of twelve men to be included in the "Roll of Honor" and was recommended for promotion in January 1863. After the only two field officers were borne disabled from the field, his commander wrote, "much of the burden of conducting the regiment devolved upon [Hyams]." He discharged this responsibility "with an activity and *efficiency* worthy of all praise, and with a gallantry which has been a universal theme of the comment of the command."[228]

In September Hyams participated in the Battle of Chickamauga, where he survived the 39th North Carolina's heavy engagement on the first day but was wounded in the leg on the second day. That day the 39th led the critical assault by McNair's brigade on two batteries of Federal guns. This feat was decisive in breaking the Federal center. Hyams was evacuated to a hospital in Atlanta. Judah Benjamin kept a watchful eye on his young cousin. On December 15 Benjamin, now secretary of state, wrote to James A. Seddon, secretary of war, reminding him of a promise he had made to promote Hyams, enclosing the letter of recommendation from his colonel. Benjamin was quite direct: "Will you be good enough to enclose to me the commission you promised?" That same day, Seddon instructed the adjutant general to appoint Hyams captain in the Provisional Army, while he still retained his second lieutenant rank in the regular army.[229]

By February 1864 Hyams had recovered enough for reassignment, and by the end of the month, he was serving as captain of Company B, Garrison Guard Battalion, at Marietta, Georgia. In May he was ordered, as a second lieutenant, Regular Army, to report to Gen. Edmund Kirby Smith in the Trans-Mississippi Department. In March 1865 he was serving as a drill officer in Maj. Gen. John

CONFEDERATE LINE OF BATTLE IN THE CHICKAMAUGA WOODS.

The Battle of Chickamauga. One of the most vicious battles of the war, Chickamauga pitted two major armies in September of 1863, both seeking control of Chattanooga. Killed were 2d Lt. Walter Mordecai of Company B, 22d Alabama, and 2d Lt. Isaiah Jacobs of Company D, 2d Carolina; Lt. Isaac S. Hyams was wounded. Numerous Jewish Confederates were there, including Maj. Alroy Jonas, who served with Gen. John Bell Hood. (*Battles and Leaders of the Civil War.*)

Austin Wharton's (Dismounted) Cavalry Corps in Texas. He was paroled at Millican, Texas, on July 5, 1865, as a captain.

Henry M. Hyams's brother Samuel Myers Hyams, who was also born in Charleston, moved to New Orleans in 1830. He later settled in Natchitoches (pronounced *Nak*-uh-tish), where he was the U.S. deputy surveyor and then clerk of the district court. In the Mexican War, Hyams raised a company in the 5th Louisiana Volunteers and served as captain, although the unit mustered out before going to Mexico. He was elected sheriff and served six years before becoming U.S. marshal of the Western District of Louisiana and register of the Land Office. He was also a successful planter. His plantation, Lac des Mures, was located on the Red River above Grand Ecore and Natchitoches.[230]

When the war began, Samuel Hyams was forty-eight years old and the head of a large family. He was nominated for secretary of the Louisiana secession convention, but was not elected. He raised a company of men, the Pelican Rangers, and became its captain. The Pelican Rangers was the largest company in the state. It traveled 479 miles to the enlistment rendezvous in New Orleans, where it was divided into two companies, the Pelican Rangers No. 1 and No. 2. Samuel Hyams retained command of No. 1. The two companies became a part of the 3d Louisiana, which mustered into service on May 17, 1861.[231]

A Louisiana "Pelican." (*Battles and Leaders of the Civil War.*)

Hyams became lieutenant colonel of the 3d Louisiana under Col. Louis Hebert when it was mustered into service in the Confederate army in May 1861. He led the regiment to Arkansas that same month. Despite the crippling effects of chronic rheumatism and a kick from a horse, Lt. Col. Hyams successfully led half of his regiment at the Battle of Oak Hills (Wilson's Creek). His command captured five of six guns in a Federal battery and, according to Tunnard's account, was "with the regiment on the march, in their ambuscades, and through the battle, coolly and calmly directing the men."[232]

Hyams was a popular officer, affable, gregarious, and hospitable to a fault. Hyams loved a horse race and participated enthusiastically in the regiment's races. His son, Samuel M. Hyams Jr., raced his horse in these races. On one occasion, a mysterious-looking wagon happened into camp with a keg of whiskey, which was promptly seized by the officers as contraband. "The Lieutenant Colonel did not, then and there, spill the whiskey," Tunnard recalled. "Not he. He had too keen an appreciation of what was good for a soldier on a cold day." Instead, the men were called to Hyams's quarters and everyone given a drink of the "forbidden nectar." The popular lieutenant colonel was vociferously cheered for his thoughtfulness toward his men.[233]

But his good humor was not equaled by good health, and Hyams was forced to retire in early 1862. He returned to Natchitoches, where he served as provost marshal, enforcing martial law. He did not, however, forget the men of his old command. When the regiment, traveling by boat, came by his plantation in August of 1864 to land a passenger, Hyams appealed to the men to sustain his authority while he prepared a feast in preparation for the whole regiment. Of course, he was upheld in these proceedings. Tunnard recalled: "The Captain was indiscriminately stuffed with a bushel of peaches, washed down with some excellent 'firewater' from a Confederate distillery; then followed a cart-load of melons, grapes *ad infinitum,* milk, fine gumbo, barbecued pork, beef, mutton, etc.—the men being likewise provided for. They bowed most *gracefully* to the *exacting* demands of the Colonel, and a scene of hilarity, joy and freedom from restraint ensued such as was seldom witnessed during the late warlike times."[234]

Samuel Hyams had two sons in the 3d Louisiana, one in the Mississippi Cavalry and one in the Missouri Cavalry. Samuel Myers Hyams Jr. rose to the rank of lieutenant colonel before the war ended.[235] Samuel Jr. was born and raised in Louisiana and joined the Pelican Rangers No. 2 (Company D), 3d Louisiana on May 17, 1861, as the junior second lieutenant. He served as adjutant in the summer of 1861 and was cited by Col. Louis Hebert for his actions at Wilson's Creek (Oak Hills), where "he left his horse and fought bravely on foot."

Hyams was also at the Battle of Elkhorn Tavern in March 1862, where he was commended by Col. Elkanah Greer, the acting division commander. By June 1862 he was aide-de-camp to now Brig. Gen. Hebert. He was again commended for gallantry in leading troops in battle at Courtland, Alabama, in July 1862, and was promoted to captain in 1863. In 1864 he was promoted to lieutenant colonel and was to assume command of the 2d Missouri Cavalry. His appointment, however, did not suit the men of the 2d, as they felt their major was entitled to the promotion. Hyams agreed to be bound by a vote of the men, which went against him, and gracefully accepted their decision. Hyams was then assigned to the command of the 1st Mississippi Partisan Rangers at Tupelo, Mississippi (later redesignated as the 7th Mississippi Cavalry). He participated in the defense of Mobile in the fall of 1864.[236] In February 1865, Hyams reported to Brig. Gen. James Ronald Chalmers, commander of Gen. Nathan Bedford Forrest's 1st Division. In early March 1865, on his way to Jackson, Mississippi, where he was sent to "hurry up" and assist Gen. William Wirt Adams in organizing his brigade, Hyams delivered a message and other orders from General Forrest to Lt. Gen. Richard Taylor. Hyams likely accompanied Forrest's command into Alabama, where it surrendered in May 1865.

The Jonas family originated in England. Abraham Jonas, the patriarch, emigrated to the United States from England in the early 1800s.[237] He served in the legislatures of Kentucky and Illinois, a grand master of Masons and an early supporter of Abraham Lincoln. He was postmaster in Quincy, Illinois, under three presidents, including Lincoln. Abraham Jonas and his second wife, Louisa Block of Virginia, had ten children.[238] The older children were born and raised in Williamstown, Kentucky, in the 1830s and 1840s and grew up with Southern sympathies. The younger children were born and raised in Quincy, Illinois, and grew up with Northern sympathies. There were at least five Jonases in uniform during the Civil War: the four eldest, Charles Henry, Benjamin Franklin, Julian J., and Sidney Alroy, wore gray, and the youngest, Edward, wore blue. Three of the five became officers. A sixth son, George, probably served briefly in the militia in Louisiana. Alroy served as a major on the staffs of Generals W. H. C. Whiting, John Bell Hood, and Stephen D. Lee. Julian fought with the Louisiana Crescent (24th) Regiment at Shiloh. He then enlisted in the Louisiana Orleans Light Horse Cavalry Company, where he became quartermaster sergeant. Benjamin Franklin, known as Frank, served with Captain Fenner's artillery battery and later with Hood. Charles was a captain and quartermaster. Edward served as a captain and aide-de-camp in the Union army. After the war, Alroy became a well-known editor and political ally of Sen. L. Q. C. Lamar; Edward, a cotton factor and commission merchant; and Benjamin Franklin Jonas, a political force in postwar Louisiana, helping to lead the Redeemer movement and becoming the first practicing Jew to serve in the U.S. Senate.

In 1838 the Jonases had moved to Quincy, Illinois, undoubtedly the first Jews in the town. Abraham Jonas was a storekeeper and studied law in the office of Orville Hickman Browning, a close friend of Lincoln and later senator from Illinois. In 1842 Jonas ran for the legislature on the Whig ticket and was elected. He was defeated for the state senate in 1844 but remained active in the Whig Party and later the Republican Party. He became a close friend and ardent supporter of Lincoln. He arranged for Lincoln to visit Quincy in 1854 to speak on behalf of the Whig candidate for Congress. When Lincoln was later accused of having attended a Know-Nothing meeting on this occasion, he wrote to Jonas to vouch for his whereabouts that night, which Jonas did. Lincoln and Jonas were both presidential electors for Fremont in 1856. When Lincoln came to Quincy as a lawyer, he did much of his legal work in the law office of Jonas & Asbury. In 1860 Jonas was a delegate to the Republican convention in Chicago, where he worked tirelessly for the nomination of his friend.[239]

The Jonas boys knew Lincoln too. In fact, before the war, Frank Jonas, then a young lawyer in New Orleans, was involved in a legal matter with Lincoln. A June 4, 1857, letter in the Lincoln papers from Frank Jonas to Lincoln discusses the arrest of a free black whom Jonas successfully represented. Lincoln must have known the client because he sent Jonas the fee. "I should never have ventured to trouble you," Jonas wrote Lincoln, "had not the boy mentioned your name, as that of one, who would take an interest in his behalf—and had I not recognized in you an old friend of my father—." The letter closes with Jonas's assurance to Lincoln—ironic in hindsight—that "any service I can render you in this part of the world will give me pleasure—."[240]

Even after the war had begun, the Jonases kept in touch with President Lincoln. "Mr. Lincoln always asked after us [the Jonas sons] when he saw anyone from New Orleans during the war," Frank Jonas recalled. In December 1860, Abraham Jonas wrote Lincoln to warn him of an assassination plot: "You perhaps are aware, that I have a very large family connection in the South, and that in New Orleans I have six children and a host of other near relatives. I receive many letters from them, their language has to be very guarded." But, he warned his old friend, he had a letter from "one who is prudent, sound and careful," and this correspondent believed there was a plot organized in New Orleans to kill the president upon his arrival in Washington.[241]

The eldest son of Abraham Jonas, Charles H. Jonas, served in the 12th Arkansas Infantry. He was captain and assistant quartermaster and was captured on July 9, 1863, at Port Hudson, Louisiana, imprisoned first in New Orleans, then

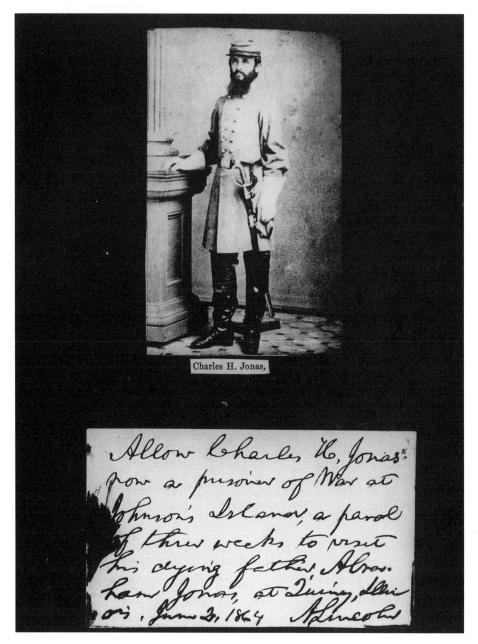

Charles H. Jonas,

Charles H. Jonas was the son of Abraham Jonas and a brother of Frank, Julian, and Alroy Jonas. He served in the 12th Arkansas as a captain. He was captured at Port Hudson, Louisiana, and was a prisoner at Johnson's Island, Ohio. When his father was dying, Sen. Orville Browning of Illinois arranged for President Lincoln to issue a parole to allow Jonas to leave the prison to visit his father in Quincy, Illinois. The note above is in Lincoln's handwriting. (Courtesy of the Jacob Rader Marcus Center, American Jewish Archives, Cincinnati, Ohio.)

sent to Fort Columbus in New York harbor, and finally to Johnson's Island, Ohio. It was while he was a prisoner of war in Ohio that news came of his dying father's wish to see him. At Sen. Orville Browning's urging, Lincoln issued a personal order in May 1864 allowing "Charles H. Jonas now a prisoner of War at Johnson's Island, a parol[e] of three weeks to visit his dying father, Abraham Jonas, at Quincy, Illinois, June 2, 1864."[242] Jonas, in turn, gave his parole: "I, *C. H. Jonas,* Cpt 12th Ark. Regt—a prisoner of war—do hereby give my parole of honor—to proceed to *Quincy, Illinois* to visit my father—and that I will do no act or thing prejudicial to the Government of the United States—while absent & further that I will *visit* no other place—But will return to this Post on the *Twenty Seventh* day of the present month." Abraham died the day his son Charles arrived "in time to be recognized and welcomed by him," as Charles later recalled. Lincoln appointed Mrs. Jonas postmaster to serve out her husband's term. Captain Jonas honored his parole. He remained a prisoner of war until exchanged on March 14, 1865, at Point Lookout, Maryland.[243]

The second son of Abraham Jonas, Benjamin Franklin ("Frank") Jonas, was born in Williamstown, Kentucky, on July 19, 1834, moved to Illinois with his family, and was educated in the public schools.[244] In 1853, at the age of nineteen, he moved to New Orleans, where his uncle George Jonas was a prominent banker. He was admitted to the bar and was offered a partnership by Henry M. Hyams, then a leading attorney and soon to be lieutenant governor. This connection also gave young Jonas a connection to Judah Benjamin, as Hyams was the senator's cousin. (Later, after the war, Jonas and Benjamin's nephew Ernest Benjamin Kruttschnitt became law partners.) Jonas was a successful lawyer and an accomplished orator, a skill which served him well throughout his career. He was active in the Jewish community, having served as one of the founders of the Jewish Orphan's Home in New Orleans. As one of the outstanding young lawyers in the city, Jonas was asked to give the dedication speech of the home.[245]

Jonas may not have been all that enthusiastic about the war. He enlisted as a private for three years on September 9, 1862, at Baton Rouge in Capt. Charles E. Fenner's Light Artillery Battery. He served under Gen. Joseph E. Johnston in the Mississippi campaign, participating in the four days' battle around Jackson. In 1863 Fenner's Battery joined Hood's corps in the Army of Tennessee, and Jonas became sergeant major and acting adjutant in the artillery regiment commanded by Col. Robert F. Beckham. Jonas's colonel requested that Jonas be promoted to first lieutenant and adjutant. He served in the terrible Atlanta campaign from May 5 to September 1, 1864, and in Hood's campaign in Tennessee. His service record describes him as "a good and faithful soldier." He apparently served at corps headquarters at the same time as his younger brother Alroy until Fenner's Battery was detached and sent to Alabama. He surrendered with Hoxton's Regiment, Smith's brigade at Citronelle, Alabama, on May 4, 1865, almost a month after Appomattox.

He was paroled at Meridian, Mississippi, on May 10. His official rank may never have risen from private, but he was considered a sergeant major and adjutant in the field by his commander.[246]

The third son of Abraham Jonas to fight for the Confederacy was Julian J. Jonas, who enlisted March 5, 1862, at New Orleans in Capt. M. A. Tarleton's company (Twiggs Guards), Crescent Regiment, for ninety days.[247] He fought with the regiment at the Battle of Shiloh, where it played an important role at the famous Hornet's Nest. Julian was promoted to fifth sergeant in June, just before his ninety days expired. On July 1, after being out of the service less than a month, he enlisted in the Orleans Light Horse Company in Tupelo, Mississippi, where the army had retired after Shiloh. He was quickly promoted to quartermaster sergeant, a month and a half after enlisting. His company was the cavalry escorts for Lieutenant Generals Leonidas Polk's and Alexander D. Stewart's corps headquarters.

It is possible, although uncertain, that Julian and his brother Edward, a Union soldier with the 50th Illinois, fought against each other at the "Hornet's Nest," so called because the bullets flew like angry hornets.[248] The Crescent Regiment made its assault at Shiloh on that portion of the line held by Brig. Gen. William H. L. Wallace, to whose division the 50th Illinois was assigned, and the division of Brig. Gen. Benjamin M. Prentiss. Edward had been detailed as an orderly to Prentiss, so he may very well have stared across the battlefield at Julian. Prentiss had lived for a while in Quincy, Illinois, in the early 1840s, so he was probably acquainted with Edward's father.

The fourth son, Sidney Alroy Jonas, left Aberdeen, Mississippi, when the war broke out.[249] He quit his job as a civil engineer working for the New Orleans, Jackson & Great Northern Railroad, enlisted in the Van Dorn Reserves, and left for Virginia. That unit afterward became Company I of the famous 11th Mississippi Volunteers.[250] When the regiment was organized at Corinth, Mississippi, Jonas's captain, W. H. Moore, was elected colonel, and Moore appointed Jonas adjutant. This appointment apparently was not legal, as military law required the detail of a lieutenant to that post. According to Jonas, his good friend Colonel Moore then "made me in the language of the opera 'Lord High Everything else.'"

Jonas served as unofficial adjutant until Harpers Ferry, where Maj. William H. C. Whiting, chief engineer of the Army of the Shenandoah, was ordered by Gen. Joseph E. Johnston to destroy the fortifications incident to evacuation. Whiting called on Colonel Moore for a civil engineer, and Moore sent Jonas. "I think I rendered good service in the work of demolition," Jonas recalled. From Harpers Ferry, Jonas's unit reinforced Gen. P. G. T. Beauregard in the Battle of First Manassas (Bull Run). "In that great battle," Jonas wrote, "Gen. Barnard E. Bee, our brigade commander who christened Jackson 'Stonewall,' was killed, and Major Whiting was promoted to succeed him and had me commissioned a Major on his staff." Jonas served as commissary of the 3d Brigade, 2d Corps, Army of the Potomac. He was appointed major and commissary of subsistence.

Gen. John Bell Hood succeeded to Whiting's command and was promoted to major general in October 1862. Jonas was transferred along with the general staff. He served on Hood's staff and served as commissary at Gettysburg. In his memoir, *Advance and Retreat,* Hood listed Jonas as among those who "rendered gallant and efficient service" in this great battle.[251] Jonas remained with Hood and went with the division from Virginia to Georgia in September 1863 for the Battle of Chickamauga. He remained in the Army of Tennessee and participated in all of its many movements and battles. By March 1864, Jonas was serving as a major and chief commissary of Hood's newly formed 2d Corps, Army of Tennessee. Hood recommended Jonas for lieutenant colonel, but apparently the appointment was never approved, as he was always referred to as "Major" or "Mage" after the war. When General Hood was promoted to temporary general and commander of the Army of Tennessee, Lt. Gen. Stephen D. Lee became commander of the 2d Corps, and Jonas was transferred to his staff. Jonas served at corps headquarters as chief commissary under Lee from the summer of 1864 until Lee surrendered with Gen. Joseph E. Johnston's forces in North Carolina in April 1865.

A fifth son of Abraham Jonas, George, may also have served the Confederacy. There are two George Jonases listed in the roll of the Confederate Guards Regiment, Louisiana Militia. One is undoubtedly George B. Jonas, the president of the Canal Bank in New Orleans and Abraham's brother, who served in Company K. The other is probably George Jonas, another son of Abraham Jonas, who served in the militia in Company B.[252]

The youngest son of Abraham Jonas fought for the Union. Edward Jonas was raised in Illinois and enlisted as a private at the age of seventeen in Company C of the Adams County Regiment, the 50th Illinois, "the blind half-hundred." He was detailed as an orderly and was captured at Shiloh (Pittsburgh Landing) while serving on the staff of Brigadier General Prentiss, who was also captured.[253] He was imprisoned at Madison, Georgia, until sent to Virginia for exchange on October 12, 1862. He rejoined the staff of General Prentiss, was promoted to lieutenant, and served as aide-de-camp during the Confederate attack on Helena, Arkansas, in July 1863. Jonas later served with Maj. Gen. Stephen A. Hurlbut and on the staff of Maj. Gen. Grenville M. Dodge. He was promoted to captain and aide-de-camp, U.S. Volunteers, in February 1865. He received a brevet promotion to major on October 13, 1865, and lieutenant colonel on June 22, 1867, for "gallant and meritorious services during the war," both to rank from March 13, 1865.[254]

The Jonas family was not the only Jewish family with officers serving in opposing armies. "I never fully realized the fratricidal character of the conflict," Charleston-born Septima Levy Collis wrote, "until I lost my idolized brother Dave [2d Lt. David Cardoza Levy Jr., 13th Louisiana Infantry killed at Murfreesboro] of the Southern Army one day, and was nursing my Northern husband [Col. Charles H. T. Collis, 114th Pennsylvania] back to life the next."[255] A captured Confederate general could not understand how Mrs. Collis, a Southern woman, could espouse the Northern cause just because she had married a Northerner. "I told him," she later recalled, "that I had only followed the example of many other Southerners— I had gone with my state, mine being the state of matrimony."[256]

The beautiful Rebecca Gratz of Philadelphia, founder of the Hebrew Sunday School Society and said to have been the inspiration for "Rebecca" in Sir Walter Scott's *Ivanhoe,* suffered a severe blow in the death of her nephew Cary Gratz. Cary was the youngest of four sons of Benjamin Gratz, Rebecca's brother and an heir to the Gratz mercantile fortune. He was one of the most distinguished citizens of Lexington, Kentucky.[257] When Benjamin's wife died, he married Anne Boswell, who had a son, Joseph ("Jo") Shelby, by her first husband. Benjamin's first wife had been Anne Boswell's aunt, so Cary and Jo were cousins as well as stepbrothers. Only one year apart, Jo and Cary were raised together as brothers. Like many Kentuckians, they moved to neighboring Missouri, and when the war came, Cary enlisted in the Union Missouri Infantry and Jo enlisted in the Missouri State Guards, Confederate Cavalry.[258] Both became captains. Jo was Joseph Orville Shelby, later a major general in the Confederate army and arguably the best cavalry general of the South.[259]

On August 10, 1861, Capt. Cary Gratz led his men under the command of Brig. Gen. Nathaniel Lyon toward Wilson's Creek, where the Federals hoped to surprise the Confederates. Capt. Jo Shelby was at Wilson's Creek with the Missouri State Guards. The Battle of Wilson Creek was an important early battle. It has been described as the Bull Run of the West, where the Southern troops prevailed but failed to pursue their victory. Soon, there "was not half a mile's distance between Capt. Cary Gratz and Capt. Jo Shelby when Lyon struck at Wilson's Creek," Daniel O'Flaherty wrote in *General Jo Shelby, The Undefeated Rebel.* "It is possible that Shelby saw the face of his stepbrother and cousin amid the smoke that rolled across the field that morning, without recognizing it. Whether he did or not will never be known; but undoubtedly he saw it afterward on the battlefield, stilled in death."[260]

The extended Levy family of Richmond was sorely divided by the war. Two sons of Jacob A. Levy served in the Confederate army: Capt. Ezekiel J. Levy and Pvt. Isaac J. Levy of the Richmond Light Infantry Blues. Jacob Levy's brother Isaac had left Richmond, and his two sons grew up in the North and served in the Union army, as did Mrs. Levy's nephew, Col. Jacob E. Hyneman. After the evacuation of Richmond, Jacob Hyneman looked up his relatives in Richmond and found a deep-seated anger.

Prominent Jewish Confederates served in many capacities in the government in addition to the armed services. Edwin Warren Moise served as a Confederate district judge in Louisiana.[261] After his retirement from the army, Samuel Hyams

Edwin DeLeon, a journalist and diplomat before the war, was asked by Jefferson Davis and Judah Benjamin to wage a Confederate propaganda campaign in France and Great Britain during the war. His efforts to win over public opinion to the Confederate cause proved futile, and he embarrassed the Confederate government in reports captured by the enemy. (DeLeon, *Belles, Beaux, and Brains of the '60s.*)

served as provost marshal in Rapides, Aroyelles, and Natchitoches. As such, he was the chief law enforcement officer in the area and charged with enforcing martial law.[262] Jacob DeCordova was collector of taxes of District 60 in Texas for the Confederacy.[263]

One interesting Confederate official was Edwin DeLeon, a member of the prominent Columbia, South Carolina, family.[264] DeLeon was living in France in 1861. Anxious to be of service to the Confederacy, DeLeon returned from Europe in the winter of 1861.[265] He traveled to New Orleans by way of Savannah on a "blockade-breaker" out of Havana and then made his way to Richmond, where he presented himself to his old friend Jefferson Davis "in sorry plight, my clothes covered with mud, and stained with travel. I was received with great cordiality and congratulation." He met with Davis for two hours, explaining the Confederacy's poor image with European governments and popular opinion. There was a crying need for an organized Confederate propaganda effort, DeLeon told the president.[266]

It took Davis some time to make a decision on Edwin DeLeon's proposal for an organized Confederate propaganda effort. When Judah Benjamin became secretary of state in March 1862, he realized the importance of such an effort. But Benjamin wanted his old friend John Slidell, then in Paris as commissioner to the French government, to head up the effort. Benjamin and Davis realized that an official diplomat would be limited in blatantly political efforts. Thus, DeLeon was chosen to lead the propaganda effort, and a dispatch was sent to Slidell which first

156 designated Slidell for the job, but a postscript from Benjamin informed Slidell of DeLeon's superior role in the matter of propaganda. "Thus," Charles P. Cullop wrote, "Benjamin planted one of the seeds of future discord between the two men." Nevertheless, this "scion of a prominent southern family, thus seemed well qualified for his new position. He would bring to the post of propaganda chief experience as a journalist, a diplomatic official, and as a traveler."[267]

Edwin DeLeon went to Europe in April 1862 as a special envoy to promote the South's cause with the French and British press, intelligentsia, and populace as well as their governments. A January 1863 letter from Benjamin to DeLeon refers to the funds sent to DeLeon as "secret service money." These accounts and vouchers were kept confidential, did not leave the department, and did not "pass through the Treasury books," Benjamin told DeLeon, and therefore DeLeon had to be scrupulous in providing receipts.[268] DeLeon states in his memoirs that at his own request, Davis and Benjamin "gave me full secret instructions, but did not label and advertise me."[269]

DeLeon returned to Europe in 1862 as a passenger once again on a "blockade-breaker," this time the *Theodora* sailing from Wilmington, North Carolina, for England. The captain gave him a cigar, and "out of bravado I lit mine; but must confess I never enjoyed my tobacco less." Chased and almost captured by a Union blockader, the captain "ground his unlit cigar to pulp between his teeth" before they made their escape.[270]

On the way to Europe, however, DeLeon made a serious error in judgment. He opened confidential diplomatic dispatches which had been entrusted to him to deliver to Confederate agents. One of the dispatches was intended only for Slidell and contained a proposal to offer the emperor of France a large bribe of cotton to break the blockade.[271]

When DeLeon arrived in England in June 1862, he went to see Lord Palmerston but was no more successful in his efforts to secure his support for the Confederacy than his predecessors had been. DeLeon was granted an interview with Palmerston through mutual friends. "Had you come to me, in any official character," the minister told DeLeon, "I must have declined seeing you . . . but as a private Southern gentleman and friend of Henry's [the grandson of Lady Palmerston], I am most happy to see and converse with you."[272]

DeLeon published a pamphlet titled "Three Letters from a South Carolinian Relating to Secession, Slavery and the Trent Case," in which he vigorously set forth the Southern position. He lambasted the views of Cassius M. Clay, Lincoln's minister to Russia, as reported in the *Times*: "Mr. Clay has drawn upon his imagination for his facts and figures," he argued, telling his readers that secession was now a "part of history; and never in the annals of mankind has such entire unanimity of sentiment and of action been manifested by any people as in the formation, deliberations, and action of the cotton States." He answered Clay's assertion that the "revolted States" could be subdued by military force by harking back to the Mexican War: "The bloody battle-fields of Mexico, where the South furnished about 45,000 and the North about 20,000 men, can attest to Southern valor and discipline. . . . The old watchword of the Jacobins in France's darkest day of blood and tears, '*Fraternite, ou la mort* (Be my brother, or I will kill you!)' is now the rallying cry of the 'free North,' not of the South, who stands with drawn sword beside her own altars." The North, he wrote, would find it impossible to subjugate twelve million people who would fight to the death against their former allies, "now their most inveterate and unscrupulous enemies."

DeLeon soon found that Henry Hotze, a Confederate commercial agent sent to London by former Secretary of State Robert M. T. Hunter in November 1861, had accomplished much of what DeLeon thought needed to be done. Hotze had already created a well-organized propaganda operation, which included publication of a pro-Confederate weekly newspaper, the *Index*.[273]

Finding Confederate efforts to influence British public opinion under way, DeLeon departed for Paris. Once settled at the Hotel du Rhin at the Place Vendôme, he wrote a pamphlet titled *La vérité sur des États Confédérés*, complete with a picture of President Davis, a positive description of slavery, and the Confederacy's argument for its place in the family of nations. He sought out members of Emperor Louis-Napoléon's entourage and made valiant efforts to influence newspapers all over France, using his contacts from his days in Egypt. He reported back that his efforts, which involved the generous use of bribes and payments to journalists, were succeeding. Imitating Hotze's success in London, DeLeon made financial arrangements with the editor of the Paris *Patrie*, which became a pro-Confederate publication until funds ran out in 1864.[274]

DeLeon's mission succeeded in the limited sense that he got the Southern message out to the French people. But it failed because the French opposed slavery and their government had no reason to become involved in the war. "It is vain to tell them," DeLeon wrote Benjamin, "how utterly impracticable [emancipation of the slaves] must be, and that the Southern people never would consent to purchase recognition [by France] at the price of such a confession of wrong doing as it would imply."[275]

DeLeon made an enemy of the powerful Slidell when Slidell was given the dispatch DeLeon had carried with the seal broken. Slidell undermined DeLeon at every turn. He refused to give him any information or introduce him to those who could help him. He wrote critical letters to his old ally, Benjamin. DeLeon reacted in kind and accused Slidell of speculating in Confederate bonds. DeLeon began to express these opinions in letters to Davis, together with descriptions of the French as money-hungry, corrupt, and a "far more mercenary race than the English."[276]

Unfortunately for DeLeon, these letters came into enemy hands in November 1863 when they were thrown overboard from the *Lady Davis*.[277] The Union officer who seized them realized their value: "This paper is interesting," he wrote Gideon Welles, "and apparently of value, as it relates to the intrigues and disappointments of the rebel emissaries abroad." When DeLeon's letters were published in the *New York Daily Tribune* on November 16, 1863, Benjamin was enraged. He had had enough of DeLeon. "As a propagandist his usefulness was over with the publication of his criticism of the French," Frank Owsley concluded, "and his criticism of Slidell made it impossible for the Confederate government to maintain them both in France."[278]

DeLeon was notified of his dismissal in February 1864. He was angry and defensive and realized he had been outmaneuvered by Benjamin, a Slidell ally. DeLeon defended his actions. He was, he told the Secretary of State, the "confidential personal friend and correspondent" of President Davis and contended he was only doing his duty in giving Davis his frank opinions. He felt that "the gallio jade is not J. W. Slidell but one of the men [that is, Benjamin!] who surround the President at home."[279] He appealed directly to the president, but Benjamin prevailed.[280]

DeLeon did not return to the Confederacy. He realized his position was indefensible and that Benjamin had far more influence with Davis than he. In June 1864 he was still in Paris. DeLeon's failure was due to Benjamin and Slidell as well as "an inordinate personal ambition" and an exaggerated view of his friendship with Davis.[281]

★ ★ ★

The South lost the flower of its young manhood in the Civil War. Its civilian population suffered grievously. It has been estimated that the Confederacy mobilized between 750,000 and 850,000 men and that 258,000 of them died on the battlefield or from disease. Another 200,000 were wounded.[282] "What had taken place," J. G. Randall and David Donald wrote, "was the collapse of a civilization."[283]

Southern Jewry also lost many a fine young officer to the cause. Hebrew officers and Israelite gentlemen were among the casualties. In addition to Col. Leon Marks, Lt. Albert Luria, Lt. Joseph Calhoun Levy, and Lt. Isaiah Jacobs, numerous other Jewish officers were killed. Capt. Madison A. Marcus of Company I, 15th Georgia, was wounded at Chickamauga and killed near Darbytown Road, Virginia, in October 1864.[284] Twenty-one-year-old 1st Lt. Will Meyer Wolf of Company G, 11th South Carolina, was killed defending Petersburg at Swift Creek, Virginia, May 9, 1864. "Although many and sad have been the casualties," his colonel wrote Wolf's father in Ridgeville, South Carolina, "few have been missed and more felt than that of your son. . . . I looked upon him as one of the most efficient, active and charming officers of his rank in my Regiment." Wolf was buried in a coffin procured by his company, and he was buried in "a patriot's grave on the battlefield upon which he fell."[285]

The Moses brothers of South Carolina. This photograph, which depicts Joshua Lazarus
Moses (*standing*), Isaac Harby Moses (*left*), and Perry Moses (*right*), was taken at the
beginning of the war. Perry is wearing his Citadel uniform. Josh Moses was killed at Fort
Blakely near Mobile. Perry Moses survived the war, was active in the Confederate Veter-
ans, and served as commandant of his camp in Sumter, South Carolina. He died in 1916.
Isaac Harby Moses served as a private in the Citadel Cadet Rangers and was known as
"Lord Shaftsbury" because of his scholarly style of writing. He saw action late in the war
and survived. As to Isaac Harby Moses, see Gary R. Baker, *Cadets in Gray* (Columbia,
S.C.: Palmetto Bookworks, 1989), 171, 199. (Courtesy of Anne F. Jennings of Charleston,
South Carolina.)

One of the Jewish community's most poignant deaths was that of Lt. Joshua Lazarus Moses. One of five Moses brothers who served the Confederacy, Joshua attended the South Carolina Military Academy (the Citadel) in the late 1850s. He enlisted in the spring of 1861 in (Palmetto Guards) Company I, 2d South Carolina, and was wounded at First Manassas. He next served in the (Wilson Light Artillery), Company C, 3d (Palmetto) Battalion, and became a first lieutenant in January 1862. In April 1865 three Moses brothers, Perry, Joshua, and Jack (Andrew Jackson) were serving in the defense of Mobile. Perry was wounded. On April 2, the Union forces surrounded Fort Blakely as Confederate forces evacuated Richmond. Josh was killed in action at Fort Blakely near Mobile on the very day Lee surrendered at Appomattox, April 9, 1865. His last words were "For God's sake, spare my men, they have surrendered."[286]

"Josh Moses the flower of our circle was killed at Blakely," Eleanor Cohen wrote in her diary. He was "a noble man, another martyr to our glorious cause."[287] He lies buried in the Confederate Rest Section of Magnolia Cemetery in Mobile. The inscription on his monument reads:

> He fired the last gun in defense of Mobile.
> He fought for the cause from its birth and
>   refusing to surrender gave his life
> to die with it.
> Oh death where is Thy Sting?[288]

In 1868, Josh Moses's mother, Octavia Harby Moses, wrote a long poem "To My Dead Son, J. L. Moses, Killed at the Battle of Blakely, Ala." She was still an unreconstructed rebel:

> Sleep sweetly in thy lonely grave,
> my good, my beautiful, my brave,
> and honored thou, and happy I
> that thus my gallant son should die.[289]

CHAPTER 4

★

Jewish Johnny Rebs

WE WILL NEVER KNOW the number of Jewish men who served in the Confederate armed forces. Neither Union nor Confederate armed services recorded men's religion; many Jewish communal records were lost or destroyed; and many Jews did not affiliate with their synagogues. Identifying Jews by their names is useful but uncertain. In the 1890s, Joseph Goldsmith, a Jewish arms contractor from Richmond, recalled a visit he and Rabbi Max Michelbacher had with Adj. Gen. Samuel Cooper to request furloughs for the Jewish boys for the 1864 High Holidays. General Cooper received his visitors kindly but declined their request for a general furlough. "Gentleman," he said, "look, we have here a roster of all our soldiers and we know, as far as possible from their names, how many of them belong to your religious denomination, and astonishing it is that we count about 10,000 to 12,000 Jews who are serving in our Army." Cooper felt that if he granted the furloughs, it would decimate certain commands in the field.[1]

There is little reason to doubt Goldsmith's recollection, although the numbers are clearly erroneous. Indeed, if the names men like Cooper *thought* were Jewish were totaled *today* from the list of more than one million Confederates, the number would be greater than twelve thousand. What was a Jewish-sounding name to nineteenth-century Americans? Most Americans believed that all German names were or could be Jewish names. For example, the Confederate secretary of the Treasury, Christopher G. Memminger, a German Protestant, was believed by many in both the North and the South to be Jewish. And there were thousands of recent German Jewish immigrants in the South. Thirty years after the war, Brig. Gen. Thomas N. Waul stated that Waul's Texas Legion contained two infantry companies with a large number of Jews. A roster of the Legion contains many German-sounding names which may or may not be Jewish, and Waul probably did not know the difference.[2]

In 1895 Simon Wolf, a prominent Jewish lawyer in Washington and national spokesman for Jewish causes, published a book, *The American Jew As Patriot, Soldier and Citizen,* in reply to anti-Semitic charges that Jews had not fought in the Civil War. He attempted to list every Jew who had served in the armed forces of the North and South as well as earlier wars. While his compilation is seriously flawed, it is the only one ever attempted. Wolf lists a total of 1,340 Jewish Confederates.[3]

Pvt. Leon Fischel was drilling with the Tensas Cavalry Company, a state militia unit from Tensas Parish, Louisiana, as early as March 15, 1861. He enlisted for the war with his company at age twenty-seven in August at Memphis. The company became Company A, Wirt Adams's Confederate Cavalry Regiment (1st Mississippi Cavalry) in October. It later became Company A, 15th Louisiana Cavalry Battalion. The battalion was still later a part of the 3d (Isaac F. Harrison's) Louisiana Cavalry. According to family tradition, Fischel was a courier or aide to Gen. Albert Sidney Johnston. (Courtesy of Bert Fischel, Dallas, Texas, and Frieda [Kline] Fischel, Vicksburg.)

Given the gargantuan nature of the task, which even today is impossible, Wolf omitted hundreds and possibly thousands of names and included some with Jewish-sounding names who were not Jews. Carolyn LeMaster points out that "well over seventy Jewish Arkansans fought on the Confederate side," as opposed to Wolf's 52.[4] Eric Brock found 78 Jewish Confederate soldiers in Shreveport, but Wolf only lists 35. Booth's *Records of Louisiana Confederate Soldiers* lists a number of Jewish Rosenthals. Wolf lists none. Using Shreveport as an example, Wolf could have omitted a thousand Jewish Confederates. He likely had less connection with the newer German, Polish, and Russian Jewish communities of Louisiana, Texas, western Tennessee, and Mississippi than he had with the eastern states, and his count is therefore low.[5]

It is possible that there were three thousand Jewish Confederate soldiers, although two thousand is a good estimate. Recordkeeping in the critical period of the 1860s in the South was unreliable. The Jewish immigrants of the 1850s and even the early 1860s (the first shot at Fort Sumter was in April 1861) were overwhelmingly single males who had come to America to seek their fortune first and marry later. These immigrants frequently lodged together or with a family. Thus, there was a disproportionately large percentage of young males in the Jewish population of 1861 compared to the general population and traditional demographics.

The typical Jewish soldier, like the typical Johnny Reb, served in the infantry. Wolf's 1895 list reflects this simple fact: Of the 1,340 men listed, 967 served in the infantry, 116 in the cavalry, 129 in the artillery, and 11 in the navy or marines.

Zalegman Phillips Moses of Sumter served as a clerk in the Navy Department. (Courtesy of Robert A. Moses, Sumter, S.C.)

(*Right*) Solomon Solomon of New Orleans. A sutler with the 14th Louisiana and the 18th Mississippi, Solomon went to Virginia to sell merchandise. Soldiers needed basic supplies, food, cigars, and other items sold by sutlers. According to his letters home, Solomon was also in combat. (Courtesy of Alice Dale Cohan of Great Neck, New York.)

Rabbi Elzas's more precise list of Jewish South Carolinians shows 117 in the infantry of a total of 167 men. Ezekiel and Lichtenstein's *The History of the Jews of Richmond* list is consistent, showing approximately 70 of 100 in the infantry, as is Brock's Shreveport list.[6] There were Jewish Johnny Rebs in every aspect of the war. They were privates in infantry units all over the South and in every major campaign. They were cooks, sharpshooters, orderlies, teamsters, and foragers. They dug trenches, cut trees, guarded prisoners, and served on picket duty.

Most of the historical data about Jewish Confederate soldiers is contained in the letters, diaries, reminiscences, and biographies of well-known, powerful, and therefore much older men, such as Judah Benjamin or Raphael Moses. Yet the average Confederate soldier was in his twenties, and this was undoubtedly true of the Jewish Johnny Rebs. We know nearly nothing about most of these young men except their names and units, but there is information on enough men in the ranks to make some generalizations.[7]

The majority enlisted in companies in their home towns with men whom they knew, often fellow Jews. The young men who enlisted in the Confederate army, like soldiers at all times and places, preferred serving in units with their

(*Left*) Pvt. Isidore Danziger was born in Paris in 1842 and came to New Orleans in 1848 with his parents. He served in the Orleans Guards Battalion at Shiloh. (Courtesy of Catherine Kahn, New Orleans.)

Sgt. Julian Levy. This portrait is reproduced from a carte de visite at the Museum of the Confederacy. Levy served in Company E, 3d Alabama Infantry. (Courtesy of the Museum of the Confederacy, Richmond, Virginia.)

friends and relatives. Jewish Johnny Rebs were no exception. There were seven Rosenbalms in Company H of the 37th Virginia. Philip Rosenheim of the Richmond militia was proud of his service and his friends: "Charley Marx and David Mittledorfer, Julius Straus, Moses Hutzler, Sam and Herman Hirsh, Simon Sycles, Gus Thalheimer, Abr. Goldback and a good many other Yuhudim all belonged to the same company, which I did." Louis Merz came to LaGrange, Georgia, from Durkheim, Bavaria, in 1853, and when the war came he enlisted in the West Point Guards, Company D, 4th Georgia, with Isaac Heyman, Jacob Friesleben, Anselm Sterne, and Levi Stern. But unlike Irish and German immigrants and their sons, who formed ethnic companies, the Jews who fought in the Civil War did not form distinctively Jewish companies. The reason is obvious: Jews fervently desired to be seen as citizens of their state and nation, not as a separate nationality. They had no desire to stand out as a group as they had been forced to do in Europe. Unlike the Irish, who also wanted to be seen as equal citizens, the Jews had been forced to live in ghettos in Europe, and true equality to them meant belonging to the gen-

Pvt. Simon Kohlman, Point Coupee Artillery (Louisiana). (Courtesy of Cecile Levine, New Orleans.)

eral population. Judaism was a religion, not a nationality, and Jews did not want to be seen as a separate nationality. Their mission, therefore, was the exact opposite of other ethnic groups, such as the Irish, who took pride in their ethnic organizations. Jewish soldiers sought to prove that they could be like everyone else. They avoided anything smacking of the ghetto. There were no Catholic or Lutheran units in the Confederate army, and, therefore, there would be no Jewish units. In addition, as a practical matter, there were few wealthy Jewish men with the military background and political influence needed to organize a company of troops. Unlike a Moise of South Carolina or a Hyams of Louisiana, the majority of Jewish Confederates were recent young immigrants. They were followers, comrades-in-arms, not leaders.[8]

The story has been told that there were two Jewish companies in the Confederate army, both from Georgia. One was supposed to have been organized at West Point, Georgia, at the start of the war and the other at Macon in 1862 for the purpose of defending Savannah.[9] But the story is not verifiable. A history of Macon Jewry by Rabbi Newton J. Friedman discounts the Macon company story, and Louis Merz, a Jewish Confederate, states that the Jewish men of West Point enlisted in the West Point Guards. Thirteen Jewish Confederates served in the Macon German Artillery, a home guard unit.

Nevertheless, there were units with many Jews in them. Because Louisiana had the largest Jewish population, it was natural that the closest thing to a "Jewish Company" was Company K, 11th Louisiana Infantry, "The Shreveport Rebels" of Caddo Parish. Doubtless, the influential Hyams family had a hand in raising the company and the regiment. Its second lieutenant was Isaac R. Hyams.[10] Other Shreveport Jews served in Companies E, F, and I, 3d Louisiana. Samuel Meyers Hyams was lieutenant colonel of the 3d Louisiana and helped raise the regiment. J. B. P. ("Pink") Hyams served with Company E and was wounded at Iuka and captured at Vicksburg, as was Pvt. David March with Company I. Julius A. Jacob served in Company F of the 3d Louisiana. The 1st Georgia contained many Jews from Savannah, including seven Cohens and four Levys.[11]

Lewis Leon's first company, the Charlotte Grays, Company C, 1st N.C. Volunteer Infantry, included 1st Lt. E. B. Cohen, Cpl. George Wolffe, and privates Jonas Engle, John R. Israel, Jacob Katz, I. C. Levi, Jacob Leopold, Sam Oppenheim, and two Wolfes in addition to Leon. His second unit, Company B, 53d North Carolina, included J. Eigenbunn, Jonas Engal, Sgt. Maj. Aaron Katz, three Markses, and Cpl. Henry Wertheim.[12] Leon spent much of his leave time with his brother Morris Leon, originally in Company I, 44th Georgia. By May 1863, the Leon brothers' regiments were assigned in brigades in Rodes's Division of Ewell's corps.[13]

The majority of Jewish Confederates served as privates or corporals in the infantry, but there were Jews in all branches of the service and in all departments. In Wolf's listing for Alabama, for example, 105 served in the infantry and 21 in the cavalry. His Arkansas list shows almost as many cavalry as infantry. Texas had 73 Jewish infantrymen and 21 cavalrymen. As the Jews went west, they apparently rode horseback more often and tended to live in small towns. One requirement of a cavalry soldier was to provide his own mount (for which he was paid sixty cents per day).[14]

Leopold Levy and his brother Sampson served in Company G, 1st Virginia Cavalry. A third brother, Solomon, was in Company C, 23d Virginia. Leopold, a native of Altenstadt, Bavaria, had married a *landsman* (fellow citizen of the same country), Rosena Hutzler of Richmond. Her parents, Abraham and Yetta Hutzler, had emigrated from Hagenbach, Bavaria. They lived in Amelia County and operated a general merchandise business. Leopold was a member of the Amelia County Troop before the war. It became part of the 1st Regiment of Cavalry commanded by Col. J. E. B. Stuart and remained in his commands as he was promoted.

Emanuel Gerst, another immigrant from Bavaria, joined Company G, 6th Virginia Cavalry Regiment. Gerst was twenty-six when he became a citizen of the United States at Williamsburg in 1845. His brother Julius was a merchant or peddler living in Richmond. Emanuel married a Gentile, Mary W. Cunningham, who owned a large plantation, "Glenmary," on the Dan River in Halifax County. Emanuel remained a lifelong member of the German synagogue in Richmond, Beth Ahabahh. He served as a sergeant in the 6th Virginia from the fall of 1861 to 1863. His unit initially served in Manassas and acted as a screen to delay the expected Federal invasion from Washington. In his forties, Gerst became ill during the war and was forced to return home, where he likely joined the home guard. He hired a substitute to replace him in the ranks.[15]

Jacob Holberg left his German homeland at age nineteen. Beginning as a peddler, he established a small store in Macon, Mississippi. In 1861 he enlisted in Company G, 1st Mississippi Cavalry, and served four years, being promoted to sergeant. According to family tradition and at least one memoir, Leon and Sam Fischel from Alsace-Lorraine served in the 15th Louisiana Cavalry Battalion. Leon Fischel was drilling with the Tensas Parish Cavalry, a state militia unit, as early as March 15, 1861. He enlisted for the war at age twenty-seven in August 1861 at Memphis. The Tensas Cavalry became Company A, Wirt Adams's Confederate Cavalry Regiment (also known as the 1st Mississippi and Wood's Confederate Cavalry) in October 1861. The company later became Company A of the 15th

Louisiana Cavalry Battalion. Leon Fischel was an aide to Gen. Albert Sidney Johnston at Shiloh, according to *Jews in Early Mississippi.* The Fischels lived in Vicksburg, and after the war Leon named his son Albert Sidney Johnston Fischel.[16]

Jews also served in artillery units such as the Washington Artillery of New Orleans. Wolf's list for Texas shows five artillerymen; five for Alabama; and eight for Arkansas. Both Edwin Kursheedt and Eugene Henry Levy served in the artillery. Marx Cohen and Gustavus A. Cohen served in James F. Hart's Company (Washington Artillery, South Carolina), initially a part of Hampton's Legion, as did five other South Carolina Cohens. Young Marx E. Cohen was killed as General Johnston made a final stand against Sherman at Bentonville. Perry Moses of Sumter served in a number of units, including Culpepper's Battery. In 1863, he was in charge of a twelve-pound Napoleon. "I fought a battery of four guns for over an hour," he wrote his mother, Octavia Harby Moses, in 1863, "giving them gun for gun."[17]

Some Jewish Johnny Rebs served in the local militia or home guards, which were organized for local self-defense. At the beginning of the war, many men who did not want to leave home or serve in the regular army joined the militia. As the war progressed and conscription instituted, the home guards consisted of those too young, too old, or too infirm to serve, as well as those exempt by virtue of their occupations or political office. Philip Rosenheim of Richmond was a youngster who served in the local militia in the summer of 1863, when Richmond was under attack. Mayor Joseph C. Mayo issued a broadsides warning of the approach of the Union army: "TO ARMS! REMEMBER NEW ORLEANS! Richmond is now in your hands. Let it not fall under the rule of another BUTLER."[18] Philip and others responded, "I, as well as all the Boys rallied to the call and we stood firmly at our Flag ready to meet the foe," he wrote his sister and brother-in-law, Amelia and Isaac Meinnart. "We were held in readiness and we drilled every afternoon from 4 til 7 in the square and our orders were at the Toll of the Bells to meet promptly at

Confederate artilleryman. (*Battles and Leaders of the Civil War.*)

our places of Rendevous." Philip was moved by the mayor's plea, as were others, "as old men with grey locks, whitened from the frosts of many winters, came forth with their muskets, ready at any moment to drive the foe from our glorious city."[19]

★　　★　　★

Like their fellow Johnny Rebs, many Jewish Confederate soldiers were anxious to enlist when the war began, believing that the war would be short and they did not want to miss it. This was a widespread Southern belief. Sen. James Chesnut told one Charlestonian "there will be no war. . . . I will drink all the blood shed in the war."[20] Albert Luria of Columbus, Georgia, enlisted within a week of the firing on Fort Sumter, as did the sons of the old established families who were expected to lead the way.[21]

Octavus S. Cohen was the son of Octavus and Henrietta Levy Cohen, members of Mikve Israel and Savannah society. (Young Octavus's mother, Henrietta, was the sister of Phoebe Yates Levy Pember and Eugenia Levy Phillips.) His father was a wealthy and distinguished commission merchant and cotton exporter with offices on Bay Street. When the war began, Octavus was a volunteer in the Savannah Artillery, a state unit, then a volunteer artillery instructor, and, finally, a volunteer aide-de-camp to Brig. Gen. William D. Smith, before he even enlisted as a private. Meanwhile, the elder Cohen and other family members attempted to secure a cadetship in the Confederate army for his son, who was only seventeen years old. (The elder Octavus served briefly as a major and quartermaster in the Georgia State Troops, but was unsuccessful in obtaining a commission in the Confederate army. G. B. Lamar wrote to George Randolph, the secretary of war, "His being an Israelite should be no objection—he has lived long in this community.")[22] Octavus Cohen's cousin, Frederick Myers, like Cohen, joined Captain Claghorn's Artillery Company (Chatham Artillery) of the 1st (Olmstead's) Georgia Infantry. He remained with it when it became Captain Weaton's Chatham Artillery Battery with the reorganization of the 1st Georgia into strictly an infantry regiment in late 1862.[23]

The Moses family had been in South Carolina for a hundred years by 1860. Their ancestors had arrived from Barbados before the Revolution, and the founding father, the colonial merchant Myer Moses, had served as a private in Bentham's Company of Militia in the American Revolution. The Moses boys from Sumter, South Carolina, joined Company D, 2d South Carolina Infantry. Henry Claremont Moses enlisted as a private on April 8, 1861; his brother Meyer B. Moses enlisted the next day; Joshua and Perry Moses both enlisted as privates on May 1. Henry was wounded at First Manassas, was discharged in October 1861, reenlisted in Company B, 15th (Lucas's) South Carolina Artillery Battalion as a lieutenant in December, and assisted in the construction of fortifications in Charleston harbor. Meyer, who rose to the rank of quartermaster sergeant, was wounded at Fredericksburg, captured at Cedar Creek, and sent to Point Lookout Prison.[24]

Leading Jewish Richmonders had been members of the Richmond Light Infantry Blues for generations. The unit participated in quelling the Gabriel slave revolt in 1800 and was called into service in 1807, when the British man-of-war *Leopard* attacked the *Chesapeake* off Norfolk. Thus, when the Richmond Blues left the city for the war on April 24, 1861, fifteen of its ninety-nine members were Jewish, including Ezekiel J. ("Zeke") Levy, fourth sergeant; Henry Adler, Bernard Goldstein, Abraham Isaacs, Thomas W. Lyon, William Lovenstein, Joseph Levy, Lewis and Calvin Myers, Hugo Plaut, Henry Rosenheim, Jacob Semon, Joseph Schoenthal, Jacob Son, and Levi Wasserman. The Blues, now in Confederate services as Company A, 46th Virginia, served in West Virginia and saw combat at Roanoke Island in February 1862. "Soon a ball [bullet] came from the Yankees," the company's record states, and "one of our boys, Mr. L. Wasserman, replied." Henry Adler was mortally wounded. Isaacs, Lyon, Levi Wasserman, and Joseph Levy were captured. They were exchanged in August. Adler, after suffering a great deal from his wounds, died at the naval hospital in Portsmouth and was buried by the Blues, who turned out en masse to honor their first private killed in the war. The Blues served throughout the war in Virginia, North Carolina, in the defense of Charleston, and later in the defense of Richmond and Petersburg. They fought to the end at Appomattox. In June 1864, the Blues' captain killed and first lieutenant wounded, Lt. Ezekiel J. Levy became commanding officer.[25]

The Richmond Grays, Company A of the 1st Virginia Volunteers (later Company G of the 12th), also contained a number of Jewish soldiers, including Ellis Ellis, Herman Hirsh, Isadore Lovenstein, Ezekiel M. Ezekiel, Philip Whitlock, and Simon Rosenfels or Rosenfield. The company was called into service in 1859, before the war began. It was ordered to Harpers Ferry to help capture John Brown, who had seized the arsenal there and taken two local planters as hostages, including Lewis Washington, a great-grandnephew of the first president. Later, it went to Charlestown, Virginia, to witness Brown's hanging. When the war began, the Grays went to Norfolk on detached service, where they became part of the 12th Virginia.[26] The Jewish boys were the sons of Jewish merchants in downtown Richmond. Rosenfield's father had a store on Seventeenth Street opposite the old market. (He later obtained a substitute and left the army.) Marx Myers was killed in action early in the war. Herman Hirsh was the son of Abram Hirsh, who kept a dry goods store on Broad Street.[27]

Myer Angle, the first president of Beth Ahabah, had six sons in the Confederate army: James Beale, Company D, 1st Virginia, who "took part in the immortal charge [presumably Pickett's charge] at Gettysburg" and was wounded; Joseph, of the Richmond Blues, who was killed in battle; Meyer, who enlisted in April 1861, in Company A, 12th Virginia, and was captured at Sayler's Creek; Montrose, who served in the Richmond Fayette Artillery, Company I, 1st Virginia Artillery; Benjamin M., in the Home Guard; and Solomon, with Company E, 23d Virginia.

The Myers brothers of Richmond. This wartime photograph shows Herman Myers (*right*), Isidore (*left*), and Marx Myers (*center*). All of the brothers served in the Confederate army. Marx served in Company A, 1st Virginia, and Company G, 12th Virginia (Richmond Grays). He was killed at Manassas. (Courtesy of the Beth Ahabah Museum and Archives, Richmond.)

Three Levy brothers of Richmond served: Leopold and Samson, with the Amelia Troop (Company G) of the 1st Virginia Cavalry, and Solomon, who died of wounds, in Company C, 23d Virginia.[28]

Eugene Henry Levy of New Orleans was born in Grand Gulf, Mississippi, in 1840. His father, like many acculturated Louisiana Jews, was born in Charleston and moved first to Mississippi and then to Louisiana. His ancestors were English Sephardim, and one was a Captain Lazarus, who fought in the American Revolution. Eugene's mother was a Marks from Philadelphia. Eugene was quite literate and graduated from the University of Louisiana with honors. The Levys had three sons who fought for the Confederacy: Eugene Henry Levy in Company C, 1st Louisiana Battalion (Rightor's) and the Donaldsonville Artillery; Julian H. "Doc"

Levy in the Donaldsonville Artillery; and Joseph Calhoun Levy in Company C, 1st
Louisiana Battalion, then in the 1st Louisiana Regulars (Strawbridge's), who was
killed at Shiloh.[29]

Young Jewish boys, like youths throughout the South, attempted to enlist
even if they were too young to serve. Fifteen-year-old Isaac Cohen of Richmond
enlisted one evening, and, early the next morning, his father found his new uniform and musket and promptly returned them to the recruiting officer. Cohen said
later he had the shortest term of service on record: two hours and a half. Simon
Sycle of Richmond enlisted, but he was underage and his father withdrew him
from the army. On his way back to school in Baltimore, he was arrested as a spy
and sent to prison. Augustus Smith enlisted upon the last call of the authorities in
1865 at the age of sixteen.[30]

Moses Jacob Ezekiel, a Sephardic Jew, the fifth of fourteen children of modest merchant parents, grew up in a Richmond neighborhood where whites and
blacks and Jews and Christians "were all jumbled together." When the war began,
young thirteen-year-old Moses, along with all the little boys in Richmond, "howled
and jumped for joy." He was so enthusiastic that he begged his grandparents to let
him go to the Virginia Military Institute (VMI) so that he could somehow get into
the war. "Mose" Ezekiel was one of the first Jewish cadets to attend VMI. A fellow
cadet said that Ezekiel "never could chisel himself into a pretty soldier . . . he looked
like a tin soldier that had been broken in the middle and mended with sealing wax.
There was but one worse soldier than myself in the world, and that was Ezekiel."[31]

According to Charles W. Joyner, the Jews of Georgetown, South Carolina,
contributed a number of men to Confederate service during the Civil War. The
Emanuel family sent at least four men into the service. Maj. W. P. Emanuel commanded the 12th Cavalry Battalion, which later formed part of the 4th S.C. Cavalry. Edwin C. Emanuel, a butcher and sergeant in Company A, 10th S.C. Infantry,
died of fever in Oxford, Mississippi, in the summer of 1862. His nephew, eighteen-
year-old Pvt. Washington Emanuel, served in the same company and was wounded
in the Battle of Atlanta in the summer of 1864. His arm was amputated and he
later died. Solomon ("Sol") Emanuel, Washington's older brother, also enlisted in
the same company and served throughout the war as a private in the infantry and
as clerk to Lt. Col. Cornelius Irvine Walker. He fought at Corinth, Mississippi, in
1862 after Beauregard's retreat from Shiloh, in the Kentucky and Tennessee
(Murfreesboro, Chickamauga, Missionary Ridge) campaigns and in the bloody
battles around Atlanta in 1864. He was admitted to the hospital in January 1865,
but when his regiment was ordered back east to resist Sherman's march through
his native state, "Sol hobbled out and took his place in ranks."[32]

Haiman Kaminski immigrated to Charleston from Posen, Prussia, in 1854 at
the age of fifteen and moved to Conwayboro, near Georgetown, two years later. He
was working as a clerk in Elkan Baum's store when the war began. Like many of

172   the men of the Georgetown area, Kaminski enlisted in the 10th South Carolina in the spring of 1861. He was promoted to sergeant and served as a commissary until his surrender at Greensboro. Sol Emanuel, who would go into business with Kaminski after the war, was clerking in his father's dry goods and general merchandise business when the war came.[33]

Young German Jewish recruits swelled the Confederate ranks, as did a substantial number of Polish and Eastern European Jews as well. Marcus Baum, a native of Schwersenz, Prussia, moved to Camden, South Carolina, just before the war and enlisted in Company E, 2d South Carolina, in July 1861, although as a foreigner he was exempt from military service. Two Oppenheim brothers, Edwin and Henry H., also enlisted in Company K, 2d South Carolina on May 12, 1861. They would later serve along with Sgt. Julius H. Oppenheim in Company B, 17th S.C. Cavalry Battalion. Levi Wasserman, a clerk in Isaac Robinson's store in Petersburg before the war, was the first member of the Richmond Light Infantry Blues to fire a shot in battle. The Jews of Petersburg, Virginia, twenty-one miles south of Richmond, enlisted many in the local Petersburg Grays, 12th Virginia. Virtually all of these men were immigrants from either England or one of the German states. Mark E. Kull, whose father, Jacob, immigrated from Germany, enlisted as a private within days of the firing on Fort Sumter. Aaron S. and Isadore Reinach, H. Seligman, and Uriah Feibelman served in the Grays. Aaron Kadden of Petersburg served in the 10th Virginia Cavalry; Alexander Myers was a private in the Confederate Guards, 9th Virginia, Pickett's division, Longstreet's corps; Simon Frankenthall and Jonas Weinburg served in Company B, 1st Virginia.[34]

The smaller communities of Virginia also furnished German Jewish immigrants to the Confederate cause. Max Guggenheimer, born in Bavaria, arrived in Lynchburg in Southwest Virginia in 1856 to study English and to visit his relatives who had settled there in 1838. He stayed, and at the age of nineteen enlisted in Company G, 11th Virginia. A cousin, Maurice Guggenheimer, served in the 2d Virginia Cavalry throughout the war. Henry Gintzberger, a peddler and a recent immigrant, arrived in Salem, Virginia, in 1860. He enlisted in the Salem Flying Artillery, which was the 1st Company A, 9th Virginia.[35] Twenty years old, Isaac Hirsh came to Fredericksburg, Virginia, in 1860. His parents had brought the family to America from Baden in 1856. They lived in New Haven and Baltimore before moving to Spotsylvania County just before the war started. In May, Isaac joined Company A, 30th Virginia and saw action.[36]

Jews from small towns in Texas, Arkansas, and Mississippi, mostly German and Polish immigrants, were no less patriotic than their eastern co-religionists and flocked to the Confederate banner. Mississippian Max Frauenthal enlisted as a private in Company A, 16th Mississippi, as a drummer. He was joined by Jews from Natchez and Woodville, which was called "Little Jerusalem" because of its large Jewish population. Solomon and Mike Loeb joined the Wilkinson Rifles (Company

K, 16th Mississippi). Joseph Kohn and F. Rosenberg joined the Wilkinson Guards (Company D, 38th Mississippi), and brothers John Cline and Henry Cline joined the Hurricane Rifles (Company E, 21st Mississippi). The smallest towns of Mississippi contributed Jewish Confederates. Sampson Weiner from Heinsheim, Baden, married a fellow passenger Caroline Forscheimer aboard the boat bringing them to America in 1852. They settled in Canton. Weiner served in Company A, 1st Mississippi Cavalry and had several horses shot out from under him, according to family legend. In the 1850s Ferdinand Krauss from Leimersheim, Rhein Pfalz, Germany, settled in Fayette, halfway between Natchez and Port Gibson. He served in Claiborne Guards, Company H, 12th Mississippi, and was wounded at Seven Pines. Isadore Moise of Portigny served in Company A, 16th Mississippi, with Max Frauenthal. Emanuel Levy of Buchsweiler joined Company A, 14th Mississippi Partisan Rangers Cavalry Battalion. Both were from Alsace-Lorraine and immigrated to Summit, Mississippi. They both served as privates.[37]

The same was true of the German Jewish immigrants to Arkansas. There were nearly two hundred Jewish merchants in the state in 1860. More than a third of them served the Confederacy. David Felsenthal of Camden, Arkansas, closed his business, lost his investment, and enlisted in Captain Purifoy's Company B, 15th (Johnson's) Arkansas. He was captured at Fort Donelson. Brothers Ferdinand, Isaac, and David Gates of Hickory Plains joined the army. Isaac Gates, like many other Jewish Confederates, served as a quartermaster and commissary. Isaac was wounded at Chattanooga and Murfreesboro. Other brothers from Arkansas, David and Samuel Bluthenthal, served in the Company K, 9th Arkansas, and Company G, 3d Arkansas Cavalry, respectively. Three Gans brothers—Morris, Jacob, and Simon—fought, as did Peter, Jacob, and Pool Cohen. Isaac Hirst of Pocahontas fought in numerous battles in Company A, 7th Arkansas, and was badly wounded in 1864. According to Dr. Junius N. Bragg, Sam Winter of Camden, who was in Company K, 6th Arkansas, was "one of the bravest Confederate soldiers I ever knew. He would walk without hesitation to the mouth of a cannon if ordered to do so." At least two Arkansas Jewish Confederates were killed: Isaac Burgauer in 1863 and Julius H. Levy of Company A, 6th Arkansas at Shiloh.[38] According to Eli Evans, Pvt. Isaac Gleitzman received the Cross of Honor for "conspicuous gallantry in the field," but he was prouder of never having eaten any nonkosher food, or "trefa."[39]

Benedict ("Ben") Oppenheimer from Tennessee had the distinction of being one of a few deaf men who enlisted in either army. According to family tradition, Oppenheimer was born in 1827 and was deaf from the age of two as a result of scarlet fever. His father died, and he and his mother immigrated from a small town in Alsace-Lorraine to Cincinnati. Ben's mother died, and he went to live with his brother in Trenton, Tennessee. When the war began, young Ben tried to enlist in various Confederate units, but they would not have him because of his disability.

174   Ben then ran away from home to join the army and was "a gallant soldier in the Confederate Army and was in 11 separate engagements."[40] Oppenheimer's great-niece recalled that he used to tell her in sign language or with pencil and paper some of his many experiences. The only way he would know that the enemy cannons were firing was when he would see a comrade on his right or left fall from his horse or see the horse shot out from under him. He told of how the company always picked him to fire the cannon because he was deaf anyway and it did not hurt his ears.[41]

Jacob Samuels of Fort Worth enlisted in June 1861 in a mounted company of the Texas State Troops, the Tarrant County Rifles. He later served in Capt. J. C. Terrell's Company F, Waller's 13th Battalion, Texas Cavalry. His friends Bero Berliner and John S. Hirchfield joined the same company. Samuels was born in Warsaw in 1836, a subject of the Russian czar and a resident of a ghetto where he and fellow Jews were strictly controlled by a hostile government. He declined the invitation to remain a third-class citizen of Russian Poland and left for America in 1847 at the age of eleven. He likely arrived in New Orleans, like many a young Jewish immigrant with only the clothes on his back, willing to risk everything for a chance to breathe the free air of America. He worked as a peddler and, at some point in the 1850s, moved to Fort Worth, Texas, where he went into general merchandising with Bero B. Berliner.[42]

Samuels's company saw action in Louisiana throughout 1862, defending Louisiana and east Texas from the invading Union army and navy. In April 1863 the Confederates under Brig. Gen. Alfred Mouton successfully defended Fort Bisland against the Union army near Morganza, Louisiana. In June, Samuels and his comrades were engaged in vicious combat in and around Bayou Teche near Pattersonville to the west of Brashear City. Samuels was with Maj. Hannibal H. Boone when he was shot and lost his arm. Samuels saw action at the Battles of Mansfield and Pleasant Hill in April 1864, where Maj. Gen. Richard Taylor's troops held back the Union advance.[43]

Shreveport, Louisiana, in 1860 is a striking portrait of the Southern Jewish immigrant's contribution to Confederate military service. Eric J. Brock has estimated that three hundred Jews lived in Shreveport in 1860 and that seventy-eight served in the Confederate armed forces. Almost all of them were recent immigrants who arrived in Louisiana in the 1850s. Most, like Marx Baer, were born in one of the German states or Alsace-Lorraine. David March of Company I, 3d Louisiana, was from Hechingen; Pvt. Henry Simon, Company K, 11th Louisiana, from Sausenheim, Bavaria; Abraham Sour of Company A, 8th Louisiana Cavalry, Leona, Germany; Marx Blum of the Donaldsonville Artillery, Sam and Nathan Weil, and the Dreyfusses from Alsace. Some were from Poland: Jack Citron, Company I, 3d Louisiana, from Koval; and Jacob Gall, Company D, 19th Louisiana, from Meschisko. And some were from France: Marx Israel of Company 5, 3d

Pvt. Lewis Leon as an older man. Leon was a German immigrant whose parents and a few siblings lived in New York City. He and his brother Morris lived in the South and fought for the Confederacy. Leon first enlisted in the 1st North Carolina Vounteers and later became a sharpshooter in the 53d North Carolina State Troops. He fought throughout the war with the Army of Northern Virginia and was captured at the Wilderness. (Author's collection, *Diary of a Tar Heel Confederate*, 1913.)

Regiment, European Brigade, Onepie, near Metz; and Gottlieb Blum of the Company F, 3d Louisiana, Hatte, Elsas.[44]

The wartime experiences of Jewish Johnny Rebs are illustrated by three men: Lewis Leon of Charlotte, North Carolina; Isaac Hermann of Washington County, Georgia; and Eugene Henry Levy of New Orleans. Leon and Hermann were immigrants. Leon had emigrated from one of the German states with his family. His father was a peddler in New York City, and Lewis and his brother Morris had left their parents, brothers, sisters, and their home on Norfolk Street on the Lower East Side in the late 1850s to seek their fortunes in the South. Lewis went to Charlotte and Morris to Georgia. Lewis worked as a clerk in a dry goods store. "Ike" Hermann had just come to America in 1859 from France. He worked in a store in rural Georgia. Eugene Henry Levy was an acculturated Sephardic Jew from Louisiana whose South Carolina ancestors included at least one Revolutionary War soldier and a grandfather who came to Charleston from Jamaica in the early 1800s.[45]

Lewis Leon was a nineteen-year-old clerk, five feet and four and a half inches tall, with a ruddy complexion and dark eyes. He enlisted on April 20, 1861, in Raleigh, and his company, the Charlotte Grays, seized the Branch Mint in Charlotte the same day. The Grays were mustered into state service for six months as Company C of the 1st N.C. Volunteer Infantry in May. The regiment was in the thick of the fighting at the first major engagement of the war at Big Bethel, Virginia, on June 10. In August, they were mustered into Confederate service at Ship Point, Virginia, for the balance of their six-month enlistment.[46]

Leon described his first months in the Confederate army in much the same way as a young college student might describe his first six months away from home: travel, girls, bad food, and some unpleasant work. Like all Johnny Rebs, Leon quickly discovered that war was unglamorous. His first tasks were digging ditches and cutting down trees, neither of which he could do very well. "Why, of course, I never thought that this was work for soldiers to do, but we had to do it. . . . I know I never had a pick or a shovel in my hand to work with in my life." While Leon was attempting to cut down a tree, his lieutenant, "seeing how nice I was marking it," asked him what he had done before becoming a soldier. "I told him I was a clerk in a dry-goods store. He said he thought so from the way I was cutting timber." Leon was then told to bring buckets of water to the men who could cut. But he quickly learned why digging breastworks was important: "If it had not been for them many of us would not be here now." Even though they had to sleep in horse stables, Leon and his comrades did not care. "They didn't even give us a looking-glass," he joked.[47]

Leon remained with his company for the six months, but after it returned to Charlotte to be mustered out; he did not rejoin when it was reorganized in the 11th North Carolina State Troops. Instead, five months later, on April 24, 1862, now twenty years old, he joined Company B, 53d North Carolina State Troops, for the duration of the war. His brother Morris enlisted on March 4, 1862, at Madison, Georgia, "for three years or the war." His unit, the 44th Georgia, arrived in Virginia just after the Battle of Seven Pines in the summer of 1862.[48]

Leon's regiment saw action all around North Carolina: at the Battle of Deep Gully, Weldon, and the Siege of Washington, North Carolina. He served in Virginia in the early defenses around Richmond and Petersburg; at Drewry's Bluff, Suffolk, Smithfield, the Blue Ridge, Warrington Springs, and Bristoe Station; and at Beverly Ford in support of J. E. B. Stuart. His unit was assigned to Daniel's brigade from 1862 to 1864 and Grimes's from 1864 to surrender. The 53d, while Leon was present, was with Lee at Gettysburg, the retreat from Pennsylvania, Mine Run, and the Wilderness.[49]

Even in the early days of the war, Pvt. Lewis Leon heard the "long roll"—the drumbeat for soldiers to wake up at 2 or 3 a.m.—fell into line at daybreak, got into the line of battle, and fought for hours, even days, in the sweltering heat and freezing cold. He and his comrades were shelled by Union artillery for days and weeks at a time. He volunteered for perilous service: going near the Yankee line as a scout and volunteering as a sharpshooter or as a skirmisher, whose job it was to go in the front of the line of infantry in battle and reconnoiter and "engage the enemy until a general engagement, then we fall in line with [the] balance of the army." Leon

Confederate sharpshooter. (*Battles and Leaders of the Civil War.*)

charged with his fellow skirmishers, giving the famous Rebel yell. He became a proficient marksman. "I hit a bull's-eye to-day," he noted proudly in April 1864.[50]

Johnny Rebs idolized Robert E. Lee, and Jewish boys were no exception. Lewis Leon referred to him reverently as "our father." He saw a lot of Lee as a soldier in the Army of Northern Virginia. He was concerned about Lee's health in May 1863. At a review, he observed a great change in Lee's appearance from the last time he saw him at Yorktown in 1861. "Then his hair was black. Now he is a gray-headed old man." He admired Lee's courage: "our father, Lee, was scarcely ever out of sight when there was danger. We could not feel gloomy when we saw his old gray head uncovered as he would pass us on the march, or be with us in a fight. I care not how weary or hungry we were, when we saw him we gave that Rebel yell, and hunger and wounds would be forgotten." On another occasion on a freezing cold winter day, when Leon was working in a sawmill, he and his detail saw Lee ride by with his daughter. Soon after a courier appeared and gave the men some woolen socks and gloves from the general's daughter. Leon believed Lee to be a very great general. The Union won, in his view, only because of greater resources and more men. "If General Lee only had half their men," he wrote in May 1864, "and those men were rebels, we would go to Washington in two weeks."[51] Like many Southerners, particularly those in the army, Pvt. Simon Mayer, even though fighting in the Army of Tennessee, believed in April 1864 that the South would win the war because of Lee's leadership. "I doubt not but that ere this reaches you, the victorious shouts of Lee's invincible heroes will be reverberated throughout the length & breadth of our land." He looked forward to the next battle, which he and his comrades believed would be "a second Chickamauga. . . . All looks bright & glowing, and soon we hope to be gathered under 'our vine & fig tree' in Peace, Happiness, & Independence."[52]

Lack of food was one of a Confederate soldier's biggest problems, and Leon's diary records the obtaining of food as a signal event. Ladies were always feeding Leon and his friends on the highways. In December 1862 he traveled by railroad to Goldsboro. "The ladies on the road, especially those at Wilson, were very kind to us. They gave us plenty to eat, which we were very much in need of." Leon, Henry Wortheim, and the Katz brothers all received packages of food from home, which were very much appreciated by the men. One Eigenbrun "came to see us to-day from home," Leon recalled, "and brought me a splendid cake from Miss Clara Phile." The Confederates lived better on the march up North than they did in the South. On the march from Virginia through Maryland and Pennsylvania to Gettysburg during June 1863, Leon ate better than he had in a long time. "So far we have lived very good in the enemy's country."[53]

But, as the war progressed, food became scarce. As early as February 1863, Leon complained that "the worst of it is we have no rations." Coffee could not be had at any price. When Leon made coffee, he meant "Confederate coffee— parched corn—that is our coffee." Like many a Johnny Reb, Leon adjusted to the deplorable conditions. "Ate our corn bread and bacon," he wrote in February 1863, "and retired to our couches and slept as good if not better than Abe Lincoln." In May, he was marching and countermarching in all kinds of weather "and very often without anything to eat." As with most Confederate soldiers, his new uniform was long gone by 1863. By June he described his misery and his comrades as "poor, ragged rebels."[54]

Disease, exposure, the strain of war, and accidents killed far more Confederates than did the enemy. Bell Wiley quotes a Tar Heel private: "they hev Been 11 Died with the fever in Co A since we left kinston and 2 died that was wounded so you now See that these Big Battles is not as Bad as the fever." Lewis Leon's experience was the same. He saw a naval officer's leg cut off in a railroad accident in which he and his friend Henry Wortheim were also injured. Leon's friend Henry Wortheim got sick during the war, possibly from constant exposure to rain and cold without sufficient shelter or food. On February 25, 1863, Leon noted: "Henry Wortheim was sent home on a sick furlough, as he is very bad off." He soon died. Leon was a tough young man, but he too suffered from the cold, exposure, and cut-up feet, as did many other Jewish Confederates. By September 1862, after Antietam, Ansel Sterne of the West Point Guards wrote from Winchester, Virginia, "The army is in poor condition, half naked and bare footed. My own clothes and shoes are in pieces and there is no chance of getting them replaced."[55]

Leon and his friends, all young men in their twenties, were interested in the girls they met along the way, especially the young ladies who worked in the factories around Petersburg, where his regiment spent much of the war. His diary, published in 1913, gives no details of his amorous adventures, but there certainly were some. Leon, Aaron Katz, Mike Etlinger, and Henry Wortheim knew their way around Petersburg. On June 21, 1862, "We reached Petersburg, Va., this morning at half-past two, and had barely laid down with a brick wall for my pillow when breakfast was announced . . . I ran the blockade [that is, sneaked away from camp without permission] with Katz." Leon's and Katz's behavior must not have been too bad. Katz was promoted to sergeant major. In July he and his friends "return[ed] to our factory girls again—all O.K., you bet." In April 1863 Leon was detailed to go to Wilson, North Carolina, to pick up the baggage for his officers. At Rocky Mount, he "[s]aw some fun with a girl and an old woman. The young one had stole a petticoat from the old one, and was compelled to take it off and return it in the presence of at least fifty men."[56]

Leon was not alone in looking for female companionship. Jacob Samuels from Texas went into Galveston with his captain and fellow soldiers in the winter of 1863–64, where they were accosted on the street by a bevy of beautiful girls who importuned the soldiers to buy tickets to a lottery to benefit war widows and orphans. Samuels told his captain that if the "dice were all right the law of gravitation would make the result, which would be providential." They won a number of necklaces, which they gave their new female acquaintances, spent two more days "in riots most uncouth," but justified their behavior because they were bachelors. Many a Jewish soldier found himself in a city or town with Jewish families and Jewish daughters, and occasional marriages resulted. It was only natural that the young men would seek out eligible girls. Others, like Harris Levin of the 2d Virginia Reserves, sought out prostitutes. "Several nights a week our lovely post [at Drewry's Bluff]," he wrote in 1864, "is visited by two sisters who are rentable for riding."[57]

Like most Confederate soldiers, Leon liked his whiskey. "Katz and myself went to Petersburg to-day," he wrote in December 1862. "We met with friends, and the consequence you can imagine. The headache we had next day was caused by too much whiskey."[58]

His brigade was transferred to General Lee's Army of Northern Virginia in May 1863. Leon marched to Gettysburg with the 53d North Carolina, a regiment in Daniel's brigade, Army of Northern Virginia. In Middleburg, the people were downhearted and "showed their hatred to us by their glum looks and silence." The townspeople shut their doors in the men's faces, including Leon's, but the Confederates proved to the Pennsylvanians that they were not "wild animals nor thieves" and procured the supplies they needed. Leon told the townspeople he dealt with that Lee had given the men strict orders not to burn the towns through which they passed.[59]

Leon's regiment arrived at Gettysburg at 1 p.m. on July 1 and met the enemy one mile south of town "and a little to the left of the Lutheran Seminary [Seminary Ridge]. We then advanced to the enemy's line of battle in double quick time. We had not gotten more than 50 paces when Norman of our company fell dead by my side. Katz was going to pick him up. I stopped him, as it is strictly forbidden for anyone to help take the dead or wounded off the field except the ambulance corps." Leon's company was now in the fight in earnest in the push to Seminary Ridge as a part of Daniel's brigade. Two of his company's lieutenants were wounded. In a fight that lasted four hours, Company B took heavy losses. The Yankees also suffered terrible losses, and Leon's company took Union prisoners. One soldier whom Leon took as a prisoner could not speak English. He asked Leon in German, "Will

I get my pay in prison?" Leon recalled that Maj. James J. Iredell, his acting regimental commander, shook his hand and complimented him for his actions.[60]

On the second day at Gettysburg, Leon's regiment was in reserve until dark but supported a battery of artillery all day. "We lost several killed and wounded, although we had no chance to fire—only lay by a battery of artillery and be shot at." At dark his division was sent into combat under terrific shelling. "Still, it was certainly a beautiful sight," he wrote. "It being dark, we could see the cannon vomit forth fire." His unit was pinned down near a fence; his friend Aaron Katz was wounded by a piece of a shell that struck him in the side, and he was sent to the rear. On the third day, July 3, Leon's brigade under General Daniel was ordered up Culp's Hill under very heavy fire. "We were on the brow of one hill, the enemy on the brow of another. We charged on them several times, but, of course, running down our hill, and then to get to them was impossible, and every time we attempted it we came back leaving some of our comrades behind." Leon's gun became so hot that the ramrod would not come out, so he picked up a gun from the ground. For a time, his regiment was trapped on the field, and the two couriers sent for help were killed. They eventually retreated safely. Pickett's charge was Lee's answer to these reverses.[61]

Leon believed that his brigade, the strongest in his division before the battle, had lost the most men. "I know that our company went in the fight with 60 men. When we left Culps Hill there were 16 of us that answered to the roll call." There had been 12 sharpshooters in his company. Now there were two, including Leon. Eleven men in Company B were killed at Gettysburg; twenty-six were wounded, three of whom would later die. Nine were taken prisoner besides the wounded. All three lieutenants were wounded and taken prisoner. "This day none will forget, that participated in the fight. It was truly awful how fast, how very fast, did our poor boys fall by our sides—almost as fast as the leaves that fell as cannon and musket balls hit them, as they flew on their deadly errand." Leon saw many men killed, heads shot off, men cut in two or their legs severed. He heard dying men begging for water or begging their comrades for "God's sake" to kill them. Like all the soldiers who fought at Gettysburg, Leon remembered the stench of rotting corpses, some of which were black and bloated. Leon helped bury the dead.[62]

Leon, his brother Morris, and his friend Aaron Katz all survived, but Katz was taken prisoner. At the time, Leon believed the great battle had been a draw. Each side, he thought, lost an equal number of men, and the South took more prisoners. "An army that has gained a great victory," he wrote, "follows it up while its enemy is badly crippled; but Meade, their commander, knows he has had as much as he gave, at least, if not more." Actually, Lee's army lost 3,903 men as opposed to Meade's 3,155. There were 18,735 Confederates and 14,529 Yankees wounded. The battle was a great victory for the North because Lee's charmed army had failed in its objective, to bring the war to Northern soil and rout the

Union army. Leon participated in the sad retreat from Pennsylvania in the rain and mud. "One consolation we have got," he noted humorously, "it is raining so hard that the mud is washed off our clothing." He would never forget Gettysburg. "We had hard marching, hard fighting, suffered hunger and privation, but our general officers were always with us."[63]

By July 13, he was crossing the Potomac. "The river was up to my chin, and very swift." He carried his cartridge box around his neck to keep the powder dry. Leon's friend J. Engle got stuck in the mud until some of the boys pulled him out. "We went six miles further, and I honestly believe more of us were asleep on our night's march than awake." Having reached Virginia, he wrote, "We are now, thank, God, on Confederate soil, but oh, how many of our dear comrades have we left behind. We can never forget this campaign."[64]

Leon spent the rest of the summer in Virginia, reaching Orange Court House on August 1. His regiment continued to see hard service in the Bristoe and Mine Run Campaigns. Leon was a sharpshooter, which required him to be at the forefront of many battles, sometimes spending a whole day in a pit with two other sharpshooters firing continually at the enemy. He recalled Mine Run as "cold, sleety, disagreeable weather," and the soldiers could not even make large fires, as it would be "a sure target for the Yankees." As the war dragged on, the early chores like cutting timber seemed like a vacation. By 1864 Leon's company, veterans of hard combat, were put to work for a time running two sawmills to make wooden planks for roads.[65]

In March 1864, when the men were at a dress parade, an order was read stating that all troops in the army would be held until the end of the war. It did not faze Leon. "This was nothing of importance to us," he wrote ,"as we enlisted for that time." Actually, on that cold March day he took more interest in a snowball fight, first between his regiment and the 43d North Carolina and then with Battle's brigade. "It was lots of fun."[66]

Letters were a very important part of the life of Confederate soldiers. "Mail call was the brightest part of a soldier's day—*if* he received a letter from home," wrote James McPherson. In April 1864, having not heard from his family up North since the war began, Leon asked a Yankee picket to put a personal advertisement in a New York newspaper to let them know that he and brother Morris were well: "To A. [Abraham] Leon or any of my relatives: Let me hear from you all through Richmond Enquirer, and let me know your address. Have not heard from you since August, 1862. Morris and myself are both well. Lewis Leon."[67]

Lewis Leon was captured at the Battle of the Wilderness, but not before he helped capture a Union sharpshooter who had positioned himself high up in a tree and was doing considerable damage to the Confederate advance with his long-range rifle. Col. James T. Morehead relates, in his history of the regiment, that "Private Leon, of Company B (Mecklenburg), concluded that this thing would have to stop, and taking advantage of every knoll, hollow, and stump, he crawled near enough for his rifle to reach, took a pop at this disturber of the peace, and he came tumbling down." Leon then discovered the sniper to be a Canadian Indian, and, "clutching his scalplock, dragged him to our line of sharpshooters." As General Daniel attempted to storm a Federal artillery battery near the Lacy House, Leon and five of his fellow sharpshooters had gotten too far in advance of their regiment. They mixed in with Gen. John Brown Gordon's men and were captured as they were moving to the right to rejoin the regiment.[68]

Now a prisoner of war, he was first sent to a battlefield collection point seven miles west of Fredericksburg, where he was kept penned up with hundreds of other Confederate prisoners for three days before moving to the main collection point at Belle Plain for three days. From there he was sent to the Point Lookout, Maryland, prisoner of war camp. His friend Engle was captured the day after he was. "They think I was killed, so does my brother, but as yet the bullet has not done its last work for your humble servant." At Point Lookout, he saw some of the men captured almost a year before at Gettysburg. On July 25 he was transferred to the notorious Elmira, New York, prison.[69]

A week after his capture and still at the battlefield collection point near Fredericksburg, Leon was surprised to see his brother Morris among the prisoners. Doles's brigade had been overrun at Spotsylvania the day before, and Morris was captured after having "sent two of the enemy to their long home with his bayonet." The brothers were separated at Belle Plain. Morris was sent to Fort Delaware, where he took the oath of allegiance on February 13, 1865, and then returned South to Augusta, Georgia.[70]

Lewis Leon faced an ordeal while at Point Lookout that was much more difficult than being in combat. He and his fellow prisoners were guarded by "negro troops, who are as mean as hell." Jewish Johnny Rebs were no more fond of African American soldiers than their Christian comrades. When Lewis Leon was captured, he noted the "terrible cursing" and abuse the Confederate prisoners took from black soldiers. One group hollered "Fort Pillow" at his group, referring to the alleged massacre of black soldiers at Fort Pillow, Kentucky, in April 1864. "I am only sorry that this brigade of negroes was not there, then they certainly would not curse us now," Leon concluded. On another occasion, Leon was delighted that one black guard accidentally killed another guard while playing with his gun and bayonet. A fellow prisoner was shot when he crossed the forbidden "Dead Line," a boundary within the perimeter fence that a prisoner could not cross. He got "five crackers with worms, a small piece of pork and coffee for breakfast and for dinner four crackers, a quarter of a pound of mule meat, and a cup of bean soup."[71]

By May 25 his friend Engle received a letter from his father, who told him they had seen Leon's parents in New York and he would hear from them soon. "This is the first time that I have heard about my parents since the commencement of the war," Leon wrote in his diary. "Thank God, my parents, as well as my sisters and brothers, are well." (They, of course, were civilians in New York, and Leon had just emerged from the Wilderness.) His family sent a box of "eatables, one or two shirts, and one pair of pants." He endured the monotony of prison life for a year until Lee surrendered in April 1865. Somehow he survived the bitter cold at Elmira, the frequent outbreaks of smallpox, and eating rats (at twenty-five cents each) to supplement his diet.[72]

According to Leon's diary, on the morning of April 12, 1865, the men learned that Lee had surrendered. Four hundred men took the "cursed oath" and were transported to wherever they wanted to go. He also told Union authorities that he had family in New York, that he was drafted, when in fact he volunteered, and that he had given himself up voluntarily rather than having been captured. These statements were obviously made in order to obtain a speedier release from a deadly prisoner of war camp. Leon went to New York City, where he was reunited with his parents and siblings, whom he had not seen for seven years. He returned to Charlotte after the war was over.[73]

Ike Hermann's war experiences were very different from Leon's. Leon was a modest soldier who did his duty, obeyed orders, fought valiantly, endured hardships without complaint, and served in hard combat throughout the war. Hermann was boastful, a soldier who sometimes did his duty, often disobeyed orders, was regularly disciplined and punished, was in and out of combat, and was out on medical disability a great deal. Like Leon, however, he too was a typical Johnny Reb.

When war came, the men of Washington County flocked to the Washington Rifles, 1st (Ramsey's) Georgia Infantry, including "Ike" Hermann, who joined in the summer of 1861. The boys met at the rural railroad station. "We were all in high spirits on the day of our departure," he recalled years later. "The people of the neighborhood assembled to wish us Godspeed and a safe return. It was a lovely day and patriotism ran high. We promised a satisfactory result as soldiers of the Confederate States of America."[74]

From Davisboro, Georgia, the group of twenty-one men went to Richmond, where they were met by President Davis, "who came to shake hands with the 'boys in gray,' and speak words of encouragement." Hermann's unit participated in Robert E. Lee's disastrous Cheat Mountain campaign in western Virginia in July 1861, and General Jackson's Romney campaign in January 1862. The 1st Georgia disbanded in March 1862, and Hermann enlisted in Captain Martin's Company of Light Artillery in the fall of 1862. He served at Fort McAllister on the Ogeechee River near Savannah, the siege of Jackson, Mississippi, and in Hood's Tennessee campaign. Hermann, of course, was a curiosity more as a Frenchman ("a rather scarce article in those days in this country") than as a Jew. His major had told the men that "we'd brought a live Frenchman with us," and many went to get a glimpse of him. Hermann then jumped up on an old stump and introduced him-

184   self to the crowd: "Gentlemen, it seems that I am eliciting a great deal of curiosity; now all of you will know me as Isaac Hermann, a native Frenchman, who came to assist you to fight the Yankees."[75]

Isaac Hermann's first brush with war in the Battle of Cheat Mountain in western Virginia was also Robert E. Lee's first operation. Hermann respected Lee, who looked, he said, "every inch a soldier. His countenance had a very paternal and kind expression. He was clean shaven, with the exception of a heavy iron gray mustache. He complimented us for our soldierly bearing." Despite Lee's leadership the battle did not go well, and it propelled Gen. George B. McClellan to command of the Union forces in the East. Hermann felt that the Confederate army was poorly led, the officers elected "on account of their cleverness at home," and that "the men and officers knew more about farming than about military tactics."[76]

In his memoir, Hermann relates a story, which is implausible at best, of how he met Judah Benjamin in Richmond during this time. He was on a mission to deliver a package to General Beauregard while on his way home to Georgia after being discharged early because of poor health. According to Hermann, he went to the Treasury Department on Saturday evening to cash his paycheck. The department was closed, but Private Hermann ran into a very affable gentleman who told him to return on Monday morning and was kind enough to lend him ten dollars until then. When he had cashed his check, he found his benefactor sitting at a desk busily at work. Hermann handed him a ten dollar bill and again thanked him for his kindness. The gentleman refused it, saying, "Never mind, you are a long ways from home and may need it." Hermann replied that he did not accept gifts from strangers, whereupon the official replied, "We are not strangers, my name is Juda [*sic*] P. Benjamin." Hermann then goes on to say that Benjamin "was at that time Secretary of the Treasury of the Confederate States." Benjamin, of course, was never secretary of the Treasury; at that time, he was secretary of war and would not even have been at the Treasury Department. Hermann was a store clerk in rural Georgia recently arrived from France, and Benjamin was the former senator from Louisiana, so it is almost inconceivable that their paths had crossed. Nevertheless, Hermann wanted his readers to believe that he personally knew the most eminent Jewish Confederate.[77]

After serving a year as a private in Virginia, Ike Hermann went home, only to rejoin an artillery company in the fall of 1862 as a bugler with the rank of sergeant.[78] In late 1862 and early 1863, he was stationed at Fort McAllister on the south bank of the Ogeechee River near Savannah. Hermann's artillery unit was a part of the heroic and dangerous defense of the fort from a series of bombardments by Union warships and Gen. Quincy Gillmore's artillery siege. Union artillery had facilitated the capture of Fort Pulaski in April 1862, and Savannah could not long resist the Union offensive if Fort McAllister fell. According to Hermann, on one occasion he was sent up the Ogeechee to report the position of the

Pvt. Isaac Hermann emigrated from Alsace in 1859 and settled in rural Georgia. He enlisted in the Washington Rifles, 1st (Ramsey's) Georgia when the war began. He served in Virginia, Georgia, and Mississippi. At one time, he was a bugler and an orderly. This photograph was taken after the war. (Courtesy of the Jacob Rader Marcus Center, American Jewish Archives, Cincinnati, Ohio.)

invading gunboats. "While thus observing I noted a strange move of one of the boats, suddenly I saw an immense flash, and a splash in the river a couple of yards in front of me." The Yankees were firing at Hermann, who was on horseback, apparently because they thought he was an officer. The fort was badly damaged—"our breast-works had been blown to atoms"—but Hermann's unit went to work, together with slaves from neighboring plantations, with spades, shovels, and pick-axes, to repair and reinforce the fort. His artillery unit was next sent to Pocotaligo, South Carolina, to defend the railroad from a Union demolition squad. At ten o'clock one night, the Yankees came out of the marshes with torches. When they came within range, "we sent canister and schrapanel [*sic*] into the ranks." Hermann next served with the artillery in the Mississippi campaign. He claimed to have twice been wounded in action in Jackson, Mississippi, in May 1863, and, following a series of medical problems, he never returned to duty with his artillery unit. He also claims to have been captured, to have escaped, been wounded again at Spring Hill, Tennessee, and to have been sent on spy missions during the last months of the war.[79]

Isaac Hermann was a true believer in the Southern viewpoint of the war. He favored secession. He believed the North had won the war because of superior manpower and paying bounties to emigrants, who were "the scum of the world." He blamed the North's refusal to exchange prisoners for the deplorable conditions at the Andersonville prison. Like Leon, Hermann wholeheartedly accepted Southern racial attitudes. After the war, Hermann derided Reconstruction measures, black officeholders, and the Freedmen's Bureau. African Americans needed no protection from white Southerners, he wrote, "as their devotion to their master and their behavior at home while every white man able to bear arms was at the front . . . leaving their families in the hands of their slaves . . . was exemplary."[80]

Hermann was, according to his own boastful account, frequently disobedient when he disagreed with the orders of his superior officers. He was reduced from bugler to the ranks on March 12, 1863, by his lieutenant for insubordination, and rather than turn over his bugle to his successor, he broke it in two, as it was his "private property." Like Leon, he had no experience at cutting wood and failed miserably when he obeyed orders to do so. Unlike Leon, however, he lost his ax and was arrested. Fortunately, the colonel to whom he reported discovered that Hermann had clerked in a store and could write well, so he was assigned a clerking position. "I had warm quarters and was relieved from camp duties for a little while," he recalled. But this was only the beginning of Ike Hermann's run-ins with authority. He was arrested by military authorities at least twice more during the war, once when he wrote a satirical song about officers drinking the army's whiskey ("That's the way Confederate whiskey goes, pop goes the Government") and for being absent without leave. When chastised for his ditty accusing officers of drinking government whiskey, Hermann denied accusing anyone by name, "but if the cap fits," he told his lieutenant, "you can wear it. I have nothing to retract." Reduced in rank and ordered to wear a ball and chain as a punishment, Hermann claims to have replied: "I volunteered in the Confederate army to do my full duty . . . but when it comes to degrading me by making me wear ball and chain, I give you fair notice that I will kill any man who attempts to place the same on my limbs."

That night he slept with one eye open and his pistol and sword by his side. Ike volunteered for a two-week assignment in Charleston, and when he returned to his unit, somehow the ball and chain disappeared. But Hermann knew exactly where it was: in the Ogeechee River. Later in the war, Hermann was accused of being a deserter. He refused to be arrested in Macon, where he was known. "I'll die first, right here, before I'll march through Macon, guarded like a horse thief," he claims to have told the arresting officer. Once again, a colonel who did not even know Hermann intervened and agreed to see that Ike showed up at the guard house. On his arrival, Hermann got in a fistfight with the Yankee prisoners but did not stay long. He was acquitted of any wrongdoing as he had a valid furlough.[81]

In December 1863 Hermann was arrested a third time for not having proper papers on a furlough. He fought with the twelve men who had arrested him. "Luckily in my school days, which were close to an army post [in France], I went twice a week to the armory to take lessons in boxing and sword exercise," he recalled. Once again, he was saved by the intervention of a lieutenant colonel who just happened by. He was returned to Atlanta under guard and turned over to a provost marshal who knew him. After being told that he was being charged with striking a superior officer, the provost asked Hermann, "What did you do it for?"

"Well, Captain," Hermann replied, "I fought for the rights of the Confederacy for the last three years and thought five minutes for myself was not too much." If Hermann has given truthful accounts in his memoirs, it is a miracle he did not land in a Confederate prison for the duration of the war.[82]

It is surprising to modern students of the Civil War to learn just how insubordinate, individualistic, rude, and hardheaded Confederate soldiers really were. According to James I. Robertson Jr., "Civil War troops were the worst soldiers and the best fighters that America has ever produced." Disrespect for authority was rampant. These observations apply to Jewish Confederates as well. Even Lewis Leon, a modest and obedient soldier, according to his diary, nevertheless freely admits to disobeying orders on occasion. In April 1863 he asked to go on picket with his company rather than stay with the colors; his colonel told him he could not, but he "went all the same."[83]

Like many a Johnny Reb, Hermann had become accustomed to sleeping on the hard ground with his knapsack as a pillow. When he was invited to stay with a Mr. Rothschild in Columbus, Georgia, in 1863, he was given a nicely furnished room and a feather bed. But he was uncomfortable and unable to sleep. So he got up, put his knapsack under his head, and fell asleep by the side of the bed on the carpet. Unfortunately, when the young servant came to his room to blacken his boots, he thought that their houseguest had fallen off the bed and lay dead on the floor, and he ran to report this tragedy to Hermann's worried hosts.[84]

Isaac Hermann never mentions his religion in his memoir, but he constantly refers to Jewish acquaintances like the Rothschilds, friends, relatives, and fellow soldiers. He stayed with the Rothschilds in Columbus; his cousin Abe Hermann, who was drafted into the Georgia militia late in the war and became a sutler in Carswell's 1st Georgia brigade; another cousin in Macon, a Mrs. Wurzbourg; a Mrs. Lyons in Yazoo City, Mississippi; and Abe Einstein, a Savannah wholesale dry goods merchant. There were a couple of other Jewish men with him in the Washington Rifles: A. H. Wessalowsky was a private, as was H. Solomon, who began the war as a private and was later promoted to captain of the 14th Georgia.[85]

The war for Hermann was as dirty and harsh as it was for Lewis Leon. The Confederate government was never able to provide adequate uniforms, and by 1863 many Southern soldiers were not even sufficiently clothed to protect them against the elements. Later in the war, Hermann, like many a Confederate soldier, lost all of his personal effects in battle and retreats, and "our wardrobes only consisted of what we carried on our backs and filth begot what we called 'creepers,'" that is, lice. By 1864 Hermann, again like most Confederate soldiers, experienced hunger. When issued rations for three days, the men "walloped" them "out of sight at one square meal on account of its meagerness." Ike did the same and "trusted to the future. I never felt any remorse of conscience to get something to eat, if I could; I felt that the people for whom I devoted my services in those days, owed

188   me a living, and when the authorities failed to supply it, I took it where I could find it." In other words, he stole food when he could.[86]

Hermann witnessed physical suffering in others. Early on he observed in the cold mountains of western Virginia that Southerners were not used to rigorous climates, and "many of our men had to succumb from exposure. My Company lost three men from pneumonia." Hermann himself was sick for much of the war. He suffered from malaria and was hospitalized near Savannah in late 1862, recovered, and went on to serve in combat at Fort McAllister. In late 1863, he complained of "Angina Pectoris" and was hospitalized in Macon. In February 1864 he was assigned by a medical examining board to hospital duty for sixty days. Then he rejoined his company only to go before another board in April, which declared him "unfit for field service." He was assigned to the medical corps as a nurse at the Fair Grounds Hospital Number 2 in Atlanta.[87]

Pvt. Eugene Henry Levy was raised in an educated, affluent, and acculturated Jewish family in New Orleans. He felt himself the social superior of Jewish immigrants in general, and German Jews in particular. His father, after all, had "married into one of the best Jewish families" of Charleston, according to Dr. Marcus. He found the Jewish girls of Richmond disappointing. By 1861 the old Jewish families were a small minority of Southern Jews. Proud, educated, affluent, and successful, accepted easily by Southern aristocrats, they were conscious of the differences between themselves and their less Americanized co-religionists. While Lewis Leon was courting factory girls at Petersburg, Eugene Levy was borrowing a volume of Shakespeare from a Miss Scribner and dropping in to visit plantation mistresses.[88]

When the war began, the Levy sons all enlisted. All served in Dreux's/Rightor's 1st Louisiana Special Battalion during its short existence. Joseph Calhoun Levy subsequently served as a second lieutenant in the 1st Louisiana Regulars (Strawbridge's). Julian H. "Doc" Levy enlisted in Dreux's Battalion with Joseph in April 1861, and Eugene joined the unit in Virginia in November. Julian's service was brief; he was discharged by the end of May. Lt. Col. Charles D. Dreux was a popular young officer, and the battalion went off to fight, first in Pensacola with the 1st Louisiana Regulars and then to Virginia in late May. In June, Dreux's companies became the 1st Louisiana Special Infantry Battalion. It included a number of companies with substantial Jewish membership, including the Shreveport Grays before they were transferred to the 1st Louisiana in June 1862.[89]

Dreux was well respected in the Sephardic community in New Orleans. When he was killed commanding an expedition on July 5 near Newport News, Virginia, he became the first Louisiana officer killed in the war. His death horrified Clara Solomon. "He was so fine, intelligent and well-liked, [a] man." His death, she

Pvt. Eugene Henry Levy, from New Orleans, joined Dreux's Battalion and later the Donaldsonville Artillery. A native Southerner whose family had deep roots in the region, Levy was committed to the preservation of the Southern way of life, including the institution of slavery. He served throughout the war, including Appomattox. (Courtesy of the Jacob Rader Marcus Center, American Jewish Archives, Cincinnati, Ohio.)

wrote, "has cast a universal gloom over the community." The funeral, one of the biggest in the city's history, jammed New Orleans. Clara and her family went down Camp Street to see the procession. "The hearse was beautifully decorated," she wrote, the Colonel's horse "draped in mourning" walked slowly behind the car.[90]

Maj. Nicholas H. Rightor was promoted to replace Colonel Dreux. As members of Company C, Eugene and Joseph Levy were likely on picket duty on the Peninsula near Richmond until February 1862. The company was involved in minor skirmishes. Joseph was discharged by order of the secretary of war in February 1862. Eugene probably remained with the company until the battalion was disbanded in May 1862. Julian returned to Virginia in March 1862 to enlist in the Louisiana Donaldsonville Artillery. Eugene joined the same unit after his release from the 1st Special Battalion.[91]

Like Leon and Hermann, Levy was a thoroughgoing Southerner. "The news from the front is glorious," he wrote in his diary in May 1864. "Our brave boys, although weary, are busily engaged in the good work of slaughtering Yanks. The enemy, under the influence of liquor, have fought desperately, charging our breastworks as frequently as eight times in succession." Like his fellow Confederates, he refers to July 4th as "the once glorious fourth." On July 4, 1864, at Petersburg, he wrote, "our brass bands and those of the enemy indulged in a musical duel. The Yanks played 'Dixie,' which we cheered; then followed 'Yankee Doodle,' which

190 elicited groans and catcalls from our boys." Levy took pleasure in noting in his diary during the Battle of Cold Harbor that the heavy fighting had caused large Union losses. "Their dead and wounded cover acres of ground in solid bloody phalanx."[92]

Private Levy was a gentleman and so his social life varied considerably from that of his poor immigrant co-religionists. For example, he relates an incident near Petersburg in 1864 when he found himself at an elegant mansion being importuned by the lady of the house to stay and visit. "She is evidently fast, vain, and frivolous," he wrote in his diary, "romantic in the extreme, fond of admiration, and disposed to hold lightly the hymenial pledge." He was frequently the guest of prominent Jewish families in Richmond and attended both Beth Shalome, the synagogue of the elite families, and Beth Ahabah, the German synagogue, but makes no mention of the Polish congregation. The Jewish soldiers were invited to Christian services and included in Christian religious celebrations. Eugene Levy spent a memorable Christmas Day in 1864 enjoying "a sumptuous dinner" at four o'clock, consisting of "turkey, mutton, and pork, a variety of choice vegetables and the usual appendage of a delicious dessert. After dinner all hands went to work to arrange the Christmas tree." After playing chess and a late eight o'clock supper, "the door of the sitting room was thrown open amid exquisite strains of music, and the tree in all its glory was displayed, each bough loaded with presents." The family did not forget their Jewish guest, "as a pair of fine woolen socks and a heart pincushion fell to my share."[93]

Levy's behavior was similar to Leon's and Hermann's in many respects. Like all Confederate soldiers, he was willing to break the rules when it came to food. He joined in a raid on a train containing commissary stores near Petersburg in 1864. "My share of the plunder," he recorded in his diary, "was ten lbs. rice, two lbs. of sugar, and a half gallon beans." In the aftermath of Cold Harbor, Levy wrote in his diary that "all was quiet in front. Doc was sent on business to the wagon yard and started designing to run the blockade [that is, leave camp without permission] and visit father." (The Levy brothers' father, Jack Levy, was in Richmond at the time.) In early July, Levy "ran the blockade" to attend a church service and have a meal with some comrades. (He was disappointed in the service, which he described as "quite flat without sacred music.") As late as March 29, 1865, Levy was anxious to visit Richmond and decided to "run the block [blockade]" on the "sick furlough" of a fellow soldier.[94]

Levy was wounded defending Petersburg. "On our left, the forces are so near each other that an incessant fusillade is kept up during the day and night. The shelling of Petersburg continues . . . and, as yet, the brutal Grant has not notified the authorities to move noncombatants," he wrote in his diary on July 8, 1864. On July 30, Levy was in the Confederate trenches when a huge explosion was set off by the Union army. For a month, coal miners of the 48th Pennsylvania had been digging a tunnel nearly six hundred feet long. When it exploded, "the earth appeared to throb beneath our feet and, a moment after, as if a volcano had burst from the bowels of the land (200 yards to my left), men, wheels, spades, logs, vast boulders of earth, and an indescribable debris obscured the rising sun. The enemy had sprung a mine, and while we yet stood transfixed with horror at the appalling spectacle, a crash of artillery came whizzing, shrieking, tearing at us." Levy was wounded in the back, on his face, and then in his ribs by a burning shell. "The shock turned me quite around, and I immediately assured my companions that I was not badly hurt. A little water soon cleared my right eye."[95]

On his way back from the Battle of the Crater, Levy realized that Gen. Robert E. Lee and his staff were approaching. He stood aside and saluted. "My noble commander . . . remarked in a tone which indicated profound sympathy: 'My friend, I hope you are not badly hurt?' This exhibition of his noble nature overcame me. I answered: 'No, General, thank God!' and pressed quickly on to avoid his beholding the tear of gratitude which coursed down my cheek. Can it be wondered at that this man has won our hearts and minds? Opposed as I am to hero worship, I shall never utter the name of Robert E. Lee unless with respect and veneration." Levy walked to the Confederate hospital on Washington Street accompanied by his brother "Doc." He was apparently not too badly hurt, as he immediately "commenced a flirtation with the good-looking Miss W . . . the matron of my ward." Doc returned to the front.[96]

Unlike Leon and Herman, Levy felt the personal horror of losing loved ones. His brother Joseph Calhoun Levy was killed at Shiloh and buried in the Dispersed of Judah Cemetery in New Orleans. We do not know his feelings firsthand because his diary from 1862 was destroyed, but on Sunday, July 31, 1864, he records in his diary the deaths of the "courteous" Captain Rush and "the gallant Lieutenant Levy." They "were numbered among many choice spirits who, on the fatal Saturday, 'slept the sleep that knows no waking.' Peace to their ashes! Poor Jacob [Levy] came to see me in the course of the day. He seems absolutely brokenhearted."[97]

In May and June of 1864 Levy described the fighting at Cold Harbor, jotting down the news as a private in the ranks heard it while Grant and Lee maneuvered for the best strategic positions to pit their armies against each other. "It is now conceded," he wrote, "that Butler's advance . . . has proved a failure; he has been slipping his force down the river and reinforcing Grant. Beauregard's army is passing through Richmond on the way to our lines." On June 3 he wrote, "A heavy engagement commenced directly East of our bivouac shortly after daylight this morning . . . we could frequently distinguish amid the din of battle the shout of the Yankees as they advanced in *drunken* array to charge the earthworks which our men had erected during the night . . . General Lee has just passed the battalion conveyed by a light Jersey wagon. The old patriot looks as calm and pleasant as if Grant's defeat has been already consummated." Levy continued to believe in Confederate victory and fought all the way to Appomattox.[98]

★ ★ ★

Lewis Leon, Ike Hermann, and Eugene Levy represent the typical Jewish Johnny Reb. They served as privates and lived to tell about it. None of them considered himself a hero, although all of them risked their lives for the Southern cause. Jewish Johnny Rebs, like most Civil War soldiers, were modest. Fischel Cohen, a telegraph operator on Beauregard's staff, once told his nephew, "Yes. I was a brave man in the war—always where the bullets were thickest—under the ammunition wagon."[99]

There were some Jewish Johnny Rebs who were genuine heroes. Max Frauenthal, Summit Rifles, Company A, 16th Mississippi was, according to Carolyn LeMaster, "an unsung hero. . . . For those who knew him and served with him during the conflict, his name became synonymous with the word *bravery*." He fought in many battles, but particularly distinguished himself at Spotsylvania Court House, Virginia, in May 1864. Southeast of the Wilderness, where a major battle had been fought the week before, Spotsylvania was the scene of the continued maneuvering between Grant and Lee. Lee's army valiantly held its position at a terrible cost against three corps sent against the entrenched Confederates. At 4:30 a.m. on May 12, after four days of ferocious fighting, Grant hurled Winfield Scott Hancock II's corps against the Confederate's "Mule Shoe" salient, the forwardmost projection of the Confederate fortifications. The armies battled for twenty hours in some of the most murderous fighting of the war. The lines were only a few yards apart, and at one point called "The Bloody Angle," where the heaviest combat occurred, stood Max Frauenthal. Col. A. T. Watts later recounted how trees with trunks from eight to ten inches were mowed down by the "leaden hail." He also recalled how "Fronthall [*sic*], a little Jew, though insignificant in appearance, had the heart of a lion.

The "Bloody Angle" at Spotsylvania. (*Battles and Leaders of the Civil War*.)

For several hours he stood at the immediate point of contact, amid the most terrific 193 hail of lead, and coolly and deliberately loaded and fired without cringing. After observing his unflinching bravery and constancy, the thought occurred to the writer—I now understand how it was that a handful of Jews could drive before them the hundred kings; they were all Fronthalls!" Years later in Texas, it was said that people referred to a courageous person as "a regular Fronthall."[100]

Spotsylvania was a terrible and bloody battle. Even those who held staff or headquarters positions were called on to risk life and limb. One "Israelite" ordnance sergeant, Morris Guggenheimer of Company C, 2d Virginia Cavalry, whose job was to manage Col. Thomas T. Munford's "mess" and write letters and reports, was

Arkansas Jewish Confederate Veterans. Little Rock residents: *top row*: Isaac Bott; Herman Ehrenberg; Simon Gans; Abraham Kempner; Isaac Levy; Samuel Lyons; *2d row*: Morris Navra; Abraham Ottenheimer; Phillip Ottenheimer; Phillip Pfeifer; Abraham Pollock; Louis Volmer; *3d row* (*statewide residents*): Simon Adler; Moses Baum; David M. Bluthenthal; Ferdinand Dreyfus; David Felsenthal; Col. Solomon Franklin; *4th row*: Max Frauenthal; David Gates; Gabriel Meyer; Henry Meyer; Charles Weil; Max Weil. Max Frauenthal, one of the heroes of "The Bloody Angle" at Spotsylvania, "had the heart of a lion," according to his colonel. (Courtesy of Charles A. Elias, North Little Rock, Arkansas.)

in the midst of a very dangerous assignment before the battle ended. In a letter to the sergeant's daughter after the war, Colonel Munford said that he sent two couriers back for ammunition; one was shot and the other "dodged." Munford sent for a third courier and "told him to tell your father to bring me some ammunition himself, and not to let anybody or thing deter him. In a very little time he came galloping to me with a big bag of ammunition before and behind him on horseback, and just as he arrived we were heavily pressed; a mince [minie] ball killed his horse and down it fell. But he went on getting out the cartridges amid the cheers of his comrades, who saw his gallant behavior. . . . He was a faithful soldier often tried."[101]

Toward the end of the war in a battle with Union forces under Gen. Hugh J. Kilpatrick, Pvt. Isaac Harby Moses, a mere cadet at the Citadel, had his horse shot out from under him. When he got up, Moses was attacked by a Union soldier wielding a saber. "Though small in stature," Gary R. Baker wrote, "Moses lowered his head and charged the bluecoat, grabbing him around the middle and wrestling him to the ground." A fellow cadet shot and killed the Federal.[102]

Many a Jewish Confederate died a heroic death. Perry Moses Jr. was mortally wounded at Malvern Hill in 1862. Aaron (Company B, 35th Mississippi) and Jacob (Company C, 13th Mississippi) Rosenbaum's names appear on the Confederate monument in the town square in DeKalb, Mississippi. Sons of Carolyn and Marx Rosenbaum, they apparently were killed on the battlefield and lie buried in unknown graves. Marcus Baum was a thirty-two-year-old Prussian immigrant serving as an orderly or aide on General Kershaw's staff. He was accompanying Brigadier Generals Kershaw and Micah Jenkins and Lt. Gen. James Longstreet as they were making arrangements for a flank attack on the southern end of the Union line in the Wilderness. In a moment of confusion, they were caught in a volley of friendly fire. General Jenkins, General Kershaw's aide-de-camp, Capt. Alfred E. Doby, and Marcus Baum were instantly killed. Lt. Gen. Longstreet was gravely wounded in the throat and right shoulder. Baum's body was never recovered. He lies in an unmarked grave on the blood-stained soil of the Wilderness. Dr. Simon Baruch wrote of this "German and a Hebrew" in *Confederate Veteran* magazine in 1914: "No braver man, none truer to the cause, no soldier more loyal to his chief ever breathed than Marcus Baum, of Camden, S.C., special aide to Gen. Joseph B. Kershaw, his friend."[103]

Several Jewish Johnny Rebs were killed alongside their Christian comrades. The Jewish community of Columbia, South Carolina, which numbered fewer than two hundred souls in the 1860s, lost three boys: Pvt. Thomas W. Mordecai died of disease at Fort Moultrie in 1861, Pvt. Samuel S. Levin at Sharpsburg in 1862, and Pvt. Clarence J. Pollock at Spotsylvania in 1864. Levin, a machinist, had enlisted as a private in Capt. Thomas W. Radcliff's Company A, 15th South Carolina, on August 15, 1861, for the war. In Augusta, Georgia, where the sole synagogue, B'nai Israel (Children of Israel), had only forty members, four Jewish Confederates were killed: 1st Lt. Jacob J. Jacobus, a former president of the congregation at Shiloh; Capt. George W. Rush and 1st Lt. Nathaniel Elcan Levy at the Battle of the Crater; and 1st Lt. Jake R. Levy (Elcan's brother) at Hatcher Run. Pvt. Conrad Weil, Company H, 16th Louisiana, a native of Lagerheim, Bavaria, was wounded at the Battle of Spanish Fort, Alabama, and died at Mobile in May 1865. He is buried in the Old Hebrew Section of Magnolia Cemetery in Mobile.[104]

There were Jewish Confederate casualties in every major engagement of the war. Ten Jewish Confederates were killed at the Battle of Shiloh (Pittsburg Landing). Capt. Isadore P. Girardey reported the death of Jacobus: "In this engagement, Lieutenant J. J. Jacobus fell mortally wounded while gallantly commanding his section." He was shot above the left eye. Second Lt. David C. Levy of Company G, 13th Louisiana, was killed at Murfreesboro (Stone's River) on December 31, 1863. In less than an hour of combat in two actions during that battle, the 13th Louisiana lost 19 officers and 332 men killed, wounded, or missing in action. According to Mel Young, seven Jewish Confederates, including Albert Luria, were killed at Seven Pines (Fair Oaks) in May 1862. At the Seven Days Battle in late June and early July 1862, 19 Jewish Confederates were killed, according to Young.[105]

The roll of the Jewish Confederate dead can be called for the remaining battles of the war: Five dead at Second Manassas; seven at Sharpsburg (Antietam) including the Bavarian immigrant Louis Merz, who had settled in West Point, Georgia. Merz was an infantryman in the West Point Guards, Company D, 4th Georgia, Ripley's brigade, D. H. Hill's division. He was killed early in the battle near the little brick church. His body was found by Union officers, who "on account of his cleanly appearance," decided to bury this particular Confederate private. They dug a hole with their swords and buried him on the battlefield in an unmarked grave. The LaGrange *Reporter* concluded his obituary as follows: "May

Louis Merz of West Point, Georgia, emigrated to the United States from Bavaria in 1853 and became a peddler. He settled in West Point, Georgia, between LaGrange and Columbus. When the war broke out, Merz enlisted in the West Point Guards and was killed in action at Sharpsburg (Antietam). (Courtesy of Cobb Memorial Archives, H. Grady Bradshaw, Chambers County Library, Valley, Alabama.)

(*Left*) Gratz Cohen of Savannah, the son of Solomon Cohen, was fatally wounded at the Battle of Bentonville, North Carolina, late in the war. He is buried in Laurel Grove Cemetery in Savannah. This is a carte de visite taken in Charleston at a time when Cohen was probably an aide with the rank of captain, on the staff of Gen. George P. Harrison, Sr. (Courtesy of Bob Marcus, Springfield, Virginia.)

Theodore Belitzer, a member of Beth Elohim, served in Company B (Wilmington Rangers) 17th South Carolina Cavalry Battalion, and in Company G (German Hussars), 3d South Carolina Cavalry. According to his family, he was captured at Wilmington and died when the Federal steamer taking prisoners to Fort Monroe caught fire at sea. (Courtesy of Selina Leidloff Rosen and K. K. Beth Elohim Archives, Charleston, South Carolina.)

---

the brave and true-hearted soldier rest in peace; and his noble spirit inspire emulation in the hearts of others."[106]

There were six Jewish Confederates killed at Vicksburg, including Col. Leon D. Marks; seven at Chancellorsville; three at Brandy Station; six at Gettysburg (three from Texas); two each at Chickamauga and the Wilderness. Six Jewish Confederates were killed at Spotsylvania and twelve defending Atlanta late in the war. Three were killed at the war's end in defense of Mobile. Some Jewish Confederates died in prisoner of war camps. There are at least twenty buried at the notorious Union prison camp at Elmira, New York. Most died from exposure during the severe winter of 1864–65.[107]

Cadet Moses Ezekiel finally realized his dream of being a Confederate soldier. He served as a cadet at the Virginia Military Institute (VMI) during the war and participated in the famous Battle of New Market. (Courtesy of the Jacob Rader Marcus Center, American Jewish Archives, Cincinnati, Ohio.)

Henry Gintzberger, the immigrant peddler, served with the Salem Flying Artillery until his death in battle in 1864. He served at Williamsport, Fredericksburg, Chancellorsville (where he was wounded), Gettysburg, and Spotsylvania Court House, and was killed at Cold Harbor in June of 1864. A fellow soldier, Pvt. N. B. Johnston, recalled that "the only Jewish soldier in the Command was shot through the head while peering over the breastworks immediately alongside him." The register of his death shows he had no money and that his only "effects" were "1 pr. shoes." The muster roll states: "Jew: killed at Cold Harbor June 2, 1864," and that he was interred at "Jews burying ground, Richmond, Virginia."[108]

Moses J. Ezekiel experienced the death of a special friend. Ezekiel, along with the entire corps of young cadets at VMI, had joined Gen. John C. Breckinridge's

198 army in May 1864 in its efforts to halt the Union invasion of the Shenandoah Valley. On their march down the valley the young lads, aged fifteen to eighteen, were met by the young ladies of Staunton and greeted with buckets full of lemonade and baskets filled with sandwiches and cakes. They had no tents. The VMI cadets fought valiantly at the Battle of New Market. Ten cadets were killed. When the battle was over, Ezekiel and a cadet officer went out on the battlefield to find their classmate Thomas G. Jefferson, a descendant of the famous president. On discovering his mortally wounded friend, Ezekiel walked to town to secure a wagon to transport the boy. The young cadets took their comrade to a nearby home and tended to him. Ezekiel put his own shirt on his dying friend. "I never closed my eyes once during the whole time of his illness," Ezekiel recalled. Jefferson asked him to read from the Bible, and Ezekiel asked him what he would prefer to hear. "Please read the chapter in St. John where there is a chapter which says: 'In my Father's house are many mansions.' So I read that for him." That evening, when everyone else was asleep, Jefferson asked Ezekiel to light a candle. "A cold chill ran over me, because I remembered once having heard my Grandmother say, that when anyone is dying they lose their sight first of all; so without telling Jefferson that the candles were burning, I went to the bedside and took hold of his hand." The sixteen-year-old VMI cadet breathed his last breath.[109]

One of the most poignant Jewish deaths of the war was that of Pvt. Isaac Levy of the 46th Virginia, who had written to his sister about Passover in Adam's Run, South Carolina, and his brother Zeke's procuring matzo. His captain endorsed him with "conduct as soldier and gentleman worth of emulation in every respect."[110]

The Battle of the Crater at Petersburg. (*Battles and Leaders of the Civil War.*)

He was twenty-one when he was killed by an exploding shell in the Petersburg entrenchments. "Gusta brought me the sad news of the death of Isaac Levy," Emma Mordecai wrote in her diary. "A fine young solder, killed in the trenches near Petersburg. He & his brother Ezekiel Levy have observed their religion faithfully, ever since they have been in the army, never even eating forbidden food." Emma Mordecai went to visit the Levy family. "Isaac was an example to all young men of any faith—to those of his own most especially," she wrote afterward. "A true Israelite without guile—a soldier of the Lord & a soldier of the South." The orthodox funeral service at the Hebrew cemetery in Richmond was filled with emotion as Isaac's brother-in-law, Rev. George Jacobs, read the ancient burial rite.[111]

Young Levy's tombstone, most of it in Hebrew, reads as follows (in its English transliteration):

> L'zekher olam
> (To Eternal Memory)
> Yiyeh Ha'tzadik Ha'bakhur
> (The righteous Youth)
> Yitzchak ben R'Yakov
> (Isaac the son of Jacob)
> Meth b'milkhamot Petersburg
> (Killed at the Battle of Petersburg)
> B'yon alef yud-teth yamim l'khodesh Menachem
> (On the First Day, 19th of the Month of Av)
> Shnath 5624 lf'k
> (In the year 5624)
> T.N.Z.B.H.
> (May His Soul be Bound up in the Bond of Eternity)
> In Memory of Isaac J.
> beloved son of
> Jacob A. & Martha Levy
> who fell in battle.[112]

Three Jewish boys were killed at the Battle of Secessionville on James Island, South Carolina, in June 1862: Robert Cohen, a private in the Company A, 22d S.C. Infantry; Gustavus Poznanski Jr., a private; and Isaac D. Valentine, a corporal in Company D (Sumter Guards), 1st South Carolina Battalion. In the summer of 1862 the Union army hoped to cross James Island, overwhelm the Confederate defenders, and capture Charleston, the Cradle of Secession. It would have been a dramatic and important victory. But the Confederate defenders of Charleston were not about to lose the symbolic capitol of the South and so when Union troops landed, a pitched battle ensued at Secessionville, a tiny hamlet on a creek that led out to the harbor.[113]

Pvt. Isaac J. Levy's letter to his sister Leonora. Written at Adam's Run, South Carolina, in April 1864, Levy's letter describes his Passover, which is spelled in Hebrew (*Pesach*) on the fifth line down (page 1). He describes his brother Zeke's purchase of matzo, also written in Hebrew (middle of page 1). (Courtesy of the Jacob Rader Marcus Center, American Jewish Archives, Cincinnati, Ohio.)

Zeke E did not bring us any meat from home. He brought some of his own, smoked meat, which he is sharing with us, he says that he supposes that Pa forgot to deliver it to him.

No news in this section at present. Troops from Florida are passing over the road enroute for Richmond. 'Tis probable that we will remain in this department, and were it not for the unhealthy season which is approaching would be well satisfied to remain here.

We received this morning Sarah's letter of the 18th and are truly sorry to learn that her sight is affected, and trust that in a few days she will have recovered entirely her perfect sight

Love to all
Your affectionate Brother
Isaac Epstein

The Charleston Battalion (1st South Carolina Battalion), made up of Charlestonians defending their homes, was a part of the vigorous Confederate defense. On June 16, 1862, according to Patrick Brennan in *Assault on Charleston,* the "sons of Charleston responded as one as Capt. Henry King led his cheering company, the Sumter Guard, up the parapet to support the decimated artillerists." King was badly wounded, as was Isaac D. Valentine, who fell in the same rifle fire that wounded his captain. Isaac's brother Hertz was shot through the arm. Defending the Tower Battery, the Charlestonians held their position against killing Union fire. Privates Cohen and Poznanski were killed in this same battle.[114]

Poznanski, the rabbi's son, had, according to the *Charleston Courier,* expressed to several friends his "solemn presentment that he was to fall in battle, and yet went forward to repel the stormers and received his death wound on the rampart." On June 21 the newspaper reported that "After serving upon other fields, [Poznanski] joined the Sumter Guard and through the campaign on James Island cheerfully labored by the side of his comrades in the trench, or exposed his life in the perilous duties of the picket. "This sad event," the *Charleston Courier* wrote of Valentine, "has poured the most agonizing sorrow into the hearts of his family, and cast a terrible gloom over a large circle of friends." The obituary noted that, through the monotony and "dull routine of camp life," he was always cheerful;

Simon and Phillipena ("Pena") Brown. The Browns (Braun in German) were immigrants from the German states. They lived in New York but moved to South Carolina to establish a new life in Blackville, South Carolina, because Pena feared Simon's involvement with Russian anarchists. Family tradition has it that Simon was a reluctant Confederate. His records show that he enlisted in the 7th South Carolina, but not until April 1864. He was captured in August. (Courtesy of Max and Marcelle Furchgott, Charleston.)

when South Carolina seceded, he sought no position, but joined his company seeking only to defend the interest and honor of his state. He "fell gallantly endeavoring to protect the former and preserve unsullied the latter."[115]

Many Jewish Confederates were captured and suffered as prisoners of war. Leopold Levy of the 1st Virginia Cavalry served at First Manassas, Williamsburg, and Winchester. He was captured in 1863 by Stoneman's raiders and was sent, under very trying conditions, to the Old Capitol prison in Washington. He was incapacitated as a result of his trials and, when paroled, he served out the remainder of the war in the quartermaster general's department.[116] A. F. Woolfe enlisted as a private in Company A (Bayou City Guards), 5th Texas, in Harris County (Houston) in July 1861. He was later wounded at the Battle of Seven Pines in June 1862, wounded again near Richmond eight days later, and mortally wounded at Antietam three months later. He died in a Federal prisoner of war hospital and is buried in the Confederate cemetery in Hagerstown, Maryland.[117] The 1st Sgt. of Company A, 33d Alabama, Julius Yaretzky, was taken prisoner and sent to Johnson's Island on Lake Erie. Pvt. Marcus Levy of the Pointe Coupee Louisiana Artillery was captured at Island No. 10. He was transported to Camp Douglas, Illinois, where he died one month later as a result of his wounds. Sergeant Isadore Lovenstein, "a gallant soldier" of Company G, 12th Virginia, was wounded at Malvern Hill in July 1862 and was captured on the retreat to Appomattox.[118]

Not all Johnny Rebs rushed out to enlist the day after Sumter was bombarded. Indeed, the majority did not. It was one thing for unmarried young clerks like Lewis Leon and Isaac Hermann to enlist, but it was quite another for married men with children to leave home. When the war broke out, Philip Sartorious was living in Milliken's Bend, Louisiana, a tiny village on the Mississippi fifteen miles north of Vicksburg. He did not enlist. He and his young wife, Rose, were working hard to support their family, and many farmers, merchants, and planters could only leave their businesses at great sacrifice. "Volunteers were called for, and all thought it was a picnic, but found it before long a sad reality," Sartorious wrote in his memoirs. He continued to operate his store, sold goods to the Confederate army, and went about his business. Once he went to New Orleans to collect on a debt for wood he had sold to the crew of a Confederate gunboat. The Federal fleet arrived that very day and Sartorious was lucky to escape with his life.[119]

By February of 1863 Grant and Sherman were literally in Sartorious's backyard. The Confederacy was drafting all men who could fight, and Sartorious, who had an exemption as postmaster, now joined the 15th Louisiana Cavalry Battalion as a private. "We had to furnish our own horses and accouterment, or march on foot to Munroe [Monroe] and join the infantry," he recalled. "I got my accouterment from a Yankee deserter." He was made steward of the unit's mess.

Milliken's Bend was located in a large bend in the Mississippi River upstream from Vicksburg. General Grant vowed to capture Vicksburg and made Milliken's

Bend his headquarters. From that base he planned his campaign from January to July 1863. Philip Sartorious went with the Confederate army into the swamps, bayous, and rivers surrounding Vicksburg to stop Grant and Sherman. His unit spent a great deal of time tracking Grant's movements. One day Sartorious attempted to visit his family, but Rose begged "me to return at once, as the Federal cavalry were expected every moment, and had been there several times looking for me. Very reluctantly I bid poor Ma good-bye and returned to camp." On March 29, 1863, General McClernand went on the march to open a road from Milliken's Bend to New Carthage, Sartorious and his comrades got in the way, and Sartorious was wounded. "I thought my arm was shattered. The gun fell out of my hand, and, after staggering some twenty feet, I fell on my face. The bullets fell around me like rain, and I thought that if the bullet that hit me would not kill me, some stray one would, and I wanted to see the sky when I died." Sartorious was captured by the Union army, and "a young excuse of a surgeon" from an Indiana regiment treated him. "He cut my clothes off. The bullet lodged under my skin at the end of my shoulder blade. He had no instruments with him but an old rusty pocket knife. Some of the soldiers that were there said: 'Doctor, don't hurt him any more than you can help.' He replied: 'Oh hell! He is nothing but a d—d Rebel s–b.'" Sartorious survived, but he could never again use his hand to write.[120]

Sartorious's family heard he had been killed because his new uniform was stolen by a Union officer. But Sartorious was treated kindly by his captors. They allowed his wife to come and visit him. The sutler of the Union regiment turned out to be his second cousin. A doctor gave him a certificate stating that he could no longer fight, and consequently he was paroled and allowed to return home rather than being sent up North to prison. Sartorious had done his duty but was glad to be excused from more of it.[121]

Of course, not all Jewish Confederates did their duty. Jewish Southerners, like all Southerners, preserved the memories of patriotic and noble deeds and tried to forget about the cowardly and unpatriotic ones. Thus, community histories are replete with the stories of heroes, but little or nothing is to be found on shirkers, deserters, and cowards. Ezekiel and Lichtenstein's *History of the Jews of Richmond* and Rabbi Elzas's *History of the Jews of South Carolina* were published in the early years of the twentieth century, when Confederate veterans and their children were still living. Both depict the loyal service of Jewish Confederates at a time when many Jews in Richmond, Norfolk, Petersburg, Charleston, Sumter, and Columbia well knew who had fought bravely and who had run from the fight. As Bell I. Wiley has written, "Cowardice under fire, being a less gratifying subject than heroism, has not received much attention from those who have written or talked of the Confederate Army."[122]

Heyman Herzberg was living in Cartersville, Georgia, when the war began. He recalled in a memoir that the excitement was great and every young man was expected to join some military organization. His brother Herz went to Pensacola, Florida, with the 36th Georgia (Villepigue's) and brother Sol joined Company B, 40th Georgia, and became a corporal. Business was at a standstill, so Heyman closed his store, packed up his young family and his merchandise, sold his house and furniture, and sent his family and all of his belongings to his brother-in-law in West Point, Georgia. Herz returned from his unit in Florida, where he participated in the bombardment of Fort Pickens, and the two brothers joined Villepigue's regiment, now designated the 1st Confederate Infantry and went to Fort Gaines on Dauphin Island on the Gulf of Mexico. Life was monotonous except for an occasional ship attempting to run the blockade. "I remember well the excitement we had one morning to see the gunboats chasing a blockade-runner who had succeeded during the night in getting close to the shore under the protection of the guns of Ft. Morgan. We were all ordered to the fort to assist in keeping off the vessels. . . . A good many of the shells came screeching over us and fell harmless in the sand on the island." The living conditions were abominable, and, had it not been for the kindness of friends in Mobile, "we would have fared badly indeed."[123]

One day, Heyman and Herz were pleasantly surprised by the arrival of brother Sol, sick from exposure as a result of the severe winter camping out in the Cumberland Mountains of east Tennessee. Sol had secured a substitute for himself, had been discharged from the Confederate army, and offered to find a substitute for Herz. Herz immediately accepted Sol's offer, and the two brothers left for Philadelphia to live with their parents. Heyman, left alone, decided to secure a substitute also. "I had to wait another month, however, as our captain would not accept more than one substitute a month. I succeeded, however, in getting an able-bodied man who was beyond the age limit of the soldier. Every male person over eighteen and up to fifty was obliged to serve in the Army unless employed in some other capacity of the government. My substitute was about sixty years, and, by giving our first lieutenant my handsome gold watch as a souvenir, I succeeded in getting my discharge from the Confederate States Army."[124]

Heyman resumed his occupation as a merchant but moved to Atlanta. In searching for goods in the country, he traveled with a friend to Lafayette, Alabama, where the two men were accosted by a recruiting officer. Not having papers showing their military status with them, Herzberg and his friend were ordered to a military camp. Herzberg asked the officer to let them first take dinner at the hotel. The officer agreed and said he would wait at the tavern next door. Herzberg recalled: "Now was our chance to escape. I gave a colored man a dollar to hitch up in the yard and place the buggy back of the hotel, paid for our dinner but did not stay to eat it, got in the buggy, and used our whip to such advantage that we soon left the town with the recruiting officer far behind." The officer fired several shots, but the men were too far away. They "never stopped until we were out of the country and got again in Lafayette. We left there to West Point the next day, having had

206   sufficient experience in trying to buy country stocks of goods." Herzberg later
traveled illegally up North to buy merchandise to sell down South, and, believing
the South doomed, eventually took his family on a long harrowing journey out of
the South.[125]

Philip Whitlock of Richmond, a Russian Polish immigrant and a tailor, was a
member of the Richmond Grays before the war. He went with his company to witness the hanging of John Brown and claimed to have stood next to John Wilkes
Booth during the execution. When the war began, Whitlock served as a private
with the Grays, then Company G, 12th Virginia. He later recalled that he "did not
see any chance to improve my condition as the profession of a 'sodier' [*sic*] was not
to my taste." By 1862 Whitlock was convinced that the South could not win. He
tried to hire a substitute so that he could quit the army "honorably if possible."
When he got sick, he somehow obtained leave and wrangled an appointment in the
Quartermaster Department in Richmond. By "being friendly" with the army doctor, he somehow continued on sick leave. "In his account," Ernest B. Ferguson
concluded, "Whitlock never uses the word *bribe,* but repeatedly hints at it in
explaining how he crossed the lines [to bring in goods from the North] and
retained his safe assignment." Whitlock wrote in his memoirs that he was not in
"any way unpatriotic but in the way things looked to me then, that it was a *lost
cause,* and every human being that lost his life was a useless sacrifice."[126]

Herman Whitlock, Philip's brother, felt no allegiance to the Southern cause
and left Richmond with his family in early 1864. Philip, now married, lived in his
brother's house and attended to his duties while his wife ran a small store they
had purchased.[127]

There were even a few Jewish "Galvanized Yankees"—that is, Confederate
soldiers recruited in Federal prisoner-of-war camps who served in the Union
army. One such "repentant Rebel" was Louis Wolf, who arrived from Germany in
1856, lived in Savannah just before the war, and fought for the Confederacy for
eighteen months when he was taken prisoner. (He lived in Lynn, Massachusetts,
after the war, and when he died the *Lynn Item* called him a "veteran of both sides
in Civil War.")[128]

And there were Jewish deserters from the Confederate army. Bernard
Rosenblatt, a native of Warsaw who lived in Charleston, was drafted into the Confederate army. According to *Hartford Jews* by Rabbi Morris Silverman, "Upon
learning that the Confederate Army was fighting to uphold slavery, he [Rosenblatt]
ran away and enlisted in the Union army in the 4th N.Y. Heavy Artillery, an Irish
Regiment." Isaac Arnold, a young immigrant and a member of Company D, 8th
Alabama, was arrested for cowardice and absence without leave in the presence of
the enemy. He was given the death sentence. Rabbi Michelbacher petitioned General Lee for mercy and enlisted a number of prominent people, including Confederate Congressmen from Alabama and Mississippi, in an effort to spare Arnold's

life. "From what we have heard," the rabbi told the general, "we fear that the fact of being an Israelite and of foreign birth, has had an injurious tendency towards the decision of his deplorable fate—we hope for the sake of the common humanity of our race, that this report may be untrue." Michelbacher argued that Arnold did not appreciate the seriousness of his behavior. However, he had confidence that Lee would not hesitate to attest "to the courage and soldier-like abilities of the Israelites in those legions of our beloved Confederacy that have aided in giving an heroic name to the army."[129]

Max Neugas was a clerk in Darlington, South Carolina, at the beginning of the war. He had two brothers in New York City and most likely came South in the 1850s seeking employment. He had no family in South Carolina. Neugas nevertheless enlisted as a private for the duration of the war in Capt. David Gregg McIntosh's Company, the Pee Dee Rifles, 1st Regiment, S.C. Volunteers, in July 1861. The regiment, originally commanded by Col. Maxcy Gregg, was later commanded by Col. Comillus W. McCreary. In March 1862 Neugas's Company D became the Pee Dee Artillery Battery and was sent to Virginia. On June 27, 1862, during the Seven Days Battle, he was severely wounded at Gaines' Mill.[130]

Neugas returned to Darlington to recuperate. He therefore missed some of his battery's hardest fighting, including Sharpsburg (Antietam) in September 1862, where McIntosh's battery was captured on the heights above Rohrbach Bridge. He soon returned to his unit and fought at Fredericksburg and Chancellorsville. His company saw heavy fighting at the former in support of Maj. Gen. Ambrose P. Hill's Division, and in the latter it was engaged after Gen. "Stonewall" Jackson's flanking move around Gen. Joseph Hooker's army on May 2 and 3.[131]

But Neugas had enough of the war and deserted on the first day of the Battle of Gettysburg, July 1, 1863. In a letter petitioning President Lincoln to pardon him, Neugas described how he hid in a shed just as his battery was going into battle, that he walked through the Confederate lines by "putting on a bold face," and slept in the woods. "After a short nights rest I got up the next morning, thankful to the Almighty of having me released, out of the clutches of the Rebel tyrants." Neugas relates how he stayed at the homes of friendly townspeople who also gave him a change of clothes. He was picked up by pickets of the 21st New York Militia at Cashtown on July 5. He offered to take the oath of allegiance but was sent to Fort Delaware as a prisoner.[132]

In his petition, Neugas told the president that prior to the "breaking out of this wicked Rebellion, I was clerking in South Carolina and as I remained longer in that State than I ought to have done, I was forced to enter the rebel army after the Conscription Act passed in April 1862." This statement was false, as Neugas enlisted on July 29, 1861. He said he "tried several plans" to leave the state, but failed. "I own no property down South," he told Lincoln, "and no slaves and I am in nothing interested there whatever, also I have no relatives in the South."

Neugas was not pardoned and was not released until the war was over. In 1863 and 1864, Neugas and several other Jewish Confederate prisoners wrote to Rabbi Isaac M. Wise in Cincinnati for help. Wise's October 16, 1863, issue of the *American Israelite* contains this story:

> MUST WAIT—Several weeks ago we received a letter from Jewish prisoners at Fort Delaware, stating that they were forced into the service of the Confederacy, and were desirous to return to civil life as loyal and peaceable citizens. We sent the letter and our remarks appended to Washington, and received the following reply: OFFICE COMMISSARY GEN. OF PRISONERS (WASHINGTON, D.C., Oct. 8, 1863) Rev. Isaac M. Wise, Rabbi of Cincinnati, Ohio—Sir: I am directed by the Commissary General of Prisoners to inform you that the petition forwarded by you, recommending the release of Henry Maas, Dalton Brannshweiger, Max Newgas, A. Wausserman, Louis Meyersburg, S. Cohen, H. Brash, prisoners of war, now confined at Fort Delaware, has been submitted to the Secretary of War, by whom the cases have not been favorably considered.
>
> Very respectfully,
>
> Your obedient servant,
>
> W. H. HUNT, Captain and A.A.G.

One year later Neugas, Louis Meyersburg of Mobile, and Aaron Waterman of Hawkinsville, Georgia, wrote to the *Israelite* again stating that they still had not been released and were now appealing "through you to your congregation to assist us. . . . We are in need of some pecuniary aid or food, especially coffee." (Henry Brash later became mayor of Marianna, Florida. On December 9, 1889, he issued a proclamation upon the death of "the illustrious chieftain of the late Confederacy"—Jefferson Davis.)

And, sad to say, there were even a few traitors. A sutler, Levi Strauss, from Lexington, Virginia, and a neighbor of Stonewall Jackson's, was discovered missing one night during one of the Valley campaigns in Virginia. His wagon was searched, and military plans and other information were discovered. He was court-martialed and hanged as a Union spy.[133]

Jewish soldiers hunted and punished deserters. Lewis Leon relates constant problems with desertion in his regiment. He witnessed men whipped and executed for desertion. In May 1863, his unit was marched to an open field and drawn up in line to see two men shot for desertion. "Their coffins were by their sides, right close to their graves, so that they could see it all." In August 1863 Leon and Si Wolf were sent on a detail looking for deserters. They went house to house, searched the woods, barns, and, at times, private homes. Leon once found a deserter in a hayloft after the owner of the house objected to his squad searching the area. They were sometimes invited for meals by the people who appreciated their fighting for the Southern cause. On one occasion, some rural Virginians, apparently never having seen a Jew, asked, "Is there a Jew in your detachment that caught a deserter yesterday?" They wanted to see him. One of the soldiers told the people that Leon was the Jew in question. "After that," he recalled, "I had a very good time there, and in fact wherever I went I was received very kindly." Indeed, Leon was sorry to leave when the time came. Pvt. Louis Merz, of the West Point Guards, was assigned to guard a deserter, but was elated when another deserter was spared execution. "What a narrow escape," he wrote in his diary, "and what a lesson to such who indulge in liquor and cannot master and govern themselves when under its influence."[134]

Jewish Johnny Rebs, or at least a portion of them, sought out religious worship services and the assistance of rabbis or Jewish "ministers," in the parlance of the Reform Jewish faith. There were no Jewish chaplains, as such, in the Confederate army, but there were laymen who ministered to the Jewish Confederate soldiers. Rabbi B. Nordlinger served the Jewish community of Macon, Georgia, and joined F. H. Burghard's Light Artillery (the Macon German Artillery). His military record shows that he served as a bugler and a musician, not a chaplain, but he likely ministered to the Jewish men in his unit. Uriah Feibelman, Company C, 12th Virginia, of Petersburg, Virginia, a musician, was recognized as "a minister of gospel in the Hebrew Church" in 1864, but enlisted as a private, and no surviving record shows him as a chaplain. Rabbi Korn speculates that both men progressed from blowing the *shofar*, the ancient ram's horn used on the Jewish New Year, to the bugle.[135]

The Confederate Congress, unlike the U.S. Congress, made no distinction between religions in the appointment of chaplains. Northern Jews were forced to launch an extensive lobbying effort against a law limiting chaplain appointments to ministers "of some Christian denominations." The Confederate law referred to "every minister of religion." Rabbi Korn concludes that, in this instance, "the Confederate Congress was more liberal and tolerant than its Washington counterpart."[136]

Like their comrades of the Christian faith, Jewish Johnny Rebs frequently brought the Holy Scriptures with them to the front. (Jews do not refer to the Holy Scriptures as the Bible.) The Holy Scriptures (which Christians call the Old Testament) consist of the Five Books of Moses (the Torah, the Law, or the Pentateuch, "five books" in Greek), the Prophets, and Writings (which include Psalms, Proverbs, and Ecclesiastes, for example). When Henry Smith (who was Jewish, despite his name) was killed at the front, his captain wrote his father, "His Bible and effects I will endeavor to have forwarded to you."[137] And like their Christian comrades, Jewish Johnny Rebs called upon God to help them achieve victory. Pvt.

Simon Mayer was a religious Jew who, like his fellow Confederate soldiers, called upon God, "the great 'Ruler of the Universe,'" to aid him, his family, and the Southern cause. "May the God of Israel guard & protect you . . . and may He vouchsafe to us all good health," he wrote his family.[138]

Many Jewish Johnny Rebs attended services at the synagogues in Richmond or at one of the Charleston, Savannah, or Memphis congregations. Some of the soldiers in Virginia were able to obtain individual furloughs on some occasions to attend services on the High Holy Days, and on at least one occasion, General Lee allowed a general furlough. Lewis Leon noted in his diary: "Brother Morris returned from Richmond yesterday, where he has been for ten days on a furlough. Before our Jewish New Year there was an order read out from General Lee granting a furlough to each Israelite to go to Richmond for the holidays if he so desired. I did not care to go." Ezekiel and Lichtenstein wrote that the commandant of the provost guard, the military police, put a detail outside the synagogue in Richmond on Friday nights to catch the Jewish soldiers absent without official leave. "The soldier boys were true to their faith," the authors concluded; a "prettier tribute could not be paid them."[139] Many a young Jewish Confederate "walked from his sweetheart," Herbert Ezekiel said in 1915, "into the arms of the guard, and the visions of a good Friday night supper melted into the stern reality of an enforced sojourn in the guardhouse."[140]

It is safe to assume that many Jewish Johnny Rebs observed the High Holidays in camp or on the field, some in small groups and others alone. Capt. Marcus Hofflin, Company K, 4th North Carolina, told of a Kippur (Day of Atonement) service held in a tent in the Shenandoah Valley in 1862 after the battle at Sharpsburg (Antietam). Stonewall Jackson, a student of religion, was said to have observed a part of the service. Lewis Leon always recorded the New Year (Rosh Hashanah), but he never attended a synagogue. On September 15, 1863, he recorded in his diary: "Still some firing in front. We are in reserve. I went to see the fight. I saw the enemy very plainly, and thus I spent my New Year's Day." On September 23 he records, "Day of Atonement to-day."[141] Ike Hermann never mentions the holidays or attending a service in his memoir, probably because his non-Jewish readers would not have been interested.

On Saturday, October 1, 1864, Eugene Henry Levy decided to attend synagogue on account of Reverend Michelbacher's appeal to General Lee for a furlough for the Jewish soldiers. He attended to demonstrate his gratitude to his commander. Levy, however, was "not sufficiently affected by the religious ceremonies to feel in the humour for praying." The next day, Rosh Hashanah, Levy attended the service at the German synagogue, Beth Ahabah. The next week Levy was "called up" for a blessing while the Torah was being read. He observed Yom Kippur by attending Beth Ahabah in the evening and "the Mayo Street Shool [that is, the Sephardic Synagogue] in time to hear Mr. [George] Jacob's excellent and appropriate sermon." Levy fasted on Yom Kippur as is the Orthodox custom. He spent from 8:30 a.m. until 1:00 p.m. at synagogue on Kippur Day, October 10, 1864. Despite the war, Jewish Confederate soldiers were still Jews and still had the traditional complaints about the length of the service. "Did not feel impressed by the Hebrew service," Levy wrote, "and am more than ever convinced of the necessity of reforms in the mode of service." He spent the rest of the day and evening visiting local Jewish families and broke his fast at 6:30 with "coffee and cakes *à la mode d'Europe.*" A devout and practicing Jew, Levy attended services at the synagogues throughout the war. On Saturday, December 17, 1864, he attended "devine services and had the honor to carry the 'scroll of the law.' Bade many of my friends farewell at the door of the synagogue."[142]

Reverend Michelbacher wrote and published a prayer, which the Jewish soldiers took with them to the front. Entitled "The Prayer of the C.S. Soldiers," it was in English except for the Shema, which Michelbacher wrote as "SHEMANG YIS-ROEL. ADONOY ELOHAINOO, ADONOY ACHOD" (Hear, O Israel. The Lord our God is one.). This prayer or proclamation called the *Shema* ("hear") is the central and most important theological statement in Judaism, its confession of faith. Its modern translation is "Hear O Israel, the Lord our God, the Lord is one," and expresses the ancient Jewish belief in monotheism.[143] The prayer connected ancient Jewish imagery with the Confederacy and linked Jewish soldiers with the Southern cause. "This once happy country is inflamed by the fury of war; a menacing enemy is arrayed against the rights, liberties and freedom of this, our Confederacy. . . . Here I stand now with many thousands of the sons of the sunny South, to face the foe, to drive him back, and to defend our natural rights. O Lord, God of Israel, be with me in the hot season of the contending strife; protect and bless me with health and courage to bear cheerfully the hardships of war. . . . Be unto the Army of this Confederacy, as thou wert of old, unto us, thy chosen people! Inspire them with patriotism! Give them when marching to meet, or, overtake the enemy, the wings of the eagle—in the camp be Thou their watch and ward—and in the battle, strike for them, O Almighty God of Israel, as thou didst strike for thy people on the plains of Canaan—guide them, O Lord of Battles, into the paths of victory, guard them from the shaft and missile of the enemy."[144]

Jewish Confederate soldiers in the field had to fend as best they could on the Jewish holidays. Obtaining kosher food was impossible and matzo, unleavened or flat bread, was difficult to find during Passover. In fact, when the soldiers were in the field, they had trouble determining the exact dates of the Jewish holidays. "No doubt you were much surprised on receiving a letter from me . . . on the 21st [April 21,1864], which was the first day of [Passover]," Isaac J. Levy of Richmond wrote his sister Leonora. "We were all under the impression in camp that the first day of the festival was the 22nd and if my memory serves me right I think that Ma wrote me that [Passover] was on the 22d inst. Zeke [Capt. Ezekiel J. Levy of Richmond]

THE PRAYER OF THE C. S. SOLDIERS.

BY REV. M. J. MICHELBACHER,

Minister of the Hebrew Congregation, "House of Love," Richmond, Va.

"SHEMANG YISROEL, ADONOY ELOHAINOO, ADONOY ACHOD!"

O God of the Universe! Although unworthy through my manifestold transgressions, I approach the Seat of thy mercy, to crave thy favor, and to seek thy protection. I supplicate thy forgiveness, O most merciful Father, for the many transgressions and the oft repeated disobedience, which caused Thee to command destruction over me. Behold me now, O my Father, supplicating Thy protection! Thou who art near when all other aid faileth! O spare me, guard me from the evil that is impending!

This once happy country is inflamed by the fury of war; a menacing enemy is arrayed against the rights, liberties and freedom of this, our Confederacy; the ambition of this enemy has dissolved fraternal love, and the hand of fraternity has been broken asunder by the hands of those, who sit now in council and meditate our chastisement, with the chastisement of scorpions. Our firesides are threatened; the foe is before us, with the declared intention to desecrate our soil, to murder our people, and to deprive us of the glorious inheritance which was left to us by the immortal fathers of this once great Republic.

Here I stand now with many thousands of the sons of the sunny South, to face the foe, to drive him back, and to defend our natural rights. O Lord, God of Israel, be with me in the hot season of the contending strife; protect and bless me with health and courage to bear cheerfully the hardships of war.

O Lord, Ruler of Nations, destroy the power of our enemies! Grant not the longings of the wicked; suffer not his wicked device to succeed, lest they exalt themselves. Selah. As for the heads of those that encompass me about, let the mischief of their own lips cover them. Let burning coals be cast upon them; let them be thrown into the fire, into deep pits, that they rise not up again." (Psalms 140.) Be unto the Army of this Confederacy, as thou wert of old, unto us, thy chosen people! Inspire them with patriotism! Give them, when marching to meet, or, overtake the enemy, the wings of the eagle—in the camp be Thou their watch and ward—and in the battle, strike for them, O Almighty God of Israel, as thou didst strike for thy people on the plains of Canaan—guide them O Lord of Battles, into the paths of victory, guard them from the shaft and missile of the enemy. Grant, that they may ever advance to wage battle, and battle in thy name to win! Grant, that not a standard be ever lowered among them! O Lord, God, Father, be thou with us!

Give unto the officers of the Army and of the Navy of the Confederate States, enterprise, fortitute and undaunted courage; teach them the ways of war and the winning of victory. Guard and preserve, O Lord, the President of the Confederate States and all Officers, who have the welfare of the country truly at heart. Bless all my fellow-citizens, and guard them against sickness and famine! May they prosper and increase!

Hear me further, O Lord, when I pray to Thee for those on earth, dearest to my heart. O bless my father, mother, brothers and sisters, (if married: my wife and children,) O bless them with all earthly and heavenly good! May they always look up to Thee, and may they find in Thee their trust and strength.

O Lord, be with me always. Show me the way I have to go, to be prepared to meet Thee here and hereafter.

My hope, my faith, my strength are in Thee, O Lord, my God, forever—in Thee is my trust! "For thy salvation do I hope, O Lord! I hope for Thy salvation, O Lord! O Lord, for Thy salvation do I hope!" Amen! Amen!

Shemang Yisroel, Adonoy Elohainoo, Adonoy Achod!

To Max Myers

from his friend & wellwisher

M. J. Michelbacher

was somewhat astonished on arriving in Charleston on Wednesday afternoon, to learn that was the first [Seder] night."[145]

Passover was difficult to celebrate on the field of battle. Isaac and Zeke Levy and their Jewish comrades were fortunate during the Passover of April 1864 to be stationed at Adam's Run, South Carolina, as it was close enough to Charleston for Zeke to buy matzo sufficient to last them for a week. Isaac noted in his letter that the "cost is somewhat less than in Richmond, being but two dollars per pound." Isaac and Zeke Levy made the best of their situation: "We are observing the festival in a truly orthodox style. On the first day, we had a fine vegetable soup. It was made of a bunch of vegetables which Zeke brought from Charleston containing new onions, parsley, carrots, turnips and a young cauliflower, also a pound and a half of fresh beef, the latter sells for four dollars per pound in Charleston."[146]

And, of course, the Jewish boys sought the comfort of their religion when they were dying. Adolph Rosenthal, Company D, 38th Georgia, a German Jew from Savannah, was severely wounded in Virginia in May 1864, at Spotsylvania Court House, and lay dying for two weeks. He was cared for by his sweetheart, Rachel Semon, at her home and by others in the Richmond Jewish community. Rachel was brokenhearted at Adolph's death and wrote Joe Rosenthal, Adolph's brother, that Adolph "died a good Jew. We even had him *benched* [blessed by the giving of a new name]. His name was *Moses*. I will tel you all som day as he told me every thing what to do four days befor he died. . . . God bless his sole. May he rest in peace. I even toock his remains to Savannah and burried him."[147]

When all is said and done, Southerners respected the willingness to fight, the bravery under fire, and sacrifices of their Jewish comrades in arms. "They were all volunteers, and I know there was not a Jew conscript in the Legion," Gen. Thomas Waul wrote. "As soldiers they were brave, orderly and well-disciplined and in no respect inferior to the gallant body of which they formed a prominent part." No Jewish soldier was court-martialed, they did not seek a disproportionate amount of leave, nor were they on the hospital rolls, according to Waul. "I will say," he concluded, "I neither saw nor heard of any Jew shrinking or failing to answer to any call of duty or danger."[148] Henry E. Henderson of Louisiana recorded in his memoirs that his unit, Company B (Stafford Guards), 9th Louisiana, consisted largely of the sons of planters, but also included a few "roughs" from the "piney wood region" north of Alexandria, Louisiana, "and perhaps half-a-dozen Jews, most of

(*Left*) "The Prayer of the C.S. Soldiers." This Jewish soldiers' prayer was written by Rev. Max Michelbacher and distributed to the Jewish boys in the Virginia theater. (Courtesy of the Museum of the Confederacy, Richmond, Virginia. Photograph by Katherine Wetzel.)

Pvt. Solomon Cohen served in Company B, 28th (Thomas's) Louisiana. He was paroled at Vicksburg in July 1863. (Courtesy of Cecile Levine, New Orleans.)

whom had carried a pack along the Red River." Henderson continued: "These Jews, singular as it may seem, proved themselves as faithful and efficient soldiers as any in the command, and shed their blood for the cause of the South as freely as the natives 'to the manner born.'"[149]

After the war, Jewish Confederate veterans passed on their guns and swords to their sons. They also passed on their good names and pride in their war record. Julius Yaretzky wrote a touching letter to his son after the war:

> You wish to know about what I, if any, had left and brought home with me from the War, such as arms or otherwise. So I will inform you fully of it. I did not bring anything home with me for the following good reasons. When I was in the army, I possessed a large knife, pistol and sword. The knife I found useless in battle and left it at Pensacola, Fla. Navy Yard, as we evacuated that place to go to Corinth, Miss. to participate in the battle of Shiloh. . . . The pistol was a Colts powder & ball and it was damaged in the battle of Perriville, Ky. and became useless. The cylinder of same was struck by a ball from grape shot and, therefore, [I] did not have any further use for it. The sword was taken from me when I was captured at the Battle of Franklin, Tenn. near Nashville. I tried to get the Yanks to let me keep it so I could bring it home but was refused and was compelled to give it up. So, dear boy, I have none of the war relics left to send you but a good record of a faithful soldier I then was.[150]

An Augusta, Georgia, editor wrote after the war that no one could "impugn their patriotism in this war." A Charleston newspaper wrote in 1892 that "the list of South Carolina Jews who remained true to their country and to their country's cause in the darkest hours and who proved their fidelity and patriotism by laying down their lives upon the field of battle could be greatly extended. . . . They possessed what Napoleon called 'the two o'clock in the morning courage,' and they followed the flag with superb loyalty to victory and defeat."[151]

PART 3

Sympathetic Soul
and Busy Hands

★ ★ ★ ★ ★ ★ ★ ★ ★ ★

THE JEWISH CONFEDERATE
HOME FRONT

'Tis mercy's self in woman's form appears,
Whose untold kindness every heart endears.
Behold in hospitals, where dread disease
Lurks . . .
    this noble woman 'midst the gloom,
Dispenses sunlight thro' each darken'd room.
Admist the suffering sick, this angel stands,
With sympathetic soul and busy hands;
Bends o'er the soldier's couch with mother's care,
And soothes the palid brow so deadly fair,
Cheers the sad heart, and hope reviving springs,
And health returning, waves her joyous wing. . . .

Col. Alfred M. Hobby
quoted in Stanley R. Brav, The Jewish Woman,
1861–1865, *AJA* (April 1965), 35–36

Touro Synagogue (Dispersed of Judah) and Canal Street block in the 1850s.
This building, formerly an Episcopal church, stood at Canal and Bourbon
Streets and was given to Dispersed of Judah by Judah Touro in the late
1840s. (Courtesy of Historic New Orleans Collection.)

CHAPTER 5

★

This Most Suffering Land

> Trembling before thy awful throne we kneel,
> Beseeching mercy at thy gracious hand,
> Praying that in compassion thou wilt heal
> The bleeding wounds of this most suffering land.
> —Capt. Samuel Yates Levy, November 2, 1863

FROM RICHMOND TO NEW ORLEANS and from Memphis to Mobile, Southern Jewish civilians—women, the elderly, the young, and the men who would not or could not serve in the armed forces—contributed to the war effort and suffered through the war alongside their neighbors. The largest Jewish populations were in the major Southern cities, which in turn were the chief objects of the Union military juggernaut. The Union navy planned the assault on the Confederacy's largest port, New Orleans, early in the war. Richmond, the capital of the new nation, was the Union army's foremost objective from the first week of the war until it fell on April 3, 1865. Charleston, the "Cradle of Secession," was a principal target of combined land and sea operations, both for its symbolic value as "the place where the Rebellion began" and for its strategic importance. The port cities of Savannah, Mobile, and Memphis, home to smaller Jewish communities, were also Union targets. Thus, the majority of Southern Jewish civilians lived in cities under siege for some or all of the war. In the peculiar demography of the South, despite their small numbers in the region, Jewish Southerners constituted a meaningful percentage of the white population of Southern cities.[1]

Many other Jews lived in smaller cities, towns, and villages in every part of the Confederacy. Some, like Sumter, South Carolina, and LaGrange, Georgia, became a refuge from the fighting in larger urban areas. Others, like Natchez, Vicksburg, and Nashville were battlegrounds and were occupied by Federal forces. Still other small towns, like Georgetown, South Carolina, and Woodville, Mississippi, were fortunate in being located away from the chief theaters of the war.

Jewish Southerners who were not serving in the military continued to engage in selling merchandise as peddlers, or in some other aspect of the mercantile trade. Many men served in the home guard or local militia. More provided services, such as innkeepers, tanners, apothecaries, doctors, or teachers. Unlike the overwhelming

220 majority of Southerners, who lived on farms in rural areas, the Jewish population was dependent on trade in urban areas and small towns for their livelihood. Therefore, once the naval blockade was implemented, Southern cities and Jewish merchants immediately began to suffer economically. When, for example, the siege of Charleston began and the city was shelled by Union artillery, Jewish merchants, store clerks, and their families were forced to close their businesses on lower King Street and either refugee inland or remove to another location beyond the shelling. In Richmond, the city's population swelled, and, at least in the early years of the war, many civilians' businesses improved. In New Orleans, the blockade disrupted commerce, and after the surrender of the city in April 1862, New Orleanians lived under military rule. Thus, each of these Jewish communities experienced a different aspect of the Civil War.

Jewish women, like Southern women generally, fervently supported the cause, tended to the wounded, knitted clothing, and were involved in a variety of war-related activities. Mary Chesnut recorded one typical event in June 1862 when her "Hebrew" friend, Miriam ("Mem") DeLeon Cohen, went to the hospital in Columbia, South Carolina, with "a beautiful Jewess friend," Rachel Lyons:

> Rachel we will call her (be it her name or not) was put to feed a very weak patient. Mem noticed what a handsome fellow he was, and how quiet and clean. She fancied by those tokens that he was a gentleman.
>
> In performance of her duties, the lovely young nurse leaned kindly over him and held the cup to his lips. When that ceremony was over and she had wiped his mouth, to her horror she felt a pair of by no means weak arms around her neck and a kiss upon her lips—which she thought strong indeed. She did not say a word. She made no complaint. She slipped away from the hospital and hereafter she will in her hospital work fire at long range no matter how weak and weary, sick and sore, the patients may be.
>
> "And," said Mem, "I thought he was a gentleman."
>
> "Well, a gentleman is a man after all—and she ought not to have put those red lips of hers so near &c&c&c."[2]

Rachel "La La" Lyons, the daughter of Jacob and Louisa Lyons of Columbia, South Carolina, had grown up as a Southern Jewish belle. Her aunt Isabel Lyons married Moses Cohen Mordecai, owner of the Mordecai Steamship Line, and her uncle Henry Lyons served as mayor. At thirteen she gave the graduation address at the annual Israelite Sunday School Examination.[3] Now at twenty-three she was the most beautiful young Jewish woman of Civil War South Carolina. Her brother, Capt. Isaac L. Lyons, commanded Company A, 10th Louisiana, in Virginia. She was described by Cooper DeLeon as "a marked woman in Columbia society and her quick wit and sinuous grace at once attracted attention at the capital."[4]

Rachel "La La" Lyons was born in Columbia in 1838 into an observant Jewish home. She was a student at Boanna Wolff's Hebrew Sunday School. During the war, she was a femme fatale who enchanted Henry Timrod, later the "poet laureate" of the Confederacy, as well as Mary Chesnut, who described her as a "beautiful Jewess." She married Confederate surgeon Dr. James Fontaine Heustis and moved to Mobile after the war. (Author's collection.)

Miriam DeLeon, first cousin to Edwin, Camden, Agnes, and Cooper DeLeon, was born and raised in South Carolina. She married Dr. Lawrence L. Cohen. Miriam and Mary Boykin Chesnut were old friends. "Mrs. Cohen was Miriam DeLeon," Mary wrote in her diary, "I have known her intimately all my life." Indeed, Mary Chesnut knew all of the DeLeons.[5] Miriam had two children, a young daughter, Isabel ("the sweetest little thing," according to Mary), and a son, Lawrence Ludlow Cohen Jr., his "mother's idol." Young Cohen served in John Chesnut's cavalry company, Boykin's Rangers, initially organized by Mary Chesnut's uncle, Capt. Alexander Hamilton Boykin.[6] The South Carolinians called it "Company A No. 1." Mem was very fond of Capt. John Chesnut and proud of his courage. "Lieutenant Chesnut's horse bolts with him," she told Mary in June 1862, "but right into the heart of the enemy." She was worried, however, about her son's safety. By June of 1862, his unit was part of Whiting's brigade, which had now been sent to Stonewall Jackson's corps. "[S]he has persistently wept ever since she heard the news," Mary recorded on June 16, 1862. "It is no child's play, she says, when you are with Stonewall. He don't play at soldiering. He don't take care of his men at all. He only goes to kill the Yankees."[7]

Mem's life in Richmond revolved around her family and her friends. She worried about everyone and assisted the ailing. In May 1862, she took Mary Chesnut scarce medicine. "Mem Cohen missed me," Mary wrote. "The Jewish angel.

Adah Isaacs Menken as a French spy. A voluptuous, witty, risqué, and mysterious actress from Louisiana, Menken may or may not have been born Jewish, but she became an active Jew after marrying Alexander Isaac Menken in 1856. She was outrageous, appearing "nude" (in a flesh-toned body stocking) while strapped to a horse in *Mazeppa*. She was active in Jewish causes even after divorcing Menken a few months after the wedding. In December 1862, just after Fredericksburg, Menken made a public spectacle of herself in Baltimore by loudly supporting the Confederate cause. She had her dressing room painted Confederate gray and decorated with pictures of Davis, Lee, Bragg, and Van Dorn. The newspapers had a field day; one of her gentlemen callers was arrested as a Confederate spy. Next, Menken was arrested "for Being a Secessionist." She retorted, "Of course, I did not deny the charge." She refused to leave for Dixie or swear an oath of allegiance. The publicity helped her career. She tried the same publicity stunt again in Baltimore in March 1864, but was arrested and sent to Washington, where the government was too busy to prosecute her. Menken has fascinated historians, but she had little real connection to the Confederacy or the war. See John S. Kendall, "'The World's Delight': The Story of Adah Isaacs Menken," *Louisiana Historical Quarterly* 21, no. 3 (July 1938): 846–68 (no, she was not born Jewish); Wolf Menkowitz, *Mazeppa: The Lives, Loves and Legends of Adah Isaacs Menken* (New York: Stein and Day, 1982), 90–92, 125–29; Allen F. Lesser, "Adah Isaacs Menken: A Daughter of Israel," *PAJHS* 34 (1937): 143–47 (yes, she was born Jewish); Leo Shpall, "Adah Isaacs Menken," *Louisiana Historical Quarterly* 26, no. 1 (January 1943): 162–68 (yes, again). (Courtesy of Bob Marcus, Springfield, Virginia.)

Sen. James Chesnut of South Carolina and his wife, Mary Boykin
Chesnut. The Chesnuts lived in Richmond for much of the war. Mr.
Chesnut was a close advisor to and confidante of Jefferson Davis.
Like many Southern aristocrats, Mrs. Chesnut had a number of Jew-
ish friends, including Miriam ("Mem") DeLeon Cohen, Rachel
Lyons, Cooper DeLeon, and Phoebe Pember. This is a prewar pho-
tograph recently found by descendants. (Courtesy of Martha
Williams Daniels, Camden, South Carolina.)

She came with healing on her wings (She found me very ill.) That is, in her hands
she bore opium."[8] Mem and Mary joked incessantly. They nicknamed Brig. Gen.
Johnson Pettigrew , who was reportedly killed at Seven Pines and lived to read his
own "splendid" obituary, "Insensible to Fear." They talked on a daily basis. One
entry in Mary's diary begins, "Miriam's story today" and relates how a friend of
Mem's heard that her son had been killed then heard it was all a mistake. She fell
on her knees with a "shout of joy," only then to see next the hearse drive up in the
midst of her family's celebration with "the poor boy in his metallic coffin."[9]

Like all Southerners, Mem was anxious for the safety of her family. She had long periods of silence and was sometimes absentminded, worrying about her son. If she were suddenly aroused, she would exclaim, "with overflowing eyes and clasped hands, 'If it please God to spare his life.'" During the Battle of Seven Pines, daughter Isabel warned Mary not to mention the battle raging around Richmond—"young Cohen is in it." Like most Jews, she was also anxious for the safety of her co-religionists. She once gave Mary a clipping about a battle. "[O]ne of her Jews is in it," Mary wrote. When there was a battle and her sons survived, "Mem takes up on her Hebrew Bible and sings that glorious hymn of her namesake Miriam: 'Sing ye to the Lord, for He hath triumphed, &c&c&c.'" (In the Torah, Miriam was said to be the sister of Moses, and the song of Miriam celebrates the victory of the Israelites over the Egyptians.)[10]

Another South Carolina Jew, Penina Moise, a poet and the first well-known Jewish woman in the field of American literature, had a different wartime experience. She left her home in Charleston for the safety of inland Sumter. She was accompanied by her widowed sister, Rachel, and Rachel's daughter, Jacqueline. They lived in a two-room cottage and eked out a bare living by running a school. Sixty-four when the war began, Penina Moise was almost totally blind and in poor health. She had been published in the local newspapers, *Godey's Lady's Book* (Philadelphia), newspapers in Boston and New York, and the national Jewish press. Her 1833 collection of poetry, *Fancy's Sketch Book*, was the first published book of poetry by an American Jewish woman.[11]

Eliza "Lize" Moses, age fourteen. She waited for the return of Lt. Albert Luria, but he was mortally wounded at age nineteen at Fair Oaks in May 1862. (Courtesy of Raphael J. Moses of Boulder, Colorado.)

Penina Moise of Charleston.
(Photograph courtesy of
Solomon Breibart, Charleston,
South Carolina.)

When the war began, Miss Moise, like the rest of the Jewish community, was excited about secession. She wrote "Cockades of Blue":

> Hurrah for the Palmetto State!
> Whose patriots the "Minute" await
> That shall summon their band
> To engage hand to hand
> Any foe that dare enter its gate!

But as the war dragged on, lives were lost and Southern fortunes declined, and she became despondent. She wrote "A Reverie":

> A chilling dream of brighter days to come,
> When peace shall be the angel of each house—
> And mapped on Freedom's atlas will be found
> The old Palmetto state with glory crowned . . .
> As with the prophet's dream in ages past
> Coming events may now their shadows cast,
> The blest design of Providence to show,
> Which sendeth balm for every chastening blow.
> Lift Carolina—proudly lift thy head,
> God, through the desert, hath thy children led.[12]

226 In Galveston, Texas, Rosanna Osterman gave so much of her time and resources to wounded soldiers that, upon her death in 1866, the *Galveston News* predicted she would never be forgotten by those she helped. Col. Alfred M. Hobby wrote, "Amidst the suffering sick, this angel stands / with sympathetic soul and busy hands." Isabel Adeline Moses was, at age fourteen, the youngest member of the Soldiers Aid Society of Columbus, Georgia. Like many a Southern girl, she nursed the wounded at the local hospital.[13]

Southern women worked in sewing circles making clothes. The "Jewess ladies" of Charlotte raised $150 to assist the volunteers of the Charlotte Grays. Even the aristocratic Eugenia Phillips considered it her duty to make garments for the soldiers "and looking to the well being of their poor families—making lint bandages as far as in our limited power doing everything to encourage the cause we thought ourselves right in espousing." Southern women were "all heroines," Eugenia Phillips wrote, "everything like dress, amusement, or frivolity was abandoned." Eleanor H. Cohen of Charleston lamented, "We struggled for freedom, but found it not."[14]

Before the war, Jewish immigrant women, like their sisters in Europe, worked beside their husbands (and often their children) in small stores and shops, in the market stalls, sewing clothes to sell, and in the petty trades in which most Jews were engaged. Most Jewish women in the 1860s were hard-working storekeepers, seamstresses, merchants, grocers, peddlers, dressmakers, and small boardinghouse operators. Frederick Law Olmsted described a German Jewess operating a small hotel with her husband in Washington, Louisiana.[15] Both Moses Ezekiel's grandfather Ezekiel and grandmother Hannah worked in their family store.[16] Judah Benjamin's mother opened her small shop on the Sabbath.[17] "Constant references in memoirs and autobiographies to Jewish female work in the nineteenth century," Hasia Din concluded, "contrast sharply with the conventional image of Jewish women of that time as predominantly middle-class . . . while official records may have only portrayed the male 'Jewish shopkeeper,' gender made little difference behind the counter."[18]

While many a well-to-do Southern woman had never learned to sew before the necessities of war introduced them to knitting and dressmaking, most Jewish women were adept at their newly important skill.[19] And while most Southern women lived on farms and experienced the Civil War as both devastating and liberating, the role of Jewish women, who lived in cities and towns and who had always worked in the same marketplace as their husbands, did not change.[20]

The Jewish women of Richmond had a special responsibility to keep families together and give comfort to Jewish soldiers from throughout the South. Beth Shalome and Beth Ahabah cooperated to provide relief especially to the Jewish poor. The women of Beth Shalome met daily in the basement of the synagogue to make clothes. The women of Beth Ahabah did likewise. Jewish women served in the hospitals and took wounded soldiers into their homes. The Jews of Richmond, Herbert Ezekiel wrote, "were just like other people. They fed the hungry, clothed the poor, nursed the sick and wounded, and buried the dead."[21] Emma Mordecai visited Richmond's Seabrook and General Winder hospitals. She wrote in her diary of the "distressing picture . . . of the condition of our brave men, now more prostrate and helpless than infants." She traveled by train from her sister-in-law's plantation, where she resided, to take a supply of buttermilk, sweet milk, and other items. She nearly fainted on one occasion while assisting a surgeon in dressing a wound, but "got over it by sitting near an open window when no longer needed." Others, like Rachel Semon, cared for Jewish soldiers in their homes. Adolph Rosenthal, wounded at Spotsylvania, died in the Semon home before his family could arrive from Savannah. Phoebe Pember, the daughter of Fanny and Jacob C. Levy of Savannah, came to Richmond to serve as matron of Chimborazo Hospital.[22] In this she was quite the exception. "A number of women of prominent background did take matron posts during the war," Drew Gilpin Faust has written. "For the most part, however, Southern ladies regarded a matron's duties as too laborious, too indelicate for women of their social standing."[23]

As the capital of the Confederacy and the chief target of the Union invasion, Richmond was sorely tested by the Civil War. Its population tripled from 37,000 in

View of Main Street, Richmond. This photograph was taken just after the war ended, but it is a good depiction of one of the main Jewish retail areas of the city. Many Jewish Confederates lived and worked on this street. (Courtesy of the Library of Congress.)

1861 to 100,000 by 1865. Housing was scarce; services were disrupted; food and goods were in short supply. The Jewish population increased as Jewish soldiers and government officials arrived. All of the city's congregations and Jewish organizations now took on much greater responsibilities. Both Rabbis Michelbacher and Jacobs ministered to the needs of Jewish boys away from home, refugees, people in want, widows, and grieving families, and they defended their co-religionists against anti-Semitic attacks on the Jewish community. Religious services continued throughout the war. In October 1864, Emma Mordecai recorded in her diary that she "passed into Richmond, where I went to attend Rosha Shannah services" on the very day of a battle raging around the city. On October 10, she went back to town "to spend several days, Monday being Yom Kippur. . . . The services on Kippur eve were solemn and impressive. Mr. Jacobs delivered a short but excellent discourse." She returned on the fifteenth to stay for a week "to keep the Feast of Tabernacles which commenced that evening." She attended "all the services at the Synagogue" and "visited most of my friends and acquaintances."[24]

The Jewish population of Richmond was caught up in the excitement, exhilaration, patriotism, and pathos of the war. The leading Jewish families were ardent supporters of the Confederacy, and their sons and husbands served in the Confederate army. Jacob Levy had come to Richmond forty years earlier and established himself in the dry good business on Main Street. His store, like those of many Jewish merchants, remained opened throughout the war. A well-respected merchant, Levy had two sons in the war, Capt. Ezekiel J. "Zeke" Levy, the eldest, and Pvt. Isaac J. Levy. Daughter Adeline was married to Rev. George Jacobs, the rabbi at Beth Shalome. Two other daughters would later marry Jewish Confederate officers they met during the war.

Jacob A. Levy, Ezekiel and Isaac Levy's father and a prominent Richmond merchant. His home, the *Richmond Dispatch* reported upon his death, "was the rendevous of Confederate soldiers of the Jewish faith." (Courtesy of Beth Ahabah Museum and Archives, Richmond, Virginia.)

(*Right*) Map of Richmond showing key Jewish Confederate sites. (Courtesy of Tim Belshaw.)

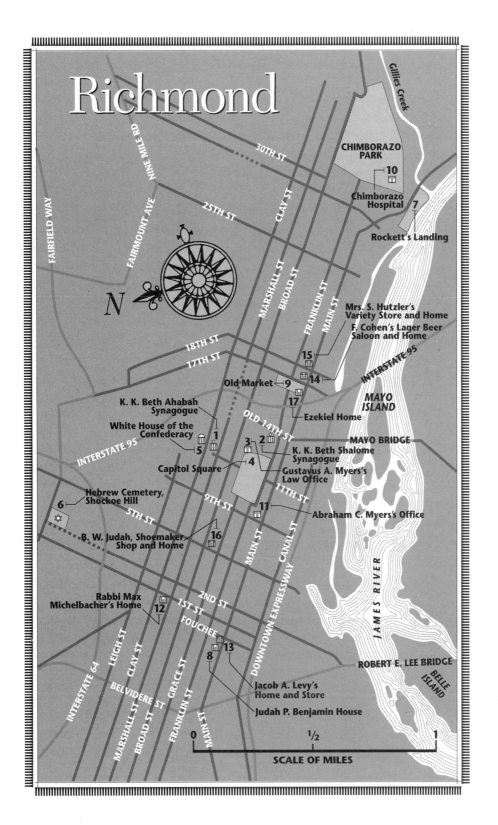

Richmond

Gillies Creek

CHIMBORAZO PARK

10

Chimborazo Hospital — 7

Rockett's Landing

30TH ST

FAIRFIELD WAY

NINE MILE RD

FAIRMOUNT AVE

25TH ST

CLAY ST

MARSHALL ST

BROAD ST

FRANKLIN ST

MAIN ST

N

Mrs. S. Hutzler's Variety Store and Home

F. Cohen's Lager Beer Saloon and Home

18TH ST

17TH ST

INTERSTATE 95

15

14

MAYO ISLAND

Old Market — 9

17

Ezekiel Home

OLD 14TH ST

K. K. Beth Ahabah Synagogue

MAYO BRIDGE

White House of the Confederacy

1

5

3 2

4

K. K. Beth Shalome Synagogue

Capitol Square

Gustavus A. Myers's Law Office

11TH ST

INTERSTATE 95

Hebrew Cemetery, Shockoe Hill

6

5TH ST

9TH ST

11

Abraham C. Myers's Office

B. W. Judah, Shoemaker Shop and Home

16

MAIN ST

CANAL ST

J A M E S   R I V E R

Rabbi Max Michelbacher's Home

12

2ND ST

1ST ST

FOUCHEE

INTERSTATE 64

LEIGH ST

CLAY ST

MARSHALL ST

BROAD ST

GRACE ST

FRANKLIN ST

MAIN ST

BELVIDERE ST

13

8

DOWNTOWN EXPRESSWAY

ROBERT E. LEE BRIDGE

BELLE ISLAND

Jacob A. Levy's Home and Store

Judah P. Benjamin House

0   1/2   1

SCALE OF MILES

Some Richmond families were divided by the war. Jacob Ezekiel, born in Philadelphia, was loyal to the Union, but his grandson, whom he raised as a son, Moses Ezekiel, was an ardent Confederate. Jacob stayed in Richmond on account of his large family, which was pro-Confederate. He contributed, however, to the relief of the Union prisoners at Libby prison in Richmond.[25]

Members of the Richmond Jewish community lived throughout the city, but many, if not most, of them lived above and behind the stores where they worked— on Main, Broad, and Franklin. The Milhisers lived at and operated a dry goods store on Broad between Fifth and Sixth. Isaac Rosenheim sold shoes and lived at 23 West Main. Mrs. C. Abram operated her grocery store on Broad near Jefferson. A. Bodecker & Company sold drugs, medicines, and spices at 10 Main Street. F. Cohen ran a "lager beer saloon" on Seventeenth Street between Main and Franklin. Jacob A. Levy's store was at 15 West Main, as was his residence. The Lichtenstein's clothing store and home was on Franklin between Seventeenth and Eighteenth. The "Old Market" on Seventeenth Street was home to German and Jewish merchants. One "might be at a loss," Samuel Mordecai wrote, "to know whether German or English is the language of the country."[26]

There were few great Jewish merchants in Richmond in 1860. Indeed, the 1860 city directory lists few Jewish names in its section showing "the best in their respective business." The same directory shows that the clothing and retail trade was dominated by small Jewish establishments and that half of the dry goods stores were owned by Jewish Richmonders. There were few doctors, lawyers, or professionals.

Beth Shalome, then still known as the Portuguese synagogue, although there were few Sephardic members, was located on Mayo Street near the state capitol. Beth Ahabah, the German synagogue, was on Eleventh between Clay and Marshall, only one block from Jefferson Davis's residence.

The Richmond rabbis, who referred to themselves as "reverend" and "minister," were ardent Confederates. George Jacobs, in the early 1860s, was a tall, handsome, outgoing young man in his late twenties. Born in Jamaica and speaking with a British accent, he was a popular figure in Richmond, active in the Masons as well as Jewish fraternal organizations. Married to Adeline Hyneman Levy, Jacobs had two brothers-in-law in combat and was committed to serving the cause which now enveloped the Levy and Jacobs families, as well as the entire Richmond Jewish community. Jacobs became the eloquent champion of Richmond's old Jewish families. Max Michelbacher ministered to the needs of Richmond's large German Jewish population. Rabbi of Beth Ahabah, he was a tireless activist on behalf of the Jewish community and the Jewish boys serving in the Confederate army in the Richmond area. His "Prayer for the C.S. Soldier" was presumably printed by Beth Ahabah and distributed to Jewish Confederate soldiers.

Michelbacher worked throughout the war to obtain furloughs for the Jewish soldiers in the Richmond area, especially during Jewish holidays. He first wrote to

Rev. George Jacobs was rabbi at Beth Shalome, Richmond's "Portuguese Synagogue" during the Civil War. Although a native of Jamaica, Jacobs embraced the Confederate cause. He had the sad duty of officiating at the funeral of his own young brother-in-law, Isaac Levy. The top hat was traditional for Sephardic rabbis of the period and was worn during the service, as Orthodox Jews cover their heads in synagogue. (Courtesy of the Beth Ahabah Museum and Archives, Richmond, Virginia.)

Rev. Maximillian ("Max") J. Michelbacher was the spiritual leader of Beth Ahabah, Richmond's "German Synagogue" during the Civil War. Although not an ordained rabbi, he was a vigorous, effective leader of Richmond Jewry, supporting the Confederate effort wholeheartedly and ministering to suffering Jewish soldiers from all over the South. (Courtesy of Beth Ahabah Museum and Archives, Richmond, Virginia.)

Robert E. Lee on August 23, 1861, seeking furloughs for the High Holidays in September. The letter, addressed to "His Excellency R. E. Lee General of CSA," reflects Reverend Michelbacher's continuing struggle to learn the English language: "Excuse me that I intrude on you but the case is important to a class of citizens, being Israelites, who take the greatest interest in the welfare of this confederacy. . . . These ten days from the 5th to the 14th of September (both days inclusive) are the 10 days of Penitence & Prayer, the most sublime of the holiest days of the year."[27]

Lee, then a general in the Confederate army, replied to Michelbacher's request in a courteous letter on August 29. "It would give me great pleasure to comply with a request so earnestly urged by you, & which I know would be so highly appreciated by that class of our soldiers," Lee wrote the rabbi. "But the necessities of war admit of no relaxation of the efforts requisite for its success." Lee continued, "I feel assured that neither you or any member of the Jewish congregation would wish to jeopardize a cause you have so much at heart by the withdrawal even for a season of a portion of its defenders."[28] In March 1863 he wrote General Lee concerning Passover. Lee agreed to comply with the rabbi's requests "as far as the public interest will permit," but he thought it "more than probable that the army will be engaged in active operations, when, of course, no one would wish to be absent from the ranks." The Battle of Chancellorsville occurred a month later in May 1863.[29]

In September 1864 Reverend Michelbacher once again wrote Robert E. Lee about furloughs for the High Holidays to allow the boys to "repair to Richmond to observe the holy days appointed by the Jewish religion." Lee patiently explained that he could not grant a general furlough to one class of soldiers, but that he would do "all in my power to facilitate the observance of the duties of their religion by the Israelites in the army and will allow them every indulgence consistent with safety and discipline."[30] Lee was a deeply committed Christian and tolerant of the religious beliefs of others. On one occasion, an application of a Jewish soldier for permission to attend synagogue was denied and endorsed by his captain: "Disapproved. If such applications were granted, the whole army would turn Jews or shaking Quakers." Lee wrote out the order: "Approved and respectfully returned to Captain —— with the advice that he should always respect the religious views and feelings of others."[31]

Jewish families in Richmond lived in constant dread of receiving news of the death of a family member. Herman J. Myers, Company G, 1st Virginia Cavalry, a cavalryman from Richmond, was wounded near Winchester, Virginia, and left for dead. According to Ezekiel and Lichtenstein, "he was carried to the residence of a fine old Virginia family nearby. There the daughter of the house nursed him back to health and strength." His family had given him up for dead and had sat *shiva*—that is, observed the seven traditional days of mourning. When Myers recovered, he set out for his home in Richmond. Stopping at a hotel in Staunton on the way, he was unable to sleep and woke up early. He went down to the office, where he happened upon his cousin, who had been sent by the family to recover the body. "The 'remains' had indeed been recovered, but in a very unusual manner," the authors concluded. Only the government could use the telegraph lines, so there was no way to inform the family, "all of whom in deep black were down at the depot [in Richmond] to meet the body when the train arrived."[32]

Like Jewish Virginians, Charleston Jewry had rejoiced at the bombardment of Fort Sumter, but the Union naval blockade disrupted the port and worried

General Lee's letter to Reverend Michelbacher, August 29, 1861. In one of his many letters to Rev. Maximillian Michelbacher, General Lee expressed his respect for "the soldiers of the Jewish persuasion in the C. S. Army," but felt he could not grant a general furlough for the High Holidays because it might "jeopardize a cause you have so much at heart." (Courtesy of the Jacob Rader Marcus Center, American Jewish Archives, Cincinnati, Ohio.)

accepted by the Most High, & their petitions answered.

That your prayers for the success & welfare of our Cause may be granted by the great Ruler of the Universe is my ardent wish—.

I have the honour to be with high esteem your obedient

B Elbe
2nd Comm[?]

236   Charlestonians. Blockade-running became big business, and Jewish merchants
joined their Christian colleagues in purchasing goods in this new wartime business
environment. Simon Fass, for example, purchased goods from blockade-runners.
The Fass children remembered stories of their young mother: "She was at a sale
carried on, when a ship would 'smuggle in' or 'run the blockade' during the war
and the folk would go to the wharf to get delicacies that the South did not have
during that time."[33]

The Union navy assault and the fall of Port Royal near Beaufort were of great
concern to the people of Charleston, who knew that the Union army would show
their city no mercy. To make matters worse, a terrible fire swept the city in December 1861, destroying much of the business and retail district. Fortunately, Beth
Elohim and Shearith Israel were just north of the burned-out areas and were
not damaged. By the summer of 1862, many Charlestonians had left the city for
safer climes. The Middleton girls went to their summer home in Flat Rock, North

David Lopez of Charleston was a member of
Beth Elohim, the builder of Institute Hall, where
the South Carolina Ordinance of Secession was
signed, and the builder of the Confederate torpedo boats called the "Davids," which were
designed to do battle with the Union "Goliaths."
(Author's collection.)

This railroad pass, allowing "two colored persons"
to travel to Columbia during the war, was signed
by David Lopez as superintendent of the state
works. (Courtesy of American Jewish Historical
Society, Waltham, Massachusetts, and New York
City.)

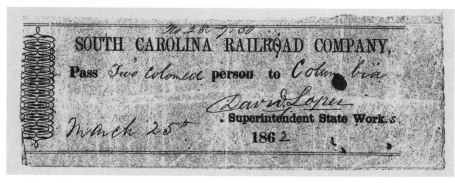

Carolina; Emma Holmes moved to Sumter; and the Smythes inland. The wives and children, and in some cases the elderly men of prominent families, left for the safety of inland towns like Sumter and Columbia. Martial law was declared in order to police a city flooded with refugees, undisciplined Confederate soldiers, and restless slaves. Half of the free black population left also. Beth Elohim's trustees did not meet from 1862 to 1865.[34]

The Union army and navy combined to lay siege to Charleston in April 1863. Much of the civilian population had left the city before the siege began. Once the huge Union guns began the terrible bombardment of the city and its civilian population, most of the residents south of Calhoun Street left their homes. This included much of Charleston Jewry because many lived in and near the retail district on King Street and near their synagogues, Beth Elohim on Hasell Street and Shearith Israel on Wentworth Street. Much of the city's business stopped. The former retail district and exclusive residential area south of Broad Street became a ghost town, known to locals as the "Shell District," on account of the Federal shelling. Most churches, homes, and businesses were closed and shuttered. A rare funeral, conducted at St. Mary's Catholic Church across the street from Beth Elohim, was interrupted by an exploding shell from Union cannons. Beth Elohim was closed, boarded up, and bombarded. Federal shells damaged its roof. The Hebrew Orphan House on Broad Street also closed down.[35]

Berith Shalome apparently remained open, possibly because of its location away from the shelling. It had a functioning board in 1863. Many of its members, including Pincus Pinkussohn, Lippman Rich, Jacob Volaske, and Simon D. Jacobowsky, served in the Confederate army or local militia.[36] Many of the churches sent their valuables to Columbia. Beth Elohim sent its Torah scrolls, the controversial organ, and its magnificent chandelier.[37] Eleanor Cohen, Dr. Philip Melvin Cohen's young daughter and a direct descendent of the first Moises, recalled "how determined the enemy were to possess dear old Charleston, how they shelled the city and we were hurried away, how my home city and forts held out." Eleanor lost her journal of these events, "but thank God," she wrote in 1865, "it lives in my heart and in the heart of every fine southern man, woman, and child."[38] Like many Charlestonians, the Cohens left Charleston for the safety of Columbia. The family remained until the capital city burned in February 1865.

Life, of course, went on, even in Charleston. Before the war, Henry Timrod, a well-known Charleston poet, was obsessed with the beautiful and witty society belle, Rachel Lyons.[39] He and Rachel developed a close relationship that was somewhat flirtatious. Timrod confided in Rachel about his personal life, enjoyed her letters, and craved her compliments about his poetry. He was frustrated with both wartime Charleston and Columbia. "Both places, to be sure, are dull enough," he wrote Rachel in September 1861, "but Columbia, being little more than a country town, is at least *legitimately* so," while Charleston suffered from "its

238 miserable metropolitan pretensions."[40] Timrod was nervous about his close relationship with a Jewish woman. His letters to Rachel contain numerous references to the Old Testament ("my spirit has become a Dead Sea into which no Jordan flows").[41] He admitted that Rachel "is rapidly conquering my old prejudices against the Hebrew."[42] Timrod, always conscious of Rachel's Jewishness, wrote a poem about her in late 1861. It was originally entitled "Rachel," and later given the title "La Belle Juive" (The Beautiful Jewess) and was published in the *Charleston Daily Courier* on January 23, 1862, and in other Southern newspapers.[43] It reads, in part:

> Is it because your sable hair
> Is folded o'er brows that wear
> At times a too imperial air;
> Or is it that the thoughts which rise
> In those dark orbs, do seek disguise
> Beneath the lids of Eastern eyes;
> Or may it be because your soul
> Looks out in features that control
> The Fancy, howso'er it stroll;
> That choose whatever pose or place
> May chance to please, in you I trace
> The noblest women of your race?

By the standards of the time it was not inappropriate for a poet to publish such a poem about an aristocratic Jewish woman, and Jewish Southerners, aware of their distinctiveness in a predominantly Christian culture, took no offense.

Timrod's health, both emotional and physical, was failing him by the fall of 1863. He could not summon up the courage to meet Rachel in Charleston while she was there on a visit in September. "I did not call upon you because I felt sure that it would be impossible for me to meet you except in the midst of the circle which you always draw around you. Once, I heard of your being in St. Michael's steeple," he admitted, but he "was not daring (God forgive me!) enough to hazard an intrusion." (During the war, the young people of Charleston would walk up the steps in the steeple of St. Michael's Church to get a look at the Union fleet and the Union army bombarding the city from the islands across the Ashley River.)[44]

Savannah's Jewish community struggled to survive. "All talk was of *war*," Rebecca Solomons Alexander of Savannah recalled years later. "It was Saturday and my nurse was putting the finishing touches to my toilet for Synagogue." When Rebecca's cousin Nellie arrived, she called to her, "Nellie, the war has begun." To which Nellie replied, "Then I am going straight back home." Rebecca recalled, "She *flew* and I felt as if war must be just around the corner." But her mother reassured her and "together she and I went to pray 'that the South would win.'"[45] Union Adm. Samuel F. Dupont vowed that he would "cork up Savannah like a bottle," and the Union army and navy did. Fort Pulaski, which guarded the mouth of the Savannah River, was captured on April 11, 1862. While the city itself was not captured until Sherman's march in December 1864, it ceased functioning as a port. Business came to a standstill. Families left. "Our commerce is perfectly prostrated," one merchant wrote. "A strange, mysterious, weird quietude reigns perpetually." A visitor wrote, "Stagnation and paralysis obstruct the channels . . . the whole town—every thing—seems to have halted."[46]

Abraham Alexander Solomons, his wife, Cecilia, and their children lived near Pulaski Square when the war began. Solomons was in the drug business with his younger brother Joseph, and his company, A. A. Solomons & Co., had been in business since 1845. When Fort Pulaski fell, little Rebecca Solomons recalled that it "meant the fall of Savannah. So all who could, left the city, our family amongst the refugees." The Solomons refugeed to Columbus, where Mrs. Solomons's sister Sarah Alexander and her brothers Isaac and Ezra Moses lived.[47] Joseph volunteered for Company C (Republican Blues), 1st (Olmstead's) Georgia. As an apothecary, he was appointed acting assistant surgeon.[48]

Mikve Israel continued to function. It remained Orthodox and, despite the large majority of Germans, it followed the Sephardic *Minhag*.[49] Wartime was not the best time for this small Jewish community to engage in its own civil war, but Rabbi Jacob Rosenfeld, who had served at Shearith Israel in Charleston (founded by Beth Elohim dissenters to return to orthodoxy), seceded from Mikve Israel and founded a new Ashkenazic congregation. This was preceded by a number of disagreements with the *adjunta*. When the rabbi requested a salary increase in August 1862 in the midst of the Union blockade, his timing could hardly have been worse. The adjunta told him he could earn more by instituting a Hebrew school. They quarreled over the activities of the school. The *shochet*, Mr. Zechariah, the rabbi, said, left the city and failed to provide kosher meat. The rabbi resigned, and the board locked him out of the synagogue. Rosenfeld then founded B'nai B'rith Jacob. Services were conducted during the war years by lay readers at Mikve Israel. B'nai B'rith Jacob met at Armory Hall.[50]

Jewish residents of Savannah lived and worked throughout the city, but most, according to Mark I. Greenberg, lived in an area stretching sixteen blocks from Bryan to Jones Streets and nine blocks from West Broad (now M. L. King Boulevard) to Abercorn. German immigrants lived along Bryan, Congress, and Broughton in the midst of shops and businesses. Elias Cohen, for example, lived at 150 Broughton; his store was next to his house. Third- and fourth-generation Savannah Jews moved south of the commercial district to Elbert, Jackson, and Brown wards. Many lived along Liberty Street between Drayton and Jefferson. There lived Solomon Cohen, Samuel Yates Levy, and Abraham Minis. Affluent Germans Abraham Einstein, Joseph Sichels, and Samuel H. Eckman lived nearby.[51] The Solomon Cohen home still stands at Barnard and Liberty.[52] Many

The home of the Minis family in Savannah. Just before the war, Abraham
Minis, who was named for his great-grandfather, one of the first settlers of
Savannah, was a leading merchant, insurance agent and cotton factor, and
an alderman in Savannah. He served as acting mayor in 1860. The Minis
family had known Robert E. Lee since his service as an army engineer in
the 1830s. "The family of Isaac Minis," Douglass Southall Freeman wrote
in *R. E. Lee,* "gave him cordial welcome, made the more delightful by the
presence of two daughters, Sarah and Philipa." Lee gave Sarah pen-and-
ink drawings of an alligator and a terrapin he had made on Cockspur
Island when he was building Fort Pulaksi. The Minises were happy to
entertain Lee again when he arrived in Savannah to arrange for its defense
early in the war. (Author's collection. Photograph by Michael Levkoff.)

Jewish residents of Savannah lived within walking distance of Mikve Israel, near
Liberty and Whitaker. This Jewish elite was well connected with and married into
the city's Christian elite. Jacob Florence Minis, for example, married Phoebe
Pember's friend, Louisa Porter Gilmer, whose father, Maj. Gen. Jeremy F. Gilmer,
served as chief of the bureau engineers of the Confederacy and for a time as second in command of the Department of South Carolina, Georgia, and Florida.
Solomon Cohen's daughter Miriam married James Troup Dent, a descendant of a
governor of Georgia.[53] Octavus Cohen and his family lived on Lafayette Square
(Macon and Abercorn).[54] His office was at 82 Bay Street near the riverfront.

The majority of Savannah's Jewish population, like Charleston's, was native-
born. Mark Greenberg estimates that 57.4 percent was born in the South. But
those born in Germany accounted for 32.5 percent. Many, like the Lippmans,
came from Bavaria. Joseph Lippman, born in Reichmandorf, came to America in

An 1856 wedding photograph of
Mr. and Mrs. Louis Haiman of
Columbus, Georgia. (From the
collection of Louis Schmier,
Valdosta, Georgia.)

1837, married Babette Eckman in Philadelphia, and moved to Savannah in 1842. He helped organize a German military company and was a leader in the local secession assembly.[55]

Some families stayed on during the war. Some who left, returned. Rebecca Solomons recalled the funerals of both Gen. Francis Bartow after Bull Run and the young Habersham brothers killed within an hour on the same day in the Battle of Atlanta. Mrs. Solomons took "such delicacies as could be had" to the sick soldiers at the Wayside Home, a Confederate hospital. The Solomons women wore calico and homespun dresses rather than the fine silk dresses Mrs. Solomons had brought back from New York just before the war began. Mr. Solomons traveled to Wilmington to purchase goods from blockade-runners and brought back "pieces of dress goods and shoes of all sizes so that the whole family, aunts and cousins, were dressed alike." Rebecca also recalled an exchange of prisoners "and everyone went out to the Park Extension and carried food to the men, so many sick and hungry." The officers were welcomed into private homes, including the home of the Solomonses. Rebecca's cousins Julius and Jacob Clarence were stationed nearby, as was her uncle Joseph M. Solomons for a time.[56]

Jewish Savannahians saw many of their own fight and die for the Confederacy. Mrs. Solomon Cohen lived to see thirty-two of her descendants enlist in the armed forces of the Confederacy. One of them was Col. Abraham C. Myers, the quartermaster general.[57] Gratz Cohen, the only son of Solomon Cohen, was killed at the Battle of Bentonville and was buried at Laurel Grove Cemetery in Savannah.[58]

There were approximately forty Jewish families in Augusta, Georgia, during the war and a small community in Columbus. Jewish Georgians were involved in the war effort and in all manner of trade. Louis and Elias Haiman had emigrated from Prussia and settled in Columbus in the 1830s. Their father owned a hardware store and, when war was declared, the Haimans began manufacturing swords. Soon, they purchased the Muscogee Ironworks. Elias traveled to Europe to buy more raw material when supplies ran out. Eventually, the Haimans produced saddles, bayonets, tin cups, and mess articles.[59] Simon Rothschild, who began as a peddler, manufactured army uniforms in Columbus. He supplied 4,000 uniforms to the Confederate army and 1,500 to the Georgia militia.[60] Henry Solomon of Augusta wrote his to brother in June 1864 that blockade-running "has been successful lately. Nine vessels arrived in one week. Business has been very dull here since November. Merchants are almost bare of goods. Very few have made or making expenses since Christmas. Confederate money buys very little of anything." Solomon blamed the economic problems on the government. "Our financial affairs," he told his brother, "are ruinously managed." He then suggested "a Yid or good merchant in the Treasury Bureau."[61] But Solomon was still optimistic that the war could be won. "'Uncle Bob,' as General Lee is called," he wrote, "becomes a greater General every day. He has the entire confidence of the people." Solomon was proud of Beauregard's "severe whipping" of Benjamin F. Butler during the Bermuda Hundred Campaign and hoped that General Johnston could stop General Sherman's march. Nevertheless Solomon believed the South "will be *macholu* [bankrupt] for many years."[62]

The small Augusta Jewish community suffered grievous losses. At least four Jewish men from the city were killed. In April 1862, when Lt. J. Julius Jacobus, a promising young attorney, was killed at Shiloh, the Richmond County Bar placed

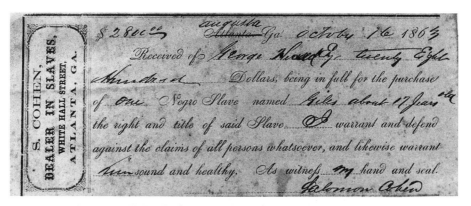

"S. Cohen, Dealer in Slaves, White Hall Street, Atlanta, Ga." This title or invoice for the sale of "one Negro Slave" was signed by Solomon Cohen on October 16, 1863, in Augusta, Georgia. (Courtesy of Paul Blatner, Savannah, Georgia. Photograph by Michael Levkoff.)

Canal Street, New Orleans, in the Civil War era. This street was home to many Jewish businesses. (Courtesy of the Louisiana State Museum.)

in its minutes a lengthy resolution praising Jacobus's "fine character, popular manners, energy and fine intellectual endowments." The resolution praised "his useful and exemplary life and glorious death." The members resolved "that we will all wear the usual badges of mourning for thirty days." The court adjourned for two days.[63]

As the war progressed and the blockade tightened, the Jewish citizens of New Orleans felt the impact of shortages and the anxiety of war. "New Orleanians," Chester G. Hearn wrote, "felt the squeeze on their accustomed freedom, as well as on their wallets and stomachs, and with each passing month they wondered when something would be done to drive off the Union blockade."[64] Rising prices and scarcity of money greatly affected the German immigrants. This was true of the Jews as well. "Yet, the business of the city," John Nau concluded, "was going in its normal way, to judge from the surface."[65] "Things are daily increasing in price," Clara Solomon wrote in her diary. "Soap which formerly was 20 cts. a bar, is now $1.00! Coffee $1. per pound, and Ma has notified us we must soon say 'good bye' to it. She tried the experiment of mixing it with rye, but we were dissatisfied with it . . . What are we coming to? The Blockade must be raised." Clara wondered how, if the war continued and the young men went off to fight, "can we have any beaus!"[66]

But these inconveniences did not dampen her enthusiasm for the cause. "Today one year ago," Clara wrote on November 6, 1861, "Abe Lincoln was elected President of the United States. How many changes since then have transpired. How much has been accomplished." Some things did not change. Clara and her family continued to "promenade" up Canal Street after synagogue services on Carondelet Street on Saturday, and shop and have lunch at Blineau's restaurant. On Saturday, November 16, 1861, Clara and her friends and family were among the thousands of New Orleanians who watched a "grand review" of the local troops. Clara was impressed with the number of soldiers—more than ten thousand, she recalled—to "keep the invader" from the soil of Louisiana. And she was proud to see her "noble Cousin" Samuel Myers of Company F, 4th Louisiana "at the head of his command, and screaming at the height of his voice, 'Forward March'!! It was a splendid turnout. How I would like to see them all 'pitch' into the Yankees and give them a sound thrashing." Many citizens visited Camp Benjamin, named for Judah P. Benjamin, and enjoyed picnicking there.[67]

New Orleans's four congregations—Gates of Mercy, the old German synagogue on Rampart Street in the French Quarter; Dispersed of Judah, the Portuguese or Sephardic synagogue on Carondelet; Gates of Prayer, the new German synagogue in Lafayette City; and Temime Derech, the Polish congregation on Carondelet Street farther uptown—continued to hold services and minister to the needs of New Orleans Jewry during the war. The rabbis of the Crescent City all supported the Confederate cause. Even the Reverend Dr. Bernard Illowy, who later cooperated with the occupation army, said in the sixth anniversary address of the Association for the Relief of Jewish Widows and Orphans: "Liberty, fraternity and equality are the precious acquisitions of this day, and the fundamental principles of our glorious Confederacy, under whose banner every one will find protection," be they a Polander, Bavarian, Frenchman, or Hungarian.[68]

The war also brought death and grief to New Orleans Jewry. J. B. Joseph, a friend of Clara Solomon, was killed at Shiloh. A native of South Carolina, he had moved to New Orleans with his family six years earlier. Rabbi Gutheim "spoke quite pathetically of the deaths of our two members, & all shed the pitying tear," Clara wrote in her diary. "My feelings were more touched," she continued, "seeing Mr. J. [Joseph], an old man, shedding such tears of bitterness, so completely bowed down with grief." Lt. Joseph Calhoun Levy of the 3d Louisiana, Eugene Henry Levy's brother, was also killed in action at Shiloh. Clara noted in her diary that "his grief-stricken parents are inconsolable."[69]

The Solomon family suffered along with their friends and relatives. Clara grieved in her diary for the loss of Gen. Albert Sidney Johnston, who was also killed

---

(*Right*) Map of New Orleans showing key Jewish Confederate sites. (Courtesy of Tim Belshaw.)

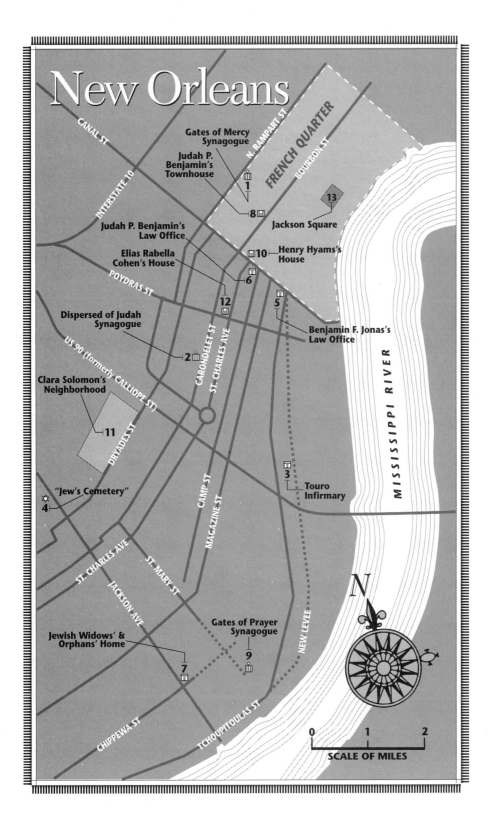

New Orleans

FRENCH QUARTER

CANAL ST

INTERSTATE 10

N. RAMPART ST

BOURBON ST

Gates of Mercy Synagogue

Judah P. Benjamin's Townhouse

1

8

13

Jackson Square

Judah P. Benjamin's Law Office

Elias Rabella Cohen's House

POYDRAS ST

10

Henry Hyams's House

6

12

5

Dispersed of Judah Synagogue

CARONDELET ST

ST. CHARLES AVE

Benjamin F. Jonas's Law Office

US 90 (formerly CALLIOPE ST)

2

Clara Solomon's Neighborhood

DRYADES ST

11

MISSISSIPPI RIVER

CAMP ST

MAGAZINE ST

3

Touro Infirmary

"Jew's Cemetery"

4

ST. CHARLES AVE

ST. MARY ST

JACKSON AVE

NEW LEVEE

Gates of Prayer Synagogue

Jewish Widows' & Orphans' Home

9

7

N

CHIPPEWA ST

TCHOUPITOULAS ST

0   1   2

SCALE OF MILES

64	Joseph Osterman	August 21 1861	January 6 1866	63	5
24	Walter son of L.C. Labatt	May 14 1863	" 29 "	8	2
64	Rosanna Osterman	February 2" 1866	February "	57	5
29	Joseph Depass	March 23 "	March 25 "	88	3
83	Sarah Joseph	May 15 "	May 16 "	64	7
2	Infant of A.H. D'Meza	" 18 "			1
69	Isaac Wolf	September 15 "	September 14 "	48	4
58	Marx Aaron Heyman	" 23 "	" 24 "	4 m.	4
44	Solomon Benjamin	" 26 "	" 27 "	53	5
82	Ulysis Abraham Cazeres	March 28 1867	March 29 1867	47 h.w	7
62	Robert Lee Block	August 9 1866	April 29 "	172 m	5
81	Joseph Calhoun Levy	April 5 1862	May 24 "		7
140	Lewis J. Winehill	June 5 1867		26	11
81	Reuben Levy	" 11 "	June 12 "	60	7
84	Jacques Olveira	" 18 "	" 19 "	31	7
80	Infant of W.A. White	August 15 "			7
84	M.C. Marcelles	" 16 "	August 17 "	40	7
84	Solomon Offner	" 26 "		22	7
84	Henry Renger	September 1 "		40	7
84	Hyman Lewis Silverstone	" 5 "	September 6 "	23	7
4	Noah J. Ellis	" 7 "	" 8 "	70	1
28	Barney Woolf	" 10 "		33	3
79	Louisa Jonas	" 10 "		58	7
84	Pauline B. Levi	" 13 "		19	7

Dispersed of Judah death record book. This New Orleans synagogue record book shows Joseph Calhoun Levy's death on April 5, 1862. He was interred on May 27, 1862, in Row 7, Grave 295. The Death Record Book, now at Tulane University, shows that Levy "died at the Battlefield of Shiloh" on "5 Nissan 5622"—that is, the fifth day of the month of "Nissan" in the Jewish year 5622. (Courtesy of Tulane University, Manuscript Department.)

at Shiloh. Many went to view the funeral procession for General Johnston, which passed through Clara's neighborhood, but Clara could not bring herself to attend. "As the sound of the sad music & muffled drums fell upon my ear, prayers for the future happiness of the great patriot, he who had died for us, ascended to the throne of the Most High."[70] But she could not avoid grief over the deaths of young Levy and Joseph, members of her congregation. Shiloh was the bloodiest day in American history to that date. It was the first great carnage of the war, "the devil's own day," according to General Sherman. But the death and destruction would be far surpassed as the war continued.[71]

brought from Galveston, Texas.	Amsterdam, Holland	15	Elul	5621	Accidental Gunshot wound
brought from Summit, Miss	New Orleans	27	Yiar	5623	Drowned.
do from Vicksburg	Mayence, Germany	17	Shebat	5624	Do
	Savannah, Ga	7	Nissan	.	General Paralysis
	New-York	1	Sivan	.	Dropsy.
	New Orleans	4	.	.	Still born.
	Prussia.	6	Tishri	5627	Asiatic Cholera.
	New Orleans	15	.	"	Meningitis
died at Fairview Plantation St Charles Parish La	Charleston S.C	18	.	.	Organic disease of the Brain, caused by an attack of malignant Fever
	New Orleans	21	Veadar	.	Diphtheria
died & was temporary buried at Mississippi City.	New Orleans	28	Ab	5626	Inflamation of the brain.
died at the Battlefield of Shiloh	New Orleans	5	Nissan	5622	Killed in Battle of Shiloh
Coroners inquest	Russia	2	Sivan	5627	Cutting his throat.
	Charleston. S.C	6	.	.	General Debility. result of long continued disease of the Kidneys.
	Amsterdam Holland	15	.	.	Phthysis Pulmonalis.
	New Orleans	14	Ab	.	Still born
	England	15	.	.	Congestive chill.
	New York	25	.	.	Yellow Fever
	Poland	1	Elul	.	do
	do	5	"	.	do
	New York	7	.	.	Apoplexy.
	England	10	.	.	Yellow Fever
		10	.	.	do
	France	13	.	.	do

The reality of the war came home to the Jews of New Orleans by the spring of 1862. "To think of soldiers, real soldiers camping in our squares, the places devoted to the gatherings of our children," Clara wrote. "Tents, real tents scattered around. Who, a few years back, would have imagined such a thing." And at the end of March, Clara wrote: "Our city is now a camp, up town and down town." New Orleans Jewry celebrated what must have been an ironic and meaningful Passover in March of 1862. Many Jewish men were in arms and away defending their country. Jewish families, like all New Orleans families, were fearful about the future and nervous about a possible Union invasion. Mrs. Solomon and many Jewish families ordered their matzo from a Mr. Da Silva, the sexton at the Dispersed of Judah synagogue. "Pasaic [Hebrew for Passover, now spelled "Pesach"] is fast approaching," Clara wrote, "and . . . our butter, our precious butter is almost gone, gone, gone." Shortages caused by the blockade even ruined the Passover matzo. Bread was impossible to buy. Bakers quit baking; the cost of flour had become prohibitive.

Emma Solomon (1824–1913). Solomon Solomon's wife and Clara Solomon's mother, Emma Solomon was born in Charleston. She and her husband were likely married at Beth Elohim and moved to New Orleans. They had six daughters: Alice, Clara, Fanny, Rosa, Sallie, and Josie. (Courtesy of Alice Dale Cohan, Great Neck, New York.)

"Our 'motzoes' are so miserably sour that I don't think I have eaten a whole one," Clara wrote. "But for form sake we must have them." The Solomons cleaned their home thoroughly, as was the Orthodox custom, to rid the house of leavened bread. By April 1862, it began to dawn on the people of New Orleans that the city could fall to the Union army and navy. A friend of the Solomon family advised Mrs. Solomon to put away provisions for some months, as, Clara wrote, "it is possible that N. O. will soon be in the hands of the cussed Yankees." Clara considered this possibility with alarm: "What a miserable state of existence to be governed by Yankee devils. Oh! God! It is too terrible to contemplate."[72]

The terrible event arrived when New Orleans fell to Comdr. David G. Farragut's fleet on April 24, 1862. In a bold attack, Farragut sent a large fleet past fortified positions at the mouth of the Mississippi and conquered the South's largest and richest city. Clara Solomon called it "the most daring naval exploit ever attempted." Philip Sartorious, a young Jewish merchant from rural Louisiana, was in New Orleans when it fell. The scene was "almost indescribable," he later recalled. Bales of cotton were cut open and set on fire. Gunboats were on fire, and "hoodlums threw balls and shells overboard." The streets were packed with people fleeing. Sartorious and his friends were lucky enough to get a ride on a railroad platform car headed inland. The Jewish community reacted as other New Orleans citizens did—with shock, anger, disbelief, and disdain. Clara wrote, "a gloom has settled o'er my spirit, a gloom envelopes our dearly-beloved city. My breaking heart but aches the more. . . . Oh! never have I experienced such emotions. . . . Oh! *never* shall I forget the 25th of Apr. 1862."[73]

(*Left*) Rabbi James Gutheim was the spiritual leader of Dispersed of Judah Synagogue of New Orleans. When the Crescent City was captured, he refused to swear allegiance to Gen. Benjamin Butler's occupation regime and left the city for Montgomery, Alabama. (Courtesy of the Jacob Rader Marcus Center, American Jewish Archives, Cincinnati, Ohio.)

Israel I. Jones of Mobile. Jones was born in London in 1810. He and his wife, Eliza, settled in Mobile in 1838. A successful merchant, Jones served as alderman and mayor pro tem. He was the president of the Mobile Musical Association and president of Gates of Heaven from 1844 to 1876. He lost a son in the Civil War. His daughter, Emilie, married Rabbi James K. Gutheim. (Portrait by Nicola Marschall. Courtesy of the Gates of Heaven Archives and Robert J. Zietz of Mobile.)

Many Jews, particularly the old Sephardic and German families, left the city. One New Orleans Jew wrote that "almost the entire Jewish population daily leave, and two-thirds of the Portuguese Congregation with their Rabbi [James K. Gutheim] have already departed." Gutheim was married in December 1858 to Emilie Jones of Mobile. Her father was I. I. Jones, the prominent merchant and leader of the Jewish community of Mobile. When New Orleans fell to the Union forces, Gutheim, his wife, and his son left for Alabama. On May 8, he wrote to his friend, Rabbi Isaac Leeser of Philadelphia: "Day after tomorrow I shall leave N[ew] O[rleans] by order of the military authorities. All those who have refused to take the oath of allegiance to the Dictator of Washington are ordered beyond the lines—that is, into Dixie. I am of that number. Nearly the whole of my congregation are similarly situated. We can now realize what a [deportation] means. Nothing but my wearing apparel and provisions for ten days are permitted. . . . I trust to God, to guide my steps. If possible I shall write you from the Confederacy."[74]

On the Sabbath before Rabbi Gutheim left, the synagogue was crowded, as many people in addition to his own congregation wanted to hear the eloquent rabbi once more. A New Orleanian wrote, "in the place which will know him no longer under the present condition of things. . . . When about to sail with his banished members and their families from their late home, he offered up a touching prayer to the throne of the Most Merciful, which moved the hearts of his hearers."[75] Gutheim served as rabbi in Montgomery, Alabama, and Columbus, Georgia, for the duration of the war. He returned to New Orleans in 1865.[76]

Joseph H. Marks was another Confederate who refused to take the oath. Born in New York City but raised in South Carolina, Marks was in the grocery business with his brother, I. N. Marks. He was banished for refusing to take the oath of allegiance and left for Columbia, South Carolina, where he was "burned out by Sherman's army." His home in New Orleans was confiscated. After the war, Marks moved to New York City for fifteen years, then returned to New Orleans.[77]

Mary Chesnut related a story in her diary about Edwin Warren Moise's escape from occupied New Orleans and "How Mr. Moise got his money out of New Orleans." Moise went to a station with his two small sons. When he arrived, the carriage he expected was not there. He had no money about him because he knew he would be searched. Some friend called out, "I will lend you my horse, but then you will be obliged to leave the children." This offer was accepted, and as Moise rode off, one of the boys called out, "Papa, here is your tobacco, which you have forgot." Moise turned back, and his son handed him a roll of tobacco, which he had held openly in his hand all the time. Mr. Moise took it, galloped off, waving his hat to them. In that roll of tobacco was encased $25,000.[78]

Many Jews living under the military rule imposed by the Union army resented the invaders and refused to have anything to do with them. Others probably welcomed the end of hostilities and the end of the blockade, which allowed business to resume. Certainly the older families and the pro-Southern immigrants resented army rule. Clara Solomon was pleased that $2 million in cotton had been burned to keep it from the Yankees, and she agreed with the city authorities' decision to refuse to lower their flag and raise the flag of the United States.[79]

The women of New Orleans resented the invaders and showed it on a daily basis. Many wore black mourning bands, and others wore clothing with the Confederate flag as a pattern. The ladies refused to sit in the same trolley car or church pew with Union soldiers. Jewish women shared this contempt, as evidenced by Eugenia Phillips's arrest and exile and Clara Solomon's strong feelings. Benjamin "Beast" Butler reacted to these insults with his infamous General Order 28, "the Woman Order." Clara could hardly believe what she had heard. "I cannot express to you the indignation this thing awakened. . . . The cowardly wretches! To notice the insults of ladies!" How could any truly Southern woman come in contact with a Yankee and "allow her countenance to retain its wonted composure." She even made faces at and sarcastic remarks to Union soldiers she encountered. As time went on, the hatred of Butler grew. By late June 1862, Clara wished that "Old

Butler" could have as many ropes around his neck as there were "ladies in the city & each have a pull! Or if we could fry him! Or give him many salt things to eat, & have water in sight, & he unable to obtain it!"[80]

Judah Benjamin's sisters Mrs. Levy, Mrs. Kruttschnitt, and Harriet Benjamin were living in New Orleans when the Federal fleet arrived. Pierce Butler wrote in his 1907 biography of Benjamin, "immunity on the part of women known to be related to the hated Confederate Secretary of State could not long be expected under the rule of such heroes as the North bestowed upon New Orleans." One night in the summer of 1862, about nine o'clock, there came a knock on the door of the Levy home. It startled the family. Riley, the black servant ("dining-room man") went to answer it and returned agitated to announce that "there's a Yankee right at the door." Mrs. Levy and Harriet fled, leaving Mrs. Levy's young daughter to face the Federal lieutenant, who told her that he had been sent to warn her family that the house was needed by the military authorities and would be taken possession of in the morning and used as a hospital for General Weitzel's men. "This will do," he said, after inspecting the rooms with a candle while Miss Levy followed, protesting vainly. "If you wish to leave at once," the officer told her, "you may take away such things as you absolutely need; a squad of men will be sent to protect you to-night." The family began packing up at once. Fortunately, when the soldiers came, the men proved to be Germans who had known Mr. Popham, Benjamin's German brother-in-law. By humoring them and plying them with what was left of Judah Benjamin's rare old bourbon and cognac, the Benjamin family prevailed on the Union soldiers to move nearly all of the furniture as well as a cow to the practically empty house of a neighbor.

All through the night they worked, packing and moving. In the morning, as Mrs. Levy was sitting on a bundle of the family's belongings on the front porch, another squad of soldiers, with an insolent young officer in command, came to relieve the complaisant guard of the past night. "Madam," said the officer, "are you the sister of the arch rebel, Benjamin?" Mrs. Levy admitted that she was. "Then you are not to remove anything from this house. It is a military necessity." Fortunately, this individual was relieved later in the day by a more reasonable officer, who permitted the Benjamin clan to remove the few remaining things. After a few days of discomfort and uncertainty, they rented two rooms in the French Quarter, where they lived for some weeks. A letter came from Mr. Benjamin advising them to make their way "out into the Confederacy, where we could be in communication with him." Mrs. Levy and her family made their way to LaGrange, Georgia, where they remained for the rest of the war. Benjamin sent them money, "as much as he could spare, and provisions, denying himself, we feared, to promote our comfort," his niece recalled.[81]

Joseph Benjamin, one of Judah P. Benjamin's brothers, served for a time with the 1st Louisiana Cavalry. His military record was uneven. For reasons which are

252   not clear, he and most of the junior officers of Col. J. S. Scott's Calvary Regiment were placed under arrest in May 1862 and later resigned. Arrests as a result of disagreements with a prickly superior officer were not uncommon during the Civil War. Joseph later formed his own cavalry company in December 1863. His company was likely a headquarters escort for Maj. Gen. Richard Taylor. In October 1864, Judah Benjamin wrote that Joseph was "still in the trans-Mississippi, and was unable to accompany Dick Taylor when he crossed to this side, in consequence of his ill health." Joseph Benjamin and his company must have remained as an escort for Taylor's successors in the District of Louisiana.[82]

Judah Benjamin's other brother, Solomon Benjamin, was clearly an embarrassment to the secretary of war. When Baton Rouge was captured, Solomon apparently took the oath of allegiance to the Union. At least this is what Gen. Benjamin Butler wrote to the secretary of war in 1862: "I brought before me some of the most violent of the rebels, and after calling their attention to the present state of things, I proposed to them the oath of allegiance, and after consideration over night, two of them, Mr. Benjamin, brother of the Rebel secretary of war, and Byam, mayor of the city, took the oath."[83] Butler later wrote that a Confederate presidential proclamation denouncing Butler "was written by Benjamin, who has an enormous grudge at me for doing a thing which he did not mention to the proclamation, i.e., so thoroughly preaching Unionism to his brother at Baton Rouge in July, that he took the oath of allegiance, declaring himself a Union man."[84] As neither Judah Benjamin nor his many biographers mention Solomon as an adult, it is likely that he was disowned by his illustrious brother, or at least they were estranged. He died shortly after the war. Joseph Benjamin, on the other hand, fled to Mexico after the war and later settled in Spanish Honduras. When asked why he would not return to the country, he is said to have answered: "I wouldn't take the oath of allegiance to the United States."[85]

In the summer of 1862, after the fall of New Orleans, Mrs. Henry Hyams, the lieutenant governor's non-Jewish wife, was walking down the street when she was accosted by Union soldiers. According to the story in the *Mobile Register* and reprinted in the *Charleston Daily Courier,* Mrs. Hyams had the misfortune to pass by a number of Union officers sitting in a doorway. One followed her and, blocking her path, told her she had not bowed to him as she passed, as required by Gen. Benjamin "Beast" Butler's infamous order. She attempted to avoid the officer, but he put his arms around her waist and, according to the news reports, "pressed his foul lips upon her face. As the villain released her from his embrace, the Southern lady coolly drew a pistol and shot him through the body, so that he fell dead at her feet." Mrs. Hyams, the story went, was spirited away by a sympathetic Union officer who helped her reach the Southern lines.[86]

Typical of the immigrant Jews of Civil War New Orleans were the Cohen and Goldstein families. Solomon Cohen and his father, Elias Rabella Cohen, emigrated

(*Left*) Elias Cohen, Solomon Cohen's father. Elias emigrated to New Orleans in the late 1840s or early 1850s from Russian Poland. He lived at St. Charles and Poydras and died in 1874 at the age of 100. This photograph was taken circa 1870. (Courtesy of Cecile Levine, New Orleans.)

Fanny Goldstein Cohen, the wife of Solomon Cohen and widow of Jacob Goldstein. An immigrant from Russia, Fanny lived in New Orleans and Mississippi. (Courtesy of Cecile Levine, New Orleans.)

from Russian Poland in the 1840s. Elias had been a rabbi in his Polish village and retained his Old World appearance well into the 1870s. By 1860, Elias was living at the corner of Poydras and St. Charles Streets in New Orleans; Solomon enlisted in March 1862 as a private "for the war." He served in Company B, 28th (Thomas's) Louisiana. In August 1862 he was in the camp hospital. He was wounded at Vicksburg. (Solomon Cohen's family tells the story that while he *was* wounded at Vicksburg, he was shot while stealing a chicken.)[87]

During the war Fanny Goldstein married Jacob Goldstein, a merchant. They lived in Liberty, Mississippi, where Fanny's father had a store. Jacob enlisted and was wounded at Shiloh. Fanny, worried about her husband, determined to bring him medicine and set out for the hospital. According to her daughter's recollection, Jacob Goldstein must have been a prisoner because the whole area was in Union hands. The "buxom and beautiful Fanny" went through Union lines, her daughter recalled, "dressed as a nun, hiding her auburn tresses, and she sewed medicines into the seams of her voluminous skirts."[88] Despite the ministrations of his devoted wife, Jacob died. Fanny took the oath of allegiance in November 1862. When Solomon Cohen, who was described by his descendants as a "scholarly and poetic gentleman" with red hair, was wounded at Vicksburg, he returned to Fanny for care and attention. They were married in 1864.

Ferdinand Goldsmith's story was also typical. He was born in Mobile in 1841. His family moved to New Orleans in 1846 and lived first on Gravier near Canal, then uptown in the 1850s to Nayades (now St. Charles). Ferdinand attended Louisiana College and worked in his father's store, Goldsmith, Haber & Co. He joined the Creole Guards but had been in camp only sixty days when New Orleans was captured. When the Confederate troops left the city, Goldsmith's unit disbanded. Goldsmith then went to Baton Rouge, where he met up with four or five comrades from his regiment, including Morris Abrams and Josh Henriquez. Apparently, the boys decided to go back to New Orleans for a little adventure. Goldsmith got involved in buying and selling sugar, which he stored in his uncle's store on Magazine Street at Poydras, a few blocks from Canal and the Levee. He prospered by shipping sugar to New York City.[89]

George Jonas, a prominent Jewish leader of New Orleans and a member of the large and influential Jonas family. He served as an officer of both the Jewish Orphan's Home and Touro Infirmary. (Courtesy of the Touro Infirmary Archives, New Orleans.)

New Orleans continued to attract Jewish immigrants while the war was in progress and the city was occupied by Federal troops. Jewish settlers came from many directions, including the North. Salomon Marx, for example, was a German immigrant from Mainz who came to New York with his parents and then to New Orleans in 1864. He operated a riverboat company between New Orleans and Shreveport. Salomon soon married eighteen-year-old Clara Marx, who had just arrived from Germany to live with her uncle and aunt, Adolph and Sophie Marx, who had come to Louisiana from France. Their children worked as "drummers," selling goods at the countryside. (Their son, David Marx, was later the well-known rabbi at the Temple in Atlanta.)[90]

The Jewish Orphan's Home continued in operation despite the departure of a number of prominent Jewish leaders, including Reverend Gutheim, who was the home's treasurer, and Joseph Magner, a board member, both of them "having come under the decree of banishment." The home's president, George Jonas, later recalled that "the evil day had come. The effect of the war between the states showed its traces everywhere. But a kind Providence watched over our Home."[91]

New Orleans Jewry, unlike Charleston and Richmond back east, was divided by the war. Rabbi Max Heller summarized the division—which came down to old families versus newer immigrants—as follows:

One rabbi, the minister of the German congregation, Rev. Dr. Bernard Illowy, is on terms of friendship with Gen. N. P. Banks, the commander of the troops of occupation, and delivers a sermon on Abraham Lincoln (as does Col. P. J. Joachimsen of New York, at the Polish synagogue); the minister of the Portuguese synagogue, Rabbi Gutheim, refusing to take the oath of allegiance, retreats with his family to the privations of "the Confederacy" . . .

A similar story could be told of the financial sacrifices that were offered. Especially to many of the Portuguese families of New Orleans the collapse of Confederate bond and Confederate money spelled utter ruin, as they had staked their all upon the fortunes of the Confederacy.[92]

The division of New Orleans Jewry in 1861—the old families enthusiastically supporting the cause and some of the more recent immigrants being less committed—continued during the Federal occupation. Eugenia Phillips, a third-generation Southerner, defied General Butler and was banished to Ship Island, while acquaintances of the Solomons such as Jacob Eisner cooperated with the occupying army. "Oh!" Clara wrote, "he is a foreigner [that is, a recent immigrant from Europe] & cannot sympathize with us."[93]

Mobile, like New Orleans, was blockaded and attacked. In the early years of the war, Jewish civilians pitched in to support the Confederate cause. Three Mobile Jewish musicians, Sigmund and Jacob Schlesinger and Joseph Bloch, all from the German states, contributed to the Confederate cause. Music teachers and composers, Sigmund and Jacob Schlesinger published "Southern Flowers," dedicated to "the Young Ladies of the Sunny South," which contained a selection of waltzes, polkas, and other dances. The "Martha Quickstep" was "a spirited march, especially in military quick time, and popular in those days," according to William Tuckman. Also included was the "Manassas Polka," written by Sigmund Schlesinger to commemorate the First Confederate Victory at Manassas. Other pieces were the "Camp Moore Polka," referring to a Confederate military post near New Orleans; "Fort Morgan Gallopade," in honor of Gen. John Hunt Morgan (the gallopade was a lively round dance popular at the time); and "Harry Macarthy's Bonnie Blue Flag," containing variations of this favorite Civil War tune. Joseph Bloch from Bingen on the Rhine came to Mobile in 1848 at the age of twenty-two. Descended from a long line of musicians, Bloch gave guitar lessons and could play almost every orchestral instrument. According to Tuckman, Bloch became a bugler with an artillery unit, blew the bugle at the Battle of Mobile Bay, and published a great amount of Civil War music.[94]

The fine hand of Israel I. Jones was probably behind the Schlesingers' and Bloch's coming to Mobile, as he was president of the Mobile Music Association, an organization which provided Mobile with concerts and sophisticated musical entertainment. And Jones's hand was also behind his daughter Emilie's and her famous husband, Reverend Gutheim's, leaving New Orleans. Jones was president of the Mobile congregation, and when the Gutheims arrived in Mobile there was quite a welcome.

In Montgomery, Mayer Lehman traded cotton as best he could and actively supported the Confederacy. In 1864, when reports reached Montgomery that Alabama soldiers were suffering from exposure and hunger at Elmira Prison in New York, the governor asked Lehman to negotiate with the Federal authorities to aid the Alabama prisoners. "He is a business man of established character and one of the best Southern patriots," the governor wrote Jefferson Davis. "He is a foreigner, but has been here fifteen years and is thoroughly identified with us." Lehman arrived in Richmond ready to go up North with supplies for his fellow Alabamaians, but General Grant would not allow it. Mayer stayed in Richmond for a month in the dead of winter, aided by a Protestant clergyman, but failed in his mission. The Lehman warehouse in Montgomery was burned as the war drew to a close.[95]

Jacob and Alexander Kohn, who had come from Bavaria in 1848, were now successful shoemakers in Montgomery. They offered their services to the Confederacy, and local tradition holds that Jacob was made the superintendent of the Confederate shoe factory on Tallapoosa Street between Coos and Commerce, which turned out tens of thousands of shoes.[96]

The Moses family of Montgomery traced its roots to Charleston. Isaiah Moses came to Charleston from Germany in 1790. A successful merchant, he eventually became a cotton planter as well. His son, Levy Moses, was not so successful, but he put his son, Alfred Huger Moses (named for the famous South Carolina Unionist, Alfred Huger), through the College of Charleston. Soon the entire Moses family moved to Montgomery, perhaps to escape the wartime conditions in Charleston. This included Alfred's mother and father, brothers Mordecai, Joseph, Judah, and Henry, and sisters Emily, Sarah, Rosannah, and Grace. (There were nine children all together.) Alfred was exempt from military service, as he served as a clerk of court, but Mordecai Moses enlisted in Company E, 46th Alabama, as a private.[97]

On May 16, 1862, Kahl Montgomery dedicated its new synagogue. Rabbi Gutheim came from New Orleans and delivered a "memorable sermon." Thomas Owen wrote in his *History of Alabama* that the dedication ceremonies were impressive, "constituting the most remarkable event up to that time in the history of Judaism in Montgomery. The congregation on that occasion felt like Solomon at the dedication of the great Temple in Jerusalem."[98] The fall of New Orleans one month later redounded to Montgomery's benefit. Rabbi Gutheim, one of the most beloved rabbis in the South, accepted the position as rabbi at Kahl Montgomery in June 1863. The B'nai Israel Congregation in Columbus, Georgia, also sought Gutheim to minister to their small congregation. He agreed to "ride circuit" and led the services in Columbus every sixth Sabbath.[99] His support for the Confederacy never wavered. He prayed from the pulpit of Kahl Montgomery:

> Regard, O Father, in Thine abundant favor and benevolence, our beloved country, the Confederate States of America. May our young Republic increase in strength, prosperity and renown; . . . Behold, O God, and judge between us and our enemies, who have forced upon us this unholy and unnatural war—who hurl against us their poisoned arrows steeped in ambition and revenge.
>
> Bless, O Father, our efforts in a cause which we conceive to be just; the defense of our liberties and rights and independence, under just and equitable laws. May harmony of sentiment and purity of motive, unfaltering courage, immovable trust in our leaders, both in national council and in the field, animate all the people of our beloved Confederate States, so as to be equal to all emergencies—ready for every sacrifice, until our cause be vindicated as the light of day.
>
> May harmony of sentiment and purity of motive, unfaltering courage, immovable trust in our leaders, both in national council and in the field, animate all the people of our beloved Confederate States, so as to be equal to all emergencies—ready for every sacrifice, until our cause be vindicated as the light of day.
>
> And we pray Thee, O God, to bless and protect the armed hosts that now stand forth in the defense of our sacred cause.[100]

Natchez, Mississippi, was home to a small Jewish community during the war. The Mayers, who met on the ship crossing the Atlantic to New Orleans, were an integral part of Natchez society. Their son, Simon Mayer, and Oscar Levy, a nephew who had recently come to live with the Mayers from Landau, enlisted in a local militia company, the Natchez Light Infantry, in the summer of 1861. When the company was called into ninety days' active service in December, these men went with it to Kentucky. After their active service was over, the two, joined by another cousin, Simon Lehman, enlisted in the Natchez Southrons, which soon became Company B, 10th Mississippi.[101] The Mayers continued to live in wartime Natchez. On September 2, 1862, the Federal gunboat *Essex* arrived, and the older men, including John Mayer, who had organized a home guard, rallied to defend the town. Believing, erroneously, that the Union army was attacking the town, the home guard fired on the *Essex* crew when some of the men came ashore for supplies. The gunboat returned fire, and after an hour of shelling and with many houses on fire, the mayor surrendered the town. The sole victim of this assault was Rosalie Beekman, a Jewish girl, aged seven. She was struck by a piece of bursting shell while she and her family fled. She died at the Mayer home on Main Street, where she had been brought for medical attention by her cousin, Miriam Wexler.[102]

Vicksburg from the North after the surrender. (***Battles and Leaders of the Civil War.***)

The Mayers, like their neighbors, took the Union military at their word when they threatened to burn Natchez to the ground. John Mayer bought a home in nearby Washington, five miles from Natchez, and moved his family there. The family's household was packed up and moved. The threatened destruction of Natchez did not occur, but Mayer continued to live in town and operate his business while his family lived in Washington.[103]

After the fall of Vicksburg in July 1863, the Union army occupied Natchez. Some of the Jewish families lived resentfully under Federal occupation. Mrs. Mayer and two of the younger daughters, Emma and Carrie, hid much-needed clothing and supplies in their hoop skirts in order to deliver these goods to friends, who would forward the supplies to Confederate soldiers. "With fear and trembling, Emma handed the guard the papers," one of the Mayer girls recalled years later. "Imagine her delight when she noticed that he was trying to read them upside down! 'Any contraband goods?' and all being fair in love and war, they answered 'No.' 'Drive on then and have a nice day with your friends,' was the pleasant rejoinder of the ignorant unsuspecting guard." One of the daughters, Ophelia Mayer, wrote a letter describing the occupying general as "a miserable tyrant," for which offense she was arrested and placed in confinement in the city hall along with twenty other women. The Mayer home was surrounded by guards and no one was permitted to leave the house for three days. The store was closed and the family threatened with confiscation of all its goods.[104]

Simon Mayer, away with his command in Dalton, Georgia, was outraged by his sister's arrest. He was concerned for his family's safety but wrote, "don't let the scoundrels intimidate you. Afraid to come out and meet us on the battlefield like men, they, like brutes, make war upon defenseless woman & children." He urged the Mayer clan to show the invaders that they were "still free and knowing your rights, dare to maintain them." Many people in Natchez had lost hope in the cause, including members of the Mayer family. But Simon urged his brother Henry to join the army "now battling for our rights and independence."[105]

Life in occupied Natchez went on. The Mayer family continued in business. With a son and nephews in the Confederate army and resentful of the occupying army, they nevertheless accepted the situation and hoped for a reversal of Southern fortunes. The occupying Union army brought with it young Jewish men from the North, including Henry Frank and Isaac Lowenburg. Frank and Lowenburg visited John Mayer in his store, and Mayer, the president of Natchez's small Chevra Kadusha (Holy Society) congregation, invited them to attend services during the High Holy Days in the fall of 1863. Isaac Lowenburg was infatuated with Ophelia Mayer, and he was helpful in convincing the Union authorities to dismiss the charges against the family and Ophelia. In January of 1865, Isaac married Ophelia in the Mayer home. Sister Melanie married Henry Frank. In fraternizing with Union soldiers, the Mayer family was a typical Natchez family. The old families of Natchez also fraternized with the enemy during the occupation. "Only people of the highest culture and dignity," Annie Harper of Natchez wrote, "can sustain themselves honorably in such an anomalous position, and Natchez was the place to find such people."[106]

As in New Orleans, the Jewish communities of Nashville and Memphis were divided over the war. Neither city had a particularly old Jewish community nor an acculturated or assimilated Jewish elite as did Charleston, Savannah, and Richmond.

View of Nashville, southwest front of the capitol looking toward the battle-field. (*Battles and Leaders of the Civil War*.)

Both were frontier towns with large immigrant populations, including a substantial number of pro-Union Germans. But when war came, Jewish Tennesseans, like their neighbors, supported the Confederacy. Once Nashville and Memphis were occupied by Union troops, some left, many remained neutral, and a few joined the Union cause.

There were Jews in Nashville as early as 1795, but in 1860 there were 105 heads of household, 42 percent of whom were single men, virtually all of whom were immigrants. Few Nashville Jews were native-born. The demography of Memphis's Jewry was similar. Twenty Jewish volunteers from Nashville had joined the rebel army in May 1861, a month before Tennessee voted to secede. At High Holiday services in September 1861, both Nashville congregations, Mogen David and Ohava Emes, prayed for Jefferson Davis and the success of the Southern cause.[107] The Young Men's Hebrew Benevolent Society and the Ladies Hebrew Benevolent Society donated clothing and raised money. Jewish women in Nashville, like their sisters in Richmond and Savannah, knitted socks and made uniforms for the Confederacy. Jewish boys from Nashville—Solomon Frankland, Herman Ehrenberg, and George Cohen, all of the 30th Tennessee—were captured when Fort Donelson surrendered in 1862. They were sent to a military prison, exchanged, and saw further service. Fedora Frank wrote that "Jewish men from Nashville served in all the Tennessee battles—Shiloh, Stones River (Murfreesboro), Chickamauga and Chattanooga, Franklin, and Nashville." Many served throughout the war. Solomon Frankland was finally released from a Union prisoner of war prison in May 1865. The 2d Lt. Joseph Lepsheets, Company G, 8th Tennessee, who enlisted in May 1861 with his brother Jacob, was killed at the Battle of Franklin on November 30, 1864.[108]

In Memphis, where the immigrant population also predominated, Rabbi Tuska introduced patriotic services, Thanksgiving, and Fast Day. At one Sabbath service at B'nai Israel (Children of Israel), a dozen Jewish Confederates in uniform, led by 2d Lt. Abraham S. Levy and Maurice A. Freeman, marched into the synagogue. "Standing round the scrolls of the law," A. E. Frankland recalled, "they recited the blessing, in chorus . . . after which they received the ancient priestly benediction from the minister [rabbi] and returned to the camps of their several commanders."[109]

Both Nashville and Memphis were captured early in the war. Nashville was occupied by the Union army from February 1862 to April 1865. The military governor, Andrew Johnson, detested secessionists. He governed the state of Tennessee with an iron fist; dissent was not tolerated. The pro-Southern Jewish men were in the army or lived in this police state run by the Federal army. Those suspected of pro-Confederate sympathies were hounded, harassed, and arrested. Indeed, when city council members refused to take the loyalty oath, they were arrested for treason.[110] This harassment, of course, included Nashville Jews who remained when the city surrendered. Some fled their homes rather than live under Yankee rule.

Many Tennesseans were involved in smuggling supplies, especially medicine and quinine, to Confederate forces. Union officials saw this as treason and profiteering. Southerners saw it as a patriotic godsend some of the time and as profiteering at other times. Bertha Ochs, for example, was considered a heroine for smuggling quinine. Jacob Bloomstein, who after the war served as president of Ohava Shalom, was arrested in May 1863 as a spy and for smuggling goods through the lines to the Confederate army. He was later released by Governor Johnson. Maier Salzkotter was arrested for smuggling and later divorced his wife, Cecelia, who turned to prostitution while he was in prison. Many other Jewish merchants were arrested for smuggling and illegally selling goods in the area. Some were acting for patriotic reasons, others for profit. Nashville was inundated with refugees, vagrants, and criminals. In 1865 three Jewish stores were looted and a Jewish peddler murdered.[111]

The Jewish tradition of firing rabbis, dissenters seceding, and the founding of new congregations did not abate during the war. Memphis Jewry did all three, before and during the war. Unhappy with Jacob J. Peres, B'nai Israel fired him in April 1860. Peres sued the congregation for breach of contract and libel. Peres won

Rabbi Simon Tuska, rabbi of B'nai Israel in Memphis. Although an immigrant himself, Rabbi Tuska supported the Confederate war effort, and, like Max Michelbacher in Richmond, he was an ardent defender of the Jews of his community. (Courtesy of the Jacob Rader Marcus Center, American Jewish Archives, Cincinnati, Ohio.)

his contract case and was awarded his salary. The congregation won the libel case. Simon Tuska was then asked to serve as rabbi in July 1860. Born in Hungary, Tuska was twenty-five years old when he came to Memphis. He was the first American sent to Europe to study at the Jewish Theological Seminary at Breslau. The congregation shifted to Reform, and Tuska became an ardent supporter of the Confederate cause.[112]

Both Nashville and Memphis experienced an influx of Northern Jews during the war years. Jewish soldiers in the Union occupation army had light duty. They could enjoy the town, meet local Jewish people, attend religious services, and become a part of the community. The local people, Jews included, had no choice but to live under military rule. Jewish immigrants who had ties, not only of religion but of national background, language, and customs, felt a natural kinship with Jews like themselves who had settled north of the Mason-Dixon line. In some instances, as in the Mayer family in Natchez, romance blossomed between local girls and Union soldiers. Capt. Adolph Loventhal of the 39th Indiana, Louis Lerman of the 4th Ohio Cavalry, and William Wolfson of the 10th Illinois all settled in Nashville after the war. Southern Jews, for their part, felt a solemn duty to bury fellow Jews—even those killed fighting for the Union army—according to Jewish law. There was, therefore, a significant amount of fraternization between Southern and Northern Jews.[113]

Lt. Col. Marcus M. Spiegel of the 120th Ohio, a German immigrant from a hamlet near Worms on the Rhine River, was stationed in occupied Memphis during Hanukkah in December 1862. "Memphis is a beautiful City," he wrote his wife, "full at present of trading Yehudim, Women and Contrabands [freed slaves]; the Cotton buying attracts many men here and often large fortunes are made in a

Marcus M. Spiegel, a Jewish Union officer in occupied Memphis. (Courtesy of the Jacob Rader Marcus Center, American Jewish Archives, Cincinnati, Ohio.)

short time." As he walked along the riverbank, Spiegel saw "a Yehudah and his wife," and, as it was the Sabbath, he decided to have a kosher lunch. Spiegel approached the Jewish couple and said, "Happy Sabbath, dear people," frightening them both. Who was this stranger offering "Happy Sabbath" while dressed in a Yankee uniform, sword, and spurs? The couple, recognizing a fellow Jew, told Spiegel he could eat a kosher lunch with them or he could go to Mr. Levy's boardinghouse. When Spiegel arrived at Levy's, he found thirty very surprised Jewish Tennesseans. He requested a Hanukkah lunch. The proprietor stared at the young officer, and believing he recognized him, asked Spiegel his name. "Dear God," Levy exclaimed, "a son of Rabbi Mosche of Abenheim, a lieutenant colonel." It turned out that Spiegel knew a number of the German immigrants who had settled in Memphis, including Levy, who had known his family in the Old Country. Spiegel was later killed in a Confederate ambush on the Red River near Alexandria, Louisiana. His brother Joseph Spiegel founded the Spiegel Catalog Company.[114]

B'nai B'rith, the Jewish fraternal order, flourished in occupied Memphis. By 1865 it had 167 members. The Southern Club, a Jewish social club, changed its name to the Memphis Club to suit the occupying army and held theatrical performances in English and German. Jewish businessmen, mainly shopkeepers, clothiers, grocers, and auctioneers, accommodated themselves to the situation. New arrivals from the North opened more Jewish businesses during the occupation. Many catered to the Union soldiers. M. Simon at 194 Main Street advertised that he "has a large lot of military goods for uniforms including brass buttons." By 1863 there were fifteen Jewish merchants selling military clothing and a number in the grocery business. Others sold liquor, tobacco, cigars, and cotton. H. Koninsky on Beale Street advertised tents: "Father Abraham of old once pitched his tent on the plains of Mamre, and the children of Abraham have pitched their tents on the hills of Vicksburg." Still others ran boardinghouses, sold jewelry, and engaged in manufacturing. "The large Jewish element of Memphis was made manifest yesterday," the *Daily Bulletin* noted on September 24, 1863, "by the number of closed stores on Main Street. The Day of Atonement was very generally observed by those of Jewish faith."[115]

Between 1860 and 1864, the Children of Israel congregation retired its debt. It had eighty-seven members in 1863. In 1862 a Polish congregation, Beth El Emeth (House of the True God) was founded and followed the *Minhag Polen.* Peres, the rabbi who sued Children of Israel, became the rabbi of the Polish congregation, and the service was "strictly Orthodox," an advertisement noted. (The name, House of the True God, obviously made a statement about Peres's former more liberal congregation.) Even the Civil War could not stop Memphis Jewry's own civil war.[116]

The Ochs family was typical, in many respects, of Tennessee's Jewry. Both Julius and Bertha Ochs had come from Bavaria, Julius from Fürth near Nürnberg, where his family had lived for hundreds of years, and Bertha from Rhenish Bavaria in the Palatinate.[117] Julius was a well-educated young man who spoke seven languages, played the guitar, was an amateur actor, and even composed light operas. He studied at a military academy in Cologne, but when his father died his older brother apprenticed him to a bookbinding firm. Julius rebelled, and in 1845 left for America to seek his fortune. He changed his name from Ochsenhorn to Ochs; settled in Louisville, where his two sisters lived; and became a peddler. When war with Mexico was declared he enlisted and, because of his military education, was made a drill sergeant. After the war he worked in a variety of jobs—as a road salesman for a jewelry company, as a small dry goods store owner, in municipal government, and even as a rabbi—in Mississippi, Kentucky, and Louisiana. He settled briefly in Natchez and ran a small store. An honest, likable, and intellectual man, he sometimes played his guitar at plantation parties.[118]

In Natchez he met Bertha Levy, an attractive and opinionated young lady who had left Bavaria for very different reasons. Bertha had been involved in the liberal politics of the 1848 revolution, and as a student in Heidelberg she had participated in antigovernment demonstrations. Her family feared she might be arrested, so she came to live with her uncle in Natchez.[119] Bertha Levy met Julius Ochs at his store in Natchez in 1851. However, they did not become involved until years later, when they met again at a reception in Nashville, where Bertha's parents had recently arrived from Bavaria. They were married in 1856.[120]

The Ochses lived in Tennessee for a time, but Julius abhorred slavery. "These sights sickened me," he wrote in a memoir for his children. "Once I saw a poor wretch so horribly beaten that tears of pity gushed from my eyes."[121] Julius and Bertha moved to Cincinnati, and Julius went back out on the road as a traveling salesman. He was evidently a failure as a businessman; at times he barely provided for his family. In 1858 Bertha gave birth to Adolph Ochs, the future publisher of the *New York Times*.

When the Civil War began, Julius joined the Union army and served as a captain. Bertha and her family remained loyal to the South. Her brother served in the Confederate army. In fact, this pro-Southern wife of a Federal officer smuggled quinine across the river from Cincinnati to Kentucky to help the beleaguered Confederates. There is a family story that Bertha pushed her baby carriage, which contained contraband material hidden under one of the little Ochs boys, across the river to the Confederates. Adolph Ochs recalled in later years that "mother gave father a lot of trouble in those days." According to their granddaughter, Bertha's smuggling drugs to the Confederates came to the attention of the Union authorities and a warrant was issued for her arrest. As a loyal Union officer, Julius was able to have the charges dismissed. In 1928, *The Confederate Veteran* wrote, "for a mother in Israel to defy her husband and an entire army was no mean assertion of militant feminism in those days."[122]

In 1864 Julius and Bertha and their young family moved to Knoxville, which was then occupied by the Union army. Adolph Ochs began his newspaper career as a paperboy in Knoxville. Julius became active in the Knoxville Jewish community and served as unofficial rabbi.[123]

Because Memphis was a large port on the Mississippi River and a center of cotton trading and illegal speculation, and because many Northern Jews flocked to Memphis, Tennessee became the flash point of the most infamous anti-Semitic event of the Civil War. Gen. Ulysses S. Grant issued Order Number 11 expelling all the Jews from the military district. This order, issued by Grant on December 17, 1862, stated: "The Jews, as a class violating every regulation of trade established by the Treasury Department and also department orders, are hereby expelled from the department of Tennessee [which included parts of Tennessee, Mississippi, and Kentucky] within twenty-four hours from the receipt of this order." Post commanders were ordered to see that "all of this class of people" be furnished with passes and made to leave the state. Jews were forced out of Paducah, Kentucky, and Holly Springs and Oxford, Mississippi, and some were imprisoned.[124] A Union colonel told one victim that he was forced to flee because "You are Jews, and are neither a benefit to the Union or Confederacy." The Jews of Paducah protested this "inhuman order" directly to Lincoln, and their leaders met with the president in Washington. Lincoln is said to have asked, "And so the children of Israel were driven from the happy land of Canaan?" Cesar Kaskel of Paducah told Lincoln, "Yes, and that is why we have come unto Father Abraham's bosom, asking protection." Lincoln replied, "And this protection they shall have at once."[125]

Henry Halleck, the Union general in chief, could not have cared less about the Jews. He wired Grant that neither he nor the president had any objection "to your expelling traitors and Jew peddlers." Atty. Gen. Edward Bates told the president he was indifferent to Jewish protests. Lincoln disagreed, stating that "to condemn a class is, to say the least, to wrong the good with the bad," and he countermanded an order which would never have been issued by Robert E. Lee or Jefferson Davis.[126]

Thus, Jewish Southerners faced all of the same perils as their fellow Confederates during the war—the death of loved ones, the collapse of the economy, want, hunger, privation, and the loss of a cause they held dear—and one unique peril their fellow Southerners did not face: anti-Semitism. When the Civil War began, many Southerners had never met a Jew. There were fewer than 25,000 Jews in the entire South, and the great majority lived in the larger cities. The average Southerner's ideas about Jews were formed by images learned in Gentile churches, or from their contact with Jewish peddlers or storekeepers. For the most part, these images and impressions were positive. Jewish merchants lived in the communities where they conducted business. Their customers knew them. Peddlers were a welcome treat in isolated Southern hamlets, farms, and plantations. They brought goods which were unavailable and they brought news of the outside world. The peddlers were unusual, interesting, and often entertaining. Thus, the image of the Jewish businessman, merchant, and peddler before the war was positive. And, of course, the few highly visible Jewish members of the Southern elite were generally accorded great respect in a hierarchical society which deferred to those of wealth and privilege.

In the first year of the war, when the South was optimistic of victory and food and goods were still available, there were no recorded anti-Semitic incidents in the South. As the war entered its second year, however, the Union blockade, inflation, hoarding, counterfeit money, the limitations on trade, the inability of planters and ordinary farmers to sell cotton and produce, the appearance of more German, foreign, and Jewish traders, and the general disruption of the Southern economy began to have an effect on the Southern people. Goods became scarce. The South was an agricultural country heavily dependent on imports for the necessities of life—clothing, coffee, tea, manufactured goods of all kinds, and, in some parts of the South, even food. Jewish merchants supplied many of these items. And most of these merchants were immigrant German Jews who spoke with a German accent. Of course, there were many merchants who were not Jews. Ironically, many merchants in the South were Christian German immigrants who also spoke with German accents and were indistinguishable from Jewish Germans in the eyes of Southerners.

German immigrants, both Jew and Gentile, were oddities in the antebellum South, and in much of the North as well. It is an irony of history that the first significant outbreak of anti-Semitism in Southern history was directed at German Jews as much because they were Germans as Jews. In many instances the dislike for German immigrants exceeded anti-Jewish discrimination. According to Daniel O'Flaherty, the German immigrants' harsh pronunciation of English, their drinking habits, differences in their observation of the Sabbath, "their heel-clicking reverence for authority, and, above all, their Teutonic industry," earned the enmity of their neighbors. E. Merton Coulter wrote that in Texas, "the Germans . . . formed nests of Unionism, which gave the Confederate authorities much trouble."[127] Some German Jews tried to distance themselves from their German roots. Lewis Leon, the dry goods clerk from Charlotte, which hardly had a Jewish population in the 1860s, gave Confederate authorities Sheffield, England, as his birthplace. As a prisoner of war at Elmira Prison, he admitted to Union authorities that he was born in Germany.[128]

To many Southerners beset by growing problems of scarcity and deprivation, these foreign-sounding people loomed much larger in their lives than they had before Fort Sumter. In August 1862, a group of disgruntled citizens met at the courthouse in Thomasville, Georgia, to protest against Jewish traders. The Union army was on the Florida Gulf Coast only fifty miles away, and the townspeople knew that Georgia's weak defenses might fail. Col. J. L. Seward, a former Congressman, warned of the military threat and of the danger of rapidly rising prices and scarcity of food and supplies. Necessities like salt, which was essential for preserving meat, were already difficult to obtain, and prices had soared. Ignoring the Union naval blockade, inflation, invasion, and the disruption of transportation caused by the war, the colonel blamed the town's woes on foreign counterfeiters and profiteers who were hoarding goods and "demanding exorbitant and ruinous prices by which the families of soldiers are likely to suffer, and be reduced to intolerable want." These villains were, according to Seward, Thomasville's German Jews conspiring with itinerant Jewish peddlers. The crowd was enraged and could have become an unruly mob but for the cool head of the meeting's chairman, W. G. Ponder, who insisted that any action taken be legal and deliberate.[129]

A committee of five, headed by Seward, drew up resolutions that condemned "German Jews traveling to and fro" in this part of the state who were "putting in circulation spurious Confederate currency" and local German Jews "engaged in extortions in trade, and in seeming complicity with the itinerant German Jews." They charged "that these Jews were 'buying up particular localities, articles of prime necessity, thereby producing a scarcity, and transferring such articles to other localities and demanding exorbitant and ruinous prices.'" The resolutions called on "every good citizen to aid in arresting their evils," and "that no German Jews be allowed to settle among us," that the local German Jews be given ten days to leave "and if they do not leave then, that we assemble and take such steps in the premises as may be deemed advisable." A Committee of Vigilance was created to enforce the resolutions.[130]

The resolutions were published in the Thomasville newspaper, and other Georgia newspapers reprinted them. In September a town meeting in Macon was called to address inflated prices and scarcity of goods. The *Macon Journal and Messenger* felt that the Thomasville resolutions were "well worthy of attention—and perhaps, of action in other communities." But, as Louis Schmier wrote, Macon was not Thomasville. Whereas Thomasville had few Jewish residents, Macon had had a sizable Jewish community for more than ten years and "the long-standing respectability of its members, acted as mitigating factors. Any lingering accusations were quickly stilled by the willingness of Macon's Jews to stand up and vouch for their peddling brothers." Moreover, no one could question the Macon Jews' devotion to the Confederacy. Their company had so many local Jews that it was nicknamed the "Macon Jewish Company."[131]

When the resolutions were reprinted in the *Savannah Daily Morning News*, the Jews of Savannah were outraged. Some of the Thomasville Jews arrived in Savannah, and the Jewish community called a meeting to protest against the "wholesale slander, persecution and denunciation of a people." Savannah Jews, many of whom were themselves German, issued a resolution condemning the

Thomasville resolutions as being "at war with the spirit of the age—the letter of the constitution—and the principles of religion—and can find no parallel except in the barbarism of the Inquisition and the persecution of the Dark Ages." The resolution defended the honor of Southern Jews as honest and faithful and condemned the citizens of Thomas County as "enemies of human liberty and freedom of conscience." The Savannah Jewish committee also took the local newspaper to task for "giving currency to this slander and intolerance," for participating in this "foul wrong," and called on Savannah Jews to boycott the newspaper. The editor of the *Daily Morning News* defended his having reprinted the story as only presenting a news story, and his failure to condemn the resolution as the result of his lack of knowledge of the facts of the case.[132]

Next, Jewish Confederate soldiers joined the fray. Members of the Tattnall Guards wrote a letter, published in the *Savannah Republican,* in which they defended the loyalty and patriotism of "the multitude who have already sacrificed the comforts and ease of civil life" and taken their places among "the heroic defenders of the South." The letter concluded in typical loquacious Southern style: "Go review the mighty hosts who are struggling to achieve our independence—recount the regiments, battalions and companies who compose the noble armies of the South—and wherever, throughout the limits of our territory, you find them arrayed, there you will behold the representatives of our sect, standing side by side with the gallant sons of the soil, enduring the privations of the camp, the hardships and toils of the march, and the dangers and perils of the battle field, to win victory for our arms."

Not to be outdone, the Jewish Confederates of the 32d Georgia Volunteers met on September 16 to protest the Thomasville incident. Pvt. Charles Wessolowsky lambasted the residents of Thomasville: "Let us look at the gentlemen from Thomasville who claim nativity to Thomas County," he proclaimed, "and see if they themselves don't partake of this extortion. Behold them coming to market, the one with fowls and the other with eggs; ask their price and 'two dollars for a pair of chickens and seventy cents for a dozen eggs,' will be the reply."

Wessolowsky pointed to the blockade, lack of labor, and the dislocation caused by the war as the problem, not the Jews. The Jews were being made scapegoats, he said, because they had far less influence than their well-connected, non-Jewish competitors. He went for the jugular of the real Thomasville extortionists, who will "push the whole of the crime upon the German Jews, including two who were present at the notorious August 1862 meeting, and clear their own skirts asserting their nativity." Wessolowsky was a charismatic speaker, and at least one soldier "sat awed, thinking for a moment that he had just heard Moses thundering down from the height of Sinai with admonishments to the Gentiles." The Jews of the 32d denounced the Thomasville resolutions, in true Southern style, as "unbecoming and unworthy of gentlemen."[133]

In retrospect, nothing much happened at Thomasville. No Jew was harmed or even personally insulted. No one was hurt. No store was ransacked. Indeed, the great majority of the Jews of Thomasville did not leave the town. The incident did not disturb Yates Levy of Savannah. He, too, looked with disdain at the peddling practices of the newly arrived German Jews. "Of course there is nothing new: there has been a battle royal between some blockheads in Thomasville and the German Jews, a struggle between the fools and the knaves, who are not, however, I believe, worse than their neighbors."[134] According to Mark Greenberg, the Jews stayed, operated their stores, purchased land, participated in social events, and fought in the Confederate army.[135] After the war, in 1866, there were five Jewish-owned dry goods stores in town. Presumably, they were all German Jews who had started out as peddlers in the area. Their being Jewish was certainly no secret. In July 1860 Benjamin F. Hubert had run an advertisement in the local newspaper announcing: "New Goods! New Goods! Cheaper than the Cheapest! Great Excitement at Receiving Better Bargains Than Jews or Gentiles Offer."[136]

When the war came, three of the seven eligible Jewish men of Thomasville joined the army: Michael Rosenfeld joined the Ochlockonee Light Infantry, Philip Schiff was a corporal in Company A/F (Thomasville Guards), 29th Georgia, and his brother Tomas served in the same unit.[137] Ironically, Tomas was discharged in 1864 when sixty-three Thomasville residents, including two who were present at the August 1862 meeting, petitioned the governor because Tomas's skills as a tanner were needed at home.[138] Certainly by the standards of nineteenth-century Europe, which were part of the experience of all German Jewish immigrants, the Thomasville incident was not dangerous. The Jews of Thomasville, or at least the local Jews who had roots in the town, did not live in fear and ignored the whole incident.

The Jews of Macon survived the war alongside their Christian neighbors. Life was difficult for the small merchants who had little to sell. There were tense moments during the war when hungry women marched on the town demanding food and goods from local storekeepers. The Macon Jewish community was well aware that a few Jews were engaged in improper activities, and when Reverend Sternheimer, who had resigned his position as *hazan*, sought to return in June 1864, he was questioned extensively by E. Einstein, the former president of the congregation, about allegations that Sternheimer had been involved in "passing spurious and counterfeit confederate States treasury notes." Einstein asked Sternheimer directly, "upon the honor of a gentleman," whether he had been involved with one Stern and Rosenberg of Columbus, who had been charged with such activities and with whom Sternheimer had boarded. The hazan had heard that Stern and Rosenberg had been arrested, and he immediately returned to Columbus from Mobile to face his accusers rather than flee the country, as he was advised to do by some. No charges were ever brought. Sternheimer cleared his name and returned to Macon to serve the Beth Israel congregation.[139]

Lazarus Straus of Talbotton, Georgia, was not as sanguine as the Jews of Thomasville. When in 1862 the grand jury issued a presentment against "evil and unpatriotic conduct of the representatives of Jewish houses," Straus decided to leave Talbotton.[140] Isidor Straus later recalled that when Jewish merchants, who were engaged in perfectly legitimate business enterprises, were called extortionists, his father immediately let it be known that he would move away from a community which "had cast such a reflection on him, as the only Jew living in their midst." Straus promptly took steps to leave Talbotton, construing the grand jury's action as a personal affront. "Father's action caused such a sensation in the whole county that he was waited upon by every member of the grand jury," Isidor recalled, "also by all the ministers of the different denominations, who assured him that nothing was further from the minds of those who drew the presentment than to reflect on father, and that had anyone had the least suspicion that their action could be construed as they now saw it clearly might be construed, it never would have been permitted to be so worded." The elder Straus was not persuaded. He moved his business and family to Columbus, Georgia. "The loyalty and good will of the people towards him was made manifest to him, as he often stated, by the customers from Talbotton who visited his store in Columbus, not a few of them never having traded with him while in Talbotton, but who became regular clients in Columbus," Isidor later recounted.[141]

Wartime Richmond, the capital of the Confederacy, was packed with soldiers, government and war workers, refugees, prostitutes, vagrants, criminals, and con artists. Goods became scarce. Prices and inflation soared. "Richmond was, by far, the most expensive, corrupt, overcrowded and crime-ridden city in the Confederacy," Ernest B. Furgurson concluded.[142] A gallon of cane syrup was one dollar in rural Georgia but fifty dollars in Richmond. To make matters worse, foreign traders, peddlers, and merchants, many of whom were German immigrants, had come to Richmond, a fertile field for small businessmen, the scrupulous and unscrupulous alike. "Temptations of profiteering were too strong for the flesh to bear," Charles P. Roland wrote, "innumerable Southerners ignored the strictures of press and public, the exhortations of the government, and the pangs of conscience and yielded themselves to the seduction of easy gain." Richmonders, in particular, were sensitive to foreigners who could be, and frequently were, spies for the Union army. And many in Richmond believed that the Union army was made up of German and Irish mercenaries.[143] Richmond was also home to the Confederate Congress, which gave vent to all of the frustrations of the entire South and contained a substantial number of demagogues and bigots, such as Congressman Henry S. Foote of Tennessee.[144]

Foote, bald, small, and of "colicky delivery," was by far the most obnoxious anti-Semitic Confederate Congressman. He was widely perceived as hotheaded, irresponsible, and foolish, although tenacious as an opponent. He detested Jefferson

Davis and attacked Judah Benjamin, whom he called "Judas Iscariot Benjamin," and Jews in general, in order to strike at the president. In January 1863, in a debate on drafting foreigners, Foote loosed a torrent of criticism against the Jews. He claimed Jews had flooded the Confederacy and controlled nine-tenths of the business, all "by official permission" and the protection of the government, an allusion to Benjamin. If "the present state of things were to continue," he said, "the end of the war would probably find nearly all the property of the Confederacy in the hands of Jewish Shylocks." The Jews of Richmond, however, did not fear Foote. "That a man like Foote should habitually denounce the Jews is to be expected," a Jewish reader wrote the *Richmond Sentinel* in January 1865. "He denounces everybody and every thing; his mouth is a 'well-spring' of slander."[145] Pvt. Eugene Henry Levy was a spectator of the Confederate Congress in December 1864. He listened "with disgust to the badinage of Foote and other buncome orators."[146]

Foote was not the only Confederate Congressman to attack the Jews. A few other members expressed anti-Semitic sentiments arising out of scarcity of supplies, inflation, speculating, and profiteering, but no legislation was ever passed directed at Jews, and no action ever undertaken against the Jews. Foote, in fact, had no following and was expelled from the Confederate Congress for fleeing to the North in February 1865.[147]

The Richmond press gave vent to the public's war-weariness and insecurity. One writer to the *Richmond Enquirer* contended that it was blasphemous for Benjamin to serve as secretary of state.[148] *Southern Punch*, published in Richmond, mocked Jews and foreigners, calling merchants "Jew and Yankee extortioners," "dirty, greasy Jew peddler," "Shylocks," and the like.[149] Alluding to the well-known fact that Jewish merchants and peddlers cheerfully sold goods to blacks, *Southern Punch* wrote: "Who are our capitalists at the present time? . . . . The dirty, greasy Jew peddler, who might be seen with a pack on his back a year or two since, bowing and cringing even to Negro servants, now struts by with the air of a millionaire."[150] The *Richmond Examiner* printed a letter in December 1862 titled "The Jews' Harvest," complaining about clothing merchants: "Specimens" of the "accursed race . . . fatten upon the calamities of the very people who are giving them a home," and claiming that Jews "are few indeed in the army, unless as camp followers, where they can follow their natural occupation." In a tirade laced with anti-Semitic clichés, this writer also charged that Jews were not productive citizens: "Did anyone ever see a Jew mechanic, a Jew farmer, or a Jew producer of any kind?" They were, in short, "the extortioners of the world." The editor agreed, describing Jews as disloyal and unpatriotic and denouncing "unkempt Israelites in our marts. . . . Every auction room is packed with greasy Jews."[151] Many a Richmonder believed the Jews dominated the retail trade, and some resented it. Sallie B. Putnam, a prominent society belle, wrote in her memoir, *Richmond During the War*, that one could "almost have imagined being in a strange city, from the signs over the doors of the shops . . . Israel and David, and Moses and Jacobs, and Hyman and Levy, and Guggenheimer and Rosenheimer, and other names innumerable of the Ancient People, were prominent, instead of the old Anglo-Saxon which had designated the most important business firms of Richmond. . . . The war was a harvest to that class of our population."[152] (In all fairness, Mrs. Putnam concluded that while the Jews were "much abused for extortion," they were "quite equaled" by "our own people," who should have set a better example.[153])

John Beauchamp Jones, a government clerk, an author, and a pathological anti-Semite, was obsessed about Jews and denounced them regularly in the safety of his private diary.[154] "Having no nationality, all wars are harvests for them," he wrote in September, 1861. Jones believed that illicit trade had depleted the country of gold "and placed us at the feet of the Jew extortioners. . . . These Jews have the adroitness to carry their points. They have injured the cause more than the armies of Lincoln. Well, if we gain our independence, instead of being the vassals of the Yankees, we shall find all our wealth in the hands of the Jews." Neither he nor his private observations had any effect on actual events, but he has been extensively quoted by historians as reflecting the prejudice against Jews in wartime Richmond.[155]

Some Richmonders believed that Jews were afraid and unwilling to fight. Coulter writes that the Jews "were especially charged with evading military service" and that "Jewish traders made desperate efforts to secure passports for the North from Judah P. Benjamin, the Jewish Secretary of State . . . . It was not unusual for them to pay as high as $10,000.00 for conveyances and bribery of frontier guards to get across the Potomac."[156] Coulter's own old-fashioned prejudice aside, the fact is that many Southerners had no desire to serve in the army, and "Jewish traders" accounted for an infinitesimal percentage of slackers. Anti-Semitism, exacerbated by fear, want, and desperation, exaggerated the failings of a few Jews. Anti-Semitic stereotypes filled many a Southerner's need to believe that looming defeat was not their fault, but that of foreigners and aliens. Thus, Jews got caught up in a general hysteria against merchants, traders, Yankees, foreigners, and Germans (often mistakenly referred to as "Dutch," a corruption of "Deutsche").

Neither the Jews of Richmond nor their Gentile friends and neighbors allowed the anti-Semitic vilification to go unanswered. The editor of the *Richmond Sentinel* criticized the "intolerant and illiberal views and prejudices" against the Jews. These allegations, he felt, "in no way [affected] their individual and personal merits and character." The *Sentinel* responded positively to Jewish pleas for fair play: "We consider it a duty to hail every good citizen as a brother. We ask him not where he was born or what his faith." The editor of the *Richmond Dispatch* agreed. While some Jews may have speculated in dry goods, Jews were not among those profiteering in food.[157]

Reverend Michelbacher publicly answered the wave of anti-Jewish invective. In Fredericksburg on May 27, 1863, a Confederate Fast Day, he gave a sermon in which he denied that Israelites were speculators or extortioners. If the Jews were guilty, he would say so, as "I always speak of your faults without fear, favor, or affection." But Jewish merchants did not hoard goods. They sold them quickly. And Jews did not sell flour, meal, wheat, corn, bacon, beer, coal, or wood, the basic commodities of speculation. Besides, if the Jews were hoarding, customers would obviously have bought supplies from honest Gentile traders. Michelbacher argued that the real speculators blamed the Jews in order to take the spotlight off their "moonshine" and evil activities.[158]

On October 18, 1863, Beth Ahabah held a congregational meeting to address the looting of merchants' shops and an incident of a rock being thrown through a synagogue window.[159] The congregation urged the Jews of Richmond to hold a mass meeting to consider raising money for the poor and the causes of the recent looting, as well as "such other matters as may be brought before the meeting to vindicate our character as Jews and good citizens."[160] Beth Shalome opposed this plan. "Beth Shalome replied to the overt pressure in a dignified and haughty manner, adumbrating the distinguished heritage of their Sephardic forebearers," Berman wrote. The quiet voice and fine hand of Gustavus A. Myers was undoubtedly at work behind the scenes when the old synagogue resolved that as citizens of Richmond they would "cheerfully" join in any endeavor to relieve the poor so long as all congregations of all religions did so. And they further resolved: "That while this meeting denounces the unfounded aspersions made against the Israelites of this city, and feels satisfied that the acts of our co-religionists can well bear the test of comparison with those of any other denomination in this community for patriotism, charity, or freedom from selfishness; yet think the best and most dignified course to be adopted, will be to treat them with silent contempt, confident that the enlightened and unprejudiced do not join in this crusade against our people."[161]

In the end, like the incident in Thomasville, the sound and fury in Richmond signified nothing. No Jew was molested, no storekeeper injured. Certainly no harm came to any Richmond Jew from the army of Robert E. Lee, the government of Jefferson Davis, or the state of Virginia, or the City Council of Richmond. It was a lot of bombast from a few demagogues and journalists and a minority of a sorely tried and increasingly frustrated populace. The Sephardic tradition of suffering in silence and working closely with those in authority prevailed over the German notion of protests. There is a local Richmond tradition that Adolphus H. Adler, said to be a colonel in the Confederate army, challenged the editor of the *Examiner* to a duel.[162] There is no record of the episode, and Adler was not a Confederate officer, but Jewish Richmonders long cherished the idea.

A few Jews may have felt threatened. Some lost faith in the cause. Philip Whitlock's brother took his family and went up North. The most embarrassing incident of the war for the Richmond Jewish community was the decision by Lewis Hyman, a jeweler and treasurer of Beth Shalome, to sell his assets, convert them to gold and precious stones, and leave for the North with his family. In February 1864, Hyman, his wife, and his party were robbed, and all of their possessions were taken while they were passing Confederate pickets. The anti-Semitic Richmond press gave the story a great deal of coverage to the consternation of the great majority of the Jews of Richmond, who remained loyal to the Confederacy to the end. Even men like Philip Whitlock, a Polish Jew who had served in the Richmond Grays and fought in the war, felt by 1862 that "there was no chance as we were getting weak and the other side were getting stronger."[163]

Other cities and towns of the South were not immune from anti-Jewish outbursts during the Civil War. Richmond was the worst, but there is evidence of other scattered incidents, such as raids on Jewish stores in Georgia by wives of soldiers away with the army and private expressions of anti-Semitism. Emma Holmes of Charleston wrote that "silver cannot be procured, as the Jews have bought up all."[165] And others wrote of Jews extorting high prices, speculating in goods, and engaging in passing counterfeit money.[165] A visitor to Charleston reported that one could "meet more Jews in Charleston than . . . in Jerusalem," there to buy goods brought in by blockade-runners.[166] Later writers romanticized blockade-running and war profiteering. Margaret Mitchell made an international hero out of Rhett Butler, who, after all, engaged in the sale of scarce goods at a very handsome profit. But Emma Holmes complained in August 1862 that when the blockade-runners arrived, the Jews outbid all others and were "setting up a quantity of little shops."[167] In Memphis, Polish Jews were accused of being involved in stealing, and Rabbi Tuska vigorously defended his co-religionists in the press. "The name of the 'Jew' has been so wantonly and unceremoniously dragged into the several reports," he wrote in the *Memphis Daily Appeal.* Before "the least particle of evidence is obtained . . . it is at once heralded abroad that Jews 'are to blame.'" "Why," he asked the editor, "were people identified as Polish Jews when Jews were, like Irish Catholics or German Protestants, citizens of their country and Jewish only in their religious beliefs."[168]

Most Southerners and particularly those in positions of authority and influence were keenly aware of the loyalty of Southern Jews. The *Charleston Courier,* for example, would have no part in anti-Jewish demagoguery:

> We have said, and shall say, and urge our opinions against extortioners and bloodsuckers and prowling beastly bipeds of prey under whatever guise they come, but we protest earnestly and emphatically against any wholesale denunciation of Germans or Jews, or of German Jews. We have no more and no less opposition to an extortioner who happens to be a German or a Jew, than one who is an Englishman, or a Frenchman, or a Welchman, or a Yankee, and a so-called Christian. If there is such an animal as a Christian extortioner, we hate and abhor it, and would gladly exterminate it. Let

the offenders and all who trouble our political Israel, and devour people, be rebuked, denounced, execrated, imprisoned, or expelled, if it can be done, but let us hear of no more abuse of a class as a class.[169]

A Confederate army chaplain wrote the *Savannah Daily Morning News* in February 1863 to express his opposition to the "many unfair, and, to my mind, very unjust, as well as injudicious *flings* at this part, no unimportant part, of our fellow citizens."[170] He wrote that there were plenty of Jews in the Confederate army and they were "good, enduring, hard-fighting soldiers" who shared in the danger, privations, battles and marches of all the other soldiers. He even suggested that the Jews of Macon establish the "first Israelite Battalion of the Confederate army. Let them take for the battle flag—*'The Lion of the tribe of Judah,'* and the God of Moses, Abraham, Isaac, and Jacob will fight their battles for them, and tread our enemies beneath His feet."[171]

Gratz Cohen, a Jewish student at the University of Virginia and scion of the prominent Cohen family of Savannah, wrote his father, Solomon Cohen, on January 9, 1864, "It is a mournful fact that in these troubled times when intolerance & prejudice cast their baneful seed throughout the land, which from one quarter of it to another rings with abuse of God's people, that we have done nothing for our religion & are so blind to our own interests." Jewish wealth had been generously given to all manner of charities, Cohen told his father, but the Jews had not looked after their own interests. The newspapers lifted up their "lying tongues against them & no defending voice has been heard. . . . Why have we no Jewish newspaper to justify us before the world & explain to us our position, to remind Israel that it is not a race of shopkeepers, but a peculiar people set apart by *Jehovah* for His service & glorification." He suggested the publication of a newspaper in the South devoted to Jewish interests.[172]

Southern Jews were frequently treated worse than other Southerners by the occupying Union army and the Northern press. New Orleans Jewry was subjected to anti-Semitic outbursts from "Beast" Butler. In 1862 he accused New Orleans "army contractors, principally Jews" of making "fortunes by the war."[173] He swore that Jews "deserve to receive at the hands of this government what is due to the Jew Benjamin."[174] All Jews, according to this Massachusetts anti-Semite, were smugglers, and he called Benjamin's brother-in-law "a Jew famed for a bargain." Later in the war, the *Jewish Record,* a partisan newspaper in New York, reported that Butler had said "he could suck the blood of every Jew, and he will detain every Jew as long as he can." Taking their cue from Butler, Northerners who came to occupied New Orleans in 1862 to run the newspapers singled out the Jews for vitriolic treatment. "The Jews in New Orleans and all the South ought to be exterminated," one Associated Press reporter wrote. "They run the blockade, and are always to be found at the bottom of every new villainy."[175] Not to be outdone, the

Chicago Times reported in July 1862, "The Israelites have come down upon the city [of Memphis] like locusts. . . . Every boat brings in a load of the hooked-nosed fraternity."[176]

Anti-Semitism, like all prejudice, is irrational. Many nineteenth-century Americans and Europeans used the word "Jew" to denote a cheap, corrupt merchant without necessarily believing all Jews were bad. For example, the British colonel, Arthur J. L. Fremantle, in his memoir, *Three Months in the Southern States,* described Matamoros, a town on the border of Texas and Mexico, as "infested with numbers of Jews whose industry spoils the trade of established merchants," and yet this same officer slept in Maj. Raphael J. Moses's tent and described Moses as "a jovial Hebrew."[177]

One of the most momentous issues of the Civil War for Northern Jews was the controversy over whether or not Jews could serve as chaplains in the Union army. Prior to the war it was not an issue, but thousands of Jews flocked to the army in 1861, and it therefore became an issue. The Volunteer Bill required that Union chaplains be "regularly ordained minister[s] of some Christian denomination," despite opposition on the floor of the House calling attention to the exclusion of "men . . . of the Hebrew faith." A controversy arose in the fall of 1861 when a YMCA worker discovered, to his horror, that one Michael Allen, a Jew, was serving as regimental chaplain for men of all faiths with the 5th Pennsylvania Cavalry.[178] Allen was not an ordained rabbi, but he was a student of theology and a competent and well-respected layman. He was forced to resign. This issue, which received widespread publicity in the Northern Jewish and religious press, precipitated a political controversy. The Jewish communities of the North petitioned Congress and the White House until, in July 1862, the law was amended to allow Jews to serve as chaplains.

In contrast to the controversy in the North, the right of Jews to serve as chaplains was never an issue for the Confederacy. Its laws referred to "clergymen," not to specific denominations. While there is no evidence that there ever was an official commissioned Confederate Jewish chaplain, there was never a legal impediment to such service. Two Confederate privates, Uriah Feibelman of Petersburg, Virginia, and B. Nordlinger of Macon, Georgia, apparently officiated as chaplains although not commissioned to do so. Feibelman, who was later ordained, served with the Petersburg Grays, Company C, 12th Virginia. Nordlinger, a bugler with the Macon German Artillery, conducted services for Temple Beth Israel in Macon in 1862.[179] In September 1862, the Confederate Congress debated the Exemption Bill, which excused "every minister of the Gospel" performing such duties from military service. The *Richmond Dispatch* editorialized against the bill if it did not include "Jewish ministers," and the final version referred to "every minister of religion." Without any debate or controversy, the Confederacy treated rabbis as equals of ministers of the Gospel.[180]

The Jews of the North and the South were bound together by ancient ethnic and religious ties, whether they were recent immigrant or third-generation Americans. Thus, while some of the Protestant churches—notably the Baptists and Methodists—divided into Southern and Northern branches, the Jews did not. Of course, American Jewry had no national religious body to divide and few national organizations of any kind. The Jewish boys in the Union army at times elicited the sympathy of Southern Jews and their hospitality, and at other times did not. As Jews, they were keenly aware of how important it was to these young men, in foreign surroundings, to attend Jewish services and celebrate the Jewish holidays. Lt. Simon S. Brucker of the 39th Illinois attended the High Holy Day services in occupied Norfolk, Virginia, and wrote his parents, "Oh! It made me feel as though I were at home among friends once more." Except that "All the Yehudin in Norfolk are so embittered against the Northern soldiers. I had several little arguments with some of them and find most of them pretty reasonable excepting the young *ladies, they* can outargue the smartest statesman in the world according to their own way." The men treated him courteously. Myer Levy, a Union soldier in another occupied Virginia town, saw a little boy eating matzo during Passover and asked him for a piece. The child ran inside and shouted "Mother! There's a 'damnyankee' Jew outside!" The mother emerged and, to his relief, invited Levy to the family Seder.[181]

For their part, Northern Jews disagreed with Southern Jews about the war, and, indeed, there were battles which pitted Jewish Confederates against Jewish Yankees. At Gettysburg, for example, the Alabama 12th, led by Major Proskauer, may have met the Illinois 82d, commanded by Lt. Col. Edward S. Salomon. But it does not appear that these feelings prevented that natural tendency of Jews of that era to come to the aid of one of their own. When Jewish Confederates were captured, for example, members of the Jewish community did what they could to relieve their suffering. The Jews of Chicago visited Jewish boys held as prisoners at Camp Douglas. Rabbi Wise attempted on a number of occasions to secure the release of Jewish Confederates from Fort Delaware. He asked the readership of his newspaper to send packages of food and published their names so that relatives in the North could assist.[182]

As the war drew to a close, the dispirited Jewish communities of Savannah, Charleston, Columbia, and Richmond reached out to Northern Jewry for desperately needed aid. They wrote appeals to national Jewish journals and newspapers such as the *Jewish Messenger,* published in New York by Samuel M. Isaacs; the *Israelite,* published in Cincinnati by Rabbi Wise; and the *Occident,* published by Rabbi Leeser in Philadelphia. Leeser, who had lived in Richmond as a young man and who had many friends and relatives in the South, was very supportive of Southern Jewry during and after the war. Indeed, upon his death in 1868, Charleston's Beth Elohim honored him in a memorial resolution: "As Southerners, we grieve over the loss of a bold defender of our rights, a true and consistent friend to

View of Richmond streets, the wounded from the Battle of Seven Pines, 1862. (*Battles and Leaders of the Civil War.*)

constitutional liberty, who, through great personal peril, remained unshaken in our vindication, undismayed by our reverses, unconquered by our defeat."[183]

In February 1865, the Jews of Savannah wrote to these Jewish periodicals seeking matzo: "Many of the inhabitants, formerly wealthy, are now in extremely straitened circumstances; and besides have entirely lost the means of baking for the ensuing Passover." Isaacs of the *Messenger* recalled the generosity of Savannah's Jewish community in its heyday and asked his readers to lay aside any enmity they might harbor and come to their co-religionists' aid. The response was overwhelming: three thousand pounds of matzo was sent from New York and two thousand pounds from Philadelphia. There was even a proposal in New York to establish a charitable organization to assist Southern Jewry. "This is no time to look back upon petty differences that may have arisen between communities," the *Jewish Record* urged. "Nor can any one now allude to political discussions or angry passions. . . . Let all of us join in tendering to our brethren a part of that wealth with which the God of Israel has blessed us.[184]

"By the latter part of 1863," William M. Robinson Jr. wrote, "Richmond in some respects resembled Chicago at the height of its gangster days." Crime was rampant. The city was full of criminals, shysters, and cheats.[185] Goods were in short supply. Philip Rosenheim wrote his sister Amelia and brother-in-law Isaac Meinnart that "check muslin could not be found at any price."[186] The population of Richmond began to suffer terribly from poverty, sickness, and war-weariness. Rev. George Jacobs of Beth Shalome could not support his family on a rabbi's salary. He engaged in business to earn additional income. In February 1863, the Jacobs's five-year-old daughter, Martha, died of scarlet fever. To make matters worse, Jacobs officiated at the funerals of six Richmond Jewish soldiers killed in the war, including that of his young brother-in-law, Pvt. Isaac J. Levy. In his funeral address, Jacobs lamented the loss of "a young man cut down in the springtime of existence, one in the plentitude of health and vigor of manhood." He spoke of faith in adversity and sorrow. "It is good for me that I have been afflicted," he quoted the words of David, "that I might better learn Thy ways." The days of darkness must come, Jacobs told the mourners, and "those whose faith is well founded" will be prepared to meet adversity.[187]

Samuel Yates Levy, writing in Savannah in November 1863, prayed for peace, victory, and humility:

> And as Thou led'st Thy chosen people forth
> From Egypt's sullen wrath, oh King of Kings!
> So smite the armies of the cruel North
> And bear us to our hopes "on eagle's wings."
> But should Thy wisdom still defer the day—
> The wish'd for day our freedom shall be won—
> Oh grant us the humility to say,
> Not human will but Thine, oh Lord, be done.[188]

Henry Timrod, the author of "La Belle Juive," died in poverty and sickness in 1867. He was later honored, more in death than in life, as the poet laureate of the Confederacy. A bust of Timrod now graces the entrance to Washington Park next to City Hall in Charleston. There for all time Henry Timrod stares at St. Michael's Church across Broad Street, where in September 1863 he dared not intrude on the Jewish beauty, Rachel Lyons.

CHAPTER 6

★

Two Jewish
Confederate Sisters

My only wish was to live and die among them, growing each
day better from contact with their gentle, kindly sympathies
and heroic hearts.
  —Phoebe Pember, *A Southern Woman's Story* (1879)

To the *women of the South* I look for approval.
—Eugenia Phillips, on her return from Union imprisonment, 1862

IF IT CAN BE SAID that there were Jewish aristocrats in the Old South, then the
Levy sisters exemplified the Southern Jewish elite. Eugenia and Phoebe Levy were
born and grew up in Charleston, South Carolina, in its heyday in the early 1800s.
T. C. DeLeon described Eugenia as "one of the most picturesque personages in
Confederate history . . . a most potent and popular one in Washington society . . .
she had great goodness of heart, and was ever loyal in her friendships [which]
included some of the most notable women." Of Phoebe he wrote: "A belle and
early a widow, she made herself loved in the army camps by that good work of her
Chimborazo Hospital." Eugenia's 1902 obituary linked the two famous Confederate sisters: "Two more brilliant women than Mrs. Phillips and her sister, Mrs. Pember, of Savannah, who frequently visited her, were not to be found in Washington,
and in those days many famous wits and beauties were gathered here." Another
recalled the sisters as "the toasts of the day." They were, without a doubt, two of
the Confederacy's most interesting women.[1]

Their parents, Jacob Clavius Levy and Fanny Yates Levy, were educated, cultured, and wealthy Charlestonians. Jacob, a Charleston native, met Fanny on a visit
to Liverpool while on a European tour. His foreign bride was, according to
Charleston Jewish tradition, the admiration of the whole city. It was said that, at
her first appearance in the dress circle of the old Charleston Theatre in Broad
Street "the whole house rose in tribute to her matchless beauty." Judging from her
portrait painted by Thomas Sully in 1842, Mrs. Levy was indeed a beautiful and
sophisticated lady.[2]

Phoebe Yates Pember was born in Charleston in 1823 into a well-to-do Jewish family. Her father, Jacob Clavius Levy, was active in Beth Elohim. She married Thomas Pember, a Gentile, who died prior to the war. A widow and feeling restless, Mrs. Pember left her parents' home in Marietta, Georgia, in December 1862 and went to wartime Richmond to become the first matron of the Chimborazo Hospital. (Courtesy of *Civil War Times*.)

Jacob Levy was prominent in the business affairs of Charleston. He was a director of the Union Insurance Company, a delegate to the Knoxville Railroad Convention in 1836, a member of the Charleston Chamber of Commerce, and was affiliated with the Union Party in the Nullification crisis. He was a pioneer in the insurance and railroad industries in the 1830s, and he pursued other interests as well. He was a member of the Charleston Library Society and, according to a great-granddaughter, was "quite literary." The soirées he gave were among the events of Charleston's social season.[3]

Levy was also a devout and practicing Jew. His father, Moses Levy, had served as president of Beth Elohim and, in 1838, in his nineties, he had rushed to

Eugenia Phillips was born in Charleston in 1819. A high-spirited
woman, she married a successful lawyer, Philip Phillips, who was
also active in Beth Elohim as a young man. The couple moved to
Mobile, where they had nine children. They moved to Washington when Mr. Phillips was elected to Congress. Mrs. Phillips was
arrested twice by Union authorities, first in Washington for spying
and then in New Orleans for mocking Union soldiers. Mary Chesnut referred to her and fellow spy Rose Greenhow as "saints and
martyrs and patriots." (Author's collection.)

the synagogue to save the sacred Torah scrolls from loss in a fire. The Jacob Levy
family worshiped at Beth Elohim, a short walk from their home on East Bay Street.
During a four-year period when there was no regular rabbi at Beth Elohim, he and
two other members of the congregation took turns officiating. He served as treasurer of the congregation; wrote one of the hymns used in the consecration of the
Temple in 1841; and wrote a book entitled *Vindicae Judearum, A History of the*

The East Bay Street home of Jacob
and Fanny Levy in Charleston.
(Author's collection. Photograph
taken by Michael Levkoff.)

Jewish People. "That history," he held, "has been the moral and religious teaching of the world; it has been the source of the national life of the most remarkable people on the face of the earth." This book apparently was never published, but Levy did publish a scholarly article on "The Reformed Israelites" in the *Southern Quarterly Review* in 1844.[4]

Jacob and Fanny Levy lived at 301 East Bay Street in a grand mansion built between 1811 and 1816 by his father, Moses Levy, a native of Krakow, Poland. Situated in Ansonborough, the house still stands. Their neighbors were the Gadsdens, the Heywards, and the Laurenses. The Levys soon filled their spacious house with seven children: the eldest was Henrietta (1818); then Eugenia (1819); Martha Sarah (1821); Phoebe (1823); Samuel Yates (1827); Emma (1832); and Fanny (1840). The children were undoubtedly raised in the Jewish religion and attended services at Beth Elohim. In 1848 the family moved to Savannah, Georgia, where Jacob Levy died in 1875. Fanny lived into her late eighties. Martha never married but was a "gifted and popular woman," according to DeLeon. Henrietta married the prominent Savannah lawyer Octavus Cohen. Emma married Samuel Prioleau Hamilton, whose father was a former governor of South Carolina. Yates Levy became a lawyer, newspaper editor, and accomplished equestrian, serving for a time as an officer in the Savannah Jockey Club.[5]

By all accounts, the youthful Eugenia Levy was the quintessential Southern belle. Given her beauty and background, Eugenia had her choice of suitors. She chose Philip Phillips, a bright, young Jewish Charlestonian from a modest background. She chose well.

Phillips was born in Charleston in 1807, the son of a German Jewish immigrant, Aaron Phillips, and a native-born mother, Caroline Lazarus, whose father had fought in the American Revolution. He studied under Isaac Harby, read law under the tutelage of the eminent Charleston lawyer John Gadsden (formerly the U.S. district attorney) and, at age twenty-two, became a successful lawyer. When he was twenty-one, he served as secretary of the Reformed Society of Israelites. His father, like Eugenia's, served as president of Beth Elohim. When Phillips joined the bar, he relocated to Cheraw, South Carolina, where he rode the circuit, as Abraham Lincoln did about the same time. In the 1830 Nullification crisis, Phillips was a staunch Unionist, a stance he maintained up to and through the Civil War. He was one of four Jewish South Carolinians who attended the Nullification Convention in Columbia, where he distinguished himself as a brave and vigorous defender of the Union. (Phillips and Chapman Levy were Unionists; Philip Cohen and Myer Jacobs favored nullification.)[6]

Many South Carolinians moved west in the 1830s, and Phillips decided to seek his fortune in Mobile, Alabama, where he lived until 1853. In 1836 Phillips returned to Charleston and, on September 7 of that year, married Eugenia Levy, aged sixteen. Phillips was then 29. Eugenia described herself as a "delicate" woman, but, as we shall see, this was hardly the case. She raised nine children, was incarcerated twice for her pro-Southern sympathies, and lived to the age of eighty-three.[7]

Phillips was a successful attorney in Mobile, where, among other clients, he represented the Bank of Mobile and numerous commercial interests. Eugenia's time was devoted to their growing family. During the eighteen years they lived in Mobile, she bore seven children: Clavius, Fanny, Caroline (Lina), Salvadora, Eugene, John Walker and John Randolph. Three more, Emma, William Hallett, and Philip, were born in Washington in the 1850s. The family first resided in the Somerville area in the western suburbs of Mobile and then on Mobile Bay. One house was destroyed by fire, and the family lost nearly every possession. Mrs. Phillips later recalled, "The picture of my two oldest children, Clavius and Fanny, was rescued from the flames by their faithful colored nurse, and now adorns our parlor at Washington." Active in Mobile society, the Phillipses entertained the Hungarian liberator, Lajos Kossuth, on his visit to their city.[8]

Phillips continued his active interest in politics and published a digest of the decisions of the Alabama Supreme Court. He was elected to the Alabama legislature in 1844, served as chairman of that body's committee on Federal relations, was reelected in 1852, and served as chairman of the committee on internal improvements. Like Judah Benjamin and David Yulee, he was a proponent of a modern

Philip Phillips, Eugenia Phillips's husband, was a moderate and opposed secession. The author of the Kansas-Nebraska Act, he was a brilliant lawyer. This photograph shows him as an older man, after the war. (Courtesy of American Jewish Historical Society, Waltham, Mass., and New York City.)

railroad system. Chairman of the Alabama Democratic Party, Phillips was a delegate to the 1852 Democratic Party Convention, where he made a speech in support of Franklin Pierce's bid for the presidency. He and President Pierce later became close friends.

In 1853 Phillips was elected to the U.S. Congress from Alabama. He was intimately involved in the negotiations and debate over the Kansas-Nebraska Act, apparently being the only Southern Representative who understood that the technical language of the Compromise of 1820 barred slavery perpetually in the territories at issue. Phillips, a moderate Democrat, was sought out by Stephen A. Douglas and John C. Breckinridge, who "begged [him] to find the least inflammatory language to accomplish modification of the Missouri Compromise." Phillips was then to clear the wording with the key Southern leaders of the Congress. They met the next day in a smoke-filled room at the Patent Office near the Phillipses' home, where all agreed on Phillips's amendments. Phillips's language, which did not repeal the Compromise of 1820, nevertheless made it "inoperative and void" in Kansas-Nebraska. "Not since the cotton gin," William Freehling has written, "had the Patent Office observed a southern invention so fateful as Phillips' phraseology."[9] It was obvious that Phillips possessed an extraordinary legal mind. His legal ability and his talent for consensus-building earned the instant respect of his colleagues and the Washington legal establishment. By 1860 he was described by Mary Chesnut and others as "a celebrated lawyer."[10]

Phillips decided not to run for reelection to the House but to stay in Washington. His law practice had suffered, and he needed to provide for his family. The family was also now part of the Washington establishment. They were close friends of President and Mrs. Pierce and socialized with them frequently. During his days in Congress, Phillips had developed personal relationships with Jefferson Davis, the senator from Mississippi; Edwin M. Stanton, the former attorney general of the United States and future secretary of war under Lincoln; as well as William H. Seward, Lincoln's future secretary of state. Seward, a neighbor, was a frequent visitor in the Phillipses' home and, as Caroline Phillips Myers recalled later, "many were the sharp and witty encounters between my Mother and this distinguished man, who afterwards became her enemy on the ever agitating question of slavery."[11] Mrs. Phillips had many friends, among them Rose O'Neal Greenhow, Washington's most notable hostess, the daughter of a prominent planter family from Maryland and the aunt of Mrs. Stephen A. Douglas. She also appeared to carry on extended flirtations with Joseph Holt, then a member of the cabinet, and Sen. Stephen R. Mallory of Florida.[12]

It is impossible for historians to know about the private lives of people, but Mary Chesnut thought Eugenia Phillips, who was after all a married woman, was more than a flirt. "I wish Mr. Mallory would not tell me so much of his flirtation with Mrs. Phillips," she wrote in her dairy in March 1861. "I do not think it as innocent as he pretends, but it's none of my business." When the Yankees seized Mrs. Phillips's correspondence, "Mallory & Holt may *tremble*," she wrote, "from what I know of the scandals."[13]

The Phillipses did not forget their Jewish roots. Mr. Phillips led the Jewish delegation to President Buchanan to seek relief for Jews from the American-Swiss Treaty of 1855, and he spoke at the laying of the cornerstone at Temime Derech, a New Orleans synagogue, in 1866.[14] Clara Solomon mentions seeing one of the Phillips daughters, whom she calls "Beauty" (probably Fanny), at Yom Kippur services at the Dispersed of Judah synagogue in September 1861 and two of the Phillips girls at Passover in April 1862. Indeed, it appears that one or both of the Phillips girls attended regularly. Clearly, the Jewish community of New Orleans perceived the Phillipses as Jews.[15]

The three Phillips girls inherited their mother's beauty and graces, "but not . . . her satiric turn." Fanny, Caroline, and Emma became popular belles and were all considered beauties in a society where plain women were exceptional. When Buchanan became president, the Phillipses visited his daughter Harriet Lane, the president's hostess at the White House. "We were present," one of the daughters recalled, "at her private entertainment given to the Prince of Wales." Mrs. Clement Clay remembered a musical performance at the White House during the Buchanan presidency. "Among the guests on that occasion," she wrote, "were

Miss Phillips of Alabama and her cousin, Miss Cohen of South Carolina, who were brilliant amateur players with a local reputation. They were the daughter and niece, respectively, of Mrs. Eugenia Phillips. . . At the invitation of Miss Lane, the Misses Phillips and Cohen took their places at the piano and performed a brilliant and intricate duet."[16]

Not since Andrew Jackson arrived in Washington had a change in administrations been so dramatic as in 1860, when Abraham Lincoln replaced James Buchanan. Southerners had held prominent places in the Buchanan cabinet, and Southern senators dominated the Senate. Indeed, Southerners dominated Washington itself in the antebellum era. Ladies like Eugenia Phillips felt that they were the leaders of "polite society" in the nation's capital. With the arrival of the Lincoln administration, however, the residents of Washington realized that the Republican political revolution was a social revolution as well. The city, Mrs. Phillips said, was "disgraced with Lincoln's low soldiery." As the Southern states began to secede and the Southern congressmen withdrew, those Southerners remaining in Washington considered themselves to be citizens of another country and no longer loyal to the old Federal Union. In response to the crises, Eugenia and Rose Greenhow organized a committee to aid Confederate prisoners and took relief packages to the Old Capital Prison.[17] Some of these Southerners began to engage in what can only be described as espionage activities—providing information to the newly established Confederate government about military affairs, troop movements, politicians, and the general activities of the Federal government. Eugenia Phillips engaged in exactly the same kind of espionage. Strictly speaking, these activities were treasonous, and the Federal government was in no mood for them, even if carried on by witty, attractive, socially prominent Southern belles. Greenhow knew what she was doing in recruiting beautiful women to extract information from gullible officers.[18]

Eugenia and Philip could not have had a greater divergence of opinion on slavery and secession. As in many marriages, the partners differed markedly in their temperament. Philip was a person of calm and moderate disposition, not inclined to radical ideas, a conservative who believed deeply in the status quo and the American legal system. Eugenia, the daughter and friend of Southern aristocrats and an enthusiastic participant in the Southern social scene, was an ardent Southern partisan who was a vociferous supporter of the Southern cause. In this, she was not alone. The entire Levy family—all of the generations—supported the war. Sister Phoebe waxed eloquent on the topic of the patriotism of Southern women. The Levy men enlisted[19]; but Philip thought secession foolhardy and had little use for the institution of slavery. He even attempted to stem the tide of secession.[20]

The Phillipses' political activities were immediately suspect because of Eugenia's vocal public support for the Southern cause, despite Philip's antisecession views. By late July 1861, despondency spread over the North when the defeat at First Manassas, or Bull Run, became known. Southern sympathizers were arrested. The most famous Southern belle to be detained was Eugenia's good friend Rose O'Neal Greenhow. She had provided the Confederates with Gen. Irvin McDowell's plans for the First Manassas campaign using a secret code provided by General Beauregard's staff. She was arrested on August 23, 1861, and on August 24, Eugenia and Philip Phillips were also arrested.[21]

Mr. Phillips's office was upstairs in their house on I Street. While he was working at his desk, a Federal officer entered the house and told Phillips that he was under arrest. Detectives searched the house, and an officer seized Phillips's papers. When the officers were finished, Eugenia and daughters Fanny and Caroline, as well as Eugenia's sister Martha Levy, were imprisoned in two dirty rooms in the attic story of Mrs. Greenhow's residence on Sixteenth Street, where officials could conveniently guard the women together. They had a broken stove, a punch bowl which could be used for a washbasin, and two filthy straw mattresses. It was later dubbed "Fort Greenhow" and "Greenhow Prison."[22]

Eugenia's innocent husband was under house arrest for a week. Mrs. Phillips and her daughters were able to receive letters and baskets of fruit from her husband and occasional visits, but Union authorities placed a guard with a musket at their table to listen to their conversation. "It is but justice to this man [the guard] to say he appeared much ashamed of the ignoble part assigned to him. Our rebel hearts, however, enabled us to rise superior to the devices of our enemies. Our conversation, which was one of the merriest, was conducted in French." She celebrated her twenty-fifth wedding anniversary while imprisoned.[23] But, she was nevertheless unrepentant: "Again I ask myself what is my crime? If an ardent attachment to the land of my birth and expression of deepest sympathy with my relatives and friends in the South constitute treason—then I am indeed a traitor! If hostility towards Black Republicanism, its sentiments and policy—is a crime—I am self-condemned . . . !"[24]

The Federal authorities could find no evidence with which to charge Eugenia, but they would not release her. Southerners were outraged at the treatment accorded Eugenia Phillips and Rose Greenhow. Mary Chesnut said: "These poor souls are jealously guarded night and day. It is a hideous tale, what they tell of their suffering. Mrs. [Robert E.] Lee punned upon the odd expression, 'Ladies of their age being confined.' These old Washington habituées say Mrs. Greenhow had herself confined and persecuted, that we might trust her the more. She sees we distrust her after all. The Manassas men swear she was our good angel."[25]

Mrs. Chesnut did blame Greenhow and Phillips, however obliquely, for causing difficulties for all Southern women. Federal authorities now began searching women's hair and clothing for contraband. Bustles, she wrote, are now "suspect. . . . Not legs but arms are looked for under hoops." Public opinion favored the prisoners. Phillip Clayton thought Mrs. Phillips's children ought not to have been hostages to fortune. "How can a motherly soul with nine children be suspected of mischief?" he wondered. But Mrs. Chesnut recounted, "She is caged up, all the same!"[26]

Philip Phillips's relationships with Edwin Stanton; Reverdy Johnson, the senator from Maryland; and Supreme Court Justice James M. Wayne, formerly mayor of Savannah, proved helpful in the crisis. The Phillips ladies were released on September 18, 1861, after three weeks of imprisonment. The family left Washington as quickly as possible. Each signed a parole agreement pledging not to take disloyal actions against the government. The document, daughter Caroline recalled, was big "with seals formidable enough to shield Federal soldiers from Southern bullets."[27]

By coincidence, the Phillips family happened to meet the secretary of state, Henry Seward, while en route to the train station. They gave him a loud "hurra for Dixie!" They then sailed for Fort Monroe in a fearful storm, which delayed their trip. Trying to decide whether to transfer to a smaller boat, Mr. Phillips consulted with the officer in charge. "But the sight of the Confederate flag was enough to inspire the enthusiastic bosoms of the women with a feeling that knows no fear, and counts no consequence." Mr. Phillips and her daughters jumped into a frail bark and sailed away. Gen. Benjamin Huger sent a steamer to bring the Phillips family ashore. Mr. Phillips caught up with them later. They were received at Norfolk, Virginia, with deep respect and emotion by Confederate officers. The next day they traveled to Richmond.[28]

The story was later widely circulated that Eugenia brought a message in code from Rose Greenhow in a ball of yarn and delivered it to Jefferson Davis.[29] After Mrs. Phillips and her daughters were freed from Greenhow prison, they were sitting at the parlor window when Rose, still a prisoner, was out walking with an officer on each side. She passed by and threw a ball of wool, saying: "You dropped your worsted, Mrs. Phillips, when you left my house." Rose went on her way, laughing and chatting with her guard. Four days later, although she had been carefully searched at Fortress Monroe, Mrs. Phillips gave Jefferson Davis the cipher letter contained in the ball. "This was," Caroline Myers recalled later, "the only treasonable act of which our Mother was guilty and of which conscientious Father never knew."[30]

From Richmond, the Phillipses traveled to Savannah and then decided to relocate to New Orleans. They arrived in the Crescent City in the winter of 1861 only to find that wartime conditions made it impossible for Mr. Phillips to open a law practice. Like others in New Orleans, the Phillipses believed that they were safe from the Yankee invasion. They were lulled into "a charming condition of safety, and our hopes buoyed up by recent victories," Eugenia recalled, "while all letters from Richmond conveyed hints of our speedy recognition by England, the surface of society seemed unruffled, and we were but little prepared for the bitter fate which was in store."[31] In April the Union fleet appeared at the mouth of the

The scene at City Hall in New Orleans when the flag was hauled down.
(*Battles and Leaders of the Civil War.*)

Mississippi River. Rear Adm. David G. Farragut commanded a fleet of twenty-four vessels, which boasted two hundred guns and mortars and nineteen mortar boats. He captured New Orleans in April, and on May 1 Union Maj. Gen. Benjamin F. "Beast" Butler took command of the city.

Butler immediately began an efficient and extremely controversial military administration of New Orleans. "Beast" Butler was the worst the Union army had to offer. He was nicknamed "Spoons" for thievery of spoons and silverware imputed to him and to his soldiers. Eugenia said Butler became "our master; *he,* intent on getting our money; *we* as determined to keep it." One of his most notorious acts was General Order No. 28, which became known as "The Woman Order." "As the officers and soldiers of the United States have been subjected to repeated insults from the women (calling themselves ladies) of New Orleans," this order read, "it is ordered, that hereafter, when any female shall, by word, gesture or movement insult or show contempt for any officer or soldier of the United States, she shall be regarded and held liable to be treated as a woman of the town plying her avocation." When the mayor of New Orleans, John T. Monroe, protested the order, he was arrested. Prime Minister Palmerston in the British House of Commons said, "An Englishman must blush to think that such an act has been committed by one belonging to the Anglo-Saxon race."[32]

Butler deliberately chose to humiliate the New Orleans aristocracy. Eugenia claimed to have kept herself as secluded as possible in order to escape any notice from Butler's henchmen. But on June 29, 1862, she unwisely showed her contempt of the occupying forces. The Phillips home, located next to City Hall, overlooked the funeral procession of Lieutenant DeKay, a Union officer. Eugenia, standing on the balcony, appeared to burst into laughter and cheers at the procession. According to her daughter Caroline, she was only reacting to the news of a Confederate victory.[33] Butler immediately ordered her to appear at his headquarters at the Customs House. Eugenia, active in raising money for the widow of a man executed by Butler for having hauled down the flag from the Federal mint, believed she was being persecuted for her pro-Southern beliefs.

Butler screamed at her, "You are *seen* laughing and mocking at the remains of a Federal officer." Eugenia replied, "I was in good spirits and felt like laughing." Butler replied, "I do not call you a common woman of the town, but an uncommonly vulgar one, and I sentence you to Ship Island for the War."[34] Mr. Phillips could not reason with the general, who threatened to have her gagged. "After making all allowance for his position as commander," Mr. Phillips recalled years later in his characteristically modest way, "I must now characterize his conduct as coarse and brutal."[35] Butler took some time writing out Mrs. Phillips's sentence. He hoped she would throw herself on his mercy. But begging pardon never occurred to Eugenia. She quietly folded her arms and looked on him contemptuously while he wrote her arrest order.[36] In truth, T. C. DeLeon later recounted, "it was Mrs. Phillips's contempt of the general and her cool sarcasm that caused her imprisonment." "If such women as you and Mrs. Greenhow are let loose, our lives are in jeopardy," General Butler said. When told she would be exiled to an island sixty-five miles from New Orleans, Eugenia retorted, "It has one advantage over the city, Sir; *you* will not be there."[37] When informed that her new home was also a Yellow Fever station, Eugenia replied, "It is fortunate that neither the fever nor General Butler is contagious!"[38]

Butler's Special Order #150, which he wrote in his own hand, reads as follows:

> Mrs. Phillips, wife of Philip Phillips, having been once imprisoned for her traitorous proclivities and acts at Washington, and released by the clemency of the Government; and having been found training her children to spit upon officers of the United States, for which act of one of those children both her husband and herself apologized and were again forgiven, is now found on the balcony of her house during the passage of the funeral procession of Lieut. De Kay, laughing and mocking at his remains, and upon being inquired of by the commanding general if this fact were so, contemptuously replies—"I was in good spirits that day."
>
> It is therefore ordered that she be not "regarded and treated as a common woman," of whom no officer or soldier is bound to take notice, but as an uncommon, bad and dangerous woman, stirring up strife and inciting to riot.

And that therefore she be confined at Ship Island, in the State of Mississippi, within the proper limits there, till further orders, and that she be allowed one female servant and no more, if she so choose. That one of the houses for hospital purpose be assigned her as quarters, and a soldier's ration each day be served out to her with the means of cooking the same, and that no verbal or written communication be allowed with her, except through this office, and that she be kept in close confinement until removed to Ship Island.[39]

Ship Island, a former quarantine station, was a mosquito-infested sandbar without amenities of any kind.[40] The summer heat in the Delta could be fatal, and the poor hygiene on the island was well known. Healthy food was hard to obtain, but Butler allowed Mr. Phillips to send some.[41] Had it not been for Phebe, her loyal servant, Eugenia may have died. Her fellow inhabitants of the island were "negroes, soldiers, contractors, sutlers, piddlars, black republicans, sailors and Officers." She was offended by everything from their manner of dress to their language. The familiarity between whites and blacks made her indignant. She described the soldiers and officers as "a crowd of drunken, low, filthy soldiers and officers." "I put the officers last as the soldiers were much more respectable. Their conversation, evidently to insult me, was of the basest and foullest character." She lived at first in a railroad boxcar, then in the former post office. Her letters were inspected by Union soldiers and were dated "From my Palace on the lake of Como." They were, her daughter recalled, "more for General Butler's edification than loving messages home."[42]

Eugenia and Phebe subsisted on beans, spoiled beef, and such food as her husband was allowed to send her, drinking saltwater made drinkable by filtering it through sand. "Entire hogshead of ice melting," she recalled, "but none for the vile Rebels." There was no place to wash. Eugenia suffered from brain fever, which was undoubtedly nervous exhaustion. She was at times very ill and even delirious. At one point, Phebe's health also broke down. Every week, General Butler inquired after Mrs. Phillips's health, hoping she would beg for mercy, a weakness she considered to be a stain on her reputation. Her family and friends wrote her often and sent her packages and books. "Send me some of Dickens' works," she wrote. "I don't care which, as I find something original whenever I read them over." She wrote copious letters. In one touching letter to her youngest children, Mrs. Phillips wrote, "You must all be satisfied with this and believe that Dear Mother never allows a day to pass without thinking of all her . . . little ones, and a night to arrive without praying to God to keep you all well and make good, obedient children of you all."[43]

The civilian population of the South, generally, and New Orleans, in particular, was outraged at Butler's treatment of Eugenia Phillips. Mary Chesnut wrote: "Mrs. Phillips, another beautiful and clever Jewess, has been put in prison again by

Beast Butler, for laughing as a Yankee funeral procession went by."[44] Newspapers all over the country were filled with particulars of her suffering. Amanda Levy wrote her, "Future historians will vie with each other for the honor of writing your biography." She reported that loyal citizens of New Orleans made pilgrimages to the Phillips home and that sympathy for her was "widespread and real." Clara Solomon was infuriated that Mrs. Phillips, "Beauty's Ma," had been mistreated. "This is one of *the outrages* of But[ler] . . . and what anyway could a woman's taunts do to them!"[45]

Mrs. Phillips's father, Mr. Levy, referred to Butler as a "Vile beast, imprisoning her body & seeking to destroy her moral character." Her husband concluded years later, "If the imprudence of my wife brought on her these difficulties she endured the consequences of them with a heroic spirit that could not be excelled."[46] William Garrett noted that "her proud Southern spirit never quailed, and she remained firm to the last in the opinions she had expressed." The newspapers at the time were filled with the story and with comments on the harsh proceedings against Mrs. Phillips. She became quite a heroine, Garrett recalled, "and to this day [1872] is remembered with admiration by all generous minds, as one of the first victims which rendered a certain *administration* in New Orleans immortal for—*eccentricity.*"[47]

How Mrs. Phillips came to be released from Ship Island after three and a half months is not known. Her daughter Caroline Myers believed that Reverdy Johnson, the family friend who came to her aid in Washington, intervened on her behalf while he was in New Orleans investigating Butler for the U.S. government.[48] As she emerged from her prison at the end of September, the Union officer in charge, Lt. Col. Charles Ruff, attempted to make amends. Mrs. Phillips was furious at this belated apology and replied: "Sir, do not imagine that my conduct during my imprisonment had for its guide any other motive than a holy and sacred respect for the cause for which I have suffered. To the *women of the South* I look for approval, while my own self-respect sustained me thro' all your persecutions. I cannot accept *your* tardy sympathy. I only hope God will forgive you for all you have done to me."[49]

Eugenia and Phebe arrived in New Orleans early in the morning and reached the Phillips home to find that her family, "true to Yankee cruelty," had been kept in ignorance of her release. "Immediately I was embraced, kissed, cried over, while Mr. Phillips, stunned by the news, not knowing whether I was dead or alive, remained in his room, overwhelmed and alarmed. I rushed upstairs. When he saw me, tears came to his release and the reaction was painful to witness."[50]

After Eugenia had been released by General Butler, her eldest son, Clavius, a Confederate soldier, wrote his mother, "I could not imagine a human being calling himself a man, could resort to so harsh treatment upon a lady. Your heart must gladden with the idea of being once more in the land of safety, where you can express your thought freely without fear of being condemned to prison. If anyone has occasion to entertain eternal enmity to the whole Yankee nation, it is our family, and I hope the time is not far distant when I may have an opportunity to avenge the insults you have undergone."[51]

Mrs. Phillips remained an unreconstructed rebel. After her release, she and her husband were summoned to take the loyalty oath or declare themselves enemies of the United States. They refused to take the oath, preferring to flee from New Orleans to LaGrange, Georgia, where they settled for the duration of the war. They stopped on the way in Mobile, where Eugenia received an ovation from the leaders of society.[52] Once in LaGrange with several other refugee families, they formed "a pleasant social circle which served to wile away the time." The men had their card club, and the ladies, musical parties. Of course, the Phillipses, like all parents with children in time of war, worried about their sons.[53]

Clavius Phillips, Eugenia and Philip's eldest child, enlisted with his cousin Octavus S. Cohen in Gallie's (Savannah Artillery) Company of the 1st (Olmstead's) Georgia on May 31, 1861, as a corporal. He was described as five feet eight inches tall, with blue eyes, brown hair, and a dark complexion. He then served in the Chatham Artillery and was detailed on special service in the Quartermaster Department of Georgia State Service. By September 1862, the twenty-four-year-old Clavius was "occupying his time in the culture of a . . . pair of Russian whiskers: a kind of cross between a civil and military beard," his Uncle Yates Levy wrote.[54] Clavius served with this artillery unit, now known as Weaton's Battery, near Savannah until July 1863. He had been detailed to the Engineering Department in Savannah in March and by August 1864 was transferred to that department. Clavius was anxious to defend his native city and undoubtedly was involved in the works defending Savannah. In January 1864, Phillips and a comrade sent a letter through military channels to the secretary of war seeking authorization "to raise a Company of heavy artillery" from the men serving in the Georgia State Guards and others whose terms were about to expire. The idea was approved by Maj. Gen. Jeremy F. Gilmer, but nothing came of it. In November 1864, young Phillips was serving as first sergeant of Company E, 2d Regiment Engineer Troops, in the Confederate army. He was promoted to second lieutenant in March 1865 and was paroled with his unit at Chester, South Carolina, on May 5, 1865.[55]

Another son, Eugene Phillips, served as a cadet in the Confederate navy. He was in Richmond at the same time as his aunt Phoebe Pember and was assigned to the *Patrick Henry,* a training vessel anchored in the James River, fourteen miles from the city, opposite Drewey's Bluff. In Richmond he had the luxury of having his laundry done by his aunt Phoebe. Yet another son, John Walker, while only about fifteen years of age, served in battle.[56]

Eugenia's family moved about during the war. A July 1862 letter from her father, Jacob Clavius Levy, finds Emma and Martha in Greenville, South Carolina;

Henrietta and grandson Clavius Phillips in Savannah; Lina Phillips in New Orleans; and the elder Levys in Marietta.[57] Things were not well in Marietta. "The privations and endurance," Mr. Levy wrote, "felt around here made us no exception for we are at present cut off from the means formerly relied on." The letter also relates that the Levys, like many elderly Southerners, left their home in Savannah in the possession of their servants and Clavius, their young grandson, "sleeping there." Henrietta's only son, Octavus Cohen, was serving as an aide to a general and was "under fire on James Island, So.Ca." This was a reference to the Battle of Secessionville on James Island across the Ashley River from Charleston. Jacob and Fanny Levy, it appears, remained firm in their Jewish faith. Jacob's letter closes with this allusion to the Scriptures, "Trusting that the time is not far distant when each may sit under his own fig tree with none to make him afraid."[58]

Mr. Phillips resumed the practice of law. He went to Mobile on one occasion and argued the question of the power of the Confederate government to tax the bonds of the Confederate states before a Confederate judge. (He argued that the Confederate government had no such power and the court agreed with him.)[59] In another case, he represented English owners of three steamers seized by the Confederate government. He successfully argued for their release. During one business trip to Richmond, it was apparent to Phillips that the Confederacy would soon collapse. He recalled, "The treasury was empty, the army worn out, the Confederate commissioners were dispirited. I saw the end approaching with rapidity, as I had long anticipated. I did not therefore, tarry. My journey homeward was embarrassed by the movements of the armies. [Confederate Vice President] Alexander H. Stephens traveled with me, and owing to his ill health, we only journeyed in the daytime. . . . We finally arrived at Washington, Georgia, where I left Mr. Stephens at the residence of Mr. [Robert A.] Toombs."[60]

Lee surrendered in April 1865. On May 10, 1865, Philip Phillips was at the depot in LaGrange waiting for the train from Atlanta. There he read a reward notice that Federal officials offered $100,000 for the apprehension of Jefferson Davis, Clement Clay, and others on the charge of being accomplices in the assassination of Abraham Lincoln. Phillips, a friend of the Clays, noticed that Mrs. Clay was at the depot at that moment. He immediately took her aside and told her of the accusation. "The distress of this good woman," Phillips recalled, "was painful to behold." Clay was innocent of any wrongdoing, and Phillips advised him to surrender to the appropriate Federal officials. Clay immediately wrote to Gen. James H. Wilson in command at Macon, Georgia, offering to turn himself in. Phillips delivered the letter himself.[61]

The Phillips family had endured a scare as the war was coming to an end. A cavalry force of fewer than three thousand Federal troops attacked West Point, Georgia, on April 16, 1865. They burned the depots, a tannery, a gristmill, and a large quantity of railroad rolling stock and engines, and looted the citizens. The

Union troops were held off for about eight hours by a ragtag command of boys, old men, convalescents from the hospital, and citizens who fought from a substantial but little fort constructed about eighteen months before. Among the captives after the battle was the Phillips's son, John, a member of the home guard. The anxious parents were relieved to receive a message from a Union colonel that John was safe but that he could not obtain a parole for ten days. The colonel added that "the boys had displayed the utmost gallantry." After ten days, John reached home, a richer if not wiser youth, the owner of the mule upon which he rode.[62]

"A few days subsequently," Phillips wrote in his understated way, "we learned the surrender of Lee's Army. This terminated a struggle in which the South lost all but honor. So far as the loss of property in slaves was involved, I regard it as the greatest blessing."[63]

★　　★　　★

The war began with a great deal less fanfare for Eugenia's younger sister, Phoebe Yates Pember. A widow, Phoebe had refugeed with her parents, Jacob and Fanny Levy, to Marietta, Georgia. But she was about to embark on the adventure of a lifetime.

In 1856 Phoebe Levy, age thirty-three, married Thomas Pember, a Christian. He was two years her junior. They removed to Boston, Massachusetts. Her letters and memoirs indicate that she was well educated. She likely had private tutors and may have attended a Northern finishing school like other daughters of her social class. Shortly after their marriage, Thomas Pember contracted tuberculosis and the couple moved South. He died in Aiken, South Carolina, in July of 1861 at the age of thirty-six.[64]

At age thirty-eight, Phoebe was unhappy living in Marietta. "You know," she wrote to Eugenia, "how unpleasantly I have been situated at Papa's house. . . . I see no chance of bettering my position while here." There were obviously some serious divisions in the Levy family, for she also wrote Eugenia that she thanked God "every night for the courage He gave me to leave those who never cared for me and I believe disliked me for the gifts [presumably, her ability to write] He had given me."[65]

One of Phoebe Pember's acquaintances was Mrs. George Randolph (whose husband served as Confederate secretary of war for eight months in 1862), according to Pember, "Foremost among Virginia women." Mrs. Randolph had been active in caring for the sick and wounded in wartime Richmond and convinced Mrs. Pember to come to Richmond and accept a position at the hospital—"rather a startling proposition to a woman used to all the comforts of luxurious life." She could hardly deny the importuning of such a lady, particularly when told of the need for "a good and determined woman's rule." She was appointed as matron of one of the divisions of Chimborazo Hospital in Richmond. The role of women in the medical profession and as nurses was just emerging at the time of the Civil War, and it was novel that a woman of Phoebe Pember's social standing would be involved in hospital management. Many thought, she wrote, that "such a life would be injurious to the delicacy and refinement of a lady." She was to become the first female administrator appointed at Chimborazo.[66]

Mrs. Pember arrived in Richmond in December 1862. She came to serve the Confederate cause in which she believed, although not quite as noisily as her fiery older sister, Eugenia. Writing years later about the women of the South, she described herself when she said the women felt "a passion of interest in every man in the gray uniform of the Confederate service; they were doubly anxious to give comfort and assistance to the sick and wounded." She began her service at Chimborazo Hospital, a sprawling series of buildings on a high hill outside of Richmond. It was to become one of the largest hospitals in the world before the Civil War ended, housing 150 wards and treating a total of 76,000 patients. Needless to say, being a woman she encountered opposition: *"one of them had come,"* a male surgeon told a friend in a tone of ill-concealed disgust on her first day.[67]

On her arrival in Richmond, she had no place to live and was forced to reside at the hospital. For a time, she lived with her friends the Randolphs, and at the home of her close friends Col. Jeremy F. and Louisa ("Lou") Gilmer. She also kept a room on Church Hill a while and boarded with the Skinner family for a time. This, of course, necessitated her making arrangements to travel back and forth to the hospital by a horse-drawn "ambulance."[68]

Chimborazo Hospital, located on Chimborazo Hill some distance from the city. This Confederate hospital, where Phoebe Pember worked, became the largest in the world during the war. (Courtesy of National Archives.)

Pember went to work for the surgeon-in-charge, Dr. James B. McCaw, and had to contend with a bureaucracy consisting of surgeons and doctors, most well-meaning but many corrupt, who knew little medicine; male nurses who were nothing more than convalescing soldiers; stewards, slaves, clerks, commissaries, quartermasters, apothecaries, baggage-masters, wagon-masters, forage-masters, cooks, carpenters, shoemakers, ambulance-drivers; "and many more forgotten hangers-on," including malingerers whom the soldiers called "hospital rats." Medical care was poor by modern standards. The huge hospital could house 8,000 patients. It was self-sufficient in some ways, containing its own dairy, bakery, brewery, ice houses, soap factory, farm, and herd of livestock.[69]

Not knowing exactly what was required of her, and on being told she was to tend to the diet of some six hundred men, her "mind could hardly grope through the darkness that clouded it, as to what were my special duties but one mental spectrum always presented itself—*chicken soup.*" She ordered the chickens and, for the first time in her life, killed the live birds and made the soup, which was a success. "Nature may not have intended me for a Florence Nightingale, but a kitchen proved my worth."[70]

Mrs. Pember went from organizing a proper diet for her patients to trying to control the dispensing of whiskey, the chief painkiller available in wartime Richmond. Confederate law provided that liquor and other luxuries used in hospitals be entrusted to the matrons. (Ladies, presumably, were less likely to drink alcohol and steal luxuries.) When she tried to take over the control of the whiskey barrels, Mrs. Pember was thwarted at every turn by those in authority, including the surgeon-in-charge. At one point, she went around the hospital with a printed copy of the law in her hand and demanded the whiskey. "So, the printed law being at hand for reference, I nailed my colors to the mast, and that evening all the liquor was in my pantry and the key in my pocket." She kept up a running battle trying to prevent the pilferage and stealing of coffee, meats, and foods of all kind in a city where inflation was horrendous and supplies could not be had at times even for those who could afford to pay inflated prices. People begged her for supplies, but she protected "every pound of coffee, every ounce of whisky, bushel of flour or vegetables."[71] "Hers was a will of steel," DeLeon recalled, "under a suave refinement, and her pretty, almost Creole accent covered the power to ring in *defi* on occasion. The friction of these attributes against bumptiousness, or young authority, made the hospital the field of many 'fusses' and more fun."[72]

The care of the wounded, of course, was her primary responsibility. She immersed herself in the daily routine of caring for wounded and dying men. By January 1863 she wrote Eugenia, "I sometimes wonder if I am the same person who was afraid to look at a dead person, for I have no timidity and hardly any sensibility left." She was involved in all hospital activities, from dressing wounds to writing letters home for the poor and illiterate common soldiers who made up the great bulk of the Chimborazo population. On one occasion, she finished writing a letter for an upcountry Georgian who had a "lean, yellow, attenuated" look with very long hair and fingernails like claws. The soldier turned to her and asked if she were married. "I am not. At least, I am a widow," she replied. "He rose higher in bed," she later recalled. "He pushed away desperately the tangled hay on his brow. A faint color fluttered over the hollow cheek, and stretching out a long piece of bone with a talon attached, he gently touched my arm and with constrained voice whispered mysteriously: 'You wait!' And readers, I am waiting still," she wrote years later.[73]

There was precious little humor in Phoebe Pember's daily life. Scenes of pathos occurred daily, "scenes," she wrote, "that wrung the heart and forced the dew of pity from the eyes; but feeling that enervated the mind and relaxed the body was a sentimental luxury that was not to be indulged in. There was too much work to be done." In her memoir, *A Southern Woman's Story*, published in 1879, Mrs. Pember relates one especially moving incident about a young Confederate soldier named Fisher.

Mrs. Pember was awakened by a nurse one very cold night in 1863 and told that something was wrong with a favorite patient of hers named Fisher. A doctor was summoned, and she hurried to the scene where the young man—he was about twenty—lay wounded. With a great deal of "hard nursing, good food and plenty of stimulant," he had had a "fair chance for recovery." A contraption had been rigged up to try and hold the bones of his broken leg together, but he had suffered a severe wound and now it appeared that the sharp edge of a splintered bone had severed his artery. Fisher "had remained," Mrs. Pember recalled, "through all his trials, stout, fresh, and hearty, interesting in appearance, and so gentlemannered and uncomplaining that we all loved him." But Fisher was now bleeding, and

I instantly put my finger on the little orifice and awaited the surgeon. He soon came—took a long look and shook his head. The explanation was easy; the artery was imbedded in the fleshy part of the thigh and could not be taken up. No earthly power could save him. There was no object in detaining Dr. —. He required his time and strength, and long I sat by the boy, unconscious himself that any serious trouble was apprehended. The hardest trial of my duty was laid upon me; the necessity of telling a man in the prime of his life, and fullness of strength that there was no hope for him.

It was done at last, and the verdict received patiently and coura-geously, some directions given by which his mother would be informed of his death, and then he turned his questioning eyes upon my face. "How long can I live?" "Only as long as I keep my finger upon this artery." A pause ensued. God alone knew what thoughts hurried through that heart and brain, called so unexpectedly from all earthly hopes and ties. He broke the silence at last. "You can let go—" But I could not. Not if my own life had trembled in the balance. Hot tears rushed to my eyes, a surging sound to my ears, and a deathly coldness to my lips. The pang of obeying him was spared me, and for the first and last time during the trials that surrounded me for four years, I fainted away.[74]

Mrs. Pember does not discuss her religion in *A Southern Woman's Story,* but, like most nineteenth-century writers relating their memories of the Civil War or even in routine letters, she makes frequent references to the Bible and to God. In a letter to her sister she wrote: "If as I was told the children of these men [her patients] will 'rise up and call me blessed' I shall have many blessings."[75] This, of course, is a reference, common in Jewish conversation and worship, to Proverbs 31 ("A woman of valour who can find? / For her price is far above rubies," 31:10–31), an ideal to which Jewish women should aspire. When once she comforted a dying soldier, she knew he would die. "What comfort could I give," she recalled. "Only silently open the Bible, and read to him without comment the ever-living promises of his Maker. Glimpses too of that abode where the 'weary are at rest.'"[76] In a letter to her sister Eugenia, however, she relates a conversation she participated in as follows:

> The feelings here against the Yankees exceeds anything I could imagine, particularly among the good Christians. I spent an evening among a particularly pious set. One lady said she had a pile of Yankee bones lying around her pump so that the first glance on evening her eyes would rest upon them. Another begged me to get her a Yankee Skull to keep her toilet trinkets in. All had something of the kind to say—at last I lifted my voice and congratulated myself at being born of a nation, and religion that did not enjoin forgiveness on its enemies, that enjoyed the blessed privilege of praying for an eye for an eye, and a life for a life, and was not one of those for whom Christ died in vain, considering the present state of feelings. I proposed that till the war was over they should all join the Jewish Church, let forgiveness and peace and good will alone and put their trust in the sword of the Lord and Gideon. It was a very agreeable evening, and all was taken in good part. I certainly had the best of the argument, and the gentlemen seconded me ably.[77]

This letter demonstrates that Mrs. Pember considered herself to be Jewish and that her friends saw her as Jewish, although there is no mention in either her published memoir or her Civil War era letters of her attending a synagogue or celebrating Jewish holidays. Of course, given her social position and acculturated background, she may well have felt out of place among the Jewish population of Richmond, most of whom were immigrants or, unlike her family, descended from recent German immigrants. She did not become a Christian. She certainly had no fear of expressing herself on the subject of the differences between Jews and Christians. Her letters show a woman quick to rise to the defense of the Jewish people.[78] In a letter to Lou Gilmer, one of her closest friends, she refers in a lighthearted way to her friend and co-religionist Thomas Cooper DeLeon's discussion of marriage with Miss Truxey Johnson's father. "Papa questioned him on his belief in the Trinity and he not responding reasonably according to Mr. Johnson's belief the old gentleman objected. It will be a new feature introduced in love affairs if the final 'parient' [*sic*] puts the lover through the catechism."[79]

Mrs. Pember's life in Richmond was not entirely dominated by her hospital duties. She had an active social life outside of Chimborazo. Indeed, her reasons for going to Richmond were to escape some unpleasantness in her family situation in Marietta and to enjoy the hospital with "half a dozen ladies who would be companionable perhaps."[80] (It certainly was not to find a man. She rejected service at another hospital because a male friend, Dr. Foster, was "very pleasant, handsome and intelligent, and as we would be comparatively alone and eat together, *that* would not do."[81]) Even though it appears that she lived at Chimborazo much of the time, Mrs. Pember had many close female friends in Richmond whom she remembered very affectionately. She not only attended but gave parties at the large hospital grounds. "I had quite a party here," she wrote Eugenia, "some of the prettiest girls in Richmond. . . . They all came at six o'clock, eat strawberries and ice cream, walked all around the Bluff and at eleven were driven home by their respective cavaliers." She participated in charades, which was a common form of entertainment.[82]

Mrs. Pember also socialized with Mary Chesnut, who recounts in her diary in January 1864 a charade with Frank Vizetelly, war correspondent for the *Illustrated London News,* and Mrs. Pember. "Mr. Vizetelly and Mrs. Pember were fun enough for one day. His part is to dandle and stifle the cries of a screaming baby while the strong-minded mother writes and dashes aside sheet after sheet of MSS. . . . Next day, they were all hoarse. When Mr. Vizetelly had exhausted all known methods of quieting an infant (in vain), his despair was comic. He threw the baby on a chair and sat on it."[83]

Life in Confederate Richmond had its dismal moments later, but before Gettysburg, in July 1863, Mrs. Pember had no hesitation in inviting her young niece, Fanny Phillips, Eugenia's daughter, to "come up during the fall and spend a couple of months with me. If she would come as my assistant I could send her a transportation ticket. All the girls here are in the different departments they make a frolic of it." She even offered to find "a sweetheart for her, though I am not much of a matchmaker." The beau she had in mind was a nephew of Robert E. Lee's, one of the well-known Virginia Carters of Shirley Plantation fame.[84]

After Gettysburg, life was not as cheerful. Mrs. Pember related in a September 1863 letter that she went to town to pay a visit, and "a gentleman stopping to hand me out of an awkward ambulance proved to be Gen. Lee. He looked much older and greatly worn."[85] By the summer of 1864, the situation in Richmond was bleak. Privations had to be endured, Mrs. Pember recalled, "which tried body and soul." Money was worthless. Theft was rampant. The railroads were cut off so often that the supplies for Chimborazo spoiled. What little food there was had to be carefully rationed: "it was almost ludicrous to see with what painful solicitude Miss G. [Mrs. Pember's assistant] and myself would count the rolls, or hold a council over the pans of corn-bread." The staff and the patients were grateful for the simplest fare and the coarsest clothing. Of course, Richmond was also under siege, and day after day, night after night, its residents heard the sounds of cannon, alarm bells, and the firing of arms.[86]

After a major exchange of prisoners, Mrs. Pember found herself comforting Confederates recently held as prisoners. Many had been starved to the point of death. One such prisoner was Richard Hammond Key, grandson of the composer of the "Star Spangled Banner." He asked Mrs. Pember to bury him in a grave apart from the crowd "in some spot where those who knew and cared for him might find him some day." The next day, with the enemy in sight of Richmond, Key died. The matron who befriended him had a coffin built, took the body to Hollywood cemetery herself, purchased a lot, and had a clergyman perform the burial service in the pouring rain.[87]

The winter of 1864 saw the beginning of the end of the Confederacy. Troops moved incessantly and rations were scarce. Government departments closed, and rumors abounded. Yet the city's social life was "unusually gay." Mrs. Pember and others realized the end was near. "Wise and thoughtful men disapproved openly of this mad gayety," she recalled. But Southerners always loved a party, and Mrs. Pember wrote, "If Spartan austerity is to win our independence, we are a lost nation." She was a careful observer of the people around her and wrote to her friend Lou Gilmer that people were not behaving very well, as "many young ladies are enjoying single blessedness with the painful accompanyments of married life." She learned in early March that Richmond would be evacuated but was sworn to secrecy. What would she do? Flee with the government and prominent Richmonders or stay at her post?[88]

She decided to stay. "My mind had been very unsettled as to my course of action in view of the impending crash, but my duty prompted me to remain with my sick, on the ground that no general ever deserts his troops." Richmond was evacuated and most, if not all, of Mrs. Pember's friends fled. The Confederate government and the military left, and those who stayed did not know what to expect from the invading Union army. Mrs. Pember stayed at Chimborazo even after all the male nurses went off to join Lee's army and the slave cooks ran away. She watched from the hill, where Chimborazo stood the turmoil and confusion of the evacuation, the fires set by the retreating Confederates, the destruction of bridges and boats, and the crowds of people leaving the old capital. Even many of the sick and lame left rather than face Yankee imprisonment. Before the hospital was taken over by Federal authorities, Mrs. Pember was set upon by some of the former malingerers, the "hospital rats" who tried to steal the whiskey left behind. An armed little matron met them, however. "Wilson," she told one, "you have been in this hospital a long time. Do you think from what you know of me that the whiskey can be taken without my consent?" When told there was now no one to protect her and to move away, Mrs. Pember responded by cocking a small pistol she had hidden in her pocket. That "sharp click, a sound so significant and so different from any other, struck upon his ear, and sent him back amidst his friends, pale and shaken. . . . 'You had better leave,' I said . . . 'for if *one* bullet is lost, there are five more ready, and the room is too small for even a woman to miss six times." The rats left.[89]

Eventually the Union army arrived. Mrs. Pember, although having no official position and liable to arrest or imprisonment, insisted on staying through the transition and caring for those Confederate soldiers who could not escape. Putting on her finest outfit to go meet the Union commander, she demanded to know whether she would be able to use her stores to feed her patients or whether the Yankees intended to "starve their captured sick." The two former enemies resolved their immediate problem, and the Union officer attempted to make pleasant conversation. He regretted "the present state of scarcity, for he could see in the pale faces and pinched features of the Richmond women, how much they had suffered during the war." While the officer may not have intended an insult, Mrs. Pember, now sounding more like her older sister, Eugenia, replied, "If my features were pinched, and my face pale, it was not caused by privations under the Confederacy, but the anguish consequent upon our failure."[90]

Phoebe Pember stayed on at Chimborazo until her sick and wounded soldiers were removed to another hospital, where she went to nurse them. She stayed on there until "all the sick were either convalescent or dead, and at last my vocation was gone."[91]

PART 4

In Our
Unhappy Land

★   ★   ★   ★   ★   ★   ★   ★   ★   ★

THE END OF AN ERA

" . . . future historians . . . will . . . attest the patriotism of the soldiers of the Lost Cause, who sacrificed all but honor in its defense, and who sought to preserve that honor alone from the dark wreck and ruin which followed their defeat."

—Senator Benjamin Franklin Jonas, address at the laying
of the cornerstone of the monument to the memory of the
Confederate dead at Baton Rouge, February 22, 1886

Belle Chasse in dilapidation. (Courtesy of Jacob Rader Marcus
Center, American Jewish Archives, Cincinnati, Ohio.)

CHAPTER 7

Lead Out the Pageant: Sad and Slow

"ATLANTA HAS FALLEN! & lucky are you that you removed your family when you did," Maj. Isaac Scherck, an assistant chief commissary on Gen. John Bell Hood's staff wrote his friend J. L. Meyer in Columbus in September 1864. "Genl Sherman *the fiend in human form,* issues an order for all Men, Women & Children, White and Black to leave Atlanta." Scherck was not ready to surrender even though he and his men were living in the woods "like hogs." Civilization, he thought, was collapsing before his eyes. "When enlightened millions of souls [in the South], raised & educated in freedom of speech & action have tamely to submit to such outrages—Liberty is gone indeed." The Jewish Confederates, like Scherck, fought on.[1] But Jewish Atlantans, many of whom had come to the city from Savannah and Charleston to escape the Union army, were forced from their homes. The David Mayer family, for example, had lived in a cellar covered with cotton bales for three weeks while Sherman's cannons shelled their city. During his family's escape from the city, Mayer was forced to leave his wife and children to find a ferry to cross a river. He gave his ten-year-old son a pistol and told him to look out for his mother and sisters.[2] Jewish Georgians long remembered Gen. William Tecumseh Sherman.

Sherman's famous March to the Sea ended on December 22, 1864, at Savannah. "I beg to present you as a Christmas gift," the general's famous telegram to Lincoln read, "the City of Savannah." The Jews of Savannah, having celebrated a rather ironic Hanukkah—a holiday commemorating a brave band of Jewish warriors' triumph over an occupying army—with the enemy literally at their gates weeks before, waited for the inevitable. There would be no miracle this time. Fanny Cohen, the twenty-four-year-old daughter of Octavus and Henrietta Cohen, detested the invader. She called them vandals, brutes, and Goths. "If we are conquered," she wrote in her diary, "I see no reason why we should receive our enemies as our friends and I never shall do it as long as I live." Her father was very concerned that Fanny's open hatred of the Yankees would get her in trouble. When she saw a family friend who was a Confederate surgeon left behind with his patients, it "was the first pleasurable moment" she had had. "I had been so surrounded by blue coats that the sight of our gray uniforms made me happy." She forced herself to be polite to the union officers who called. "I was obliged to receive [Captain Poe] and never was so embarrassed in my life," she wrote. "My hatred for the Army in which he was an officer and my desire to be polite made me almost speechless—the contending feelings were more than I could control."[3]

The Cohens were told that their home on Lafayette Square was being taken by the army for officers' housing. When Mr. Cohen complained that there were ladies in the house and that it would be exceedingly inconvenient for them to move, the response was: "Well! I suppose *it will inconvenience* you but you know you Rebs *will* fight and when you are conquered you must submit to what ever will contribute to our comfort." Mr. Cohen was extremely upset at having his family threatened in this fashion. "I have never seen a man so annoyed and unnerved as my Father is," Fanny confided to her diary. Mrs. Cohen was sick, her illness brought on, Fanny supposed, by "worry and excitement." Somehow Cohen convinced the Union authorities to take an empty house across the street with the promise of allowing the army to keep their horses in the Cohen stable. Soon, however, the Cohens were required to house Brig. Gen. William Babcock Hazen, one of Sherman's top lieutenants.[4]

The Octavus Cohen house, Abercorn Street, Savannah. The Cohen house in Lafayette Square was commandeered by the Union Army after Sherman captured the city in December 1864. Fanny Cohen railed against the "vandals" and "Goths" who intruded on the Cohen family. The house was demolished in the twentieth century, and a condominium stands there now. (Courtesy of the Georgia Historical Society, Savannah.)

On December 25, Fanny wrote in her diary, "This is the saddest Christmas that I have ever spent and my only pleasure during the day has been in looking forward to spending my next Christmas in the Confederacy." The whole Levy and Cohen extended family was despondent. Jacob and Fanny Levy, now back in Savannah, were sick and "very much dispirited." Things had not improved by January 1, when Fanny wrote, "How sad this beginning of the year to us surrounded by our enemies without any prospects of seeing our friends."[5]

From Savannah, Sherman marched into South Carolina, keeping the Confederates in doubt as to his real objective. "Charleston," Sherman told Grant, was "now a mere desolated wreck," and the conqueror of Georgia turned his army inland and headed for Columbia, South Carolina's capital. "I look upon Columbia as quite as bad as Charleston," Sherman wrote Maj. Gen. Henry Halleck on December 24, "and I doubt if we shall spare the public buildings there as we did at Milledgeville [Georgia]." Charleston's supply lines having been cut by Sherman's army, the Confederate army evacuated the city on February 17, 1865. Charleston surrendered the next day.[6]

Charleston was a defeated city. "A city of ruins, of desolation, of vacant houses, of widowed women, of rotting wharves, of deserted warehouses, of weed-wild gardens, of miles of grass-grown streets, of acres of pitiful and voiceful barrenness—that is Charleston," Sidney Andrews, a reporter for the *Boston Advertiser,* wrote. "The splendid houses are all deserted," another visitor noted, "the glass in the windows broken, the walk dilapidated, the columns toppled over." The description undoubtedly applied to M. C. Mordecai's grand mansion on Meeting Street, a few blocks from the Battery, and to the city's synagogues and many Jewish homes and businesses.[7] Sixteen-year-old Lee Cohen, Isaac Harby's granddaughter, watched the evacuation of Charleston. Cotton was burned in a public square; rice was set on fire. "As the day wore on," she recalled, "explosions were heard on every side; the gunboats 'Charleston' and 'Chicora' were blown up at the wharves; the 'big gun' at the corner of South and East Battery was exploded. . . . Fires started everywhere . . . the city was helpless and expecting its foe. . . . It was a terrible, heartbreaking awful night." Late on the night of the seventeenth, Lee watched the firing of the *Palmetto State,* a gunboat built with contributions from the ladies of Charleston. "Women who had worked and striven and contributed to its building stood at their windows and viewed the flames," she later recalled, "and lo! As the last detonation sounded, the smoke arose, and upon the red glare of the heavens, formed a palmetto tree, perfect and fair, that stood out against the sky, then wavered and broke apart as we watched it through our tears." The next day, she went to Meeting Street near Ann Street to see the last of the Confederate soldiers evacuate Charleston. "Yet, even then," she recalled, "some laughed and jested, for, God pity us, we were hopeful still, and they were brave, and we could not think that the end had really come." The *New York Herald* reported on March 25, 1865,

K. K. Beth Elohim in 1886. This photograph was taken twenty-one years after the war ended, and following the Charleston earthquake. It is the oldest known photograph of the temple. (Courtesy of K. K. Beth Elohim Archive, Charleston, South Carolina.)

that the "Hebrew congregation of Charleston sustained a heavy loss in the destruction of their splendid organ, the five Books of Moses, and other valuables. It is a noteworthy fact that not an Israelite left with the Yankees."[8]

Charlestonians believed that Sherman's army would destroy Charleston, and they sent their valuables to Columbia for safekeeping. The trustees of Beth Elohim packed up its Torahs, chandelier, and other valuables and sent them to the capital. Now Sherman's army was in Columbia.[9]

Eleanor Cohen was twenty-six years old when Sherman's troops arrived in Columbia. The daughter of Dr. Philip Melvin Cohen and Cordelia Moise Cohen, Eleanor could trace her ancestry back to the founders of the Moise clan in South Carolina, Abraham and Sarah Moise, who escaped from Haiti (Santo Domingo) in 1791 in the midst of the slave insurrection. Seventy-five years later, in 1865, another Moise found herself in the middle of the collapse of the old regime and the end of another slave society.

Small, dark-complexioned, pretty, with black eyes and "a grand figure," Eleanor also described herself as quick-tempered and intelligent. She was to have been married in April, but her intended, Benjamin Mendes Seixas, was forced to leave Columbia on February 7 and had not returned when the city was shelled by Union troops. "Oh! God, can I ever forget that day," Eleanor wrote in her diary, "Can time with Lethean draughts ever efface from my memory the deep sorrow, the humiliation, the agony of knowing we were to be under the Yankees, that our beloved flag was to be pulled down and the U.S.A. flag wave over the city." Eleanor recorded in her diary the Union army's arrival in Columbia, "the bands playing 'The Star Spangled Banner,' and the shouts of the soldiers filled the air."[10]

Eleanor H. Cohen grew up in
Charleston, the daughter of Dr. P.
Melvin Cohen, a dentist. She and her
family moved to Columbia during the
war. The Cohens were living in Columbia when it was burned by Sherman's
troops. (Courtesy of the Jacob Rader
Marcus Center, American Jewish
Archives, Cincinnati, Ohio.)

Columbia was badly damaged by both the Union troops and the retreating
Confederate army. Main Street, according to Eleanor, "was a fearful sight." The
stores were looted; lawless mobs roamed the streets. Then the fires started. The
Cohens gathered in a room at the top of their home and watched as the fires grew.
The flames were "leaping and dancing assisted by the wind . . . and the air was
filled with torpedoes, shells, hand grenades and all the most cruel instruments of
evil doers." The Cohens did not think the fire would reach them, but they were
mistaken. Soon the burning inferno reached their neighborhood and they fled, taking only a change of clothes and leaving behind all of their possessions, the "letters
of loved absent ones, pictures of our precious relations, tokens and souvenirs of
childhood."[11]

The destruction, angry mobs, and drunken Union soldiers that fearful night
were terrifying to all who lived through it. Philip S. Jacobs was at home when three
soldiers came into his home and demanded his watch. "They put a bayonet before
my breast and pulled the watch and chain from my body." Union soldiers also
invaded the home of Moses Winstock on Assembly Street while the family was in
the midst of their Sabbath dinner. They invited the soldiers to join them and
learned, after dessert, that the soldiers planned to loot and torch their home! The
Winstocks fled and were separated in the confusion. It took Moses Winstock three
days to find his family.[12] Mordecai DeLeon's library was, Edwin DeLeon recalled

years later, "one of the holocausts offered up to the Union at the burning of Columbia."[13] Rabbi Henry S. Jacobs, who like many Charlestonians who had come to Columbia to escape Sherman, found he had come to the wrong place. All of his possessions were destroyed in the fire. He and his family were "driven forth from our home to a park in the suburbs, where wrapped in blankets we passed Friday night [February 17], and nearly the whole [Sabbath]. . . . I lost everything in the world—clothing, furniture, books, manuscripts, provisions, even my canonicals and [prayer shawls]—every-thing except hope and confidence in our Heavenly Father."[14]

Columbia, South Carolina, after being burned by Sherman's army, the retreating Confederate army, and others. (*Battles and Leaders of the Civil War.*)

The streets were crowded with Union soldiers, freed slaves, and fleeing Columbians. Eleanor Cohen recalled being taunted by the invaders with jeers: "How do you like secesh now?" and "curses too fearful to be entered in my book." The flames did not abate. Instead, they seemed to Eleanor "to encircle us like a belt and the heat was so great that our faces were scorched and blackened by smoke!" The Cohens went to the country with barely enough food for one day, but the drunken soldiers and the lawless conditions there convinced Dr. Cohen to return to the burned city. Back in town, the Cohens, like their fellow townspeople, wandered about homeless, without food or change of clothing. "In one night," Eleanor wrote, "we were brought from comparative wealth and luxury to abject poverty." Advised to go to the state asylum on Bull Street, the Cohens joined hundreds of other families there. Everyone was shocked and in a desperate condition. Old men and young women were weighted down with bundles. There was no water. The Cohens stayed five days without a bed to lie on and little to eat. "I never imagined," Eleanor recalled, "I should be so near actual starvation."[15] The day after the fire, Rabbi Jacobs rushed to the synagogue on Assembly Street, where he had stored the Torahs and other treasures from Charleston. He found the building burned to the ground. He rummaged through the debris only to find the remnant of a Torah and a single Torah bell, which he sent to Charleston "as Sacred Relics."[16]

The Jews of Columbia, like all Southerners, were bitterly resentful of the occupying Union troops. "No words of mine," Eleanor concluded, "can give any idea of the brutality of the ruffians; they swore, they cursed, plundered and committed every excess . . . oh my God, teach me to bear my burden."[17] The Cohens next stayed at Eleanor's uncle's house, which had survived the fire. By March 7 the family was "comfortably fixed," with twenty-three family members. Eleanor was doing nearly all of the housekeeping and waiting anxiously for word of her fiancé.

Moses Henry Nathan lost his home and took up residence in an abandoned school. He asked to "beg a great favor" of an associate "to let me have some meat, grist, and potatoes," as "we are almost at the point of starvation here." Jacob C. Lyons, the president of the gas company and a successful merchant, lost all he had, his home at Marion and Gervais destroyed.[18]

Despite their massive losses, Columbia Jewry rose to the occasion. On the Monday morning after the fire, local citizens met at the home of Elizabeth Lyons, Mayor Henry Lyons's widow, as her property (the block bounded by Lady, Bull, Gervais, and Pickens) had escaped destruction. Lyons's building housed the local relief effort, and Jewish leaders led the effort to bring in food and supplies. Moses Cohen Mordecai, the former state senator, came to Columbia to serve as its food administrator. Augusta, Georgia's Jewish community, sent provisions and funds. The *Daily Phoenix* lauded "the handsome conduct of the Israelites of Columbia. . . . No people could have been more active in their efforts to assist the sufferers during the fire."[19]

The Southern nation began to dissolve. Casualties were high in Lee's army. Survivors deserted. The end was near. But some young Jewish Southerners did not give up. Marx Cohen Jr. of Charleston, whose grandfather had been a Polish immigrant but whose father was a successful landowner, enlisted in the cavalry early in the war. By 1864 he was apparently impatient to join the fray in Virginia, so he enlisted in an artillery company, Hart's battery, which served in Hampton's cavalry brigade. (The fieldpieces were drawn by six horses and the artillerist rode on his own mount, thereby increasing the speed of the unit.) Hart's battery had attracted a number of Jewish Charlestonians, and, at one time, five Cohens served in the company.

Young Cohen was a true Southerner. In March 1865, when words were exchanged with one Thomas R. Chew, one of the soldiers challenged the other to a duel. At daybreak, the two young Confederate soldiers fired at each other in the last duel in the Confederacy. Because their seconds had placed blanks in the pistols, neither duelist was hurt. As soon as the men returned to camp, they heard the bugle sound, rushed to their horses, and rode into battle, the Battle of Bentonville, March 19, 1865. Tragically, both Chew and Cohen were killed by artillery fire in this, the last major battle of the Civil War.[20]

Richmond's government was now in a state of desperation. There is circumstantial evidence that in the early months of 1865, Jefferson Davis and Judah Benjamin were involved in desperate plans to blow up the White House and kidnap Lincoln and other high-ranking Federal officials. William A. Tidwell, the author of *Come Retribution* and *April '65,* contends that Davis and Benjamin decided in the early spring of 1865 to send a team of undercover operators to Washington and that it was financed by Secret Service gold drawn on the Treasury as late as April 1, 1865. John H. Surratt, one of John Wilkes Booth's lieutenants, whose mother, Mary Surratt, was later executed for her role in the assassination, had been a courier for Benjamin. Benjamin had sent Surratt on a mission to Canada two weeks before the assassination and had given him two hundred dollars in gold to defray his expenses. (Surratt later testified that neither Davis nor Benjamin had any knowledge of Booth's plans to kill Lincoln.) Surratt left Richmond on April 1, 1865, the day before its evacuation, with dispatches from Benjamin to be delivered to Brig. Gen. Edwin G. Lee in Montreal. Lee had replaced Jacob Thompson and Clement C. Clay as the head of the Canadian operation.[21]

In Tidwell's view, Booth was not a lunatic, but rather was a responsible undercover agent recruited by the Confederate secret service as a part of the kidnapping plot. The plot failed in March. The Confederate government, including its spymaster, Judah Benjamin, fled Richmond on April 2, leaving Booth and his undercover team with no direction. Lee surrendered. The assassination of the president on April 14 and attempts to assassinate other high Federal officials were not approved by Davis or Benjamin, or even known by them. Booth only concocted his scheme a few days or perhaps even hours before the commission of the crimes. The assassination and attempted assassinations were Booth's idea alone, but consistent, Booth erroneously thought, with his mission to disable the Union leadership. There is no direct evidence linking either Davis or Benjamin to the bombing and kidnapping plot, but there is convincing circumstantial evidence that Davis and Benjamin set in motion a plot which ended in a rogue agent killing the president. All of these desperate schemes and many others failed.

By late March 1865, the siege of Petersburg was coming to an end and General Lee was waiting for the roads to dry out so that he could combine his army with General Johnston's army in North Carolina. Gen. Lee sent a message to Maj. Gen. John C. Breckinridge, the secretary of war, at 10:40 a.m. on April 2 warning him that the army would have to evacuate their position that night. This took place at about the same time General Lee sent information to President Davis, who had to be called out of Sunday morning church service.[22]

Secretary of State Judah Benjamin methodically destroyed all documents, correspondence, official records, files on covert operations, and anything else which would prove embarrassing if found by the Yankees. He personally destroyed the department's Secret Service records. Like others in the government, Benjamin anticipated that this hour might arrive and had sent his clerk and six boxes of key documents south to Charlotte. At 2:00 p.m. on April 2, Benjamin was visited by Alfred Paul, the French Consul. "I found him extremely agitated . . . his hands shaking, wanting and trying to do and say everything at once," Paul told his superiors. "Mr. Benjamin said to me in a trembling voice, 'I have nothing in particular to say to you, but I wanted to be sure to shake your hand before my departure.'"[23]

On Sunday afternoon, April 2, 1865, the Confederate government announced it was departing Richmond. On Sunday night, Emma Mordecai heard a "terrific explosion, which jarred the house to its foundation." She and her sister-in-law and her niece all got in bed together, terrified and trembling. The Confederates had set fire to ships, ammunition magazines, and ordnance. The arsenal was ignited. Soon, however, the women, alone on the family plantation and surrounded by slaves, decided that they had best begin making plans to hide their valuables and food.[24]

Two trains left Richmond that night, one carrying over a half a million dollars worth of gold and silver, all that was left of the Confederate Treasury, and the other carrying the presidential party: Mr. and Mrs. Jefferson Davis; Judah P. Benjamin; Stephen R. Mallory, secretary of the navy; George Davis, attorney general; Judge John H. Reagan, postmaster general; and George A. Trenholm, secretary of the Treasury. "Now," Ernest B. Furgurson wrote, "legislature and governor, Congress and president were gone," and Richmond "was capitol of nothing."[25] Benjamin had regained his composure from the afternoon. His "Epicurean philosophy was ever at command," Stephen Mallory recalled, "and his hope and good humor inexhaustible . . . with a 'never-give-up-the-ship' sort of air, [he] referred to

The Confederate cabinet escaping in April 1865. Judah P. Benjamin kept President Davis and his fellow cabinet members amused as they traveled south from Richmond. Benjamin is just behind Davis, wearing a silk hat. (Courtesy of the Library of Congress.)

other great national causes which had been redeemed from far gloomier reverses than ours." A. J. Hanna wrote: "The morale of the official family was strengthened by [former Texas governor Francis R.] Lubbock's large stock of Texas anecdotes, Mallory's Seminole Indian war stories, and Benjamin's inexhaustible wit and good humor."[26]

Richmond was now at the mercy of the rabble. Looters roamed the streets. The Confederate army had evacuated, but the Union army had not yet arrived. Stores were ransacked. Fire swept the city. "The city was wrapped in a cloud of densest smoke, through which great tongues of flame leaped in madness to the skies," one Federal officer recalled.[27] Philip Whitlock, still in the Quartermaster Department, stayed to the end, packing records to be sent south. "It is hard to describe the condition of this country at *this time*," he recalled. The people of Richmond "did not know what will become of us. Some of us expected to be put in prison and all our property taken away." Whitlock saw rioters and robbers plundering and setting fire to downtown Richmond, "people carrying away the goods on their Heads and rolling out Barrels of Licquor in the Streets."[28]

When Whitlock finished his packing job around midnight, he tried to leave the building but was prevented from doing so by a sentinel who told Whitlock he had orders to form all the men into a company to follow Lee's army. "This *did not suit* me," he later wrote. "I knew that there would be no use," so he went down to the basement, found an unguarded door, and escaped. It was on his way to his home and shop at the corner of Mayo and Franklin that Whitlock encountered the rioters. He determined to save his goods. When he arrived, his wife met him with "a whole Apron full of Confederate money," she had earned selling tobacco and cigars. Whitlock carried box after heavy box of tobacco up three flights of stairs to hide them from the looters.[29]

The next morning, the Whitlocks were awakened at 6 a.m. by the great explosion from the arsenal which broke several windows in their home. Fortunately, the fire did not destroy their building, and the arrival of Federal troops restored order. "That was a day," he wrote, "which was remembered by the people that were here as long as they lived."[30]

On Tuesday, April 4, John A. Campbell, formerly a justice of the U.S. Supreme Court, asked a number of prominent Richmonders to accompany him on a visit to see President Abraham Lincoln.[31] Lincoln had come to the city a day after the Confederate government left. Accompanied only by sailors, the president walked through downtown Richmond, passing Philip Whitlock's store on Franklin Street and likely passing near Beth Ahabah on his way to the mansion Jefferson Davis had only just abandoned.[32] Campbell hoped to convince the president to be lenient. Gustavus Myers had heard from many citizens that they opposed taking an

Richmond at the end of the war. The Confederate army and many civilians flee Richmond as the Union army is poised to enter. (Courtesy of the Library of Congress.)

Citizens of Richmond in Capitol Square during the conflagration. (*Battles and Leaders of the Civil War.*)

enforced oath of allegiance and he hoped to convince Lincoln to dispense with it. He also wished "to ascertain the tone and temper existing on the part of the Federal authorities towards the Citizens," and went also out of respect for Campbell, who did not wish to go alone. On the morning of April 5 Campbell and Myers met with Lincoln aboard the *Malvern.* The president was friendly and told the two men that he knew that they came in no official capacity and that they were not authorized to act on behalf of the government. He handed Campbell a paper outlining his conditions, which included that the authority of the United States would be recognized in all parts of the nation, that his sentiments on slavery would be respected, and that all fighting must end and all hostile forces disbanded. Lee, of course, had not yet surrendered and the war was still ongoing. The president said that he was disposed to exercise his authority with regard to the return of confiscated property "in the spirit of sincere liberality," that he hoped "to see an end of the struggle," and that he was considering a plan to ask the Virginia legislature to meet in Richmond. Myers expressed his concern about the oath to the president, who said "he had never attached much importance to the oath of allegiance being required." The men talked about the president's policy of leniency and lack of vindictiveness. Campbell gave the president a draft of proposed articles for a military convention to be held by Lee and Grant, which the president accepted. "Throughout," Myers recalled later, "it was conducted with entire civility and good humor."[33]

Nothing came of the conference. Lincoln was assassinated nine days later, on April 14, 1865.

Gustavus A. Myers was Civil War Richmond's most prominent Jewish citizen after Judah P. Benjamin. He served on the city council and was active in civic affairs. He befriended Benjamin and, together with former Supreme Court Justice John A. Campbell, met with President Lincoln aboard the *Malvern* when the Union army occupied Richmond. His son, Will, was an adjutant to major generals Samuel Jones and William W. Loring. (Courtesy of the Virginia Historical Society, Richmond.)

Meanwhile, the train carrying the Confederate leaders from Richmond pulled into Danville, Virginia, where the cabinet stayed for a week. It was obvious to Benjamin that the cause was now definitely lost, and he determined to escape or die trying. A fellow refugee later recalled, "I will never forget the expression of his countenance or the pitiless smile which accompanied his words when he said, 'I will never be taken alive.'" The train proceeded to Greensboro, North Carolina, and then to Charlotte. Burton Harrison recalled: "I could see from afar the occasional bright glow of Benjamin's cigar." While the other travelers were "perfectly silent, Benjamin's silvery voice was presently heard as he rhythmically intoned for their comfort verse after verse of Tennyson's 'Ode on the Death of the Duke of Wellington.'"

> Mourning when their leaders fall,
> Warriors carry the warrior's pall,
> And sorrow darkens hamlet and hall . . .
> Lead out the pageant: sad and slow,
> As fits an universal woe,
> Let the long procession go,
> And let the sorrowing crowd about it grow.[34]

After Pvt. Eugene Henry Levy recuperated from his wounds, he returned to his artillery unit and participated in the last desperate defense of Richmond. "Oh, ever-memorable day of horror!" he wrote in his diary on April 3, 1865, "I heard of the capture of Petersburg, the evacuation of Richmond, and the retreat of Lee's army. . . . May God protect our noble commander, for the name of Lee will act as a talisman for the recall of the army." He retreated with his company from Richmond. On Saturday, April 8, "a lovely day," he fell in behind the artillery and marched twenty-two miles until dark, "by which time we had arrived at the base of the hill on which is situated the pretty town called Appomattox C.[ourt] H.[ouse]. Here we parked for the night." Levy was captured and became a prisoner of war. Pressed into service to drive wagons, he met several fellow prisoners from the New Orleans Washington Artillery "bragging as usual in a disgusting manner." When the Yankee officers tried to convince Levy and his comrades that Lee would soon surrender, they "hooted at the idea" and its "fabricators." Of course Lee did surrender the next day.[35]

After Lee's surrender, neither Greensboro nor Charlotte was particularly hospitable to Jefferson Davis and the Confederate cabinet. The Union army was advancing in their direction, and the citizenry feared Yankee wrath in Charlotte. Benjamin lodged with the Abram Weill family. Weill was an ardent Confederate who not long before had offered his home to Varina Davis. When Benjamin was leaving, he presented the Weills with a gold-headed cane he had when he made his farewell speech to the U.S. Senate.[36]

Before leaving Charlotte, the full Confederate cabinet held its last meeting on April 26. Only President Davis wanted to continue the fight. The cabinet members saw the reality of the situation. The leaders of the Confederacy now had to consider their personal situations. Benjamin feared that, should he be captured, he would be blamed for acts committed by Confederate Secret Service agents. Lincoln's assassination had occurred on April 14, after Lee's surrender, but while the Confederate leaders were in flight. Federal authorities searched for Booth and his co-conspirators throughout the next twelve days. Booth was captured and killed on April 26, when the Confederate cabinet was in North Carolina. Davis had learned of Lincoln's death by telegram on April 19, when he arrived in Charlotte.[37]

There was talk of hanging the Confederate leaders. Gen. George Boutwell wrote General Butler that, if there were any evidence connecting any of "the rebel leaders with the plot," they should be pursued. "It is not unlikely," he concluded, "that Davis, Breckenridge and Benjamin had a hand in the business." The Jewish secretary of state, the man after Jefferson Davis most detested in the North, would almost certainly be a target. He was described by the former Speaker of the House, James G. Blaine, as the "Mephistopheles of the Rebellion, the brilliant, learned, sinister Secretary of State." Lincoln's secretary of state, William H. Seward, who disliked Benjamin, thought him, alone of the Confederate cabinet, guilty of complicity in Lincoln's assassination. Orville Browning recalled: "Mr. Seward expressed his belief that Booth and Surratt had conferred with Benjamin upon the subject, and that Benjamin had encouraged and subsidized them; but he did not believe that the matter had ever been under discussion before the Richmond Cabinet or received the countenance of other members of the Cabinet than Benjamin." Seward had unsuccessfully debated Benjamin when they served in the Senate before the war. When cornered by Benjamin in those years, Seward could only plead that he was not a lawyer. Seward, in fact, was likely the only Senator Benjamin had truly disliked.[38]

As it turned out, Federal prosecutors attempted to use the perjured testimony of one Sandford Conover, who claimed that he knew of letters from Davis and Benjamin authorizing the assassination. This attempt failed, but Benjamin could not know this in April and May of 1865. During the military trial of the Booth conspirators, the prosecutors continually claimed that the Confederate government was the real culprit. Writing in 1895, David M. Dewitt claimed in *The Judicial Murder of Mrs. Surratt* that scoundrels and perjurers attracted by the scent of reward money "flocked like buzzards, around the doors of the old Penitentiary . . . to swear that Davis and Benjamin were the instigators of Booth and Surratt."[39]

Years later, L. Q. Washington, Benjamin's secretary, wrote to Francis Lawley,

> I was present at the time when Mr. Thompson [Jacob Thompson, a Confederate secret agent serving in Canada] received his instructions from Mr. Benjamin. They were oral and largely suggestive and informal. Much was left to his discretion and wisely; for he was an experienced and conservative man. But there was not a word or a thought that looked to any violations of the rules of war, as they exist, among civilized nations. As a matter of fact, Mr. Davis, Mr. Benjamin, General Lee and the other leaders of the Confederacy believed to the last that it was not merely right, but the wisest and best policy to maintain and respect every one of the humane restrictions in the conduct of war which are upheld by the publicists.[40]

Like Davis, Benjamin determined to escape. Unlike Davis, he determined to leave the South. The cause had been lost. Only Benjamin and Breckinridge escaped imprisonment, although no member of the Confederate cabinet was ever executed. Benjamin left Davis and the dwindling presidential party after crossing into Georgia. Other cabinet members had already left. Benjamin decided not to make the next leg of a proposed escape on horseback. "Thus," Varina Davis recalled in later years, "these two master minds . . . parted with mutual respect and affectionate esteem . . . after breasting as one man the heavy storm which beat upon them for five bitter years." Benjamin had left a trunk of his personal belongings in Abbeville together with money for his sisters, now refugees in LaGrange, Georgia. He traveled disguised as a Frenchman who could not speak English, M. M. Bonfals. He had had the foresight to prepare a false passport describing himself as a French national. "The name itself," Eli Evans wrote, "showed a kind of

Judah Benjamin disguised as
"Monsieur Bonfals" during his
daring escape through Florida.
(Reprinted from A. J. Hanna,
Flight into Oblivion. Courtesy of
Louisiana State University Press,
Baton Rouge.)

bravado—probably a play on the Cajun French for 'a good falsification' or 'a good disguise.' It must have given him a certain pleasure to tease his pursuers with a Cajun word-game." He traveled with Col. Henry J. Leovy of New Orleans, who had served the Confederacy in espionage matters. Leovy "translated" for Benjamin. He made his way to the west coast of Florida, which he supposed would be an easier place from which to escape the country, and parted from Leovy, who later recalled that never was Judah Benjamin so great "as during the time of adversity. Traveling in disguise, sleeping at night in log huts, living on the plainest fare, subjected to all the discomforts of such a journey, with all his plans shattered and without definite hope for the future, his superb confidence and courage raised him above all."[41]

After a harrowing four-month flight to avoid capture, which included hiding in swamps, Benjamin took passage on a ship that sank not long after sailing and spent weeks at sea in another smaller boat and even sailed into a dangerous storm. "I had never seen a waterspout," he wrote his sister. "I got, however, more than I bargained for." When he finally landed in Southampton, England, he was bereft of assets and an occupation, but not of friends and hope.[42]

When the war ended, the business affairs of Benjamin's former Senate colleague David Yulee were in shambles. His home at Homosassa, Margarita, "the most beautiful in the land," was destroyed by fire in a Union naval assault. He had removed his family inland to Archer, thirteen miles west of Gainesville, where he built Cottonwood, a humbler structure. Another home was taken over by strangers. "Nearly all my means of support [were] lost," he wrote, "by acts of force of *both* the Governments during the war." Although he was not a diehard Confederate, Yulee was fiercely opposed to freeing the slaves to the bitter end. No other issue gave him as much concern. He wrote Davis in October of 1864 opposing the use of slaves as soldiers. Fighting for the Confederacy meant that slaves would be entitled to "the prerogatives of the citizen," which could not be, because "This is a white man's Government. To associate the colors in the camp, is to unsettle castes."[43]

Now, Yulee counseled peace, acceptance of the Union victory and the end of slavery, and reconciliation between the sections. "The conflict of arms is ended," he wrote one correspondent, "ended by the unconditional surrender of the South: and thereby, as practical facts, Slave labor is abolished. . . . It is bootless to look back. . . . The great duty, then, of the day, is Pacification. Not a partial, and constrained, but a solid, true, enduring pacification; thus restoring, as soon as practicable, a complete and earnest reconciliation." Yulee may have wanted peace, but his many enemies wanted revenge for his role in the events leading up to secession. He was arrested a few weeks later.[44]

The Yulee family had one other connection with the Confederacy: The Confederate baggage and treasure train. When the Confederate government fled Richmond, they took with them officials records, baggage, and the Confederate Treasury. Traveling at first by train, and then by wagon, carriage, and horse, the presidential party went to Danville, Virginia, through North Carolina, and on to Abbeville, South Carolina, where the last war council was held. Some papers were left in Abbeville with Mrs. Henry J. Leovy, the wife of Judah Benjamin's friend Col. Leovy. With the cabinet dissolved, Davis and one cabinet member, John H. Reagan of Texas, and a few aides continued on with a wagon and two ambulances. Davis separated from the wagon train in Georgia and was soon captured. The wagon train, however, continued on to Florida, and the last remnant of the Confederate cabinet's records arrived at Yulee's plantation, Cottonwood, in Archer, Florida, near Gainesville on May 22, 1865. While at Cottonwood, the young soldiers escorting the train learned of the surrender of Gen. Joseph E. Johnston. "A general gloom," Tench Tilghman recalled in his diary, "pervades our camp. Of course the last hope is gone of the Confederacy." Yulee was not at home when the wagon train arrived, which was prior to his arrest and imprisonment. In his absence, Mrs. Yulee and young Wickliffe helped the soldiers hide and bury the valuable trunks and records. One of the trunks contained Jefferson Davis's personal papers. When the senator returned, two of the young soldiers asked his advice as to what they should do. He told them to obtain their parole, "return home to their families, and resume the duties of civil life." The trunks were eventually discovered by the Union troops.[45]

After his parole, and with other young Confederate officers from Johnston's army, Alroy Jonas hopped aboard the top of a railroad boxcar and traveled from North Carolina to Richmond, hoping to secure transportation back home. He and his comrades stopped at the Powhatan Hotel, run by fervent Confederates, where a theatrical company and its leading lady, a Miss Annie Rush, were also staying. One day Miss Rush came into the sitting room where Jonas and his friends were assembled, with a handful of Confederate $500 bills, blank on the back, which someone had given her, and requested that each officer write "a sentiment" for her on the back of the bills. "Well, I had been doing a good deal of doggerel during our sojourn," Jonas recalled, "and so I had the whole load dumped upon my shoulders and performed the required task for each as speedily as possible." He wrote poems for each of his friends, but, for his own contribution, he wrote a sentimental poem entitled "Lines on the Back of a Confederate Note," which was published shortly thereafter in the *New York Metropolitan Record,* a Copperhead (pro-Southern) newspaper, under the heading "Something Too Good To Be Lost." The author was not identified until years later, but the poem was an instant success, appealing in a sentimental way to the tragic frame of mind of Southerners in 1865. The idea of a hungry, penniless man giving away a $500 bill was a bit of grim humor for many Southerners. According to the *Aberdeen Examiner,* Major Jonas's newspaper, to write the lines of this verse on the back of a Confederate bill and send it to "some woe-begone friend" became a fad.[46] As Jonas later put it, he had "unwittingly . . . touched a subtle heart chord that gains vibration as the days pass by, and like Banquo's ghost, it will not 'down.'" The famous lines are as follows:

Lines on the Back of a Confederate Note

Representing nothing on God's earth now,
And naught in the waters below it,
As the pledge of a nation that's dead and gone,
Keep it, dear friend, and show it.
Show it to those who will lend an ear,
To the tale that this trifle can tell,
Of a liberty born of the patriots dream,
Of a storm-cradled nation that fell.
Too poor to possess the precious ores
And too much of a stranger to borrow,
We issued today our promise to pay
And hoped to redeem on the morrow.
The days rolled by and the weeks became years,
But our coffers were empty still;
Coin was so rare that the treasury'd quake
If a dollar should drop in the till.
But the faith that was in us was strong indeed,
And our poverty well we discerned
And this little check represented the pay
That our suffering veterans earned.
We knew it had hardly a value in gold,
Yet as gold each soldier received it.
It gazed in our eyes with a promise to pay
And each Southern patriot believed it,
But our boys thought little of price or of pay,

Or of bills that were overdue;
We knew if it bought us our bread today
'Twas the best our poor country could do.
Keep it, it tells all our history o'er
From the birth of the dream to its last;
Modest and born of the angel Hope,
Like our hope of success, it passed.[47]

Simon Mayer had enlisted in 1861 in the Natchez Light Infantry. He had served throughout the war in various Mississippi regiments, surrendered, and was paroled at Greensboro, North Carolina, on May 1, 1865.[48] He wrote his family, "At sunrise this morning we turn our faces homeward." He was joyous about seeing his family again, "but how sad the reflection that all our efforts for the last four years have been in vain. Eager and anxious as I am to once more be at home, yet willingly would I forego that pleasure if I thought we could alter the present circumstances of our return." He still believed fervently in the justice of the Southern cause. He was "proud and defiant," believing that the South succumbed to overwhelming numbers. "We have still made an honest and glorious fight and as the boys express it 'have kept the flies off the Yanks for the past 4 years.'" He hoped that "ere the month of June shall have passed that the 'major' will be able to present himself to you in 'proper person.'" By May 25, "Maj. Simon Mayer AAG Sharp's brigade paroled prisoner of the Army of Tennessee" was given permission "to proceed to his home in Natchez, Mississippi."[49]

Lt. Simon Mayer was the son of immigrants who settled in Natchez. He served in the Natchez Southrons of the 10th Mississippi and was an ardent Confederate soldier. (Courtesy of Joan and Thomas H. Gandy, Natchez, Mississippi)

Most of Richmond's Jewish families were devastated by the war. Emma Mordecai visited Richmond in the early days after the end of the war and found the "pavement was covered with the plate glass from the fire doors and windows, reduced to powder by the explosions while rough boards supplied its place. All stores were closed and the street filthy." Later when she returned, she found it a "strange looking place . . . sidewalks thronged with Yankee soldiers and saucy Negro women." She was, needless to say, mortified and devastated by the fall of the Confederacy and concerned about its leaders. She wrote in her diary, "When I think of our President [Jefferson Davis], the victim of their petty tyranny, my heart aches, and fervently my prayers ascend to Heaven, that he may be sustained in these dark days, by a high and unfaltering trust in God!"[50]

Even the mild-mannered Mrs. Jacob A. Levy could not abide Yankees. When her nephew Jacob Ezekiel Hyneman came to visit her, she met him at the door. "Oh, Jacob, Jacob," the grieving mother of a dead Confederate son exclaimed, "I have made a vow never to touch the hand of a man who wears that uniform; but how can I keep it with my own flesh and blood, my sister's son?" Poor Hyneman had more to come. He went outside to see his cousin, in whom he had a definite romantic interest. She would not see him until he took off his sword. "The war is over," he said. "I guess I can surrender." His cousin then introduced the disappointed Jacob to her fiancé, 1st Lt. Edwin Kursheedt of the Washington Artillery, with the words, "This is my traitor cousin, Jacob Hyneman, from Philadelphia." Kursheedt rose to his former enemy's defense by telling young Miss Levy that she ought not call Jacob a traitor, as he had left Richmond as a little boy and was raised up North. Finally Jacob gave up. "I had an old briar-wood pipe sticking in my cap," he later recalled. "Edwin said: 'Comrade, let's smoke a pipe of peace together,' producing his tobacco pouch."[51]

On April 9, 1865, Perry Moses of Sumter married Rosalie Levy of Mobile. They had met earlier, when Perry and his brother Jack were invited to dinner at the Levy home. "As the two young men came up the walk to the house," Dorothy Bultman wrote, "Rose and Adele peeped through the blinds at them. Rose promptly chose 'that one' and Adele 'the other'—a choice that was to end in marriage for both couples." But on April 9, the war was not quite over and a squad of Yankees came looking for Lieutenant Moses. "Run, Cap'n run, the Yankees are after you," an old servant yelled. Moses fled and did not see his bride for three months until they were reunited. They settled in Louisiana and later in Sumter, South Carolina, and had seven children.[52]

Raphael Moses Jr., Master, CSN, attached himself to the 20th Georgia Volunteers and served as a courier in Benning's brigade during the retreat from Petersburg. He was with Lee's army on that fateful April 9 and surrendered and was paroled at Appomattox Court House. He either marched the eight hundred miles home with Benning's brigade or "walked home." In early May his father, Raphael Moses, was ordered to Washington, Georgia, and he and another son, Israel Moses Nunez ("Major"), were staying with Moses's old friend Robert Toombs. One day a cavalryman rode up and delivered a sack containing $5,000 in gold for Toombs's personal use, presumably to make his escape from the Union army. Toombs handed the money to "Major" and told him to buy corn and provisions and distribute it among the returning soldiers, which he did. Toombs said he would not defile his hands with "any of the damn stuff." Not long thereafter, Union soldiers arrived at Toombs's home to arrest him, but young Major met the Union officer between the gate and the house while Toombs escaped. Toombs barely got away but eventually made his way with his wife to Paris, where he lived in exile. He was never pardoned and, years later, paid a call on President Grant and told him, so the story goes, that it was his practice, whenever he visited a foreign country, to call on the chief magistrate of the land.[53]

Davis was determined not to surrender. On May 5, the last fragments of the Confederate government met in Washington, Georgia. Present were Davis; John C. Breckinridge, secretary of war; John C. Reagan, former postmaster general and now secretary of the Treasury; A. R. Lawton, quartermaster general; I. M. St. John, commissary general; and Raphael J. Moses, major, Confederate army. The government had ceased to exist, and most of the treasury had been disbursed on May 2. It now became necessary to dispose of the remaining gold bullion in the possession of the government. As the remnant of the government dissolved, one of the final orders of the Confederate States of America was given by W. F. Alexander, assistant to the quartermaster general: "Major R. J. Moses will pay Ten thousand dollars, the amount of bullion appropriated to the Q.M. Department by Secretary of War to Major R. R. Wood./May 5th, 1865. By order of Q.M. General/W. F. Alexander, Maj. & Assist./to the Q.M. General."[54]

Moses was faced with what to do with this gold bullion in the midst of what can only be described as anarchy. The war was over. Soldiers were discharged. Union troops were nearby. Many were desperate for food and money. Local government was in disarray. Toombs gave Moses the names of ten reliable soldiers to guard the funds. He took a squad to destroy all the liquor in the shops. Then he put the gold in an unoccupied wooden building with a keg of powder under it and a guard around it. He passed the word that a trail of powder led outside and that, if the guard was challenged, the fuse would be lit. After a sleepless night, Moses and his detail boarded a train for Augusta but were met at the train depot in Barnett, Georgia, by a large group of unruly former Confederate soldiers. Rumor had it that the car containing the gold would be stormed. Moses's guard stood by him, but the men certainly had to consider whether they were willing to die protecting gold in a war that was over.[55]

328   Moses determined to go out into the crowd and talk quietly but directly to the men. He read his orders and told them he had no interest in protecting the bullion except to fulfill his orders; that every dollar of it would be devoted to feeding their fellow soldiers and caring for the wounded; that he would do his best to carry out these orders; that they might kill him and his guard but that would be murder; and that if he and his men killed any of them, which they "would certainly endeavor to do," they would be justified on grounds of self-defense and, he added, "the discharge of a sacred duty." A number of the men who knew Moses spoke up and assured the rest that Moses would not steal the money. The bullion was successfully delivered to the commanding general of the Union army in Augusta.[56] Raphael J. Moses had carried out one of the Confederacy's final orders.[57]

Jewish soldiers who had fought for the Confederacy straggled home to rebuild their lives. But David Yulee *was* home and the end of the war brought him his greatest suffering. The governor of Florida had appointed Yulee as one member of a commission to negotiate Florida's reentry into the Union. In May he met with Salmon P. Chase, secretary of the Treasury, and Whitelaw Reid, a journalist and Chase confidant, who let Yulee know in no uncertain terms that neither Yulee nor any Southern white man was going to negotiate for or reorganize the government of Florida. Disappointed, Yulee went home to Archer; martial law was declared on May 22, and a few days later Yulee and Gov. Abraham K. Allison were arrested. Yulee was sent to Jacksonville as a prisoner. Gen. Israel Vodges treated him with great courtesy and gave him the run of the city. Higher authorities, however, soon ordered Yulee to Fort Pulaski near Savannah.[58]

At the war's end, President Lincoln had not decided on the fate of the Southern leadership. Many believed that treason should be punished severely. There was substantial sentiment, particularly in the aftermath of Lincoln's assassination, to hang Davis, Lee, Benjamin, and other high-ranking officials. Thus when Yulee was taken off to prison, no one could know his fate. In fact, he had no idea what he was to be charged with until early January 1866, when Secretary of War Stanton reported to President Johnson that Yulee was charged with treason "while holding a seat in the Senate of the United States."[59]

Mrs. Yulee and the children visited him in prison on their way to Washington to plead his case. They stayed with family in Maryland, where Mrs. Yulee's father, Governor Wickcliffe, joined her crusade to free her husband. There were rumors that Yulee would be court-martialed and hanged. The family hoped to utilize their contacts in the government to free the imprisoned former senator. Few Confederates had been arrested or imprisoned. Lee was paroled by General Grant. Along with Davis and Sen. Clement Clay, Yulee, however, remained imprisoned longer than any of the other Confederates. He was still a prisoner after Robert Toombs and Alfred Iverson, Confederate senators from Georgia; Howell Cobb and George A. Trenholm, secretaries of the Treasury; Francis W. Pickens,

David Yulee. (Courtesy of Frank and Marie-Therese wood print collections, Alexandria, Virginia.)

governor of South Carolina; John A. Campbell, assistant secretary of war; Wade Hampton, Confederate lieutenant general; and many others had been released.[60]

The reasons are not readily apparent. Robert L. Clarke contends that Yulee's Northern partners in the Florida Railroad Company kept him in prison "until they were satisfied that he would cooperate with them." Professor Thompson agrees that this may have been a factor. It does appear that a notorious carpetbagger lawyer, Lyman D. Stickney, came to Fernandina after it was captured and influenced local events. Serving as a Federal tax commissioner and lawyer for one of the northern creditors of the Florida Railroad, he sought out Union major-general Joseph Holt, now judge advocate general, and urged him to keep the "proslavery men, the active rebels during the rebellion" from resuming power. One way to do that—and take over the Florida Railroad at the same time (which Stickney attempted)—was to keep David Yulee in prison. No contemporary or historian has suggested that Yulee's Jewish lineage played any part in his outrageous treatment, but Yulee's fate was certainly not lost on his old colleague Judah Benjamin.[61]

The Yulee family had a more personal and more credible explanation: Yulee's former brother-in-law and old nemesis, Union Maj. Gen. Joseph Holt. Margaret Crepps Wickliffe, one of the Wickliffe sisters, had, in Mrs. Clay's words, "married Joseph Holt, [who] rose high in Federal honours after the breaking out of the War, having sold his Southern birthright for a mess of Northern pottage." Holt had been a stereotypical prosecutor as a young man. His loyalty to the Union caused him to reject not only his wife's family, but also his own brother in Mississippi and mother in Kentucky. As Holt was a staunch Unionist, Lincoln had appointed Holt judge advocate general of the Union army and had offered to appoint him attorney general. He had seriously considered him to head the War Department. During the war, Holt ferreted out spies, traitors, and, at times, political dissenters, and was conspicuously loyal to Edwin Stanton, his superior, in his various political difficulties. It was Holt who headed the investigation into the Copperhead and Order of American Knights movements, and it was Holt who was the chief judge in the military-style trial of Booth's co-conspirators. Holt and Yulee had known each other for decades, first as brothers-in-law until Holt's wife's death just before the war, and second as political allies during the Buchanan administration.[62]

Holt now accused Yulee of treason, and Holt was now the nation's chief prosecutor of traitors. He was also a bitter man rejected by his own family and little concerned about the rights of his victims. Holt felt he had been used by both Yulee and Stephen Mallory, and he now had both of them arrested and accused both of "overt acts of treason" and "skulking treachery." It was clear from gossip passed on by another Wickliffe brother-in-law, Judge William Merrick, that Holt was behind the arrest and detention of Yulee. Yulee, of course, was no more guilty of treason than millions of other Southerners and considerably less guilty than thousands who served more actively than he in the armed forces and the Confederate government.[63]

Holt based his accusations of treason on Yulee's attempt to learn about the condition of the Federal military in Florida while he was still a senator. Holt cited Yulee's January 1861 letter in which he promised to give "the enemy a shot" and "that I am willing to be their masters but not their brothers" in his continuing efforts to keep Yulee in prison and put him on trial for treason.[64]

Holt was so bitter he accused Mallory and Yulee of cowardice. He wrote, "Many of the most conspicuous of these modern conspirators—and this was especially true of Yulee and Mallory . . . —seem to have shrunk away from the bloody conflicts of the war in which they had so eagerly involved the deluded States and people they represented." Wickliffe Yulee described Holt as suffering from a "diseased vanity," a man "who sought to bite the hand that had aided him, and shine, in artificial light, as a spurious Brutus. He had been degraded, by the noble-minded Lincoln from his cabinet place" to the position he now occupied, where he "resembled the notorious Fouché," the French revolutionary. There was much truth to these allegations. Holt detested not just Yulee and Mallory but all of his former Southern friends and colleagues. He was willing to use perjured testimony in order to convict Davis and Clement Clay of complicity in the Lincoln assassination.[65]

Yulee's family and friends flooded Stanton and Johnson with letters and petitions and called in person. Mrs. Yulee went to Maryland so that she could work for her husband's release in person. In July she wrote that Holt "has gone to the White Mountains. If only he would stay there. The temperature would suit his heart."

Yulee's old friends in high places, such as his former friend and lawyer Edwin Stanton and William Seward, refused to help. They were waiting to see which way the political wind would blow, and, in Stanton's case, he may have felt an obligation to support Holt as Holt had once supported him. President Andrew Johnson wrote a now thoroughly worried Governor Wickliffe: "Tell Mrs. Yulee that not one hair of her husband's head shall be touched—but for me to do anything now in his behalf, while passions remain excited, would only injure his cause."[66]

While passions cooled, the family continued to hope. When advised that a letter from General Grant would help, the Yulees turned to an old friend, Joseph E. Johnston, the former Confederate general whom Yulee had helped become quartermaster general of the U.S. Army under Buchanan. Johnston wrote Grant. "Wires flashed," Wickliffe Yulee recalled, "and magically the prison doors were thrown open; as were the hearts of Senator Yulee and his family, for the great and simple soldier, who had enemies only in time of war." He was pardoned by President Johnson and released on March 25, 1866, having been imprisoned for ten months.[67]

Emma Mordecai of Richmond spoke for her fellow Jewish Confederates when she wrote, "I feel as if there was nothing more to live for in this world. My very heart and soul were bound up in our cause and while I can truly say I do not murmur at God's will, I feel utterly cast down, at our failure."[68]

CHAPTER 8

★

We Are Passing through Another Captivity

THE CIVIL WAR BROUGHT a social revolution to the South. Millions of slaves were freed, and those who had invested in the South's "peculiar institution" lost a great proportion of their wealth. White Southerners had expended their capital in a failed war for independence. Political power ebbed from antebellum elites to their former slaves, free blacks, and newcomers to government, both Northern and native-born, "carpetbaggers" and "scalawags," respectively, as native white Southerners called them. Much of the South lay devastated by the war, particularly Richmond and Charleston. Jewish Confederates who had shared in the glories, the honors, and the triumphs of the war now shared the despair and gloom of defeat.

The old Southern Jewish families, the few Sephardim remaining, those most committed to the cause, suffered the greatest losses. Judah P. Benjamin was in exile, having literally lost everything he had—his land, his home, his law practice, his fortune, and the comfort of his family. David Yulee spent almost a year in prison, uncertain of his fate. Abraham C. Myers lost his military career, his health, and his reputation, as did Camden DeLeon. Judith Hyams Douglas, recalling her Aunt Ann in 1936, remembered that she "wore her poverty as a badge of honor as all loyal Southerners did."[1]

Raphael J. Moses, Longstreet's commissary, returned to The Esquiline in Columbus. He had lost a son as well as a way of life. The war had taken a heavy toll on the extended Moses family. In addition to their son Albert, Raphael and Eliza Moses lost three nephews: Pvt. Perry Moses Jr., mortally wounded at Malvern Hill; Lt. Joshua L. Moses, killed at Fort Blakely; and Lt. David Cardoza Levy, killed in action at Murfreesboro (Stone's River), Tennessee. Five cousins were killed: Saul Magnus, Van Den Corput's Company, Georgia Light Artillery, at Resaca, Georgia; Alexander Hilzheim, Bradford's corps of Scouts and Guards, at Kennesaw Mountain, Georgia; Gratz Cohen, Bentonville, North Carolina; and two brothers, Cpl. Isaac Phillip Goldsmith, 17th South Carolina Cavalry Battalion, at James Island, South Carolina, and Lt. Mikel Myers Goldsmith, 1st South Carolina Regiment, Charleston Guard, at Macon, Georgia.[2]

Maj. Raphael J. Moses of Columbus, Georgia, served as a major and was Longstreet's commissary at Gettysburg. Douglas Southall Freeman called Moses "the best commissary of like rank in the Confederate service." He lost one son, Albert Luria, in the war, as well as several nephews. He was a vigorous opponent of the carpetbagger government of Georgia after the war. (Courtesy of the Jacob Rader Marcus Center, American Jewish Archives, Cincinnati, Ohio.)

Yet life went on for the Moses clan. On June 28, 1865, less than three months after Appomattox, Nina Moses, Raphael's daughter, married William Moultrie Moses, who had served in Company G, 2d Georgia in Longstreet's corps. It was likely no coincidence that the patriotic Moses family from South Carolina, whose daughter was marrying a man named for the great hero of the American Revolution, chose "Carolina Day" as the day of the wedding. (On June 28, South Carolinians celebrate the colonists' first victory of the Revolution, the defeat of the British fleet off Sullivan's Island, when Gen. William Moultrie led the victorious troops.) The couple was married at the family plantation before sundown under a *huppah,* the canopy prescribed by Jewish custom. The huppah, held up by four friends, was made of evergreens and white flowers. The proud father performed the ceremony himself, as no rabbi was available.[3]

Henry Hyams, who had gone west to Louisiana in the 1820s to seek his fortune, lost it in the war. "As Israelites," the former lieutenant governor of Louisiana wrote a family member in April 1868, "we are passing through another captivity which relives and reenacts all the troubles so pathetically poured forth by the inspired Jeremiah. Let us hope with him that the days of Bondage will have a permanent end and that freedom will again reign in our unhappy land." Hyams and the defeated Jewish Confederates saw in the Union occupation and Reconstruction a modern-day version of the Jewish exile in Babylonia after the destruction of the Jewish state. Hyams believed that the spirituality of the Jewish faith had been adopted by its political conquerors and, in that sense, "Jerusalem has prevailed." So he now hoped that the "pure patriotism of the Southern mind must *one day* conquer and overcome its present vanquishers—despite our present degradation."[4]

Hyams lost three plantations and two hundred slaves in the war. His land was confiscated. At first, he accepted the results of the war philosophically. He moved to New Orleans. By September 1865, he had opened a law practice, and he worked diligently to have his friend, former Governor Moore, restored to his political rights. His interest in Governor Moore was personal. His son Kosciusko ("Kossie") married Moore's daughter, Emma Jane.[5]

By April 1868 Hyams, along with the rest of the white population of Louisiana, bore the yoke of the Reconstruction government. The Federal government, controlled by the Radical Republicans, at first denied the Southern states representatives in the Congress and divided the South into military districts. Later, rigorous laws were passed ensuring the right to vote to the former slaves and effectively taking control of the state governments away from native whites. The former leadership of the Southern states—planters, businessmen, lawyers—were removed from office and new leaders, loyal to the Union, took their place. This was revolution in the eyes of white Southerners, a revolution they did not accept.[6] Hyams wrote a family member, "I hope that we will all live long enough to see the end of our personal and political suffering. So far there is scarcely any ray of light ahead." Despite his troubles, he felt he had done his duty and that sustained him. Like most native whites, Hyams was aghast at the tactics of the carpetbaggers, the Union occupying army, and the Reconstruction government.[7]

Hyams did not live to see the end of Reconstruction. He died on June 25, 1875. Some of the district courts in Louisiana adjourned out of respect for his memory, and the next day a hundred members of the legal profession assembled in the Louisiana Supreme Court to offer a tribute. The *Daily Picayune* relayed the sad circumstances of Hyams's last years: "The downfall of the South—the death of his fair and accomplished daughters and of two sons—the latter within one year—and recently the demise of the worthy and cherished wife of his bosom, all contributed to break his noble spirit. He had devoted all his affection to these beings, too dear to him, and their loss, to use Irving's phrase, was the bankruptcy of his heart. This good, and true and chivalrous old man had died overwhelmed with grief!"[8]

Abraham Myers, the former quartermaster general, never accepted his fall from grace. He contended after the war that his removal from office was illegal, that he had been the Confederacy's only quartermaster general, and that he had been promoted to general. Indeed, the words "Gen. A. C. Myers" are the most prominent ones on his original headstone.[9]

Many Southerners left the South; many Jewish Southerners did the same. Moses Cohen Mordecai, his shipping business destroyed by the war and his eyesight gone, moved to Baltimore. His son-in-law, Marks H. Lazarus, who had served in the Washington Artillery (South Carolina), handled his business affairs in Charleston. Eleanor Cohen of Columbia finally married Benjamin Mendes Seixas on August 2,

1865, in Columbia. The sun shone. The bride was radiant. She was dressed plainly in "white swiss muslin high & long sleeves." All "passed off well, the glass broke [the Jewish custom of breaking a glass], the ring was on my finger & from every side I received kisses & congratulations." After the wedding, Eleanor moved to New York City despite her concerns about living among those who were so recently her enemies. Her heart, she confided to her diary, was filled with "Southern fire" and bitterness toward the North. Returning to Charleston in 1866 to have her first child, she was shocked by the crowds of Yankees, freedmen, and "colored soldiers." Many of her friends were dead; some were still refugees. She eventually had four children and died, a New York resident, at age thirty-four in 1874.[10]

Slavery was at an end, and Jewish slave owners experienced the same exodus of their slaves as their fellow Southerners. In some instances slaves stayed on as paid servants. In most cases, they left, searching for a new life. Emma Mordecai, living with her sister-in-law Rose on a plantation, witnessed the rapid deterioration of the relationship between the former masters and their slaves. Cy, now a freedman, demanded part of the farm on account of all the work he had done. Emma's nephew Willie Mordecai told Cy "he would give him three days to find a place to move." The Mordecais bargained for the former slaves to work until new servants could be hired. Cy did return and "expressed to Rose his regret for his improper conduct . . . and was very much affected at parting with her. She could not take leave of him without emotion and has felt miserable ever since." This, of course, left Rose and Emma with all the housework. "I have been doing drudgery for the greater part of the week," Emma complained, "assisted unwillingly and inefficiently by a little white girl from town."[11]

Gratz Cohen of Savannah died at the battle of Bentonville. (From the collection of Louis Schmier, Valdosta, Georgia.)

Emma Mordecai's experience with the freeing of her own slaves was more friendly. Like many city dwellers, Emma owned slaves whom she hired out to others for a portion of their wages. Moses, her former slave, was now a bricklayer. She remained on good terms with him. "No servant," she wrote, "could behave better than he has done. He shewed great interest in me and all of us, and begged me to call upon him whenever he could do anything for me." Emma was, in a sense, relieved at the turn of events, because she had the expense of Moses, his sickly wife, and young children, and it took nearly all of the wages Moses could earn to pay his family's medical and clothing expenses.[12]

Eleanor Cohen of Charleston and Solomon Cohen of Savannah lamented the end of slavery. All of Eleanor Cohen's clothing, she wrote, was saved from the fire in Columbia by Rose, "our faithful servant. She and Helen were true, so was Lavinia. I shall ever remember her devotion to us. She gave us cotton homespun and behaved like a friend. Ben, who we believed faithful, left us; he says, or said, he was forced to."[13]

Many Jewish communities and congregations were decimated by the war. Although life went on in Norfolk, New Orleans, and Memphis, Charleston was practically destroyed by the Civil War. More dependent on slavery and the planter class than Richmond, besieged by an invading army for years, more remote from railroad lines, and bound to an agricultural economy, Charleston's economic life came to a standstill. The ranks of the old Charleston Jewish families and the new German and Polish immigrant families were shattered by the war. Many had died: Thomas W. Mordecai, 4th South Carolina, in 1861 at Fort Moultrie; R. Blankensee, Hampton Legion, at First Manassas; Jacob Blankenstein, 15th South Carolina, near Richmond; Mikell. M. Goldsmith, 1st South Carolina Charleston Guard, killed accidentally in 1864; Isacc P. Goldsmith, 5th South Carolina, of disease; Jacob M. Hoffman, 10th South Carolina, at Franklin; Isaiah Jacobs, 2d South Carolina, at Chickamauga; 1st Lt. W. Myer Wolff, Co. G, 11th South Carolina, at Swift Creek; Mendel Brown, 10th South Carolina, at Atlanta; 5th Sgt. Jacob B. Cohen, Company A, 21st South Carolina, at Fort Fisher; Marx E. Cohen Jr., Hart's (South Carolina) Battery, at Bentonville. Add to this partial list a much longer list of the wounded, disabled, impoverished, the widows, the orphans and the grieving survivors, and it is apparent that the old Jewish elite of Charleston was no more.[14]

The leaders of congregation Shearith Israel took advantage of the military occupation to take over Beth Elohim's synagogue. The military authorities, now administering the laws and acting as the local government, gave possession of the temple to the Wentworth Street congregation until the Beth Elohim trustees petitioned Brig. Gen. William Gurney, the provost judge, "that they be put in possession and control of their Synagogue in Hasell Street." The military judge agreed with Benjamin D. Lazarus and B. F. Moise that the "congregation to which Mr. Moise belongs" had the right to the building on account of a decision by the state courts before the war.[15]

The once proud Jews of Charleston, like their fellow Charlestonians, were reduced to poverty and misery. Many prominent businessmen left the city to find work elsewhere. One-third of Beth Elohim's congregation were stricken from the rolls in 1867 for their inability to pay dues. A fund established before the war by Abraham Ottolengui for "poor Israelites" of the city, had among its applicants some of the formerly well-to-do, including Ottolengui himself.[16]

In January 1866, Beth Elohim's building was still not repaired and was so dilapidated and damaged that its few members met in the Hebrew Orphan Society building. The minutes noted that the "Organ, Chandeliers, Sepherim and

Remonim . . . removed for safety" to Columbia for safekeeping were destroyed when "that City was invaded by the ruthless Army under command of General Sherman." Beth Elohim and Shearith Israel, soon voted to combine the two synagogues "on a basis of mutual concessions." The membership of Beth Elohim, the minutes noted, had been "disastrously diminished by death, and removals and by the ravages of War, its property . . . seriously damaged, and its finances greatly reduced." Charleston Jewry no longer had the luxury to debate the merits of Reform versus Orthodoxy. It had to survive. The new constitution was a compromise: the service would be a shortened version of the Orthodox Portuguese Minhag. The Wentworth Street synagogue would be sold; the two cemeteries on Coming Street would be combined. Secession on one level had ironically led to union on the congregational level.[17]

When the indefatigable journalist Rabbi Isaac Leeser visited Charleston in the summer of 1866, he found Shearith Israel "so greatly injured during the war, as almost to render it useless as a place of worship." He found Beth Elohim "much disfigured by the explosion of shells fired indiscriminately into Charleston during the protracted siege it underwent, and, by being so long closed, it suffered likewise by natural dilapidation." When Leeser went to Beth Elohim to preach on Saturday morning, June 2, 1866, he saw "the unwashed floor, the dust resting on the furniture and benches, many panes of glass broken, [and] the ceiling crushed in many places by the explosion of shells that penetrated the roof." The "Polish synagogue" on St. Philips Street, Lesser found, was "without a permanent minister." Leeser found that many of the assimilated Charleston Jews were dead or gone.[18] Charles Henry Moise, a grandson of Abraham and Sarah Moise from Haiti, served as president of Beth Elohim for four years. Moise spent a great deal of time raising funds up North to rebuild the Jewish community. Because he could not make a living in Reconstruction Charleston, Moise went to live with his brother Edwin in Sumter.[19]

The Jewish community of Richmond was in deep despair after Appomattox. The old Virginia Jewish families could not abide the invaders. "Richmond is a strange looking place," Emma Mordecai confided to her diary, "with its heap of ruins, its streets transversed by U.S. Army wagons, sidewalks thronged with Yankee soldiers and saucy Negro women." Mordecai could not bear the thought of Yankees in Richmond. "Everything looks unnatural and desecrated," she wrote, "and the eye is offended by all it sees, and the ear by all it hears."[20] Like the Jews of Charleston, the members of Richmond's Jewry were subject to grinding poverty. Rosena Hutzler Levy recalled that all she and her husband Leopold Levy "had worked for & as he thought saved it . . . was swept away."[21] Jacob Ezekiel could not make a living and was forced to move in order to support his family. Richmonders, like Charlestonians, grieved for the many killed and wounded.[22]

Rabbi Leeser described Richmond in October 1865: "Suffering had been familiar to them in every shape, and the deprivation of many comforts of life had become habitual, and it is only wonderful that all this had left so few traces in them. It must be recorded to the credit of the Israelites of Richmond, that they kept up all their various organizations during the trials through which they had passed."[23] The returning soldiers took their places in the community. For four years, Beth Ahabah had been without its secretary, Capt. Ezekiel Levy. The congregational minutes of May 1865 reflected that Levy had returned to his congregational post.[24]

In 1866 Beth Shalome's Franklin Street cemetery was "a vacant lot, overrun with rank weeds and grass, showing the track of wagons and bearing the hoofmarks of horses and which is washed into deep ruts and gullies by the rains of many a season." The city had been badly damaged and, indeed, in some places destroyed, by the shelling and the fires set by looting mobs and the departing Confederate army in 1865.[25]

The Jewish women of Richmond formed the Hebrew Ladies' Memorial Association for the Confederate Dead. Many a Southern Jewish youth had died and been buried in Richmond. Jewish Richmonders took on the responsibility of caring for their graves. Their notice in the newspaper read as follows: "HEBREW LADIES MEMORIAL ASSOCIATION FOR CONFEDERATE DEAD.—A society has been formed by the Hebrew ladies of this city for the purpose of caring for the graves of the Israelitish soldiers of the Confederate army who have been interred in their cemetery on Shockoe Hill. This society will not come in conflict with the others already formed, but is merely intended for the deceased of their own persuasion, while they have all joined in the general associations for Hollywood and Oakwood, recently established. We will publish their proceedings shortly." A circular was sent out "To the Israelites of the South" asking for funds to "mound and turf each grave," to place simple stone markers, and eventually to erect a monument to the Jewish Confederate dead. Time was of the essence, the circular said. "While the world yet rings with the narrative of a brave people's struggle for independence," it began, and while the story of their noble sacrifices for liberty was fresh, the graves themselves were neglected. This was not a situation which Southern Jewry should allow. Southern Jews should remember "the myriads of heroes who spilled their noble blood" in defense of the "glorious cause." The circular was also designed to appeal to the Southern Jewish readers' fear of anti-Semitism: "In time to come," it concluded, "when the malicious tongue of slander, ever so ready to assail Israel, shall be raised against us, then, with feeling of mournful pride, will we point to this monument and say: '*There* is our reply.'"[26]

Tending to graves became an important event. William B. Myers, Gustavus A. Myers's son and a former Confederate officer, designed the railing around the Confederate graves in the Hebrew Cemetery on Shockoe Hill, complete with furled flags, stacked muskets, and a Confederate flag. Every May the Jewish ladies would, like their Christian counterparts, "decorate" the graves of the Confederate

TO THE ISRAELITES OF THE SOUTH.

Richmond, Va. June 5th, 1866.

While the world yet rings with the narrative of a brave people's struggle for independence, and while the story of the hardships so nobly endured for Liberty's sake is yet a theme but half exhausted, the countless graves of the myriads of heroes who spilled their noble blood in defence of that glorious cause, lie neglected, not alone unmarked by tablet or sculptured urn, but literally vanishing before the relentless finger of Time. Within the past four weeks, there have been formed by the ladies of Richmond two Associations, viz: the "Hollywood" and the "Oakwood," having for their object the care and renovation of the soldiers' graves in those cemeteries.

Cotemporaneously with the above, we, the Hebrew Ladies, formed a similar Association, with the view of caring for the graves of Jewish soldiers; which, of course, would not be embraced in the work of either of the first named Societies.

In our own cemetery repose, alas! the sacred remains of many a loved brother, son and husband, to whose relatives, in the far sunny South, it would be a solace to know that the pious duty of preserving from decay the last resting place of their lost ones, although denied to them to perform, is yet sacredly fulfilled by the members of the "Hebrew Ladies' Memorial Association."

It is our intention to mound and turf each grave, and to place at the head of each a simple stone, inscribed with the name, State, and time and place of death; subsequently, to rear a monument commemorative of their brave deeds.

In order, however, to successfully accomplish our object, we need some pecuniary assistance. Our scant and somewhat needy community, already so heavily taxed, has done well; but we find "this work is too great for us:" therefore, with a full confidence in the sympathy and co-operation of our people elsewhere, we make this appeal for aid, well knowing that as Israelites and true patriots, they will not refuse to assist in rearing a monument which shall serve not only to commemorate the bravery of our dead, but the gratitude and admiration of the living, for those who so nobly perished in what we deemed a just and righteous cause; and while as Israelites we mourn the untimely loss of our loved ones, it will be a grateful reflection that they suffered not their country to call in vain.

In time to come, when our grief shall have become, in a measure, silenced, and when the malicious tongue of slander, ever so ready to assail Israel, shall be raised against us, then, with a feeling of mournful pride, will we point to this monument and say: "*There* is our reply."

MRS. ABRAHAM LEVY.
Corresponding Secretary of the Hebrew Ladies' Memorial Association.

Contributions can be forwarded to Mrs. Abraham Levy, Box 289, Richmond, Va.

Circular sent to Southern Jews in 1866 by the Hebrew Ladies' Memorial Association. The Jewish women of Richmond raised funds to care for the graves of "the glorious dead" at the Hebrew Cemetery on Shockoe Hill. (Courtesy of Beth Ahabah Museum and Archives, Richmond, Virginia.)

dead with wreaths of roses and magnolias. In May 1869, the *Richmond Dispatch* contained this notice: "Hebrew Memorial Day. This is the day set apart by the Hebrew Ladies Memorial Association for the decoration of the graves of the young men of their nationality who fell in the Confederate struggle. They cordially invite the people of Richmond to unite with them in the sad but pleasing exercises, and contribution of flowers will be thankfully received. The Hebrew cemetery is in the northern part of the city—a pleasant walk or ride."[27]

The war certainly did not bring the contentious factions of Nashville Jewry together. A story in a Jewish periodical in 1867 described Nashville's 250 Jewish families as "divided into three groups [who] . . . do not cooperate. . . . The spirit of unity did not move them to establish and build a united synagogue, but each has bought a place to build its own house of worship, and that which one planned to build, the others plotted to destroy."[28] In 1868, two prewar synagogues united to form Khal Kodesh Ohava Sholom, later known as the Vine Street Temple. Former President Andrew Johnson, who had so many anti-Semitic things to say about Judah P. Benjamin and David Yulee, was one of the speakers at the dedication of the Temple in 1874. He told his listeners that he hoped the temple "would ever remain a monument to the industry, prosperity and welfare of the Jewish citizens of Nashville."[29]

Of course the Jewish South after the Civil War did not belong exclusively to native Southern Jewry. More Jewish immigrants from Germany, Poland, Russia, and the North came South during the Reconstruction years. Often poor, like the previous generation of peddlers, these new settlers, rejuvenated many moribund congregations and helped rebuild the shattered Southern economy.[30] These new settlers did not share the same feelings about the war as those who had lived through it, but there is little evidence that they played any significant political role in the Reconstruction era. Clearly, however, Jewish immigrants from abroad and the North played a substantial role in rebuilding Atlanta, Memphis, and Richmond.

Janice O. Rothschild wrote of these newcomers to Atlanta: "These enterprising young men [peddlers for Northern merchants] perceived that Atlanta, a booming hub of trade and transportation, would be a good place to go into business for themselves. By 1866 they were sufficiently prosperous to organize a social club, the Concordia Society, forerunner of the present Standard Club." In 1867 Rabbi Leeser returned to Atlanta to again urge the formation of a congregation. This time he succeeded. "The Israelites of the place," he wrote, "have rented a hall, purchased a Sepher [Torah] and intended holding services. . . . We expect much from Atlanta. The city has been fearfully devastated during the late war. . . . Still, it is a center of commerce. . . . Israelites will, to a certainty, take their share in the regeneration of Georgia."[31]

★　★　★

Before the war, Dr. Simon Baruch had courted Isabelle ("Belle") Wolfe, the daughter of a prominent Jewish planter, Saling Wolfe. Belle was the granddaughter of Charleston Rabbi Hartwig Cohen and the niece of Baruch's mentor, Mannes Baum. When the war ended, the Wolfes, like their fellow South Carolinians, were ruined and impoverished. Their fortune had been invested in Confederate money. The Wolfe plantation in Winnsboro—the home, the crops, the outbuildings—were all burned by Sherman's army. A neighbor found Mr. and Mrs. Wolfe "with all their little children gathered around them offering up prayers in Hebrew."[32] Simon Baruch married Isabelle Wolfe on November 28, 1867.[33] They lived in Camden, in the Midlands of South Carolina. Life was difficult in Reconstruction South Carolina. Baruch was a country doctor who soon had four children, including the second son, Bernard, born in Camden in 1870. (Bernard Baruch later became one of the most prominent Jews of the twentieth century, a friend and advisor to Franklin D. Roosevelt.)[34]

John and Jeanette Mayer continued to live in Natchez. Their son, Simon, returned from the war a hero. He had narrowly escaped being killed at the Battle of Franklin when a bullet passed through his hat but missed his head as he carried a message to Gen. Jacob H. Sharp when he served as acting adjutant. The Mayers's home was, according to their daughter, "the center of all Jewish festivities, and at the long dining table . . . there were often seated as many as thirty-five guests on Passover Eve, the feast of Seder, which was always celebrated with much 'pomp and ceremony.'" In 1865 the Jewish community was small. It had an Orthodox congregation, Chevra Kadusha (Holy Society), made up mainly of Polish Jews. The older families and German Jews soon established a Reform congregation, and a new temple was dedicated in 1871.[35]

When the war ended, the Lehman brothers were in business as Lehman, Durr & Co., still at Court Square in Montgomery. The business had to be rejuvenated, and the family worked diligently to rebuild its fortune. By 1866 Emanuel Lehman reactivated the New York office of Lehman Brothers at 176 Fulton Street. They also opened a New Orleans office the same year. In 1868 Mayer Lehman moved to New York, and Lehman Brothers soon became one of the largest brokers of commodities in New York City. The firm traded petroleum, coffee, and sugar as well as cotton.[36]

After the war, Thomas Cooper DeLeon moved to Baltimore, where he served as the editor of the *Cosmopolite Magazine,* lending a hand to his poverty-stricken colleagues from the South, including Phoebe Pember. The *Cosmopolite* published some portions of Pember's memoir, *A Southern Woman's Story.* DeLeon moved to New York City in 1866, where he wrote for newspapers and magazines and was a translator of French novels. He collected and edited *South Songs,* a collection of war poems of the South in 1866. In 1868, DeLeon moved to Mobile to become the managing editor of the *Mobile Register.* There, he became

Thomas Cooper DeLeon served as a clerk in the Confederate government in Richmond. After the war, he became a noted Southern author, writing *Four Years in Rebel Capitals* and *Belles, Beaux, and Brains of the '60s*, two Civil War classics. He also wrote Confederate poetry and, in later years, was known as "the Blind Poet of the Confederacy." The Civil War–era DeLeons abandoned Judaism. They proved to be more Southern than Jewish, according to Jacob Rader Marcus (Gergel and Gergel, *Tree of Life*, 35). (Courtesy of South Caroliniana Library, University of South Carolina, Columbia.)

a well-known member of society, creating and managing the Mobile Mardi Gras Carnival for twenty-five years. He became the owner and editor of the *Register* in 1877 and also owned and edited the *Gossip* and the *Gulf Citizen*. He was a prolific writer, publishing plays, novels, and memoirs of the war. His Confederate poems included "Asleep with Jackson," an ode to Stonewall Jackson, and "Paladin and Poet," a tribute to Robert E. Lee. He wrote two journalistic memoirs of the Civil War, which have become classics: *Four Years in Rebel Capitals*, published in Mobile in 1890, and *Belles, Beaux, and Brains of the '60s*.[37]

Yates Levy resumed the practice of law after the war and became the outspoken pro-Southern editor of the *Daily Advertiser*, a Savannah newspaper. His editorials during the Union occupation were not acceptable to General Meade, and he was forced to resign. His father wrote in 1868, "I should not be surprised if he again finds himself one of these days in prison." He resumed the practice of law and was active in Mikve Israel, serving as the congregation's attorney.[38]

Jacob and Fanny Levy survived the war and moved back to Savannah. Former Alabama Sen. Clement C. Clay and Jefferson Davis were among a group of prisoners that passed through Savannah on their way to Northern prisons on May 14, 1865. Clay and Davis were sent to Fort Monroe on the tip of the Virginia Peninsula.[39] Mrs. Clay followed them to Savannah so that she could be close to her husband. She relates in her charming memoir, *A Belle of the Fifties* (1904), a story of the Levy family:

> Just before leaving the hospitable coast city [Savannah], I was the guest of Mrs. Levy, mother of the brilliant Mrs. Philip Phillips, of Washington, of

Mrs. Pember, and of Miss Martha Levy, one of the readiest wits I have ever known. During the evening . . . many guests were introduced, among them some of Savannah's prominent Hebrews. For an hour Miss Martha had been busy presenting her friends, both Christian and Jew, when one after another came Mr. Cohen, Mr. Salomon, Dr. Lazarus and Dr. Mordecai. At this remarkable procession my risibles proved triumphant. I glanced slyly at Miss Martha. Her eyes shown with mischief as she presented Dr. Mordecai. "And is Hayman here, too?" I asked.[40]

The extended Levy family cared passionately about the welfare of Varina and the imprisoned Jefferson Davis. The Davises were old friends of Eugenia and Philip Phillips and Henrietta Levy Cohen and her husband, Octavus Cohen. One of the Phillipses's daughters, Carolina Meyers, remembered in 1900 how much she valued her association with "that dear martyr Mr. Davis. As a girl, I often sat on his lap with my arms around his neck." After the war, Octavus Cohen took a leading role in raising funds for Mrs. Davis.[41]

The Levy family regrouped in Savannah and the younger members adjusted to the new order. By 1868 Clavius Phillips was socializing every night and even attending the opera. Like his fellow Southerners, Jacob C. Levy was devastated economically by the war and bitter about the Reconstruction government. He detested Republican rule. "There may be some choice to be sure in the Quality of the Scamps," he wrote his daughters in 1868, "for the invading Yankees always make one believe they confer a favor on you in all that is done."[42]

In later years after his presidency, Ulysses S. Grant made a tour of the South and stopped in Fernandina and visited for several days with the Yulees. David Yulee spent his later years pursuing his railroad and farming ventures. He continued to be an officer or director of the Florida Railroad Company until his death. Not only did time cool the hatred of his captors, but Yulee was even compensated in later years for his efforts on behalf of the railroad during the Civil War. The company prospered in the postwar era, and the rail lines over which two armies made war were gradually absorbed by bigger companies. Yulee retired with a comfortable income. He had been the great Floridian of antebellum Florida history, and he had mapped out his state's internal improvement system and its railroads.[43]

When Maj. Alroy Jonas returned to Aberdeen, Mississippi, in 1865, he was, like most Southerners, broke. On a shoestring budget, he established the *Aberdeen Examiner*, which was published weekly, and Jonas was its editor for fifty years. He married a Methodist woman of Aberdeen, and their children were raised in the Methodist church. The major apparently never joined a church, but must have ceased the practice of Judaism. Yet he was always considered to be Jewish.[44]

Jonas became something of a local character. His office was a curiosity shop, having, one local newspaperman said, "more the appearance of an agricultural

Maj. Alroy Jonas, the author of the famous poem "Lines on the Back of a Confederate Note." (Courtesy of Mel Young, Chattanooga, Tennessee.)

museum than newspaper establishment." When Sen. L. Q. C. Lamar of Mississippi was appointed chairman of the senate committee on the Mississippi River and Tributaries, Jonas was appointed clerk and Lamar's secretary. Jonas's fortunes in Washington, like those of all white Southerners of the period, rose and fell with those of the Democratic Party. He moved to Washington for a time, where his brother, Frank Jonas, was a senator from Louisiana. Then he served on the staff of the sergeant at arms, as secretary to the Assistant Secretary of the Interior Colonel Muldrew, and as Lamar's clerk when Lamar became secretary of the interior.[45]

Jewish Southerners who had served in the Confederate army and who had supported the South's war for independence were outraged by the Federal military occupation and Reconstruction. In 1868 Octavia Harby Moses of Sumter, South Carolina, wrote a poem about her dead son, Josh Moses, containing these lines:

> The lovely land thou died'st to save,
> Is ruled by traitor and by slave,
> Wretches who in their thirst for gain,
> An eminence of guilt attain.[46]

Some of the old Southern Jewish elite, like some of their former comrades in arms, returned to power at the end of Reconstruction. Indeed, a number of Jewish Confederates were active in the Conservative (or "Bourbon" or "Redeemer") Movement, which returned the old antebellum elite and a new business elite to power. Three Jewish Confederate officers in particular played prominent roles in the Reconstruction era: Edwin Warren Moise of South Carolina, who had served with Wade Hampton in Virginia and North Carolina; Raphael J. Moses, who had served with Longstreet at Gettysburg; and Benjamin Franklin Jonas of Louisiana, who was sergeant major of Fenner's battery.

When the war ended, Frank Jonas returned to New Orleans, where he practiced law with Henry Hyams. He became a key leader of the Democratic Party in Reconstruction Louisiana. Elected to the Louisiana House of Representatives in 1865, Jonas served as chairman of the finance committee. The *Picayune* observed that the legislature was charged with nothing less than the reorganization of the

Sen. Benjamin Franklin Jonas. Frank Jonas's father, Abraham,
served in the Illinois legislature with Abraham Lincoln. Frank
Jonas moved to New Orleans and fought in Fenner's battery. He
was elected city attorney of New Orleans and then to the U.S.
Senate in 1876, becoming the first practicing Jew elected to the
Senate. (Courtesy of Tulane University.)

entire civil government. Louisiana whites intended to control the state government
and keep the black population from exercising many of their newly created rights.
The Federal government disagreed, and the legislature was dissolved by Maj. Gen.
Philip Sheridan of the occupation army. In 1872 Jonas was nominated as lieutenant
governor on a ticket with John McEnery, when the native white Louisianians
attempted unsuccessfully to take the reigns of power from the Republican regime.
But with the formation of the "fusion ticket," Jonas withdrew in favor of another
candidate. He was elected to the state senate in the same year and sat in that body
as long as McEnery was governor. When the Federal courts declared that the
Republican candidate had been elected governor, Jonas refused to serve, even
though he was chosen by the election boards of both Republicans and Democrats.
In the colorful language of Louisiana politics, Jonas's supporters later boasted that

"he refused to sit in the Legislature created by fraud, by the midnight order of a drunken Federal Judge, and maintained by the bayonets of United States troops." Jonas later told the U.S. Senate, "I never entered the door or took my seat by the grace of military permission."[47]

Louisiana politics was among the most turbulent in the Southern states during Reconstruction. Military rule was accompanied by violent and at times deadly factionalism and racial confrontation. For a time after the 1872 election, the state had two governors and two legislatures which even the U.S. Army could not subdue. Jonas was regarded as a key leader of the old regime by the opposition. A carpetbagger from Vermont, Marshall H. Twitchell, who would have served in the Louisiana Senate with Jonas, wrote: "In the Senate a party of newly elected extremists under the leadership of a little wizened-faced person by the name of Jonas decided they would not take the oath" written by the carpetbag regime. "Little Jonas never forgave me," Twitchell concluded.[48]

Jonas was a brilliant attorney. He became city attorney of New Orleans in 1875 and was elected to the state legislature in the tumultuous year of 1876. He served as chairman of the Judiciary Committee in 1877 and 1878 and was an ally of Governor Nicholls in his efforts to expel the Republicans from the state supreme court, framing and offering the legislative resolutions on this controversial issue. He undoubtedly helped to organize the crowd of armed citizens who went to the supreme court to "install" the newly elected justices and eject the Republican court.[49] At the height of his political power, Jonas was elected U.S. senator in 1879. No doubt many in the Louisiana legislature saw in Benjamin F. Jonas a reincarnation of Judah P. Benjamin.

Capt. Edwin W. Moise surrendered with Wade Hampton at Greensboro, North Carolina. He returned to Columbus, Georgia, but saw no future there and then moved to Sumter, South Carolina, where some of his family lived. He arrived, Harold Moise wrote, "riding a wounded horse and paid the first month's board for his family of a wife and five children from the sale of that horse." He built a law practice, went into politics, and wrote for the local newspaper. The charismatic Moise, now in his early thirties, became one of the most successful trial lawyers in the region and a noted orator as well. A physically powerful, energetic man, he was a natural leader who campaigned effectively for his many political friends. He was involved in community affairs and even represented the Episcopal Church. While he himself was a practicing Jew, he was invited to become an honorary member of the vestry, an invitation he declined.[50]

Like Jonas, Moise was a bitter opponent of the Reconstruction government. South Carolina, like Louisiana, suffered under one of the most corrupt state governments in American history. Indeed, Gov. Franklin J. Moses Jr., the son of a Jewish father (but raised as a Protestant) became known as the "Robber Governor" on account of his acceptance of bribes and misappropriation of funds. He was, wrote

Edwin Warren Moise, a South Carolina native, raised a company of men
for the Confederate army in Columbus, Georgia, where he resided. Known
as the "Moise Rangers," it was one of the few Confederate companies
named for a Jewish Confederate. A captain, Moise served with the 7th
Cavalry under Gen. Wade Hampton and was one of the commanders of
"the Great Beefsteak Raid" in 1864. After the war, he was an energetic
Hampton lieutenant in Reconstruction South Carolina and commander of
the Red Shirts. He was elected adjutant general of the state in the tumultuous 1876 election. (Courtesy of the Jacob Rader Marcus Center, American Jewish Archives, Cincinnati, Ohio.)

R. H. Woody, "the most perfect scalawag, perhaps, in all the South." Moses served
as governor in the early 1870s, and after his two-year term ended, the Republicans
would not renominate him. When he was elected a circuit judge for the Sumter
area by his cronies in the legislature, Edwin Moise, by then a well-respected Sumter
lawyer, threatened to shoot and kill Moses if he came to Sumter. (Gov. Daniel
Chamberlain refused to issue the commission, and Moses never served.) The Jewish Moses families of Sumter changed their names to DeLeon and Harby to avoid
any identification with the governor.[51]

Franklin J. Moses Jr., the "Robber Governor" of South Carolina, was the very essence of a scalawag. He is depicted here in a political carton by Thomas Nast. Despite the fact that he had been raised as a Christian, the public and the press identified him with the Jewish religion because of his name and background, and indeed Moses had many connections to the South Carolina Jewish community. (Author's collection.)

Franklin J. Moses Sr. had been a distinguished lawyer and state senator for twenty years before the war. After the war and during Reconstruction, he was elected chief justice of the South Carolina Supreme Court. Like his son, he was alienated from the white majority. But, unlike his son, he was an honest and competent jurist. "He was a man of recognized ability," Simkins and Woody wrote, "and served with distinction until his death."[52] The *News and Courier* lamented his death while deploring his connection with the Reconstruction government. "It is pleasantest to know," the Charleston paper concluded, that Judge Moses was about to rule in favor of Wade Hampton's contested election as governor, but death prevented Moses from delivering the opinion. "The act that would have blotted out the past he was not, in God's Providence, allowed to perform. From the heights, like the Hebrew lawgiver, he might look down upon the land where reigned plenteousness and peace, but he had not kept the faith, and in the flesh he might not enter in."[53]

In the dramatic election of 1876 in which the fate of Republican rule, and indeed the continuation of Reconstruction, was at stake, Moise enthusiastically supported his former commander, Wade Hampton, for governor. This campaign—which pitted Hampton's Red Shirts, a volunteer armed organization, against the Republicans led by carpetbagger Daniel H. Chamberlain—included intimidation of blacks by some and the wooing of black voters by others. Moise ran for adjutant general on Hampton's ticket and commanded the Red Shirts, who engaged in armed intimidation at times. He made numerous appearances and speeches to rally South Carolinians to elect Hampton and overthrow Republican rule. While Moise counseled moderation and nonviolence, he directed the armed might of Hampton's followers. Moise stumped the state and spoke to black audiences on behalf of Hampton's candidacy. "The only brand Wade Hampton's slaves ever wore," he exclaimed, "was the name of their master stamped on their loving hearts."[54] The office of adjutant general was especially critical in 1876 because the successful candidate would command the state's militia. The election was permeated by fraud, bribery, and intimidation. Both candidates claimed to have been elected. In fact, as had happened in Louisiana earlier, rival general assemblies existed. This time, though, the outcome was different. As part of a bargain in the disputed presidential election of 1876, Rutherford B. Hayes withdrew the last of the Federal troops from South Carolina and the Reconstruction government collapsed.

Moise was elected adjutant general and commanded the militia in a fair and evenhanded way. He was now a general. Like Hampton, Moise was a moderate on racial issues, inviting black South Carolinians to join the militia even in the racially charged atmosphere of the 1870s. Moise served a second term as adjutant general but declined reelection in 1880. He ran for Congress in 1892 but was defeated. By then, Moise had become a fierce opponent of "Pitchfork" Ben Tillman, the Populist demagogue. He retired from the law to tend his little farms near Sumter but remained active in civic affairs.[55]

Like his brother Confederate officers, Raphael Moses detested the Reconstruction regime in Georgia: "we were," he wrote, "surrounded by spies, carpetbaggers, a class of politicians, men without character who came from the North in swarms seeking whom they might devour." Columbus society, like Southern society generally, was "upheaved and the bottom turned on top by the revolution." Moses felt that his fortunes, like those of other members of the gentry, were destroyed by the war and the bitter reconstruction. "No one except one who had passed through the ordeal can realize the changes of fortune . . . [and] change of position, that takes place in a generation following a revolution."[56] Ironically, because Moses had never held elective office, he was one of the few prominent men in Muskogee County eligible to serve in the legislature under the early Reconstruction laws. He was elected to the Georgia House of Representatives and was appointed chairman of the Judiciary Committee. He was described in *The Occident* in April 1866 as the acknowledged leader of the House, "a short, heavybuilt Israelite—proud of his tribe—with raven hair . . . and dark eyes, languid in repose, but which when aroused kindle with Promethean fire. . . . Being chairman of the Committee on the Judiciary, he is often called to address the House, and never fails to command attention."[57]

Moses was regarded as an outstanding orator and a man of integrity. When the state decided to create a lottery designed, ostensibly, to fund a Confederate orphan's home, Moses opposed it because he believed it would result in corruption, and he knew and distrusted the proponents. Unable to defeat the bill, he offered an amendment at the last minute replacing all of the trustees, except the bill's proponent, with Confederate widows. He eulogized their dead husbands, and the amendment passed by an overwhelming majority. Moses took on the oversight of the lottery by acting as advisor to the widows on the board, all of whom were paid handsome salaries for the times. Eventually, Moses was able to catch the manager and his staff in corrupt practices and did his best to keep the lottery honest.[58]

Moses remained active in politics after the war, but, except for another brief term in the Georgia House in 1877, he never held another elective office, although he was a candidate for several. He was in the thick of the resistance to the Reconstruction regime in Georgia, in one instance acting as counsel for a group of young white men, the "Columbus Prisoners," accused of killing a carpetbagger politician, George W. Ashburn. When funds were raised to pay the legal fees, Moses and his fellow Columbus lawyers gave the money to the Democratic Club. (The trial was suspended and never concluded.)[59]

Moses was pugnacious when defending his religion, and, as he was both an experienced soldier (and presumably a good shot) and hot-tempered, few chose to antagonize him. Once, in the 1870s, Moses took on the case of a Jewish immigrant to Columbus named Koerneker who had saved a thousand dollars to visit his mother in Germany. He obtained a check with his cash to be used in New York. Unbeknownst to Koerneker or anyone else, the bank was in the midst of collapse, and the local bankers, who took the poor immigrant's money, knew full well the check would not be honored in New York. Koerneker had to abandon his trip. The bank went into bankruptcy. Moses fought the bankruptcy and "had no hesitancy in saying on the streets that if [the banker] had purchased a check from Koerneker, a Jewish Banker, under the same circumstances, the Jew would have been hung to a lamp post."[60]

In 1877 he was reelected to the Georgia House. In 1878, he campaigned vigorously for a candidate named Harris in the congressional race. At a campaign rally when Moses was not present, Harris's opponent, Tuggle, attacked Moses as a Jew. Moses was livid. He published an open letter to Tuggle in which he took the candidate to task: "You could not have honored me more highly, nor distinguished me more gratefully than by proclaiming me a Jew," he began. "I am proud of my lineage and my race; in your severest censure you cannot name an act of my life which dishonors either, or which would mar the character of a Christian gentleman." The letter continued: "Would you honor me? Call me a Jew. Would you place in unenviable prominence your own unchristian prejudices and narrow minded bigotry? Call me a Jew. Would you offer a living example of a man into whose educated mind toleration can not enter—on whose heart the spirit of liberty and the progress of American principles have made no impression? You can find it illustrated in yourself."[61]

Moses's finances declined after the war. Like many Southerners, he lost a fortune. He had invested money in forty-seven slaves. When the war ended, he wrote, "I had forty-seven free men. All left me except one—old London, he stayed with me until he died." His crops could not be sold. He owed money he could not repay. He had earned nothing from his law practice for years.[62]

Finally, he retired to The Esquiline, where he lived quietly with his wife, Eliza; his daughter Isabel; her husband, Lionel Levy; and their children. Moses kept in touch with his children and his grandchildren. When William Moultrie Moses died in 1879, his widow, Raphael's daughter Penina, came to live at The Esquiline with her children. Among the children was seven-year-old Stanford. Years later, when Stanford Moses entered the Naval Academy at Annapolis, Raphael Moses wrote him a long letter filled with advice. He instilled in his grandson pride in being Jewish: "You can point to your ancestry and show the wisdom of Solomon, the poetry of David, the music of Miriam and the courage of the Maccabees. Who can excel you in your past?"[63]

The greatest of the Jewish Confederates had gone to England. Judah Benjamin wrote a former colleague, Senator Bayard of Delaware, that he had arrived "on the 30th of August, nearly four months after my separation from the President, during which time I had spent twenty-three days seated in the thwart of an open boat, exposed to the tropical sun in June and July, utterly without shelter or change of clothes. I never, however, had one minute's indisposition or despondency but was rather pleased by the feeling of triumph in disappointing the malice of my enemies."[64]

Benjamin Disraeli offered to assist him. Shortly after his arrival, he visited with Sir Frederick Pollock, lord chief baron of the exchequer, and his family. When Sir Frederick's daughter asked him what the Northerners would have done to him if they had caught him, he replied that they probably would have put him to death. When the young lady exclaimed "in horror at such an atrocity, he said *apologetically* that party feelings ran so high just then that his side might have done the same, had the circumstances been reversed." The former attorney general of the Confederacy and nominee to the Supreme Court of the United States now became a law student again at age fifty-five at Lincoln's Inn. He wrote for newspapers to earn a living, and at one low point despaired of making a living. But Benjamin persevered at his first and only love of his life: the law.[65]

The English bar quickly accepted Benjamin, and he became a member of the esteemed Charles Pollock's chambers. He wrote an authoritative treatise on the law of sale of personal property, which came to be known as *Benjamin on Sales*, and gradually advanced to the front ranks of the bar. He became a queen's counsel and developed a profitable commercial and appellate law practice in the Northern Circuit, Liverpool, the port to which the South exported its prewar cotton and a city where he was well known to the business, legal, and political communities.

352   He was so successful that he eventually limited his practice to the highest courts in the land, the House of Lords and the Judicial Committee of the Privy Council. His cases involved important legal issues or substantial financial interests. He became an acknowledged expert on international commercial law. His cases involved appeals from former French colonies ceded to England, the supreme courts of Canada and New Zealand, the consular courts of Constantinople, and the court of appeals of Malta, among other exotic jurisdictions.[66]

Despite Benjamin's resolve to stay out of political matters and never look back to his former life, he was compelled in September of 1865, only months after arriving in England, to come to the defense of Jefferson Davis. The former president was being held under deplorable circumstances as a prisoner in Fort Monroe, shackled to the wall in a damp cell. His health was failing. Benjamin, outraged by this barbaric mistreatment of his former chief, wrote a long letter to the *London Times* defending Davis's record, his integrity, and his honor. He knew Davis better, he wrote, "than he is known by any other living man," and he told the readers of the *Times* (and readers in the United States, because he knew the letter would be reprinted widely), "Neither in private conversation nor in Cabinet council have I ever heard him utter one unworthy thought, one ungenerous sentiment." Davis consistently rejected any plan to inflict atrocities on the enemy, Benjamin argued. Davis, for his part, told the prison doctor that Judah Benjamin had been "the ablest and most faithful member of his advisory council."[67]

In 1868 Jefferson and Varina Davis traveled to England and spent considerable time in the company of their fellow former Confederates. Benjamin met the Davises in Paris and attended a round of parties and receptions in their honor. Benjamin helped Davis in the preparation of his memoirs, but only on the condition that he be left out of it.[68]

When at the age of seventy-two Judah Benjamin retired, the *London Times* called him "almost the leader of the English Bar in all heavy appeal cases, and 'in the widest sense of the term, an international lawyer.'" Lamenting that he was not made a judge, the *Times* noted that Benjamin had "equal authority with a standard text-book." He was so popular with the English bar that its leaders all gathered for a farewell dinner in his honor at the Inner Temple Hall in London. More than two hundred lawyers and judges, including the lord chancellor, the attorney general, the lord chief justice, the solicitor general, and other distinguished guests, came to pay tribute to one of Great Britain's greatest advocates.[69]

Benjamin remained married to Natalie, and he continued supporting her and their daughter Ninette. He gave up all of his savings to create a dowry for his daughter when she wed Henri deBousignac, a French army captain, in a Catholic ceremony in Paris. He determined to retire to Paris one day. He built a mansion there, on the Avenue d'Iena. While on a brief visit to Paris in 1880, he was severely injured as he attempted to jump off a moving trolley car, as he was used to doing

Judah P. Benjamin in his barrister's wig after the war. (Author's collection.)

thirty years earlier in New Orleans. He died at home in Paris in his mansion near the Arc de Triomphe on May 6, 1884.[70]

Solomon Benjamin, Judah's older brother, had died shortly after the war. Brother Joseph Benjamin also left the country and settled in Spanish Honduras. "And here," Robert Douthat Meade concludes, "after various vicissitudes, this cultured graduate of the University of North Carolina operated a store and plantation near Puerto Cortes." Joseph's descendants, still living in Honduras in the 1940s, are perhaps Judah P. Benjamin's nearest relatives.[71]

Benjamin never forgot the South. When he resided in England, he never claimed British citizenship, and in his application to study law at Lincoln's Inn he stated simply that his father was a merchant of Charleston, South Carolina. In his letters home, he said he could not bring himself to return to New Orleans and see firsthand the carpetbaggers in power. Toward the end of his life, he told a visitor from home: "Louisiana . . . remember me there."[72]

★

It Seems Like a Dream
As We Look Back

Remember the days of old, consider the years of many generations: ask thy father, and he will show thee; thy elders, and
they will tell thee.

Moses' song of farewell to the Israelites, Deuteronomy 32:7

Judah P. Benjamin lies buried in Père Lachaise Cemetery in Paris. The official
record card reads as follows: "BENJAMIN, Judah Philip, sénateur de la louisiane,
Jefferson DAVIS, président de la confédération le nomma ministre de la guerre
poste qu'il conserva jusqu'a la défaite des sudistes" (senator from Louisiana,
named secretary of war by Confederate President Jefferson Davis, he served until
the Southerners were defeated.) The gravesite gave no indication of who he was
until, in 1938, the United Daughters of the Confederacy, Paris chapter, placed a
plaque on his grave identifying him as attorney general, secretary of war, and secretary of state of the Confederate States of America.[1] He wanted history to forget
him. He had discouraged biographers and destroyed his papers.

The record of Judah Benjamin's burial at
Père Lachaise Cemetery in Paris. (Author's
collection.)

But people did not forget him. In 1889, Benjamin's nephew Ernest Benjamin Kruttschnitt was asked by Varina Howell Davis to serve as a pallbearer at the funeral of her husband. She had not forgotten Benjamin and wanted to honor his memory as her husband would have wished. In 1906, when Kruttschnitt died, the *New Orleans Item* editorialized, "His mother was sister of that orator, statesman and lawyer, Judah P. Benjamin, and it is the inherited qualities of his ancestors that irradiated his life."[2]

In 1911 Confederate Veterans celebrated the centennial of Benjamin's birth. In Florida in 1925, the United Daughters of the Confederacy saved from destruction the Gamble Mansion, where Benjamin had hidden out during his escape through Florida. (The house has since been deeded to the State of Florida.) In 1927 Stephen Vincent Benét published his monumental poem *John Brown's Body,* referring to Benjamin as "the dapper Jew / Seal-sleek, black-eyed, lawyer and epicure / aide, well-hated, face alive with life." In 1930 the City Council of Richmond granted approval to the Stonewall Jackson Camp, Sons of Confederate Veterans, to erect a monument to Benjamin at the intersection of Monument and Malvern Avenues "to perpetuate the character and services of the Honorable Judah P. Benjamin." In the 1930s, the Louisiana State Museum made an effort to preserve Belle Chasse but failed. In 1942 the United Daughters of the Confederacy arranged for the erection of a memorial marker in Sarasota, Florida. The governor of Florida attended the ceremony. In 1948 the two Jewish congregations of Charlotte made a gift of a monument to Benjamin on South Tryon Street (between Third and Fourth Streets) to the North Carolina Division of the UDC.[3]

Why did Judah Benjamin's memory survive? "Without a question," Rabbi Korn wrote, "he achieved greater political power than any other Jew in American history." Rabbi Calisch of Richmond explained his meaning for Southern Jews in 1902: "I stand here in the name of the Jewish community of this city. . . . Judah P. Benjamin was born of Jewish parents and reared as a Jewish child. I have not been able to discover if he was an observing Jew or not. But this I know, had he been a traitor we would have had to bear the ignominy of his wrong doing—but as he was a hero, a statesman, a gentleman and a patriot, we claim the privilege of sharing in the reflection of his glory."[4]

In 1886 Sen. Benjamin F. Jonas gave the main address at the laying of the cornerstone of the monument to the Confederate dead at Baton Rouge. Representatives of the regiments and military organizations Louisiana sent into the field were present. "Over twenty years have past since the last gun was fired in the civil war," he told his listeners, "and since the last soldier who gave his life to the cause which he espoused was gathered to his rest." Looking back to 1861, Jonas said, "the call to arms, North and South—all of these strange things passed with the rapidity

Invitation to the ceremonies laying the cornerstone of the Confederate
memorial monument in Baton Rouge, 1886. "Hon. B. F. Jonas will deliver
the oration." (Author's collection.)

of a dream, and it seems like a dream as we look back upon them after the lapse of twenty-five years." The old soldiers, now in "the afternoon of life . . . with the shadows of evening gathering," the former Confederate continued, "look back through the twenty years of trials and struggles . . . without regret over precious years wasted and sacrifices made in vain, but with feelings of melancholy satisfaction and pride over duty done." He closed on a personal note, recalling his own wartime experience: "In memory, I see again these regiments and battalions starting for the front, with music and banners and all the panoply of war, and memory brings back to me, and to all of you, the recollection of loved faces and brave hearts of many who were marching in the ranks. . . . We cannot strew flowers upon their scattered graves; we cannot mark their unknown resting places with stone or monument . . . but we erect this monument in their honor that all people in all time to come may know that the soldiers who died for the Confederate cause are not without love and honor and reverence in the land which gave them birth."[5]

One by one the old Jewish Confederates passed into history.

In 1866, Edwin Kursheedt of the Washington Artillery married "Miss Sallie" Levy of Richmond. They returned to New Orleans, where Kursheedt resumed his occupation as a merchant. He was later in the hardware business and served as assistant postmaster of New Orleans. He continued to serve in the Washington Artillery. Active in the Jewish community, he was president of the Jewish Orphan's Home and treasurer of the Touro Infirmary. Upon his death, he was buried with full military honors attended by the members of his old company. His casket was wrapped in the battle flag of the Washington Artillery.[6]

Solomon and Fanny Cohen alternated between living in New Orleans and Meridian, Mississippi, where they operated stores selling boots, shoes, saddles, and custom-made leather goods. "In both," his daughter remembered, "Solomon sat reading and studying while Fanny took care of the customers." The 1880 census shows Solomon married to Fannie, living in New Orleans with three daughters, Cecelia, Laura, and Minni, and two elderly servants, both Irish. Their descendants live in New Orleans today.[7]

The young Polish immigrant who settled in Cold Springs, Texas, Harris Kempner, returned to his general merchandising business. He had invested his funds, Jacinto County's funds, and his neighbors' funds wisely during the war. In the 1870s, Kempner

Harris Kempner of Galveston, Texas. (Courtesy of the Jacob Rader Marcus Center, American Jewish Archives, Cincinnati, Ohio.)

moved to Galveston, where he went into the wholesale grocery business. He later owned a cotton factory, a merchant bank, hotels, manufacturing plants, cotton baling plants, and interests in railroads and shipping. He was an early and enthusiastic member of the Confederate Veterans. In 1885 he organized and supported a militia unit, the Kempner Rifles. By his death in 1894, Harris "Herschell" Kempner was one of the wealthiest men in Texas.[8]

Leopold Levy returned to Richmond after the war and went into the supply and grocery business. He was one of the first members of the Robert E. Lee Camp Number One of the Confederate Veterans and became a director in the Veteran Cavalry Association of the Army of Northern Virginia. He was an early member of the Tobacco Exchange and a prominent businessman. He died in November 1897. The R. E. Lee Camp reported "the death of our beloved and esteemed comrade." His funeral took place from his residence at 15 East Marshall Street, Rabbi Calisch presiding. He was buried in the Hebrew Cemetery. Eight members of the camp were detailed to attend Levy's funeral.[9] In January 1988 the descendants of Leopold Levy were included in a commemoration of the birthday anniversaries of Robert E. Lee and "Stonewall" Jackson at the Virginia State Capitol in Richmond.[10]

Eliza Moses died in June of 1892 at the age of eighty. Raphael Moses survived her by sixteen months. In 1893 the old soldier embarked on a pleasure trip to Europe with his daughter Mathilda and her husband, Robert Samuel. He died in Brussels, Belgium. His calling card still read, "Major Raphael J. Moses, C.S.A."[11]

William Mallory Levy served in Virginia as a captain in the 2d Louisiana. The Confederate cause, he wrote his wife, "is a righteous one." He later served in Louisiana as a lieutenant colonel and adjutant under Lt. Gen. Richard Taylor. Levy was elected to Congress from Louisiana and served one term from 1875 to 1877. He later served on the Supreme Court of Louisiana. He died in Saratoga, New York, on August 18, 1882, and was buried in Natchitoches, Louisiana. (Courtesy of the Historic New Orleans Collection.)

Adolph Proskauer remained in Mobile after the war. He was active in his synagogue and served in the Alabama legislature. He moved to St. Louis in 1895, served as president of the Merchants' and Cotton Exchanges, was engaged in the life insurance business, and was active in social clubs and the Confederate Veterans Association. He died at age sixty-two in 1900 and was buried in Mount Sinai Cemetery, St. Louis. Joseph Proskauer, Adolph Proskauer's nephew, became a prominent New York lawyer, a judge, an adviser to Alfred E. Smith, and a leader in Jewish affairs.[12]

On March 28, 1878, Mayer Lehman's eighth and last child was born. He named the boy Herbert, in honor of his friend Hilary A. Herbert, colonel of the 8th Alabama, and his lawyer in Montgomery. Herbert H. Lehman, the namesake of a Confederate officer and a New Yorker, later became the first Jewish governor and a U.S. senator.[13]

Col. Henry J. Leovy, the military judge and confidant of Judah Benjamin, returned to the practice of law in New Orleans. He was the executor of the estate of William R. Hunley, the builder of the famous Confederate submarine CSS *Hunley*. Elected city attorney of New Orleans, he built a successful commercial law practice representing railroad and insurance companies.[14] He was prominent at the bar and was a partner with Judah Benjamin's nephew E. B. Kruttschnitt in the 1870s. Leovy was an exceptional lawyer. He had the confidence of the leading members of the former Confederate government and army. They may have met Leovy through Judah P. Benjamin, and with Benjamin gone, they turned to the lawyer to whom Benjamin himself had entrusted his legal affairs. Both Jefferson and Varina Howell Davis were his clients, as was Gen. Albert Sidney Johnston's son, Col. William Preston Johnston. In 1877 Johnston wrote to Leovy to ascertain the facts about General Butler's opening of his famous father's tomb on the pretext of searching for treasure. Leovy died in 1902.[15]

Octavus S. Cohen as an older man. The Cohens were a prominent Jewish family in Savannah before, during, and after the war. "Octy" Cohen served in the 32d Georgia at Morris Island and in the Battle of Olustee, Florida. (Courtesy of Bob Marcus, Springfield, Virginia.)

When Wade Hampton died in the same year, Edwin W. Moise was asked to give the oration at the memorial services in Sumter. "Wade Hampton with his latest breath," Moise told his fellow townspeople, "had given his blessing to all his people, white and black. Who here does not feel that he is richer for

Monuments to a Jewish Confederate colonel, Leon Dawson Marks, and a Jewish Union colonel, Marcus H. Spiegel, at the Vicksburg Battlefield. This is undoubtedly the only instance of monuments to Jewish colonels of the Confederate and Union armies on the same battlefield. (Courtesy of the Vicksburg National Park.)

362   blessing of so good, so great, so pure a man?" Let Harold Moise, his grandson, conclude the story of Captain Moise's life: "Eight months later in the twilight of December 12, 1902, coming out [of] a coma, his eyes unclosed to see the fading light, Hampton's faithful lieutenant uttered his last words, 'What a beautiful sunset!'"[16]

Col. Leon Dawson Marks of Shreveport was remembered at Vicksburg in 1903 when a bronze relief portrait case by Tiffany was mounted on a granite base and placed on the battlefield. It overlooks the area were Marks was mortally wounded. In 1992 the Col. Leon D. Marks Camp of the Sons of Confederate Veterans was formally chartered.[17]

Maj. Alexander Hart of the 5th Louisiana was presented with a handsome sword by the residents of New Orleans in recognition of his service during the war. He soon returned to Richmond, where he married Leonora Levy and went into business. He and Leonora had four children. They lived in Staunton for a while and then in Norfolk. Hart was active in the Confederate Veterans, serving as commander of the Pickett-Buchanan Camp in Norfolk in 1906. His family belonged to the Ohef Shalom Temple, where Hart conducted services in the absence of the rabbi. His tombstone in Norfolk reads, "Major Alexander Hart, 5th La. Inf. C.S.A."[18]

David Levy Yulee died in 1886. Fernandina suspended all business, and the church bells rang during the hour appointed for the funeral service. The *Washington Post* remembered that before the Civil War, "as Senator from Florida, he was better known than the state he represented." The *Florida Times-Union* regarded him as "by far the ablest man that Florida ever sent" to Congress. Florida has remembered its first senator in the name of Levy County, and the towns of Yulee and Levyville. The Wickliffe Madonna from Kentucky and the Father of

Maj. Alexander Hart, a native of New Orleans. Hart became major of the Louisiana 5th. He met one of Jacob A. Levy's daughters in wartime Richmond, married her, and settled in Virginia after the war. He is pictured here in 1893 as the president and minister of the Staunton, Virginia, synagogue. (Courtesy of the Jacob Rader Marcus Center, American Jewish Archives, Cincinnati, Ohio.)

Florida Statehood are buried beneath a marble angel in Oak Hill Cemetery in Georgetown in Washington, D.C. In 1939 the United Daughters of the Confederacy erected a bronze plaque at Cottonwood Plantation in honor of the "First United States Senator from Florida" and the officers who accompanied the Confederate baggage and treasure train. A great-grandson of Moses Levy, Samuel Yulee Way, was mayor of Orlando, Florida, in the 1940s. The remnants of Yulee's plantation at Homosassa are now a Florida state park, the Yulee Sugar Mill Ruins State Historic Site.[19]

Despite his heroic efforts as the religious leader of Beth Ahabah before, during, and after the war, the synagogue board declined to reelect Max Michelbacher as its minister. The reason, apparently, was Michelbacher's guttural German accent, which the board felt was not appropriate for the more acculturated English-speaking congregation. Michelbacher stayed in Richmond, remained active in the Jewish community, taught, and conducted weddings and other services. He died in 1879. In 1904 Beth Ahabah placed a stained glass window in the synagogue depicting the Eternal Light "to symbolize," Allan Creeger wrote, "the illumination which came from Michelbacher." Michelbacher's descendants are active members of Beth Ahabah today.[20]

New Orleans escaped the ravages of war. Its Jewish community prospered. Rabbi James Gutheim returned to New Orleans but left again in 1868 to officiate

Rabbi James Gutheim. This portrait of the distinguished rabbi was painted in 1884, two years before his death and long after the war. As can be seen by comparing an earlier likeness at page 249, he had come a long way from his immigrant roots. His funeral in 1886 was reputedly the largest in the Crescent City since the Civil War. (Courtesy of Louisiana State Museum.)

at Temple Emanuel in New York City. He returned to New Orleans in 1872 to become rabbi at Temple Sinai on St. Charles Avenue. In 1882 the South's most distinguished rabbi spoke to the Southern Historical Society, then meeting in New Orleans, about the history of the Lost Cause, a cause "which had enlisted the warm sympathies and active participation of our noblest, purest and ablest minds." He talked to the delegates, who included Jefferson Davis, about sectional reconciliation, citing the history of ancient Israel. "The eloquent Rabbi was loudly applauded," the minutes noted.[21] Gutheim became a venerated figure in both Jewish and Christian circles, and when he died in 1886 his funeral was reputedly the largest in the Crescent City since the Civil War. His body, guarded by young men of the synagogue, lay in state at Temple Sinai. Jewish businesses in New Orleans closed, as did the Louisiana legislature. "The funeral cortege was the largest ever seen in New Orleans," the *Israelite* reported. Rabbis came from throughout the South, as did local Christian ministers. The governor of Louisiana and the mayor of New Orleans were pallbearers. "It was," reported the *Israelite*, "the greatest demonstration of respect ever shown to a Jew in the United States."[22]

In 1869 George Jacobs left Richmond to assume the pulpit left vacant by the death of Isaac Leeser. He returned to Richmond often to visit his wife's family, the Levys, and returned in 1870 at the request of the entire Jewish community when fifty-six people were killed in the collapse of a balcony at the capitol building. He died suddenly in 1884, still in his late forties. Among the mourners were Jacob E. Hyneman and Edwin J. Kursheedt of New Orleans, who had met and smoked a peace pipe at the Levy home in Richmond in 1865.[23]

Miriam DeLeon Cohen's son, Lawrence Ludlow Cohen, the young lieutenant in the Boykin Rangers who fought for Stonewall Jackson, survived the war unhurt. In 1870, however, he was killed in a duel fought near Savannah, falling at the fourth exchange of shots. The seconds were indicted for murder, but the case was dismissed for lack of evidence. The affair, according to Perry M. DeLeon, "put an end to dueling in Georgia, so young Cohen did not die in vain."[24] It must have ended Mem Cohen's life, however, because she died soon thereafter. Her old friend Mary Chesnut lived on in sadly reduced circumstances in Camden, South Carolina, until her death in 1886. Her famous memoir was published posthumously as *A Diary from Dixie* in 1905.[25]

Thomas Cooper DeLeon lost his sight in 1903 but continued to write articles and books and attend to his many social obligations. He became known as "The Blind Laureate of the Lost Cause."[26] Edwin DeLeon remained in Europe, writing for English periodicals. He was a part of the literary world that included Dickens and Thackery. In 1881 he was involved in bringing the telephone to Egypt, and he published several books and novels, including *The Khedive's Egypt*. He died in New York in 1891 while on a lecture tour. His wife survived him by a few days.[27]

Miss Alice Kruttschnitt as Queen of Comus (Mardi Gras) in 1896. The caption on the reverse of this photograph at Tulane reads: "Miss Kruttschnitt was the daughter of John Kruttschnitt and Penina Benjamin K. (sister of Judah P. Benjamin)." (Courtesy of Howard-Tilton Library, Tulane University, New Orleans, Louisiana.)

Julius Ochs died in 1888. He was buried in Chattanooga, with members of the Grand Army of the Republic at his graveside. As he had requested, the Stars and Stripes was placed over his coffin. Bertha Levy Ochs died in 1908. She was a charter member of the A. P. Stewart Chapter of the United Daughters of the Confederacy, and members of her chapter attended the funeral. She was buried next to her husband. Bertha Ochs's coffin was, at her request, draped with the Confederate flag.[28]

Pvt. Simon Kohlman of the Point Coupee Artillery in later years. He was active in the Confederate Veterans. (Courtesy of Cecile Levine, New Orleans.)

Their son Adolph Ochs went to Chattanooga in 1877 and became a successful newspaperman. He owned and operated the *Chattanooga Times* for years and became the city's most prominent citizen. In 1896 he saw an opportunity to buy a floundering newspaper, the *New York Times*. By the early 1900s it was one of the nation's leading newspapers. In 1928 Adolph Ochs made a gift of a new temple to Congregation Mizpah in Chattanooga.[29]

Sen. Benjamin F. Jonas died in December 1911. He was buried near his brother

Graves of Solomon and Emma Solomon, Dispersed of Judah Cemetery, New Orleans. (Photograph by Susan Rosen. Author's collection.)

George in the Dispersed of Judah Cemetery on Canal Street, several miles from the French Quarter. The Solomon family remained in New Orleans. In the 1870s the family lived on Magazine Street. Their fortunes declined. Alice married in 1866. Clara married a much older man in 1866; the following year he died. Solomon Solomon died in 1874 at age fifty-eight. Clara next married Dr. George Lawrence, a former Confederate doctor, in 1872; the couple had four daughters. Clara died in New Orleans in 1907. Emma Solomon, Clara's mother, outlived her husband by almost forty years, dying in Atlanta in 1913.[30]

Alroy Jonas lived to be seventy-seven, telling one correspondent that "Time's hand has fallen gently upon me, and I have changed but little in nature or appearance since the days I wore the gray." He died in 1915, survived by two children. He is buried in Aberdeen, Mississippi. The R. E. Lee Chapter of the United Daughters of the Confederacy erected a monument to him on the Parkway in Aberdeen where James Street crosses Commerce. The inscription reads: "United Daughters of the Confederacy, In Memory of Major S. A. Jonas, Editor, Journalist, Poet." The lines of his famous poem were inscribed on the back.[31] His poem lives on. Margaret Mitchell quoted from it in *Gone with the Wind* ("Oh, how beautiful! How touching!" cried Melanie when she read it).[32]

Simon Mayer of Natchez married Emma Roos. They named their first child Robert E. Lee Mayer.[33] On January 19, 1898, the anniversary of Robert E. Lee's birthday, Simon Mayer spoke to the Confederate veterans about the Lost Cause, the honored dead "with the rest of Heaven upon their cheeks & the fire of liberty in their eyes." But time was running out for the Confederate veterans. The war had been over for more than thirty years, and the "majority of that vast army are fast joining their grand old comrades on the other shore, but what a precious legacy they can leave to their children and posterity."[34] In 1915 Herbert T. Ezekiel of the distinguished old Richmond Ezekiels gave an address to a Jewish group. (The son of a Jewish Confederate, Ezekiel good-naturedly told the group that he had no idea why "one who was not born in the United States" was asked to give the talk. Ezekiel was born in 1863 in Richmond—then in the Confederate States of America.) "Confederate Jews," he concluded, "are becoming scarce. Most of them are resting quietly in our home of the dead."[35]

Lewis Leon lived to see his *Diary of a Tar Heel Confederate Soldier* published in 1913. After the war, he returned to his job as a store clerk. He later owned his own store in Charlotte, North Carolina. He died in 1919 at the age of seventy-eight in a home for old Confederate soldiers. Isaac Hermann apparently learned to obey orders, became a pillar of his community, and rose to the rank of Captain in the Georgia militia. He died at age seventy-nine in 1917.[36] Herman Kaminski returned to Georgetown, South Carolina, where he became a highly respected businessman, owning a hardware company and a steamship company, and becoming a bank officer.[37]

Moses Ezekiel graduated from VMI in 1866, and, after consulting with Robert E. Lee, then president of Washington College, decided to pursue his dream of becoming a sculptor. "Whatever you do," Lee told the aspiring artist, "try

Sir Moses Ezekiel, Virginia's internationally renowned sculptor. After the war, with the encouragement of Robert E. Lee, then president of Washington College, Ezekiel pursued his dream of becoming a sculptor. (Courtesy of American Jewish Historical Society, Waltham, Massachusetts, and New York City.)

Moses Ezekiel's Confederate monument at Arlington National Cemetery. (Courtesy of Andrew Felber, Bethesda, Md.)

to prove to the world that if we did not succeed in our struggle, we were worthy of success." He left for Europe, where he achieved international celebrity as an artist. He later lived in Rome, was decorated by European royalty, and was knighted by the king of Italy. He never forgot that he was a Virginian and a Confederate. His works stand now in the Old Dominion: Thomas Jefferson before the Rotunda at the University of Virginia, *Virginia Mourning Her Dead* (1903) at VMI, and the monument to the Confederate War dead at Arlington National Cemetery, dedicated by Woodrow Wilson in June 1913. Ezekiel died in Rome in 1917 and was buried in his home state, at the base of his monument at Arlington. President Warren G. Harding eulogized the famous sculptor from Richmond's Jewish community as a great American and a great Virginian.[38] The simple inscription on his grave reads: "Moses J. Ezekiel, Sergeant of Company C, Battalion of Cadets of the Virginia Military Institute." "And now," the *Confederate Veteran* reported, "the eye that saw is closed, the hand that executed is still." The "soldier lad who fought so well" was lauded in foreign lands, but dying "his last request was that he might rest among his old comrades at Arlington."

Eugene Henry Levy returned to New Orleans, where he joined his father in the banking and brokerage business. In 1875 he left New Orleans and bought a sugar plantation at Vermillionville, Lafayette Parish. In 1886 he moved to New York, where he was a stockbroker. A victim of the perils of the stock market, he became a correspondent on financial matters for the *New Orleans Item* and the *Picayune.* He later opened a rare-books store on Liberty Street called the Dixie Book Shop, which served a great many Wall Street businessmen. He never missed a Confederate reunion or the meeting of the Confederate Camp, of which he was a member. His bookstore was a place where "those who were interested in the cause he loved so well could foregather and obtain the books which told of the Confederacy." He died at eighty-one and is buried at the Confederate Veterans Cemetery at Mount Hope, New York. Prior to his death in June 1921, he claimed the honor of being the only surviving private of the Confederate army.[39]

Alfred Huger Moses and Mordecai Moses of Montgomery became prominent citizens after the war. Mordecai served three terms as mayor from 1875 to 1881, and the brothers became successful businessmen, building the tallest building in Alabama in 1887, the six-story Moses Building on Court Square, near the offices of Lehman, Durr and Company.[40] By 1880, according to Kenneth Libo, "Moseses brothers was the largest real estate, insurance, and retail banking institution in the state." Alfred's daughter Adeline married Carl M. Loeb, a young man who boarded with her aunts. Their son John, Alfred's grandson, married Frances Lehman, Mayer's granddaughter, thereby joining two exceptional Jewish families from Alabama, the Moseses and the Lehmans.[41]

Philip Whitlock of Richmond died in 1919 at the age of eighty-one. His tobacco business had grown mightily since the war. He had pioneered the manufacture of inexpensive cigars, inventing and producing the "Old Virginia Cheroot." He eventually sold his company, one of the largest employers in Richmond, to the American Tobacco Company, and retired. He was buried at the Hebrew Cemetery, Rabbi Edward N. Calisch of Beth Ahabah presiding.[42]

In 1867, only two years after the war ended, Eugenia and Philip Phillips returned to Washington, where Mr. Phillips became a successful lawyer practicing before the U.S. Supreme Court. He argued hundreds of cases before that Court and published scholarly articles on the law and a treatise on the Supreme Court. Before the war, he had proposed the creation of the court of claims and is credited with being one of the fathers of that federal court.

In 1876, when Phillips wrote his memoirs, he remembered Eugenia's arrest as a noble moment: "If the imprudence of my wife brought on her these difficulties, she endured the consequences of them with a heroic spirit that could not be excelled." It also afforded Phillips amusement "to look over the letters of my daughters as I prepare this [memoir]. These two young girls of amiable disposition wrote under the excitement which then pervaded the public mind like two

370   viragos. If they could read them now they would themselves laugh heartily at their extravagant expressions. It is no less amusing to note the extravagant excitement of the Provost Marshal, who gravely endorses the tattle of these two children as 'Rank treason.'"[43] Philip Phillips died in 1884 at the age of seventy-seven. He was buried in Laurel Grove Cemetery in Savannah, Georgia, the last home of the Levy family.

Eugenia Phillips lived on in Washington, the irascible leader of the old Washington society. She had been a part of the "best" Washington society since the 1850s. One newspaper, before her death, described her as "the most remarkable of the hostesses of the old Washington regime. . . . Her brilliant sallies, caustic wit, kind and generous heart . . . have been the wonder and despair of the other social celebrities."[44] Three of her children preceded her to the grave: William Hallet, who lived with his mother, was a prominent international lawyer in Washington. He accidentally drowned several years earlier. Eugene, the Confederate navy veteran, had died in New Orleans; and Randolph had died in Savannah.

After the war, Fanny Phillips married Capt. Charles S. Hill, nephew of the wealthy banker W. W. Corcoran. (Hill had served as chief of ordnance on General Forrest's staff.)[45] Clavius Phillips married a Cohen of Savannah, and John Walker Phillips married Nellie Jonas of New Orleans, the daughter of Sen. Benjamin Franklin Jonas.[46]

Eugenia Phillips died in 1902 at the age of eighty-three, being, her daughter Caroline remembered, "the last of the old regime and the grand old ladies of the day."[47] Newspapers ran fanciful obituaries recalling her famous brushes with the Union authorities. Her famous exploits grew with time. One newspaper lamented that "Washington society has suffered a great loss by the death of Mrs. Eugenia Levy Phillips. . . . During the Civil War Mrs. Phillips acquired fame as a Confederate spy and once she slapped Gen. "Ben" Butler in the face." She was buried next to her husband in Savannah, Georgia.

Phoebe Pember returned to Georgia after the war. She was appointed, with the help of Raphael J. Moses, to the Georgia Lottery Commission. She spent many of the postwar years traveling at home and abroad and writing articles for magazines such as the *Atlantic Monthly, Harper's New Monthly Magazine,* and the *Independent.*[48] She wrote her memoir, *A Southern Woman's Story,* in the 1870s. She moved to New York and died in Pittsburgh on March 4, 1913. She is buried next to her husband in Laurel Grove Cemetery in Savannah. Maj. Gen. Jeremy F. Gilmer and Mrs. Gilmer, Phoebe's dear friend "Lou," are buried nearby.[49]

In 1995 the U.S. Postal Service issued twenty stamps commemorating the Civil War. A committee of historians chose the battles and famous persons to be depicted. Among them was Phoebe Pember, Confederate nurse. The back of the postage stamp reads: "Confederate Nurse, Phoebe Yates Levy Pember, 1823–1913, Directed care and dietary needs of over 10,000 soldiers at Richmond's Chimborazo,

one of CSA's largest hospitals. Speciality: chicken soup. Criticized poor care in her
A Southern Woman's Story."

The Straus family left Georgia after the war and moved to New York City. In the 1890s, Isidor and Nathan Straus took over R. H. Macy and Company. In 1912 Isidor Straus refused a lifeboat while women still remained on the *Titanic.* Mrs. Straus stayed with her husband, and they died at sea.[50]

Dr. Simon Baruch moved his family up North to pursue his medical career. By the early 1880s the Baruchs were living on West Fifty-seventh Street, in those days the northernmost fringe of Manhattan. Dr. Baruch soon became a prominent physician, surgeon, and public health reformer. (He once described Manhattan as a "body of land surrounded by sewage.") He wrote books on hydrotherapy and taught at Columbia University. His son Bernard grew up in New York City and became the most successful financier of his time and one of the best-known American Jews of the twentieth century. He was chairman of the War Industries Board during World War I, an adviser to Woodrow Wilson at Versailles, and a close friend of Franklin Roosevelt.[51]

Simon Baruch never forgot his Southern heritage. He was an active member of the Confederate Veterans and a frequent contributor to the *Confederate Veteran.*[52] Belle Baruch also remained a staunch Southerner, becoming a member of the United Daughters of the Confederacy. The Baruchs raised their children with pro-Southern views. If a band struck up "Dixie," no matter where he was, Dr. Baruch would jump up and give the rebel yell. Bernard recalled that as soon as the tune started, the whole family knew what was coming. "Mother would catch him by the coattails and plead, 'Shush, Doctor, shush!' But it never did any good. I have

Dr. Simon Baruch as an older man. (Courtesy of American Jewish Historical Society, Waltham, Massachusetts, and New York City.)

seen Father, ordinarily a model of reserve and dignity, leap up in the Metropolitan Opera House and let loose that piercing yell."[53] Dr. Baruch died in New York on June 3, 1921.

★   ★   ★

In the 1890s, the few remaining old Southern Jewish families still revered their Confederate ancestors and joined the Sons of Confederate Veterans and the United Daughters of the Confederacy. Joseph Proskauer wrote in *Boyhood in Mobile* of his veneration for his Uncle Adolph. "My grandmother's attic was a storehouse of worthless Confederate bills," he recalled. "[M]y uncle's partner, Leopold Straus, was known as 'Johnny' because he had been a fighting Johnny Reb. . . . Until my entrance into college in 1892 I was never quite sure that a 'Yankee' could be anything but damned."[54]

Irene Goldsmith was born in 1868 in Charleston, the daughter of Abraham A. Goldsmith, who had been seriously wounded at Antietam. Four Goldsmith boys had fought in the war. Her mother's only brother, Alexander Hilzheim, was killed at Kennesaw Mountain during Sherman's campaign against Atlanta. His body was

The leadership of the South Carolina division of the United Daughters of the Confederacy. President Irene Goldsmith Kohn, wearing a dark hat, is standing at the far left of the five women in the very front row. (Courtesy of Julian Hennig Jr., Columbia, South Carolina.)

never recovered, but his name is inscribed on a monument in the Coming Street
Cemetery, "A victim at 18 years to the horrors of war." In her application to the
Wade Hampton Chapter of the United Daughters of the Confederacy, she noted
that she had four uncles in Confederate service as well as her father. After marrying August Kohn, Corporal Theodore Kohn's son, in 1894 at Beth Elohim, the
couple moved to Columbia, where they helped organize a new congregation, Tree
of Life. Irene Kohn, like Joseph Proskauer, also revered her Confederate relatives, and in the 1890s became a charter member of the UDC. In 1909 she was
elected president of the South Carolina Division, believing that the war reflected
the "sacrifice, devotion to duty, courage, and struggle for conviction" of Confederate soldiers. "In honoring our sires and their patriotism," she wrote, "we honor
ourselves."[55]

In the 1880s Alexander III, the czar of Russia, began a campaign of terror
against the Jews of his empire. His pogroms and anti-Semitic brutality drove hundreds of thousands and then millions of poor Russian, Polish, and Ukranian Jews
to America, that "fabled land of freedom" that the German Jews had sought fifty
years before. By the early twentieth century, these immigrants, like the wave of
German Jewish immigrants before them, had overwhelmed the American Jewish
community. Like a great ship passing a small boat in a foggy night, the wave of Jewish immigrants from Russia and Eastern Europe came to the South and founded
their own communities and institutions. Many never knew the Jewish families in
their own cities and towns who had fought and died for the Confederacy.

The old congregations were gradually taken over by the newcomers, who
knew little or nothing about Robert E. Lee, Jefferson F. Davis, Judah P. Benjamin,
Henry M. Hyams, Edwin W. Moise, or Benjamin Franklin Jonas. Nor did they
share the communal loss of Joshua L. Moses, Isaac Levy, Albert Luria, Isaac Valentine, Gustavus Poznanski Jr., Joseph Calhoun Levy, or Leon Marks. They knew little or nothing of the sacrifices made on their behalf on the battlefields of Shiloh
and Antietam, Vicksburg, Gettysburg, Cold Harbor, or Atlanta. Indeed, the Confederate War, as their Southern neighbors then called it, was as remote to them as
Joshua at the Battle of Jericho. And as the years passed and the Confederate War
receded into memory for all Southerners, the Jewish Confederates, many of their
descendants no longer members of the ancient faith, disappeared from the communal memory of Southern Jewry. Theirs was a lost world as well as a lost cause.

Little remains of the Jewish Confederate South. Both of Richmond's ante-
bellum synagogues, Beth Ahabah on Eleventh Street and Beth Shalome on Mayo
Street, are gone, as are many of the Jewish homes and shops that crowded Main
Street in the 1860s, victims of "progress" and Richmond's urban growth. In 1891
Beth Shalome Synagogue was sold to a newly organized Russian congregation and

Lt. Joshua Lazarus Moses, Company C, 3d (Palmetto) Battalion, South Carolina Light Artillery. (Painting courtesy of Robert Moses, Sumter, S.C.).

was demolished in 1935.[56] All of New Orleans's antebellum synagogues are gone as well, and for the same reason. The old commercial district near Canal Street has been rebuilt. Belle Chasse was demolished. Judah Benjamin's law office is no more, nor is Frank Jonas's. Clara Solomon's house is gone, and the neighborhood has fallen into decay. The Jackson Street synagogue has been sold, is now boarded up, and is in danger of destruction.

Octavus Cohen's home on Lafayette Square in Savannah, where his daughter excoriated the Yankee invaders, has been replaced by a condominium. Shearith Israel in Charleston was torn down.

Yet some remnants of the Southern Israelites still survive: the Hebrew Cemetery on Shockoe Hill in Richmond; Moses Cohen Mordecai's house and Phoebe Pember's childhood home in Charleston; the Solomon Cohen house and the Minis house in Savannah, where Robert E. Lee was charmed by Sarah and Phillipa Minis. And Kahal Kadosh Beth Elohim—where Gustavus Poznanski promised that the sons of Jewish South Carolinians would defend their temple, their city, and their land—still stands on Hasell Street in Charleston, facing east toward Jerusalem.

★ ★ ★

Gates of Prayer, then and now. The Jackson Street Synagogue in New
Orleans just after the war and today. (Courtesy of Touro Infirmary
Archives, New Orleans, Louisiana; Photograph by Susan Rosen.)

The Hebrew Cemetery, Confederate Section, at Shockoe Hill, Richmond.
(Courtesy of Beth Ahabah Museum and Archives, Richmond, Virginia.)

The home of Moses Cohen Mordecai on Meeting Street in Charleston today. (Author's collection, courtesy of Robert and Susan Prenner. Photograph by Michael Levkoff.)

The home of Solomon Cohen at Barnard and Liberty in Savannah today. (Author's collection. Photograph by Michael Levkoff.)

Monument to Marx E. Cohen Jr. at the Coming Street Cemetery, Charleston, South Carolina. The two flags are the South Carolina flag and the Confederate battle flag. (Author's collection. Photograph by Michael Levkoff.)

(Left) Mikve Israel in Savannah, built after the war in 1875. (Author's collection. Photograph by Michael Levkoff.)

Robert E. Lee. This Mathew Brady photograph was taken one week after the surrender. Jewish Confederates continued to venerate Lee. They even named their children for him: "Throughout the Southland today," Simon Mayer of Natchez told his fellow veterans in 1898, "the birth of the immortal Lee is being celebrated." "I was brought up to believe that Robert E. Lee was the epitome of all virtues," Bernard Baruch wrote. "Father often quoted a maxim of Lee's as a guide to my own conduct: 'Do your duty in all things. You could not do more. You would not wish to do less.'" (Courtesy of Mathew Brady Collection, Prints and Photos Division, Library of Congress.)

NOTES

★

PREFACE

1. There are two people named Edwin Warren Moise in this work. One was born in Charleston in 1811 and lived in Louisiana; the other was born in Charleston in 1832 and lived in Columbus, Georgia, at the beginning of the war and in Sumter, South Carolina, afterward. Harold Moise, *The Moise Family of South Carolina and Their Descendants* (Columbia, S.C.: R. L. Bryan, 1961), 48–50, 83–126.

2. Bertram W. Korn, preface to paperback edition to *American Jewry and the Civil War*, 2d ed. (Cleveland and New York: Meridian Books/World Publishing, and Philadelphia: JPSA, 1961), xx–xxi.

3. Lawrence Fuchs, "Introduction," *AJHQ* 66, no. 2 (December 1976): 187.

4. Nathaniel Weyl, *The Jew in American Politics* (New Rochelle, N.Y.: Arlington House, 1968), 54–55. Many Jewish historians, reflecting their own beliefs and preconceived notions and reading history from the present to the past, cannot bring themselves to believe that Jews voluntarily fought for the Confederacy. Typical of this disbelief is Jordan Schwarz in *The Speculator: Bernard M. Baruch in Washington, 1917–1965* (Chapel Hill: University of North Carolina Press, 1981). Simon Baruch, Bernard's father, Schwarz writes, "feeling the social pressure of watching other Camden men enlist for the Southern cause . . . became a Confederate army medical officer" (11). Baruch was, however, one of the most ardent of the Jewish Confederates. He was active in Confederate Veteran affairs even after he moved to New York after the war.

5. See, for example, Thomas Cahill, *The Gifts of the Jews* (New York: Nan A. Talese/Doubleday, 1998), 120–22, 154.

6. Tony Horwitz, *Confederates in the Attic: Dispatches from the Unfinished Civil War* (New York: Pantheon Books, 1998), 63.

7. See chapter 1 below for a discussion of the motivation of Jewish Confederates. The literature on the causes of the Civil War is immense. See the following for an introduction: Allan Nevins, *The Emergence of Lincoln: Prologue to Civil War, 1859–1861* (New York: Scribner's, 1950), chap. 11; David M. Potter, *The Impending Crisis, 1848–1861* (New York: Harper & Row, 1976); and Potter, *The South and the Sectional Conflict* (Baton Rouge: Louisiana State University Press, 1968). The best single explanation of the relationship between the war and slavery is a minor classic, Charles E. Cauthen's *South Carolina Goes to War, 1860–1865* (Chapel Hill: University of North Carolina Press, 1950), chap. 5 ("Much has been written on the causes of secession, but one who reads the contemporary literature can have no doubt of the fundamental issue in South Carolina" [71]).

8. On the history of early anti-Semitism and Judeophobia, see Klaus Fischer's excellent work, *The History of an Obsession: German Judeophobia and the Holocaust* (New York: Continuum, 1998), chaps. 1 and 2. (Anti-Semitic pamphlets in Germany in the eighteenth and nineteenth centuries claimed that Jews "belonged to an absolutely different nation" [46].) Benjamin F. Perry, quoted in Lewis Jones, *South Carolina: A Synoptic History for*

380   *Laymen* (Lexington, S.C.: Sandlapper Press, 1978), 169. On Lee's actions and opinions on slavery, see Douglass Southall Freeman, *R. E. Lee* (New York: Scribner, 1934), 4:400–401.

9. Lee quote, Freeman, *R. E. Lee*, 4:401.

10. Rabbi Saul Jacob Rubin, *Third to None: The Saga of Savannah Jewry, 1733–1983* (Savannah: Congregation Mikve Israel, 1983), 68.

PROLOGUE

1. Gene Waddell, "An Architectural History of Kahal Kadosh Beth Elohim, Charleston," *South Carolina Historical Magazine* 98, no. 1 (January 1997): 6–55, *Charleston Daily Courier* quote, 55; Solomon Breibart, "The Rev. Mr. Gustavus Poznanski: First American Jewish Reform Minister," paper delivered at Congregation Beth Elohim on the 100th anniversary of Reverend Poznanski's death, College of Charleston, January 19, 1979. James W. Hagy, *This Happy Land: The Jews of Colonial and Antebellum Charleston* (Tuscaloosa: University of Alabama Press, 1993), 236–39. "Kahal Kadosh" (Holy Congregation), traditionally the first two words of all early Sephardic congregations, is usually abbreviated "K. K.," as in K. K. Beth Elohim.

2. Barnett A. Elzas, *The Jews of South Carolina from the Earliest Times to the Present Day* (Philadelphia: J. B. Lippincott Co., 1905; reprint, Spartanburg, S.C.: Reprint Co., 1983), chap. 12; Charles Reznikoff and Uriah Z. Engelman, *The Jews of Charleston: A History of an American Jewish Community* (Philadelphia: JPSA, 1950), 157–60; Compiled service record (CSR), Gustavus Poznanski Jr.

3. Raphael J. Moses, *Last Order of the Lost Cause—The Civil War Memoirs of a Jewish Family from the "Old South,"* edited by Mel Young (Lanham, Md.: University Press of America, 1995), 94–101. The Columbus Light Guards became a part of Wright's brigade in November 1862.

4. Moses, *Last Order*, 98.

5. Ibid., xv, 111, 94.

6. Ibid., 162–63.

7. C. Vann Woodward, ed., *Mary Chesnut's Civil War* (New Haven: Yale University Press, 1981), 378.

8. Moses, *Last Order*, 165–66.

9. The *Charleston Mercury*, June 10, 1862. For the *Charleston Daily Courier*, see Mel Young, *Where They Lie Someone Should Say Kaddish* (Lanham, Md.: University Press of America, 1991), 40.

CHAPTER 1

1. Sermon, November 29, 1860, James K. Gutheim, Manuscript Collection, No. 224, AJA, 23.

2. Abraham Barkai, *Branching Out: German-Jewish Immigration to the United States 1820–1914* (New York: Holmes & Meier, 1994), passim; Hasia R. Diner, *A Time for Gathering: The Second Migration, 1820–1880* (Baltimore: Johns Hopkins University Press, 1992), 9.

3. Naomi W. Cohen, *Encounter with Emancipation: The German Jews in the United States, 1830–1914* (Philadelphia: JPSA, 1984), 11.

4. Sermon, November 29, 1860, J. K. Gutheim Manuscript Collection, No. 224, AJA.

5. Cohen, *Encounter*, 11.

6. Ibid., 13.

7. "Both sides in the American Civil War professed to be fighting for freedom," James M. McPherson wrote in *Battle Cry of Freedom* (New York: Oxford University Press, 1988). Jefferson Davis exclaimed in 1863 that the South was "forced to take up arms to vindicate the political rights, the freedom, equality, and State sovereignty which were the heritage purchased by the blood of our revolutionary sires" (vii).

8. Benjamin's farewell speech is described by all of his biographers. See Pierce Butler, *Judah Benjamin* (Philadelphia: W. G. Jacobs & Co., 1907), 205–13; Robert Douthat Meade, *Judah P. Benjamin: Confederate Statesman* (London: Oxford University Press, 1943), 152–55; Eli N. Evans, *Judah Benjamin: The Jewish Confederate* (New York: Free Press, 1988), 109–12 (Mrs. Davis's quote).

9. Meade, *Judah P. Benjamin*, 116.

10. Thompson, "David Yulee," 494; Joseph G. Adler, "The Public Career of Senator David Levy Yulee" (Ph.D. diss., Case Western Reserve University, 1973), 160.

11. Davis, *A Government,* 223.

12. Malcolm M. Stern, *Americans of Jewish Descent* (Reprint, New York: KTAV Publishing House, 1971); Walter E. Burke Jr., *Quartermaster: A Brief Account of the Life of Colonel Abraham Charles Myers, Quartermaster General C.S.A.* (February 14, 1976), 24 (copy in possession of author and available from the city of Fort Myers and the Fort Myers Historical Museum).

13. Louis Schmier, "Georgia History in Pictures. This 'New Canaan': The Jewish Experience in Georgia," *Georgia Historical Quarterly* 73, no. 4, pt. 2 (winter 1989): 820 (Cohen quote); Isaac Hermann, *Memoirs of a Veteran Who Served as a Private in the 60s in the War between the States, Personal Incidents, Experiences, and Observations* (Atlanta: Byrd Printing Co., 1911), 192–93. Hermann's CSR; see also chapter 3 below.

14. See CSRs of Kaminski, Emanuel, the Levy brothers, and Proskauer. As to Leon, see his CSR and his memoir, *Diary of a Tar Heel Confederate Soldier* (Charlotte: Stone Publishing Co., 1913); Morris U. Schappes, ed., *Documentary History of the Jews in the United States, 1654–1875*, rev. ed. (New York: Citadel Press, 1952), 709n. 17; Herbert Ezekiel and Gaston Lichtenstein, *The History of the Jews of Richmond from 1769 to 1917* (Richmond: Herbert Ezekiel, 1917), 161. As to Kempner, see Harold M. Hyman, *Oleander Odyssey: The Kempners of Galveston, Texas, 1854–1980s* (College Station: Texas A & M University Press, 1990), chap. 1.

15. Ezekiel and Lichtenstein, *The History of the Jews*, 148–93; Myron Berman, *Richmond's Jewry, 1769–1976: Shabbat in Shockoe* (Charlottesville: University Press of Virginia, 1979), 175–77; John H. Neblett and Roberta C. Neblett, "Emanuel Gerst—A Gentleman of Virginia," *Generations: Journal of Congregation Beth Ahabah Museum and Archives Trust* 5, no. 1 (November 1992); Louis Ginsberg, *History of the Jews of Petersburg, 1789–1950* (Petersburg, Va.: privately printed, 1954), 42–56; Allan Schoener, *The American Jewish Album: 1654 to the Present* (New York: Rizzoli, 1983), Guggenheimer on 44–45.

16. Yates Levy to J. C. Levy, March 16, 1865, Phillips-Myers Papers, # 596, UNC.

17. Elzas, *Jews of South Carolina,* 18–19; Richard Gergel of Columbia pointed out to the author that South Carolina's constitution was the first to guarantee freedom of religion to the Jews.

18. Hagy, *This Happy Land,* 9, 34–36; Elzas, *Jews of South Carolina,* 68–77; Leonard Dinnerstein, *Anti-Semitism in America* (New York: Oxford University Press, 1994), 6.

19. Abram V. Goodman, "South Carolina: From Shaftesbury to Salvador," in Leonard Dinnerstein and Mary Dale Palsson, eds., *Jews in the South* (Baton Rouge: Louisiana State University Press, 1973); Ira Rosenwaike, "The Jewish Population of the United States as Estimated from the Census of 1820," *AJHQ* 53, no. 2 (December 1963): 131–49; Rev. Isaac Leeser, "The Jews in the United States—1848," *AJA* 7, no. 1 (January 1955): 82–84; Uriah Z. Engelman, "Jewish Statistics in the U.S. Census of Religious Bodies (1850–1936)," *Jewish Social Studies* 9 (1947): 127–32.

20. Rubin, *Third to None*, 1–25; Berman, *Richmond's Jewry*, chap. 1;, Melvin I. Urofsky, *Commonwealth and Community: The Jewish Experience in Virginia* (Richmond: Virginia Historical Society and Jewish Community Federation of Richmond, 1997), 1–16, 30, 36, 55.

21. Eli Faber, *A Time for Planting: The First Migration, 1654–1820* (Baltimore: Johns Hopkins University Press, 1992), 127–28.

22. Samuel Proctor, "Jewish Life in New Orleans 1718–1860," *Louisiana Historical Quarterly* 40 (1957): 110–32.

23. Korn, *American Jewry and the Civil War,* 15–31, and *Jews and Negro Slavery in the Old South, 1789–1865* (Elkins Park, Pa.: Reform Congregation Kenesseth Israel, 1961), published also as a chapter entitled "Jews and Negro Slavery in the Old South, 1789–1865," in Leonard Dinnerstein and Mary Dale Palsson, eds., *Jews in the South* (Baton Rouge: Louisiana State University Press, 1973), 89–134; Hagy, *This Happy Land,* 93; Barkai, *Branching Out,* 109–11.

The 1850 census, which records all slaveholders and the number of slaves they owned, gives the names of 51 Jewish Charlestonians who owned a total of 288 slaves. Twelve Jewish Charlestonians owned 10 slaves or more. David Lopez owned 14, and, as he was a builder, he likely employed his slaves in construction work. Abraham Ottolengui owned 13, Hannah Myers, 15, and Morris Goldsmith, 16. There were approximately 500 Jews living in Charleston in 1850. In the same year, there were 3,441 free blacks in Charleston, of whom 266 owned 1,087 slaves, more than three times the number owned by Charleston Jewry. Some free blacks, like Louisa R. DaCosta and William Penceel, owned a substantial number of slaves. "Indeed, so widespread was black slaveholding in the City of Charleston," Larry Koger wrote, "that the majority of free black heads of household owned slaves from 1820 to 1840." See Larry Koger, *Black Slaveowners: Free Black Slavemasters in South Carolina, 1790–1860* (Jefferson, N.C.: McFarland & Co., 1985), 23; Bernard E. Powers Jr., *Black Charlestonians: A Social History, 1822–1885* (Fayetteville: University of Arkansas Press, 1994); Hagy, *This Happy Land,* 91–93. See also Michael Johnson and James L. Roark, *Black Masters: A Free Family of Color in the Old South* (New York: W. W. Norton & Co., 1984); and Michael Johnson and James L. Roark, ed., *No Chariot Let Down: Charleston's Free People of Color on the Eve of the Civil War* (Chapel Hill: University of North Carolina Press, 1984). A Northern visitor to Charleston noted that "a number [of blacks] are free and own slaves themselves. This may seem strange to many Northern people, especially to that class who cannot understand nor appreciate that system of labor known as slave labor" (Koger, *Black Slaveowners,* 23). Both the free black and Jewish slave owners of Charleston utilized slaves as domestic servants, as artisans, and in small commercial and manufacturing businesses. Many free blacks were engaged in the garment trade and utilized slave labor to sew and make clothes. Jewish Charlestonians sold clothing and dry goods, and it is possible there was an economic tie between the two antebellum minority communities. Mark Greenberg points out that the Jews of Savannah generally utilized slaves as domestics or hired them out. Henry and Isaac Meinhard put most of their sixteen slaves to work in their wholesale dry goods business. Solomon Cohen and Dinah Minis, the largest Jewish slaveholders in the city, with 23 and 18, respectively, hired most of them out. (Greenberg, "Becoming Southern," 61).

For a discussion of the minor role played by Jews in the slave trade in the colonial era, see Eli Faber, *Jews, Slaves and the Slave Trade* (New York: New York University Press, 1998).

24. Greenberg, "Becoming Southern," 57–58 and passim.

25. Richard C. Wade, *Slavery in the Cities: The South, 1820–1860* (Oxford: Oxford University Press, 1964), 20, appendix and passim; Robert N. Rosen, *A Short History of Charleston* (Columbia: University South Carolina Press, 1997), 67–79.

26. Korn, "Jews and Negro Slavery," 111–13. He was apparently a kindly master. After the war, his former slave came with his family to Philadelphia. See Korn, *American Jewry,* 29.

27. Korn, *American Jewry,* 29; Berman, *Richmond Jewry,* 163, 166. Frederick Law Olmsted described blacks in Richmond wearing "the cast-off clothes of the white people . . . purchased of the Jews, whose shops show that there must be considerable importation of such articles, probably from the North." Olmsted, who was blatantly anti-Semitic, wrote that Jews in the South engaged in "an unlawful trade with the simple Negroes, which is found very profitable" (Korn, *American Jewry,* 104). The Ezekiels operated a dry goods store in Richmond, which Moses Ezekiel recalled "was filled with Negro clothing [including] ready-made dresses of all sizes." Moses's grandparents, the store owners, "were monopolists in the sense that every Negro who was brought to Richmond from the South to be sold at auction was, on the morning of the sale, brought to our store to be dressed" (Zebulon Vance Hooker II, "Moses Jacob Ezekiel—The Formative Years," *Virginia Historical Magazine* 60 [April 1952]: 241–54, 243).

28. Barkai, *Branching Out,* 1–31; I. J. Benjamin, *Three Years in America, 1859–1862,* edited by Oscar Handlin and translated from the German by Charles Reznikoff (Philadelphia: JPSA, 1956), 1:75. The history of German Jewry is rich and complicated. See Michael A. Meyer, ed., *German-Jewish History in Modern Times,* 4 vols. (New York: Columbia University Press, 1996–1998).

29. Barkai, *Branching Out,* 93–94; Malcolm M. Stern, "Preface," *Americans of Jewish Descent* (New York: reprint KTAV Publishing House, 1971). Ironically, American German Jews were proud of their German heritage, culture, and language. One writer observed that "nowhere [exists] a truer tribe for Germany than in the Jews. . . . On the prairies of America we hear the Jew speaking German; he carries the German fatherland along everywhere and can never leave it" (Howard M. Sacher, *A History of the Jews in America* [New York: Alfred A. Knopf, 1992], 61). Hasia Diner points out in *A Time for Gathering* that many so-called German Jews actually came from Poznań (Posen) or Silesia, which were part of Poland annexed by Prussia. Joseph Proskauer always said his parents were German, but they actually came from Hungary and Breslau in Silesia. German ancestry was clearly more prestigious than Polish ancestry (see pp. 9, 49–50). In her autobiography, Kitty Carlisle Hart said that her mother, who was born in Shreveport, falsely claimed that her family came from Alsace-Lorraine "because she thought it was more exotic. (She would have preferred France, but since [her father's] name was Holtzman, Alsace was as near as she dared get.)"

384 *Kitty: An Autobiography* (New York: Doubleday, 1988), 3. It seems her mother and father both tended to exaggerate a bit. Her grandfather Holtzman claimed to have been a gunner on the *Merrimack,* to have sold a tie to President Lincoln after the war, and to have been at Ford's Theater when Lincoln was shot. Kitty Hart's father did, however, marry Stella Baer (pronounced "Barr"), the daughter of Max Baer, who signed the pro-Confederate letter of the Shreveport congregation, which denounced *The Jewish Messenger.* For a detailed history of nineteenth-century anti-Semitism in Germany, see Klaus Fischer, *The History of an Obsession: German Judeophobia and the Holocaust* (New York: Continuum Publishing Co., 1998).

30. Marcus, *United States Jewry, 1776–1985,* 4 vols. (Detroit: Wayne State University Press, 1989–93), 3:14–15.

31. Reznikoff and Engelman, *Jews of Charleston,* 148, 208; Jacob Rader Marcus, *To Count a People: American Jewish Population Data, 1585–1984* (Lanham, Md.: University Press of America, 1990), 208, 204; Ford's Census, Charleston, 1860, South Carolina Historical Society, Charleston. The condescending attitude of the Jewish elite at Beth Elohim and elsewhere toward the newer Polish immigrants is reflected in a statistical report of Jewish congregations that dismissed Berith Shalome as "a Polish congregation . . . numbering a few foreigners" (Reznikoff and Engelman, *Jews of Charleston,* 148). In 1905 Rabbi Elzas wrote that Charleston had "a Polish congregation," but it had "no history, communal or otherwise, worth recording" (Elzas, *Jews of South Carolina,* 261n. 1). Solomon Breibart has pointed out that Berith Shalome was the first Ashkenazi congregation in the South. Belinda Gergel and Richard Gergel, *In Pursuit of the Tree of Life: A History of the Early Jews of Columbia, South Carolina, and the Tree of Life Congregation* (Columbia, S.C.: Tree of Life Congregation, 1996), 8–34.

32. Marcus, *To Count a People,* 204–5; Steinberg, *United for Worship and Charity: A History of Congregation Children of Israel* (Augusta, Ga.: privately printed, 1982). The demographics of this era is a maddening subject. Modern historians still rely on contemporary estimates of the Jewish population made by the eminent rabbi and editor Isaac Leeser of Philadelphia. Steven Hertzberg, in *Strangers within the Gate City: The Jews of Atlanta, 1845–1915* (Philadelphia: JPSA, 1978), claims that some of Leeser's estimates "may have been high" (281n. 18). Elliott Ashkenazi in *The Business of Jews in Louisiana, 1840–1875* (Tuscaloosa: University of Alabama Press, 1988), states that Leeser's figures "are little more than estimates, and I believe that they err on the low side" (183n. 15). Jacob Rader Marcus, in *To Count a People,* continues to give Leeser's estimates as the only information available. Like Hertzberg and Ashkenazi (in the "absence of more concrete data"), I have accepted Leeser's numbers as estimates, but like Ashkenazi, I believe them to be low.

33. Joseph B. Mahan, *Columbus: Georgia's Fall Line "Trading Town"* (Northridge, Calif.: Windsor Publications, 1986), 48.

34. Rabbi Newton J. Friedman, "A History of Temple Beth Israel of Macon, Georgia" (Ph.D. diss., Burton College and Seminary, 1955), 11–25.

35. Hertzberg, *Strangers within the Gate City,* 10–18; interview with Jacob Haas, Atlanta; Franklin M. Garrett, *Atlanta and Environs: A Chronicle of Its People and Events,* reprint, 3 vols. (Athens: University of Georgia Press, 1969–1987; originally published New York: Lewis Historical Publishing Co., 1954), 1:214–55. Apparently, Sarah was pro-Union. The family recorded a story that after the battle on the Columbus bridge on April 16, 1865, friends ran to her to compliment her on a conspicuous act of courage of her son, Julius M. Alexander. She is said to have replied, "Pity it was not done in a better cause" (Henry Aaron

Alexander, *Notes on the Alexander Family of South Carolina and Georgia and Connections* 385
[privately printed, 1954], Atlanta Jewish Federation Archives and CC, 59).

36. *Pittsburgh Evening Leader,* Merz file, Pittsburgh, March 31, 1875, AJA; Fannie Herzberg, "Pioneer Members and History of Temple Beth-El, 1859–1959," *Chattahoochee Valley Historical Society Bulletin,* November 1959 (reprinted in the *Newsletter of the Southern Jewish Historical Society*).

37. The Moses family were prominent, prosperous, and cosmopolitan for the place and times. When Hannah, a Moses daughter, married Isaac I. Moses, the Moseses had a large wedding with more than three hundred guests, thirty of whom spent the night at the plantation. Moses's children visited relatives and friends in South Carolina and Pennsylvania. One daughter, Penina, met the famous rabbi Dr. Isaac Leeser on a visit to Philadelphia. She was expecting her brother, Lea, when Rabbi Leeser arrived. "I rushed to the door," she later recalled, "and finding my mistake was much embarrassed and said 'Oh! I thought you were Lea, sir' to which he laughingly replied 'It is Lee—ser'" (Moses, *Last Order,* 70–82).

38. Isaac Wheeler Avery, *The History of the State of Georgia* (1881; reprinted New York: AMS Press, 1972), 155–56.

39. Berman, *Richmond's Jewry,* 10, 36–50; *Second Annual Directory for the City of Richmond* (1860), microfilm, VSL.

40. Urofsky, *Commonwealth,* 63–65; *Our First Century and a Quarter, 1844–1969,* a history of Ohef Sholom Temple by Elise Levy Margolius (privately printed, 1970). My thanks to Jennifer Gregory Priest, Ohef Sholom's archivist, for her kind assistance in sending me this work. *Hazzan* is Hebrew for cantor. In the nineteenth century, hazzan sometimes meant "reader" as well as "cantor." It even meant "rabbi" at times, because there were few ordained rabbis.

41. *The Oxford Dictionary of the Jewish Religion,* 440; *Washington Daily National Intelligencer,* August 27, 1861, front page, quoting the *Richmond Enquirer.* The *Enquirer* pointed out that *Manassa* and *Manassas* were both corruptions of *Manasseh.* In 1991 the town of Manassas debated the question of whether or not it was named for a Jewish innkeeper or an Indian (Native American). Although there was little or no evidence for the Indian origin, in the interest of political correctness, the town put up a marker saying it could be either (*Washington Jewish News,* December 5, 1991).

42. Marcus, *To Count a People,* 204–5; Urofsky, *Commonwealth,* 79.

43. Moses, "Jews of Mobile," 120, 121–22; Robert J. Zietz, *The Gates of Heaven, Congregation Sha'arai Shomayim: The First 150 Years, Mobile, Alabama, 1844–1994* (Mobile: Congregation Sha'arai Shomayim, 1994), 11–33.

44. Elliot Ashkenazi, *A Centennial, Lehman Brothers, 1850–1950* (New York: Lehman Brothers, 1950); Harry's name change courtesy of Kenneth Libo; Cotton quote in Harriet E. Amos, *Cotton City: Urban Development in Antebellum Mobile* (Tuscaloosa: University of Alabama Press, 1985), xiii. On Civil War Montgomery, see William W. Rogers, Jr., *Confederate Homefront: Montgomery during the Civil War* (Tuscaloosa: University of Alabama Press, 1999).

45. Allan Nevins, *Herbert H. Lehman and His Era* (New York: Charles Scribner's Sons, 1963), 7–8.

46. Leo E. Turitz and Evelyn Turitz, *Jews in Early Mississippi* (Jackson: University Press of Mississippi, [1983]), 12, 18, 35–36, 43, 121; Carolyn Gray LeMaster, *A Corner of the Tapestry: A History of the Jewish Experience in Arkansas, 1820s–1990s* (Fayetteville: University of Arkansas Press, 1994), 7; Clara L. Moses, *Aunt Sister's Book* (New York: privately printed, 1929), 2–3.

47. William Howard Russell, *My Diary North and South* (Boston, 1863), 242.

48. Marcus, *Memoirs*, 3:104.

49. Ashkenazi, *Business of Jews*, 9–11, citing Hertzberg, *Strangers within the Gate City* (see note 49); Wade, *Slavery in the Cities*, appendix ("Population of Major Southern Cities, 1820–1860"). Norfolk's population was 14,620.

50. Eric Brock, preface to "The Jewish Cemeteries of Shreveport, La." (privately printed, 1995); Proctor, "Jewish Life," 123. Rabbi Max Heller states in "Jubilee Souvenir of Temple Sinai, 1872–1922" (New Orleans: Temple Sinai, 1922) that the second Touro synagogue was opened in 1857 on Carondelet near Julia. Cathy Kahn says 218 (old numbering system) Carondelet, river side, between Julia and St. Joseph (letter to author).

51. Bobbie Malone, "New Orleans Uptown Jewish Immigrants: The Community of Congregation Gates of Prayer, 1850–1860," *Louisiana History* 32, no. 3 (summer 1991): 239–65; Proctor, "Jewish Life," 126; Malone, "New Orleans Uptown," 242–56.

52. Ashkenazi, *Diary of Clara Solomon*, 1–4, 142, illustrations and captions between pages 342 and 344. Drew Gilpin Faust describes the Solomons in *Mothers of Invention: Women of the Slaveholding South in the American Civil War* (Chapel Hill: University of North Carolina Press, 1996). Indeed, the title of her book is taken from Clara's diary ("Necessity & war is the mother of invention," *Diary* [May 18, 1862]; see page 2 for epigram). Ironically, Clara Solomon was atypical of Jewish Southern women because, first, she was not an immigrant and, second, she came from a more affluent segment of society (as Faust acknowledges). Faust points out that Clara's emotional extravagance, her fantasy life, and her interest in other women were not unusual or deviant in the 1860s. Such expressions, she writes, "represented a sensitivity and authenticity of feeling celebrated in this sentimental mid-Victorian era as appropriate to true friendship as much as true love" (144).

53. "The Story of the Jewish Orphan's Home of New Orleans" (New Orleans: Louisiana State Museum, 1905); Malone, "Uptown," 242.

54. Ashkenazi, *Business of Jews*, 8–11; Malone, "Uptown," 242–43.

55. Ashkenazi, *Business of Jews*, 13; Rabbi Martin I. Hinchin, *Fourscore and Eleven: A History of the Jews of Rapides Parish, 1828–1919* (Alexandria, La.: McCormick Graphics for Congregation Gemiluth Chassodim, 1984), 2–4; my thanks to Nancy Greenberg and Rabbi Task of Alexandria for providing me with this local history. Korn, *Early Jews*, 189; Marcus, *Memoirs*, 3:104.

56. Brock, "Shreveport," 57, preface and passim; Schappes, *Documentary History*, 439–40.

57. Bernard Postal and Lionel Koppman, "Tennessee," in *A Jewish Tourist's Guide to the U.S.* (Philadelphia: JPSA, 1954), 585–95; Rabbi James A. Wax, "The Jews of Memphis: 1860–1865," *West Tennessee Historical Society Papers* 3 (1949): 39–89; Selma S. Lewis, *A Biblical People in the Bible Belt: The Jewish Community of Memphis, Tennessee, 1840s–1960s* (Macon, Ga.: Mercer University Press, 1998), 1–54; Fedora Small Frank, "Nashville Jewry during the Civil War," *Tennessee Historical Quarterly* 39, no. 3 (fall 1980): 310; Frank, *Five Families and Eight Young Men (Nashville and Her Jewry, 1850–1861)* (Nashville: Tennessee Book Co., 1962), 9.

58. Cecilia Felsenthal, *The Felsenthal Family*, 2nd ed. (Memphis, Tenn: Goldberger Printing & Publishing, 1939), 13–42. In 1732 a Felsenthal ancestor named Isaac (so the family legend goes) went to a local meeting. When he announced "Isaac" to a roll call, he was asked "From where?" He answered, "Ich komme uber fels und thal" (I came over rock and dale). He became Isaac Felsenthal.

59. Ruthe Winegarten and Cathy Schechter, *Deep in the Heart: The Lives and Legends of Texas Jews* (Austin: Eakin Press and Texas Jewish Historical Society, 1990), 7, 12–13; Juliet George, "By the Brazos and the Trinity They Hung Up Their Harps: Two Jewish Immigrants in Texas" (master's thesis, Texas Christian University, 1991), 4.

60. Harold M. Hyman, *Oleander Odyssey: The Kempners of Galveston, Texas, 1854–1980s* (College Station: Texas A & M University Press, 1990), 3–13.

61. Winegarten and Schechter, *Deep in the Heart*, 16–22; George, "By the Brazos," passim; Frances R. Kallison, "100 Years of Jewry in San Antonio" (master's thesis, Trinity University, 1977).

62. Sacher, *A History of the Jews in America*, 72.

63. Elzas, *Jews of South Carolina*, 244; Rubin, *Third to None*, 119; I. J. Benjamin, "Introduction," *Three Years in America, 1859–1862*, vol. 1, edited by Oscar Handlin and translated from the German by Charles Reznikoff (Philadelphia: JPSA, 1956).

64. Benjamin, *Three Years*, 76.

65. Greenberg, "Becoming Southern," 72–74. Greenberg astutely points out that, by every indicator, Jews were more accepted in antebellum Savannah than the Irish. ("Nativism directed primarily against Irish immigrants restricted their access to political office to a far greater degree than anti-Semitism affected Savannah Jews.")

66. Woodward, *Mary Chesnut*, 288.

67. Ibid., 459: "They say," Mary quoted a Mrs. Goodwyn, "there has never been a fallen woman among them." "Rachel—a shining light to the contrary," Mary jokingly replies, referring to the beautiful Rachel Lyons.

68. Ibid., 317, 346, 359.

69. Mary was attracted to Mem's lively personality and enjoyed her many stories. She recorded one in her diary:

> Some man was terribly angry with his son, who had a weakness for some beautiful Jewess, swore at all Jews, and used bad language freely. Being high church and all that, he read the service for them on Sunday.
>
> Son: "I do not want to hear anything from Isaiah or Solomon or Moses and the prophets—or Matthew, Mark, Luke, or John."
>
> "Silence, sir—with your ribaldry."
>
> "But, my father—you know they are only 'damned old Jews' anyhow." (359)

70. Oscar S. Straus, *Under Four Administrations* (Boston and New York: Houghton Mifflin Co., 1922), 10. "In the Bible Belt," Selma S. Lewis writes in *A Biblical People*, "the dominant community felt more tolerant of Jews" (33).

71. William R. Taylor, *Cavalier and Yankee: The Old South and American National Character* (New York: George Braziller, 1961), 325. See, generally, Eugene D. Genovese, *A Consuming Fire: The Fall of the Confederacy in the Mind of the White Christian South* (Athens: University of Georgia Press, 1998), 9, 38–39 ("we have provoked the Holy One of Israel to anger"; "bless our future Zion" [55]), ("The divines preached the model of the Abrahamic household" [70]; Heb. 6:4–8, the fate of Babylon).

72. Woodward, *Mary Chesnut*, 217, 233, 548.

73. "The Civil War Music Collector's Edition," notes by Charles K. Wolfe (Alexandria, Va.: Time-Life Music, n.d.): "And lift thou up thy rod, and stretch out the hand over the sea

388   and divide it," God commands Moses (Exod. 14:15). Moses, of course, was a hero to the Union as well. "O, Let My People Go" was sung by the freed slaves ("O, go down Moses / Away down to Egypt land / and tell King Pharaoh / to let my people go").

74. "Civil War Music Collector's Edition," notes by Charles K. Wolfe.

75. Rev. J. William Jones, *Personal Reminiscences of General Robert E. Lee* (reprint, Richmond: U.S. Historical Society Press, 1989), 419.

76. Capt. R. E. Lee, *Recollections and Letters of General Robert E. Lee* (Garden City, N.Y.: Garden City Publishing Co., 1904), 105–6; Jonathon Kirsch, *Moses: A Life* (New York: Ballentine Books, 1998), 187–89.

77. See "Biographical Sketches of Jews Who Have Served in the Congress of the United States," in *The American Jewish Yearbook,* vol. 2, 1900–1901 (Philadelphia: JPSA), 517–24. (The Southerners were Benjamin of Louisiana, Yulee of Florida, Philip Phillips of Alabama, and, for added measure, likely David S. Kaufman of Texas. The *Jewish Year Book* included him as a Jew.)

78. Bertram Wallace Korn, *Eventful Years and Experiences: Studies in Nineteenth Century America Jewish History* (Cincinnati: AJA, 1954), 114–15; Frederic Cople Jaher, *A Scapegoat in the New Wilderness: The Origins and Rise of Anti-Semitism in America,* (Cambridge: Harvard University Press, 1994), 177.

79. Abraham J. Peck, "The Other Peculiar Institution: Jews and Judaism in the Nineteenth Century South," *Modern Judaism* 7, no. 1 (February 7, 1987): 106. Hammond was, to say the least, a curmudgeon of the highest order. He disliked Jews—but then, Hammond disliked everyone.

80. Carol Bleser, ed., *Secret and Sacred: The Diaries of James Henry Hammond, a Southern Slaveholder* (New York: Oxford University Press, 1988), 94–95 (June 1842); Jaher, *Scapegoat,* 187.

81. John F. Marszalek, ed., *The Diary of Miss Emma Holmes, 1861–1866* (Baton Rouge: Louisiana State University Press, 1979), 162, 209, 306; Carol Bleser, ed., *Tokens of Affection: The Letters of a Planter's Daughter in the Old South* (Athens: University of Georgia Press, 1996), 343. Bleser refers to this remark as anti-Semitic, which it does not appear to be. After all, the family had a Jewish houseguest, and the letter was simply a private expression of the writer's surprise at what was a strange custom in the South—or the Western world generally—refusing to eat pork and ham.

82. Jaher, *Scapegoat,* 91. "The guilt of the bloud [*sic*] of the Lord of Heaven and Earth lyeth upon that Jewish nation," Increase Mather bellowed in 1669 (Marcus, *Colonial American Jew,* 3:1113–14). Rhode Islander John Bannister referred to Moses Lopez as "a Jew, the offscouring of the human species" (Rubin, *Third to None,* 10).

83. See, generally, Jacob Rader Marcus, *Early American Jewry* (Philadelphia: JPSA, 1951), 1: chap. 5 ("it is . . . a matter of record that the New Englanders, with rare exception, had no use for Jews. The original Puritans were interested in Hebrew and in ancient Hebrews . . . but not in their descendants as long as they remained Jews"). Unlike Southerners, the Puritans "frowned at the thought of tolerating or assimilating others" (103). Rabbi Marcus correctly refers to "the bigots of Massachusetts" (116) in *The Jews in America: Four Centuries of an Uneasy Encounter, a History* (New York: Simon and Schuster, 1989). Arthur Hertzburg points out that the Massachusetts Bay colony "had chased professing Jews out of Boston" (34). Of course Puritans *hanged* Quakers (see John T. Noonan, Jr., *The Lustre of our Country* [Berkeley: University of California Press, 1998]). Lee Friedman tries

to whitewash early Massachusetts anti-Semitism in *Early American Jews* (Cambridge: Harvard University Press, 1934), and succeeds at muddying the water somewhat. Friedman apparently did not know that the South existed, as he fails to mention colonial South Carolina, Georgia, or Virginia. In 1821, Massachusetts narrowly approved a constitutional revision removing a declaration of belief in Christianity as a qualification for election to public office. Old New Englanders like Leverett Saltonstall, true to their anti-Semitic ancestors, objected that "jews, mahometans, deists, and atheists" were "opposed to the common religion of the Commonwealth and believe it an imposition, a mere fable, and that its professors are under a wretched delusion." Jews, he thought, were not "suitable members of a Christian state" (Jaher, *Scapegoat*, 131). Leonard Dinnerstein agreed with this general assessment in *Anti-Semitism in America*, 8.

84. Charles Francis Adams, ed., *Memoirs of John Quincy Adams*, 12 vols. (Philadelphia: J. B. Lippincott, 1874–77), 10:483; 11:155, 162, 500; 12:164; Jaher, *Scapegoat*, 131, 190; Korn, in *Jews in the South*, 139; Dinnerstein, *Anti-Semitism*, 11. Adams wrote in 1780 that the Jews of Amsterdam "would steal your eyes out of your head if they possibly could."

85. Korn, *Eventful Years and Experiences*, 104; Dinnerstein, *Anti-Semitism*, 31–32.

86. Gergel and Gergel, *Tree of Life*, 33–35.

87. *Confederate Veteran*, 23:8, 343, August 1915. This is in a letter from Simon Baruch to *The Confederate Veteran*.

88. Samuel Proctor and Louis Schmier, eds., with Malcolm Stern, *Jews of the South: Selected Essays from the Southern Jewish Historical Society* (Macon, Ga.: Mercer University Press, 1984), 37; Schmier, "Georgia History in Pictures."

89. Greenberg, "Becoming Southern."

90. Lewis, *A Biblical People*, 34.

91. The lithograph of Lilienthal is at the Judah L. Magnes Museum (Western Jewish History Center), Berkeley, California; see p. 36. The lithograph was purchased for $110,000 in 1996. See *Maine Antique Digest*, "Pacific Currents," *Pacific Book Auction Galleries Quarterly* (April 1996): 8-A.

92. Lewis, *A Biblical People*, 32; Frank, *Five Families*, 87.

93. *Sinai* 7 (1862), 158–63, AJA; Korn, *Jews and Negro Slavery*, 26, 56–57; Berman, *Richmond Jewry*, 372n. 77. The author acknowledges the kind assistance of Andrea Mehrländer in translating this article, which has been cited by previous historians but has never been accurately translated into English. As to Jewish abolitionists, see Jayme A. Sokolow, "Revolution and Reform: The Antebellum Jewish Abolitionist," *Journal of Ethnic Studies* 9, no. 1 (1981): 26–41.

94. Korn, "Jews and Negro Slavery," 123.

95. Ibid., 131–32; Korn, *American Jewry*, 17. The American Jewish community generally avoided the debate over slavery in the antebellum years. Too small, vulnerable, and foreign to affect the outcome; too insecure in their social, political, and economic strength; suspicious of the abolitionist movement; and anxious to assimilate, neither organized Jewry and few Jews individually had anything to say on the controversy, North or South. National Jewish publications such as Isaac Leeser's *Occident* maintained a policy of silence or strict neutrality. National organizations, such as they were, took the same position: these were political issues and inappropriate for official Jewish comment. B'nai B'rith, a Jewish fraternal organization, ignored the issue. The American and Foreign Anti-Slavery Society issued an Annual Report in 1853 in which it found that the "Jews of the United States have never

390   taken any steps whatever with regard to the Slavery question." Korn, *American Jewry,* 15–16.

When Rabbi David Einhorn of Baltimore's Har Sinai congregation preached the abolition of slavery, he was forced to flee Baltimore. In May 1861 he was threatened during riots between Confederate and Union mobs. His board advised him that he should avoid "the excitable issues of the time" (Barkai, *Branching Out,* 110; Cohen, *Encounter,* 135). Another abolitionist rabbi, Bernard Felsenthal of Chicago, preached against the evils of slavery (Barkai, *Branching Out,* 113).

Numerous rabbis and Jewish leaders in the North answered Rabbi Raphall's defense of slavery. The majority of Jews in the North opposed slavery, and there were a number of Northern Jewish abolitionists. Michael Heilprin, a Polish Jewish-American writer, was outraged by Raphall's "sacrilegious words." "Have we not had enough of the 'reproach of Egypt?' Must the stigma of Egyptian principles be fastened on the people of Israel by Israelitish lips themselves?" (Felsenthal felt so strongly about slavery that he refused to even apply for a position at the Mobile congregation; Korn, *American Jewry,* 18–23.)

96. Solomon Cohen to "My Dear Aunt," transcription courtesy of Lewis Schmier, copy in possession of author.

97. Marcus, *Memoirs,* 2:295.

98. Schappes, *Documentary History,* 436–41.

99. Korn, *American Jewry,* 250n. 48; Jaher, *Scapegoat,* 138, 200–203, 215. For a different view of the abolitionists, see Louis Ruchames, "The Abolitionists and the Jews," *PAJHS* 42 (September 1952–June 1953): 131–55. Ruchames moderated his views in "The Abolitionists and the Jews: Some Further Thoughts," in *A Bicentennial Festscrift for Jacob Rader Marcus* (Waltham, Mass: AJHS, New York KTAV, 1976), 505–17. (See "The Abolitionist and the Jews," 145.) Jaher concedes that the abolitionists occasionally had positive things to say about the Jews. See page 310. See also Dinnerstein, *Anti-Semitism,* 16. Of course, white Southerners generally detested New Englanders and abolitionists. "Nothing on earth shall ever induce us to submit to any nation," one South Carolinian said in 1861, "with the brutal, bigoted blackguards of the New England States" (*Battle Cry of Freedom,* 234–35).

100. John Weiss, *Life and Correspondence of Theodore Parker* (New York: D. Appleton, 1964): Theodore Parker, "Journal," March 1843, 1:214, and Parker to Dr. Francis, May 26, 1844, 1:236, "Letter to the Members of the 28th Congregational Society of Boston" (1859), 2:497, and "Some Thoughts on the Charities of Boston" (1858), 1:397, and to Rev. David Wasson, December 12, 1857, 1:395–96. See also Egal Feldman, *Dual Destinies: The Jewish Encounter with Protestant America* (Urbana and Chicago: University of Illinois Press, 1990), 56–59; Jaher, *Scapegoat,* 200–203.

101. *Liberator* 15 (May 20, 1842): 1; 19; (May 18, September 21, 1849): 77, 751; Jaher, *Scapegoat,* 201.

102. Edmond Quincy, "A Jew and a Christian," *Liberator* 18 (August 11, 1848): 126; *Liberator* 15 (May 20, 1842): 1; 19 (May 18, September 21, 1849): 77, 751. Quincy, a Boston Brahmin and a cousin of John Quincy Adams, was an officer of the Massachusetts and American Anti-Slavery Society, editor of the Massachusetts *Abolitionist,* and a contributor to the *Liberator.* He wrote a novel, *Wensley: A Story without a Moral,* published in 1854, in which the villain is a forger and cheat named Aaron Abrahams. The book is laced with every cliché of old-fashioned Boston anti-Semitism: the Jew as a liar, cheat, and

coward (see pages 275–91). See also Jonathon D. Sarna, "The 'Mythical Jew' and the 'Jew Next Door' in Nineteenth-Century America," in David A. Gerber, ed., *Anti-Semitism in American History* (Urbana and Chicago: University of Illinois Press, 1986), 57–78; for a detailed treatment of Child, James Russell Lowell, and others; and David A. Gerber, "Cutting Out Shylock: Elite Anti-Semitism and the Quest for Moral Order in the Mid-Nineteenth Century American Market Place," *Journal of American History* 69, no. 3 (December 1982): 615–37, for the anti-Semitic credit reporting of Arthur and Lewis Tappan, leading abolitionists and merchants. Of course, not all New England intellectuals were anti-Semites. Henry Wadsworth Longfellow, for example, wrote philo-Semitic works, including "Tales of a Wayside Inn" and "Judas Maccabaeus."

Lydia Maria Child, *Letters from New-York* (New York: Charles Francis, and Boston: James Munroe, 1843), 12–13, 26–29, 31, 33–34, 217–18, 225 (Judaism was rife with superstition, vengeance, blindness; its ceremonies "strange . . . spectral and flitting"). Child, of Boston, was one of the most famous female writers of her time and a vocal abolitionist. Her husband was a member of the Massachusetts legislature and an early member of the New England Antislavery Society. She wrote numerous antislavery tracts and edited the "Anti-Slavery Standard." Her *Letters from New-York* was a best-seller in the 1840s. See also Patricia G. Holland and Milton Meltzer, eds., *Guide to the Collected Correspondence of Lydia Maria Child, 1817–1880* (New York: Kraus Microform, 1980), s.v. "Jews," especially letters to Louisa Gilman Loring (September 4, 1846) and Ellis Gray Loring (March 5, 1854).

As to Henry Wilson's views, see *The Congressional Globe,* 36th Cong., 2d sess., February 21, 1861, 1091; and 37th Cong., 2d sess., February 13, 1862, 789; Korn, *American Jewry,* 168 ("The race that stoned Prophets and crucified the Redeemer of the World"; "the Jew brokers"; "curbstone Jew broker"); Meade, *Judah P. Benjamin,* 139; Marcus, *U.S. Jewry,* 3:36.

103. Ibid. See notes 84 and 102, above.

104. Sacher, *A History of the Jews of America,* 73.

105. *History of the Jews of Louisiana, Their Religious, Civic, Charitable and Patriotic Life* (Jewish Historical Publishing Company of Louisiana, 1903), 33; Scherck to J. L. Meyer, Columbus, Ga., September 9, 1864, AJA; *Charleston Daily Courier,* March 11, 1861.

106. Dauber, 2, 927.

107. Harry Simonhoff, *Jewish Notables in America, 1776–1865: Links of an Endless Chain* (New York: Greenberg, 1956), 297–300; Woodward, *Mary Chesnut,* 11.

108. Edwin DeLeon, *Thirty Years of My Life on Three Continents* (London: Ward and Downey, 1890), 1:13.

109. William L. King, *The Newspaper Press of Charleston, S.C.* (Charleston, 1872), 159–61.

110. Avery, *History of Georgia,* 115.

111. Greenberg, "Savannah Jews," 238; *Journal of the Public and Secret Proceedings of the Convention of the People of Georgia* (Milledgeville, Ga., 1861), Georgia Historical Society, Savannah.

112. Some sources claim that Hyams presided over the Louisiana Secession Convention, but this is erroneous. *Louisiana History* 2 (winter 1961): 7–105 (*Journal of the Convention*); *New Orleans Daily Picayune,* March 26, 1861; John D. Winters, *The Civil War in Louisiana* (Baton Rouge: Louisiana State University Press, 1963), 9.

113. Bernard Lemann Diary, Lemann Family Papers, Tulane Special Collections, TU; Ashkenazi, *Business of Jews,* 31–38, 42–43.

114. Thus, while one can barely find a single opponent of the war among Charleston, Savannah, or Richmond Jewry, there was identifiable opposition to secession in New Orleans. Clara Solomon, for example, was highly critical of one immigrant: "Mr. E. [Elburger] is a very intelligent, well informed man, full of information. He expressed *strong* union sentiments. He said that Lincoln was *our* President, and if not we then were 'Rebels,' thus endorsing Lincoln's words. His interests are with the North, and had better be guarded in his speech." (75)

These sentiments were more likely to be expressed by the most recent German and Polish immigrants.

115. Ralph A. Wooster, *The Secession Conventions of the South* (Princeton, N.J.: Princeton University Press, 1962), 101.

116. John Frederick Nau, *The German People of New Orleans, 1850–1900* (Leiden: E. J. Brill, 1958), 38.

117. Weil's views were not shared by his brother Henry, who took a more moderate view. Henry did not even enlist in the Home Guard, although he did purchase Confederate bonds, an investment Jake thought unwise. His friends Lehmann and Durr also felt that Jake was unwise to involve himself in the controversy. (Jake Weil to Josiah Weil, May 16, 1861, Jake Weil Papers, Alabama Dept. of Archives & History, Montgomery, Ala., copy in possession of author, courtesy of Bert Fischel, and at Touro Infirmary Archive, courtesy of Catherine Kahn.) A second copy in the author's possession states as follows: "This is a copy of a letter made by the Father of Peter Weil (a student at the University of Texas) from an original in private hands in Montgomery, Alabama, and loaned to Dr. Barnes F. Lathrop, December 1, 1961." This copy is at the LBJ Library, University of Texas, according to Bert Fischel. Maurice Kahn Weil of Shreveport has the original, according to Catherine Kahn.

118. Berman, *Richmond's Jewry*, 177–78.

119. Ibid., 172–74; Stanley L. Falk, "Divided Loyalties in 1861: The Decision of Major Alfred Mordecai," *PAJHS* 48:3 (March 1959), 168.

120. Phoebe Yates Pember, *A Southern Woman's Story: Life in Confederate Richmond*, ed. Bell Irvin Wiley (Jackson, Tenn.: McCowat-Mercer Press, 1959; reprint, Wilmington, N.C.: Broadfoot Publishing Co., 1991), 24; Phillips-Meyers Papers, Philip Phillips Diary, Southern Historical Collection, University of North Carolina, Chapel Hill, 38; Jacob Rader Marcus, *Memoirs*, 3:151.

121. Rosen, *Confederate Charleston* (Columbia: University of South Carolina Press, 1997), chap. 4; I. Valentine obituary, *Charleston Daily Courier*, June 21, 1862; Young, *Where They Lie*, 1–2, 41; Hagy, *This Happy Land*, 200–201; Samuel Wylie Crawford, *The Genesis of the Civil War: The Story of Sumter, 1860–1861* (New York, 1887), 429. Lieutenant Valentine's report is in OR, ser. 1, 1:53; Elzas, *Jews of South Carolina*, 236. Col. Roswell S. Ripley also cited Valentine for his prompt and energetic performance of duties. (OR ser. 1, 1:30–53; see page 39, "Operations Charleston Harbor"). Gen. Samuel W. Crawford, an eyewitness, described the enfilade battery in *The History of Fort Sumter*, published after the war. "Taking the most important battery upon the parapet reverse, its guns were so actively worked, and at such short intervals of fire, that six hundred and eleven shots were fired from it alone. 'The object of our firing,' said the officer who immediately commanded it, Lieutenant Jacob Valentine, in his official report, 'was to sweep the crest of the parapet, the roofs of the quarters within Fort Sumter, to dismount the barbette guns, if practicable, and to drive the enemy from the parapet.' The latter object was accomplished." Crawford,

The Genesis of the Civil War, 429; Young, *Where They Lie,* 1-2. Lieutenant Valentine's report is in OR, chap. 1, 53; Elzas, *Jews of South Carolina,* 236. Beauregard agreed that Valentine's battery had been effective and prevented the use of the Sumter's barbette guns. In his official report of April 27, 1861, the general praised his men and mentioned, "in the highest terms of praise," two captains and the eight commanders of batteries of Sullivan's Island, including Lieutenants Wagner, Rhett, Yates, and Valentine.

122. Crawford, *Genesis,* 434; OR, ser. 1, vol. 1, 31, 53–54.

123. OR, ser. 1, vol. 1, 32, 34; Elzas, *Jews of South Carolina,* 205; Dorothy Bultman, *The Story of a Good Life* (Sumter, S.C, 1963).

124. On Sunday afternoon, after Governor Pickens, General Beauregard, and their staffs had started from Sullivan's Island to take possession of Fort Sumter, they were told that a fire had broken out. Their boat returned to Sullivan's Island and took two fire engines on board. Later that day, more equipment was sent to the fort "in charge of our very efficient chief, M. H. Nathan, Esq.," the local press reported. ("The Battle of Fort Sumter and First Victory of the Southern Troops," pamphlet, 1861 [1961 reprint], 24.)

The local press also reported that the first Palmetto flag was raised over Fort Sumter by Colonels Franklin J. Moses Jr. and J. L. Dearing of Governor Pickens's staff (pamphlet, 27). Although he was raised as a Jew and never converted to Christianity, young Moses's father, Franklin J. Moses Sr., married a Christian and raised his son in the Protestant faith. Franklin Jr. was born and raised in Sumter, studied at South Carolina College, and began his career as the Civil War began, as private secretary to Gov. Francis W. Pickens. He was fervent for secession (*DAB,* 112). His service during the war was varied. He was private secretary and/or the aide to the governor, but was terminated by the Executive Council because he was unable to perform satisfactorily (Charles E. Cauthen, ed., *Journals of the South Carolina Executive Councils of 1861 and 1862* [Columbia: S.C. Archives Dept., 1956], passim; John B. Edmunds, Jr., *Francis W. Pickens and the Politics of Destruction* [Chapel Hill: University of North Carolina Press, 1986], 166, 168, 220n. 26; Woodward, *Mary Chesnut,* 406). He served at Fort Moultrie and at Battery Gregg on Morris Island as second lieutenant in Company F, 1st Regiment of South Carolina Regulars, which served as an artillery unit. He was absent from his unit for extended periods of time because of illnesses, and he apparently ended the war as a colonel, serving as "an enrolling officer" pursuant to the Conscription Act. He was almost certainly under fire on Morris Island, as the records show him reporting in August 1863 "with special instructions to receive and forward ordnance stores" and, by September, he was "mounting the Dahlgren gun at Gregg" (OR, ser. 1, vol. 28, pt. 1, 468–69, 479–80, "Operations on Morris Island").

After the war, Franklin J. Moses Jr., whose father had been a respected member of the prewar general assembly, turned his back on his community and became a Radical Republican, a scalawag, and, in 1872, governor of South Carolina. Known to American history as "the Robber Governor," he was, according to R. H. Woody, "the most perfect scalawag, perhaps in all the South" (R. H. Woody, "Franklin J. Moses, Jr.: Scalawag Governor of South Carolina, 1872–74," *North Carolina Historical Review* [April 1933]: 111). The Jews of South Carolina were so mortified by Moses that the Moseses of Sumter changed their names to Harby and Moses's wife resumed her maiden name, Richardson, and renamed their children Richardson (Herbert A. Moses, "Pertaining to the Moses Family" ["The less said of him the better. He was dishonest, dishonorable, and dissolute"]); interview, Belinda Gergel, Columbia, August 1999).

125. Henry Steele Commager, *The Blue and the Gray* (New York: Bobbs-Merrill Co., 1950), 1:607. See Cauthen, *South Carolina Goes to War, 1860–1865*, chap. 5, for a full treatment of the reasons South Carolina seceded.

126. Wooster, *The Secession Conventions of the South*, 131. For the relationship between secession and slavery, see McPherson, *Battle Cry*, 242, 255, 283–84.

127. Winters, *The Civil War in Louisiana*, 8.

128. Letter of Solomon Cohen to "My Dear Aunt," transcription courtesy of Louis Schmier, Valdosta, Georgia; copy in the possession of the author.

129. Marcus, *Memoirs*, 3:308–9; see James M. McPherson, *For Cause and Comrades: Why Men Fought in the Civil War* (New York: Oxford University Press, 1997), for the motivation of Civil War soldiers, especially 108–10, 309.

130. April 17, 1864, letter, Simon Mayer Papers, Box 1, TU; see chapter 7, note 48, below, for the details of Mayer's military service. He became a lieutenant late in the war.

131. McPherson, *For Cause and Comrades*, chap. 1

132. *Charleston Mercury* obituary, June 19, 1862, 1; *Charleston Daily Courier* obituary, in Young's *Where They Lie*, 39–40.

133. McPherson, *For Cause and Comrades*, 23; Young, *Where They Lie*, 39.

134. Letter dated July 8, 1863, addressed to "Dear Brother Isaac and Sister Amelia" (Mr. and Mrs. Isaac Meinnart) in Richmond from Philip Rosenheim, AJA.

135. Turitz and Turitz, *Jews in Early Mississippi*, xvii.

136. Typewritten autobiography of Sir Moses Ezekiel, 75–76, BA. See also Joseph Gutman and Stanley F. Chyet, eds., *Moses Jacob Ezekiel: Memoirs from the Baths of Diocletian* (Detroit: Wayne State University Press, 1975); *VMI Alumni Review* (Spring 1973): 1; Stanley F. Chyet, "Moses Jacob Ezekiel: A Childhood in Richmond," *PAJHS* 62 (1973): 286–94.

137. *VMI Alumni Review* (Spring 1973): 1.

138. Berman, *Richmond's Jewry*, 194–95.

139. J. Gottlieb to Mr. J. Abeles, Philadelphia, June 12, 1861, Personal Papers, Confederate Miscellany, Acc. 22812, VSL (Gottlieb may be listed in the *Roster* as Isaac Gottlieb, a corporal in Company H, 14th Mississippi).

140. Autobiography of Moses Ezekiel, BA.

141. Woodward, *Mary Chesnut*, 350.

142. Pember, *A Southern Woman's Story*, 24.

143. Ezekiel and Lichtenstein, *History of the Jews of Richmond*, 186; Schmier, *Reflections of Southern Jewry*, 4–7.

144. Helen Kohn Hennig, *August Kohn: Versatile South Carolinian* (Columbia: Vogue Press, 1949), 9–10. Philip Kohn evidently had strong pro-Union views: "If I think about the fact that your eager demagogues, parsons, hussies and wenches neglect nothing to make you inexperienced boys afraid for their failure, then I can only regret that I have a son among them" (10); William Valmore Izlar, *A Sketch of the War Record of the Edisto Rifles, 1861–1865* (Columbia: The State Co., 1914; reprint, Camden, S.C.: J. J. Fox, 1990), 53.

145. Gary W. Gallagher, *The Confederate War*, (Cambridge, Mass.: Harvard University Press, 1997), 28.

146. Bernard M. Baruch, *My Own Story* (New York: Henry Holt & Co., 1957), 5.

147. Lewis Leon, *The Diary of a Tar Heel Confederate Soldier* (Charlotte: Stone Publishing Co., 1913), 1; Schappes, *Documentary History*, 481. *The Diary of a Tar Heel*

Confederate Soldier was kept during the war, or, at least according to Lt. Col. James T. Morehead, "kept by [Leon] from the organization of the regiment [which was a year after the war commenced] up to May 1864, when he was captured." It was published when Leon was seventy-two years old and still an unreconstructed Confederate. There is additional information on Lewis Leon in J. R. Marcus, *Memoirs*, 3:197, and Schappes, *Documentary History*, 481, 707–8. My research assistant, Lt. Col. James A. Gabel, an experienced Civil War researcher, writes of Leon's book, "I must say that his little volume is one of the best accounts of life in the ranks I have read." I have also utilized Lewis and Morris Leon's service records at the National Archives. Men were paid a fifty-dollar bounty to join the army. See Albert B. Moore, *Conscription and Conflict in the Confederacy* (New York: Hillary House Publishers, 1963), 7, 14, 308.

148. Schmier, "Reflections of Southern Jewry," 11. The spelling of Wessolowsky obviously created transcription problems. An A. H. Wessalowsky is shown in 1st Georgia (Ramsey's) Company E as well as an A. H. Wessolowsky in Company E, 32d Georgia. There is an A. B. Wessalowsky in Companies E and G, 32d Georgia. Asa Wessolowsky, then, likely joined the 1st Georgia (Ramsey's) in March 1861, served at Pensacola, then went to (West) Virginia before being mustered out in Augusta, Georgia, in March 1862, just in time to reenlist in the 57th/32d Georgia in May 1862.

149. Gerald Sorin, *A Time for Building: The Third Migration, 1880–1920*, vol. 3 of *The Jewish People in America* (Baltimore: The Johns Hopkins University Press, 1992), 49–50, as to Castle Garden; Schappes, *Documentary History*, 495–96, 86; Hermann, *Memoirs*, 192–93. Isaac Hermann's *Memoirs of a Veteran Who Served as a Private in the 60s in the War Between the States* is full of braggadocio, boasting, and outlandish and blatantly untrue tales. There is no way to prove or disprove many of these stories written nearly fifty years after the war. "After reading Isaac Hermann's *Memoirs of a Veteran*," James Gabel wrote, "I came away with the impression that he was the Forrest Gump of the War Between the States, but with a really bad attitude. He was everywhere, and despite the fact that he was a lowly private, he was frequently in the company of the colonels and generals who often relied on his advice and counsel." *Civil War Books: A Critical Bibliography*, volume 1, notes that "much of the material is of questionable accuracy." Jacob Rader Marcus wrote more generously in *Memoirs of American Jews*: "Were only half of the adventures which Isaac Hermann [1838–1917] relates true—and there is no reason to discount his narrative—then he was indeed a hard-bitten Confederate soldier." Marcus, in a rare lapse of judgment, let his sympathies get the better of him. Harry Simonhoff in *Jewish Participants in the Civil War* (New York: Arco Publishing Co., 1963) is equally forgiving: "Cautious readers may suspect that some of the adventures might have been exaggerated, yet they cannot be dismissed merely as tall tales." Bell I. Wiley in *The Life of Johnny Reb* warns that memoirs must be used with great care "on account of the caprices of recollection, particularly its tendency to minimize weaknesses and to magnify virtues." He categorizes Hermann's memoirs with those "surcharged with romanticism." The story of Hermann's meeting with Judah Benjamin, for example, is not credible, not to mention all of Hermann's brushes with military justice and his close personal relationships with generals and colonels; his military records do not corroborate his memoirs. Unlike Rabbi Marcus, I think there is good reason to discount much of the memoir and, unlike Simonhoff, I think there are many tall tales. Nevertheless, it is known that Hermann did serve in the Washington Rifles (Company E,

1st [Ramsey's] Georgia) and Martin's Light Artillery Company, and much of the essentials of his military career is corroborated by his military records at the National Archives. There is additional information on Hermann in Marcus, *Memoirs*, 3:236, and Schappes, *Documentary History*, 495–96, 712–13.

150. Jaher, *Scapegoat*, passim, especially 3–4, 117–18, 135–36; *Oxford Dictionary of the Jewish Religion*, s.v. "Wandering Jew," 718. Many German Jews welcomed World War I, Klaus Fischer wrote in *The History of an Obsession*, "for the same reasons as their fellow Germans, but perhaps especially because it provided them with the opportunity to prove convincingly that, by laying their lives on the line for Germany, they were loyal German citizens" (120). "All Jews," one German Jewish group stated during World War I, "must do their duty, but the German Jews must do more than their duty" (120). Fischer points out that German Jews sacrificed more in World War I than other Germans. One hundred thousand Jews served in the army; two thousand became officers; twelve thousand were killed (120). The same was true for the Jews of Alsace-Lorraine, who were "more French than the French" (Vicki Caron, *Between France and Germany: The Jews of Alsace and Lorraine 1871–1918* (Stanford, Calif.: Stanford University Press, 1988), 192.

151. Letter dated April 17, 1864 to "My dear Parents, Bros. & Sisters," Simon Mayer Papers, Box 1, TU.

152. Ezekiel and Lichtenstein, *History of the Jews of Richmond*, 183.

153. Philip Whitlock, MS, autobiography, Virginia Historical Society, 92.

154. Ezekiel and Lichtenstein, *History of the Jews of Richmond*, 183, 16, 175.

155. Jonathon D. Sarna, "American Jewish Political Conservatism in Historical Perspective," *AJH* 87 (June and September 1999), 113–22.

156. Bertram W. Korn, introduction to "The Jews of the Confederacy," *AJA* 13, no. 1, "Civil War Centennial Southern Issue" (April 1961): 4. Korn felt that the old Jewish families of the South, both in cities and small towns, "achieved a more genuinely integrated status with their neighbors than has seemed possible in any other part of the United States then or now" (4–5).

CHAPTER 2

1. Meade, *Judah P. Benjamin*, 4; Evans, *Judah Benjamin*, 4–5.

2. Benjamin Kaplan, "Judah Philip Benjamin," in Dinnerstein and Palsson, eds., *Jews in the South*, 76; Butler, *Judah Benjamin*, 24.

3. Butler, *Judah Benjamin*, 22–24; Evans, *Judah Benjamin*, 5; Burton J. Hendrick, *Statesmen of the Lost Cause* (New York: Literary Guild, 1939), 169; Meade, *Judah P. Benjamin*, 11; Ernest B. Kruttschnitt, Benjamin's nephew, to Pierce Butler, November 3, 1905, Manuscript Department, TU; draft of a letter dated August 13, 1897, from Kruttschnitt to F. C. Lawley, TU. Remarkably, Malcolm Stern's genealogy is incorrect.

4. Evans, *Judah Benjamin*, 11–14; Richard S. Tedlow, "Judah Benjamin," in *"Turn to the South," Essays on Southern Jewry*, edited by Nathan M. Kaganoff and Melvin I. Urofsky (Charlottesville: AJHS, University Press of Virginia, 1979), 64–65.

5. Leon Hühner, "David L. Yulee, Florida's First Senator," *PAJHS* 25 (1917), 1–29, 18; 18; Joseph Gary Adler, "The Public Career of Senator David Levy Yulee" (Ph.D. diss., Case Western Reserve University, 1973), 2.

6. George R. Fairbanks, "Moses Elias Levy Yulee," *Florida Historical Quarterly* 18, no. 3 (January 1940): 165–67; Arthur W. Thompson, "David Yulee: A Study of Nineteenth

Century American Thought and Enterprise" (Ph.D. diss., Columbia University, 1954), 4;
Mills B. Lord, "David Levy Yulee: Statesman and Railroad Builder" (master's thesis, University of Florida, 1940), 1–3. In another version, he was quartered alive and burned, and, in a third version, he was imprisoned. See Heller, "Yulee," 2–4. The vizier's name was Jacob Attal or Attar but was given the name Yulee, which may have been an honorary title or official name of some kind. In one version of the facts, the family had always been known as Yulee. In another version, the vizier's widow used her own maiden name, Levy. In 1846 Moses Levy wrote a Florida newspaper, "sirnames [*sic*] are little thought of by orientals; . . . a Levite with the Jews is called but Levy." See Thompson, "David Yulee," 4–5. It may well be that the entire story is fictional. In the Bible, Joseph was freed from prison and made vizier, second in command of all Egypt (see Cahill, *The Gift of the Jews,* 96–97); this story may be the origin of the Yulee tale. Chris Monaco clarifies the facts in "Moses E. Levy of Florida: A Jewish Abolitionist Abroad," *AJH* 86, no. 4 (December 1998): 377–96. He cites Norman A. Stillman and Yedida K. Stillman, "The Jewish Courtier Class in Late Eighteenth Century Morocco as Seen Through the Eyes of Samuel Romanelli," in *Essays in Honor of Bernard Lewis: The Islamic World from Classical to Modern Times* (Princeton, N.J.: Princeton University Press, 1989), 845–51, and other sources to show that Eliahu Levy was "an influential Jewish courtier of Sultan Sidi Muhammad (1757–90)." See 382n. 27.

7. Adler, "Public Career," 158; Thompson, "David Yulee," 5. David Yulee's mother, Hannah Abendanone, was also Sephardic, a member of the large St. Thomas Jewish community. In addition to their son David, the couple had three other children, Elias, Rahma, and Rachel. Yulee's parents separated in 1815 and divorced in 1818. (This required the approval of the king of Denmark, as St. Thomas was then a Danish colony.) The children stayed with their mother on St. Thomas. The sons eventually were sent to schools in North America; the daughters stayed and married. In 1816 Moses Levy moved to Havana, where he secured military contracts, and it was there that he became interested in settling in Florida. See Thompson, "David Yulee," 5.

8. Leon Hühner, "Moses Elias Levy: An Early Florida Pioneer and the Father of Florida's First Senator," *Florida Historical Quarterly* 19, no. 4 (April 1941). Moses Elias Levy was also an author and speaker on religious subjects and controversies, and the friend of prominent Jews in America, Europe, and the Caribbean. Fairbanks, in a sketch written in 1901, recalled that "His whole name was Moses Elias Levy Yulee. Moses designated his personal name, Elias a race name, Levy his tribal name and Yulee his father's name." Because this name was too cumbersome for business, he shortened it. See note 6 above.

9. Joseph Gary Adler, "Moses Elias Levy and Attempts to Colonize Florida," in *Jews of the South: Selected Essays from the Southern Jewish Historical Society,* edited by Samuel Proctor and Louis Schmier, with Malcolm Stern (Macon, Ga.: Mercer University Press, 1984), 21. Moses Levy became a member of the Kariate sect, which rejected the Talmud but believed the literal interpretation of the Scriptures. Mrs. Levy remarried and lived in St. Thomas. In her later years she was forced to rely on financial assistance from her two sons, who supplemented the support she received from her former husband. The two daughters married Sephardic Jewish husbands and continued to live on St. Thomas. Adler, "Moses Elias Levy," 4; Thompson, "David Yulee," 226.

10. Meade, *Judah P. Benjamin,* 31–33.

11. Louis Gruss, "Judah Philip Benjamin," *Louisiana Historical Quarterly* 19, no. 4 (October 1936): 988; Meade, *Judah P. Benjamin,* 43–45.

12. Charles Curran, "The Three Lives of Judah Benjamin," *History Today* 17, no. 9 (September 1967): 583–85; Meade, *Judah P. Benjamin,* 34–36.

13. Gruss, "Judah Philip Benjamin," 987; Evans, *Judah Benjamin,* 47–48.

14. Evans, *Judah Benjamin,* 28–29.

15. Marcus, *Memoirs,* 3:306.

16. Butler, *Judah Benjamin,* 44–47.

17. Butler, *Judah Benjamin,* 47; Bertram W. Korn, "Judah Benjamin as a Jew," *PAJHS* 38 (September 1948): 153–71, quote at 168, emphasis in original.

18. Butler, *Judah Benjamin,* 99.

19. Thompson, "David Yulee," 7–8; Hühner, "Florida's First Senator," 8.

20. Thompson, "David Yulee," 17–25; Lord, "Yulee," 121. Yulee had a talent for making enemies, and his enemies pursued him with unusual zeal. When he was first elected to the constitutional convention, his foes raised the issue of his citizenship, a problem that haunted him throughout his early political career. He was challenged again upon his election as territorial delegate, and extensive hearings were held on the matter. At issue was the citizenship of Moses Levy on July 17, 1821. Although he was onboard a ship in sight of land off the Florida coast at the time (the date set for the exchange of Florida to the United States, on which date all residents were declared U.S. citizens), Moses Levy was not actually on land and residing in Florida. Because Moses Levy was not legally a citizen, his children, then minors, were not citizens either. A strict interpretation of the law would leave Yulee a noncitizen. The spirit of the law prevailed, however, and Yulee was seated.

It appears from the congressional record that although Yulee's father cooperated and supplied necessary testimony, he was completely estranged from both of his sons. The reason apparently was David's and his brother's rejection of the Jewish faith, or at least his father's peculiar version of it. This is the explanation given by Yulee's daughter, Florida Yulee Neff. It may have been due also to the father's unorthodox ideas about life in general, what his son called "the peculiar character of his opinions." Thompson, "David Yulee," 223–26.

21. Thompson, "David Yulee," 220–21. Moses Levy lived to see his son elected to high office. It is ironic that David Levy Yulee, the first person of Jewish ancestry elected to the U.S. Senate, did not acknowledge his Judaism, and yet was raised in a traditional Jewish family by an observant Jewish father whose goal was to provide a homeland for Jews in Florida, the state which sent Yulee to the Senate. Clearly, Yulee's marriage to a non-Jew was fatal to the relationship between father and son. Moses Levy wrote, "Every Jew who contributes knowingly to the . . . amalgamation of the House of Israel is an enemy to his nation, to his religion, and consequently, to the world at large." Quoted in Monaco, "Moses E. Levy," 12; Jacob Toury, "M. E. Levy's Plan for a Jewish Colony in Florida—1825," in *Michael: On the History of the Jews in the Diaspora,* edited by Lloyd Gartner (Ramat-Aviv, Tel Aviv: ha-Universitah ha-petuhah, 1975), 23.

22. C. F. Adams, *Memoirs of John Quincy Adams,* 10:304, 483; 11:62, 155, 162, 294, 500–2; Jaher, *Scapegoat,* 190; Hühner, "Florida's First Senator," 14–17; Thompson, "David Yulee," 40. In Leon Hühner's view, Yulee's "most important work . . . on which his whole heart and soul centered, was that of obtaining the admission of Florida into the Union." Another historian, Joseph G. Adler, calls him the "architect of Florida Statehood." Arthur Thompson, a professor of history at the University of Florida, agrees, stating that Yulee was one of Florida's two major leaders from the 1840s to 1861 and that Yulee spearheaded the

drive for the admission of Florida to the Union. Thompson, "David Yulee," 17, 28, 749; Adler, "Public Career," 20.

23. Hühner, "Florida's First Senator," 19; Adler, "Public Career," 38–39; Thompson, "David Yulee," 605n. 21.

24. Adler, "Public Career," 38–39; Thompson, "David Yulee," 749.

25. Adler, "Public Career," 38, 39; Lord, "Yulee," 121–22.

26. C. Wickliffe Yulee, "Senator David L. Yulee," *Florida Historical Society Quarterly* 2, no. 1 (April 1909): 35–36; 2, no. 2 (July 1909): 3–22; Adler, "Public Career," 87. See, for example, Clyde N. Wilson, ed., *The Papers of John C. Calhoun,* vol. 20, 1844 (Columbia: University of South Carolina Press, 1990), 15–16, 48, 56.

27. Dorothy Dodd, "The Secession Movement in Florida, 1850–1861," pt. 1, *Florida Historical Society Quarterly* 12, no. 1 (July 1933): 4; Proctor and Schmier, *Jews of the South,* 163–64; Adler, "Yulee," 63–64.

28. Hühner, "Florida's First Senator," 22; Dodd, "Secession," 6, 10; Adler, "Public Career," 67.

29. Thompson, "David Yulee," 73; Robert L. Clarke, "The Florida Railroad Company in the Civil War," *Journal of Southern History* 19, no. 2 (May 1953): 180–92. ("More than a decade before the Civil War," Clarke wrote, "Senator David L. Yulee of Florida had envisioned a railroad that would cross the state from a point on the Atlantic just north of Jacksonville to Cedar Keys on the Gulf of Mexico. His plan was to provide a short land route that would eliminate the tricky passage through the Florida Keys and tap the lucrative trade between New Orleans and New York.") For an excellent discussion of the Whig and Democratic Party rivalry in this period, see Michael F. Holt, *The Rise and Fall of the American Whig Party* (New York: Oxford University Press, 1999), chap. 16 (Yulee's defeat at 564).

30. Meade, *Judah P. Benjamin,* 84–85; Jacob R. Marcus, "Jew Who Refused Supreme Court Seat," *Jewish Advocate,* January 13, 1972 (also at AJA in typescript).

31. Gruss, "Judah Philip Benjamin," 1003, 1018–28. By Southern lights, Sumner deserved the beating because in a speech on the Senate floor he, in effect, called the older, courteous, and popular senator Andrew P. Butler of South Carolina a liar. The speech was tasteless, deplorable, and "pure rant." See Allan Nevins, *Ordeal of the Union: A House Dividing, 1852–1857* (New York: Charles Scribner, 1947), 437–44.

32. Butler, *Judah Benjamin,* 62.

33. Meade, *Judah P. Benjamin,* 96.

34. Evans, *Judah Benjamin,* 93.

35. Meade, *Judah P. Benjamin,* 100–104.

36. Evans, *Judah Benjamin,* 96–97.

37. Adler, "Public Career," 119–20, 161.

38. Robert W. Johannsen, *Stephen A. Douglas* (New York: Oxford University Press, 1973), 721; Thompson, "David Yulee," 121; Adler, "Public Career," 121, 129–32

39. Yulee, "Senator David L. Yulee," 1:38; Thompson, "David Yulee," 481.

40. Dorothy Dodd, "The Secession Movement in Florida, 1850–1861," pt. 2, *Florida Historical Society Quarterly* 12, no. 2 (October 1933): 45–66, at 52–53, 64; Hühner, "Florida's First Senator," 23–24.

41. Hühner, "Florida's First Senator," 25–26.

42. Adler, "Public Career," 149.

43. Ibid., 151, 154–55.

44. Ibid., 155–57; OR 52:15.

45. Adler, "Public Career," 113; Clarke, "Railroad Company," 182; Bertram Korn Collection, no. 99, folder 34, p. 8, AJA. (The undated clipping is from a Jewish periodical, which quotes the *New York Times* in an article entitled "Attacks on the Jewish Name."). The *New York Times* article appeared on the front page of the "Supplement to the New York Times" on Saturday, March 15, 1862. It is the last paragraph in an article entitled "From the Southern Coast."

46. Dorothy Dodd, "The Secession Movement in Florida, 1850–1861," *Florida Historical Quarterly* 12, no. 1, pt. 1 (July 1933), and 12, no. 1, pt. 2 (October 1933), 53; Adler, "Public Career," 165.

47. Butler, *Judah Benjamin*, 193.

48. Meade, *Judah P. Benjamin*, 139.

49. Ibid., 145.

50. S. I. Neiman, *Judah Benjamin: Mystery Man of the Confederacy* (Indianapolis: Bobbs-Merrill Co., 1963), 101; Meade, *Judah P. Benjamin*, 153.

51. Meade, *Judah P. Benjamin*, 159–60; Butler, *Judah Benjamin*, 226–28.

52. See note 102, chap. 1; Thomas Cooper DeLeon, *Belles, Beaux, and Brains of the '60s* (New York, 1909), 91–93.

53. Evans, *Judah Benjamin*, 110–11; Hans L. Trefousse, *Andrew Johnson*, 414n. 22; Johnson quoted in *Charles Francis Adams, 1835–1915: An Autobiography* (1916; reprint, New York, Russell and Russell, 1968), 94; Jaher, *Scapegoat*, 190–91.

54. Neiman, *Judah Benjamin*, 88.

55. Butler, *Judah Benjamin*, 231; William Howard Russell, *My Diary North and South* (Boston, 1863), 175.

56. Meade, *Judah P. Benjamin*, 161.

57. Butler, *Judah Benjamin*, 234.

58. DeLeon, *Belles, Beaux, and Brains*, 91–93; Meade, *Judah P. Benjamin*, 175.

59. Meade, *Judah P. Benjamin*, 177–79; *DAB*.

60. Meade, *Judah P. Benjamin*, 179–81; Evans, *Judah Benjamin*, 134.

61. Neiman, *Judah Benjamin*, 124–33; Meade, *Judah P. Benjamin*, 185–207.

62. Butler, *Judah Benjamin*, 232–53; Meade, *Judah P. Benjamin*, 219–27.

63. Neiman, *Judah Benjamin*, 131, 134; Meade, *Judah P. Benjamin*, 220–37.

64. Tedlow, "Benjamin," 46; Evans, *Judah Benjamin*, 147–49.

65. Neiman, *Judah Benjamin*, 145–46; Meade, *Judah P. Benjamin*, 235; George C. Rable, *The Confederate Republic* (Chapel Hill: University of North Carolina Press, 1994), 130.

66. Thompson, "David Yulee," 558; Yulee, "Senator David L. Yulee," 2:4.

67. Yulee, "Senator David L. Yulee," 1:38; Mrs. Clement C. Clay Jr. (Virginia Clay-Compton), *A Belle of the Fifties* (New York: Doubleday, 1904), 202. The records of the Washington (Georgia) Rifles show no Elias Yulee. There is an Elias Yulee, captain and commissary, and a Lt. E. Levy, an ordnance officer in Lee's Corps, either of which could be Yulee's brother.

68. Robert C. Black III, *The Railroads of the Confederacy* (Chapel Hill: University of North Carolina Press, 1952), 209; Thompson, "David Yulee," 560.

69. Black, *Railroads*, 37, 200.

70. Thompson, "David Yulee," 519, 526; Lord, "Yulee," 150.

71. Thompson, "David Yulee," 150–53; 525–58; OR I, 6:292–93.

72. Thompson, "David Yulee," 525–28; OR I, 53:214; Lord, "Yulee," 150.

73. Thompson, "David Yulee," 153–56, 533, 556; ORN I, 12:573–76; Lord, "Yulee," 151.

74. A. J. Hanna, *Flight into Oblivion* (Richmond, Va.: Johnson Publishing Co., 1938), 194.

75. Gruss, "Judah Philip Benjamin," 1046; Butler, *Judah Benjamin,* 332; Robert Selph Henry, *The Story of the Confederacy* (Indianapolis, Ind.: Bobbs-Merrill, 1931), 85, 87.

76. Roland, *The Confederacy* (Chicago: University of Chicago Press, 1960), 83, 111.

77. Neiman, *Judah Benjamin,* 112; Butler, *Judah Benjamin,* 332.

78. Meade, *Judah P. Benjamin,* 261.

79. Evans, *Judah Benjamin,* 175–97; Meade, *Judah P. Benjamin,* 253–69.

80. Evans, *Judah Benjamin,* 196–97.

81. Ibid., 196–97; *Statesmen of the Lost Cause,* 222–23; Meade, *Judah P. Benjamin,* 253–69.

82. Evans, *Judah Benjamin,* 197.

83. Meade, *Judah P. Benjamin,* 258–59; Evans, *Judah Benjamin,* 156, 196.

84. Roy Z. Chamlee Jr., *Lincoln's Assassins: A Complete Account of Their Capture, Trial, and Punishment* (Jefferson, N.C.: McFarland & Co., 1990), 401.

85. Meade, *Judah P. Benjamin,* 297–305. For more on Henry J. Leovy, see p. 412, n. 195 below; Evans, *Judah Benjamin,* 193.

86. Meade, *Judah P. Benjamin,* 301–4; William A. Tidwell, *Come Retribution: The Confederate Secret Service and the Assassination of Lincoln* (Jackson: University Press of Mississippi, 1988), chap. 8; Tidwell, *April '65: Confederate Covert Action in the American Civil War* (Kent, Ohio: Kent State University Press, 1995), 127–9.

87. *Yulee v. Canova,* 11 Florida 9; *Florida Reports,* xi, 11–17.

88. Thompson, "David Yulee," 154–55.

89. Black, *Railroads,* 137, 209; Clarke, "Railroad Company," 182–84.

90. Black, *Railroads,* 208, 210; Thompson, "David Yulee," 546 (quote is incorrect in Black).

91. Black *Railroads,* 211–12, 190; Clarke, "Railroad Company," 189–91.

92. Black *Railroads,* 201; Yulee, "Senator David L. Yulee," 2:7–8; Thompson, "David Yulee," 64.

93. Yulee, "Senator David L. Yulee," 2:7– 9; Thompson, "David Yulee," 164.

94. Joseph G. Adler, "The Public Career of Senator David Levy Yulee," 171.

95. Evans, *Judah Benjamin,* 279–80.

96. Ibid., 282.

97. Ibid., 284–85; Meade, *Judah P. Benjamin,* 307.

98. Chamlee, *Lincoln's Assassins,* 403, 532; William Hanchett, *The Lincoln Murder Conspiracies* (Urbana: University of Illinois Press, 1986), 52; Tidwell, *Come Retribution,* 419, 430, and passim; Tidwell, *April '65,* chap. 5; Chamlee, *Lincoln's Assassins,* 403 ("the evidence linking the Confederate leaders to the kidnap plot is undeniable").

CHAPTER 3

1. Letter dated April 17, 1864, to "My Dear Parents, Bros. & Sisters," TU, Simon Mayer Papers, Family Papers, #815, Box 1; CSR, Simon Mayer. Mayer served officially as a private for most of the war. He served as a clerk in the assistant adjutant general's office in Chalmers's brigade and became acting assistant adjutant general of Sharp's Brigade by

402   war's end. He was promoted to first lieutenant, and his parole records show him as a first lieutenant in the Consolidated 9th Mississippi. Nevertheless, he may have been unofficially promoted to major in the field as befitted the position of division AAG, as Sharp's Brigade was composed of the consolidated remnants of three brigades. Local histories refer to him as major, but this rank is not reflected in his CSR.

2. Berman, *Richmond's Jewry,* 126.

3. Gallagher, *The Confederate War,* 96–111, 144.

4. Adolph's grandfather, Mayer Ben Halevey Proskauer, was, according to family tradition, a professor at the University of Proskau. Prior to Napoleon's edict that all Jews should have surnames (or "Christian names"), the professor's name was Joseph Mayer Ben Halevey (Hah-LAY-vey). One day, so the family story goes, the professor stopped at a toll gate to talk to one of his fellow members of the goldsmith and silversmith guild, who called each other "brother" (Brudder). The keeper of the tollgate asked who the professor was, and, as he had failed to comply with the law requiring a surname, his fellow guild members said "almost in unison, that is brother Proskauer, because he was known for teaching at the University of Proskau. So the tollman wrote down, Joseph Mayer Proskauer." (Jenny Proskauer Recollections, October 28, 1948, St. Louis, Mo., AJA, p. 2); see note 59, p. 406.

5. As to Triest, see note 131, p. 410; Baruch, see note 180, pp. 411–12; Kursheedt, see note 72, p. 407; Fischel, see Turitz and Turitz, *Jews in Early Mississippi,* 48–49.

6. Simonhoff, *Jewish Participants in the Civil War,* 193; Young, *Where They Lie,* passim; as to Hyams, see notes 226–235, pp. 413–14; E. J. Levy, notes 29–32, p. 403; Moise, note 86, p. 408; Valentine, note 2, ch. 1, p. 392; Yates Levy, notes 33–40, pp. 403–5; Luria, note 3, prologue, p. 380; n. 137, ch. 3, p. 410.

7. Jewish officers undoubtedly encountered some anti-Semitism. One Jewish officer, according to Bell I. Wiley, encountered so much resistance he could not effectively command the unit to which he was assigned. "Although there were many foreigners in the Rebel Army," Wiley wrote, "prejudice against officers on the score of non-nativity was sometimes a factor in their unpopularity." The Jewish officer was a colonel, assigned command of a Texas regiment sent east to Richmond. The men began making remarks in his presence, "What?" said one. "What is it? Is it a man, a fish, or a bird?" "Of course it is a man," said another, "don't you see his legs?" The men opposed him on a daily basis, until he awoke to find his horse without his tail, when he gave up. See Bell I. Wiley, *The Life of Johnny Reb,* 236–37, citing Nicholas A. Davis, *The Campaign from Texas to Maryland with the Battle of Fredericksburg* (Richmond, 1863), 18–19. But there is very little evidence of anti-Semitism in the Confederate army, and this one example is atypical.

8. Robert K. Krick, *Lee's Colonels: A Biographical Register of the Field Officers of the Army of Northern Virginia* (Dayton, Ohio: Morningside House, 1992), introduction (14–18); Gary Gallagher, *Confederate War,* 98.

9. Karl H. Grismer, *The Story of Fort Myers: The History of the Land of the Caloosahatchee and Southwest Florida.* ([Fort Myers, Fla.]: Southwest Florida Historical Society, 1949; reprint, Fort Myers Beach, Fla.: Island Press Publishers, 1982, 60–61); Burke, "Quartermaster," 13–19; see note 90 below.

10. Grismer, *Fort Myers,* 60–61; *Historical Times Illustrated Encyclopedia of the Civil War,* 767; Burke, "Quartermaster," 22 and 40.

11. Elzas, *Jews of South Carolina,* 207, 236; Wolf, *American Jews,* 380.

12. Krick, *Lee's Colonels,* 236.

13. Leonard G. Dauber, M.D., "David Camden DeLeon, M.D.: Patriot or Traitor," *New York State Journal of Medicine,* December 1, 1970 (2927–33), 2929; and *Twentieth Century Biographical Dictionary.*

14. Young, *Where They Lie,* 175–270.

15. CSR of Michael Levy (6th Arkansas, Company E, and M. Levy General & Staff, Lt. Ord. Off.; Roster of Company A, 6th Arkansas [J. H. Levy]).

16. Young, *Where They Lie,* 23, 214, 223.

17. CSR of Michael Levy. Gen. Braxton Bragg's chief of ordnance, Lt. Col. Hypolite Olandowski, wrote Maj. J. T. Champney, "Lieut. W. M. Levy [*sic*] is ordered to report to you for duty. I cannot say he is entirely posted in ordnance manual, but permit me to introduce him as an intelligent and energetic young officer, and I hope, with your instructions and teachings he will be efficient." Presumably, Levy had served under Olandowski and was therefore a part of Bragg's staff. By September 1862 Levy was post ordnance officer. By December 1862 he was stationed in Bridgeport, Alabama, where he was an ordnance officer. He wrote Olandowski requesting an examination by a board so that he could be promoted to first lieutenant of artillery. He apparently had substantial responsibilities, as he sent carloads of ordnance to Brig. Gen. John Hunt Morgan and Gen. Nathan Bedford Forrest. Levy remained at Bridgeport until March 1863 and was promoted to first lieutenant of artillery in September 1863. His salary was ninety dollars per month plus ten dollars in "hazardous duty pay." He was on detached duty with Brig. Gen. Gideon Pillow's Volunteer and Conscription Bureau from October to December 1863. (His military records end in December 1863, but his family referred to him as a captain after the war, so he may very well have been promoted to captain.) See *Confederate Veteran* 18, no. 6 (June 1910): 265, and his CSR.

18. All of these letters are contained in the CSR of Octavus Cohen.

19. June 10, 1862 letter from Octavus Cohen, Phillips-Myers Papers, Southern Historical Collection, UNC.

20. July 5, 1862 letter, Phillips-Myers Papers, UNC; CSR, O. Cohen.

21. CSR, O. Cohen; John Johnson, *The Defense of Charleston Harbor, including Fort Sumter and Adjacent Islands, 1863–1865* (Charleston, 1890), 256.

22. June 13, 1863 letter, Phillips-Myers Papers, UNC.

23. Letter dated July, 1863, Phillips-Myers Papers, UNC.

24. Wise, *Gate of Hell,* 93, 11, 115–16, 175.

25. Letter dated August, 1863, Phillips-Myers Papers, UNC.

26. Letter dated February 25, 1863, Phillips-Myers Papers, UNC; 545, *Historical Times Illustrated Encyclopedia of the Civil War; The Atlas of the Civil War,* 147.

27. Phillips-Myers Papers, UNC; CSR of O. Cohen.

28. James I. Robertson Jr., *Tenting Tonight* (Alexandria, Va: Time-Life Books, 1984), 48.

29. John A. Cutchins, *A Famous Command: The Richmond Light Infantry Blues* (Richmond: Garrett & Massie, 1934), 130; CSR, E. J. Levy.

30. Isaac Levy, letter, AJA; CSR, E. J. Levy.

31. Cutchins, *A Famous Command,* chap. 19; CSR, E. J. Levy.

32. *Historical Times Illustrated Encyclopedia of the Civil War,* 190; James M. Day, *Death in the Trenches* (Alexandria, Va: Time-Life Books, 1986), 75–78; CSR of E. J. Levy.

33. CSR, S. Y. Levy.

34. September 29, 1862, letter, Phillips-Myers Papers, UNC.

35. Ibid., 1–2.

36. Ibid., 4.

37. CSR, S. Y. Levy.

38. Levy to Jacob C. Levy, September 29, 1862, Phillips-Myers Papers, UNC; CSR, S. Y. Levy. Levy's eloquent Prayer for Peace is set forth below in its entirety:

A Prayer for Peace

Captain Samuel Yates Levy
Savannah, November 2, 1863

Almighty God! Eternal sire and king!
Ruler supreme who all things did'st create,
Whose everlasting praise the angels sing,
Whose word is mercy and whose thought is fate:
Trembling before thy awful throne we kneel,
Beseeching mercy at thy gracious hand,
Praying that in compassion thou wilt heal
The bleeding wounds of this most suffering land.
We know our sins are manifold, oh Lord,
And that thy wrath against us is but right,
For we have wandered wildly from thy word
And things committed wrongful in thy sight.
But thou, oh Lord, art powerful to save
And full of mercy, full of love art thou;
Else had we not the courage thus to brave
Thy righteous wrath — thus at thy feet to bow.
O'er all our fields, where late the joyful air
Struck rustling music from the waving grain,
Now the sad earth is lying stark and bare,
or groaning 'neath the burden of our slain.
In sackcloth robed, disconsolate and wild,
With ashes strewed upon her lovely breast,
The Country mourns her hearths and homes defiled,
Weeps for her bravest and bewails her best.
From the cold hearths where lately genial fires
Beamed upon scenes of innocent delight,
The little children vainly call their sires
Or fly their burning homes with wild affright.
Our punishment is very hard to bear:
We droop and faint beneath thy chast'ning rod:
Oh list in mercy to our earnest prayer
And move thy anger from us, oh, our God.
Throw, Lord, thy buckler thick 'twixt us and harm.
Bid the destruction and the carnage cease.
Outstretch in power thy all protecting arm,
Roll back the clouds of War and give us Peace.
And as thou led'st thy chosen people forth

From Egypt's sullen wrath, oh King of Kings!
So smite the armies of the cruel North
And bear us to our hopes "on eagles' wings."
But should thy wisdom still defer the day —
The wish'd for day our freedom shall be won —
Oh grant us the humility to say,
Not human will but Thine, oh Lord, be done.
                    (*AJA,* 10, no. 2 [October 1950]: 133–34).

The allusion to "bear us to our hopes 'on eagles' wings'" is from Exodus 19:4–6 ("Ye have seen what I did unto the Egyptians, and how I bore you on eagles' wings and brought you unto Myself").

39. *Historical Times Illustrated Encyclopedia of the Civil War,* 115, 117.

40. Letter dated March 16, 1865, from Johnson's Island, Phillips-Myers papers, UNC; CSR, S. Y. Levy.

41. Eric J. Brock, "An Exhaustive Study of Hebrew Rest Cemetery Number One, Shreveport, Louisiana," 1992, HNOC; "The Jewish Cemeteries of Shreveport, Louisiana," 1995; Maude Hearne O'Pry, *Chronicles of Shreveport and Caddo Parish* (Shreveport: Journal Publishing Co., 1928), 166; as to Mrs. Grant: *Southwestern,* March 16, 1859.

42. Louisiana Ordinance of Secession and Minutes of Secession Convention (see note 112, ch. 1, p. 391); O'Pry, *Chronicles,* 169; W. N. King, "Journal of W. N. King: A Private Soldier in the La. Infantry," MS, Texas State Archives; *Shreveport (La.) Times,* September 24, 1863; *Confederate Veteran,* 29:357. The author wishes to thank Eric Brock of Shreveport for his kind assistance and his file on Colonel Marks.

43. Maj. Alexander Hart's military record is derived from his compiled service record, which is quite extensive; Hart Diary (July 6, 1864–May 7, 1865), AJA; Andrew B. Booth, *Records of Louisiana Confederate Soldiers and Louisiana Confederate Commands,* 3 vols. (New Orleans, 1920; reprinted Spartanburg, S.C.: Reprint Co., 1984), "Hart, Alexander," 210; Hart obituary in the *Norfolk Landmark,* September 22, 1911; Krick, *Lee's Colonels,* 159; *Confederate Veteran,* December 1911, 589; Arthur W. Bergeron Jr., *Guide to Louisiana Confederate Military Units, 1861–1865* (Baton Rouge: Louisiana State University Press, 1996), 82–84; Jones, *Lee's Tigers,* 128–31, 150–60, 214–17; Stephen W. Sears, *Landscape Turned Red: The Battle of Antietam* (New Haven: Ticknor & Fields, 1983; reprinted Norwalk, Conn.: Easton Press, 1988), 188–89; Jeffry D. Wert, *From Winchester to Cedar Creek: The Shenandoah Campaign of 1864* (Carlisle, Pa.: South Mountain Press, 1987; reprinted New York: Simon & Schuster, 1989), 47–101. Mel Young kindly provided the author with copies of Special Order No. 16 and Report dated January 25, 1864, relative to Hart's brief service in the Department of Henrico (the military prison unit in Richmond).

44. Jones, *Lee's Tigers,* 236–38.

45. Sears, *Landscape Turned Red,* 188; Ezekiel and Lichtenstein, *History of the Jews of Richmond,* 157.

46. Hart Diary, August 1864, AJA.

47. Jones, *Lee's Tigers,* 216.

48. Hart Diary, November 12, 13, 1864, AJA.

49. Hart Diary, November 16–20, 1864, AJA; CSR, Hart.

50. This sketch of William Mallory Levy is based almost entirely on his compiled service record, the OR (ser. 1, vol. 11, pt. 1, 420–21, "Report of Col. Wm. M. Levy, April 18, 1862"); and a few letters in the Levy Family Papers, 1840–1889, Box 2, MSS 408, Williams Research Center, Historic New Orleans Collection: April 23, 1862, and July 5, 1862, to his wife. See also Gen. Richard Taylor's article "The Last Confederate Surrender," in *Southern Historical Society Papers* (1877) and his memoir, *Destruction and Reconstruction* (1879).

51. Levy to his wife, letter dated April 23, 1862, Levy Family Papers, 1840–1889, Box 2, MSS 408, Williams Research Center, HNOC.

52. Levy to his wife, July 5, 1862, HNOC.

53. Letter, June 12, 1862, in compiled service record of W. M. Levy.

54. Letter dated May 1, 1862, in CSR.

55. Letter dated July 5, 1862, in CSR.

56. *Historical Times Illustrated Encyclopedia of the Civil War.*

57. Report of General Taylor, April 18, 1864 (Red River Campaign). OR I, 34, part I, 569–70.

58. Taylor, *Destruction and Reconstruction* (1879); Taylor described his surrender as "The Last Confederate Surrender" in an 1877 article in the *Southern Historical Society Papers*: "Accompanied by a staff officer, Colonel William M. Levy (now a member of Congress from Louisiana), and making use of a 'hand car' I reached the appointed spot, and found General Canby with a large escort."

59. There is very little written about Adolph Proskauer. His nephew Judge Joseph Proskauer wrote a brief account of his uncle's life in his memoir, *A Segment of My Times* (New York: Farrar, Straus, 1950). Adolph Proskauer's daughter Jenny Proskauer wrote an unreliable recollection in 1948, which is at the AJA. The chief source of this material is Robert Emory Park, *Sketch of the Twelfth Alabama Infantry of Battle's Brigade, Rodes Division, Early's Corps, of the Army of Northern Virginia* (Richmond: W. E. Jones, 1906), originally printed in *Southern Historical Society Papers* 33, pp. 193–296. This work is generally reliable and well written, but Park erred in his description of Proskauer at Gettysburg. Proskauer was neither wounded nor captured at Gettysburg. He was wounded three times, and each is referred to in Proskauer's compiled service record, which also includes a letter from Proskauer himself in 1865 stating that he had been wounded three times. The details of Proskauer's military career are derived from his compiled service record as well as the OR, where his name is misspelled "Proskaner." See ser. 1, vol. 25, pt. 1, 960 (Reports of Col. Samuel B. Pickens, 12th Alabama, May 5, 1863); ser. 1, vol. 36, pt. 1, 1083 (May 9, 1864); 1:27, 563; 1:25, 950–53 (Reports of Col. Edward A. O'Neal, May 12, 1863); 1:29, 891–92 (Reports of Maj. A. Proskaner, January 22, 1864). Also see Young, *Where They Lie,* 76, 78–79; Krick, *Lee's Colonels,* 266; Korn, *American Jewry,* 176; obituary of Adolph Proskauer, AJA (the AJA has an extensive file on Proskauer); Park, *Sketch,* 5.

60. Park, *Sketch,* 16–17.

61. Ibid., 31.

62. *Historical Times Illustrated Encyclopedia of the Civil War,* 18.

63. Park, *Sketch,* 10.

64. Korn, *American Jewry,* 176.

65. Park, *Sketch,* 53–54; Champ Clark, *Gettysburg* (Alexandria, Va.: Time-Life, 1985), 53–54.

66. Park, *Sketch,* 54; Foote, *The Civil War: A Narrative* (New York: Random House, 1974) 2:488, 528.

67. Clark, *Gettysburg,* 127–28; *Historical Times Illustrated Encyclopedia of the Civil War,* 196.

68. Park, *Sketch,* 55.

69. Park, *Sketch,* 62–69, CSR, Adolph Proskauer.

70. CSR, Adolph Proskauer.

71. Joseph H. Crute Jr., *Units of the Confederate Army,* 2d ed. (Gaithersburg, Md.: Olde Soldier Books, 1987), passim.

72. Edwin I. Kursheedt's career is described in his compiled service records, the OR (ser. 1, vol. 11, pt. 11, chap. 23, 925–26; chap. 63, 39–40, 222–24); William Miller Owen, *In Camp and Battle with the Washington Artillery of New Orleans* (Boston: Ticknor & Co., 1885), 17, 134–35, 180–191, 308–9, 314–17, 361; Napier Bartlett, *Military Record of Louisiana* (Baton Rouge, 1875; reprint, New Orleans: Louisiana State University Press, 1992), 225–31 (Muster Roll of Washington Artillery); and Ezekiel and Lichtenstein, *History of the Jews of Richmond.* Both the OR and the CSR erroneously refer to Kursheedt as E. J. Kurshudt or R. J. Kursheedt.

73. Ashkenazi, *Diary of Clara Solomon,* 86, 89; see muster roll of First Company in Napier Bartlett, *A Soldier's Story of the War; Including the Marches and Battles of the Washington Artillery and of Other Louisiana Troops* (New Orleans, n.p., 1874), 228–29.

74. Ashkenazi, *Diary of Clara Solomon,* 79.

75. Report of Lt. Charles W. Squires, September 4, 1861, OR I, 151, 39–40, part 1, chap. 63, (Skirmish at Great Falls, Md.); CSR, E. J. Kursheedt.

76. April 27, 1862, letter, Edwin I. Kursheedt papers #2805Z, Southern Historical Collection, UNC.

77. Undated letter, probably May 1862, to "Miss Sallie" ("Bivouac 1 mile from Lebanon Church"), Southern Historical Collection, UNC.

78. Letter to "My Dear Miss Sarah," June 25, 1862, Kursheedt Papers, UNC.

79. Ibid.

80. Ibid.

81. Owen, *Washington Artillery,* 134–35.

82. Ibid., 189–91.

83. Eshleman may have been born a Jew, or he may have had Jewish ancestors. He was well known in the New Orleans Jewish community, and the name Eshleman is a German-Jewish name. He married Fanny H. Leverich, who also had a possible Jewish name. Elliot Ashkenazi, the editor of Clara Solomon's diary, states that Eshleman was "one of several Jewish members of the Washington Artillery," but Eshleman was a member of the Episcopal Church after the war and served on the vestry of Christ Church for twenty-seven years (*Diary of Clara Solomon,* 81n. 21); biography of Col. B. F. Eshleman in "Historical Military Data of Louisiana Militia, Washington Artillery, July–Dec. 1861," Hill Memorial Library, Louisiana State University Collection. All genealogical research to date has failed to prove Eshleman was Jewish. Box 1 of the Craig, Fanny Leverich Eshleman Collection (#225) at Tulane's Special Collection yielded a 1770 edition of *The Book of Common Prayer.* Fanny and her siblings were confirmed in the church in April 1861. Clara Solomon, however, generally wrote about Jews in her diary, and Eshleman's initial romance was with a Jewish woman, Charlotte da Ponte or Brooks. Letter from Elliott Ashkenazi to Mel Young dated

February 20, 1997. Kursheedt may have known Eshleman before the war, as the major asked the young sergeant to become his adjutant. "I am under especial obligations," Eshleman reported after Gettysburg, "to Sergeant Major E. J. [*sic*] Kursheedt, who (having no adjutant) acted as my aide. He was always at hand, frequently under the heaviest fire, performing his duty with coolness and efficiency."

84. Owen, *Washington Artillery*, 314.

85. Korn, *American Jewry*, 90; letter, December 28, 1864, AJA ; see Korn, note 105, 265.

86. This sketch of E. W. Moise is based primarily on *The Moise Family*, 75, 108–26, as well as his compiled service record. His records are cataloged under Company A, 7th Confederate Cavalry, and the 10th Georgia Cavalry.

87. William Frayne Amann, ed., *Personnel of the Civil War* (New York: Yoseloff, 1961), 100; Marcus Wright, *Local Designations of Confederate Troops* (1876).

88. *Supplement to OR, Record of Events*, vol. 5, *Georgia Troops (Confederate) Cavalry*, 553–54; Sifakis, *Compendium of the Confederate States Armies*, 170–71, 159; Crute, *Units of the Confederate States Army*, 70, 90; OR, 1:18 chap. 30, 142 (February 4, 1863); OR Navy, 1:9, 424–34 (February 2, 1864) (*Smith Briggs* incident); OR, 1:33 chap. 65, 103 (January 29–February 1, 1864); OR, 1:33, chap. 65, 273–74; Richard W. Lykes, "The Great Civil War Beef Raid," *Civil War Times Illustrated* (February 1967): 4; OR, 1:36; 3:421 (May 1864); Mark L. Bradley, *Last Stand in the Carolinas: The Battle of Bentonville*, 92–104, 376–96; John G. Barrett, *Sherman's March through the Carolinas* (Chapel Hill: University of North Carolina Press, 1956), 204. While the family history shows Moise as a major, his compiled service record does not. He was never officially promoted to major, or if he was, the records do not reflect it.

89. "The Great Civil War Beef Raid," 47.

90. The best source on Abraham C. Myers is Richard D. Goff, *Confederate Supply* (Durham, N.C.: Duke University Press, 1969), an excellent scholarly work on the Confederate supply bureaus. Walter Burke Jr. has written a useful pamphlet entitled "Quartermaster: A Brief Account of the Life of Colonel Abraham Charles Myers, Quartermaster General C.S.A," published in 1976. William C. Davis, *Breckinridge: Statesman, Soldier, Symbol* (Baton Rouge: Louisiana State University Press, 1974); Davis, *Jefferson Davis: The Man and His Hour* (New York: Harper Collins, 1991); and Davis, *A Government of Our Own: The Making of the Confederacy* (New York: Free Press, 1994). Thomas Cooper DeLeon, the irrepressible author of *Belles, Beaux, and Brains of the '60s* and *Four Years in Rebel Capitals: An Inside View of Life in the Southern Confederacy, from Birth to Death* (Mobile: Gossip Printing Co., 1890), knew Myers personally and was well acquainted with his family, as both DeLeon and Myers had been born and raised in the Jewish community in South Carolina, DeLeon in Columbia and Myers in Georgetown. The same was probably true of Mary Chesnut, who was also from South Carolina and knew the Jewish community through her close friendship with Miriam DeLeon Cohen. Thus, her diary, *Mary Chesnut's Civil War*, is a good source on Myers.

See also Grismer, *Fort Myers;* Samuel Bernard Thompson, *Confederate Purchasing Operations Abroad* (Chapel Hill: University of North Carolina Press, 1935); Clement Eaton, *A History of the Southern Confederacy* (New York: Macmillan Co., 1954); Patricia L. Faust, ed., *Historical Times Illustrated Encyclopedia of the Civil War* (New York: Harper Collins, 1991); Ellsworth Eliot Jr., *West Point in the Confederacy* (New York: G. A. Baker and Co., 1941); Frank E. Vandiver, ed., "Proceedings of the First Confederate Congress

[1723–1726]," *Southern Historical Society Papers* 50 (1953): 109–12; Black, *Railroads;* DeLeon, *Four Years* and *Belles, Beaux, and Brains;* John Beauchamp Jones, *A Rebel War Clerk's Diary at the Confederate States Capital,* 2 vols., edited by Howard Swiggett (New York: Old Hickory Bookshop, 1935); Elzas, *Jews of South Carolina.* I wish to thank Diane Kremski of the City of Fort Myers for providing material on Col. Abraham C. Myers, and my mother-in-law, Mrs. Joyce Ann Corner of Naples, Florida, for finding Ms. Kremski.

91. Goff, *Confederate Supply,* 6–10.

92. Ibid., 3–4.

93. DeLeon, *Belles, Beaux, and Brains,* 120; Goff, 16–21.

94. Woodward, *Mary Chesnut,* 271, 428–29, 496–97.

95. Goff, *Confederate Supply,* 127–30; Burke, "Quartermaster," 27–28.

96. Geoffrey C. Ward, *The Civil War: An Illustrated History* (New York: Knopf, 1990), 62.

97. Goff, *Confederate Supply,* 23–26; Woodward, *Mary Chesnut,* 124.

98. DeLeon, *Four Years,* 114.

99. Goff, *Confederate Supply,* 50–51; Pollard, *Southern History of the War,* 1:535–56.

100. Goff, *Confederate Supply,* 27, 29, 33, 34, 52, 72–75.

101. Ibid., 54–62.

102. Ibid., 69–71.

103. Ibid., 75–76, 85–86; "Tax in Kind," in *Historical Times Illustrated Encyclopedia of the Civil War,* 74.

104. Richard E. Beringer, *Why the South Lost the Civil War* (Athens: University of Georgia Press, 1986), 14–16.

105. Goff, *Confederate Supply,* 40.

106. Ibid., 104–7, 110–11, 41–42.

107. Ibid., 44–46.

108. Ibid., 132, 142.

109. McPherson, *Battle Cry,* 319; Goff, *Confederate Supply,* 143–44.

110. Burke, "Quartermaster," 29–30.

111. *DAB*; Charles Roland contends that Davis rightly declared the Senate's action unconstitutional (Roland, *The Confederacy,* 133).

112. James G. Randall and David Donald, *The Civil War and Reconstruction,* 2d ed. (Lexington, Mass.: D. C. Heath & Co., 1969): 253.

113. Quoted in Eaton, *A History of the Southern Confederacy,* 138.

114. Goff, *Confederate Supply,* 186.

115. Ibid., 142.

116. Eaton, *A History of the Southern Confederacy,* 138; Davis, *Jefferson Davis,* 537–38.

117. Davis, *Jefferson Davis,* 537; Goff, *Confederate Supply,* 142.

118. Woodward, *Mary Chesnut,* 437n. 5.

119. Ibid., 437, 447.

120. Ibid., 438.

121. Ibid., 524.

122. Goff, *Confederate Supply,* 142.

123. Woodward, *Mary Chesnut,* 532; Sallie B. Putnam [A Richmond Lady], *Richmond during the War: Four Years of Personal Observation* (New York, 1867; reprinted in Collector's Library of the Civil War, Alexandria, Va.: Time-Life Books, 1983), 275.

410   124. Jones was a native of Baltimore. *A Rebel War Clerk's Diary,* condensed edition, edited by Earl Schenck Miers (New York: Sagamore Press, 1958); see 1:186; 2:8; Berman, *Richmond's Jewry,* 187.

125. Woodward, *Mary Chesnut,* 551.

126. Goff, *Confederate Supply,* 150–51.

127. *DAB.*

128. Burke, "Quartermaster," 34.

129. *DAB.*

130. Burke, "Quartermaster," 35–36.

131. CSR, Maier Triest; William J. Rivers, *Rivers' Account of the Raising of Troops in South Carolina for State and Confederate Service 1861–1865* (Columbia: Bryan Publishing Co., 1899), 29–30.

132. Elzas, *Jews of South Carolina,* 235. The compiled service record neither corroborates nor contradicts this statement.

133. Jerry Korn, *War on the Mississippi* (Alexandria, Va.: Time-Life, 1985), 109.

134. Eugene W. Jones Jr., *Enlisted for the War: The Struggles of the Gallant 24th Regiment, South Carolina Volunteers, 1861–1865* (Hightown, N.J.: Longstreet House, 1997); on Triest, see 15, 91, 214; Capers letter dated May 17, 1863, South Caroliniana Library, University of South Carolina; Elzas, *Jews of South Carolina,* 171, 235.

135. Elzas, *Jews of South Carolina,* 235.

136. Freeman, *Lee's Lieutenants,* 2:439; G. Moxley Sorrell, *Recollections of a Confederate Staff Officer,* 126.

137. Moses's three sons all served in the Confederate armed forces. The youngest, Raphael J. ("Lea") Moses Jr. joined the Confederate navy. Albert Moses Luria joined the Columbus Light Guards, transferred to the 13th/23rd North Carolina, and served and died in the Army of Northern Virginia. The oldest, Israel Moses Nunez, born in Florida in 1838, was nicknamed "Major." Major took care of the family plantation and businesses when his father and younger brother Albert went off to war. By virtue of the Confederate "Twenty-Negro Law," a plantation owner with twenty slaves or more was entitled to an exemption allowing one white male to stay at home, which Major did until 1863. The Confederate Congress revised the law in May 1863 and required planters to pay $500 for the exemption. In December 1863, "Major" Nunez enlisted as a private in Parker's Virginia Battery of Artillery in his father's corps and reported for duty at Bean Station, Tennessee, near Knoxville. Probably on account of his father's influence, Major was sent to corps headquarters; he rejoined Parker's battery in the summer of 1864 and served in the trenches with the artillery defending Petersburg, Virginia. At the end of the war in May 1865, Major had rejoined his father in Georgia. See, generally, Moses, *Last Order,* xiv, 77, 220; McPherson, *Battle Cry,* 611–12.

138. Nevins, *Emergence,* 2:434.

139. Rosen, *Confederate Charleston,* 66.

140. Nevins, *War,* 1:98; Marcus, *Memoirs,* 1:146–47; Moses, *Last Order,* 113–14; CSR, R. J. Moses.

141. Moses, *Last Order,* 157–59.

142. Ibid., 161–62.

143. Ibid., 114–15, 175.

144. Wert, *Longstreet,* 208–9; Moses, *Last Order,* 170.

145. Wert, *Longstreet,* 211.

146. Moses, *Last Order,* 170–71.

147. Ibid., 174.

148. Ibid., 175.

149. Wert, *Longstreet,* 224.

150. Moses, *Last Order,* 178.

151. D. S. Freeman, *Lee's Lieutenants,* 2:477–78.

152. Moses, *Last Order,* 180–82.

153. Fremantle, *Three Months in the Southern States: April-June, 1863.*

154. Ibid.

155. Ibid.

156. Moses, *Last Order,* 185–86.

157. Marcus, *Memoirs,* 1:4; G. Moxley Sorrel, *Recollections of a Confederate Staff Officer* (New York: Smithmark Publishers, 1994), 126, 178.

158. Wert, *Longstreet,* 83.

159. Moses, *Last Order,* 115–16.

160. CSR, R. J. Moses.

161. Moses, *Last Order,* 187.

162. Fremantle, *Three Months,* 240.

163. Ibid., 271.

164. Moses, *Last Order,* 188.

165. Ibid., 201–4.

166. Ibid., 206–7.

167. Wert, *Longstreet,* 393.

168. H. H. Cunningham, *Doctors in Gray: The Confederate Medical Service* (Baton Rouge: Louisiana State University Press, 1958), 27.

169. DeLeon, *Belles, Beaux, and Brains,* 121.

170. Woodward and Muhlenfeld, *The Private Mary Chesnut,* 29–31.

171. Dauber, 2932; catalog, *AJHS* (1962): 406.

172. Cullop, *Confederate Propaganda,* 80n. 40 (DeLeon to Benjamin January 8, 1863 [Pickett Papers]).

173. Dauber, 2932n. 40.

174. C. Vann Woodward and Elisabeth Muhlenfeld, eds., *The Private Mary Chesnut: The Unpublished Civil War Diaries* (New York: Oxford University Press, 1984), 29.

175. Ibid., 78.

176. Ibid., 114.

177. Dauber, 2929.

178. Baruch, *My Own Story,* 5.

179. Ibid., 1–12.

180. Baruch's war record is based on his compiled service record, and his recollections contained in *Confederate Veteran Magazine* 12 (December 1914): 22, 545–48; and "Bernard Baruch's Father Recounts His Experiences as a Confederate Surgeon," a reprint of a newspaper account in the *Long Branch Record* of an address Baruch made on September 23, 1915, before a historical society in Long Branch, New York. The reprint is titled "Experiences as a Confederate Surgeon" in *Civil War Times Illustrated* 4, no. 6 (October 1965): 40–47. Simon Baruch's service records are cataloged under the 13th Mississippi, Surgeon (where his name is sometimes "S. Barnet"); 3rd S.C. Battalion; and "General & Staff Surgeon, 3rd S.C. Battalion," which yielded a typewritten summary and correspondence.

412   181. Baruch, "Experiences as a Confederate Surgeon," 40–47.

182. Ibid., 42.

183. Baruch, *My Own Story,* 7–9; Baruch, "Experiences as a Confederate Surgeon," 42.

184. Baruch, *My Own Story,* 8.

185. Simon Baruch, "A Surgeon's Story of Battle and Capture," *Confederate Veteran* 22, no. 12 (December 1914): 545–48; Baruch, "Experiences as a Confederate Surgeon," 43.

186. Baruch, "Experiences as a Confederate Surgeon," 43.

187. Baruch, "A Surgeon's Story," 545.

188. Baruch, "Experiences as a Confederate Surgeon," 43.

189. Ibid., 44–45.

190. Baruch, "A Surgeon's Story," 546–47.

191. Baruch, *My Own Story,* 10; Baruch, "Experiences as a Confederate Surgeon," 45–46.

192. Baruch, "Experiences as a Confederate Surgeon," 46.

193. Ibid., 46–47.

194. William M. Robinson, Jr., *Justice in Grey: A History of the Judicial System of the Confederate States of America* (Cambridge, Mass.: Harvard University Press, 1941), 408, 460.

195. Col. Henry J. Leovy's activities are briefly described in Robinson, *Justice in Grey,* 409–11. His activities as a special commissioner are described in the OR IV, 4: 802–15 and Kenneth W. Noe, "Red String Scare: Civil War Southwest Virginia and the Heroes of America," *North Carolina Historical Review* 69, no. 3, July 1992, 301–22. Noe has Leovy's name as "Leory" because the OR made the same mistake. On the flight of the cabinet, see Hanna, *Flight into Oblivion.* See Leovy's obituary, *Daily Picayune,* October 4, 1902; 10, col. 2; letters from Jefferson Davis to Leovy dated May 26, 1877, and November 10, 1883, Historic New Orleans Collection (Henry J. Leovy Papers, 1859–1900).

196. Letter dated October 31, 1863, to Leovy, Henry J. Leovy Papers, HNOC.

197. Noe, "Red String Scare," 301–22. Charles Frazier mentions the Red Strings in his popular novel, *Cold Mountain.*

198. Noe, "Red String Scare," 315–16.

199. OR IV, 3:802–15, 805, 812. The OR refers to him as "Leory."

200. OR IV, 3,:802.

201. Robinson, *Justice in Grey,* 411.

202. Ledger book of Confederate commissions in the National Archives, chap. 1, vol. 94 (confirmed January 12, 1865, to rank from December 26, 1864). My thanks to Bruce Allardice for providing this information on Leovy.

203. *Register of Officers of the Confederate States Navy, 1861–1865* (Washington: GPO, 1931), 48.

204. ORN, I, 2:822–24; Raimondo Luraghi, *A History of the Confederate Navy* (Annapolis: Naval Institute Press, 1996), 312.

205. *Historical Times Illustrated Encyclopedia of the Civil War,* 5; Luraghi, *History of the Confederate Navy,* 277–78, 291–99, 329–31.

206. "Military Record of the DeLeon Family and of Captain Perry M. DeLeon," *PAJHS* 1, no. 4 (June 1961).

207. Harby's military career is confusing. He trained troops in artillery in Harrisburg, Texas, near Galveston early in the war. (H. S. Lubbock to Col. X. B. Debray, October 15, 1862, has Lieutenant Harby stationed at Harrisburg. Debray to Lieutenant General Pemberton, November 12, 1862, has Harby training men in artillery practice. OR I,

15:830–31; 864–65.) He was an officer, not in the Confederate army or navy, but in the Texas Maritime Department or Service. He apparently was commissioned a lieutenant and was later promoted to captain. Harby did not turn the *Henry Dodge* over to the Confederates; he may have resigned and allowed Lt. William F. Rodgers to do so. See ORN I, 16:867–68; 18:85; *Confederate Military History Extended Edition*, vol. 6, *South Carolina* (Wilmington, N.C.: Broadfoot Publishing Co., 1987), 628–29; Charles W. Hayes, *History of the Island the City of Galveston* (Cincinnati, 1879), 550–77. Henry J. Harby and J. O. Harby are listed in *The Roster of Confederate Soldiers; The Jewish Texans*, 7; Simonhoff, *Jewish Participants in the Civil War*, 261; Simonhoff, *Deep in the Heart*, 24. Harby was married to Leonora R. DeLeon of Savannah (*Confederate Military History*, 629).

208. Edward T. Cothan Jr., *Battle on the Bay* (Austin: University of Texas Press, 1998), 108–11; Donald S. Frasier, *Cottonclads! The Battle of Galveston and the Defense of the Texas Coast*, (Fort Worth, Tex.: Ryan Place Publishers, 1996), 46–77; Sharf, *History of the Confederate Navy*, 506–13; *Confederate Veteran* 2 (1998); Campbell, "Victory at Galveston," 16–26.

209. Magruder's official report dated February 26, 1863; OR Series I, 15:211–20 (chap. 27).

210. Frasier, *Cottonclads!*, 73.

211. Cothan, *Battle on the Bay*, 124.

212. Ibid., 125.

213. Frasier, *Cottonclads!*, 75.

214. OR I, vol. 15, chap. 27, p. 211.

215. OR I, vol. 15, chap. 27, p. 217.

216. Letter to F. R. Lubbock from J. B. Magruder, February 11, 1863; OR I, vol. 15, chap. 27, p. 974–75.

217. *Confederate Military History*, 629.

218. Moses, *Last Order*, xiv–xv.

219. Ibid., 119–21; Civil War Dictionary, "Tattnall."

220. *Historical Times Illustrated Encyclopedia of the Civil War*, 304; Luraghi, *History of Confederate Navy*, 231–32. In May 1864, the ship was sold at Liverpool. Moses, *Last Order*, 223; 1909 obituary.

221. Moses, *Last Order*, 223–24.

222. Ibid., 224.

223. Luraghi, *History of Confederate Navy*, 60. Simonhoff, *Jewish Participants in the Civil War*, 259. Solomon Breibart contends that this was "wishful thinking" on Simonhoff's part.

224. Ruth H. Duncan, *The Captain and Submarine C.S.S.* Hunley (Memphis, Tenn.: S. C. Toof & Co., 1965), 60.

225. Ibid., 79.

226. The Hyams family has a remarkably undocumented history. Even Simon Wolf misspelled their names in his listing of Confederate soldiers. There is not a biographical essay on Lt. Gov. Henry M. Hyams, who was one of the most prominent *practicing* Jews of nineteenth-century America. The glaring omission of Hyams and Benjamin F. Jonas in American Jewish historiography is curious. Korn gives a sketch of Hyams in *The Early Jews of New Orleans* (188–89), as does Elzas in *Jews of South Carolina* (191). See also Young, *Where They Lie*, 6–7, 38–9, 158–62; Ashkenazi, *Diary of Clara Solomon;* Marcus, *Memoirs*, 3:104 (Rothschild letter); Malcolm H. Stern, *Americans of Jewish Descent* (New York: KTAV Publishing

414   House, 1971), 87; *The Jewish Encyclopedia* (New York, 1901–5), 1:512; AJA (obituaries, Korn files, Elzas manuscript, and Judith Hyams Douglas material); obituary, *New Orleans Daily Picayune,* June 26, 1875; *Dictionary of Louisiana Biography,* vol. 1 (Louisiana Historical Association). Rabbi Task and Nancy Greenberg of Alexandria, Louisiana, kindly provided me with a brief typewritten recollection of Hyams family members.

The wartime activities of all of the Hyamses is derived from their extensive compiled service records at the National Archives, the Official Record, and various secondary sources on units and battles. A number of Hyamses appear in Andrew W. Booth's *Records of Louisiana Confederate Soldiers and Louisiana Confederate Commands.*

Despite the fact that Hyams was a lieutenant governor, his wartime career is difficult to reconstruct. He was not at the secession convention. Much of the material used herein is contained in obituaries, letters, and memoranda at the AJA. As to Hyams's life after the war, see letters at AJA and a letter to former Governor Moore, published in the *Louisiana Historical Quarterly* 13 (January 1930): 20–22.

227. As to Isaac S. Hyams, see his compiled service record, which includes the Benjamin letter; OR I, 20:976; I, 20:762–767; OR Supplement, *Record of Events,* 23:660–61; Glen Tucker, *Chickamauga: Bloody Battle in the West* (Indianapolis: Bobbs-Merrill, 1961), 270; *History of the Confederate States Marine Corps,* 22–39, 184–225.

228. CSR, I. S. Hyams, letter of D. Coleman, January 1863.

229. CSR, I. S. Hyams.

230. CSR, Samuel Myers Hyams; William H. Tunnard, *A Southern Record: A History of the Third Regiment, Louisiana Infantry* (reprint, Fayetteville: University of Arkansas Press, 1997), 28–39, 64–67, 108–18, 184–85, 324–25, 529; OR Supplement, *Record of Events,* vol. 23, Louisiana Troops (Confederate), 740; *Guide to Louisiana Military Units,* 77; OR IV, 1:748–9; I, 53:808–9; I, 3:113–16; I, 3:588–89; *Louisiana History* 2 (winter 1961): 7–105 (Journal of Proceedings).

231. Tunnard, *A Southern Record,* 29–30.

232. Ibid., 64.

233. Ibid., 36, 108.

234. Ibid., 324.

235. CSR, Samuel M. Hyams Jr.; OR Supplement, *Record of Events,* vol. 32, *Mississippi Confederate Troops,* 345, 339 (Confederate); 38:149, 140; Robert Selph Henry, *"First with the Most" Forrest* (Indianapolis: Bobbs-Merrill, 1944), 312–15; OR I, 49:1030–31 (Forrest to Taylor, March 6, 1865); I, 49:956; I, 39:315, 609, 648, 676, 805–6, 809; I, 3:113–16; I, 30:496–97; I, 23:23, 191; I, 16:827–28; I, 8:293–94; I, 41:171. OR Supplement, *Record of Events,* vol. 32, *Mississippi Troops (Confederate)—Cavalry,* 141–49; 338–45; Report of Col. Louis Hebert, August 10, 1861.

236. Young, *Where They Lie,* 7.

237. Abraham Jonas followed his brother Joseph from England to America. Joseph, a native of Exeter, arrived in Cincinnati in 1817 at the age of twenty-five, the first Jew in that town and, indeed, the first Jew in Ohio. The leaders of the congregation in New York warned him that "in the wilds of America and entirely amongst Gentiles, you will forget your religion and your God." An old Quaker woman came to see him. She asked: "Art thou a Jew? Thou art one of God's chosen people. Wilt thou let me examine thee?" She turned him around and finally said, with a tinge of disappointment in her voice: "Well, thou art no different to other people." Joseph prospered as a watchmaker, silversmith, and mechanic. He was elected to the Ohio legislature and was a founder of the first synagogue in the west,

K. K. B'nai Israel. Despite his move to the "wilds of America," he continued to be an observing Orthodox Jew. When the Civil War was over, Joseph moved to Mobile, Alabama, where his son practiced law and where he died in 1869 (*Universal Jewish Encyclopedia*, 179; Marcus, *Memoirs*, 1:203–13).

Joseph's brother Abraham Jonas was a Henry Clay Whig. He believed in the national government and disliked the "Slave Oligarchy." Like many pioneers of the West, he moved about. He followed his brother to Cincinnati in 1819 with a group of Jews from Plymouth and Portsmouth and aided in the founding of the synagogue. His first wife was Lucia Orah Seixas, the daughter of Rabbi Gershom Seixas of New York, the Revolutionary War hero and friend of George Washington (Ira L. Harris, "Abraham Jonas, Lincoln's Most Valued Friend," paper at AJA). She died tragically in 1826. To escape his grief, Jonas moved to Williamstown, Kentucky, in 1827 (Simonhoff, *Jewish Notables in America*, 348–52.). There he met and married Louisa Block.

Jonas was elected four times to the Kentucky House of Representatives in the late 1820s and 1830s (Korn, *American Jewry*, 189–91). He knew Henry Clay and believed in him. Writing in 1858 to Sen. John K. Crittenden, whom Jonas had known when Crittenden was Speaker of the House of Representatives in Kentucky, he said, "Permit an old friend to express his satisfaction and delight, at reading your recent able speech on Kansas affairs . . . I am quite sure that had Mr. Clay been alive and by your side in the Senate, he would have spoken as you did" (Korn Papers, AJA, letter dated March 22, 1858). Half of the Jonas children were born in Kentucky in the 1830s and 1840s.

238. Rabbi Bertram Korn was particularly interested in Abraham Jonas and his family. He appended the Jonas-Lincoln correspondence to *American Jewry and the Civil War* and hoped one day to publish a "sizable monograph" on the patriarch. He regarded Abraham Jonas as "one of the most fascinating Jewish figures of the period" and found it "exceedingly significant that Mr. Jonas's sons achieved positions of importance" (letters in Korn manuscript collection, AJA, no. 99, folder 13/15 to H. E. Pratt, 3–19–52 and Mrs. S. A. Jonas, 3–18–52). On Abraham Jonas and the family generally, I have relied on the following: Korn, *American Jewry* and *The Early Jews of New Orleans* (Waltham, Mass.: American Jewish Historical Society, 1969), as well as Korn's manuscript collection at AJA (Collection 99, folder 13/15 Jonas, Abraham; folder 13/18 Jonas Family; Jonas Family and Abraham Jonas Nearprint Box—Biographies; Carl Landrum's series in *The Quincy Herald-Whig* [especially 1–31–1971, "Lincoln and the Jonas Family"; 2–12–67, "Quincy men helped Lincoln"; 2–6–77, "Lincoln and his friends in Quincy"; 8–29–82, "Abraham Jonas—early leader here"]). While there are entries for both Abraham and Benjamin Franklin Jonas in the *Universal Jewish Encyclopedia*, there is nothing of substance on Benjamin F. Jonas, the first practicing Jew in the U.S. Senate. This reflects the lack of scholarly work on Louisiana Jewry generally.

239. David C. Mearns, *The Lincoln Papers*, 3:516; see also Isaac Markens, "Lincoln and the Jews," *AJHS* 17 (1909): 123–28. *Quincy Herald*, February 12, 1867, Carl Landrum Series, Korn Papers, AJA.

240. David C. Mearns, *The Lincoln Papers* (Garden City, N.J.: Doubleday, 1998), 1:203–4 (June 4, 1857).

241. Korn, *American Jewry*, 228–29. The letter is reproduced in Isidor S. Meyer, ed., *The American Jew in the Civil War: Catalog of the Exhibit of the Civil War Centennial Jewish Historical Commission* (New York: AJHS, 1962), entry 160.

242. Korn, *American Jewry*, 194.

243. CSR, Charles H. Jonas; Korn, *American Jewry;* AJA, Korn Papers.

244. On Benjamin Franklin Jonas, I have utilized his compiled service record, standard references such as the *National Cyclopedia of American Biography* 4:544; *Biographical Directory of the United States Congress, 1774–1949* (1950); *A Dictionary of Louisiana Biography,* 1:442; *Confederate Military History,* 459–60; *American Jewish Yearbook* ("Biographies of Members of Congress"), 1901; and *Who Was Who in America, 1897–1942: A Component of Who's Who in American History* (Chicago: Marquis Publications, 1968).

Jonas's military record is confusing. His compiled service records conflict with his obituary in essential areas. The records show that he enlisted in September 1862, although perhaps he enlisted sooner.

245. The firms were Farrar, Jonas & Kruttschnitt; Farrar, Jonas, Kruttschnitt & Goldberg; and later Farrar, Jonas, Kruttschnitt & Gurley. The firms are mentioned in more than two hundred reported cases. See, for example, *Edrington v. Louisville, N.O. & T.R. Co.,* 6 So. 19 (La., 1889); *State v. Meyer,* 6 So. 590 (La., 1889); *Stackhouse v. Zuntz,* 6 So. 666 (La., 1889)(dealing with Judah Benjamin's former plantation, Belle Chase). My thanks to prominent Nevada attorney Leigh Goddard, Esq., for this information. Korn, *Early Jews,* 334n. 28. Jonas was likely a member of the Dispersed of Judah congregation, and, when that synagogue went out of existence, he joined the new Reform Temple Sinai, where he served as a member of the Board of Governors and vice president from 1894 to 1904. He was described as "an Israelite by nationality and religion" and was a member of the prestigious Boston Club of New Orleans and the Manhattan Club of New York. He married Josephine Block, whose parents were both Virginians. Many members of the Block family married members of the Cincinnati–Quincy–New Orleans Jonas family, according to Rabbi Korn. Korn, *Early Jews,* 228; *National Cyclopedia of American Biography,* 4:544; *American Biography* (but *Confederate Military History* says of New Orleans, 459); Korn, *Early Jews,* 326.

246. Obituary, *New Orleans Daily Picayune,* December 22, 1911, p. 1; CSR, B. F. Jonas.

247. CSR, Julian J. Jonas. There are a number of listings on file for J. J. Jonas: Captain Greenleaf's company (Orleans Light Horse), Louisiana Cavalry; Stewart's Corps, QMSgt; and LA. Inf. Crescent Regiment Company E. Sgt. They all represent Julian Jonas.

248. *Historical Times Illustrated Encyclopedia of the Civil War,* 370.

249. S. A. Jonas is known to Civil War historians as the author of the famous poem "Lines on the Back of a Confederate Note." A biographical sketch in *Confederate Veteran* quotes it in its entirety. The Mississippi Department of Archives and History has a collection of biographical and autobiographical material on Jonas (Acc. No. 2109, Boxes 1–2; MS 60–2439 in Nat'l. Union Catalog of Manuscript Collections). The best source, which is repeated almost verbatim in *Confederate Veteran* and other summaries, is a letter he wrote to Mrs. Fred Cullum dated March 24, 1908, in response to a request for a sketch of his life (Box 2, folder 8, Acc. No. 2109, reprinted in *Aberdeen (Miss.) Examiner,* August 13, 1936, AJA). He closes with these words: "Now if you had dreamed of the infliction impending, you would never have ventured the request for this life sketch."

The AJA has substantial material on S. A. Jonas in the Korn Collection and its Nearprint Box-Biographies (Jonas, Major S. A.). Korn's files contain letters about Jonas from descendants as well as newspaper clippings, especially from the *Aberdeen (Miss.) Examiner.* Major Jonas has an extensive service record at the National Archives, including a summary (marked "CARDED") of his record. See also John B. Hood's memoir, *Advance and Retreat: Personal Experiences in the United States and Confederate Armies* (New Orleans, 1880); Crute, *Confederate Staff Officers, 1861–1865;* Young, "The Sons of Abraham," *North and*

South Magazine 1, no. 6, 94 (1999); "The Story of a Poem," *North and South Magazine* 1, no. 4 (April 1998): 44.

250. March 24, 1908, letter from S. A. Jonas, Miss. Dept of Archives and History Acct. 2109; reprinted in *Aberdeen (Miss.) Examiner,* August 13, 1936, AJA.

251. Hood, *Advance and Retreat,* 60.

252. CSR, George B. Jonas and George Jonas.

253. Obituary in Quincy newspaper attached to letter from Frederick Wells III, to Carl Landrum, February 16, 1868, Korn Papers, AJA; "Lincoln and the Jonas Family," *Quincy Herald-Whig,* January 31, 1871, Korn Papers, AJA.

254. OR, Series I, vol. 22, pt. 1, p. 385; CSR, Edward Jonas.

255. Stanley R. Brav, "The Jewish Woman, 1861–1865," *AJA* 17, no. 1 (April 1965): 61.

256. Ibid., 63

257. Daniel O'Flaherty, *General Jo Shelby, Undefeated Rebel* (Chapel Hill: University of North Carolina Press, 1954), 18. The Gratz family was German, from Langensdorf in Upper Silesia. They had migrated in 1755 and settled in Pennsylvania. The legend of Rebecca Gratz is that one of her closest friends, Matilda Hoffman, was engaged to Washington Irving. When Matilda fell ill, Rebecca Gratz nursed her and spent considerable time with Irving. When Matilda died, Irving traveled to England. There he met Sir Walter Scott, who asked Irving to pen a description of a beautiful Jewess for Scott's use in *Ivanhoe.* Irving described Rebecca Gratz. Gratz Cohen's mother of Savannah was raised by her aunt, Rebecca Gratz. See David Philipson, ed., foreword, *Letters of Rebecca Gratz* (Philadelphia: JPS, 1929); *DAB; The Universal Jewish Encyclopedia;* Dianne Ashton in *Jewish Women in America* dismisses the *Ivanhoe* connection as "a legend" and "a popular tale." However, Stephen Birmingham in *The Grandees: America's Sephardic Elite* (New York: Harper & Row, 1971) believes the story is "probably true" (178–80).

258. Young, *Where They Lie,* 4–6.

259. O'Flaherty, *General Jo Shelby,* vii.

260. Ibid., 79.

261. OR II, 2:1421.

262. OR I, 53:808–809.

263. James M. Day, *Jacob DeCordova: Land Merchant of Texas* (Waco: Texan Press, 1962), 124.

264. The best treatment of Edwin DeLeon's mission to Europe is chapter 5, "The DeLeon Mission," in Charles P. Cullop, *Confederate Propaganda in Europe, 1861–1865* (Coral Gables, Fla.: University of Miami Press, 1969), also published as "Edwin DeLeon: Jefferson Davis' Propagandist," *Civil War History* (State University of Iowa), 8, no. 4 (December 1962): 386. Cullop gives a detailed and balanced account. Frank Owsley treats the subject in *King Cotton Diplomacy: Foreign Relations of the Confederate States of America* (Chicago: University of Shicago Press, 1959), 2d ed. There are a number of references in the Official Records. See ORN II, 3:971–73.

There are numerous references to the DeLeons throughout Mary Chesnut's diaries. See Woodward, *Mary Chesnut's Civil War,* and Woodward and Muhlenfield, *The Private Mary Chesnut.* DeLeon wrote his memoirs, *Thirty Years of My Life on Three Continents* (London, 1890), which deal superficially with his service to the Confederate States. There are sketches of him in Elzas, *Jews of South Carolina,* 332 (Perry DeLeon); *DAB; Twentieth Century Biographical Dictionary; Universal Jewish Encyclopedia;* Simonhoff, *Jewish Notables;* and *National Cyclopaedia.*

418

265. Cullop, *Confederate Propaganda,* 67; DeLeon, *Thirty Years,* 320.

266. DeLeon, *Thirty Years,* 296–325.

267. Cullop, *Confederate Propaganda,* 68–72.

268. ORN II, 3:657, no. 3, January 16, 1863.

269. DeLeon, *Thirty Years,* 2:3.

270. Ibid., 2:7–8.

271. Owsley, *King Cotton,* 162–63.

272. DeLeon, *Thirty Years,* 2:24–31.

273. Ibid., 2:38–40; Cullop, *Confederate Propaganda,* 108–9; *Historical Times Illustrated Encyclopedia of the Civil War,* 214.

274. Cullop, *Confederate Propaganda,* 74; DeLeon, *Thirty Years,* 2:47; Owsley, *King Cotton,* 163–64.

275. Cullop, *Confederate Propaganda,* 75–76.

276. Owsley, *King Cotton Diplomacy,* 164–65.

277. ORN, I, 9:276, North Atlantic Blockading Squadron, November 11, 1863.

278. Owsley, *King Cotton Diplomacy,* 165.

279. Cullop, *Confederate Propaganda,* 82–83.

280. ORN, II, 3:971, December 9, 1863.

281. Cullop, *Confederate Propaganda,* 83.

282. Gallagher, *The Confederate War,* 28–29.

283. Randall and Donald, *The Civil War and Reconstruction,* 545.

284. Muster Roll of Company I, 15th Georgia. Marcus commanded the 15th Georgia at the assault on Fort Gilmer. See *Confederate Veteran,* June 1905, 269.

285. Letter to Simon Wolf from Col. F. Hay Gantt, November 7, 1864, copy courtesy of Mel Young, in possession of author. W. M. Wolf's CSR is filed under Will Wolff.

286. Obituary ("Perry Moses Passes Away"), *Sumter* [S.C.] *Daily Item, 1916* in possession of author, courtesy of Anne F. Jennings; Arthur W. Bergeron, *Confederate Mobile* (Jackson: University Press of Mississippi, 1991), 193; Young, *Where They Lie,* 130–238.

287. "Diary of Eleanor Cohen Seixas," in Penelope Franklin, ed., *Private Pages: Diaries of American Women, 1830s–1970s* (New York: Ballantine Books, 1986), 314.

288. Young, *Where They Lie,* 130.

289. Octavia Harby Moses, *A Mother's Poems, A Collection of Verses* (privately printed, 1915), 54.

CHAPTER 4

1. Wolf, *The American Jew,* 102–4; Ezekiel and Lichenstein, *History of the Jews of Richmond,* 163. This remark, contained in a letter to Simon Wolf in the early 1890s, later became the basis of the "fact" that there were ten thousand Jews in the Confederate army, which there absolutely were not.

2. Wolf, *The American Jew,* 100–101.

3. Wolf's total for all states appears at page 424. The eleven Confederate states total 1,216, which is approximately the number reached by counting each soldier in these states. At page 410 are 104 men unclassified as to commands. Three listed in an addenda at page 423 must be added, for a total of 1,323. Several Confederate staff officers, such as Abraham C. Myers, are listed at pages 114–15 and are not included in the state lists. Others are included. Finally, eleven naval officers are listed on pages 116. Wolf thus lists approximately 1,340 Confederate soldiers and sailors.

4. Wolf, *The American Jew,* 46; LeMaster, *A Corner of the Tapestry,* 46.

5. Letter to author from Eric Brock; list of Shreveport Jewish Confederate soldiers compiled by Eric Brock in possession of author; Eric Brock, "The Jewish Cemeteries of Shreveport, Louisiana" (available at Historic New Orleans Collection, AJA, and CC). Moses Rosenthal, as an example, was a member of "the Hebrew church," according to *The History of Louisiana,* 588. Jonas Rosenthal was an immigrant from Alsace-Lorraine. Affidavit dated November 8, 1926, in possession of author courtesy of Nancy Greenberg, Alexandria, Louisiana. Ms. Greenberg identified Mires Rosenthal as her great-grandfather and Moses, Jonas, and Isaac as his brothers.

6. Elzas wrote, "The complete record of the part played by the Jews of South Carolina in the war between the States will never be known" (*Jews of South Carolina,* 122). He examined 70,000 names and positively identified 167. The list, he noted, could be "largely extended, had accounts been taken of the sons of South Carolina Jews who fought in the war," meaning that many, like Franklin J. Moses, had been raised as Christians (237n. 33). The list excluded dozens he could not positively identify, the Home Guard, the Regiment of Reserves, men listed by Wolf he could not verify, and men with Jewish-sounding names (David Jacobs, Isaac Abrahams) who were likely Jewish Confederates. There were forty-two in the artillery, seventeen in the cavalry, and two in the navy. Ezekiel and Lichtenstein, *History of the Jews of Richmond,* 176–88. The authors, writing in 1916, believed their list of Jewish Confederate soldiers to be "the best that has ever been printed, and it is safe to assume that no more complete or accurate one will ever be published" (176).

7. Wiley, *The Life of Johnny Reb,* 331.

8. Roster, 37th Virginia; AHA, letter from Philip Rosenheim to the Meinnarts, July 8, 1863; Fannie Herzberg, "Pioneer Members and History of Temple Beth-El, 1859–1959," paper published in *Chattahoochee Valley Historical Society Bulletin* 4 (November 1959), and by the Southern Jewish Historical Association. AJA file as *Pittsburgh Evening Leader,* March 31, 1875; Barkai, *Branching Out,* 112; Korn, *Civil War,* 121ff.

9. Korn, *Civil War,* xiii, preface, paperback ed., 119; Friedman, *Jews of Macon;* Louis Schmeir, "Diary of Louis Merz."

10. OR Supplement, *Record of Events,* Louisiana Troops, 24:235. CSR, I. R. Hyams.

11. Amann, *Personnel of the Civil War,* 139; Brock, *The Jewish Cemeteries of Shreveport,* 57, and "Shreveport Jewish Confederate Soldiers," in possession of author; *Roster of Georgia Troops in Confederate Service.*

12. Eigenbrun is listed erroneously as J. Engenbrun on the roster (Schappes, 708n. 9); Oppenheim is listed incorrectly as Oppenheimer in Wolf (Schappes, 707–8n. 6); as to Engle, see Schappes, p. 708n. 9, although he is not on the roster.

13. "Moons" for Morris is in Ezekiel and Lichtenstein, *History of the Jews of Richmond,* 161; CSR, Lewis Leon, Company B, 53rd North Carolina; Morris Leon, Company I, 44th Infantry (Georgia); Leon, *Diary of a Tarheel Confederate.*

14. Wolf, *The American Jew; Encyclopedia of the Confederacy,* 266–67.

15. John H. and Roberta C. Neblett, "Emanuel Gerst—A Gentleman of Virginia," *Generations, Journal of Congregation Beth Ahaba Museum and Archives Trust* 5, no. 1 (November 1992). See p. 11n. 11.

16. Turitz and Turitz, *Jews in Early Mississippi,* 48.

17. Wolf, *The American Jew,* passim, as to Cohens, see 374; Ashley Halsey Jr., "The Last Duel in the Confederacy," *Civil War Times Illustrated* 1, no. 7 (November 1962): 7; Elzas, *Jews of South Carolina,* 226; Crute, *Units of the Confederate States Army,* 271–72;

420   Dorothy Phelps Bultman, "The Story of a Good Life" (November, 1963, Sumter, S.C.), 1 (Courtesy of Thomas Bultman, Esq.).

18. Ernest B. Furguson, *Ashes of Glory: Richmond at War* (New York: Alfred A. Knopf, 1996), 212.

19. Letter dated July 8, 1863, from Philip Rosenheim to the Meinnarts, Korn file, AJA.

20. Rev. A. Toomer Porter, *Led On! Step by Step* (1898).

21. Albert Moses Luria, Maj. Raphael J. Moses's son, joined the 2d Georgia Battalion on April 19, 1861, arrived in Portsmouth, Virginia, in May 1861, and fought in the Battle of Sewell's Point. On June 17, 1861, he was elected second lieutenant of his new company in the 13th North Carolina Volunteers (NCV). He had transferred to be with a fellow cadet from Hillsboro Military Institute in North Carolina. (The unit entered Confederate service on July 12, 1861. It was redesignated the 23d Regiment North Carolina State Troops in November 1861.) Luria was reelected second lieutenant on April 16, 1862. Wounded in the head on May 31, 1862, at the Battle of Seven Pines, he was treated at Byrd Island Hospital in Richmond (General Hospital No. 3).

22. CSR, Octavus Cohen. Octavus Cohen has an extensive and interesting CSR. There are files under Gallie's Company, 1st (Olmstead's) Georgia Infantry; Company G, 32d Georgia Infantry; Company C, 22d Battalion Georgia Heavy Artillery.

23. Kole, *The Minis Family,* 115–16.

24. Mac Wyckoff, *A History of the 2nd South Carolina Infantry: 1861–65* (Fredericksburg, Va.: Seargeant Kirkland's Museum and Historical Society, 1994), 218. The extended family included Franklin J. Moses, chief justice of the South Carolina Supreme Court during Reconstruction, and his son, the notorious "Robber Governor," Franklin J. Moses Jr.

25. Cutchins, *A Famous Command,* passim; Berman, *Richmond's Jewry,* 93–97; Ezekiel and Lichtenstein, *History of the Jews of Richmond,* 129, 149–52; Collins, *46th Virginia Infantry,* 151.

26. Ezekiel and Lichtenstein, *History of the Jews of Richmond,* 153; David M. Potter, *The Impending Crisis 1898–1861* (New York: Harper & Row, 1976), 369–71; Furguson, *Ashes of Glory: Richmond at War* (New York: Knopf, 1996), chap. 1.

27. Whitlock MS, autobiography, 97–98, VHS.

28. Ezekiel and Lichtenstein, *History of the Jews of Richmond,* 154.

29. Letters dated April 14, 1954, and February 3, 1954, from Charles B. Levy to J. R. Marcus, AJA.

30. Ezekiel and Lichtenstein, *History of the Jews of Richmond,* 178, 186–87.

31. *VMI Alumni Review* (Spring 1973): 1.

32. Joyner, "Georgetown"; Walker, *Rolls and Historical Sketch of the Tenth Regiment, So. Car. Volunteers,* introduction and 9.

33. Elzas, *Jews of South Carolina,* 230; J. C. Hemphill, *Men of Mark in South Carolina* (Washington, D.C., 1907), 1:201–3.

34. Wycoff, *A History of the 2nd South Carolina Infantry,* 158; *Confederate Veteran* 22 (1914): 170, 221; Louis Ginsberg, *History of the Jews of Petersburg, 1789–1950* (Petersburg, Va., privately printed, 1954), 29, 41; Collins, *46th Virginia,* 30, 37–43.

35. *Confederate Military History* 4 (Va.): 914–15; J. Ambler Johnston, "Not Forgotten, Henry Gintzberger, Private, CSA," paper, BA.

36. Ruth Friedman, *A Portrait of Jewish Life, Fredericksburg, Virginia 1860–1986* (copy at VHS), prologue and chap. 1.

37. LeMaster, *A Corner of the Tapestry*, 43; Turitz and Turitz, *Jews in Early Mississippi*, 3, 117–18, 29, 85–86, xvii, 109, 112.

38. LeMaster, *A Corner of the Tapestry*, 46, 45, 42–44; Felsenthal is listed as David "Felamthall" at the NA.

39. His family, according to Eli Evans, still has his two mess kits—one for meat and one for milk (Evans, *The Provincials: A Personal History of Jesus in the South* [New York: Athenaeum, 1974], 63). The author could locate no record of Gleitzman. Some of LeMaster's information is not found in the various rosters.

40. Notes from family members provided by a descendant, Van Harte of Montgomery, Alabama (1995), in author's file. Oppenheimer's obituary on the front page of the *Memphis News Scimitar*, complete with a photograph of him in his Confederate uniform, called him "a picturesque character" who was one of the original California "Forty-niners," fought the Indians with Custer in the Black Hills, and "Was With Gen. Beauregard at Shiloh," all of which may or may not have been true. The story states that "Mr. Oppenheimer had served under [Gen. P. G. T.] Beauregard and [Gen. Albert Sidney] Johnston against Grant and Bull at Shiloh. He was captured by federal troops and imprisoned in the courthouse at Trenton. Upon his release he went to Mobile in the latter part of 1863 and participated in the defense of that city against the terrific naval onslaughts of Admiral Farragut." Another newspaper account has him as "a personal friend of Gen. Custer and Buffalo Bill Cody." His family's tradition had him serving in Company D, 3d Alabama Cavalry at Shiloh, Murfreesboro, Chickamauga, Knoxville, and Atlanta, but army records do not confirm this.

41. Oppenheimer told his fellow Confederate Veterans in later years that he was near Gen. Albert Sidney Johnston when he was killed at the Battle of Shiloh and saw him fall. These stories were apparently credible to the Confederate Veterans of Montgomery, who asked him to attend their reunion (undated clipping from newspaper, dateline Montgomery). In his "Soldier's Application for Pension," dated October 13, 1908, Oppenheimer states that he enlisted in the army at Pensacola with the Georgia infantry but was soon transferred to Captain Judkin's Company of the 2d Alabama Cavalry, "where I remained until some time in 1863 when I came home on furlough from Gen. Joe Wheeler." He stated that he was captured at Bolivar, Tennessee, and imprisoned in Jackson, Tennessee. His brother secured his release, and he returned to Alabama to rejoin his command. Ben had a half-brother named Simon Oppenheimer who peddled during the war in the North and the South. It may have been this brother who rescued him from the Union army.

42. Juliet George, "By the Brazos and the Trinity They Hung Up Their Harps: Two Jewish Immigrants in Texas" (master's thesis, University of Texas, Austin, 1991), 88, 90–93. Berliner is listed as "Berlener" and Samuels as "Samuel" at NA.

43. Ibid., 99–100; John D. Winters, *The Civil War in Louisiana*, 212, 284–99; *Historical Times Illustrated Encyclopedia of the Civil War*, 587.

44. Eric Brock, "The Jewish Cemeteries of Shreveport, Louisiana."

45. Leon, *Diary*, 11–4; Charles B. Levy to J. R. Marcus, February 3, 1954, Levy Family Papers, AJA.

46. CSR, Lewis Leon; "Regimental History, 1st Regiment, N.C. Infantry"; Crute, *Units*, 211–12, 238. Lewis Leon's record is filed under North Carolina 53d Infantry, Company B. Morris Leon's record is Georgia, 44th Georgia Infantry, Company I.

47. Leon, *Diary*, 1–4.

48. Ibid., 58; CSR, Morris Leon; Crute, *Units*, 109.

422

49. Leon, *Diary*, 29; Crute, *Units*, 238; CSR, Morris Leon.

50. Leon, *Diary*, 19–31, 59.

51. Ibid., 39, 28, 41, 56, 61.

52. Simon Mayer Papers, Letter, April 17, 1864, TU.

53. Leon, *Diary*, 13, 14, 33.

54. Ibid., 15–16, 26, 32.

55. Wiley, *The Life of Johnny Reb*, 244; Leon, *Diary*, 17, 27; letter to "Dear Friend" (probably Herman Heyman, September 23, 1862) Merz Papers, AJA; Herzberg, "Pioneer Members and History of Temple Bethel, 1859–1959."

56. Leon, *Diary*, 7, 76, 8, 25.

57. George, "By the Brazos," 101; Thomas Lowry, M.D., *The Story the Soldiers Wouldn't Tell: Sex in the Civil War* (Mechanicsburg, Pa.: Stackpole Books, 1994), 28; Leon, *Diary*, 27.

58. Leon, *Diary*, 12.

59. Ibid., 27–28, 32–33; Crute, *Units*, 238.

60. Leon, *Diary*, 34–35; OR Series I, vol. 27, pt. 2, 342, 564–71, 576–77.

61. Ibid., 35–36.

62. Ibid., 36–39.

63. Ibid., 39, 41; *Historical Times Illustrated Encyclopedia of the Civil War*, 307.

64. Ibid., 41.

65. Ibid., 43, 53–56.

66. Ibid., 58.

67. McPherson, *For Cause and Comrades*, 132; Schappes, *Documentary History*, 709n. 17; Leon, *Diary*, 59; Ezekiel and Lichtenstein, *Jews of Richmond*, 16.

68. Leon, *Diary*, 72; Gordon C. Rhea, *The Battle of the Wilderness, May 5–6, 1864* (Baton Rouge: Louisiana State University Press, 1994), 164–65; Edward Steere, *The Wilderness Campaign: The Meeting of Grant and Lee* (Harrisburg, Pa.: Stackpole Co., 1960; reprinted Mechanicsburg, Pa.: Stackpole Books, 1994), 162, 172–73.

69. Leon, *Diary*, 61–63.

70. The date one took the oath of allegiance was important to Southerners after the war. Obviously, if a soldier refused the oath, he was considered more patriotic. Thus Leon had a motive to write that, *after Lee surrendered* on April 9, he was among 400 Confederate prisoners at the Elmira Prison to take "the cursed oath." But Union prisoner of war records show that Leon took the oath and was released on February 7, 1865. A letter from the military archives dated August 3, 1953, to Dr. Jacob R. Marcus shows that Dr. Marcus was aware of the February date, but he chose to use Leon's version in *Memoirs of American Jews*. Of course, the military records could be wrong. See Leon's compiled service record; Leon, *Diary*, 62, 64; Schappes, *Documentary History*, 708.

71. Leon, *Diary*, 61–65.

72. Ibid., 61–65.

73. Ibid., 70.

74. Isaac Hermann, *Memoirs*, 12. His pension records show that he enlisted in Company E, 1st Regiment, Georgia Infantry, on June 30, 1861. Schappes, *Documentary History*, 712n. 4; Herman's records are filed under Georgia, Capt. Howell's Company, Georgia Light Artillery and 1st (Ramsey's) Georgia Infantry, Company E. His pension record is Confed. Arch., chap. 6, file 751, 58 (April 8, 1916).

75. Stan Cohen, *The Civil War in West Virginia: A Pictorial History* (Charleston, W.Va.: Pictorial Histories Publishing Co., 1982): 26, 28, 49, 77; OR, series 1, vol. 5, 389–96; Hermann, *Memoirs*, 15.

76. *Historical Times Illustrated Encyclopedia of the Civil War*, 135; Hermann, *Memoirs*, 39, 19.

77. Hermann, *Memoirs*, 69–71.

78. Hermann, *Memoirs*, 74. According to Schappes, Hermann was discharged from the 1st Georgia on January 25, 1862, and reenlisted May 10, 1862, in Martin's Battery, Georgia Light Artillery. The author's research shows September 1862. He was appointed a musician. Schappes, *Documentary History*, 712n. 4.

79. Hermann, *Memoirs*, 83, 86, 99; Schappes, *Documentary History*, 712. None of his claimed wounds are substantiated by the available records.

80. Hermann, *Memoirs*, 173, 233–34.

81. Ibid., 64, 89, 91–95, 138–41.

82. Ibid., 163–64.

83. James I. Robertson Jr., *Soldiers Blue and Gray* (Columbia: University of South Carolina Press, 1988), 122–24; Leon, *Diary*, 24.

84. Hermann, *Memoirs*, 98.

85. Ibid., 227–28; 179; 118; 248; Schappes, *Documentary History*, 712.

86. Wiley, *The Life of Johnny Reb*, 108; Hermann, *Memoirs*, 121, 176.

87. Hermann, *Memoirs*, 67, 155; CSR, I. Hermann.

88. Marcus, *Memoirs*, 3:302–6.

89. Obituary says he joined the Donaldsville Artillery, later known as Dreux's Battalion, which is erroneous; Young, *Where They Lie*, 23, 223; Marcus, 3:299; Ashkenazi, *Diary of Clara Solomon*, 62, 69–73; Bergeron, *Guide to Louisiana Confederate Military Units*, 148–49; see CSR, the Levy brothers.

90. Ashkenazi, *Diary of Clara Solomon*, 62–73, 77.

91. Bergeron, *Guide to Louisiana Confederate Military Units*, 148; CSR, Eugene and Julian Levy.

92. Marcus, *Memoirs*, 3:301; Diary of Eugene Henry Levy, AJA, 17 (6–3–1864).

93. Marcus, *Memoirs*, 3:303; Levy Diary, AJA, 112–13 (December 26, 1864).

94. Marcus, *Memoirs*, 3:301; Levy Diary, AJA, 19 (June 6, 1884); 33–34 (July 2, 1864).

95. Marcus, *Memoirs*, 3:302–4.

96. Ibid., 3:304.

97. Levy Diary, 305.

98. Levy Diary, 16–17 (June 1, 1864).

99. Baruch, *My Own Story*, 36.

100. LeMaster, *A Corner of the Tapestry*, 43; *Historical Times Illustrated Encyclopedia of the Civil War*, "Bloody Angle," 68; "Spotsylvania," 709; Simonhoff, *Jewish Participants in the Civil War*, 263–64. His name has had many other spellings in various writings: Frankenthal, Fahrentold, Fronthall. His CSR is under Mark Fraunthall.

101. Thomas T. Murford to Hortense G. Moses, March 22, 1905. The soldier was "Maurice" from Lynchburg, Virginia, Botetourt Dragoons, Company C, 2d Virginia Cavalry, AJA.

102. Gary R. Baker, *Cadets in Gray: The Story of the Cadets of the South Carolina Military Academy and the Cadet Rangers in the Civil War* (Columbia, S.C.: Palmetto Book-

works, 1989), 171. Moses was nicknamed "Lord Shaftsbury" because of his "scholarly style of composition."

103. Obituary, *Charleston Daily Courier,* September 21, 1862; Wycoff, *A History of the 2nd South Carolina Infantry,* 218, 117; Turitz and Turitz, *Jews in Early Mississippi,* 87–88; Young, *Where They Lie,* p.111; *Confederate Veteran* 22 (1914): 170.

104. Gergel and Gergel, *Tree of Life,* 36; Young, *Where They Lie,* 57; Jack Steinberg, "United for Worship and Charity: A History of Congregation Children of Israel" (1982), 8.

105. Young, *Where They Lie,* 23–24, 27, 36, 46, 49, 222; OR Series I, vol. 10, pt. 1, 565 (Shiloh); Obituary, *Charleston Daily Courier,* July 12, 1864; OR I, 20, pt. 1, 799 (Stone's River).

106. Young, *Where They Lie,* 54, 56; Merz file, AJA; Herzberg Papers, AJA; Merz Papers, Cobb Memorial Archives, Valley, Alabama; Herzberg, "Pioneer Members and History of Temple Bethel, 1859–1959." Henry Blankenesee is listed on the granite monument in Washington Park in Charleston as a casualty. Robert Blankensee, Company A, Hampton Legion, was killed at First Manassas, not Second. Robert was confused with Henry, according to Kirkland, *Broken Fortunes.*

107. Young, *Where They Lie,* 68, 74, 76, 82, 100–101, 115, 128; Mel Young, "Jewish POWs Buries at Andersonville," *The [Atlanta] Jewish Georgian,* November–December 1995, 27.

108. J. Ambler Johnston, "Not Forgotten, Henry Gintzberger, Private, CSA," paper, BA. Johnston was chairman of the Richmond Civil War Centennial Committee and a descendent of Pvt. N. B. Johnston, who wrote about "the only Jewish soldier" being killed while peering over the breastworks. He was moved to write this paper by the pathos of the death of this poor Jewish peddler, who was then buried under the wrong name, Henry Gersberg, in the Hebrew Cemetery in Richmond. Through Mr. Johnston's efforts in 1963, Gintzberger's correct name was placed on a marker at the cemetery.

109. Ezekiel autobiography, 62–65.

110. Darrell L. Collins, *46th Virginia Infantry* ([Lynchburg, Va.]: H. E. Howard, 1992), 123.

111. Diary of Emma Mordecai, August 30, 1864; Berman, *Richmond's Jewry,* 177.

112. Levy Family Papers, BA.

113. Brennan, *Assault on Charleston;* Young, *Where They Lie,* 39, 187, 245, 263.

114. Brennan, *Assault on Charleston,* 184; Young, *Where They Lie,* 40, 187, 245.

115. *Charleston Daily Courier,* June 18 and 21, 1862; Brennan, *Assault,* 185; Young, *Where They Lie,* 39–40; *Charleston Daily Courier,* June 21, 1862.

116. Saul Viener, "Rosena Hutzler Levy Recalls the Civil War," *AJHQ* 62, no. 3 (March 1973): 306–13.

117. Young, *Where They Lie,* 57.

118. Young, *Where They Lie,* 21–22; Ezekiel and Lichtenstein, *History of the Jews of Richmond,* 182.

119. Korn, *War on the Mississippi,* 63, 90; Marcus, *Memoirs,* 2:33–34.

120. Marcus, *Memoirs,* 2:39–41.

121. Ibid., 42–43.

122. Wiley, *The Life of Johnny Reb,* 83.

123. Marcus, *Memoirs,* 3:116–17.

124. Ibid., 117.

125. Ibid., 118–32.

126. Furguson, *Ashes of Glory*, 6, 12, 182–85. Whitlock's memoir, "The Life of Philip Whitlock," is at the Virginia Historical Society. These facts are understandably omitted from Berman's *Richmond's Jewry* and Ezekiel and Lichtenstein's *History of the Jews of Richmond*, which states that Whitlock "was disabled in the service April, 1862 and transferred to the Quartermaster's Department" (188). Whitlock wrote his memoir after Ezekiel and Lichtenstein's book was published and he may not have been as candid with his contemporaries as he was in his memoir.

127. Whitlock MS, 122–24.

128. *Lynn Item,* August 3 or 8, 1918, clipping courtesy of Mel Young.

129. Morris Silverman, *Hartford Jews, 1659–1970* (Hartford: Connecticut Historical Society, n.d.), 247; Korn, *American Jewry,* preface, xvi; Jones, *Personal Reminiscences,* 443. There is no listing for Rosenblatt in the Confederate Roster.

130. CSR, Private Max Neugas (Company D, 1 [McCreary's] S.C. Inf. [1 S.C. Inf. Prov. Army]; Pee Dee Light Artillery, Zimmerman's Company, South Carolina Light Artillery; OR I, 2, pt. 2, chap. 23, 860 ("Private Neugas severely wounded"). My thanks to Tom Brooks of Ontario, Canada, for sending me material on Neugas from the Fort Delaware Society.

131. OR I, vol. 21, 649–50; OR I, vol. 25, pt. 1, 937–39.

132. *American Israelite* (October 16, 1863): 122; and 11 (October 14, 1864): 124; Bernard Postal and Lionel Koppman, *Jewish Delaware: History, Sites, Communal Services* (Wilmington: Jewish Federation of Delaware, 1976), 26; "Celebrating the Sites of Jewish Delaware," 26; letter from Dean E. Nelson, Delaware Bureau of Museum and Historic Sites to William Craven, president, Fort Delaware Society, enclosing Neugas's letter or petition to Lincoln (April 9, 1864), Archive of Fort Delaware Society. The Boston Athenaeum Library owns a number of prints by Neugas, who was an engraver. The library published a catalog titled "Citizens in Conflict" by Sally Pierce, which contains additional material on Neugas.

133. Young, *Where They Lie,* 53; *Confederate Veteran,* January 1908.

134. Leon, *Diary,* 18, 27, 46; *Pioneer Members and Diary of Louis Merz,* 31.

135. Korn, "Was There a Confederate Jewish Chaplain?," *American Jewish Historical Quarterly* 53, no. 1 (September 1963): 63–69; *AJA* 1, no. 1 (June 1948): 6–22; Ezekiel and Lichtenstein, *History of the Jews of Richmond,* passim.

136. Korn, *American Jewry,* 57. "My suggestion . . . that the Confederate Congress was more liberal than its Federal counterpart has caused a few eyebrows to be raised fairly high," Korn wrote in his preface to the paperbound edition (page xiv). See his article, "Jewish Chaplains during the Civil War," *AJA* 1, no. 1 (June 1998): 7, for the same quote.

137. Ezekiel and Lichtenstein, *History of the Jews of Richmond,* 187.

138. Simon Mayer Papers, letter dated May 3, 1865, TU.

139. Leon, *Diary,* 49; Ezekiel and Lichtenstein, *History of the Jews of Richmond,* 155.

140. Herbert T. Ezekiel, "The Jews of Richmond during the Civil War," address delivered to Rimmon Lodge No. 68, International Order of B'nai B'rith (I.O.B.B.), February 28, 1915, 1 (Published Richmond, Va: Press of H. T. Ezekiel; copy at VHS).

141. Ezekiel and Lichtenstein, *History of the Jews of Richmond,* 171; Leon Diary, 47–48.

142. Marcus, *Memoirs,* 3:306–7; Levy Diary, 107, December 17, 1864.

143. *The Oxford Dictionary of the Jewish Religion.*

144. A photograph of the prayer is reproduced on page 212; Korn, *American Jewry,* 88–90.

145. Korn, *American Jewry,* 92.

146. Ibid., 92.

147. "Death of a Soldier" (Adolph Rosenthal) in "Civil War Centennial, Southern Issue," *AJA* 13, no. 1 (April 1961): 61–72; Berman, *Richmond's Jewry*, 180.

148. Wolf, *American Jew*, 100–101.

149. Ibid.; Clyde L. Cummer, *Yankee in Gray: The Civil War Memoirs of Henry E. Handerson* (Cleveland, Ohio: Press of Western Reserve University, 1962), 31.

150. Turitz and Turitz, *Jews in Early Mississippi*, xvii.

151. E. Merton Coulter, *The Confederate States of America*, vol. 1 of *A History of the South*, 6th ed. (Baton Rouge: Louisiana State University Press, 1987), 228; Elzas, *Jews of South Carolina*, 220.

CHAPTER 5

1. Jewish Southerners were more visible than their small numbers suggest. While it is true that of the 4 million of foreign-born in the United States, only 500,000 lived in the South, they clustered in the coastal and larger river towns. As Herbert Weaver has pointed out in "Foreigners in Ante-Bellum Towns of the Lower South," *JSH* 13 (1947): 62–73, "They [all foreigners] comprised a considerable portion of the free population, and their impact upon the society in these centers of concentration produced some significant results." For example, 67 percent of the foreign-born in South Carolina lived in Charleston; 63 percent in Alabama lived in Mobile. "The concentration in larger towns, such as Mobile, Savannah and Memphis," Weaver concludes, "was so great that on the basis of total free inhabitants the percentage of foreigners in these cities was comparable to that in Philadelphia and Boston." Weaver also points out (correctly in my view) that the foreign-born tended to concentrate in specific neighborhoods. "In 1860," he writes, "almost a third of the foreigners in Mobile, lived in a single downtown ward" (66–67). While Jews did live throughout all of the Southern cities, the immigrants did tend to cluster in the commercial district. In 1861, upper King Street in Charleston and parts of Main Street in Richmond were definitely Jewish neighborhoods.

There is an excellent bibliography and discussion of this issue in Mark I. Greenberg's perceptive article, "Becoming Southern: The Jews of Savannah, Georgia, 1830–1870," *AJH* 86, no. 1 (March 1998): 55–56. Greenberg points out that 350 Jews constituted 2.5 percent of Savannah's white population in 1861.

2. Woodward, *Mary Chesnut*, 368–69.

3. Stern, *Americans of Jewish Descent*, 130; Gergel and Gergel, *Tree of Life*, 35, 17–18.

4. DeLeon, *Belles, Beaux, and Brains*, 144; Gordon Grey, "The Ancestry of Nathalie Fontaine Lyons," edited by Jo White Linn (Salisbury, N.C.: privately published, 1981), copy in possession of author, courtesy of Belinda Gergel.

5. Woodward, *Mary Chesnut*, 346.

6. Ibid., 91n. 5.

7. Ibid., 358, 387; Hagy, *Happy Land*, 299; Cohen is erroneously listed in the roster as Ludlow L. Cohen in Company A, 2d Cavalry. The unit did not become Company A, 2d Cavalry until August 22, 1862.

8. Woodward, *Mary Chesnut*, 344.

9. Ibid., 366, 371.

10. Ibid., 346, 354, 359. In Exodus, Miriam, the prophetess, "took a timbrel in her hand" and led the Hebrew women in a celebratory dance. Her song, believed by many scholars to be the oldest part of the Hebrew Bible, at Exod. 15:20–21, is as follows:

Sing ye to the Lord for He is highly exalted;
The horse and his rider hath He thrown into the sea.
　　　　See Jonathan Kirsch, *Moses: A Life*
　　　　(New York: Ballantine Books, 1998), 192–97.

11. Moise, *Moise Family,* 65; Solomon Breibart, "Penina Moise, Southern Jewish Poetess," in Proctor and Schmier, *Jews of the South,* 34–35.

12. "A Reverie," copy in possession of author, courtesy of Solomon Breibart. This poem was written during the Civil War and published in the Charleston *World* (June 21, 1891); "Cockades of Blue" was reprinted in *The American Jewish Yearbook* (1906) in an article titled "Penina Moise, Woman and Writer" by Lee C. Harby; Brav, "The Jewish Woman," 36.

13. Brav, "The Jewish Woman," passim; Korn, *American Jewry,* 99.

14. Brav, "The Jewish Woman," 35; Schappes, *Documentary History,* 707n. 3; Marcus, *Memoirs,* 3:366.

15. Diner, *A Time for Gathering,* 12, 76, 81–85; Sue Eakin, *Washington, Louisiana* (Bossier City, La.: Everett Co., 1988), 105–7.

16. Zebulon Vance Hooker II, "Moses Jacob Ezekiel: The Formative Years," *Virginia Magazine of History and Biography* 60 (April 1952): 241–43.

17. Evans, *Judah Benjamin,* 7.

18. Diner, *A Time for Gathering,* 81–82.

19. Drew Gilpin Faust, *Mothers of Invention: Women of the Slaveholding South in the American Civil War* (Chapel Hill: University of North Carolina Press, 1996): 46–51.

20. Faust, *Mothers of Invention,* 4–8; 134–38; Diner, *A Time for Gathering,* 81–82.

21. Ezekiel, "The Jews of Richmond during the Civil War," 1.

22. Urofsky, *Commonwealth and Community,* 84; Berman, *Richmond's Jewry,* 179–80.

23. Faust, *Mothers of Invention,* 99.

24. Berman, *Richmond's Jewry,* 193–94.

25. *Generations, Journal of Congregation Beth Ahabah* 3, no. 3 (May 1991).

26. Samuel Mordecai, *Virginia, Especially Richmond, in Bygone Days* (Richmond: West and Johnson, 1858), 246. All locations from *Second Annual Directory for the City of Richmond* (1860) on microfilm at the Library of Virginia Archives, Richmond.

27. Creeger, "Michelbacher"; *Generations* 5, no. 2 (April 1993): 3–4.

28. Ezekiel and Lichtenstein, *History of the Jews of Richmond,* 162; Korn, *American Jewry,* 94.

29. Ezekiel and Lichtenstein, *History of the Jews of Richmond,* 162.

30. Ibid., 162–63.

31. Ezekiel and Lichtenstein, *History of the Jews of Richmond,* 164–65; Rev. J. William Jones, *Personal Reminiscences,* 442–44. This account also contains Lee's letters to Michelbacher dated August 29, 1861, April 2, 1863, and September 20, 1864. Jones quoted the venerable Dr. White as to Lee's Christian character. "His love for the truth, and for all that is good and useful, was such as to render his brotherly kindness and charity as boundless as were the wants and sorrows of his race" (445).

32. Ezekiel and Lichtenstein, *History of the Jews of Richmond,* 156–57; Berman, *Richmond's Jewry,* 202.

33. Reznikoff and Engelman, *The Jews of Charleston,* 163; Fass memoirs, CC.

34. Rosen, *Confederate Charleston,* chap. 6; Moise, *Moise Family,* 8.

35. Rosen, *Confederate Charleston,* 99, 144; Reznikoff and Engelman, *The Jews of Charleston,* 157.

36. Solomon Breibart, "BSBI Celebrates 140th Anniversary," *Charleston Jewish Journal,* April 1995. Jeffrey Kaplan wrote a history of Berith Shalom Beth Israel in 1948 for its 130th anniversary booklet.

37. Reznikoff and Engelman, *The Jews of Charleston,* 152; Gergel and Gergel, *Tree of Life,* 42.

38. Moise, *Moise Family,* 8. Eleanor Cohen's diary has also been printed in Penelope Franklin, *Private Pages: Diaries of American Women 1830s–1870s.*

39. William Fidler, "Henry Timrod: Poet of the Confederacy," *The Southern Literary Messenger* 2 (Revised) (October 1940): 527–35; "Unpublished Letters of Henry Timrod," *Southern Literary Messenger* 2 (November 1940): 605–11, and 2 (December 1940): 645–51.

40. *Southern Literary Messenger* 2 (November 1940), 608.

41. William Fidler, "Notes and Documents: Seven Unpublished Letters of Henry Timrod," *Alabama Review* (April 1949): 146.

42. H. Timrod to his sister Emily, June 11, 1861, H. Timrod Papers, South Caroliniana Library, University of South Carolina, Columbia (courtesy of Belinda Gergel).

43. *Southern Literary Messenger* 2 (December 1940): 645; *Charleston Daily Courier,* January 23, 1862.

44. Fidler, "Seven Unpublished Letters," 148–49; Rosen, *Confederate Charleston,* passim.

45. Rebecca Ella Solomons Alexander Memoir transcript, Alexander Papers, Atlanta Jewish Federation Archives, p. 7.

46. Russell and Hines, *Savannah,* 104–10.

47. Rebecca Alexander transcript, 6–8.

48. *Confederate Veteran,* August 1921, 304.

49. Greenberg, "Creating Ethnic, Class, and Southern Identity," 178.

50. Rubin, *Third to None,* 115–17; F. O. Lee and J. C. Agnew, *Historical Record of the City of Savannah* (Savannah, 1869), 171–73.

51. Greenberg, "Creating Ethnic, Class, and Southern Identity," 165–68.

52. Rubin, *Third to None,* 135. It was formerly the Liberty Inn.

53. Greenberg, "Creating Ethnic, Class, and Southern Identity," 164.

54. "Fanny Cohen's Journal of Sherman's Occupation of Savannah," *Collections of the Georgia Historical Society,* 407–16.

55. Greenberg, "Creating Ethnic, Class, and Southern Identity," 64, 236–38.

56. Russell and Hines, *Savannah,* 114; Rebecca Alexander transcript, 9–10; *Confederate Veteran* 8 (1921): 304.

57. Foreword to Proctor and Schmier, *Jews of the South.*

58. Rubin, *Third to None,* 213.

59. Mary A. DeCredico, *Patriotism for Profit: Georgia's Urban Entrepreneurs and the Confederate War Effort* (Chapel Hill: University of North Carolina Press, 1990), 33; Joseph B. Mahan, *Columbus, Georgia's Fall Line Trading Town* (Northridge, Calif.: Windsor Publications, 1986), 48–9, 52, 57.

60. DeCredico, *Patriotism,* 50.

61. *AJA* 13, no. 1 (April 1861): 73–74.

62. Ibid, 74.

63. Jack J. Steinberg, "The Jews of Augusta" (article in *Ancestoring* 12 in possession of author); "United for Worship and Charity: A History of Congregation Children of Israel."

64. Chester G. Hearn, *The Capture of New Orleans, 1862* (Baton Rouge: Louisiana State University Press, 1995), 65.

65. Nau, *The German People*, 37.

66. Ashkenazi, *Diary of Clara Solomon*, 233, 273.

67. Ibid., 243, 263–64, 289–90.

68. Records of the Association for the Relief of Jewish Widows and Orphans, bound volume at Louisiana State Museum, New Orleans.

69. Ashkenazi, *Diary of Clara Solomon*, 325–26, 329, 332; Young, *Where They Lie*, 223; Congregation Book of Records of Dispersed of Judah, Howard Tilton Library, TU.

70. Ashkenazi, *Diary of Clara Solomon*, 325.

71. David Nevins, *The Road to Shiloh* (Alexandria, Va.: Time-Life Books, 1983); *Historical Times Illustrated Encyclopedia of the Civil War*, 684–85.

72. Ashkenazi, *Diary of Clara Solomon*, 295, 310, 326, 331, 334n. 24, 340.

73. Ibid., 343–45.

74. Korn, *American Jewry*, 48.

75. Ibid.

76. Max Heller, "Jubilee Souvenir Booklet," 48–53, 71–75; Jewish Historical Publishing Company of Louisiana, comp., *The History of Jews of Louisiana: Their Religious, Civic, Charitable and Patriotic Life* (New Orleans: Jewish Historical Publishing Company of Louisiana, 1905), 29.

77. *The History of Jews of Louisiana*, 176.

78. Woodward, *Mary Chesnut*, 371–72.

79. Ashkenazi, *Diary of Clara Solomon*, 350–51.

80. Ibid., 354, 369–70, 395, 424, 419–20; Faust, *Mothers of Invention*, 207–14.

81. Butler, *Judah Benjamin*, 336–38.

82. Joseph Benjamin is listed in the *Roster of Confederate Soldiers* in Benjamin's Company Cavalry, a company he formed in December 1863. The only record is the company muster roll for "Dec. 24, 1863 to Feb. 29, 1864," which shows that the company was enlisted on December 24, 1863, at Rapides, Louisiana, by Maj. William M. Levy. The supposition that it was a headquarters escort is based on comments by Judah Benjamin when Taylor gave up his command and moved east of the Mississippi in August 1864, and the fact that William M. Levy was on General Taylor's staff from July 1862 until the end of the war. A notation on the surrender rolls for H. M. Hyams says he was paroled with Lt. Gen. Simon Bolivar Buckner's escort, commanded by Capt. Joseph Benjamin at Natchitoches in June 1865.

83. James Parton, *General Butler in New Orleans* (New York, 1864).

84. Benjamin Butler, *Butler's Book: A Review of His Legal, Political and Military Career*, (Boston, 1892).

85. Evans, *Judah Benjamin*, 381; Meade, *Judah P. Benjamin*, 362.

86. Young, *Where They Lie*, 152.

87. The CSR for Solomon Cohen shows him in Company B (Thomas's), 28th Louisiana Infantry. His son's application for membership in the Sons of Confederate Veterans in 1951 shows Captain Sloan's Company. E. B. Sloan was commander of Company C. The story about the chicken, courtesy of Cathy Kahn and Cecile Levin of New Orleans, December 6, 1997. He is listed as "S. Cohen" in *Booth's*, 372. (The official 28th Louisiana was Gray's

Regiment. Thomas's is listed as the 29th Louisiana, yet in the OR, Thomas's is designated as the 28th. This confusion was not uncommon in the Confederate Army.)

88. Memoir in possession of Cecile Levine of New Orleans, the great-granddaughter of Fanny Goldstein Cohen; copy at the Museum of the Southern Jewish Experience.

89. "Life and Doings of Ferdinand Goldsmith," courtesy of Moise Steeg, Esq., of New Orleans; copy in the possession of the author.

90. A. Metz Kahn, "From the Rhine to Dixie and Beyond," 1992, TU, Metz Papers.

91. *The Story of the Jewish Orphan's Home of New Orleans* (New Orleans, 1905); Malone, "New Orleans Uptown," 245n. 11. This institution, funded in large part by Judah Touro, was necessitated by the death toll caused by the yellow fever epidemics of 1847 and 1853.

92. Heller, "Jubilee Souvenir Booklet," 11, 39.

93. Ashkenazi, *Diary of Clara Solomon*, 352.

94. William Tuckman, "Sigmund and Jacob Schlesinger and Joseph Bloch: Civil War Composers and Musicians," *AJHQ* 53, no. 1 (September 1963): 70–75. A Joseph Block is listed in Company C, Alabama State Artillery, stationed at Mobile.

95. Gov. T. H. Watts to Jefferson Davis, OR II, vol. 8, 1222–24; Nevins, *Herbert H. Lehman and His Era*, 10; Ashkenazi, *A Centennial*; Elliott Ashkenazi, "Jewish Commercial Interests between North and South: The Case of the Lehmans and the Seligmans," *AJA* 63, no. 1 (Spring/Summer 1991): 25–39; "Mayer Lehman in Correspondence with General U.S. Grant, Jefferson Davis and Governor T. H. Watts of Alabama," *PAJHS* 20 (1911): 154–57 (also in OR II, 7, 1223–24 and II, 8, 69–70, 166, 365).

96. Postal and Koppman, *A Jewish Tourist's Guide to the U.S.*, 7.

97. Kenneth Libo, "The Moses of Montgomery: The Saga of a Jewish Family in the South," *Alabama Heritage* 35 (spring 1995): 18–25; Loeb book.

98. Owen, *History of Alabama*, 813.

99. Korn, *American Jewry*, 49.

100. Ibid., 49; *AJA* 13, no. 1 (April 1961): 40–42.

101. The Natchez Light Infantry was Company A of the 1st (Patton's) Mississippi, Army of 10,000. The Natchez Southrons was first Company O, then new Company B, 10th Mississippi. During the major reorganization of the Army of Tennessee, most of the 10th Mississippi became Company G, 9th Mississippi (consolidated).

102. ORN I, 19, 181–82. Report of Commodore Porter, commanding USS *Essex*, Blockading Squadron; *Aunt Sister's Book* (New York, 1929), 5–6; Turitz and Turitz, *Jews in Early Mississippi*, 11–12.

103. *Aunt Sister's Book*, 6.

104. Ibid., 8–12.

105. April 17, 1864, letter, Simon Mayer Family Papers, No. 815, Box No. 1, TU.

106. *Aunt Sister's Book*, 7–8, 15; Faust, *Mothers of Invention*, 207.

107. Fedora Small Frank, "Nashville Jewry during the Civil War," *Tennessee Historical Quarterly* 39, no. 3 (fall 1980): 310–13; *Nashville Daily Gazette*, September 8, 1861.

108. Frank "Nashville Jewry," 313.

109. Rabbi James A. Wax, "The Jews of Memphis: 1860–1865," *West Tennessee Historical Society Papers* 3 (1949): 39–43. Levy was a second lieutenant in the 1st Alabama, Tennessee and Mississippi infantry, also known as the 4th Confederate. He was second lieutenant of Company I, 42d Tennessee, and captain, AQM. He is referred to as a major, which he may have been late in the war.

110. Frank, "Nashville Jewry," 315–16.

111. Ibid., 317–18.

112. *Children of Israel v. Peres,* 42 Tenn 620; Wax, "The Jews of Memphis," 41; Lewis, *A Biblical People,* 24.

113. Frank, "Nashville Jewry," 318–20.

114. Frank L. Byrne and Jean Powers Soman, ed., *Your True Marcus: The Civil War Letters of a Jewish Colonel* (Kent, Ohio: Kent State University Press, 1986), 175–203, 335. This book has been reissued as *A Jewish Colonel in the Civil War: Marcus M. Spiegel of the Ohio Volunteers,* edited by Soman and Byrne (Lincoln, Tenn.: University of Nashville Press, 1994).

115. Wax, "The Jews of Memphis," 57, 61, 63, 64.

116. Ibid., 46, 48.

117. Iphigene Ochs Sulzberger, *From Iphigene: The Memoirs of Iphigene Ochs Sulzberger,* edited by Susan W. Dryfoos (privately printed, 1979); on Julius and Bertha Ochs see, generally, *Twentieth Century Biographical Dictionary of Notable Americans* [s.v. "Adolph Ochs"]; "Southern Jew as Businessman," *AJH* 71, no. 3 (March 1982): 347; *Confederate Veteran* 36, no. 5 (1928): 164; Gay Talese, *The Kingdom and the Power* (New York: World Publishing Co., 1966); Gerald W. Johnson, *An Honorable Titan: A Biographical Study of Adolph S. Ochs* (New York: Harper & Brothers, 1944); Susan E. Tifft and Alex S. Jones, *The Trust: The Private and Powerful Family Behind the New York Times* (Boston: Little, Brown, 1999).

118. Gay Talese, *The Kingdom and the Power,* 81–82; Susan E. Tifft and Alex S. Jones, "The Family," *New Yorker* 75, no. 8 (April 19, 1999): 44–52.

119. Sulzberger, *From Iphigene,* 4.

120. Talese, *The Kingdom and the Power,* 83.

121. Sulzberger, *From Iphigene,* 3.

122. Ibid., 4; *Confederate Veteran* 36, no. 5 (1928): 164.

123. The 1864 date is given in G. E. Govan and J. W. Livingood, "Adolph S. Ochs: The Boy Publisher," *East Tennessee Historical Society's Publications* 17 (1945); other sources say the family moved in 1865.

124. John Y. Simon, ed., *The Papers of Ulysses S. Grant* (Carbondale, Ill.: Southern Illinois University Press, 1967–81), 7:58; Jaher, *Scapegoat,* 198–9; Korn, *American Jewry,* 122–25.

125. Korn, *American Jewry,* 122–25; Lewis, *A Biblical People,* 37–42; Schappes, *Documentary History,* 472–75. Schappes, a New Yorker who compiled this one-volume documentary history in the 1940s, omitted Grant's infamous Order Number 11, despite the fact that it was the most blatant anti-Semitic document ever issued by the U.S. government. Northern Jews of the 1950s were clearly embarrassed by this episode in American history. Schappes did, however, include documents relating to the revocation of Order Number 11 by President Lincoln. "Resembling a Czarist ukase more than an American governmental decree, Grant's order," Jaher wrote, "was the severest attempted official violation—civil or military, federal, state or local—of the rights of Jews in the history of this nation" (*Scapegoat,* 199).

126. Grant's order was not an isolated event, as his many apologists have argued. Earlier in November, he had issued two orders forbidding travel to all persons, "the Israelites especially," because they were "such an intolerable nuisance." Korn, *American Jewry,* 126; William S. McFeely, *Grant: A Biography* (New York: W. W. Norton & Co., 1981), 123–24; Schappes, *Documentary History,* 472. One of Grant's orders instructed all railroad con-

432   ductors "that no Jews are to be permitted to travel on the railroad." See Selma S. Lewis, *A Biblical People,* 38–43; Jaher, *Scapegoat,* 198–99; Joakim Isaacs, "Ulysses S. Grant and the Jews," in Johanthan D. Sarna, *The American Jewish Experience* (New York: Holmes and Meier, 1986), 62–71; Brooks D. Simpson, *Ulysses S. Grant: Triumph Over Adversity, 1822–1865* (Boston: Houghton Mifflin, 2000), 163–65 ("Some of his statements were clearly anti-Semitic").

Gen. William T. Sherman was, unlike Grant (who was simply reflecting the ignorance about Jews prevalent at the time), a genuine anti-Semite. "The country will swarm with dishonest Jews who will smuggle powder, pistols, percussion-caps, &c., in spite of all the guards and precautions we can give," he wrote in August 1862 (Korn, *American Jewry,* 148–49). See Sherman to Ellen Ewing Sherman, September 18, 1858, in *Home Letters of General Sherman,* edited by M. A. DeWolfe Howe (New York: Charles Scribner's Sons, 1909), 155, 229–30, to Salmon Chase, August 11, 1862, in *Memoirs of General William T. Sherman* (New York: Appleton, 1875), 1:267, and to the adjutant general of the army, August 11, 1862, OR III, vol. 2, 350. One of Sherman's biographers, Michael Fellman, agrees that Sherman was a genuine anti-Semite. See his *Citizen Sherman: A Life of William Tecumseh Sherman* (New York: Random House, 1995), 153–54. The notorious Benjamin F. "Beast" Butler was also known to be an anti-Semite (see Jaher, *Scapegoat,* 192, 198, 200). Korn treats General Order No. 11 at length in chap. 6, "Exodus 1862," (*American Jewry,* 121–55). He does not believe that Grant was an anti-Semite and that he was instead the victim of unconscious prejudices. To his credit, Grant as president was a good friend to the Jews and had many Jewish supporters. Jewish Tennesseans, however, were not among them. Sacher provides a good summary of the episode in *A History of the Jews in America,* 78–80.

127. Coulter, *Confederate States,* 85.

128. CSR, Lewis Leon.

129. Louis Schmier, "An Act Unbecoming: Anti-Semitic Uprising in Thomas County, Georgia," *Civil War Times Illustrated* 23 (October 1984), 21–25; Louis Schmier, "Notes and Documents on the 1862 Expulsion of Jews from Thomasville, Georgia," *AJA* 32 (April 1980): 9; Mark I. Greenberg, "Ambivalent Relations: Acceptance and Anti-Semitism in Confederate Thomasville," *AJA* 65, no. 1 (Spring/Summer 1993): 13–29. Greenberg and Schmier disagree as to the seriousness of the incident.

130. Schmier, "Notes and Documents," 12–15.

131. Schmier, "An Act Unbecoming," 23.

132. Ibid., 15–16; Schmier, "An Act Unbecoming," 23.

133. Schmier, "An Act Unbecoming," 24.

134. Letter dated September 29, 1862, 4, Phillips-Myers Papers, UNC.

135. Schmier, "Notes and Documents," 15; Greenberg, "Ambivalent Relations," 15–18.

136. Schmier, "Notes and Documents," 17.

137. Ibid., 18.

138. Ibid., 25.

139. Friedman, "History of Temple Beth Israel," 35–39.

140. Jaher, *Scapegoat,* 200; Bertram Wallace Korn, "American Judeophobia: Confederate Version," in Dinnerstein and Palsson, *Jews in the South,* 147.

141. Marcus, *Memoirs,* 2:304.

142. Furguson, *Ashes of Glory,* 191; Emory M. Thomas, *The Confederate State of Richmond: A Biography of the Capitol* (Austin: University of Texas Press, 1971), passim.

143. Korn, "American Judeophobia," in *Jews in the South,* 135; Roland, *The Confederacy,* 89.

144. Henry S. Foote was a relative of the famed Civil War historian Shelby Foote, whose maternal grandfather was a Viennese Jew, Morris David Rosenstock, who immigrated to the South in the 1880s and worked as a plantation bookkeeper. See Tony Horwitz, *Confederates in the Attic: Dispatches from the Unfinished Civil War* (New York: Pantheon Books, 1998), 148.

145. Korn, "American Judeophobia," in *Jews in the South,* 139–44; Roland, *The Confederacy,* 99.

146. Marcus, *Memoirs,* 3:309.

147. Korn, in *Jews in the South,* 148–49.

148. Ibid., 137.

149. Jaher, *Scapegoat,* 224.

150. Berman, *Richmond's Jewry,* 185.

151. Jaher, *Scapegoat,* 224.

152. Putnam, *Richmond during the War,* 105; see also Coulter, *Confederate States,* 227.

153. Putnam, *Richmond during the War,* 105.

154. Earl Schenck Miers edited *A Rebel War Clerk's Diary* in 1958 and eliminated "Jones' constant harping on Jews," which, Miers wrote, "reaches a point of offensiveness," xxi. For the unedited, unexpurgated version, see John Beauchamp Jones, *A Rebel War Clerk's Diary at the Confederate States Capital* (New York, 1935; reprint, Baton Rouge: Louisiana State University Press, 1993).

155. Jaher, *Scapegoat,* 197–98; Korn, *American Jewry,* 179, 184.

156. Coulter, *Confederate States,* 227.

157. Korn, *American Jewry,* 185; Korn, in *Jews in the South,* 153.

158. Korn, in *Jews in the South,* 144.

159. Berman, *Richmond's Jewry,* 188.

160. Ibid., 189; Korn, in *Jews in the South,* 150.

161. Korn, in *Jews in the South,* 150.

162. Ibid., 85.

163. Furguson, *Ashes of Glory,* 182–83.

164. Marszalek, *Diary of Miss Emma Holmes,* 209.

165. Korn, in *Jews in the South,* 142; Coulter, *Confederate States,* 223–29.

166. Coulter, *Confederate States,* 227.

167. Marszalek, *Diary of Miss Emma Holmes,* entry for August, 22, 1862.

168. Wax, "The Jews of Memphis," 73.

169. Korn, *American Jewry,* 186–87.

170. Korn, in *Jews in the South,* 143.

171. Korn, *American Jewry,* 185–86; 295n. 173; Korn, in *Jews in the South,* 152. In the Book of Joshua, seven priests bore seven rams' horns before the Ark of the Covenant and, when all the people shouted in unison, the wall of Jericho fell (Josh. 6:1–21).

172. Korn, *American Jewry,* xx; Young, *Where They Lie,* 185.

173. Butler to Edwin M. Stanton, October 1862, in James Parton, *General Butler in New Orleans* (Mason Bros., 1864); Jaher, *Scapegoat,* 198.

174. Parton, *General Butler in New Orleans,* 391–92; Jaher, *Scapegoat,* 192.

175. Korn, *American Jewry,* 163–66.

176. Coulter, *Confederate States,* 228n. 27.

177. Korn, in *Jews in the South,* 149n. 45; Moses, *Last Order,* 14.

178. Korn, *American Jewry,* 57–58.

179. Ibid., 57. In the introduction to the 1961 paperbook edition of this book, Korn revisited this conclusion, which had caused "a few eyebrows to be raised fairly high," and found evidence "which ought to satisfy all but the most rabid anti-Confederate historians." See also Korn, "Was There a Confederate Jewish Chaplain?" *AJHQ* 53, no. 1 (September 1963), 63–69, and "Jewish Chaplains during the Civil War," *AJA* 1, no. 1 (June 1998): 6–22.

180. Preface to the paperback edition of Korn, *American Jewry and the Civil War,* xiv.

181. Korn, *American Jewry,* 92–93.

182. Ibid., 112; Young, *Where They Lie,* 76.

183. Korn, *American Jewry,* 45–46, 112–13.

184. Ibid., 112–13. One enigmatic Northern Jew, Isachar Zacharie, President Lincoln's chiropodist (he removed the president's corns and bunions), took on special missions in the South. The press had a field day with Zacharie's treatment of the president, the secretary of war, and prominent Union generals. How could the president "put his foot down firmly when he was troubled with corns?" they asked. Jackson's "bare-footed rebels, who do not know the need or value of a chiropodist," got the better of Zacharie's patients, but "Dr. Zacharie has shown us precisely where the shoe pinches" (Korn, *American Jewry,* 194–96). Lincoln sent his chiropodist friend, whose family was in Savannah, on a number of secret missions, including a meeting with Judah Benjamin and other Confederate cabinet members to discuss possible cessation of hostilities in 1863 (197–200). Zacharie wrote Gen. Nathaniel Banks that "Benjamin said he was under many obligations to you for your kindness towards his *sister.*" Lincoln may have believed that Zacharie, being Jewish and having a Southern connection, could somehow reach an agreement with the Jewish Confederate secretary of state (198). Lincoln also sent Zacharie to occupied New Orleans to learn the state of affairs directly from a man he trusted, as he had done in 1861, when he sent friends to Charleston to learn the state of affairs there.

Zacharie took a special interest in the Jews of New Orleans. Some were Northerners trapped by the war. Most were Southerners who resented the occupying army. Zacharie apparently helped them cope with the Federal authorities. On another occasion, Zacharie came to the aid of Goodman L. Mordecai, who was arrested and imprisoned as a Confederate commercial agent. Goodman was the son of Benjamin Mordecai of Charleston, who had given $10,000 to the state of South Carolina when it first seceded. Zacharie went to Washington personally to ask the president to release young Mordecai, who was engaged to be married to the niece of a prominent New Yorker, Samuel A. Lewis. Upon his release, young Mordecai insisted on thanking President Lincoln personally. The president shook his hand and, in his humorous way, said, "I am happy to know that I am able to serve an enemy!" (Korn, *American Jewry,* 199).

185. Robinson, *Justice in Grey,* 418.

186. Philip Rosenheim to Amelia and Isaac Meinnart, July 8, 1863, AJA.

187. Emilie V. Jacobs, "Biography of George Jacobs," George Jacobs Papers, AJA.

188. *AJA* 10, no. 2 (October 1950): 150, 133–34.

CHAPTER 6

1. DeLeon, *Belles, Beaux, and Brains,* 178, 230; Phillips-Myers Papers, UNC.

2. K. K. Beth Elohim, *Centennial Booklet* (Charleston, 1924), 42–43.

3. Elzas, *Jews of South Carolina*, 194; K. K. Beth Elohim, *Centennial Booklet*, 42–43.

4. Biographical sketch by Solomon Breibart and Carolyn Rivers in possession of author; Hagy, *This Happy Land*, 245; Allison Demoff, "Phoebe Pember" (thesis, College of William and Mary, 1993).

5. DeLeon, *Belles, Beaux, and Brains*, 178; Woodward, *Mary Chesnut*, 707; Rubin, *Third to None*, 92.

6. David T. Morgan, "Eugenia Levy Phillips: The Civil War Experiences of a Southern Jewish Woman," in Dinnerstein and Palsson, *Jews of the South;* Proctor and Schmier, *Selected Essays*, 95–106; David T. Morgan, "Philip Phillips: Jurist and Statesman" in Dinnerstein and Palsson, *Jews in the South*, chap. 8, p. 107–20; Marcus, *Memoirs*, 3:133–60; Hagy, *This Happy Land*, 104.

7. Marcus, *Memoirs*, 3:161.

8. Ibid., 145.

9. Phillips Diary, Phillips-Myers Papers, UNC, 28–33; William W. Freehling, *The Road to Disunion: Secessionist at Bay, 1776–1854* (New York: Oxford University Press, 1990), 553–56; Morgan, "Philip Phillips," 117.

10. Woodward and Muhlenfeld, *The Private Mary Chesnut*, 186.

11. Caroline Myers, "Events Which Befell Us in 1861," Phillips-Myers Papers, UNC.

12. Woodward and Muhlenfeld, *The Private Mary Chesnut*, 24.

13. Ibid., 24, 183.

14. Marcus, *Memoirs*, 3:134; Korn, *The Jews of Mobile*, 46–47. Korn points out that Phillips, unlike Benjamin and August Belmont, "the other two notable Jewish figures of the day," identified with the Jewish people and religion. Temime Derech was a Polish immigrant synagogue, yet Phillips, an acculturated Reform Jew, had no qualms about identifying himself with the congregation. See Korn, *The Jews of Mobile*, 46–47n. 30.

15. Ashkenazi, *Diary of Clara Solomon*, 290, 310.

16. Clay, *A Belle of the Fifties*, 104–5.

17. *UDC* [United Daughters of the Confederacy] *Magazine*, October 1993, 8.

18. *Spies, Scouts, and Raiders: Irregular Operations* (Alexandria, Va.: Time-Life Books, 1985), 23; Ishbel Ross, *Rebel Rose: Life of Rose O'Neal Greehow, Confederate Spy* (New York: Harper, 1954), chs. 10 and 11.

19. Pember, *A Southern Woman's Story*, 25–26.

20. Phillips Diary, 38. Mrs. Phillips states in her memoirs that her husband "had no sympathy with the Confederacy." "Mrs. Phillips: A Southern Woman's Story of Her Imprisonment in 1861 and 1862," Library of Congress, Manuscript Division, 4.

21. Ross, *Rebel Rose*, chaps. 10 and 11.

22. Ibid.

23. Ibid., 169, 173.

24. August–September 1861, Journal of Eugenia Phillips, Philip Phillips Papers, Library of Congress.

25. Woodward and Muhlenfeld, *The Private Mary Chesnut*, 172.

26. Ibid., 172, 176.

27. Phillips Diary, 44; Caroline Myers, "Events Which Befell Us," Phillips-Myers Papers, UNC.

28. Phillips Diary, 49; Morgan, "Eugenia Levy Phillips," 99; Marcus, *Memoirs*, 3:176–77.

29. Myers, "Events"; Morgan, "Eugenia Levy Phillips," 99.

30. Myers, "Events."

31. Marcus, *Memoirs,* 3:178, 179.

32. Ibid., 3:184; *Civil War Dictionary,* 109, 945.

33. Myers, "Events," 4.

34. Marcus, *Memoirs,* 3:187.

35. Phillips Diary, 50.

36. Marcus, *Memoirs,* 3:187.

37. DeLeon, *Belles, Beaux, and Brains,* 177.

38. *UDC,* October, 1993, 9.

39. Phillips Diary, 50.

40. Myers, "Events," 4.

41. Phillips Diary, 51.

42. Morgan, "Eugenia Levy Phillips," 102–5; Marcus, *Memoirs,* 3:189; Myers, "Events," 4.

43. Marcus, *Memoirs,* 3:192–93; Morgan, "Eugenia Levy Phillips," 104; Phillips-Myers Papers, UNC, letters dated July 10, 1862 and September 1, 1862.

44. Woodward, *Mary Chesnut,* 411.

45. Morgan, "Eugenia Levy Phillips," 104; Ashkenazi, *Diary of Clara Solomon,* 430.

46. Phillips-Myers Papers, UNC, letter dated July 24, 1882; Phillips Diary, 52. For more on Phillips and his memoir, see p. 369.

47. William Garrett, *Reminiscences of Public Man in Alabama for Thirty Years* (reprint, Spartanburg, S.C.: n.p., 1972), 407.

48. Myers, "Events," 4; Morgan, "Eugenia Levy Phillips," 104–5 .

49. Marcus, *Memoirs,* 3:194.

50. Ibid., 195.

51. Clavius Phillips to Eugenia Phillips, November 11, 1862, Phillips-Myers Papers, UNC.

52. DeLeon, *Belles, Beaux, and Brains,* 179; Phillips Diary, 51.

53. Marcus, *Memoirs,* 3:154.

54. Letter of Yates Levy to J. C. Levy, September 1862, Phillips-Myers Papers, UNC.

55. CSR, Clavius Phillips (Chatham Artillery, Weaton's Co.; 2d Confederate Engineers, Co. E; 1st [Olmstead's] Infantry).

56. Pember, *A Southern Woman's Story,* 159; Coulter, *Confederate States,* 299; DeLeon, *Belles, Beaux, and Brains,* 179.

57. Phillips-Myers Papers, UNC, letter dated July 17, 1862.

58. Letter from Jacob C. Levy, July 1862, Phillips-Meyers Papers, UNC.

59. Marcus, *Memoirs,* 3:155.

60. Ibid., 155–56.

61. Ibid., 156.

62. Ibid., 158; Phillips Diary, 56–58.

63. Phillips Diary, 60.

64. Pember, *A Southern Woman's Story,* 4.

65. Ibid., 149, 157–58.

66. Woodward, *Mary Chesnut,* 537n. 16; Pember, *A Southern Woman's Story,* 4, 25.

67. Pember, *A Southern Woman's Story,* 4–6, 26 (emphasis in original).

68. Phoebe Pember to Eugenia Phillips, September 13, 1863, Philip Phillips Collec-

tion, Manuscript Division, Library of Congress, Washington, D.C.; Phoebe Pember to Louisa Gilmer, October 20, 1863, Pember Papers, UNC.

69. Pember, *A Southern Woman's Story,* 4–5, 23–24, 28; Robertson, *Tenting Tonight,* 95–97.

70. Pember, *A Southern Woman's Story,* 28–29.

71. Ibid., 6–7, 36–40.

72. DeLeon, *Belles, Beaux, and Brains,* 385.

73. Pember, *A Southern Woman's Story,* 42–44, 156.

74. Ibid., 66–68.

75. Ibid., 157–58.

76. Ibid., 56.

77. Ibid., 168.

78. Alison Demoff, "Phoebe Pember," 110.

79. Pember, *A Southern Woman's Story,* 137.

80. Ibid., 151–52.

81. Ibid., 151.

82. Ibid., 161–62.

83. Woodward, *Mary Chesnut,* 537.

84. Pember, *A Southern Woman's Story,* 164–67.

85. Ibid., 164–66.

86. Pember, *A Southern Woman's Story,* 82–83.

87. Ibid., 82–83.

88. Ibid., 185–92.

89. Ibid., 127–8, 136–41.

90. Ibid., 142–43.

91. Ibid., 143–44.

CHAPTER 7

1. Isaac Scherck to J. L. Meyer, Esq., September 9, 1864, Scherck Papers, AJA. A biographical sketch of Scherck appears in *History of the Jews of Louisiana,* 33.

2. Mayer Family Memoir, Atlanta Jewish Federation Archives.

3. Spencer B. King, "Fanny Cohen's Journal of Sherman's Occupation of Savannah," *Georgia Historical Quarterly* 41 (December 1957): 414.

4. King, "Fanny Cohen's Journal," 410. According to Georgina L. Phillips, Mrs. Octavus Cohen's granddaughter, General Sherman's adjutant ordered the Cohen family out of their home within twenty-four hours so that it could be used by General Sherman as his headquarters. While Mr. Cohen was remonstrating with the adjutant, General Hazen happened by and recognized Mr. Cohen. He settled the dispute over the use of the Cohen home by using the front drawing room as his office. According to Miss Phillips, General Hazen used the drawing room as his office until he left Savannah. Note dated November 18, 1949, in the Cohen-Phillips Papers, Collection 162, Folder 2, GHS.

5. King, "Fanny Cohen's Journal," 412.

6. Rosen, *Confederate Charleston,* 133–34.

7. Ibid., 142.

8. Mrs. Lee Cohen Harby, quoted in *Voices of the Civil War: Charleston* (Alexandria,

Va.: Time-Life Books, 1997), 158; Lee Cohen was born in 1849 and married Jacob De La Motta Harby in 1869. Hagy, *This Happy Land*, 322; front page, *New York Herald*, March 25, 1865, courtesy of Mel Young.

9. Gergel and Gergel, *Tree of Life*, 40–44.

10. Eleanor Cohen Diary, AJA, 8–9; see also Marcus, *Memoirs*, 3:357–64; Gergel and Gergel, *Tree of Life*, 40; Franklin, *Private Pages*, 304–23.

11. Cohen Diary, 9; Charles Royster, *The Destructive War* (New York: Knopf, 1991), ch. 1.

12. Gergel and Gergel, *Tree of Life*, 40–41.

13. DeLeon, *Thirty Years*, 1:4–5.

14. Gergel and Gergel, *Tree of Life*, 41–42.

15. Cohen Diary, 9–10.

16. Gergel and Gergel, *Tree of Life*, 42n. 42; Korn, *American Jewry*, 53.

17. Cohen Diary, 10.

18. Gergel and Gergel, *Tree of Life*, 43.

19. Ibid., 42–43.

20. Ashley Halsey Jr., "The Last Duel in the Confederacy," *Civil War Times Illustrated* 1, no. 7 (November 1962): 6–8, 31; *Confederate Veteran* 9 (1901): 500–501 (Hart's Battery); Randolph W. Kirkland, Jr., *Broken Fortunes: South Carolina Soldiers, Sailors, and Citizens Who Died in the Service of Their Country and State in the War for Southern Independence, 1861–1865* (Charleston: South Carolina Historical Society, 1995), 69; Baker, *Cadets in Gray*, 192; *Roster of Confederate Soldiers;* Wolf, *American Jew*, 374.

21. Tidwell, *Come Retribution*, 24, 65, 89, 213, 337–41; Tidwell, *April '65*, 12–13, 28, 162–64; Chamlee, *Lincoln's Assassins*, 532; Hanchett, *Lincoln Murder Conspiracies*, 52.

22. A. A. Hoehling and Mary Hoehling, *The Day Richmond Died* (San Diego: A. S. Barnes & Co., 1981), 105–15.

23. Axelrod, *The War Between the Spies*, passim; Evans, *Judah Benjamin*, 294.

24. Marcus, *Memoirs*, 3:327; Furguson, *Ashes of Glory*, 326–33.

25. Furguson, *Ashes of Glory*, 325.

26. Meade, *Judah P. Benjamin*, 312; Hanna, *Flight into Oblivion*, 31.

27. Furguson, *Ashes of Glory*, 332.

28. Whitlock MS, 125–27; Furguson, *Ashes of Glory*, 328–29. Whitlock believed the fires were set by escapees from the penitentiary who did it to mask their crimes. "I saw this with my own Eyes" (127).

29. Whitlock MS, VHS 127–29.

30. Ibid., 130.

31. Furguson, *Ashes of Glory*, 344–46.

32. Whitlock MS, VHS, 131. He correctly describes Lincoln as being guarded by "a few marines or sailors."

33. *Virginia Magazine of History and Biography* 41 (October 1933): 318–22.

34. Meade, *Judah P. Benjamin*, 314. Alfred, Lord Tennyson, wrote his famous ode in 1852.

35. Marcus, *Memoirs*, 3:312–15.

36. Evans, *Judah Benjamin*, 308; Hanna, *Flight into Oblivion*, 45.

37. Long, *The Civil War Day by Day*, 679–80; Foote, *The Civil War*, 3: chap. 8.

38. Evans, *Judah Benjamin*, 303, 306, 334; Gruss, "Judah Philip Benjamin," 999, 1002; John M. Taylor, *W. H. Seward: Lincoln's Right Hand* (New York: HarperCollins, 1991), 261.

39. Hanchett, *Lincoln Murder Conspiracies*, 72, 107.

40. Evans, *Judah Benjamin*, 271–72.

41. Evans, *Judah Benjamin*, 312–15; Meade, *Judah P. Benjamin*, 318; Neiman, *Judah Benjamin*, 190.

42. Meade, *Judah P. Benjamin*, 322.

43. Thompson, "Yulee," 556, 602, 567.

44. Ibid., 580.

45. A. J. Hanna, "The Confederate Baggage and Treasure Train Ends Its Flight in Florida," *Florida Historical Quarterly* 24, no. 3 (January 1939): 158–80 (an introduction to the diary of Tench Francis Tilghman).

46. Alroy Jonas letter, November 19, 1936, Korn Papers, AJA.

47. See pp. 152–53 and n. 249, ch. 3, p. 416.

48. Mayer enlisted originally in the 5th Mississippi Army of 10,000, later redesignated Patton's 1st Mississippi. When his original enlistment expired, he joined the Natchez Southrons, Company O of the 10th Mississippi. Later, it was redesignated Company B. He served as a clerk in the assistant adjutant general's office of Brig. Gen. James R. Chalmer's brigade, then in the same capacity on the division staff. He was promoted to first lieutenant on April 8, 1865. Because of the various consolidations of regiments, Mayer ended the war in Company D, 9th Mississippi (consolidated). See CSR, Company O, 10th Mississippi; Company A, 1st Mississippi; *Military History of Mississippi*, 208–18. When he was paroled, he was officially recognized as a first lieutenant in the Consolidated 9th Mississippi. However, a provost marshall pass given him in Montgomery three weeks later shows him as a major and assistant adjutant of Sharp's brigade. In a letter dated May 3, 1865, he addresses himself as "Major" with the quotation marks. Thus, he may have been promoted to major unofficially in the field by General Sharp or assumed the rank temporarily, as befits an assistant adjutant general of a unit composed of the remains of three brigades.

49. Letter dated May 3, 1865, Sharp's Brigade, TU; Order of Provost Marshall, May 25, 1865, Simon Mayer Papers, Box 1, TU.

50. Jacobs, *Biography of George Jacobs;* Ezekiel and Lichtenstein, *History of the Jews of Richmond,* 177; Berman, *Richmond's Jewry,* 196–98.

51. Ezekiel and Lichtenstein, *History of the Jews of Richmond,* 158.

52. Bultman, "The Story of a Good Life," 2.

53. Moses, *Last Order,* 224, 249, 264, 265; obituary of Raphael Moses Jr., 1909.

54. Moses, *Last Order,* 249, 251, 252.

55. Ibid., 253.

56. Ibid., 255.

57. It could not have been the last order because the last significant land battle was fought at Palmito Ranch, Texas, on May 13; Stand Watie surrendered June 23; the Trans-Mississippi surrendered May 26; and the CSS *Shenandoah* surrendered at Liverpool, England, on November 6. Nevertheless, it was the last order of the Confederate army in the main theater of the war, and arguably the last order of the Confederate government.

58. Thompson, "David Yulee," 166.

59. Ibid., 172.

60. Yulee, "Senator David L. Yulee," 2:2, 12–15; Thompson, "David Yulee," 171, and n. 23.

61. Clarke, "Florida Railroad," 191; Thompson, "David Yulee," 169–70, 174, 575.

62. Clay, *A Belle of the Fifties,* 54; Mary Bernard Allen, "Joseph Holt, Judge Advocate

General (1862–1875): A Study in the Treatment of Political Prisoners by the United States Government during the Civil War" (Ph.D. diss., University of Chicago, 1927), 48, 66; on Holt, see also Roger J. Bartman, "The Contribution of Joseph Holt to the Political Life of the United States" (Ph.D. diss., Fordham University, 1958); David Donald, *Lincoln* (New York: Simon and Schuster, 1995), 313, 325, 333, 550; Thompson, "David Yulee," 173.

63. Thompson, "David Yulee," 173.

64. OR II, 8, 668–893, especially 862.

65. Yulee, "Senator David L. Yulee," 14.

66. Ibid., 594.

67. Thompson, "David Yulee," 175; Hühner, "David L. Yulee," 28.

68. Berman, *Richmond's Jewry*, 196–97.

CHAPTER 8

1. Notes by Judith Hyams Douglas, October 19, 1936, AJA.

2. Moses, *Last Order*, 243–44, roster of Confederate soldiers.

3. Ibid., xvi, 268–69.

4. Letter from Hyams dated April 19, 1968, to "My Dear Caroline," AJA.

5. "Thomas O. Moore, Governor 1860–1," *Louisiana Historical Quarterly* 13 (January 1930): 20–22, Hyams letter dated September 10, 1865, to Moore.

6. The literature on Reconstruction is massive and controversial. E. Merton Coulter gives the traditional Southern viewpoint in *The South during Reconstruction* (Baton Rouge: Louisiana State University Press, 1947).

The most recent revisionist view which rehabilitates (or tries to rehabilitate, depending on one's point of view) the carpetbaggers and scalawags is represented by Richard Current in *Those Terrible Carpetbaggers* (New York: Oxford University Press, 1988) and Eric Foner in *Reconstruction, 1863–1877: America's Unfinished Revolution* (New York: Harper and Row, 1988). Three works on South Carolina illustrate the debate: Francis Butler Simkins and Robert Hilliard Woody give a balanced account in *South Carolina during Reconstruction* (Chapel Hill: University of North Carolina Press, 1932); Richard Zuczek in *State of Rebellion Reconstruction in South Carolina* (Columbia: University of South Carolina Press, 1996) describes Reconstruction as a continuation of the war and emphasizes the white Redeemers' use of fraud, coercion, and terrorism. Edmund L. Drago gives the "postrevisionist" version in *Hurrah for Hampton! Black Red Shirts in South Carolina during Reconstruction* (Fayetteville: University of Arkansas Press, 1998), which argues that some blacks did indeed support the Redeemer movement. The historiography of Reconstruction reflects the emotions and politics of the times. See Zuczek's excellent introduction to *State of Rebellion*.

7. Letter from Hyams dated April 19, 1868, to "My Dear Caroline," AJA.

8. *New Orleans Daily Picayune* and the *New Orleans Times*, June 26, 1875.

9. See chapter 3, note 90, pp. 408–9.

10. Elzas, *Jews of South Carolina*, 231, 265; Penelope Franklin, ed., *Private Pages: Diaries of American Women, 1830s–1970s* (New York: Ballantine Books, 1986), 318–21 (diary at 304–23); Moise, *Moise Family*, 7.

11. Marcus, *Memoirs*, 3:342–34.

12. Ibid., 3:346.

13. Ibid., 3:364.

14. Reznikoff and Engelman, *Jews of Charleston*, 303–4; Elzas, *Jews of South Carolina*, 223–37.

15. Reznikoff and Engelman, *Jews of Charleston*, 305n. 235; 163–67.

16. Ibid.

17. Ibid., 163–64.

18. Ibid., 162–63.

19. Moise, *Moise Family*, 91; Jacob S. Raisin, *Centennial Booklet* (Charleston: KKBE, 1925).

20. Marcus, *Memoirs*, 3:341.

21. Saul Viener, "Rosena Hutzler Levy Recalls the Civil War," *AJHQ* 62, no. 3 (March 1973): 313.

22. Ibid., 200; Berman, *Richmond's Jewry*, 198.

23. Viener, "Rosena Hutzler," 202–3.

24. Herbert Ezekiel, "The Jews of Richmond during the Civil War"; Minutes of Beth Ahabah, BA.

25. Berman, *Richmond's Jewry*, 45; Furguson, *Ashes of Glory*, chap. 26.

26. Undated clipping, George Jacobs scrapbook, AJA. The circular is reproduced on page 339. See also Korn, *American Jewry*, 110–12.

27. Berman, *Richmond's Jewry*, 200, 206, 377n. 76.

28. Frank, "Nashville Jewry," 319.

29. Postal and Koppman, *A Jewish Tourist's Guide to the U.S.*, 587, 594.

30. Libo and Howe, *We Lived There Too*, 150–51.

31. Janice O. Rothschild, *As But a Day: The First Hundred Years, 1867–1967* (Atlanta: Hebrew Benevolent Congregation, The Temple, 1967), 2–3.

32. James Grant, *Bernard M. Baruch: The Adventures of a Wall Street Legend* (New York: Simon & Schuster, 1983), chap. 1, "A Doctor's Son." (Deborah Marks, whose father, Samuel Marks, arrived in South Carolina about 1800, married Rabbi Hartwig Cohen. Their daughter Sarah Cohen married Prussian immigrant Saling Wolfe. Simon Baruch married their daughter Isabelle.)

33. Even though Simon had courted Belle for years, the marriage was not a foregone conclusion. When Sherman's troops were setting fire to the Wolfe home, Belle, then fifteen, ran to save a portrait she had painted of Simon. A Yankee soldier took it from her and ripped it with his bayonet. When she protested, the soldier slapped her. A Union officer, Capt. John J. Cantine, came to her rescue and beat the soldier with the flat of his sword. A romance ensued between Belle and Cantine. But Simon persisted. Bernard Baruch later wrote in his memoirs that when he was chairman of the War Industries Board during World War I, he was visited by a young man seeking help to get overseas to the fighting front. He carried a letter of introduction from Baruch's mother. "The bearer of this," she wrote, "is a son of Captain Cantine. I know you will do what you can for him." Baruch, *My Own Story*, 20–21.

34. Baruch, *My Own Story*, 32, 34.

35. *Aunt Sister's Book*, 3, 14, 17; Marcus, *Memoirs*, 1:269 (portions of *Aunt Sister's Book* are printed in Marcus).

36. Ashkenazi, *A Centennial: Lehman Brothers*, 11, 13, 20.

37. Korn, "The Jews of the Confederacy," 6; DeLeon, *Four Years*, 10-11, "Sketch of the Author"; *Who Was Who*, 312.

38. Rubin, *Third to None*, 88, 145, 175; Jacob C. Levy letter dated March 24, 1868, in Phillips-Myers Papers, UNC.

39. Clay, *A Belle of the Fifties,* 277.

40. Ibid. The reference is to Haman, the minister of Ashasuerus, who plotted to kill the Jews in Persia. He was thwarted by Queen Esther, a Jewish woman, who saved her people at the risk of her own life. The holiday of Purim celebrates this event. See "Purim" in glossary. This story illustrates how well-versed Southerners were in the Old Testament. The story is told in the Book of Esther.

41. "Some Memories," Phillips-Myers Papers, UNC, October 1900, p. 2; Rubin, *Third to None,* 134.

42. Letter of J. C. Levy, March 24, 1868, in Phillips-Myers Papers, UNC.

43. Yulee, "Senator David L. Yulee," 15–17; Thompson, "David Yulee," 219.

44. Julia McFarlane to Korn, March 19, 1962, Korn Papers, AJA; *Aberdeen (Miss.) Examiner,* October 15, 1936 ("Major Jonas Corner") clipping in Korn Papers (Jonas).

45. *Aberdeen (Miss.) Examiner,* April 28, 1966, Korn Papers (Jonas), AJA.

46. *Poems of Octavia Harby Moses* (privately printed).

47. *New Orleans Daily Picayune,* November 3, 8; December 6, 10, 16, 1865; Jonas Executive Committee memo, December 12, 1903, Stephens Memorial Library, Southwestern Louisiana Institute; "Speech of Honorable Benjamin F. Jonas of Louisiana in the Senate of the United States, May 20, 1879" (Washington, 1879). While Jonas's own election was undisputed, he and a fellow senator were met at the door of the capitol by an "insolent" Federal officer demanding to know his name. The officer let Jonas pass as the court order affirmed his election, but refused admission to his colleague.

48. Ted Tunnell, ed., *Carpetbagger from Vermont* (Baton Rouge: Louisiana State University Press, 1989), 131–33.

49. "Speech of Honorable Benjamin F. Jonas . . . ," May 20, 1879, 14–15.

50. Moise, *Moise Family,* 112–15; CSR, E. W. Moise.

51. *DAB;* Harry Simonhoff, *Saga of American Jewry, 1865–1914* (New York: Arco, 1959), 21–27; R. H. Woody, "Franklin J. Moses, Jr.: Scalawag Governor of South Carolina, 1872–74," *North Carolina Historical Review* (April 1933): 111; Elzas, *Jews of South Carolina,* 197–99; Moise, *Moise Family,* 116–25; interview with Robert Moses of Sumter, South Carolina. Even Richard Zuczek in his revisionist work *State of Rebellion: Reconstruction in South Carolina* concedes Moses was corrupt (136). See also Francis Butler Simkins and Robert Hilliard Woody, *South Carolina during Reconstruction.* Much to the horror of South Carolina Jewry, Franklin J. Moses continues to be identified with the Jewish people. Richard N. Current in *Those Terrible Carpetbaggers: A Reinterpretation* identifies Moses as a "descendent of a prominent South Carolina Jewish family" (145). Walter Edgar gives a balanced account in *South Carolina: A History* (Columbia: University of South Carolina Press, 1998), but still refers to Moses as "the infamous scalawag" (402). Moise's warning that he would kill Moses is confirmed by the Moses family in Sumter. R. H. Woody in his article on Moses confirms that Charles H. Moise threatened in a public speech to march to the courthouse with "a band of determined men" with "muskets on our shoulders" (129).

52. Simkins and Woody, *South Carolina during Reconstruction,* 142–43; obituary, *News and Courier,* March 7, 1877.

53. Obituary, *News and Courier,* March 7, 1877; see also Simonhoff, *Saga,* 21–28. Moses was the first Jew to serve as chief justice of the supreme court of any American state. But, in the eyes "of white Carolinians, Franklin J. Moses, Sr., became a scalawag, guilty of

treachery to his state and to the white race" (24); Elzas (*Jews of South Carolina*, 197–99) was adamant that "the notorious Governor" was not "brought up as a Jew, nor were his affiliations Jewish in any way" (199).

54. Manley Wade Wellman, *Giant in Gray: A Biography of Wade Hampton of South Carolina* (reprint, Dayton, Ohio: Morningside Bookshop, 1980), 262.

55. Moise, *Moise Family*, 123–25.

56. Moses, *Last Order*, 280, 287.

57. Quoted in Simonhoff, *Saga*, 7.

58. The ladies he had appointed were, of course, all grateful to him, except one— Phoebe Yates Pember. Moses had her appointed at the request of her brother-in-law, Octavus Cohen of Savannah, who was Eliza Moses's cousin. "When I had her appointed," Moses recalled, "she wrote me a letter profuse with grateful acknowledgments in giving her a competence when she said she was earning her bread by her needle." Afterward, Mrs. Pember was dissatisfied with her $2,000 annual salary, which, according to Moses, "didn't satisfy her extravagance." She attempted to sell her interest to an investor and make a substantial profit, but Moses scotched her plan. "I have heard of several of her tongue lashings," Moses later wrote, "but I have always regarded her enmity as lightly as I did her friendship." Moses, *Last Order*, 269–80.

59. Ibid., 280–82; Derrell C. Roberts, *Joseph E. Brown and the Politics of Reconstruction* (Tuscaloosa: University of Alabama Press, 1973), chap. 7.

60. Moses, *Last Order*, 297.

61. Ibid., 302–4.

62. Ibid., 263.

63. Ibid., 311, 321.

64. Evans, *Judah Benjamin*, 321.

65. Gruss, "Judah Philip Benjamin," 969–70, 1049.

66. Evans, *Judah Benjamin*, chap. 18.

67. Meade, *Judah P. Benjamin*, 340–41; Davis, *Jefferson Davis*, 656–57.

68. Evans, *Judah Benjamin*, 369.

69. Meade, *Judah P. Benjamin*, 377.

70. Neiman, *Judah Benjamin*, 209; Evans, *Judah Benjamin*, 381.

71. Meade, *Judah P. Benjamin*, 362. Benjamin's only child, his daughter, never had children.

72. Gruss, "Judah Philip Benjamin," 1068.

EPILOGUE

1. Visit to Père Lachaise Cemetery; copy of card in possession of author; Evans, *Judah Benjamin*, 402–3. Evans writes, "It is as if he tried to escape notice even in Paris." The United Daughters of the Confederacy (UDC), founded in 1895, is sometimes referred to as the Daughters of the Confederacy. See *Encyclopedia of the Confederacy*, 3:1027–28 ("Memorial Organizations").

2. Clipping, April 16, 1906, in "In Memoriam" book of clippings, Kruttschnitt Papers, HNOC.

3. Judah Benjamin Papers, Memorabilia, AJHS. "The Life of Judah Philip Benjamin," a pamphlet published by the Louisiana State Museum (March 27, 1937), is in the possession of the author. The granite marker in Charlotte is still there. It marks the site of Abram Weil's home on the main street of downtown Charlotte, where Benjamin stayed.

4. Bertram W. Korn, "Judah Benjamin as a Jew," *PAJHS* 38, pt. 1 (September 1948): 170. Korn believed Benjamin to be "one of the most distinguished Jews in all American history" (169); Rabbi Calisch's remarks in *Southern Historical Society Papers* 40 (September 1915): 240.

5. "Address of Honorable B. F. Jonas at the Laying of the Corner Stone of the Monument to the Memory of the Confederate Dead at Baton Rouge, February 22, 1886" (New Orleans, 1886), Favrat Collection, TU.

6. *History of the Jews of Louisiana* (1903); obituary at Touro Infirmary Archive, New Orleans.

7. Census data in possession of Cathy Kahn, New Orleans.

8. Hyman, *Oleander Odyssey,* 13–48.

9. Obituary, *Pittsburgh Evening Leader,* November 16, 1897, in Levy File, BA; Report of Robert E. Lee Camp, No. 1, November 19, 1897, Leopold Levy File, BA.

10. Lee-Jackson Memorial Service Program, January 19, 1988, Leopold Levy File, BA.

11. Moses, *Last Order,* 324–32; Simonhoff, *Saga,* 6. Raphael Jr. and his wife, Georgina, moved to New York in 1871. The former Confederate naval officer from Georgia became a successful New York lawyer. He died in 1909 (*Columbus Enquirer-Sun,* December 14, 1909, p. 8, Confederate Naval Museum). "Major" Israel Nunez and his wife, Anna Moses, moved to Austin, Texas. Stanford, Raphael's grandson, graduated from Annapolis and was a career naval officer. He retired as a captain in 1927. Belle Moses, Mrs. Lionel C. Levy, continued to reside at The Esquiline into the twentieth century. She resided there when Raphael Jr.'s body was returned from New York so he could be buried on his father's and mother's plantation in Columbus, Georgia.

12. Obituary, Proskauer Papers, AJA; Sacher, *A History of the Jews in America,* 459, 468, 471, 564–65.

13. Nevins, *Herbert H. Lehman,* 11, 13, 20.

14. Letters to Leovy from Jefferson Davis and William Preston Johnston, Leovy Papers, HNOC.

15. Obituary, *New Orleans Daily Picayune,* October 4, 1902; 10, col. 2.

16. Moise, *Moise Family,* 126.

17. *Shreveport (La.) Times,* February 13, 1869; interview with Eric Brock, Shreveport, in *Shreveport Magazine,* February 1977, 29.

18. Obituary, *Norfolk Landmark,* September 22, 1911.

19. Yulee, "Senator David L. Yulee," 17; Korn Collection, folder 34/8, AJA.

20. Creeger, "Michelbacher," 5–6.

21. *Southern Historical Society Papers,* 10:248–50.

22. Yvonne Strug, pamphlet titled "History of Temple Sinai, New Orleans, 1870–1995"; quoted by Leo Shpall, "Rabbi James Koppel Guttheim [*sic*]," *Louisiana Historical Quarterly* 22 (1939), 169–70.

23. *The American Hebrew,* clipping, July 18, 1884, G. Jacobs Scrapbook, AJA.

24. DeLeon, "Sketch"; Greenberg, "Becoming Southern," 59–60.

25. Woodward, *Mary Chesnut,* xv, xii–xiv.

26. *Confederate Veteran* 18 (1910): 379; *Who Was Who,* 312.

27. DeLeon, "Sketch"; Elzas, *Jews of South Carolina,* 273.

28. Sulzberger, *Iphigene,* 4–5.

29. Simonhoff, *Saga,* 289–96; Johnson, *An Honorable Titan,* passim. See chap. 5, note 117, p. 431. *The Confederate Veteran* recalled Ochs as "modest and genteel" and recalled

that "Mr. Ochs's Southern friends rarely have a wish that is not developed in the *New York Times*" (13, no. 12 [December 1905]: 578–79).

30. Ashkenazi, *Diary of Clara Solomon,* 439–44.

31. The monument was later moved to the Jonas family plot at Oddfellows Rest Cemetery in Aberdeen (*Aberdeen [Miss.] Examiner,* April 28, 1966).

32. Margaret Mitchell, *Gone with the Wind* (New York: Scribner, 1996; originally published New York: Macmillan, 1936), 485.

33. *Aunt Sister's Book;* Stern, *Americans of Jewish Descent;* Marcus, *Memoirs,* 1:261.

34. "Speech on the Anniversary Birth, Gen. Lee," January 19, 1898, Simon Mayer Papers, Box 1, TU.

35. Ezekiel, "The Jews of Richmond during the Civil War."

36. Marcus, *Memoirs,* 3:197, 236.

37. J. C. Hemphill, ed., *Men of Mark in South Carolina* (Washington D.C.: 1907), 206–8.

38. Simonhoff, *Saga,* 137–42; Arthur Coe, "Sir Moses J. Ezekiel: A True Son of the Confederacy," *Jewish Veteran* (Winter 1995): 17; Guy R. Swanson, "Sir Moses Ezekiel: The Contribution of a Sculptor," *Southern Jewish Historical Society Journal* 3–4 (Lee quote); *Confederate Veteran,* May 17, 1917, 235–6.

39. Obituary, Levy Papers, AJA.

40. Libo, "The Moses of Montgomery," 20–25.

41. Ibid., 25.

42. Obituary in Whitlock MS, VHS.

43. Philip Phillips Diary, Phillips-Myers Papers, UNC; Marcus, *Memoirs,* 3:153–54.

44. Phillips-Myers Papers, UNC, undated clipping.

45. DeLeon, *Belles, Beaux, and Brains,* 178; *Roster of Confederate Soldiers.*

46. Obituaries of Eugenia Phillips and other family members. Phillips-Myers Papers, UNC. Stern, *Americans of Jewish Descent.*

47. Morgan, "Eugenia Levy Phillips," 105; C. Myers, Phillips-Myers Papers, UNC.

48. Demoff, "Phoebe Pember."

49. Pember, *A Southern Woman's Story,* 16; *Civil War News,* September 1995, 71.

50. Simonhoff, *Saga,* 238–43.

51. Grant, *Adventures of a Wall Street Legend,* chap. 1, 24; *Universal Jewish Encyclopedia; DAB.*

52. In 1914 Baruch wrote an article titled "The Heroic Death of Marcus Baum," about the brother of his benefactor Mannes Baum. General Longstreet's book *From Manassas to Appomattox* had mentioned an orderly named "Bowen" of Kershaw's staff who was killed at the Wilderness in May 1864. Baruch knew that "Bowen" was a mispronunciation of "Baum" (pronounced "Bomb") and recalled young Marcus's dashing into camp on a white horse. "Do you hear that volley, Marcus?" Baruch had told young Baum. "The General is always in the front." "I must go to him at once," Marcus cried, and sped off. Marcus Baum reached Longstreet and was killed at his side. "It is but just," Dr. Baruch wrote for the benefit of the Confederate veterans still living, "to chronicle this historic fact and correct the name . . . [Marcus Baum] was a German and a Hebrew. Though exempt from military duty as a foreigner, he enlisted early. No braver man, none truer to the cause, no soldier more loyal to his chief ever breathed than Marcus Baum" (*Confederate Veteran* 22, no. 4 [April 1914]: 170).

53. Grant, *Adventures of a Wall Street Legend,* ch. 1; Baruch, *My Own Story,* 35; *Confederate Veteran* 29 (1921): 433. A resolution of the Bedford Forrest Camp, U.C.V., Arling-

446   ton, Texas, said Baruch was a great friend of Lee, which he was not; that he was "always at the front," which he was not; and that he was captured because he was at the front, which he was not.

54. Quoted by Eli N. Evans, *The Provincials*, 43.

55. Belinda F. Gergel, "Assimilated 'New South' Daughter: Irene Goldsmith Kohn and the Widening Sphere of Jewish Women in Early Twentieth Century South Carolina," a paper for presentation at the Conference on Southern Women's History, Charleston, June 1, 1997; copy of Irene Kohn's UDC application courtesy of Belinda F. Gergel and Julian Hennig Jr., Columbia, S.C. The inscription to Hilzeim reads, in full, as follows:

In Memoriam of Our Dear Son Alexander M. Hilzeim

A victim at 18 years to the horrors of war. Wounded at Kennesaw Mountain, Georgia, he fills an unknown grave. We do not mourn his loss as God gave and God hath taken away. Truly the works of God are incomprehensible.

(Elzas, *The Old Jewish Cemeteries at Charleston, S.C.* [Charleston, 1903], 42).

56. Berman, *Richmond's Jewry*, 44.

GLOSSARY

★

Abraham   Father of the Jewish people as described in Genesis. Father of Isaac.

Acculturation   The transfer of culture from one group to another. In this context, many Jews of the nineteenth century became Americans and Southerners without assimilating; that is, they adapted to the majority culture without losing their Jewish identity.

Adjunta   The board of trustees of a Sephardic synagogue, also called a *junta.*

Anti-Semitism   Hostility and prejudice against Jews, who are a Semitic people.

Ashkenaz   The Hebrew word for Germany.

Ashkenazim   Jews of Germany, Northern France, Central and Eastern Europe, Poland, and Russia, and their descendants. These Jews eventually settled in France, Great Britain, and Western Europe as well, although generally after the Sephardic expulsion from Spain. By 1860 the word *Ashkenazic* was applied to all Jews from Europe, except Spanish and Portuguese Jews, who came from a different tradition. The language of the Ashkenazi Jews was Yiddish. (*Ashkenazim* is the plural form.)

Assimilation   The merging of diverse cultures. In this context, the loss of Jewish identity in the majority Christian culture, usually by the Jew abandoning his or her religion and marrying a Christian. See *acculturation.*

Bayers   Bavarians.

Bimah   The pulpit in a synagogue.

B'nai B'rith   "Sons of the Covenant," a national Jewish fraternal organization.

Cantor   The leader of chanting and singing in the synagogue. *Hazzan* in Hebrew.

Chanukah   See **Hanukkah.**

Chevra Kadisha   Hebrew for Holy Society. A Jewish burial society. Jewish tradition regards service in such a society as especially praiseworthy.

Chuppah   See **huppah.**

Gabbai   Hebrew for "collector." It came to mean the treasurer of the synagogue or other Jewish organization.

448   ***Ghetto***   A Jewish residential district in Europe. The earliest ghetto is in Venice and dates from the thirteenth century.

Hanukkah   Hebrew for "dedication." This winter Festival of Lights lasts eight days and celebrates the victory of the Jewish Maccabees over the Hellenists and the miracle of the holy oil in the synagogue lamp lasting for eight days.

Hazan or ***hazzan***   Hebrew for "cantor." Originally a caretaker of the synagogue who also performed religious ceremonies; one who leads the congregation in song. In the nineteenth century, the word *hazan* had a different meaning: a congregational official who carried out a variety of nonmusical functions, including reading prayers and leading the congregation, much like a rabbi or Protestant minister of the time. In the 1850s, a hazan was not considered as learned as a rabbi, but because there were few ordained rabbis, the hazan acted as the leader, rabbi, and reader of the congregation.

Hebrew   The language of the ancient Jews. The Torah is written in Hebrew.

Huppah   Marriage canopy.

K. K.   Kahal Kadosh, Holy Congregation, as in K. K. Beth Elohim. The names of all Sephardic synagogues begin with K. K.

Kaddish   Prayer for the dead said for a parent, spouse, child, or sibling.

Kol Nidre   "All Vows"; refers to the Yom Kippur Eve service and the opening prayer.

Kosher   *Kashrut,* Hebrew for "fit" or "fitness." The body of dietary laws set forth in the Torah (for example, Deuteronomy 14 and Leviticus 11) governing what observant Jews may and may not eat. As almost all observant Jews in the nineteenth century were Orthodox, keeping kosher was a hallmark of being Jewish. Larger Jewish communities in the South went to great lengths to provide kosher food by hiring *shochets* (Hebrew for "ritual slaughterer") to properly prepare the food.

Landsman   German or Yiddish for a fellow citizen, male or female, of the same country in Europe. Immigrants enjoyed being in the company of their fellow "landsmen."

Magen David   Hebrew, "Shield of David." Six-pointed Jewish star, the symbol of Judaism in medieval and modern times. It became popular in the nineteenth century.

Matzo   Unleavened bread used in the Passover service, or Seder. (Also, *matzah, matsah,* or *matzoth.*)

Menorah Hebrew, "candelabrum," a seven-branch candlestick. The eight-branch candelabrum is used for Hanukkah celebrations.

Minhag The service or ritual used in prayer or in synagogue. There are Polish, Sephardic, Ashkenazic, and American Minhags.

Minyan Ten men who are necessary to form a Jewish worship service.

Mohel Ritual circumciser.

Parnass President of a Sephardic synagogue or congregation.

Passover *Pesah* in Hebrew. The Festival of Matsah, unleavened bread, celebrating the exodus from Egypt. It is celebrated at a dinner called the Seder.

Purim Hebrew, "Lots." The Feast of Esther, this holiday commemorates the victory of Esther and Mordecai over Haman, King Ahasuerus's most powerful adviser, who wanted to kill all the Jews in the kingdom. "So many Hamans," a Yiddish proverb goes, "and only one Purim."

Rabbi Hebrew for "my master." A teacher and learned man who interprets the law; a spiritual leader of a congregation. In the nineteenth century, there were few ordained rabbis in America, and the leader of the synagogue was variously described as rabbi, hazan, minister, or reverend.

Reform Judaism A branch of Judaism that believes in using the vernacular instead of Hebrew, an abbreviated service, and a less literal understanding of the Holy Scriptures.

Rosh Hashanah Hebrew for New Year. The Jewish High Holy days (or High Holidays) begin with Rosh Hashanah and end with the Day of Atonement, Yom Kippur. Jews believe that on Rosh Hashanah God judges all human beings, and the virtuous are inscribed in the Book of Life. The shofar is blown on Rosh Hashanah to call Jews to repent of their sins.

Seder Passover dinner and service celebrating the exodus from Egypt.

Sephardim Jews of Spanish, Portuguese, or North African origin, descended from those who lived on the Iberian Peninsula before the expulsion of 1492. Ladino is the language of the Sephardim.

Sepharad Hebrew word for Spain.

Sh'ma The central statement and belief of Jews: "Hear, O Israel, the Lord our God, the Lord is One" (Deut. 6:4). "In just six Hebrew words," Rabbi Joseph Telushkin wrote, "it sums up Judaism's belief in monotheism, and its rejection of all idols."

450   *Shamash*   Sexton.

Shabbat   The Sabbath. The Jewish Sabbath begins on Friday evening and concludes on Saturday evening. Judaism holds the Sabbath to be a holy and important day of rest and prayer. Orthodox Jews are not allowed to ride or work on the Sabbath.

Shiva   A period of seven days of mourning for the dead.

Shochet/shohet   Ritual butcher or slaughterer who prepares meat and fowl according to Jewish kashrut (kosher) laws.

Shofar   The ram's horn blown like a trumpet on a special occasions such as Rosh Hashanah.

Shul   Yiddish for synagogue. It also means "school."

Synagogue   House of worship where the Torah or scrolls are kept in the ark. The dais is called a *bimah* in Hebrew. In Orthodox synagogues, men and women must sit separately. Reform synagogues are frequently known as temples.

Talmud   Commentaries on the Torah and Holy Scripture, written in the Middle Ages.

Temple   Reform Jews often refer to their synagogues as temples.

Torah   The scroll containing the five books of Moses, the first five books of the Holy Scriptures (or Old Testament or Hebrew Bible, according to Christians); namely, Genesis, Exodus, Leviticus, Numbers, and Deuteronomy. Orthodox Jews believe that the Torah (or Pentateuch, "five scrolls") was given to Moses on Mount Sinai.

Yarmulke   Yiddish for a small skullcap worn by traditional Jews in a synagogue or elsewhere to show respect for God. The Hebrew word is *kippah*.

Yehudah   Yiddish for Jew. *Yehudim* is the plural.

Yiddish   The language spoken by Ashkenazic Jews. Written in Hebrew letters, Yiddish was a combination of Hebrew and German. Many nineteenth-century immigrants spoke Yiddish and German.

Yom Kippur   Hebrew for Day of Atonement, the holiest and most important day of the Jewish year. Orthodox Jews fast from sunset of the Kol Nidre until twenty-five hours later.

BIBLIOGRAPHICAL NOTE

★

All bibliographical information for *The Jewish Confederates* is contained in the endnotes. The purpose of this note is to give an overview of the bibliography, to discuss the major works I have relied upon, and to discuss important bibliographical issues in Jewish Confederate history. The following bibliography lists the major works cited in the endnotes. All abbreviated citations in the endnotes are set out in full in the bibliography.

More than fifty thousand books have been written about the American Civil War. The most readable and helpful general histories are James M. McPherson, *Battle Cry of Freedom: The Civil War Era* (New York: Oxford University Press, 1988); Emory M. Thomas, *The Confederate Nation 1861–1865* (New York: Harper & Row, 1979); Allan Nevins, *Ordeal of the Union,* 2 vols. (New York: Scribners, 1947), Nevins, *The Emergence of Lincoln,* 2 vols. (New York: Scribners, 1950–1951), and Nevins, *The War for the Union,* 4 vols. (New York: Scribners, 1971); Bruce Catton, *The Centennial History of the Civil War,* 3 vols. (New York: Doubleday, 1961–1965); Shelby Foote, *The Civil War: A Narrative,* 3 vols. (New York: Random House, 1958–74); E. Merton Coulter's good, old-fashioned Southern volume, *The Confederate States of America, 1861–1865* (Baton Rouge: Louisiana State University Press, 1987). Excellent illustrated histories are William C. Davis, ed., *The Image of War,* 6 vols. (Garden City, N.Y., 1981–1988) and the Time-Life Civil War Series (Alexandria, Va.: Time-Life Books, 1983–1987).

Interpretations about the causes of the war and the war itself abound. This work has been influenced by the following: Nevins's works cited above; David M. Potter, *The Impending Crisis, 1848–1861* (New York: Harper & Row, 1976); Steven A. Channing, *Crisis of Fear: Secession in South Carolina* (New York: Simon & Schuster, 1970); James M. McPherson, *For Cause and Comrades: Why Men Fought in the Civil War* (New York: Oxford University Press, 1997); Gary W. Gallagher, *The Confederate War* (Cambridge, Mass.: Harvard University Press, 1997); and David Herbert Donald, *Lincoln* (New York: Simon & Schuster, 1995).

The foremost work on American Jewry in the Civil War is Rabbi Bertram Wallace Korn's *American Jewry and the Civil War* (Philadelphia: AJPS, 1957). A paperbound edition was published in 1961, and the author's preface to that edition contains additional information. Rabbi Korn was and remains the foremost historian of nineteenth-century Southern Jewry. He also wrote *Jews and Negro Slavery in the Old South, 1789–1865,* reprinted in Leonard Dinnerstein and Mary Dale Palsson, eds., *Jews in the South* (Baton Rouge: Louisiana State University Press, 1973); *Eventful Years and Experiences: Studies in Nineteenth Century American Jewish History* (Cincinnati, 1954); and *The Early Jews of New Orleans* (Waltham, Mass.: American Jewish Historical Society, 1969), as well as excellent articles on Judah Benjamin and other topics.

This work also owes a great debt to Jacob Rader Marcus, the editor of *Memoirs of American Jews, 1775–1865,* 3 vols. (Philadelphia: JPSA, 1956), which I have used extensively. Dr. Marcus had the foresight to collect and preserve numerous nineteenth-century manuscripts at the American Jewish Archives at Hebrew Union College in Cincinnati. Harry Simonhoff was also a pioneer in American Jewish history. While flawed, inaccurate in places, and incomplete, his *Jewish Participants in the Civil War* (New York: Arco, 1963) was a helpful starting place, as were his *Jewish Notables in America, 1776–1865* (New York: Greenberg, 1956) and his *Saga of American Jewry, 1865 to 1914* (New York: Arco, 1959).

Mel Young of Chattanooga has made a major contribution to this subject. Young's pioneering work, *Where They Lie Someone Should Say Kaddish* (Lanham, Md.: University Press of America, 1991), chronicles the Jewish soldiers, Union and Confederate, killed in the Civil War. Young has conducted more research in this field than anyone else. He has edited Raphael J. Moses's memoir and other Moses family documents in *The Last Order of the Lost Cause* (Lanham, Md.: University Press of America, 1995).

I have utilized a variety of works on American Jewish history. The most helpful to this work were the following: Eli Faber, *A Time for Planting: The First Migration, 1654–1820,* and Hasia R. Diner, *A Time for Gathering: The Second Migration, 1820–1880* (Baltimore: Johns Hopkins University Press, 1992); volumes 1 and 2 of *The Jewish People in America;* Naomi Cohen, *Encounter with Emancipation: The German Jews in the United States, 1830–1914* (Philadelphia: JPSA, 1984); Abraham Barkai, *Branching Out: German-Jewish Immigration to the United States, 1820–1914* (New York: Holmes & Meier, 1994); J. Abraham Karp, *Haven and Home: A History of the Jews in America* (New York: Schoken, 1985); Howard M. Sachar, *A History of the Jews in America* (New York: Knopf, 1992); Arthur Hertzberg, *The Jews in America: Four Centuries of an Uneasy Encounter* (New York: Simon and Schuster, 1989); and various editions of *The American Jewish Yearbook.*

On Southern Jewish history, I have relied on Eli N. Evans, *The Provincials: A Personal History of Jews in the South* (New York, 1974); Samuel Proctor and Louis Schmier, eds., *Jews of the South, Selected Essays from the Southern Jewish Historical Society* (Macon, Ga.: Mercer University Press, 1984); Dinnerstein and Palsson, *Jews in the South;* Nathan M. Kaganoff and Melvin I. Urofsky, *Turn to the South: Essays on Southern Jewry* (Charlottesville: AJHS, University Press of Virginia, 1979); Civil War Centennial Southern Issue, *AJA* 13, no. 1 (April 1961); and Mark I. Greenberg's work on Savannah, especially his perceptive "Becoming Southern: The Jews of Savannah, Georgia, 1830–1870," *AJH* 86, no. 1 (March 1998).

The local histories of Southern Jewish communities are critical to an understanding of the Jewish Confederates. Although these histories vary in reliability, the classic works are still valuable. Rabbi Barnett A. Elzas wrote *The Jews of South Carolina* (Philadelphia: Lippincott, 1905; reprint, Spartanburg, S.C.: Reprint Co., 1983) in 1905. It was reprinted in 1983. Elzas was a careful historian who prided himself on his accuracy. Charles Reznikoff and Uriah Z. Engelman wrote *The Jews of Charleston: A History of an American Jewish Community* (Philadelphia: JPSA, 1950) to commemorate the 200th anniversary of the founding of Beth Elohim. Most recently, James W. Hagy, professor of history at the University of Charleston, has written *This Happy Land: The Jews of Colonial and Antebellum Charleston* (Tuscaloosa: University of Alabama Press, 1993), which, while ponderous, is useful, although it ends in 1850.

Richard and Belinda Gergel have written an excellent short history of Columbia Jewry titled *In Pursuit of the Tree of Life: A History of the Early Jews of Columbia, South*

Carolina, and the Tree of Life Congregation (Columbia, S.C.: Tree of Life Congregation, 1996). Solomon Breibart, the preeminent modern historian of Charleston Jewry, has written a number of excellent articles and essays on topics ranging from Poznanski to Penina Moise.

The first significant book on the Jews of Richmond was Herbert T. Ezekiel and Gaston Lichtenstein's *The History of the Jews of Richmond from 1769 to 1917*, published in Richmond in 1917. While this work cannot be compared to Elzas's *The Jews of South Carolina*, it nevertheless contains valuable information. A later excellent work, Rabbi Myron Berman's *Richmond's Jewry, 1769–1976: Shabbat in Shockoe* (Charlottesville: University Press of Virginia, 1979) is much more comprehensive. Melvin I. Urofsky has written a useful popular history of the Jews of Virginia entitled *Commonwealth and Community: The Jewish Experience in Virginia* (Richmond: Virginia Historical Society and Jewish Community Federation of Richmond, 1997). Louis Ginsberg published two books, *History of the Jews of Petersburg, 1789–1950* (Petersburg, Va., privately printed, 1954) and *Chapters on the Jews of Virginia, 1658–1900* (Petersburg, 1969).

On Savannah, I relied upon Rabbi Saul Jacob Rubin, *Third to None: The Saga of Savannah Jewry*, as well as Mark I. Greenberg's comprehensive dissertation, "Creating Ethnic, Class, and Southern Identity in Nineteenth-Century America: The Jews of Savannah, Georgia, 1830–1880" (Ph.D. diss., University of Florida, 1997) and "Becoming Southern: The Jews of Savannah, Georgia, 1830–1870," *AJH* 86, no. 1 (March 1998), 55–75, both of which give a great deal of information about Civil War–era Savannah Jewry.

Atlanta has been fortunate in having attracted a competent scholar to write a history of its Jewish community: Steven Hertzberg, *Strangers within the Gate City: The Jews of Atlanta, 1845–1915* (Philadelphia: JPSA, 1978). Macon, Georgia, is also fortunate in having a well-researched dissertation written by Rabbi Newton J. Friedman. This dissertation should be published, as Macon is typical of the larger towns and smaller cities in the antebellum South. Jack Steinberg was kind enough to share a copy of his history of Augusta's Children of Israel congregation with me.

Mobile Jewry has been documented in another good local history by Robert J. Zeitz titled *The Gates of Heaven, Congregation Sha'arai Shomayim, The First 150 Years, Mobile, Alabama 1844–1994*. Rabbi Korn's *The Jews of Mobile, Alabama, 1763–1841* (Cincinnati: Hebrew Union College Press, 1970) is helpful, although it does not address the Civil War period. Rabbi James A. Wax wrote an extensive essay titled "The Jews of Memphis, 1860–1865," published in the *West Tennessee Historical Society Papers* 3 (1949). On Tennessee, I relied on Fedora Frank, *Five Families and Eight Young Men: Nashville and Her Jewry, 1850–1861* (Nashville: Tennessee Book Co., 1962), *Beginnings on Market Street: Nashville and Her Jewry, 1861–1901* (Nashville: Jewish Community of Nashville, 1976), and her excellent article, "Nashville Jewry during the Civil War," *Tennessee Historical Quarterly* 39, no. 3 (fall 1980). Leo E. and Evelyn Turitz authored *Jews in Early Mississippi* (Jackson: University Press of Mississippi, [1983]), which contains a great deal of information, although the authors are so embarrassed by Jews owning slaves and fighting for the Confederacy that it must have affected their work. In all fairness to the authors, they admit as much in the introduction. Why, they asked, did Jews support the Confederacy? "Was it that he was afraid to show his neighbor his real feelings?" This is historical anachronism at its worst.

There is no book-length history of the Jews of Montgomery. Rabbi Alfred G. Moses of Mobile wrote a brief essay, "The History of the Jews of Montgomery," which was published in the *Proceedings of the American Jewish Historical Society* in 1905. It is based primarily on a sketch by longtime resident Leopold Young and is full of errors. The Moses family was ably described by Kenneth Libo in *Alabama Heritage* magazine, no. 36 (Spring 1995).

The biggest disappointment in the literature of Southern Jewish history is the lack of a reliable history of Jewish Louisiana during the antebellum and Civil War years. Bertram Korn's *Early Jews of New Orleans* describes the Crescent City prior to the sectional conflict, but it contains some information on the Civil War era. *History of the Jews of Louisiana, Their Religious, Civic, Charitable and Patriotic Life* (1903), compiled by the Jewish Historical Publishing Company of Louisiana, and W. E. Myers's *The Israelites of Louisiana* (New Orleans: published by W. E. Myers, 1905) are not reliable, although they contain much information. (*History of the Jews of Louisiana* is not a real history, but a combination of a Jewish *Who's Who* and a lot of advertisements.) See also Max Heller, "Jubilee Souvenir of Temple Sinai, 1872–1922" (New Orleans, La.: Temple Sinai, 1922). Neither Julien B. Feibelman's dissertation, "A Social and Economic Study of the New Orleans Jewish Community" (University of Pennsylvania, 1941) nor Leo Shpall, *The Jews of Louisiana* (New Orleans: Steeg Printing & Publishing Co., 1936) contain much information on the Civil War.

There is no complete history of the Jews of New Orleans, which is difficult to comprehend in view of the importance of this sizable Jewish community. Nor are there biographies or even biographical essays on Benjamin Franklin Jonas or Henry M. Hyams, two important figures in American Jewish history. Elliot Ashkenazi has done a great service in writing *The Business of Jews in Louisiana, 1840–1875* (Tuscaloosa: University of Alabama Press, 1988) and in editing *The Civil War Diary of Clara Solomon: Growing Up in New Orleans, 1861–1862* (Baton Rouge: Louisiana State University Press, 1995). It would be a great mitzvah if Ashkenazi would bring his formidable talents to bear on the general history of the Jews of Louisiana. Other Louisiana sources include Rabbi Martin I. Hinchin, *Fourscore and Eleven: A History of the Jews of Rapides Parish, 1828–1919* (Alexandria, La.: McCormick Graphics for Congregation Gemiluth Chassodim, 1984) and Eric Brock's pamphlet, "The Jewish Cemeteries of Shreveport, Louisiana" (privately printed, 1995).

On Texas Jewry, I have relied on Ruthe Winegarten and Cathy Schechter, *Deep in the Heart: The Lives and Legends of Texas Jews* (Austin: Eakin Press and Texas Jewish Historical Society, 1990); Natalie Ornish, *Pioneer Jewish Texans* (Dallas: Texas Heritage Press, 1989); Juliet George's excellent work, "By the Brazos and the Trinity They Hung Up Their Harps: Two Jewish Immigrants in Texas" (master's thesis, Texas Christian University, 1991); Frances R. Kallison, "100 Years of Jewry in San Antonio" (master's thesis, Trinity University, 1977); and *The Jewish Texans* (San Antonio: University of Texas Institute of Texan Culture, 1974), compiled by a team of researchers headed by W. Phil Hewitt. Arkansas Jewry has been blessed with Carolyn Gray LeMaster's *A Corner of the Tapestry: A History of the Jewish Experience in Arkansas, 1820s–1990s* (Fayetteville: University of Arkansas Press, 1994).

On the subject of anti-Semitism, I have relied on the voluminous scholarly literature, especially Rabbi Korn's chapter in *American Jews in the Civil War,* "American Judeophobia: Confederate Version," which was reprinted in Dinnerstein and Palsson's *Jews in the South;* Abraham J. Peck, "That Other Peculiar Institution: Jews and Judaism in the Nineteenth

Century South," *Modern Judaism* 7, no. 1 (Feb. 7, 1987): 99–104; Frederic Cople Jaher, *A Scapegoat in the New Wilderness: The Origins and Rise of Anti-Semitism in America* (Cambridge, Mass.: Harvard University Press, 1994); Leonard Dinnerstein, *Anti-Semitism in America* (New York: Oxford University Press, 1994); and (surprisingly) the standard Southern version of the war in *The Confederate States of America, 1861–1865,* vol. 7 of *A History of the South* by E. Merton Coulter (Baton Rouge: Louisiana State University Press, 1987).

I have utilized a number of original sources. The American Jewish Archives at Hebrew Union College in Cincinnati is the chief repository of American Jewish history of this period. The AJA has collections pertaining to the Jonases, Proskauer, Hart, and many others. Bertram Korn's papers at the AJA include a great deal of information. Other institutions that have material on Jewish Confederates include the American Jewish Historical Society in Waltham, Massachusetts, and New York City; the Virginia Historical Society, the Virginia State Library, and the Beth Ahabah Museum and Archives in Richmond; the Southern Historical Collection at the University of North Carolina; the College of Charleston; Tulane University's Special Collections, and the Historic New Orleans Collection.

Fortunately for this study, a number of famous, prominent, or highly successful Jews were Confederate soldiers or otherwise involved with the Confederacy in their youth. Thus, their stories have been preserved. They include Harris Kempner in Texas; Isidor Straus in Georgia and New York; the Lehman family in Alabama and New York; Adolph Ochs's parents in Tennessee; and Bernard Baruch's father, Simon Baruch, from South Carolina.

Although all of Judah P. Benjamin's biographers lament the fact that their subject destroyed his papers and did all he could to impede the writing of a biography, a great deal of information is available about him. He inspired numerous biographies, including three excellent and readable major biographies, each quite different from the other. The first, *Judah P. Benjamin* (Philadelphia: W. G. Jacobs & Co., 1907), was written in the early years of the twentieth century by Pierce Butler, a well-connected New Orleans professor. It is the most eloquent biography. Professor Butler was closer to his subject as a planter, Southerner, and Louisianian because he himself was a product of Benjamin's world. Butler's writing is witty and charming for the reader willing to get past the flowery and often stilted language of the era.

Benjamin's second biographer, Robert Douthat Meade, was a professor of history and a descendant of Confederate officers as well. He wrote *Judah P. Benjamin: Confederate Statesman* (New York: Oxford University Press, 1943), a scholarly, comprehensive, and meticulously researched volume. Meade focused on Benjamin's political career and researched Benjamin's post–Civil War legal career in England. The third biographer, Eli Evans, the dean of Southern Jewish writers, filled the void of the Jewish aspects of Benjamin's life. Meade was both uncomfortable with and ignorant of the Jewish world from which Benjamin sprang. Evans gives us as much insight as the records will allow and sometimes more. Readable and well researched, Evans's *Judah P. Benjamin: The Jewish Confederate* (New York: Free Press, 1988) is indispensable to an understanding of the subject. Other useful biographies include Rollin Osterweis, *Judah P. Benjamin: Statesman of the Lost Cause* (New York: G.P. Putnam's Sons, 1933) and S. I. Neiman, *Judah Benjamin, Mystery Man of the Confederacy* (Indianapolis: Bobbs-Merrill, 1963).

456   Because of the great interest in Benjamin as a key Confederate cabinet member, there are numerous articles about him. The most informative are as follows: Louis Gruss's "Judah Philip Benjamin," *Louisiana Historical Quarterly* 19, no. 4 (October 1936): 964–1068. This 100-page article is actually a scholarly biography containing a vigorous attack on writers and scholars who have demeaned Benjamin as a Jew or otherwise in the eyes of the author. "The Three Lives of Judah P. Benjamin," by Charles Curran in *History Today* (London) 17, no.9, (September 1967): 583–92, portrays Benjamin as Calhoun's successor as defender of the South and a cynical British lawyer from the very beginning of the Civil War.

Because of the interest of Jews in Benjamin as a Jew, there are a number of articles about his religious views and connection to Judaism. The best by far, and a fine piece of historical research by a master historian, is "Judah Benjamin as a Jew" by Bertram Wallace Korn, published in *Publications of the American Jewish Historical Society* (PAJHS) 38 (September 1948): 153–71. Because Rabbi Korn proves that various "traditions which link [Judah Benjamin] with Jewish religious worship" are false, I have not included them in this book. (Korn proves false the tradition that Benjamin once spoke at a synagogue in San Francisco, concluding, "Is it not ironic that the only instance in which Benjamin was supposed to have spoken in a synagogue turns out to be one of the many occasions when he spoke in, or for the benefit of, a church?" [157]). He never attended services in wartime Richmond, according to Rabbi Korn, despite statements in Ezekiel and Lichtenstein's *History of the Jews of Richmond* that he did. (The short answer is that Benjamin lived in New Orleans for more than thirty years, in Washington for seven years, and in London for eighteen years, and there is no record that he ever joined a synagogue or even attended a service [161–65]. Nor is there a record in Rabbi George Jacob's Civil War scrapbook, Jacobs being the rabbi at the synagogue where Benjamin was alleged to have attended services.)

An early but excellent article by the lawyer-historian Max J. Kohler titled "Judah P. Benjamin: Statesman and Jurist" appeared in *PAJHS* 12 (1904). Another useful article, by Richard S. Tedlow, appeared in Kaganoff and Urofsky's *Turn to the South* (1979). It begins: "The most important American-Jewish diplomat before Henry Kissinger, the most eminent lawyer before Brandeis, the leading figure in martial affairs before Hyman Rickover, the greatest American-Jewish orator, and the most influential Jew ever to take a seat in the United States Senate were all one and the same man—Judah Philip Benjamin of Louisiana." Dinnerstein and Palsson's *Jews in the South* contains a workmanlike article by Benjamin Kaplan, who saw Benjamin as a disillusioned hero. He accepts Rabbi Korn's judgments but cannot quite resist telling at least one of those good but fictional stories about Benjamin's Judaism, namely the proud retort to an anti-Jewish remark: "It is true that I am a Jew, and when my ancestors were receiving the Ten Commandments from the immediate hand of Deity, midst the thunderings and lightnings of Mount Sinai, the ancestors of my opponent were herding swine in the forest of Great Britain." Rabbi Korn dismisses the story in a footnote. "Four different sources are referred to, each detailing a different time, place and opponent; all this in addition to the coincidence that the retort is also credited to Disraeli. Benjamin was reticent to the extent of self-effacement; it is extremely unlikely that he ever made this or any other reply to an anti-Jewish attack."

Eli Evans attempts to prove that Judah Benjamin had close ties to Judaism and the Jewish community. Thus, a substantial portion of Evans's *Judah Benjamin: The Jewish Con-*

federate, relating to Benjamin's Judaism, is creative speculation. For example, compare Evans's treatment of whether or not Benjamin attended a synagogue service in wartime Richmond to Bertram W. Korn's article "Judah P. Benjamin as a Jew." Korn gets the better of the debate on the facts. But Evans should not be faulted for what I would describe as educated speculation. Still, despite Evans's efforts, he did not convince me that Benjamin's relationship to Judaism was anything other than as Rabbi Korn described it: He "had no positive or active interest in Jews or in Judaism."

There is no biography of David Levy Yulee. This is quite remarkable given his important role in Florida statehood. The biographical essay is a two-part article by Senator Yulee's son, C. Wickliffe Yulee, entitled "Senator David L. Yulee," in *Florida Historical Society Quarterly* 2, no. 1 (April 1909): 26–43 and vol. 2, no. 2 (July 1909): 3–22. As promised by the author, it suffers from the adage that "every man is a hero to his child." But, since the son was an eyewitness to some events and had a unique opportunity to obtain information, the articles are useful. A short memoir by Moses Levy's friend and lawyer, George R. Fairbanks, sheds some light on the mysterious origin of the Yulee family. See *Florida Historical Quarterly* 18, no. 3 (January 1940): 165–67.

An article entitled "David L. Yulee, Florida's First Senator," by Leon Hühner, a lawyer and historian, was published in *Publications of the American Jewish Historical Society* 25 (1917): 1–29. This article was reprinted in Dinnerstein and Palsson's *Jews of the South*. Hühner also wrote an article on Yulee's father, "Moses Elias Levy: An Early Florida Pioneer and the Father of Florida's First Senator," published in *Florida Historical Quarterly* 19, no. 4 (April 1941).

Hühner unfortunately did not have the benefit of the extensive Yulee manuscripts and papers, which were deposited at the P. K. Yonge Library of Florida History at the University of Florida in 1948 by his daughter Florida Yulee Neff. These papers provide the basis of an extensive and excellent dissertation titled "David Yulee: A Study of Nineteenth Century American Thought and Enterprise," by Arthur W. Thompson (Columbia University, 1954). A second and equally helpful dissertation written by Joseph G. Adler, "The Public Career of Senator David Levy Yulee" (Case Western Reserve University, 1973), sheds light on Yulee's connection to Judaism as well as his political career. I have relied in great measure (but not entirely) on Adler's interpretation of Yulee's family and religious background. Adler also wrote an essay on Yulee's father: "Moses Elias Levy and Attempts to Colonize Florida," in *Jews of the South: Selected Essays from the Southern Jewish Historical Society*, edited by Samuel Proctor and Louis Schmier (Macon, Ga.: Mercer University Press, 1984). Chris Monaco's article "Moses E. Levy of Florida: A Jewish Abolitionist Abroad," *AJH* 86, no. 4 (December 1998): 377–96, is also useful on Yulee's family. A thesis by Mills M. Lord Jr., "David Levy Yulee: Statesman and Railroad Builder" (University of Florida, 1940) is also an excellent, readable, and, at times, moving account of Yulee's life. The author interviewed Yulee's daughter, Florida Yulee Neff, and many others and had access to Yulee's letters.

Another two-part article in the *Florida Historical Quarterly* is informative on the question of Senator Yulee's positions on secession: Dorothy Dodd, "The Secession Movement in Florida, 1850– 1861," *Florida Historical Quarterly* 12, no. 1, pt. 1 (July 1933): 3–24 and 12, no. 1, pt. 2 (October 1933): 45–66. On the history of the presidential party and its wagon

458   train, see A. J. Hanna, *Flight into Oblivion* (Richmond, Va.: Johnson Publishing Co., 1938) and an introduction to and the diary of Tench Francis Tilghman, "The Confederate Baggage and Treasure Train Ends Its Flight in Florida," *Florida Historical Quarterly* 24, no. 3 (January 1939): 158–80. On the history of the Florida Railroad Company, I have relied on Robert C. Black III's classic work, *The Railroads of the Confederacy* (Chapel Hill: University of North Carolina Press, 1952), and "The Florida Railroad Company in the Civil War," by Robert L. Clarke, in *Journal of Southern History* 19, no. 2 (May 1953): 180–92.

On Joseph Holt, I have utilized Mary Bernard Allen, "Joseph Holt, Judge Advocate General (1862–1875): A Study in the Treatment of Political Prisoners by the United States Government during the Civil War" (dissertation, University of Chicago, 1927) and William Hanchett, *The Lincoln Murder Conspiracies* (Urbana and Chicago: University of Illinois Press, 1983).

A sketch in *The Universal Jewish Encyclopedia* is, as is typical of that work, full of errors. It states that Yulee served in the Confederate Congress, which he did not, and the author and publisher outdid themselves by publishing a photograph of Judah P. Benjamin with the caption "David L. Yulee."

The story about Yulee's grandfather as grand vizier in Morocco and his being exiled or executed when he fell out of royal favor strikes this writer as not believable in the least. It has, however, been accepted by all of the historians who have studied Yulee, and so I have included it. I would point out, as a kind of humorous "reality check," the amazing similarity between the story of Yulee's grandfather and that of the great-grandfather of Isaac Harby, the well-known Jewish writer and religious reformer. Gary Phillip Zola, in his biography, *Isaac Harby of Charleston, 1788–1828: Jewish Reformer and Intellectual,* states that this great-grandfather was "reputedly the 'secretary to the King of Morocco,' who, as the family legend went, was robbed of his wealth shortly after his death 'for a supposed crime alleged against him.'" Another version of the Harby ancestry included a fifteenth-century non-Jewish English nobleman. People obviously make up fantastic stories about their ancestry. And in the eighteenth and nineteenth centuries, it was difficult, if not impossible, to verify the facts.

A great portion of this work is based on traditional Civil War sources, particularly the compiled service records of Jewish Confederate soldiers at the National Archives. Individual records vary enormously. Some, such as Octavus Cohen's and Adolph Proskauer's, contain letters and orders as well as basic records. Others, such as Lewis Leon's, contain minimal information. These records are important, but they are not definitive. As Jim D. Moody points out in *Rolls and Historical Sketch of the Tenth Regiment, So. Car. Volunteers,* Washington Emanuel's service records end in 1862, yet he was killed in the Battle of Atlanta in 1864. "This is a glaring example of the inadequacy of the Confederate service records in the National Archives, particularly for the last year of the war." Broadfoot Publishing Company has published a multivolume series entitled *Roster of Confederate Soldiers, 1861–1865,* which lists in sixteen volumes each Confederate soldier who has a record at the National Archives.

Other sources are *War of the Rebellion Official Records of the Union and Confederate Armies* and the *Official Records of the Union and Confederate Navies in the War of the Rebellion* (OR and ORN), but as with the service records, both works are seriously lacking in Confederate records for the last year of the war. There are a number of regimental histories, both modern and those written by participants. Both contemporaneous and reflective accounts can be found in the fifty-two-volume *Southern Historical Society Papers*. Firsthand accounts vary enormously in reliability. Lewis Leon's *Diary of a Tar Heel Confederate* (Charlotte, N.C.: Stone Publishing Co., 1913) is excellent, whereas Isaac Hermann's *Memoir* (Atlanta: Byrd Printing Co., 1911) is absurd. Marcus's *Memoirs* contains a number of firsthand accounts.

The secondary literature on the subject of Jewish Confederate soldiers is almost non-existent. The pioneering works are Korn's *American Jewry and the Civil War* and Mel Young's *Where They Lie*. Korn's focus was the organized Jewish community mostly in the North, and Young's goal was only to record those killed in battle. I have relied on the standard works on Confederate soldiers: Bell Irvin Wiley, *The Life of Johnny Reb: The Common Soldier of the Confederacy* (Garden City, N.Y.: Doubleday, 1971) and James I. Robertson Jr., *Soldiers Blue and Gray* (Columbia: University of South Carolina Press, 1988).

Ella Lonn's *Foreigners in the Confederacy* (Chapel Hill: University of North Carolina Press, 1940; reprinted Gloucester, Mass.: Peter Smith, 1965) pays little attention to foreign-born Jews and reflects the author's lack of research into Jewish sources. She advances the simplistic notion that, because it "cannot be disputed that Jews were interested in the slave trade," it follows that "the Jews [were] foremost among all the foreign element in advocacy of secession." She cites no source or evidence for this statement because there is none. She has, however, located every anti-Semitic observation in the Confederacy. She relies on Henry Foote on the subject of disreputable Jewish businesses when she certainly knew that Foote was regarded as a crackpot by the Davis administration and most of the Confederate Congress. She is complimentary of foreigners who she does not realize are Jewish, such as Isaac Hermann and Herman Kaminski.

In 1895 Simon Wolf, a prominent Jewish attorney in Washington, D.C., published *The American Jew as Patriot, Soldier, and Citizen,* in which he attempted to catalogue every Jew who had served not only in the armed services of the United States but of all of the countries of the Americas. The 1890s was a time when German notions of anti-Semitism were being exported to the United States and began to take hold. Among those who jumped on this anti-Semitic bandwagon was one J. M. Rogers, who wrote an article in the *North American Review* in 1891 alleging that the Jews had not fought for their country in the Civil War. Wolf was outraged. He replied in the pages of the *North American Review* and determined to write his book in reply to the slander that Jews were not patriots. The result was *The American Jew as Patriot, Soldier and Citizen,"* a tome 576 pages in length. It contains a list of every Jewish soldier and sailor who fought on the Union or the Confederate side.

While Wolf's work has long been out of print, it is the only work that attempted a comprehensive list of every Jewish soldier in the Civil War. But the task of identifying every Jewish soldier who fought in the Civil War is an impossible one. A number of scholars have pointed out flagrant errors in Wolf's work. For example, Sylvan Morris Dubow wrote an article published in *American Jewish Historical Quarterly* 59, no.3 (March 1970), titled "Identifying the Jewish Serviceman in the Civil War: A Re-appraisal of Simon Wolf's *The American Jew as Patriot, Soldier and Citizen,"* in which he said that although the book "performed a valuable service" when it first appeared, "its value to modern scholarship is questionable." Dubow correctly pointed out that the list of soldiers and sailors is both incomplete and very often inaccurate. Wolf erred in identifying Jews, in misspelling names, and in misidentifying the military organization to which the person belonged.

These are substantial criticisms of Wolf's work, and they make it impossible to rely solely on Wolf without further verification. However, Rabbi Barnett A. Elzas, hardly a shy man when it came to criticizing other historians, relied on Wolf's list as a starting point and had this to say about him in *The Jews of South Carolina:a* "Mr. Wolf in his book, *The American Jew as Patriot, Soldier and Citizen,* perhaps the greatest monument, even if least appreciated, of his services to the cause of the Jew, has given many more names, many of which we have not been able to identify, though many months have been given to the task, and it is with regret that we must leave them for future investigation." Elzas felt that "while many of [Wolf's] names may be erroneous, the majority of them are doubtless correct."

Neither Union nor Confederate armies or navies kept records of a soldier's or sailor's religion. Thus, one cannot positively identify a particular soldier or sailor as a Jew from Civil War military records alone. The historian is then remitted to an examination of the local records of each and every Jewish congregation, organization, and newspaper in the South and to an examination of each individual soldier, a task which is extremely onerous and indeed impossible, even for a researcher willing to attempt it. The records of Beth Elohim in Charleston, for example, were destroyed when Sherman burned Columbia, and therefore whether or not a particular Jewish soldier from South Carolina was a member of K. K. Beth Elohim will never be known. If the soldier is buried in a Jewish cemetery or if he had Jewish ancestors or descendants, one might then be able to verify his religion. But there are many Civil War soldiers, in fact the great bulk of them, who do not fit into that category. Abraham Barkai points out in *Branching Out: German-Jewish Immigration to the United States, 1820–1914* that congregational and institutional histories focus almost exclusively on a dozen or so prominent families, that many Jews were not congregants, and that identifying Jews by Jewish-sounding names is, while "a passable expedient," full of shortcomings. "In the United States," he concludes, "biblical names among Gentiles are even more usual than in Europe, and the 'Anglicization' of names was widespread not only among Jewish immigrants. When individuals proven to be of pure Christian stock are known under the name Israel Israel, and when German-born Jews appear as Bennett King, Henry Jones, and John Middleton, caution is in order."

Wolf was working from various lists of soldiers, sailors, and veterans, and he took every Jewish-sounding or Jewish-looking name he could find. Some of Wolf's information was derived from letters sent to him in response to newspaper ads taken out in 1891 seeking "Hebrews in the Civil War." Eugene Levy, a Confederate veteran, searched Southern archives. Undoubtedly Wolf received letters with information now no longer verifiable or perhaps even available. As Dubow points out, Wolf mistakenly believed that a number of soldiers were Jews just because of their names. He listed seven Jewish recipients of the Medal of Honor when three is more likely.

Despite the criticism, however, Wolf is entitled to a great deal of credit for attempting a difficult task. He did produce a list, which is more than one can say for his critics. Dubow, for example, could have produced a better list but did not do it. Wolf's list remains a good starting point. One day, a dedicated and diligent historian will produce a more accurate and comprehensive list of Jewish Confederate soldiers. Today, however, is not that day.

With regard to soldiers, local Jewish histories vary enormously in reliability. Some contain material on Jewish Confederate soldiers. First and foremost is *The History of the Jews of Richmond* by Herbert T. Ezekiel and Gaston Lichtenstein (Richmond, 1917). Both men were sons of Jewish Confederate soldiers writing fifty years after the end of the war, when Confederate veterans were still living. "A close acquaintance of more than forty years with the Jewish people of this city," Ezekiel wrote, "with a large stock of information . . . has enabled [me] to prepare a list of Confederate soldiers from Richmond, as near correct as such could be. . . . The list given is undoubtedly the best that has ever been printed, and it is safe to assume that no more complete or accurate one will ever be published." The weakness of the work is that the authors would not publish anything negative about the Richmond Jewish Confederates even though they undoubtedly were privy to such information.

Rabbi Elzas's *The Jews of South Carolina* declines the invitation to exaggerate the number and heroic deeds of Jewish Confederates. Elzas recognized Simon Wolf's great contribution but sets out only those names he could verify as Jewish soldiers in the Confederate armies. Charles Reznikoff and Uriah Z. Engelman take the easy way out in *The Jews of Charleston* by repeating local lore rather than conducting research. They assert that more than 180 Jews of Charleston served in the armies of the Confederacy and that, of these, 25 or so were killed. This is not correct. Elzas lists more than 180 South Carolinians, not Charlestonians, and Reznikoff's footnote does not back up the statements in the text.

Regimental histories written by the participants and works about particular regiments by historians are extremely valuable when they mention Jewish Confederates, which is not often enough. I have utilized the following regimental histories by men who served in the war: William V. Izlar, *A Sketch of the War Record of the Edisto Rifles, 1861–1865*, originally published by August Kohn, Theodore Kohn's father (Columbia, S.C.: August Kohn, 1914; reprint Camden, S.C.: J. J. Fox, 1990); C. I. (Irvine) Walker, *Rolls and Historical Sketch of the Tenth Regiment So. Car. Volunteers in the Army of the Confederate States to Which Is Added an Historical Sketch of the Georgetown Rifle Guards, Company A, 10th South Carolina*, by Sol. Emanuel (Charleston, S.C.: Walker, Evans & Cogswell, 1881; reprint, with an excellent introduction by Jim D. Moody, Alexandria, Va.: Stonewall House, 1985); Robert Emery Park, *Sketch of the Alabama 12th Infantry* (Richmond, 1906). I have utilized the following histories written by historians at a later date: Mac Wyckoff, *A History of the 2nd South Carolina Infantry, 1861–1865* (Fredericksburg, Va.: Sergeant Kirkland's Museum and Historical Society, 1994), on Kershaw's brigade and men from Sumter, Charleston, and other parts of South Carolina; Darrell L. Collins, *46th Virginia Infantry*, on the Richmond Blues ([Lynchburg, Va.]: H. E. Howard, 1992); Lee A. Wallace Jr., *1st Virginia Infantry*, on the Richmond Grays ([Lynchburg, Va.]: H. E. Howard, 1984); John A. Cutchins, *A Famous Command: The Richmond Light Infantry Blues* (Richmond: Garret & Massie, 1934).

Other good sources on soldiers are Isadore S. Meyer, "The American Jew in the Civil War," Catalog of the Exhibit of the Civil War Centennial, *PAJHS* 50, no. 4 (June 1961); Bertram W. Korn, "Jewish Chaplains during the Civil War," *AJA* 1, no. 1 (June 1948); and Korn, "Was There a Confederate Jewish Chaplain?," *AJHQ* 53, no. 1 (September 1963): 63–69.

The Levy and Phillips families have not been entirely ignored by historians, but there is little in the published literature. First and foremost is the brief but excellent introduction

462   to *A Southern Woman's Story: Life in Confederate Richmond* (Wilmington, N.C., 1991). Written by one of the great Civil War historians, Bell Irvin Wiley, this sketch focuses on Phoebe Pember, the author of *A Southern Woman's Story*, and gives an outline of the Levy family. The volume also contains Pember's Civil War letters from Richmond.

Two excellent but brief biographical essays on Eugenia and Philip Phillips appear in Proctor and Schmier's *Jews of the South*. Both essays are written by David T. Morgan and are titled "Eugenia Levy Phillips: The Civil War Experiences of a Southern Jewish Woman" and "Philip Phillips: Jurist and Statesman." Jacob Rader Marcus included excerpts of the Phillipses's diaries and memoirs in *Memoirs of American Jews, 1775–1865* (Philadelphia: JPSA, 1956), vol. 3, together with very brief biographical information. Charles Fairman discusses Phillips in *Mr. Justice Miller and the Supreme Court 1862–1890* (Cambridge: Harvard University Press, 1939).

On Eugenia Phillips, I have also utilized Ishbel Ross, *Rebel Rose: Life of Rose O'Neal Greenhow, Confederate Spy* (New York: Harper & Brothers, 1954). As to Philip Phillips's career in Alabama: William Garrett, *Reminisces of Public Men in Alabama for Thirty Years* (1872; reprint, Spartanburg, S.C., n.p., 1975); and regarding the Kansas-Nebraska Act: William W. Freehling, *The Road to Disunion: Secessionist at Bay, 1776–1854*, vol. 1 (New York: Oxford University Press, 1990). Other brief but useful sketches of the Phillipses are contained in the following: Elzas, *The Jews of South Carolina;* Reznikoff and Engelman, *The Jews of Charleston;* Hagy, *This Happy Land;* Simonhoff, *Saga of American Jewry from 1865 to 1914;* and *Jewish Participants in the Civil War.*

On the Levy family and other members of the Phillips family, I have relied on Rubin, *Third to None;* DeLeon, *Belles, Beaux, and Brains of the '60s;* a brief history of 301 East Bay Street written by Carolyn Rivers; interviews with Solomon Breibart; and a biographical sketch of Moses C. Levy in *Eleven Gentlemen of Charleston: Founders of the Supreme Council of Ancient and Accepted Scottish Rite of Freemansonry* (Washington, D.C., 1959) by Ray Baker Harris. The Phillips-Myers Collection, Southern Historical Collection, University of North Carolina, contains voluminous letters, clippings, and memoirs of the Levy, Phillips, and Myers families. I relied on letters from Jacob Clavius Levy to his daughters; Eugenia Phillips's memoirs; Philip Phillips's autobiography, which he calls a diary; Caroline Phillips Myers's memoirs; and letters of Octavus Cohen. I have also quoted Mary Chesnut's diary, now available in a splendidly annotated version entitled *Mary Chesnut's Civil War*, edited by C. Vann Woodward (New Haven, Conn.: Yale University Press, 1981); *The Private Mary Chesnut: The Unpublished Civil War Diaries*, edited by C. Vann Woodward and Elisabeth Muhlenfeld (New York: Oxford University Press, 1984); and Virginia Clay-Compton, *A Belle of the Fifties* (New York: Doubleday, 1904).

Slavery is a controversial topic that has generated a great deal of heat as well as some light. The best work relative to Jews is still Bertram Wallace Korn, *Jews and Negro Slavery in the Old South, 1789–1895* (Elkins Park, Pa.: Reform Congregation Kenesseth Israel, 1961), republished in Dinnerstein and Palsson, eds., *Jews in the South*, 89–134. See also Abraham J. Karp, ed., *The Jewish Experience in America* (Waltham, Mass.: American Jewish Historical Society, 1969) and Eli Faber, *Slavery and the Jews: A Historical Inquiry* (New York: New York University Press, 1995). Korn concludes that Jews were such a small minority in the South that the "history of slavery would not have differed one whit from historic reality if no single Jew had been resident in the South." Hagy treats the subject briefly in *This Happy Land,* where he provides a summary of the 1850 Census. Berman also treats it briefly.

BIBLIOGRAPHY

★

PRIMARY SOURCES

Manuscripts and Manuscript Collections

American Jewish Archives, Cincinnati, Ohio
    Gutheim, James K. Papers.
    Hart, Alexander. Papers.
    Heustis, Rachel Lyons. Papers.
    Jacobs, George. Papers and Scrapbook.
    Korn Family Papers.
    Levy Family Papers (Levy Diary).
    Proskauer Family Papers.
    Tobias, Thomas J. Papers.
American Jewish Historical Society, Waltham, Massachusetts, and New York
    Photograph collections.
Atlanta Jewish Federation
    Alexander, Rebecca Ella Solomons. Memoir Transcript. Alexander Papers.
Beth Ahabah Museums and Archives, Richmond, Virginia
    Beth Shalome. Minutes.
    Ezekiel, Moses. Autobiography.
College of Charleston, Jewish Heritage Collection, Charleston, South Carolina
    Fass, Simon. Memoirs.
Georgia Historical Society, Savannah, Georgia
    Cohen-Phillips Papers.
    Minis Family Papers.
Louisiana State Museum, New Orleans, Louisiana
    Association for the Relief of Jewish Widows and Orphans.
    Gates of Prayer Synagogue Papers.
South Carolina Historical Society, Charleston, South Carolina
    Ford's Census. Charleston, 1860.
South Caroliniana Library, Columbia, South Carolina
    Kohn Family Papers.
    Timrod, Henry. Papers.
Southern Historical Collection, University of North Carolina, Chapel Hill
    Kursheedt Papers.
    Phillips-Myers Papers.
Tulane University, New Orleans, Louisiana
    Congregation Book of Records of Dispersed of Judah.
    Congregation Gates of Prayer Records, 1850–1990.

466   Eshleman, Craig. Papers.

Lemann, Bernard. Diary.

Lemann Family Papers.

Mayer Family Papers.

Metz-Kahn Family Papers.

Moise Family Papers.

Temple Sinai Records.

Touro Synagogue Records.

Virginia Historical Society, Richmond, Virginia

Whitlock, Philip. Manuscript.

Virginia State Library, Richmond, Virginia

Hirsh, Isaac. Diary.

Personal Papers, Confederate Miscellany.

Second Annual Directory for the City of Richmond, 1860 (microfilm).

Williams Research Center, Historic New Orleans Collection, New Orleans, Louisiana

Kursheedt, Edwin J. Papers.

Leovy, Henry J. Papers, 1857–1900.

Levy Family Papers, 1840–1889. Box 2, MSS 408.

Published Memoirs and Letters

Baruch, Bernard M. *My Own Story.* New York: Henry Holt & Co., 1957.

Baruch, Simon. "A Surgeon's Story of Battle and Capture." *Confederate Veteran* 22, no. 12 (December 1914).

Benjamin, I. J. *Three Years in America, 1859–1862.* Vol. 1. Ed. Oscar Handlin. Trans. from German by Charles Reznikoff. Philadelphia: JPSA, 1956.

Bleser, Carol, ed. *Secret and Sacred: The Diaries of James Henry Hammond, a Southern Slaveholder.* New York: Oxford University Press, 1988.

Bleser, Carol, ed. *Tokens of Affection: The Letters of a Planter's Daughter in the Old South.* Athens: University of Georgia Press, 1996.

Butler, Benjamin. *Butler's Book: A Review of His Legal, Political, and Military Career.* Boston, 1892.

Clay, Mrs. Clement C., Jr. (Virginia Clay-Compton). *A Belle of the Fifties.* New York: Doubleday, 1904.

Cummer, Clyde L. *Yankee in Gray: The Civil War Memoirs of Henry E. Handerson, with a Selection of His Wartime Letters.* Cleveland, Ohio: Western Reserve University Press [c. 1962].

Cumming, Kate. *A Journal of Hospital Life in the Confederate Army of Tennessee from the Battle of Shiloh to the End of the War.* Louisville: J. P. Morton & Co; New Orleans, W. Evelyn, [c. 1866].

DeLeon, Edwin. *Thirty Years of My Life on Three Continents.* London: Ward and Downey, 1890.

DeLeon, Thomas Cooper. *Belles, Beaux, and Brains of the '60s.* New York, 1909.

DeLeon, Thomas Cooper. *Four Years in Rebel Capitals: An Inside View of Life in the Southern Confederacy, from Birth to Death.* Mobile: Gossip Printing Co., 1890.

Fremantle, Arthur J. *Three Months in the Southern States: April–June, 1863.* Edinburgh   467
and London: W. Blackwood and Sons, 1864.

Garrett, William. *Reminiscences of Public Men in Alabama for Thirty Years.* 1872. Reprint,
Spartanburg, S.C.: n.p., 1975.

Golden Jubilee Souvenir, Congregation Gates of Prayer, Shaara Tefilah, 1851–1901. 1901.

Hermann, Isaac. *Memoirs of a Veteran Who Served as a Private in the 60s in the War
between the States, Personal Incidents, Experiences, and Observations.* Atlanta: Byrd
Printing Co., 1911.

Herzberg, Fannie. *Pioneer Members and History of Temple Beth-El, 1850–1959,* and *Diary
of Private Louis Merz, C.S.A. of West Point Guards, 1862.* Chattahoochee, Ala.: Chattahoochee Valley Historical Society, 1959.

Jones, John Beauchamp. *A Rebel War Clerk's Diary at the Confederate States Capital.* 2
vols. Ed. Howard Swiggett. New York: Old Hickory Bookshop, 1935.

Jones, Rev. J. William. *Personal Reminiscences of General Robert E. Lee.* 1875. Reprint,
Richmond: U.S. Historical Society Press, 1989.

King, Spencer B. "Fanny Cohen's Journal of Sherman's Occupation of Savannah, Georgia."
Georgia Historical Quarterly 41 (December 1957): 414.

Lee, F. O., and J. C. Agnew. *Historical Record of the City of Savannah.* Savannah, 1869.

Leon, Lewis. *The Diary of a Tar Heel Confederate Soldier.* Charlotte, N.C.: Stone Publishing Co., 1913.

Marcus, Jacob Rader, ed. *Memoirs of American Jews, 1775–1865.* 3 vols. Philadelphia:
JPSA, 1955–56.

Mearns, David C. *The Lincoln Papers.* Vol. 1. (Garden City, N.Y.: Doubleday, 1948).

Miers, Earl Schenck, ed. *A Rebel War Clerk's Diary.* New York: Sagamore Press, 1958.

"Military Record of the DeLeon Family and of Captain Perry M. DeLeon." *PAJHS* 1, no.
4 (June 1961).

Moses, Clara L. *Aunt Sister's Book.* New York: privately printed, 1929.

Park, Robert Emory. *Sketch of the Twelfth Alabama Infantry of Battle's Brigade, Rodes
Division, Early's Corps of the Army of Northern Virginia.* Richmond: W. E. Jones,
1906. Reprinted in *Southern Historical Society Papers* 33.

Pember, Phoebe Yates. *A Southern Woman's Story: Life in Confederate Richmond.* Ed. Bell
Irvin Wiley. Jackson, Tenn.: McCowat-Mercer Press, 1959. Reprint, Wilmington,
N.C.: Broadfoot Publishing, 1991.

Porter, Anthony Toomer. *Led On! Step by Step: Scenes from Clerical, Military, Educa-
tional, and Plantation Life in the South, 1828–1898; An Autobiography.* New York and
London: G. P. Putnam's Sons, 1898.

Putnam, Sallie B. *Richmond during the War: Four Years of Personal Observation.* New
York, 1867. Reprint, Alexandra, Va.: Time-Life Books, 1983.

Rivers, William J. *Rivers' Account of the Raising of Troops in South Carolina for State and
Confederate Service, 1861–1865.* Columbia, S.C.: Bryan Publishing Co., 1899.

Soman, Jean Powers, and Frank L. Byrne, eds. *A Jewish Colonel in the Civil War: Marcus
M. Spiegel of the Ohio Volunteers.* Lincoln, Tenn.: University of Nashville Press, 1994.

Sorrel, G. Moxley. *Recollections of a Confederate Staff Officer.* 1905. Reprint, New York:
Smithmark Publishers, 1994.

"The Story of the Jewish Orphan's Home of New Orleans." New Orleans: n.p., 1905.

Straus, Oscar S. *Under Four Administrations.* Boston and New York: Houghton Mifflin Co., 1922.

Sulzberger, Iphigene Ochs. *From Iphigene: The Memoirs of Iphigene Ochs Sulzberger.* Ed. Susan W. Dryfoos. Privately printed, 1979.

Taylor, Gen. Richard. "The Last Confederate Surrender." *Southern Historical Society Papers* 3 (March 1877): 155–58.

Tunnell, Ted, ed. *Carpetbagger from Vermont.* Baton Rouge: Louisiana State University Press, 1989.

Walker, C. I. *Rolls and Historical Sketch of the Tenth Regiment, South Carolina Volunteers, in the Army of the Confederate States.* Charleston, S.C.: Walker, Evans and Cogswell, 1881. Reprint, with introduction by Jim D. Moody, Alexandria, Va.: Stonewall House, 1985.

Unpublished Memoirs

Bultman, Dorothy P. "The Story of a Good Life." Sumter, S.C., November 1963. Courtesy of Thomas Bultman, Esq., Sumter, S.C.

Goldsmith, Ferdinand. "Life and Doings of Ferdinand Goldsmith." Courtesy of Moise Steeg, Esq., New Orleans, La.

Published Diaries

Ashkenazi, Elliott, ed. *The Civil War Diary of Clara Solomon: Growing Up in New Orleans, 1861–1862.* Baton Rouge: Louisiana State University Press, 1995.

Franklin, Penelope, ed. *Private Pages: Diaries of American Women, 1830s–1970s.* New York: Ballantine Books, 1986. Eleanor Cohen diary at pp. 304–23.

Marszalek, John F., ed. *The Diary of Miss Emma Holmes, 1861–1866.* Baton Rouge: Louisiana State University Press, 1979.

Russell, William Howard. *My Diary North and South.* Boston: T.O.H.P. Burnham, 1863.

Woodward, C. Vann, ed. *Mary Chesnut's Civil War.* New Haven: Yale University Press, 1981.

Woodward, C. Vann, and Elisabeth Muhlenfeld, eds. *The Private Mary Chesnut: The Unpublished Civil War Diaries.* New York: Oxford University Press, 1984.

Other Published Primary Sources

"The Battle of Fort Sumter and First Victory of the Southern Troops." 1861. Reprint, Charleston, S.C.: n.p., 1961. Pamphlet containing newspaper reports.

Child, Lydia Maria. *Letters from New-York* (New York: Charles Francis; Boston, James Munroe, 1843).

Commager, Henry Steele. *The Blue and the Gray.* Vol. 1. New York: Bobbs-Merrill Co., 1950.

Fidler, William, ed. "Unpublished Letters of Henry Timrod." *Southern Literary Messenger* 2 (October 1940): 527–35, 2 (November 1940): 605–11, and 2 (December 1940): 645–51.

Gardner's New Orleans Directory (New Orleans: Charles Gardner, 1861).

Harwell, Richard B., ed. *The Civil War Reader* (New York: Mallard Press, 1991).

Journal of the Public and Secret Proceedings of the Convention of the People of Georgia.
    Milledgeville, Ga., 1861.

Moses, Octavia Harby. *A Mother's Poems: A Collection of Verses.* Privately printed, 1915.

"Notes and Documents: Seven Unpublished Letters of Henry Timrod." *Alabama Review*
    (April 1949), pp. 139–49.

Hewett, Janet B., ed. *Roster of Confederate Soldiers, 1861–1865.* 16 vols. Wilmington,
    N.C.: Broadfoot Publishing Co., 1995–1996.

*Proceedings of the Convention of the State of Louisiana in English and French Together
    with the Ordinances.* New Orleans, 1861.

Schappes, Morris U., ed. *Documentary History of the Jews in the United States, 1654–1875.*
    Rev. ed. New York: Citadel Press, 1952.

Whittington, E. P., "Thomas O. Moore, Governor of Louisiana 1860–1864." *Louisiana His-
    torical Quarterly* 13 (January 1930): 5–31.

SECONDARY SOURCES

Dictionaries, Encyclopedias, and Reference Works

The American Jewish Yearbook. Philadelphia, Pa.: JPSA. Vol. 2, 1900–1901.

Americans of Jewish Descent.

Biographical Directory of the Congress, 1774–1949. 1950.

Biographical Directory of the United States Congress, 1774–1989 (Washington, D.C.:
    USGPO, 1989).

Confederate Military History.

Cyclopedia of Eminent and Representative Men of the Carolinas of the Nineteenth Century.

The Dictionary of American Biography.

Dictionary of Jewish Biography (New York: Simon and Schuster, 1991).

A Dictionary of Louisiana Biography.

Encyclopedia of the Confederacy.

Historical Times Illustrated Encyclopedia of the Civil War.

History of Alabama and Dictionary of Alabama Biography.

National Cyclopedia of American Biography.

The Oxford Dictionary of the Jewish Religion.

Twentieth Century Biographical Dictionary.

The Universal Jewish Encyclopedia.

Who Was Who in America, 1897–1942: A Component of Who's Who in American History.

Books

Amos, Harriet E. *Cotton City, Urban Development in Antebellum Mobile.* Tuscaloosa: Uni-
    versity of Alabama Press, 1985.

Ashkenazi, Elliott. *The Business of Jews in Louisiana, 1840–1875.* Tuscaloosa: University of
    Alabama Press, 1988.

———. *A Centennial: Lehman Brothers, 1850–1950.* New York: Lehman Brothers, 1950.

470　　Avery, Isaac Wheeler. *The History of the State of Georgia* (1881). Repr. New York: AMS Press, 1972.

Axelrod, Alan. *The War between the Spies: A History of Espionage during the American Civil War.* New York: Atlantic Monthly Press, 1992.

Barkai, Abraham. *Branching Out: German-Jewish Immigration to the United States, 1820–1914.* New York: Holmes & Meier, 1994.

Bartlett, Napier. *Military Record of Louisiana.* New Orleans, 1875. Reprint, Baton Rouge: Louisiana State University Press, 1992.

Bergeron, Arthur W., Jr. *Guide to Louisiana Confederate Military Units, 1861–1865.* Baton Rouge: Louisiana State University Press, 1996.

———. *Confederate Mobile.* Jackson: University Press of Mississippi, 1991.

Beringer, Richard E. *Why the South Lost the Civil War.* Athens: University of Georgia Press, 1986.

Berman, Myron. *Richmond's Jewry, 1769–1976: Shabbat in Shockoe.* Charlottesville: University Press of Virginia, 1979.

Black, Robert C., III. *The Railroads of the Confederacy.* Chapel Hill: University of North Carolina Press, 1952.

Booth, Andrew B. *Records of Louisiana Confederate Soldiers and Louisiana Confederate Commands.* 3 vols. New Orleans, La.: n.p., 1920. Reprint, Spartanburg, S.C.: Reprint Co., 1984.

Butler, Pierce. *Judah P. Benjamin.* Philadelphia: W. G. Jacobs & Co., 1907.

Cauthen, Charles Edward. *South Carolina Goes to War, 1860–1865.* Chapel Hill: University of North Carolina Press, 1950.

Chamlee, Roy Z., Jr. *Lincoln's Assassins: A Complete Account of Their Capture, Trial, and Punishment.* Jefferson, N.C.: McFarland & Co., 1990.

Chattahoochee Valley Historical Society. *Pioneer Members and History of Temple Beth-El, 1859–1959,* and *Diary of Private Louis Merz, C.S.A., of West Point Guards, 1862.* Chattahoochee, Ala.: Chattahoochee Valley Historical Society, 1959. Courtesy Fannie Herzberg.

Clark, Champ. *Gettysburg.* Alexandria, Va.: Time-Life, 1985.

Cohen, Naomi, W. *Encounter with Emancipation: The German Jews in the United States, 1830–1914.* Philadelphia: JPSA, 1984.

Collins, Darrell L. *46th Virginia Infantry.* [Lynchburg, Va.]: H. E. Howard, 1992.

Cooper, William J., Jr. *Liberty and Slavery, Southern Politics to 1860.* New York: Alfred A. Knopf, 1983.

Cothan, Edward T., Jr. *Battle on the Bay.* Austin: University of Texas Press, 1998.

Coulter, E. Merton. *A History of the South.* Vol. 7, *The Confederate States of America, 1861–1865.* 6th ed. Baton Rouge: Louisiana State University Press, 1987.

Crawford, Samuel Wylie. *The Genesis of the Civil War: The Story of Sumter, 1860–1861.* New York, 1887.

Crute, Joseph H., Jr. *Emblems of Southern Valor: The Battle Flags of the Confederacy* (Louisville: Harmony House, 1990).

Crute, Joseph H., Sr. *Units of the Confederate Army.* 2d ed. Reprint, Gaithersburg, Md.: Olde Soldier Books, 1987.

Cullop, Charles P. *Confederate Propaganda in Europe, 1861–1865.* Coral Gables, Fla.: University of Miami Press, 1969.

Cunningham, H. H. *Doctors in Gray: The Confederate Medical Service.* Baton Rouge: Louisiana State University Press, 1958.

Current, Richard N. *Those Terrible Carpetbaggers: A Reinterpretation.* New York: Oxford University Press, 1988.

Cutchins, John A. *A Famous Command: The Richmond Light Infantry Blues.* Richmond: Garrett & Massies, 1934.

Davis, William C. *A Government of Our Own: The Making of the Confederacy.* New York: Free Press, 1994.

———. *Breckinridge: Statesman, Soldier, Symbol.* Baton Rouge: Louisiana State University Press, 1974.

———. *Jefferson Davis: The Man and His Hour.* New York: HarperCollins, 1991.

Davis, William, and the editors of Time-Life Books. *Death in the Trenches: Grant at Petersburg.* Alexandria, Va.: Time-Life Books, 1986.

Day, James M. *Jacob DeCordova, Land Merchant of Texas.* Waco: Texan Press, 1962.

DeCredico, Mary A. *Patriotism for Profit: Georgia's Urban Entrepreneurs and the Confederate War Effort.* Chapel Hill: University of North Carolina Press, 1990.

Diner, Hasia R. *A Time for Gathering: The Second Migration, 1820–1880.* Vol. 2 of *The Jewish People in America.* Baltimore: Johns Hopkins University Press, 1992.

Dinnerstein, Leonard, and Mary Dale Palsson, eds., *Jews in the South.* Baton Rouge: Louisiana State University Press, 1973.

Duncan, Ruth H. *The Captain and Submarine C.S.S. H. L. Hunley.* Memphis, Tenn.: S. C. Toof & Co., 1965.

Eakin, Sue. *Washington, Louisiana.* Bossier City, La.: Everett Co., 1988.

Eaton, Clement. *A History of the Southern Confederacy.* New York: Macmillan Co., 1954.

Edgar, Walter. *South Carolina: A History.* Columbia: University of South Carolina Press, 1998.

Eliot, Ellsworth, Jr. *West Point in the Confederacy.* New York: G. A. Baker and Co., 1941.

Elzas, Barnett. A. *The Jews of South Carolina from the Earliest Times to the Present Day.* Philadelphia: Lippincott, 1905. Reprint, Spartanburg, S.C.: Reprint Co., 1983.

Evans, Eli N. *Judah P. Benjamin: The Jewish Confederate.* New York: Free Press, 1988.

———. *The Provincials: A Personal History of Jews in the South.* New York: Athenaeum, 1974.

Ezekiel, Herbert, and Gaston Lichtenstein. *The History of the Jews of Richmond from 1769 to 1917.* Richmond: Herbert Ezekiel, 1917.

Faber, Eli. *A Time for Planting: The First Migration, 1654–1820.* Vol. 1 of *The Jewish People in America.* Baltimore Baltimore: Johns Hopkins University Press, 1992.

Faust, Drew Gilpin. *Mothers of Invention: Women of the Slaveholding South in the American Civil War.* Chapel Hill: University of North Carolina Press, 1996.

Felsenthal, Cecelia Fesenthal. *The Felsenthal Family.* 2d ed. Memphis, Tenn.: Goldberger Printing & Publishing, 1939.

Foote, Shelby. *The Civil War: A Narrative.* Vol. 1. New York: Random House, 1974.

Ford, Francis A. *Civil War Sutlers and Their Wares.* New York: T. Yogeloff, 1969.

472   Frank, Fedora S. *Five Families and Eight Young Men: Nashville and Her Jewry, 1850–1861.* Nashville: Tennessee Book Co., 1962.

———. *Beginnings on Market Street: Nashville and Her Jewry 1861–1901.* Nashville: Jewish Community of Nashville, 1976.

Frazier, Donald Shaw. *Cottonclads! The Battle of Galveston and the Defense of the Texas Coast.* Fort Worth, Tex.: Ryan Place Publishers, 1996.

Freeman, Douglass Southall. *R. E. Lee: A Biography.* Vol. 1. New York: Charles Scribner's Sons, 1934.

Furguson, Ernest B. *Ashes of Glory: Richmond at War.* New York: Alfred A. Knopf, 1996.

Gergel, Belinda, and Richard Gergel. *In Pursuit of the Tree of Life: A History of the Early Jews of Columbia, South Carolina, and the Tree of Life Congregation.* Columbia, S.C.: Tree of Life Congregation, 1996.

Ginsberg, Louis. *Chapters on the Jews of Virginia, 1658–1900.* Petersburg, Va.: privately printed, 1969.

———. *History of the Jews of Petersburg, 1789–1950.* Petersburg, Va., 1954.

Goff, Richard D. *Confederate Supply.* Durham, N.C.: Duke University Press, 1969.

Grant, James. *Bernard M. Baruch: The Adventures of a Wall Street Legend.* New York: Simon and Schuster, 1983.

Grismer, Karl H. *The Story of Fort Myers: The History of the Land of the Caloosahatchee and Southwest Florida.* [Fort Myers, Fla.]: Southwest Florida Historical Society, 1949. Reprint, Fort Myers Beach, Fla.: Island Press Publishers, 1982.

Gutman, Joseph, and Stanley F. Chyet, eds. *Moses Jacob Ezekiel: Memoirs from the Baths of Diocletian.* Detroit: Wayne State University Press, 1975.

Hagy, James W. *This Happy Land: The Jews of Colonial and Antebellum Charleston.* Tuscaloosa: University of Alabama Press, 1993.

Hanchett, William. *The Lincoln Murder Conspiracies.* Urbana: University of Illinois Press, 1986.

Hanna, A. J. *Flight into Oblivion.* Richmond, Va.: Johnson Publishing Co., 1938.

Hayes, Charles W. *History of the Island and the City of Galveston.* Cincinnati, 1879.

Hemphill, J. C. *Men of Mark in South Carolina.* Vol. 1. Washington, D.C., 1907.

Hennig, Helen Kohn. *August Kohn, Versatile South Carolinian.* Columbia: Vogue Press, 1949.

Henry, Robert Selph. *"First with the Most" Forrest.* Indianapolis: Bobbs-Merrill, 1944.

Hertzberg, Steven. *Strangers within the Gate City: The Jews of Atlanta, 1845–1915.* Philadelphia: JPSA, 1978.

Hinchin, Rabbi Martin I. *Fourscore and Eleven: A History of the Jews of Rapides Parish, 1828–1919.* Alexandria, La.: McCormick Graphics for Congregation Gemiluth Chassodim, 1984.

Horwitz, Tony. *Confederates in the Attic: Dispatches from the Unfinished Civil War.* New York: Pantheon Books, 1998.

Hyman, Harold M. *Oleander Odyssey: The Kempners of Galveston, Texas, 1854–1980s.* College Station: Texas A & M University Press, 1990.

Izlar, William Valmore. *A Sketch of the War Record of the Edisto Rifles, 1861–1865.* Columbia, S.C.: August Kohn, 1914; reprint Camden, S.C.: J. J. Fox, 1990).

Jaher, Frederic Cople. *A Scapegoat in the New Wilderness: The Origins and Rise of Anti-Semitism in America.* Cambridge, Mass.: Harvard University Press, 1994.

Jarrell, Hampton M. *Wade Hampton and the Negro.* Columbia: University of South Carolina Press, 1949.

Jewish Historical Publishing Company of Louisiana, comp. *The History of Jews of Louisiana: Their Religious, Civic, Charitable and Patriotic Life.* New Orleans: Jewish Historical Publishing Company of Louisiana, 1903.

Johannsen, Robert W. *Stephen A. Douglas.* New York: Oxford University Press, 1973.

Johnson, Gerald W. *An Honorable Titan: A Biographical Study of Adolph S. Ochs.* New York: Harper & Brothers Publishing, 1944.

Johnson, John. *The Defense of Charleston Harbor, Including Fort Sumter and the Adjacent Islands, 1863–1865.* Charleston, 1890.

Johnson, Michael P., and James L. Roark. *Black Masters: A Free Family of Color in the Old South.* New York: W. W. Norton & Co., 1984.

———, eds. *No Chariot Let Down: Charleston's Free People of Color on the Eve of the Civil War.* Chapel Hill: University of North Carolina Press, 1984.

Jones, Eugene W., Jr. *Enlisted for the War: The Struggles of the Gallant 24th Regiment, South Carolina Volunteers, 1861–1865.* Hightown, N.J.: Longstreet House, 1997.

Jones, Lewis. *South Carolina: A Synoptic History for Laymen.* Lexington, S.C.: Sandlapper Press, 1978.

Kaplan, Bernard. *The Eternal Stranger: A Study of Jewish Life in the Small Community.* New York: Bookman Associates, 1957.

King, William L. *The Newspaper Press of Charleston, S.C.* Charleston, 1872.

Kirkland, Randolph W., Jr. *Broken Fortunes: South Carolina Soldiers, Sailors, and Citizens Who Died in the Service of Their Country and State in the War for Southern Independence, 1861–1865.* Charleston, S.C.: South Carolina Historical Society, 1995.

Koger, Larry. *Black Slave Owners: Free Black Slave Masters in South Carolina, 1790–1860.* Jefferson, N.C.: McFarland & Co., 1985.

Kole, Kaye. *The Minis Family of Georgia, 1733–1992.* Savannah: Georgia Historical Society, 1922.

Korn, Bertram Wallace. *American Jewry and the Civil War.* Philadelphia: AJPS, 1957. 2d ed., Cleveland and New York: Meridian Books/World Publishing, and Philadelphia: JPSA, 1961.

———. *Eventful Years and Experiences: Studies in Nineteenth Century America Jewish History.* Cincinnati: AJA, 1954.

———. *The Jews of Mobile, Alabama, 1763–1841.* Cincinnati: Hebrew Union College Press, 1970.

———. *Jews and Negro Slavery in the Old South, 1789–1865.* Elkins Park, Pa.: Reform Congregation Kenesseth Israel, 1961.

———. *The Early Jews of New Orleans.* Waltham, Mass.: AJHS, 1969.

Korn, Jerry. *War on the Mississippi.* Alexandria, Va.: Time-Life Books, 1985.

Krick, Robert K. *Lee's Colonels: A Biographical Register of the Field Officers of the Army of Northern Virginia.* Dayton, Ohio: Morningside House, 1992.

LeMaster, Carolyn Gray. *A Corner of the Tapestry: A History of the Jewish Experience in Arkansas, 1820s–1990s.* Fayetteville: University of Arkansas Press, 1994.

Lewis, Selma S. *A Biblical People in the Bible Belt: The Jewish Community of Memphis, Tennessee, 1840s–1960s.* Macon, Ga.: Mercer University Press, 1998.

474 Libo, Kenneth, and Irving Howe. *We Lived There Too.* Marek, N.Y.: St. Martin's, 1984.

Lowry, Thomas P., M.D. *The Story the Soldiers Wouldn't Tell: Sex in the Civil War.* Mechanicsburg, Pa.: Stackpole Books, 1994.

Luraghi, Raimondo. *A History of the Confederate Navy.* Annapolis, Md.: Naval Institute Press, 1996.

Madison, Charles A. *Eminent American Jews.* New York: Frederick Unger, 1970.

Marcus, Jacob Rader. *Early American Jewry.* Vol. 1. Philadelphia: JPSA, 1951.

———. *Early American Jews.* Cambridge: Harvard University Press, 1934.

———, ed. *Memoirs of American Jews, 1775–1865.* 3 vols. Philadelphia: JPSA, 1955–1956.

———. *To Count a People: American Jewish Population Data, 1585–1984.* Lanham, Md.: University Press of America, 1990.

———. *United States Jewry, 1776–1985.* 4 vols. Detroit: Wayne State University Press, 1989–93.

McPherson, James M. *The Atlas of the Civil War.* New York: MacMillan, 1994.

———. *Battle Cry of Freedom.* New York: Oxford University Press, 1988.

———. *For Cause and Comrades: Why Men Fought in the Civil War.* New York: Oxford University Press, 1997.

Meade, Robert Douthat. *Judah P. Benjamin: Confederate Statesman.* London: Oxford University Press, 1943.

Meyer, Isidore S., ed. *The American Jew in the Civil War: Catalog of the Exhibit of the Civil War Centennial Jewish Historical Commission.* New York: AJHS, 1962.

Moise, Harold. *The Moise Family of South Carolina and Their Descendants.* Columbia: privately printed, 1961.

Moore, Albert B. *Conscription and Conflict in the Confederacy.* New York: Hillary House Publishers, 1963.

Moses, Raphael J. *Last Order of the Lost Cause: The Civil War Memoirs of a Jewish Family from the "Old South."* Edited by Mel Young. Lanham, Md.: University Press of America, 1995.

Nau, John Frederick. *The German People of New Orleans, 1850–1900.* Leiden: E. J. Brill, 1958. Reprint, Hattiesburg, Miss.: USM Publication & Printing Services, n.d.

Neiman, S. I. *Judah Benjamin: Mystery Man of the Confederacy.* Indianapolis: Bobbs-Merrill Co., 1963.

Nevins, Allan. *Herbert H. Lehman and His Era.* New York: Charles Scribner's Sons, 1963.

Nevins, David. *The Road to Shiloh.* Alexandria, Va.: Time-Life Books, 1983.

O'Flaherty, Daniel. *General Jo Shelby, Undefeated Rebel.* Chapel Hill: University of North Carolina Press, 1954.

O'Pry, Maude Hearne. *Chronicles of Shreveport and Caddo Parish.* Shreveport: Journal Publishing Co., 1928.

Ornish, Natalie. *Pioneer Jewish Texans, Their Impact on Texas and American History for Four Hundred Years, 1590–1990.* Dallas: Texas Heritage Press, 1989.

Owsley, Frank. *King Cotton Diplomacy: Foreign Relations of the Confederate States of America.* Chicago: University of Chicago Press, 1959.

Parton, James. *General Butler in New Orleans.* New York, 1862.

Postal, Bernard, and Lionel Koppman. *A Jewish Tourist's Guide to the U.S.* Philadelphia: JPSA, 1954.

Potter, David M. *The Impending Crisis, 1848–1861.* New York: Harper & Row, 1976.

Powers, Bernard E., Jr. *Black Charlestonians: A Social History, 1822–1885.* Fayetteville: University of Arkansas Press, 1994.

Proctor, Samuel, and Louis Schmier, eds., with Malcolm Stern. *Jews of the South: Selected Essays from the Southern Jewish Historical Society.* Macon, Ga.: Mercer University Press, 1984.

Randall, James G., and David, Donald. *The Civil War and Reconstruction.* 2d ed. Lexington, Mass.: D. C. Heath & Co., 1969.

Regan, William B. *Irish Jewry.* Dublin, Ireland: Mendelsohn Press, 1975.

Reznikoff, Charles, and Uriah Z. Engelman. *The Jews of Charleston: A History of an American Jewish Community.* Philadelphia: JPSA, 1950.

Robertson, James I., Jr. *Soldiers Blue and Gray.* Columbia: University of South Carolina Press, 1988.

————, and the editors of Time-Life Books. *Tenting Tonight: The Soldier's Life.* Alexandria, Va.: Time-Life Books, 1984.

Robinson, William M., Jr. *Justice in Grey: A History of the Judicial System of the Confederate States of America.* Cambridge, Mass.: Harvard University Press, 1941.

Rosen, Robert N. *A Short History of Charleston.* Columbia: University of South Carolina Press, 1997.

————. *Confederate Charleston.* Columbia: University of South Carolina Press, 1997.

Ross, Ishbel. *Rebel Rose: Life of Rose O'Neal Greenhow, Confederate Spy.* New York: Harper & Brothers, 1954.

Rothschild, Janice O. *As But a Day: The First Hundred Years, 1867–1967.* Atlanta: Hebrew Benevolent Congregation, The Temple, 1967.

Rubin, Rabbi Saul Jacob. *Third to None: The Saga of Savannah Jewry, 1733–1983.* Savannah: Congregation Mikve Israel, 1983.

Sachar, Howard M. *A History of the Jews in America.* New York: Alfred A. Knopf, 1992.

Schoener, Allan. *The American Jewish Album, 1654 to the Present.* New York: Rizzoli, 1983.

Shpall, Leo. *The Jews of Louisiana.* New Orleans: Steeg Printing & Publishing Co., 1936.

Silverman, Morris. *Hartford Jews, 1659–1970.* Hartford: Connecticut Historical Society, n.d.

Simkins, Francis Butler, and Robert Hilliard Woody, eds. *South Carolina during Reconstruction.* Chapel Hill: University of North Carolina Press, 1932.

Simonhoff, Harry. *Jewish Participants in the Civil War.* New York: Arco, 1963.

————. *Saga of American Jewry, 1865–1914: Links of an Endless Chain.* New York: Arco, 1959.

————. *Jewish Notables in America, 1776–1865: Links of an Endless Chain.* New York: Greenberg, 1956.

Sorin, Gerald. *A Time for Building: The Third Migration 1880–1920.* Vol. 3 of *The Jewish People in America.* Baltimore: The Johns Hopkins University Press, 1992.

Stern, Malcolm M. *Americans of Jewish Descent.* Reprint, New York: KTAV Publishing House, 1971.

The Story of the Jewish Orphan's Home of New Orleans. New Orleans: n.p., 1905.

Talese, Gay. *The Kingdom and the Power.* New York: World Publishing Co., 1966.

476   Taylor, John M. *William Henry Seward: Lincoln's Right Hand.* New York: HarperCollins, 1991.

Taylor, William R. *Cavalier and Yankee: The Old South and American National Character.* New York: George Braziller, 1961.

Thomas, Emory M. *Robert E. Lee: A Biography.* New York: W. W. Norton & Co., 1995.

———. *The Confederacy as a Revolutionary Experience.* 1971. Columbia: University of South Carolina Press, 1992.

Thompson, Samuel Bernard. *Confederate Purchasing Operations Abroad.* Chapel Hill: University of North Carolina Press, 1935.

Tidwell, William A. *April '65: Confederate Covert Action in the American Civil War.* Kent, Ohio: Kent State University Press, 1995.

———. *Come Retribution: The Confederate Secret Service and the Assassination of Lincoln.* Jackson: University Press of Mississippi, 1988.

Tucker, Glen. *Chickamauga: Bloody Battle in the West.* Indianapolis: Bobbs-Merrill, 1961.

Tunnard, William H. *A Southern Record: The History of the Third Regiment, Louisiana Infantry.* Reprint. Fayetteville: University of Arkansas Press, 1997.

Turitz, Leo E., and Evelyn Turitz. 2d ed. *Jews in Early Mississippi.* Jackson: University Press of Mississippi, 1995.

Urofsky, Melvin I. *Commonwealth and Community: The Jewish Experience in Virginia.* Richmond: Virginia Historical Society and Jewish Community Federation of Richmond, 1997.

Wade, Richard C. *Slavery in the Cities: The South, 1820–1860.* Oxford: Oxford University Press, 1964.

Wallace, Lee A., Jr. *1st Virginia Infantry.* [Lynchburg, Va.]: H. E. Howard, 1984.

Ward, Geoffrey C. *The Civil War: An Illustrated History.* New York: Knopf, 1990.

Wellman, Manley Wade. *Giant in Gray: A Biography of Wade Hampton of South Carolina.* 1949. Reprinted Dayton, Ohio: Morningside Bookshop, 1980.

Wiley, Bell I. *The Life of Johnny Reb: The Common Soldier of the Confederacy.* Garden City, N.Y.: Doubleday & Co., 1971.

Winegarten, Ruthe, and Cathy Schechter. *Deep in the Heart: The Lives and Legends of Texas Jews.* Austin: Eakin Press and Texas Jewish Historical Society, 1990.

Wolf, Simon. *The American Jew as Patriot, Soldier, and Citizen.* Philadelphia: Levytype Co., 1895.

Wooster, Ralph A. *The Secession Conventions of the South.* Princeton, N.J.: Princeton University Press, 1962.

Wyckoff, Mac. *A History of the 2nd South Carolina Infantry, 1861–1865.* Fredericksburg, Va.: Sergeant Kirkland's Museum and Historical Society, 1994.

Young, Mel. *Where They Lie Someone Should Say Kaddish.* Lanham, Md.: University Press of America, 1991.

Zietz, Robert J. *The Gates of Heaven, Congregation Sha'arai Shomayim: The First 150 Years, Mobile, Alabama, 1844–1994.* Mobile: Congregation Sha'arai Shomayim, 1994.

Zuczek, Richard. *State of Rebellion, Reconstruction in South Carolina.* Columbia: University of South Carolina Press, 1996.

Pamphlets

Breibart, Solomon. "The Rev. Mr. Gustavus Poznanski: First American Jewish Reform Minister." Charleston, S.C.: privately printed, 1979.

Brock, Eric. "The Jewish Cemeteries of Shreveport." Shreveport, La.: privately printed, 1995.

Burke, Walter E., Jr. *Quartermaster: A Brief Account of the Life of Colonel Abraham Charles Myers, Quartermaster General C.S.A.* February 14, 1976.

"An Exhaustive Study of Hebrew Rest Cemetery Number One, Shreveport, La." N.p., 1992.

Heller, Rabbi Max. "Jubilee Souvenir of Temple Sinai, 1872–1922." New Orleans, La.: Temple Sinai, 1922.

Grey, Gordon. "The Ancestry of Nathalie Fontaine Lyons." Edited by Jo White Linn. Salisbury, N.C.: privately printed, 1981.

Margolius, Elise Levy. "Our First Century and a Quarter, 1844–1969." A history of Ohef Sholom Temple. 1970.

Mearns, Frances. "The Jewish Background and Influence in the Confederacy." Charleston, W. Va., privately printed, 1965.

Moses, Herbert A. "Pertaining to the Moses Family." (1963), CC.

"Portraits in the Collection of the Virginia Historical Society." Catalogue published for the Virginia Historical Society by University of Virginia Press, Charlottesville, Va.

Raisin, Jacob S. "Centennial Booklet." Charleston: K. K. Beth Elohim, 1925.

Rosenbaum, Claire Millhiser. *Universal and Particular Obligations.* Richmond: Beth Ahabah Museum & Archives Trust, 1988.

Steinberg, Jack. "United for Worship and Charity: A History of Congregation Children of Israel." Augusta, Ga.: privately printed, 1982.

Strug, Yvonne. "History of Temple Sinai, New Orleans, 1870–1995." New Orleans, La.: Temple Sinai.

Articles and Chapters

"Abraham Lincoln in Richmond." *Virginia Historical Magazine* 41 (October 1933), pp. 318–22.

Adler, Joseph Gary. "Moses Elias Levy and Attempts to Colonize Florida." In *Jews of the South: Selected Essays from the Southern Jewish Historical Society,* edited by Samuel Proctor and Louis Schmier. Macon, Ga.: Mercer University Press, 1984.

Amann, William Frayne, ed. "Introduction." *Personnel of the Civil War.* New York: Yoseloff, 1961.

"Biographical Sketches of Jews Who Have Served in the Congress of the United States," in *The American Jewish Yearbook,* vol. 2 (Philadelphia: JPSA, 1900–1901), 517–24.

Brav, Stanley R. "The Jewish Woman, 1861–1865." *AJA* 17, no. 1 (April 1965): 34–75.

Breibart, Solomon. "Penina Moise, Southern Jewish Poetess." In *Jews of the South: Selected Essays from the Southern Jewish Historical Society,* edited by Samuel Proctor and Louis Schmier. Macon, Ga.: Mercer University Press, 1984.

———. "The Synagogues of Kahal Kadosh Beth Elohim, Charleston." *South Carolina Historical Magazine* 80 (1976): 215–35.

478   Clarke, Robert L. "The Florida Railroad Company in the Civil War." *Journal of Southern History* 19, no. 2 (May 1953), 180–192.

Coe, Arthur. "Sir Moses J. Ezekiel: A True Son of the Confederacy." *Jewish Veteran* (winter 1995).

Creeger, Allan D. "Maximilian J. Michelbacher (1810–1879): His Times and His Legacy." *Generations, Journal of Beth Ahabah Museum and Archives* 5, no. 2 (April 1997).

Curran, Charles. "The Three Lives of Judah P. Benjamin." *History Today* (London) 17, no. 9 (September 1967): 583–92.

Dauber, Leonard G., M.D. "David Camden DeLeon, M.D.: Patriot or Traitor." *New York State Journal of Medicine* (December 1, 1970), 2927–33.

Dodd, Dorothy. "The Secession Movement in Florida, 1850–1861." Pt. 1. *Florida Historical Society Quarterly* 12, no. 1 (July 1933), 3–24; pt. 2, *FHSQ* 12, no. 2 (Oct. 1933), 45–61.

Engelman, Uriah Z. "Jewish Statistics in the U.S. Census of Religious Bodies (1850–1936)," *Jewish Social Studies* 9 (1947): 127–32.

Ezekiel, Herbert T. "The Jews of Richmond during the Civil War." Address delivered to Rimmon Lodge No. 68, I.O.B.B., February 28, 1915 (VHS).

Fairbanks, George R. "Moses Elias Levy Yulee." *Florida Historical Quarterly* 18, no. 3 (January 1940), 165–67.

Falk, Stanley L. "Divided Loyalties in 1861: The Decision of Major Alfred Mordecai." *PAJHS* 48:3 (March 1959), 147–69.

Frank, Fedora Small. "Nashville Jewry during the Civil War." *Tennessee Historical Quarterly* 39, no. 3 (fall 1980), 310–322.

Govan, G. E., and J. W. Livingood. "Adolph S. Ochs: The Boy Publisher." *East Tennessee Historical Society's Publication* 17 (1945), 84–104.

Greenberg, Mark I. "Becoming Southern: The Jews of Savannah, Georgia, 1830–1870." *AJH* 86, no. 1 (March 1998): 55–75

Gruss, Louis. "Judah Philip Benjamin." *Louisiana Historical Quarterly* 19, no. 4 (October 1936): 964–1068.

Halsey, Ashley, Jr. "The Last Duel in the Confederacy." *Civil War Times Illustrated* 1, no. 7 (November 1962), 6–8, 31.

Hanna, A. J. "The Confederate Baggage and Treasure Train Ends Its Flight in Florida." *Florida Historical Quarterly* 24, no. 3 (January 1939): 158–80.

Herzberg, Fannie. "Pioneer Members and History of Temple Beth-El, 1859–1959." *Chattahoochee Valley Historical Society Bulletin,* November 1959.

Hooker, Zebulon Vance, II. "Moses Jacob Ezekiel: The Formative Years." *Virginia Historical Magazine* 60 (April 1952).

Hühner, Leon. "Moses Elias Levy: An Early Florida Pioneer and the Father of Florida's First Senator." *Florida Historical Quarterly* 19, no. 4 (April 1941).

———. "David L. Yulee, Florida's First Senator." *PAJHS* 25 (1917), 1–29.

———. "David L. Yulee, Florida's First Senator." In *Jews in the South,* edited by Leonard Dinnerstein and Mary Dale Palsson, 52–74. Baton Rouge: Louisiana State University Press, 1973.

Joyner, Charles. "A Community of Memory, Assimilation and Identity among the Jews of

Georgetown [S.C.]." In *Shared Traditions, Southern History and Folk Culture* (Urbana: University of Illinois Press, 1999).

Korn, Bertram W. "American Judeophobia: Confederate Version." In *Jews in the South,* edited by Leonard Dinnerstein and Mary Dale Palsson, 135–56. Baton Rouge: Louisiana State University Press, 1973.

———. "Jewish Chaplains during the Civil War." *AJA* 1, no. 1 (June 1998): 6–22.

———. "The Jews of the Confederacy." *AJA* 13, no. 1 (April 1961), 3–90.

———. "Judah P. Benjamin as a Jew." *PAJHS* 38 (September 1948): 153–71.

———. "Factors Bearing upon the Survival of Judaism in the Ante-Bellum Period." *AJHQ* 53 (1964): 341–51.

———. "Jews and Negro Slavery in the Old South, 1789–1865." In *Jews in the South,* edited by Leonard Dinnerstein and Mary Dale Palsson (Baton Rouge: Louisiana State University Press, 1973), 89–134.

———. "Was There a Confederate Jewish Chaplain?" *American Jewish Historical Quarterly* 53, no. 1 (September 1863), 63–69.

Leeser, Rev. Isaac. "The Jews in the United States—1848." *AJA* 7, no. 1 (January 1955).

Leigh, Mrs. Townes Randolph. "The Jews in the Confederacy." *Southern Historical Papers* 39 (1914): 177–180.

Libo, Kenneth. "The Moses of Montgomery: The Saga of a Jewish Family in the South." *Alabama Heritage* 35 (spring 1995).

Malone, Bobbie. "New Orleans Uptown Jewish Immigrants: The Community of Congregation Gates of Prayer, 1850–1860." *Louisiana History* 32, no. 3 (summer 1991).

Marcus, Jacob R. "Jew Who Refused Supreme Court Seat." *Jewish Advocate,* January 13, 1972.

Marks, Henry, and Marsha Kass. "Jewish Life in Alabama: The Formative Stages." *Alabama Heritage* 36 (spring 1995).

"The Minis Family." *Georgia Historical Quarterly* 1 (March 1917).

Monaco, Chris. "Moses E. Levy of Florida: A Jewish Abolitionist Abroad." *AJH* 86, no. 4 (December 1998): 377–96.

Morgan, David T. "Eugenia Levy Phillips: The Civil War Experiences of a Southern Jewish Woman." In *Jews of the South: Selected Essays from the Southern Jewish Historical Society,* edited by Samuel Proctor and Louis Schmier. Macon, Ga.: Mercer University Press, 1984.

———. "Philip Phillips: Jurist and Statesman." In *Jews of the South: Selected Essays from the Southern Jewish Historical Society,* edited by Samuel Proctor and Louis Schmier. Macon, Ga.: Mercer University Press, 1984.

Moses, Rabbi Alfred G. "The History of the Jews of Montgomery." *AJHS* (November 13, 1905).

———. "A History of the Jews of Mobile." *AJHS* 12 (1904).

Neblett, John H., and Roberta C. Neblett. "Emanuel Gerst—A Gentleman of Virginia." *Generations: Journal of Congregation Beth Ahabah Museum and Archives Trust* 5, no. 1 (November 1992).

Noe, Kenneth W. "Red String Scare: Civil War Southwest Virginia and the Heroes of America." *North Carolina Historical Review* 69, no. 3 (July 1992).

Peck, Abraham J. "The Other Peculiar Institution: Jews and Judaism in the Nineteenth Century South." *Modern Judaism* 7, no. 1 (February 7, 1987): 99–104.

Proctor, Samuel. "Jewish Life in New Orleans, 1718–1860." *Louisiana Historical Quarterly* 40 (1957): 110–32.

Rosenwaike, Ira. "The Jewish Population of the United States as Estimated from the Census of 1820." *AJHQ* 53, no. 2 (December 1963): 131–49.

Ruchames, Louis. "The Abolitionists and the Jews." *PAJHS* 42 (September 1952–June 1953): 131–55.

———. "The Abolitionists and the Jews: Some Further Thoughts." In *A Bicentennial Festscrift for Jacob Rader Marcus*, 505–17. Waltham, Mass.: AJHS; New York: KTAV, 1976.

Schmier, Louis. "An Act Unbecoming: Anti-Semitic Uprising in Thomas County, Georgia." *Civil War Times Illustrated* 23 (October 1984).

———. "Georgia History in Pictures. This 'New Canaan': The Jewish Experience in Georgia." *Georgia Historical Quarterly* 73, no. 4, pt. 2 (winter 1989).

———. "Notes and Documents on the 1862 Expulsion of Jews from Thomasville, Georgia." *AJA* 32 (April 1980).

Steinberg, Jack J. "The Jews of Augusta." *Ancestoring* 12 (1986).

Tuckman, William. "Sigmund and Jacob Schlesinger and Joseph Bloch: Civil War Composers and Musicians." *AJHQ* 53, no. 1 (September 1963).

Vandiver, Frank E., ed. "Proceedings of the First Confederate Congress." *Southern Historical Society Papers* 50 (1953).

Viener, Saul. "Rosena Hutzler Levy Recalls the Civil War." *AJHQ* 62, no. 3 (March 1973).

Waddell, Gene. "An Architectural History of Kahal Kadosh Beth Elohim, Charleston." *South Carolina Historical Magazine* 98, no. 1 (January 1997): 6–55.

Wax, Rabbi James A. *"The Jews of Memphis: 1860–1865." West Tennessee Historical Society Papers* 3 (1949).

Weaver, Herbert. "Foreigners in Ante Bellum Towns of the Lower South." *JSH* 13 (1947): 62–73.

Woody, R. H. "Franklin J. Moses, Jr.: Scalawag Governor of South Carolina, 1872–74." *North Carolina Historical Review* (April 1933): 111–32.

Young, Mel. "Jewish POWs Buried at Andersonville." *The [Atlanta] Jewish Georgian*, November –December 1995, 27.

Yulee, C. Wickliffe. "Senator David L. Yulee." *Florida Historical Society Quarterly* 2, no. 1 (April 1909): 26–43 and no. 2 (July 1909): 3–22.

Dissertations and Unpublished Papers

Adler, Joseph G. "The Public Career of Senator David Levy Yulee." Ph.D. diss., Case Western Reserve University, 1973.

Allen, Mary Bernard. "Joseph Holt, Judge Advocate General (1862–1875): A Study in the Treatment of Political Prisoners by the United States Government during the Civil War." Ph.D. diss., University of Chicago, 1927.

Bartman, Roger J. "The Contribution of Joseph Holt to the Political Life of the United States." Ph.D. diss., Fordham University, 1958.

Demoff, Allison L. "Strategies of an Independent Woman: The Life of Phoebe Pember." Undergraduate thesis, College of William and Mary, 1993.

Feibelman, Julien B. "A Social and Economic Study of the New Orleans Jewish Community." University of Pennsylvania, 1941.

Friedman, Rabbi Newton J. "A History of Temple Beth Israel of Macon, Georgia." Ph.D. diss., Burton College and Seminary, 1955.

George, Juliet. "By the Brazos and the Trinity They Hung Up Their Harps: Two Jewish Immigrants in Texas." Master's thesis, Texas Christian University, 1991.

Gergel, Belinda F. "Assimilated 'New South' Daughter: Irene Goldsmith Kohn and the Widening Sphere of Jewish Women in Early Twentieth Century South Carolina." A paper presented at the Conference on Southern Women's History, Charleston, June 1, 1997.

Greenberg, Mark I. "Creating Ethnic, Class, and Southern Identity in Nineteenth-Century America: The Jews of Savannah, Georgia, 1830–1880." Ph.D. diss., University of Florida, 1997.

Johnston, J. Ambler. "Not Forgotten, Henry Gintzberger, Private, CSA." Unpublished paper, Beth Ahabah Archive, Richmond, Virginia.

Kallison, Frances R. "100 Years of Jewry in San Antonio." Master's thesis, Trinity University, 1977.

Lord, Mills B. "David Levy Yulee, Statesman and Railroad Builder." Master's thesis, University of Florida, 1940.

Thompson, Arthur W. "David Yulee: A Study of Nineteenth Century American Thought and Enterprise." Ph.D. diss., Columbia University, 1954.

INDEX

★

Italicized page numbers refer to illustrations and captions of illustrations.